THE WHOLEFOOD BOOK

THE WHOLEFOOD BOOK

George Seddon / Jackie Burrow

Galley Press

Executive Editor Glorya Hale
Editors Gail Howell-Jones
Sally Walters
Art Editor Sue Casebourne
Assistant Editor Nicola Hemingway
Assistant Art Editor Javed Badar
Designers Suzanne Stevenson
Jackie Whelan
Picture Research Editor Susan Pinkus
Picture Researcher Bridget Alexander
Editorial Assistant Charlotte Kennedy
Production Barry Baker

Publisher Bruce Marshall
Art Director John Bigg
Production Director Michael Powell

Consultant John Rivers

ISBN 0 86136 771 5

Filmset by Servis Filmsetting Limited,
Manchester
Reproduction by Sackville Press,
Billericay Limited
Printed and bound in Spain by
Printer Industria Grafica S.a., Barcelona
D.L.B. 28533-1984

Eating is one of the great pleasures of life. It is not just a source of pleasure, however, because life itself depends on it. The food we eat greatly affects how we feel, so it is wise to discover what constitutes a healthy diet; but to allow concern about eating the right food to become an obsession is fatal to enjoyment. This book, therefore, is about eating good food, enjoying it and avoiding the worry.

Anyone who is desperately hungry will eat the most unpalatable food, and will stop as soon as the pangs of hunger have been appeased. Appealing food, however, tempts us to go on eating after our needs are satisfied. We all eat too much sometimes, with no harm done, but if we consume even a little more than we need day after day we are in grave danger of becoming unhealthily fat. So the first target is to control our greed.

The next step is to realize that our affluent Western diet is not as healthy as it should be. Food processing, for example, has decreased the amount of roughage in our diet and our overdependence on animal products means we eat too much rich, fatty food that may also be high in cholesterol. The answer is not only to cut down on fat consumption, but to have a more varied diet.

The authors of this book firmly believe that the basis of a good meal—one that tastes good as well as being nutritious—is wholesome, natural food that is prepared at home. But they have no desire to turn anyone into a kitchen slave. You will find that only a little extra effort will be needed to end dependence on the supermarket deep-freeze and on the can opener—and it will be

amply rewarded by the extra pleasure you will have. In fact, cooking wholesome food can soon become part of the enjoyment of eating it.

The plan of the book is as straightforward as its aim. It begins with an outline of the foods we require and goes on to explain where, and why, our diet has gone wrong. It explodes many of the popular myths about various foods, and tells you how bad eating habits can be easily corrected.

The heart of the book, however, is a survey of the cornucopia of good ingredients that are available and shows you how you can use them to make delectable dishes.

The recipes are comparatively low in cholesterol, fats and sugar and they use wholesome foods, unadulterated by processing techniques. The cooking methods used in the recipes ensure that as much flavour and as many vitamins and minerals as possible are retained for maximum nutritional benefit and the greatest enjoyment.

Finally, the fact-finding charts provide an easy-to-follow guide to some of the essential information you will need to eat well and stay healthy.

Nutritional Measurements

Throughout this book the nutritional value of each of the foods has been given as the number of grams (g) of each nutrient in one hundred grams of food (shown as a cube divided into one hundred squares). One hundred grams (which is equivalent to about three and a half ounces) is the standard amount of food used in food tables because it is the simplest way of calculating the percentage of protein, fat, carbohydrate and water in a particular food.

Although the amount of major nutrients can be expressed in grams per hundred grams of food, minerals and vitamins must be given in milligrams (mg), which are thousandths of a gram, or, for even more minute quantities, in micrograms (mcg), which are millionths of a gram.

There are complications, however, with vitamin A. This has often been expressed in international units (i.u.), but it is now given in retinol equivalents. Retinol is the form of vitamin A found in animal products. Carotene, which is contained in fruit and vegetables, can be converted into vitamin A in the body, but less efficiently; so while one milligram of retinol provides one milligram of retinol equivalent, it takes six milligrams of carotene to provide one milligram of retinol equivalent.

It is simple to convert international units into retinol equivalents. One milligram of retinol equivalent is equal to 3,330 international units of retinol, or 10,000 international units of carotene.

For large weights, such as the amount of sugar a person consumes in a week or how much a person should weigh, the metric measurements must be in units of thousands of grams, or kilograms (kg). One thousand grams is equal to one kilogram, which is about 2.2 pounds.

Calories as an expression of the energy values of foods are already being abandoned by scientists in favour of the Système International unit (SI), the joule, but calories are too well established in popular use to disappear immediately.

One thousand calories make up the Calorie in general use. The Calorie, also called a kilocalorie (kcal), represents the amount of heat required to raise the temperature of a kilogram of water one degree centigrade. The joule, abbreviated to J, is such a small unit that the kilojoule (kJ), which is one thousand joules, is more widely used. One Calorie equals 4.186 kilojoules. For larger amounts than a kilojoule, the megajoule (MJ), one thousand kilojoules, or one million joules, is used.

Recipe Measurements

All the ingredients in the recipes in this book are given in both Imperial and metric quantities. Use either the Imperial or the metric quantities; do not mix them. The metric quantities are not exact conversions of the Imperial quantities, but are in correct proportion to the other metric quantities in the same recipe.

Standard measuring spoons have been used to measure small quantities of liquid and dry ingredients. All spoon measurements are level. British Standard Imperial spoons of a quarter teaspoon, a half teaspoon, one teaspoon and one tablespoon and standard metric spoons of two and a half, five, ten and fifteen millilitres (ml) capacity have been used.

The recipes have been tested in Imperial-sized baking dishes. Although the equivalent metric measurements have been given, dishes in these sizes may not be easy to obtain and the nearest-sized dish available may have to be substituted.

Fish is one of the most wholesome of foods and the more recently caught it is the more delicious it will taste.

TASTE IS A PRECIOUS SENSE that we shamefully neglect. Indeed today's average Western diet corrupts it. Natural honest flavours are replaced by blandness or by artificial flavourings whose impact has all the subtlety of a sledge hammer. Many of the foods we eat have lost not only their agreeable flavour but some of their nutritional value as well. A return to wholesome food would give us more enjoyment as well as a sense of well-being—the most desirable sixth sense we can hope for. Eating, unlike some human activities, can be good for us and can also be extremely pleasurable.

The basis of good, pleasurable eating is honesty —natural ingredients, their natural flavours and nutrients retained as much as possible. Nothing you like need be excluded from your diet. Some foods, of course, are more nutritious than others and some should be eaten in moderation, but there is nothing that a healthy person need avoid completely. Even sugar is maligned for the wrong reasons. Its virtue is that it can help to make some other foods palatable; but that virtue can be turned into a vice if sugar is eaten to excess. The same can be said of fats and oils; they are not harmful until excess makes them so. It is our eating habits rather than the foods we eat that are bad for us.

Although in theory we may accept that all food is good, only a person who is starving will put the belief into practice. For most of us there are a vast number of foods we reject with feelings that range from slight distaste to revulsion. Because they are largely irrational, our prejudices are all the more firmly held and harder to overcome. Local customs, submerged taboos, fads, aversions acquired in childhood and a fear of experimenting impose quite unnecessary restrictions on our diet. It is unrealistic to expect that overnight we can sweep away all these self-imposed barriers, but we might occasionally demolish a few and explore new areas of taste.

The first step is to realize how sloppy and uncritical most people have become over the last two decades about the food they buy and eat. The growth of vast chains of supermarkets epitomizes the decline. But supermarkets are obviously here to stay and are the places to shop if you want predictable, prepacked and processed food. They have made shopping faster but impersonal. They have made food safer, so that our stomachs and our palates are unlikely to be upset. They can almost guarantee unchanging quality by the control they exercise over the growing, processing and transporting of the food they sell. They have cut time spent in the kitchen by as much as three-quarters since Grandma's day. But in the process much of the individuality of our diet has been lost and the great variety of flavours which were enjoyed only a generation ago has now been reduced to a comparative few. Creativity in the kitchen has, unfortunately, been sacrificed for convenience.

It is still possible, however, to break out of the straitjacket of taste imposed by technology. If you are lucky enough to have a garden you can grow vegetables and eat them when they are at their best. If not, there are still greengrocers and markets that sell vegetables that are not sweating heavily under their plastic wraps. There are still butchers who sell excellent meat, although fresh fish becomes harder to find. In larger towns you can still find exciting, though expensive, speciality food shops that sell wholesome food. For some delicious "unfashionable" foods you may have to search in "health-food" shops. Although their prices are often inflated, their booming business may be a sign that a growing number of people think it worth the extra trouble and expense to shop for honest-to-goodness food and worth the extra time to cook it, too.

A wholesome diet is not just a question of taste. Even Brillat-Savarin, the eighteenth-century lawyer and gourmet, who argued that of all the senses taste gives most delight, added that along with the pleasure of eating there is the satisfaction of knowing that the wear and tear on the body is being made good and life is being prolonged.

A wholesome diet is not a cranky health-food regime, conjuring up the image of devotees endlessly chewing raw vegetables. While some foods can be enjoyed raw, many are more digestible and palatable when they are cooked. A chart of the nutritive value of food shows that raw asparagus, for example, has a reasonably high vitamin C content and that half of it is lost when the stalks are cooked. But unless asparagus is cooked it is not fit to eat and when it is cooked it is fit for the gods. Similarly, sound though it might be nutritionally, it would be very difficult to savour such foods as raw globe artichokes, beetroot, kale, lentils, turnip tops, marrow or potatoes.

Wholesome cookery, like the ingredients it uses, is honest. It does not dress nut cutlets up as lamb. It makes no pretence of imitating *haute cuisine*, but that does not mean that it is crude fare. Appreciation of the natural flavours of food, and doing justice to them, demand considerable skill on the part of the cook. Like French provincial cooking its appeal will be to those who have, or who develop, fairly sophisticated palates and to those for whom eating is something more than filling a ravenous hole in the stomach. A healthy gourmet does not demand elaborate meals, but can appreciate, for example, the simple flavours of home-baked bread, a bowl of crisp crudités or tart homemade preserves.

As Elizabeth David, the great English cook and writer, wrote in her highly acclaimed book *French Provincial Cooking*: "The feeling of our time is for simpler food, simply presented; not that this is necessarily easier to achieve than *haute cuisine*; it demands less time and expense, but if anything a more genuine feeling for cookery and a truer taste."

Traditional butcher shops, such as this famous one in London, hang meat properly so that it is tender and flavoursome.

THE ENERGY GIVERS

According to many experts our diet should include many more polyunsaturated fatty acids than saturated ones. Generally, this means using vegetable or fish oils instead of animal fats.

More than fifty per cent of the fatty acids in sunflower seed oil are polyunsaturated. Only safflower seed oil, popular in the United States, has a marginally higher percentage.

Most vegetable oils are high in polyunsaturated fatty acids, but coconut oil and olive oil are the exceptions. Coconut oil contains only two per cent, and olive oil contains from four to fourteen per cent, depending on the particular crop. All vegetable oils are, however, superior to animal fats from a health point of view, because they do not contain cholesterol, which is thought to contribute to heart disease.

WE EAT FOOD, but our bodies absorb nutrients. Therefore to help us to decide what to eat we must know what nutrients our food contains. Although it is easy to get bogged down in the details of nutritional research the basic outline is fairly simple.

Our diet contains carbohydrates, fats, proteins, minerals and vitamins, plus water, alcohol and fibre, or roughage. Each has a role, separately or in co-operation with another. Carbohydrates and fats are the body's main sources of energy. The role of proteins, minerals and vitamins is in body building and maintenance. Proteins can also provide energy. Fibre is needed for the efficient functioning of the digestive system, while water is necessary for all the body's functions.

As a rough guide it can be reckoned that carbohydrates and proteins provide a similar amount of energy (110 Calories per ounce or 4 Calories from every gram), while fat provides more than double that amount (250 Calories per ounce or 9 Calories from every gram). In practice, even in the fat-rich diets of the Western world, the greater part of most people's energy is derived from carbohydrates.

Carbohydrates are chemical substances made up of carbon, hydrogen and oxygen. They are manufactured in the green leaves of plants from carbon dioxide and water through the action of sunlight. This process is known as photosynthesis. Carbohydrates that plants do not need for energy accumulate in fruits and seeds and in roots and tubers. Animals cannot carry out the remarkable process of photosynthesis, and obtain most of their carbohydrates by eating plants.

Sugars, starch and cellulose are the main forms of carbohydrates produced by plants. The two simplest sugars in the diet are glucose, which occurs in such plants as sweetcorn and onions and

is formed in the body during the digestion of other carbohydrates, and fructose, a sweeter sugar found in honey and fruit. Other sugars are sucrose, obtained from sugar cane and sugar beet, lactose, found in the milk of cows and humans, and maltose, which is produced from the starch of grain when it germinates.

Starches, chemically more complex than sugars, are the main source of carbohydrate throughout the world—although in industrialized countries sugars come a close second. In Europe, for example, some forty per cent of the carbohydrates eaten are sugars, and sixty per cent are starches, mainly from cereals and potatoes.

A large proportion of the fibrous parts of plants consists of cellulose, which humans cannot digest. The virtue of cellulose in the human diet is that it provides bulk or roughage to help in the working of the bowel. But ruminants such as cattle and sheep have rumen bacteria in one of their stomachs which can digest cellulose, and when we eat beef and lamb we are eating the cellulose that they have converted into protein and fat.

All carbohydrates, except cellulose, are broken down in the body during digestion into simple

Slimmers should beware of the avocado, which is a nutritional rogue. It contains seventeen per cent fat, whereas most vegetable fruits contain less than one per cent.

COOKING MEANS CALORIES

Although raw potatoes provide 87 Calories per hundred grams, the calorific value of a potato rises when it is cooked. The explanation is simple—the potato loses some of its water content. Frying in oil or butter increases the calorific value even more. One hundred grams of raw potato produces 85 grams of baked potato (which provide 87 Calories). The same amount of raw potato makes 50 grams of chips (which provide 120 Calories) or 44 grams of potato crisps (which provide as many as 245 Calories).

sugars, mainly glucose. In a complicated series of chemical reactions the glucose is broken down and combined with oxygen to form carbon dioxide, water and energy.

Fats are a more concentrated source of energy than carbohydrates. In a Western diet they may provide forty per cent or more of the energy requirement, while in the rest of the world, either because of poverty or choice, they contribute ten per cent or less. Fats and oils are provided by both animals and plants, and although the basic constituents of all of them are carbon, hydrogen and oxygen, the way in which these are chemically linked and the number of hydrogen atoms in the molecule alters the character of the fat, even when it does not affect the energy value. An understanding of these differences will clarify current concern about the types of fat that should and should not be eaten.

Almost all the fats we eat are triglycerides, which are made up of one glycerol molecule and three fatty acid molecules. Of the forty or more fatty acids found in nature, those with a full quota of hydrogen atoms are called "saturated". These form a large proportion of animal fats and are held responsible for the high blood cholesterol levels that increase the risk of coronary disease. Cholesterol itself is essential for the functioning of the body. It is important in the manufacture of sex hormones and vitamin D. But because the body makes all the cholesterol it requires we do not need it in our diet. Common saturated fatty acids, which make up a high proportion of animal fats, include palmitic acid, found in all fats and oils, but especially in mutton fat; stearic acid, found in beef fat, mutton fat and lard; and butyric acid, found in butter. Most saturated fats are solid at room temperature.

Fatty acids with fewer hydrogen atoms and with carbon atoms joined together by double instead of single bonds are called "unsaturated". These form a high proportion of the fatty acids in most vegetable oils. Those fatty acids with two or more double bonds (polyunsaturated acids) tend to lower the cholesterol level of the blood. Those fatty acids that have only one double bond (monounsaturated fatty acids) do not have this effect. Most unsaturated fatty acids are liquid at room temperature. Unsaturated fatty acids include the monounsaturated fatty acid oleic acid, found in all oils, the polyunsaturated fatty acid linoleic acid, which is in all vegetable oils, particularly soybean, safflower, sunflower and cotton-seed oil, the polyunsaturated fatty acid linolenic acid, which is in some vegetable oils, and the polyunsaturated fatty acid arachidonic acid, found in unsaturated animal fats, especially eggs, liver and the "invisible" fat of meat. Linoleic acid cannot be synthesized in the body and is therefore described as an essential fatty acid.

Besides providing energy, fats add to the flavour of food, give a feeling of fullness after a meal and, since they are digested more slowly, stave off hunger for a longer period of time than carbohydrates. Like carbohydrates and proteins, fats that are not needed for immediate conversion into energy are used to build up body fat. Some body fat is invaluable because it forms an insulating layer under the skin, a protective covering for such organs as the kidneys, and a reserve of energy. Body fat should average fifteen to eighteen per cent of an adult's weight.

Animal and vegetable fats and oils are the most obvious sources of fat. Visible fat—such as that on meat, and in butter and cream—accounts for up to half of the average fat consumption in the Western diet. The rest—"invisible" fat—comes from such foods as lean meat, fish and eggs.

THE VALUE OF PROTEINS

DO YOU GET ENOUGH OF THE RIGHT KIND OF PROTEIN?

Most protein in the average Western diet comes from animal products.

Vegetables contribute about ten per cent of the daily protein requirement.

Cereals are surprisingly rich in protein and because most people eat so much of them, they may supply almost one-third of the protein in the diet.

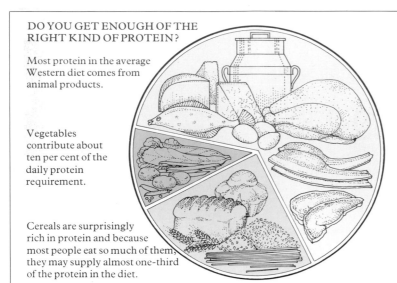

Most vegetable proteins lack one or more of the essential amino acids and are considered second-class proteins. But a pairing of certain foods, each of which makes up for the other's deficit, produces a first-class protein with the full complement of amino acids.

Bread is low in lysine, but is fairly rich in methionine. Baked beans are the reverse and on toast are a good protein meal.

Cornflakes and milk are an excellent protein combination. Milk contributes tryptophan and maize methionine.

PROTEINS ARE PRIMARILY BODY BUILDERS, and we need them not only when we are growing up but all our lives. The tissues of the body are always being renewed, although diminishingly so as we get older. Between one and two per cent of the tissue protein is replaced each day, but the rate varies for different parts of the body. The renewal of heart, liver and kidney tissue, for example, is rapid; that of muscle and bone much slower.

The word protein was first used in 1837 by a Dutch chemist, G. J. Mulder, who made the error of thinking of it in terms of an unvarying nitrogen-rich substance. The great German chemist Justus von Liebig perpetuated the error which became accepted doctrine. Later research showed that proteins vary greatly according to the different combinations and amounts of the basic building blocks, or amino acids, of which they are composed.

The building blocks, like those of carbohydrates and fats, are constructed of carbon, hydrogen and oxygen, but in addition they include nitrogen. In some proteins there may be other elements present, such as sulphur. Of the hundreds of amino acids present in proteins only about twenty commonly occur and are of particular importance to us. Some of these are described as "essential" because they cannot be manufactured in the body and must therefore be included in the diet. Eight such amino acids are essential for adults. These are isoleucine, leucine, lysine, methionine, phenylalanine, threonine, tryptophan and valine. Very young children need an additional two—arginine and histidine. The "nonessential" proteins are just as important, but these are made in the body.

The value of protein foods depends on the relative amounts of essential amino acids they contain, and the value may be limited simply by a shortage of one amino acid. Bread protein, for example, is deficient in lysine, maize and legumes are deficient in tryptophan and leafy vegetables in methionine. The protein we eat is broken down in digestion into its constituent amino acids in order to be recreated as body protein. Body protein can only be formed if all the necessary amino acids are available at the same time. There is no store to call upon, for excess amino acids are used up as energy or converted into fat. By eating a mixture of protein-rich foods in the same meal, however, you can help to ensure that you get enough of the essential amino acids needed to form body protein.

Estimates of the daily requirements of protein vary widely, but both estimates and consumption in the West are way above the minimum. This, for most adults, ranges between one to one and a half ounces (about 25 to 45 g); for mothers who are breastfeeding it rises to almost two ounces (55 g). Usually the recommended daily intakes are based on the calculation that ten per cent of an individual's energy requirements should be provided by protein. By this rather arbitrary calculation the recommended intakes for adults range between two to three ounces (55 to 85 g). A varied diet will include more than enough protein, with adequate amounts of the essential amino acids.

To talk of a food as being rich in protein may be true but it is, nonetheless, misleading; it all depends on how much of that food we eat. Lobster, for example, is undoubtedly rich in protein, but the contribution it makes to most people's protein needs is minimal. Potatoes, however, which we think of as a starchy food, give most people about five per cent of their daily protein. More surprisingly, twenty-seven per cent of the protein in the average British diet, and twenty per cent in the average American diet

It's difficult to persuade people to try new foods, particularly the new protein foods, which frequently masquerade as meat.

A GROWING SOURCE OF PROTEIN

In the future the new vegetable protein foods, such as soya products, are likely to become more important in our diet because they are so much cheaper to produce than animal protein. An acre of soya can produce almost thirty times the amount of protein as an acre on which beef cattle are reared.

comes from bread and other flour products, which are always regarded as carbohydrate foods. The percentage of protein from vegetables is about ten per cent for both the United States and Britain. The rest of our protein comes from animal products—meat, fish, milk, cheese and eggs.

Researchers are now urgently looking for new sources of protein which will add to or substitute for such protein-rich foods as meat, fish, eggs and milk, which are both scarce and expensive. So far the alternative protein foods intended for human consumption have been manufactured from existing food sources, notably soya beans. In one process soya flour is made into a dough, heated and extruded through a nozzle under pressure, dried and then cut into pieces that have a texture similar to meat. Another method produces fine threads of soya protein, which can be spun to give different textures. Flavour, colour and fat can be added at will and the end product can be dried, canned or frozen. Soya protein is also used to make nonmilk coffee whiteners.

Beans and other seeds now generally used for animal feeds will in the future undoubtedly also be used to provide human food with a high crude protein content of at least fifty per cent.

Even more novel protein foods may be in the offing. Since green leaves are so efficient in synthesizing food it is a pity that humans cannot digest the inedible fibre of such plants as grass. The protein-rich juice, however, can be extracted and processed, but the result is as yet unattractive.

All our food ultimately comes from plant life and researchers have even learned how to obtain food from plant life that died millions and millions of years ago and now exists as oil. Yeasts, bacteria and fungi can all manufacture protein by being cultivated on waste petroleum products. Some of these proteins are already being used experimentally in Britain and abroad as animal feeds. A group of Dutch researchers have for some years been feeding yeast/petroleum protein to pigs and poultry. As a sign of the courage of their convictions they and their families have been eating the meat and eggs of their experimental animals, and no harm has befallen them.

The ever increasing demand for protein can never be solved through meat—the world's resources are too limited to squander on the uneconomical conversion of plant to animal to human protein. Increasingly, people all over the world will have to rely on vegetable protein.

Various forecasts are that by 1980 between five and ten per cent of meat will have been replaced by textured vegetable proteins, largely because they are cheaper. This estimate is probably optimistic because people are not willing to accept a product that pretends to be something it isn't. The novel proteins so far introduced are being projected in the image of meat, even though they do not taste or even chew like meat. That is the prerogative of meat alone. Until the new protein foods stop being produced as "meat" and their own worth is established in a palatable form, people will not willingly use them as a source of protein.

Vitamin A is needed to make the pigment that enables the retina of the eye to adjust from a bright to a dim light. It is found in such animal products as eggs and such vegetables as spinach and carrots. Two average-sized carrots, for example, supply our daily needs.

Vitamin D is the vitamin that nearly isn't, because provided that we get sunlight we do not need it. We produce compounds in our skin that are changed by even dull sunlight into vitamin D. Without sun, we depend on such foods as fatty fish and dairy products, with our daily requirement coming, for example, from one egg.

There are seven B vitamins that are important in our diet— niacin, riboflavin, folic acid, pantothenic acid, B_6 and B_{12}. Two ounces of peanuts and two ounces of liver, for instance, give us all the B vitamins that we need in one day.

Vitamin C, or ascorbic acid, is provided by fruit and vegetables. Recommended daily amounts vary from thirty to sixty milligrams— the upper limit can be obtained from a glass of orange juice. However, many people take from ten to fifty times as much in the hope that excess vitamin C will prevent or at least ameliorate the common cold. The theory arose originally out of the observation that in scurvy—vitamin C deficiency—infections were more common. It was regarded as untrue by most nutritionists until in 1970 Nobel prizewinner Professor Linus Pauling published a book backing what he called megavitamin therapy—the idea that very large doses of vitamin C specifically protect you against the common cold. Despite the boost give by Pauling's reputation the theory still remains "unproven".

MAN CANNOT LIVE by carbohydrates, fats and proteins alone; but scientists were a long time discovering why. It is only since the beginning of the twentieth century that the other essential elements in food have been tracked down; some of them little more than twenty years ago. These other essential elements are minerals and vitamins, and although the amounts we need of them are small, their importance to our health is immense. Lack of vitamins is responsible, for example, for such deficiency diseases as anaemia, scurvy, rickets, pellagra, beriberi and blindness.

The minerals needed in the largest amounts are known as the major elements. They include calcium and phosphorus, the chief elements in the bones of the body. Of the total weight of our bones, more than two pounds (just less than a kilogram) is calcium and about one and a half pounds (just over half a kilogram) is phosphorus. For the body to absorb calcium vitamin D has to be present. Absorption is reduced by the presence of phytic acid, which is found particularly in wholewheat. Calcium is unavoidably removed in the milling of white flour and in many countries it is put back to ensure that there is no lack of calcium in the diet. Milk and cheese are excellent sources of calcium, and water in hard-water areas also makes a fair contribution. There is little risk of shortage of phosphorus because it is present as phosphate in many of the foods we eat.

Other elements which are needed are iron, magnesium, sodium, chlorine, potassium and sulphur. Liver and eggs are the best sources of iron. Bread, however, provides much of most people's daily requirement not because it is rich in iron but because they eat so much of it.

Magnesium is found in almost all foods and particularly in cereals, pulses, fish, green vegetables and potatoes. Sodium and chlorine, largely provided by common salt (sodium chloride), are also found in most foods. Meat, milk and green vegetables are rich sources of potassium. Sulphur is supplied by meat, fish, poultry, eggs and the cabbage family (hence the smell). Minerals needed in the diet in only minute quantities, and found in many foods, are called trace elements; these are iodine, fluorine, zinc, copper, manganese, chromium, cobalt and molybdenum.

It is hard to believe that before 1911 there was no such word as vitamin. More than half a century and the discovery of thirteen major vitamins later there are still great gaps in the knowledge of vitamins; even the precise function of the first to

be named, vitamin A, is not known. Recommendations of the amounts we should eat are largely guesswork and are generous, to be on the safe side. But the knowledge we do have has meant that scurvy can be cured with vitamin C, beriberi with thiamine, pellagra with niacin, and rickets with vitamin D. These are the more dramatic aspects of the part vitamins play, but just as important is their everyday role in the body's functions.

Unlike minerals, which are inorganic, vitamins are organic substances. Although essential they are not magical, at least no more than anything else in our diet. The amounts we eat range from minute to merely small, and it is a fallacy to believe that because small amounts of vitamins are good for us more would be better. A well-balanced diet provides a generous amount of vitamins, and it is a waste of money to stuff our bodies with vitamin pills. Indeed an excess of vitamin A and vitamin D may be harmful.

Vitamin A is needed for vision, healthy skin and the linings of the throat and bronchial tubes. The most important sources of vitamin A include liver, butter and fortified margarine. While most vegetables contain no vitamin A, they provide carotene, from which the body can make vitamin A.

There are, so far, seven B vitamins known to be necessary in our diet. One of the main roles of B vitamins is the part they play in the release of energy from carbohydrates, fats and proteins. They are also involved in the making of red cells in the blood and the working of the nervous system. B vitamins include thiamine (B_1), found in flour, cereals, meat and vegetables, especially potatoes. There can be heavy losses of thiamine during cooking. The richest sources of riboflavin (B_2) are liver and kidney, but we get our largest supplies from other meats and from milk. While niacin is found in meat, fish and whole grains, in practice the main sources are meat, vegetables and enriched flour. Beer drinkers consume a fair amount. Vitamin B_6 is found in many foods; rich sources include nuts, meat, fish and wholewheat flour. Pantothenic acid is found in almost all foods, folic acid in green vegetables and liver and B_{12} is found most notably in liver, kidney, fish, milk and eggs.

Vitamin C helps to make the tissue that binds the cells of the body together. For some reason it is given star rating by many people, who swallow vitamin C pills in the mistaken belief that they will cure all ills. Good sources of vitamin C are soft fruits and citrus fruits, peppers, vegetables of the cabbage family, potatoes and fresh beans. Regrettably, this vitamin dissolves in water, and much is lost in cooking. Further losses occur by exposure of cut fruit and vegetables to the air.

The role of vitamin D is to assist the body to build bones and teeth, and it controls the absorption of calcium from the digestive system and excretion of calcium from the kidneys. The body can make vitamin D through the action of the sun's ultraviolet rays on the skin. Food sources are such fatty fishes as kippers, herrings and sardines, and also dairy products.

The effect of vitamin E on the fertility of mice, rabbits and turkeys and unsupported claims for its value in treating heart disease are scarcely reasons for it to become one of the pet vitamins of food faddists. Little of certainty is known about the vitamin, but the body does seem to need it, although in what quantity no one can say. It is present in most foods, notably vegetables, fats and the germ of cereal grains.

Vitamin K is required for the clotting of blood. It is found particularly in green leafy vegetables and is manufactured by bacteria in the intestine.

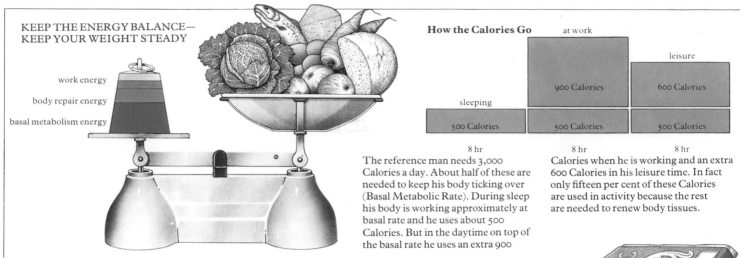

KEEP THE ENERGY BALANCE—
KEEP YOUR WEIGHT STEADY

work energy

body repair energy

basal metabolism energy

How the Calories Go

	at work	leisure
	900 Calories	600 Calories
sleeping		
500 Calories	500 Calories	500 Calories
8 hr	8 hr	8 hr

The reference man needs 3,000 Calories a day. About half of these are needed to keep his body ticking over (Basal Metabolic Rate). During sleep his body is working approximately at basal rate and he uses about 500 Calories. But in the daytime on top of the basal rate he uses an extra 900 Calories when he is working and an extra 600 Calories in his leisure time. In fact only fifteen per cent of these Calories are used in activity because the rest are needed to renew body tissues.

There has to be a balance between the amount of food energy (calories) we eat and the amount we expend. Even if we take in only a few more calories than we use up— protein calories, fat calories or carbohydrate calories—we become fat.

HAVING DIGESTED THE basic facts of nutrition and diet, the next step is to turn this knowledge into meals that you enjoy and from which you will benefit. If only nutrition were an exact science it might be possible to establish a theoretically "perfect diet", but even that would not work in practice because it would ignore individual likes and dislikes. There are, however, certain guidelines to be followed to achieve a balanced diet.

Food and health are indissolubly related. Too often, however, our approach to a healthy diet is negative. We are always lectured about the foods that are "bad" for us and, according to which nutritional theory is currently in favour, we give up potatoes, bread, fat, sugar, eggs or meat, hoping thereby that we will put off illness for as long as possible. But health is more than the state of not being ill.

The World Health Organization has ambitiously defined health as "a state of complete physical, mental and social well-being and not merely the absence of disease or infirmity". Not even a "perfect diet" would achieve that, whatever food faddists claim, but there is no doubt that a reasonably balanced diet makes a major contribution to overall health.

The first balance that has to be achieved in a diet is between the energy your food provides and the energy your body uses up. The reason why people become fat is that carbohydrates, fats and proteins—in excess of the body's needs—are turned into fat.

Appetite, controlled by two small areas in the lower part of the brain, is one way of regulating how much you eat, but it is easily led astray. A pair of scales is far more reliable, for if you overeat you will gain weight. The eighteenth-century scholar Dr Samuel Johnson, speaking with the authority of one who was grossly overweight, was perfectly right when he said to his chronicler Boswell, "Nay sir, whatever may be the quantity

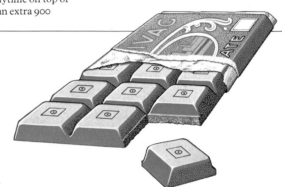

Obesity does not necessarily come from gluttony or sloth. A half ounce piece of chocolate in excess per day, for example, is equal to a gain of 28,000 Calories per year or eight pounds (3½ kg) of body fat.

that a man eats it is plain that if he is too fat he has eaten more than he should have done."

But how fat is "too fat"? The chart on page 225 indicates the considered optimum weights for people of various ages, heights and builds. If you are reasonably close to the suggested figures, regular weighing will act as a check on your energy balance. If you are already overweight you should aim to slim gradually by losing no more than two pounds (about 1 kg) a week. It should be possible to achieve this with a daily intake of 1,000 fewer Calories than you expend.

Although the energy output of each individual differs, averages have been calculated for people of the same age and weight living in comparable conditions and engaged in a whole range of activities. One such set of calculations has been made by the World Health Organization, taking as the basis a hypothetical reference man. He lives in a temperate zone with a mean annual temperature of 50°F (10°C), is twenty-five years of age and weighs an unchanging ten stone three pounds (65 kg). He works eight hours a day, not too strenuously, and for the rest of the day he spends six hours sitting around and in light activity, a total of two hours walking and in active leisure and then he sleeps. The reference woman

A NUTRITIOUS MEAL

People cannot live by bread alone, or indeed on any other single food apart from breast milk. No one food combines all of the vitamins, minerals, amino acids and essential fatty acids in the amounts that we need. Thus it is fortunate that we eat meals rather than food, because it is often the mixture of foods that we choose to eat which provides the balance we need. Even relatively cheap combinations can be well balanced—fish and chips, spaghetti bolognese or moussaka, for example. On its own the versatile American hamburger is not a balanced meal; but in a bun (which adds extra B vitamins and the carbohydrate that is not found in meat) and eaten with a layer of cheese (which has the calcium and vitamins A and D that meat lacks) and a garnish of red and green peppers (for added vitamin C) it is a perfectly balanced meal

A balanced diet in tablet form would require at least six hundred tablets a day.

is also twenty-five, weighs eight stone eight pounds (55 kg), and is busy doing housework or is employed in a moderatively active job.

The reference man is reckoned to have an energy output of 3,000 Calories a day, and the woman one of 2,200 Calories. These estimates are similar to official British standards. Even 100 Calories a day more than you need can add ten pounds (about 5 kg) a year to your weight.

Energy is needed simply to keep your heart, lungs, and other organs and tissues working, and this, calculated under precisely defined conditions, is known as the Basal Metabolic Rate. Energy output rises as soon as you indulge in any activity, from thinking (a negligible increase) to running upstairs (a large upsurge). Researchers have estimated that playing Beethoven's *Appassionata Sonata* on the piano takes almost twice as much energy as playing Mendelssohn's *Songs Without Words* for the same length of time, but less than playing Liszt's *Tarantella*.

Fats, proteins and carbohydrates are our sources of energy. But fats and proteins have nutritional roles that carbohydrates cannot fulfil. So a diet must have a balance between the three nutrients. Proteins are essential for body maintenance, but to consume more than is needed is pointless, for excess protein is converted into fat; one gram of protein provides the same number of Calories (four) as one gram of carbohydrate.

The amount of protein required each day varies considerably according to age. It reaches a peak among teenagers, drops marginally in adulthood and decreases in old age. By the time you are seventy your needs are the same as those of a seven-year-old. The estimated figure for an adult man's daily intake of protein is nearly three ounces (85 g) in the United Kingdom. A simple rule of thumb for ensuring an adequate (indeed generous) supply of protein is to reckon it as about one-tenth of total energy intake. Thus if you need

3,000 Calories a day proteins should provide 300 Calories—that is nearly three ounces (85 g) at 110 Calories an ounce.

But some proteins, depending on the relative amounts of essential amino acids they contain, are more valuable than others. A balance of amino acids is needed in a balanced diet. Wheat, for example, is low in the amino acid lysine, but this can be made good by combining it with such lysine-rich foods as cheese or beans. A diet should be varied to ensure an adequate intake of amino acids. Vegetarians, especially those who do not include milk, cheese and eggs in their diet, must be particularly careful to eat a wide range of vegetables and cereals.

In the West we eat too much fat. Nutritionists generally agree that fats should contribute between thirty to forty per cent of our energy intake. In Britain the proportion has reached over forty per cent of the daily Calorie intake—that means about four ounces (120 g) of fat a day. Fortunately, we are beginning to eat more vegetable fats than animal fats. This means that the diet is less likely to be short of one of the essential fatty acids, linoleic acid, which is low in most visible animal fats but high in vegetable fats. The invisible fats of animal products do, however, contain some of the other essential fatty acids.

No diet is balanced unless it has an adequate supply of minerals and vitamins. In the main, if we balance our diet by eating a wide range of carbohydrates and proteins plus a discriminating choice of fats we need not worry about consuming enough minerals or vitamins. What we have to guard against is that we do not, by the careless preparation and cooking of food, destroy too many of those precious vitamins.

One other balance has to be achieved—the balance between eating what we like and what is best for us. The solution is to try to make them the same thing.

TABOOS AND ADDICTIONS

Our diets are limited by our refusal to regard all that is edible as food. Most Europeans, for example, refuse to eat horseflesh, not knowing that the origin of the taboo was a directive from the Pope in the eighth century AD.

Economics and fashion interact. In the nineteenth century oysters, then plentiful, were eaten by London's poor.

Fish Fridays, illustrated in this detail from a nineteenth-century painting by Walter Sadler, began as a day of abstaining from meat. Originated by the Roman Catholic Church during the Middle Ages, now it survives as a habit few people question.

SEVERAL MILLION YEARS OF HISTORY have shaped our diet. To go back about seventy-five thousand years, Neanderthal man hunted and fished and gathered plants and was not averse to eating his fellow men, although possibly only in times of dire need. The Neanderthals lasted some forty thousand years, and by the end of that time the foundations had been laid for the Neolithic revolution in which man basically changed from hunter-gatherer to farmer.

Experts have rival theories to explain why and how domestication of plants and animals began and developed. But there is no doubt that domestication shifted the emphasis in man's diet from animal to vegetable. Even in the modern, affluent, meat-loving West that has not changed. Indeed it cannot be otherwise if there is to be any hope of feeding soaring populations.

Some of our food habits are entirely irrational, since they merely perpetuate ancient taboos and myths, that have now lost any relevance. They are frequently of religious origin. Throughout recorded history, and probably before, the gods have taken a hand in deciding what we may eat. According to the book of Leviticus in the Old Testament the Lord gave to Moses and Aaron an enormously complex list of forbidden foods. The meat of pig, camel, hare and rock badger was unclean. So was the flesh of any swimming creature without fins and scales. Forbidden birds ranged from eagles to ostriches, with bats included. Winged creatures that "creep, going upon all four" were an abomination unless they also had legs; this let out the locust—a wise provision since more than fifty per cent of dried locust is protein and about twenty per cent is fat.

The Jewish and Muslim prohibition of pork is based on its being an "unclean" meat, but in India the taboo against beef arose because the cow was

Unfortunately a childhood aversion to certain foods may last through a lifetime.

considered sacred. The prohibition goes back more than three thousand years, and survived the country's conquest by two beef-eating invaders—Muslims in the Middle Ages and the British in the nineteenth century. In ancient Egypt religious taboos limited the meat eaten by royalty to veal and goose.

While most of the taboos and myths apply to animal products there are also aversions to eating certain vegetables. The Jains, for example, an ancient religious sect in India, will not eat vegetables that grow underground.

The choice of food may also be circumscribed for reasons that have lost any validity. Most Britons, for example, have an aversion to eating horsemeat. By contrast, the early Britons were avid eaters of horse, and it was Pope Gregory III who put a stop to that. In the eighth century, in support of St Boniface's great missionary campaigns in Germany and England, he ordered that Christians should abstain from eating horseflesh so that they would stand apart from the uncon-

WEALTH VERSUS HEALTH

During the last century, increasing economic wealth has not only encouraged us to eat more but also to eat the wrong kinds of foods. We now tend to eat an excessive amount of fat, which because of its high calorific value can easily lead to obesity. Even worse there has been a trend towards eating less vegetable oil and more animal fat, thus unfortunately shifting the balance towards the high cholesterol, saturated kind. Furthermore, we now obtain more calories from sugar than from starchy foods, which do at least contain other nutrients.

Ice-cream sums up what is wrong with modern eating. A super non-food made from sugar and saturated fat, it has no other nutrients and provides energy in its least nutritious form.

On average we eat about five ounces (140 g) of fat a day—two and a half tons in a lifetime.

We eat about four and a half ounces (130 g) of sugar a day—more in two weeks than in a year a century ago.

---

verted pagans. (The British, however, readily send horses to be slaughtered and eaten abroad.)

The English now eat far less fish than they do meat. In the Middle Ages it was the other way around, because the Roman Catholic Church dictated that all Fridays, certain Wednesdays and Saturdays, other occasional days and the forty days of Lent were days on which meat was forbidden but fish was allowed. With the Reformation official fish days disappeared. This change had such disastrous effects on the fishing industry that eventually two fish days were restored, but by the end of the sixteenth century the attempt to enforce them was abandoned. Friday remains the popular unofficial fish day even though today it has little religious significance even for Catholics.

Our choice of staple foods—wheat, rice, potatoes, maize and other grains—is largely decided by where we live and what will grow in that climate. Our food habits are also under strong pressures from national and regional eating habits. Just as important are the likes and dislikes acquired in childhood or as we grew up. Of all the irrational factors that decide what we eat, our fads and fancies can be the most treacherous.

In the affluent West the most obvious dietary vice we have is that we eat so much of what we like that we grow fat. Gluttony and obesity are not, of course, the prerogative of twentieth-century man. The ancient Egyptians overate, but believed that by setting aside three days during each month for vomiting they would remain healthy. (The modern equivalent is to flee periodically to a health farm.) Medieval man was an enormous eater, but he compensated by leading an energetic life. Similarly, although the gluttony of well-to-do Victorians almost matched that of ancient Romans, the Victorians may have been reprieved by the non-existence of the motor car.

Modern Western man not only overeats, he is also sedentary and a worrier. His current dietary obsessions centre mainly on his obesity and on his fear of early death from heart troubles. The Western woman is also worried about growing fat, as much concerned with her figure as with her health.

While animals in their natural state tend not to overeat, the human appetite may need to be consciously regulated, for there are siren foods that will lead it astray. The most seductive of these are fat and sugar; even monkeys in captivity will quickly develop an excessively sweet tooth.

The Western diet is high in both fat and sugar. Sugar, once an expensive luxury, is now a cheap and large part of our diet. Since the beginning of the twentieth century world consumption of sugar has trebled. The British and Americans are notorious addicts; on average each man, woman and child eats about two pounds of sugar every week. Sugar may be a good source of energy, but it contains no vitamins or minerals. Taken in such large quantities it spoils the appetite for more balanced foods and plays havoc with teeth.

More fat is now being eaten, but the rise in its consumption has been less spectacular than that of sugar. Even in the wealthy United States consumption of fat has risen only twelve per cent since the beginning of the twentieth century, while sugar consumption has shot up by one hundred and twenty per cent. It is, however, the combined increase in the amounts of sugar and fat eaten that is important; for example, there are large amounts of both sugar and fat in cakes, puddings, sticky pastries and ice-cream. It is unfortunate that sugar and fat are so attractive to the palate and so satisfying to the appetite, and that the penalty for overindulgence in these nutrients is obesity and ill health.

The free-range chicken is rapidly becoming a food of the past. Factory farming (inset right) is economically so successful that it produces ninety-eight per cent of the chicken sold in the United States. The argument for factory farming is simple—that chicken is no longer a luxury food but one that is relatively cheap and available. The argument against is just as clear—for cheaper chicken we have sacrificed flavour.

Perhaps it is fortunate that food labels are often imprecise: food technologists may be able to spray-dry blood plasma and mix it with locust bean kernel, thus producing an acceptable alternative to egg white. But would you enjoy eating meringues labelled "containing blood protein"?

IN THE AFFLUENT WESTERN WORLD it is not only historical influences and personal prejudices that determine our diet. There are other insidious factors. Recent developments in the growing, processing and retailing of food are of the greatest significance to our eating habits and health, even though we may be only dimly aware of them.

Immediately disturbing is the quality and taste of the food produced by "factory farming". This cliché describes the new intensive system of rearing animals. Pigs, for example, are raised along factory lines, and with machinery for feeding and manure removal one person can look after as many as three thousand pigs. Veal calves are reared intensively and fed solely on milk substitutes until they are killed at three months old. Beef calves may never be allowed out to graze, but are fed lavishly indoors and sold soon after they are a year old.

Intensive production of meat has a considerable, but generally unrealized, effect on our diet. Cattle which graze at large have a high proportion of muscle—that is, lean meat—and very little fat. Intensively fed beef may be one-third fat, even when it looks lean, because of the fat embedded in the muscle—the marbling, which gives much of the succulence to meat. Thus, while we worry about our own obesity we are eating obese meat.

Heavy use of artificial fertilizers, particularly if no organic fertilizers are used as well, can, by affecting the amount of nutrients absorbed by the plants from the soil, reduce the amount of trace elements in our diet. While nitrogen, used by plants to make protein, will increase yield, excessive nitrogen will lower the percentage of protein in a crop, decrease the vitamin content and affect the taste.

Plant breeders have never been so preoccupied with developing varieties that crop heavily, resist disease, mature rapidly, can be harvested by machines and travel well. This may seem praiseworthy, but not when texture and flavour are ruined, as has happened, for example, with potatoes, strawberries and tomatoes.

It was less than two centuries ago that people started eating canned food and barely half a century since their pets did. People had to get along without instant coffee until 1900, frozen vegetables until the 1920s and instant potatoes until 1939. Frozen fish fingers and frozen chips did not exist fifteen years ago. And we have had to wait until the last few years before being able to "enjoy" substitute meat spun out of soya beans. How did mankind ever survive?

Some methods of preserving food have an incredibly long history. Early man observed that food that was dried either by sun or wind did not putrefy or rot. This is because bacteria, yeast and moulds that cause food to go bad need moisture to develop. Meat, fish, green vegetables and fruit are now dried in a mechanically produced current of hot air. In the more expensive freeze-drying the food is first frozen, then dried in a near-vacuum, causing the ice to be driven off as vapour without first turning into water. The dearest instant coffee is made in this way.

Freezing is both the oldest and almost the newest method of preserving food. But until ways of making ice artificially were discovered, reliable refrigeration was out of the question. One of the most radical changes in the eating habits of the Western World came about because an American named Clarence Birdseye went on a fur-trading expedition to Labrador in 1912, and realized the commercial possibilities of frozen food. After years of experimenting, in 1924 he put his packaged frozen food on the market and went on

Technological improvements in food processing are efficient but unromantic. Butter advertisements may feature rural landscapes (below) and farmhouse settings to imply their butter is "naturally" produced. Today, commercial butter is never made in such pastoral settings. A modern dairy (right) resembles an operating theatre more than a rural landscape by Constable. Technology makes food production more efficient, and hence reduces cost. It also minimizes the chance of bacterial contamination of food and the danger of food poisoning. But the price we have to pay for cheaper, more hygienic food is the loss of much of its original taste and texture.

The proliferation of convenience foods can all too easily seduce you away from good wholefood.

to make millions. If you seek a monument to the father of frozen food, look around you in any supermarket.

The convenience food explosion of the last two decades has changed the Western diet as much as frozen foods have. A convenience food is something that is almost literally handed to you on a plate. All you have to do to the cooked, dried, frozen or canned product is to warm it, add water or milk to it and eat or drink it (the most strenuous part of the operation). The appeal starts early in life; on average every baby in the United States and Europe eats more than one can or packet of baby food a day.

Many people are becoming rightly suspicious about what goes into convenience food. There has, of course, hardly ever been a time when someone has not been tampering with food. It was usually done to cheat, and it was called adulteration. It reached a scandalous peak in the first half of the nineteenth century. There was alum and ground bones in bread, chalk in milk, vitriol in beer and in sugar, floor sweepings in pepper, verdigris and black lead in tea, brick dust in cocoa powder, copper in pickles and red lead in Gloucester cheese.

Today there is less reason to fear such adulteration, but now we have what is called enrichment,

which means adding to food substances that have been lost in processing. White bread, for example, is supplemented with iron, calcium, thiamine and niacin; just some of the nutrients lost in the production of flour. Never have so many permitted substances been added to food. Many countries throughout the world add vitamins and calcium to their basic cereals on nutritional grounds. But additives may also be used to make food acid or alkaline, ensure that it stays moist, or glazed to give an appealing shine, while some merely prevent the food from sticking to surfaces while it is being processed. Additives can enhance the flavour of food, or change it completely, and give it irresistible colour. The result is that the end product has little resemblance to the original.

To the raw meat basis of "luncheon meat" may be added potato starch (to give texture), sodium caseinate (a stabilizer), salt, emulsifying fats, spices, monosodium glutamate (a flavour enhancer), sodium nitrite (a preservative) and colouring. At least luncheon meat has some meat in it, but artificial cream has none of the ingredients of real cream: instead it is refined sugar, methyl ethyl cellulose, polyoxyethylene, sorbitan stearate, salt, sodium alginate, colouring and, of course, synthetic mouth-watering flavouring.

The greater the amount of food that is processed the more additives we are going to consume. While there is no doubt that many additives have a corrupting influence on our appreciation of the true taste of food it is impossible to say with certainty that they are either harmful or harmless; the danger is that we are woefully ignorant about many of the additives we use. A quarter of a century ago about one thousand five hundred processed foods were being sold; now the number has increased more than sixfold. Give us this day our daily additives.

Technological Fish

The modern fisherman hunts with all the paraphernalia of modern technology. Huge trawlers track down their quarry with electronic devices, hauling in ton after ton of fish to be quick-frozen by the accompanying factory ship. Back in port, skinned fillets are moulded and frozen into solid blocks of fish, then sawn into steaks to boil in the bag or cut into strips. The strips progress through a curtain of batter, a shower of brightly coloured crumbs, a half-minute dip in a tank of hot fat and finally another quick freeze down to —40°F (—40°C) in a blast of cold air. Ten fish fingers weigh about two hundred and twenty grams, of which about one hundred and fifty grams are water, thirty-five protein and twenty fat. Each fish finger, therefore, provides nearly 40 Calories as well as an unidentifiable texture. To label them fish is an affront to one of nature's most wholesome foods.

THE GROWING REVOLT against the way commercialism desecrates our food is a healthy sign. Unfortunately, the forms the reaction takes are often irrational. One of Brillat-Savarin's aphorisms was: "Animals feed: man eats: only the man of intellect knows how to eat." How wrong he was. People who are otherwise intelligent readily take leave of their senses over their diet, and turn eating first into a fad, then into a cult, then, possibly, into a way of life and even into a religion. There are no cranks so impervious to reason as food cranks.

History is littered with them. In the second century AD the Greek Athenaeus reports in his food guide and cookery book *The Sophists at Dinner* that two of the Sophists lived entirely on figs. Even the fact that they were ostracized at the public baths because they smelled so rank did not persuade them to change their diet.

At the end of the fifteenth century the Venetian Luigi Cornaro decided, after forty years of excessive eating and drinking, to give abstemiousness a chance. For years afterwards his diet consisted of exactly twelve ounces of food and fourteen ounces of wine a day. As he grew older he was able to subsist, he claimed, on one egg a day. He lived to be a hundred.

Although vegetarianism attracts innumerable food faddists, the vegetarian diet is a perfectly valid and acceptable one. You may be a vegetarian because, like the Greek philosopher Pythagoras, you believe in the transmigration of souls and respect the sanctity of animals: "Beware, I implore you in the name of the Gods, of expelling their souls, which are cognate to you, from their housings, in order that blood might not be nourished by blood." Many of the world's religions have the deepest respect for animal life, but in the West it is rare. Western vegetarians are more likely to have other motives; they may have

an ethical objection to slaughtering animals, a revulsion to the idea of eating their flesh or the belief that, in a world short of food, it would be more economical if grain was fed directly to people. These reasons are to be respected; the argument, however, that it is healthier to eat only vegetables is not proven. Nor is there any evidence that vegetarians are less aggressive and more sweet-tempered than meat eaters. They are in fact often violent in expressing their views.

Dr Sylvester Graham, the nineteenth-century American "natural" food faddist whose name lives on in Graham flour, declared: "The enormous wickedness and atrocious violence and outrages of mankind immediately preceding the Flood, strongly indicate, if they do not prove, an excessive indulgence in animal food." His perfect diet went even further back, to that of the Garden of Eden. "Fruits, nuts, farinaceous seeds and roots, with perhaps some milk and it may be honey, in all rational probability, constituted the food of the first family and the first generations of mankind." He pointed out that the only processing needed in that diet was to crack the nuts.

In the nineteenth century in both Britain and the United States there were strongly religious and puritanical elements in vegetarianism. Dr Graham, described by the nineteenth-century American writer Ralph Waldo Emerson as "the poet of bran bread and pumpkins", advocated not only natural foods but temperance, chastity, hard mattresses, cold showers and cheerfulness at meals. When he was dying he weakened somewhat and accepted stimulants and submitted to a tepid bath.

Vegetarianism is closely connected with the Seventh Day Adventists. Dr J. H. Kellogg, when he was the director of the Battle Creek Sanitarium in Michigan towards the end of the nineteenth

Grapefruit has no magic properties, although some people believe that eating a grapefruit before a meal will burn up all the calories they'll consume afterwards.

Zen Macrobiotics are based on the traditional diet of the vegetarian Zen Buddhist monks in Japan (right). Unfortunately the diet has too often been taken to extremes, notably by Western youth in the 1960s, until the devotee has finished up on an unnourishing diet exclusively of brown rice. Such a diet inevitably leads to malnutrition. Zen Macrobiotics in fact recognizes the importance of vegetables in the diet and even considers small amounts of fish and poultry to be acceptable secondary foods.

century, invented eighty or more grain and peanut products to give variety to the patients' vegetarian diet. These included peanut butter and cornflakes, the basis of the vast food industry developed by his brother, W. K. Kellogg.

One of the pioneers of the vegetarian movement in Britain was the nineteenth-century Scot Dr George Cheyne, who was disgustingly obese. When he reached thirty-two stones (203 kg) he decided that something must be done, and for several months he adopted a light diet of vegetables and milk. Of course he lost weight, but this was because he was eating less, not because he had given up meat. In fact many of the claims for all kinds of diets are more likely to be arguments against overeating.

Some food cults concentrate on the eating of raw vegetarian foods. The twentieth-century Swiss physician Dr Bircher-Benner did so because he held that all heating of food was bad.

Many modern fads are connected with the obsession to be thin. Various foods—peanuts, honey, bananas and milk—have their bigoted disciples. The myth attached to grapefruit is the most odd; to it is attributed the magical quality of burning up fat inside the body. Even seemingly reasonable people believe this.

Americans are particularly susceptible to fad diets and their commercial exploitation is one of the country's great growth industries. The Germans are not far behind, and some of their cults are based on American fads. In the 1950s the American "Separating Diet" fad was introduced into Germany. Various foods could not be mixed, and had to be taken separately in three meals a day: one of milk, vegetables and fruit; one of starchy foods; and one of such protein foods as meat and eggs. The concept is ridiculous if only because many natural foods contain all three types

of nutrient. The "Point Diet" was introduced in the late 1960s and had some resemblance to the "Drinking Man's Diet" in the United States. It was high in fat and alcohol and low in vegetables and fruits, so cutting down the intake of vitamins and minerals.

The United States Food and Drug Administration blames the addiction of Americans to food cults on four "myths" which are said to have misled the American public. These are that faulty diet is the cause of all disease; that foods are over-processed; that chemical fertilizers are bad for health; and that depletion of the soil leads to malnutrition.

Yet in each of those "myths" there is some truth. A faulty diet is likely to cause ill health. Food is overprocessed to the point of boredom, if nothing more. Chemical fertilizers and depletion of the soil do affect the composition of foods. It is the irrational conclusions drawn from such facts that make people fall prey to health quacks and commercial operators, who make fortunes out of the fears of the gullible.

"It would be a good deal better for these people", said the British nutrition expert Sir Jack Drummond, who became well known during the Second World War, "if they would adopt a simple and more rational diet in their everyday life." But a "simple diet" must not involve restricting the variety of foods eaten, as Dr William Stark demonstrated. In 1769 he set out to discover whether "a pleasant and varied diet is equally conducive to health with a more strict and simple one". The simple diets he chose included bread and water for two weeks, bread, water and sugar for a month, bread and olive oil, and finally honey puddings and Cheshire cheese. The honey pudding and Cheshire cheese diet was his last because after suffering from scurvy and digestive troubles for six months he died at the age of thirty. One obituary notice read that "he fell a victim to his enthusiasm".

There could be no clearer evidence of the need for eating as wide a range of foods as possible. In such a diet the only restraint to be exercised is in the amount you eat.

THE GOOD INGREDIENTS

"NOTHING TO EAT BUT FOOD" runs one line of a nineteenth-century poem called *The Pessimist*, and what a fantastic choice that still gives us. But the staple food of most of the world is derived from a handful of grasses. Grains, therefore, which are plentiful and nutritious, have pride of place among the good ingredients.

The climate of the part of the world in which we live usually decides what grains we eat. In temperate climates they will be mainly wheat and rye, with some oats and barley. In the tropics and subtropics they will be rice, maize and millet. Only from wheat and rye can a good bread flour be obtained; the other crops are eaten as grains, or are ground to make gruels and porridges or flat breads.

Whatever the grain, and however it is eaten, it is the cheapest and most important source of our energy. But because we eat grain products in large amounts they also contribute a fair proportion of the proteins we require.

The major sources of protein in Western countries are animal products. These foods are high in good-quality protein, but whereas there is comparatively little fat in most fish and poultry, there is a substantial amount in meat and only a small proportion of it is polyunsaturated. So while meat can be considered to be among the good ingredients, except by vegetarians, most people who can afford it probably eat too much of it.

The importance given to meat in Western diets is curious considering that the choice of meat is limited almost to the point of monotony; beef, lamb, pork and chicken—only a minority of people venture beyond these. By comparison plants can give an infinite variety of natural flavours to a diet, without the need of elaborate artifice by the cook.

Some vegetables that are dug out of the ground rate as staple foods in many parts of the world. These include potatoes, yams, cassava, taro and sweet potatoes, all of which are rich in carbohydrates. Other roots and tubers—carrots, turnips, swedes, parsnips, beetroots, Jerusalem artichokes—provide sweetness and different flavours. They are invaluable, too, because they can be stored for use in the winter. They are not particularly rich in vitamins, but these can be found in greater profusion in leaf vegetables and brassicas. Cabbage, kale, turnip tops, broccoli and spinach are, above all, good sources of vitamin C.

The onion family is in a class of its own among vegetables, and has been for thousands of years. Quite why is not clear. A boiled onion contains precious little protein, even less fat, few calories and only a token amount of vitamins. Even its showing on minerals is only fair and is beaten hands down by celery. In spite of that it is hard to envisage a diet that lacks the flavour of onions. Substituting ethyl thiocyanate for real onions and diallyl disulphide for garlic is a bad second best.

Delicious and satisfying, the seeds and pods of leguminous plants—peas, beans and lentils—are rich in protein and can help us to escape from our overdependence on meat. They are also delicious and satisfying, either fresh in summer or dried in winter.

Stalks and shoots—asparagus, globe artichokes, seakale and, of course, celery—give us some of the most delicate and desirable flavours. The fruits of vegetable plants—tomatoes, courgettes, aubergines, peppers, cucumbers and avocados—contribute pleasure as well as nutrients to the diet. For the overfed tomatoes have the negative virtue of being low in carbohydrate, while avocados and olives are unique among fruits in having up to seventeen per cent fat, instead of the usual trace amount.

There are many vegetables that can be eaten raw, thus avoiding the loss of nutrients in cooking. They add variety to the established salad plants— the inevitable lettuce and cress, chicory and endive, or to the more unusually encountered dandelion, corn salad and celtuce.

Without doubt vegetables rank high among the good ingredients. There is one great drawback. They are never as good, either in food value or in flavour, when you buy them as when they were freshly harvested. The answer is to grow your own vegetables.

If you can grow some fruit as well, so much the better but, unfortunately, few people can or do. In Britain on average a miserable one and a half ounces (43 g) of fruit per person is grown in gardens or allotments, and rhubarb accounts for a fair proportion of that. In fact, the average Briton eats little more than one and a half pounds (about $\frac{3}{4}$ kg) of fruit a week. He would be healthier, livelier and slimmer if only he could be persuaded to abandon starchy, sugar-saturated desserts in favour of fruit, preferably uncooked.

Completing the cornucopia of good ingredients are herbs, spices and flavourings. Tactfully used they will enhance or complement the flavours of other foods. Although chemists can identify and imitate their flavours, the imitations are but crude approximations of the originals.

It would be pointless taking all the care in the world to eat wholesome food if we swilled it down with poison. With the proliferation of synthetic soft drinks and bad beers there is every opportunity to do so.

Furthermore, as Socrates used to remind his pupils, we should eat only when we are hungry and stop long before we feel bloated. The Christian grace before meals could well be changed to make us truly thankful for what we are about to receive—in moderation.

THE WORLD WE KNOW TODAY could not have come into existence without grain; no other food could have supported such vast populations. The six main crops—wheat, rice, rye, oats, maize and barley—would provide enough grain, if shared out equally, for each person in the world to have nearly six hundred pounds (270 kg) a year. Western town dwellers may take their bread and pasta for granted, but to the peasant the grain harvest is as worthy of veneration as it was to the ancients.

Of all the grains wheat is the most venerable and valuable. Although barley is as ancient it is not so widely used, and rice has a shorter history. Only rye approaches wheat as a bread grain.

From the wild species of wheat that evolved at the end of the last Ice Age came the first cultivated wheat, einkhorn, and the first bread wheat, emmer. Selective breeding of emmer has produced today's two great wheats—*Triticum aestivum*, which, in its thousands of varieties, is the wheat used in bread making, and *Triticum durum*, the basis of pasta.

A field of ripe wheat is staggeringly beautiful, but totally inedible. Before humans can digest it the grain has to be threshed to separate it from the stalks and chaff, and then milled and cooked.

In milling the first of a succession of rollers breaks open the whole grain and the outer coat is sifted out. What is left is then passed through more rollers, each grinding being followed by a sifting. The fineness of the sieve decides the so-called extraction rate, which is simply the percentage of the original wheat that remains in the flour. If nothing, not even the coarse bran, is sieved out, the extraction rate is one hundred per cent and the flour is used for wholewheat bread. Other brown bread is baked from flour with extraction rates of between eighty and ninety per cent. The whitest bread has an extraction rate of about seventy-two per cent. Usually all bread, except wholewheat, is enriched with calcium, iron, niacin and thiamine.

Most people prefer white bread. Yet brown bread is certainly more nutritious because it contains more protein, fat, iron, thiamine, riboflavin and niacin. Protagonists of white bread point out that wholewheat bread has more indigestible fibre and that the phytic acid in the fibre combines with the calcium in the flour to prevent the absorption of calcium in the intestine. The brown-bread supporters retort that roughage is good for you, that it is far cheaper eaten in bread than in breakfast cereals, and that in any event the amount of bread we eat does not raise phytic acid to dangerous levels. Actually the choice between brown and white bread is usually made as a matter of taste, and there is no reason why we should not enjoy the flavours and textures of both.

To taste bread as it should be, however, you should make your own. Most of the bread sold in shops is made by a process in which a prefermented brew is mixed into the flour by blades working at very high speeds. The operation takes about sixty seconds and produces a continuous stream of oven-ready dough. Such technologically processed bread can be relied on not to vary greatly from day to day.

Home-baked bread has no such uniformity. Two people making bread according to the same recipe are liable to produce loaves of widely different taste and texture, each having an individual character that is totally lacking in mass-produced, sliced and wrapped bread.

The magic ingredient, shared by wheat and rye

a head of durum wheat

a head of bread wheat

a head of English wheat

flour, is gluten, a complex of two proteins, which becomes viscous when water is added and so produces a dough. The dough is made to rise by the use of carbon dioxide, traditionally produced by the slow fermentation of yeast; the trapped bubbles of gas are responsible for the mass of small holes in the bread. Kneading stretches the gluten fibres and this, combined with the action of carbon dioxide gas, gives the dough elasticity and a fine, smooth texture.

Soft water gives a better dough than hard water, which slows down the fermentation of the yeast. Salt may make a dough sticky but, on the other hand, it gives flavour and helps to form a crisp crust.

STRUCTURE OF WHOLEWHEAT

The germ, or seed, of a wheat grain is nourished by a starchy endosperm and protected by a coat of indigestible fibre, or bran. In the milling of wholewheat flour the bran and germ are retained; wholewheat bread, therefore, provides roughage and is a good source of B vitamins and iron as well as starch. White flour is often fortified with nutrients.

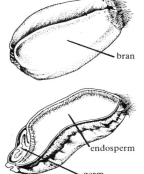

bran

endosperm

germ

The Nutrients in Wheat
Wheat contains more protein than any other cereal and is high in calories. Three and a half ounces (100 g) provide about 330 Calories.

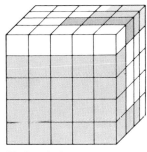

Carbohydrate	70 %
Protein	13.5
Water	10
Fat	3
Vitamins and minerals	2
Fibre	1.5

Wheat is a versatile grain. From the harvested wheat can come a great variety of products.

Wheat can be bought not only in its processed forms but also as a whole grain. The grain must be cooked in water or other liquid before it can be eaten.

Pasta in its simplest form is made from semolina and water. Semolina is the endosperm removed from coarsely ground durum wheat. Pasta comes in innumerable shapes, from tubular macaroni to flat lasagne.

Ready-to-eat cereals are made from wheat grains that have been cooked as they are processed. To make good the nutrient losses in processing, some cereals are enriched with vitamins, iron or protein. The high-gluten content of wheat makes it the best cereal grain for bread-making. The type of bread made depends upon the variety of wheat used and the amount of bran and germ removed in the manufacture of the flour.

THERE IS SOMETHING immensely gratifying about producing a loaf of bread, from kneading the dough and seeing it rise to finally removing the baked loaf from the oven, brown, crusty and fragrant.

The basic ingredients for bread-making are flour, yeast, salt and water or milk.

FLOUR

Use strong white flour, made from hard wheat which has a high gluten content, for the lightest bread; and wholewheat, granary or rye flour for the tastiest. Gluten absorbs liquid and makes the dough strong and expansile. Bread made only with wholewheat or rye flour is rather heavy textured, while a mixture of wholewheat or rye and strong white flour produces a lighter loaf with a rich colour and flavour. Plain white or self-raising flour are unsuitable for bread-making because they are made from soft wheat and lack the gluten necessary to make good bread.

YEAST

Yeast is a living organism which grows when it is provided with warmth and moisture. As it grows it produces carbon dioxide, which causes the bread dough to rise.

Fresh yeast is available from some bakers and health-food shops. It looks like pale cream-coloured putty and should be smooth and moist. It can be stored in a sealed polythene bag in the refrigerator for up to two weeks, or in the freezer for up to one year.

Dried yeast, which is widely available, must be reconstituted before it can be used in bread-making. Dissolve one teaspoon of sugar in a little tepid water, then add the yeast. Leave it in a warm, draught-free place for ten to twenty minutes, or until the mixture becomes frothy. Dried yeast will keep for up to six months if it is stored in an airtight container in a cool place.

When substituting dried yeast for fresh yeast, two teaspoons of dried yeast equal one half ounce of fresh yeast.

Although yeast is the most commonly used raising agent, or leavening, baking powder, sour milk or bicarbonate of soda are also used.

SALT

A little salt, about two teaspoons to every pound of flour, is added to improve the flavour of the bread. Too much salt will, however, slow down the growth of the yeast.

LIQUID

The liquid used to bind the dough is usually water, but milk or a mixture of milk and water may be used. Always use tepid liquid—if it is too hot it will kill the yeast—and add it all at one time. Extra flour may be added if the dough is too sticky.

A batter may be made from the yeast, the liquid and one-third of the flour specified in the recipe. Leave the mixture to stand for twenty minutes, or until it is puffed up and frothy, then add the rest of the flour with the other ingredients. This method of incorporating the yeast is best suited to enriched doughs.

ENRICHED DOUGH

Fat, molasses or honey, malt and eggs may also be added to bread dough. Butter or oil improves the flavour of bread and helps it to stay fresh longer, but polyunsaturated margarine, which has the same effect, can always be substituted. Molasses, honey and malt also add flavour and give the bread a good, dark colour. Eggs may be added to bread dough to give it a yellow colour and a rich flavour.

MIXING THE DOUGH

Put the flour and salt into a mixing bowl. Make a well in the flour and pour in the yeast liquid, then stir thoroughly with a wooden spoon. Continue to bind the dough with your hands until it comes away cleanly from the sides of the bowl.

KNEADING

Thorough kneading of the dough is very important to develop the elasticity of the gluten. Turn the dough out on to a lightly floured surface and knead by lifting and folding one end of the dough towards you into the centre, then pushing it down and away from you with the heel of your hand. Give the dough a quarter turn after each fold and continue kneading for ten minutes, or until the dough is firm and elastic and no longer sticks to your hands.

RISING

Shape the dough into a ball and put it into a lightly greased bowl. To prevent the dough from drying out while it is rising, cover it lightly with greased polythene. Alternatively, grease the inside of a large polythene bag with oil, and put the dough into it.

Leave the dough to rise in a warm place until it has doubled in bulk and springs back into shape if you press it lightly with a floured finger.

In a warm place the dough will rise in forty-five to sixty minutes. At room temperature it will take about two hours, in a cool larder it will take twelve hours and in a refrigerator it will take about twenty-four hours.

Dough that has risen in the cold should be brought back to room temperature before it is knocked back.

KNOCKING BACK

When the dough has risen, knead it again for two to three minutes to knock out the air bubbles and to reduce the dough to its original size.

SHAPING

Roll the dough up, or shape it into a rectangle by folding each side under, to fit into a loaf tin. The dough should come no higher than halfway up the sides of the tin.

Alternatively, the dough may be formed into a variety of shapes such as a cottage loaf, a round cob, a plait, a French loaf or individual rolls and placed on a greased baking sheet.

PROVING

After shaping the dough, cover it lightly with greased polythene and leave it to rise in a

MAKING BREAD DOUGH

Make a well in the flour and pour in the yeast liquid.

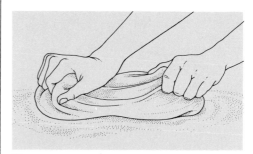

Knead the dough; push away with the heel of the hand.

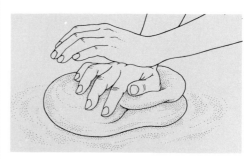

Lift and fold the end of the dough towards you. Repeat.

Leave the dough in a warm place to double in bulk.

warm place for twenty to thirty minutes, or until it has doubled in bulk or has reached the top of the loaf tin.

GLAZES AND FINISHES
The top of the loaf may be left plain, dusted with flour to give a soft crust, or glazed with beaten egg mixed with a little milk to give a shiny crust. A saltwater glaze gives a crisp, hard crust. The loaf may also be sprinkled with cracked wheat, sesame or poppy seeds.

BAKING
Bread must be baked in a very hot, pre-heated oven. A shallow baking tin filled with water and placed in the bottom of the oven hardens the crust and improves the texture of the bread.

Bread is done when it shrinks slightly from the sides of the tin and sounds hollow when it is removed from the tin and tapped sharply with the knuckles underneath. Leave the loaf on a wire rack until it is cool.

STORAGE
Risen dough may be wrapped in a greased polythene bag and stored in the refrigerator for a couple of days before it is shaped and baked.

Baked loaves must be thoroughly cooled before being stored in a covered, but venti-lated, container.

FREEZING
Risen or unrisen dough may be frozen, but it is advisable to use fifty per cent more yeast than is given in the recipe.

Place the dough in a greased polythene bag, insert a straw into the opening and suck out the air before sealing the bag.

Unrisen, plain dough may be frozen for two months and enriched dough for one month. Risen dough may be frozen for up to one month.

Baked, plain bread may be frozen for one month and enriched bread for two months. The bread must be left to cool thoroughly before being wrapped in foil or sealed in a polythene bag.

Basic Bread
Wholewheat flour, white flour or a mixture of flours may be used for this easy-to-make traditional bread.

In a large bowl mix 1½ pounds (750 g) of wholewheat flour and 1 tablespoon (15 ml) of salt. Add ½ ounce (15 g) of margarine or butter and rub it into the flour.

Blend ½ ounce (15 g) of fresh yeast with ¾ pint (450 ml) of tepid water until the yeast has dissolved. Make a well in the flour and pour in the yeast liquid. Mix the ingredients together until they form a firm dough. After the initial stirring with a wooden spoon it is best to bind the dough with your hands.

Turn the dough out on to a lightly floured surface. Knead the dough well for 10 minutes, or until it becomes firm and elastic and no longer sticks to your fingers.

Lightly grease a large bowl. Shape the dough into a ball and put it into the bowl. Cover the bowl with greased polythene and leave the dough in a warm place to rise for 45 to 60 minutes, or until it has doubled in bulk.

When the dough has risen, turn it out on to a floured surface and knead it again for 2 to 3 minutes. Shape the dough into a loaf and place it in a well-greased 2-pound (1-kg) loaf tin or 2 smaller tins.

Preheat the oven to 450°F (230°C, Gas Mark 8).

Cover the tin with greased polythene. Leave the dough to rise in a warm place for 20 to 30 minutes, or until it has risen to the top of the tin.

Remove the polythene. Bake the loaf in the centre of the oven. If overbrowning after 15 minutes, lower the oven temperature to 400°F (200°C, Gas Mark 6) and continue baking for 15 to 25 minutes more.

Remove the loaf from the oven and turn it out of the tin. Tap the base of the loaf. If it sounds hollow it is ready. Leave the loaf on a wire rack to cool.

INGREDIENTS TO MAKE ONE LARGE LOAF:
1½ lb (750 g) wholewheat flour
1 tablespoon (15 ml) salt
½ oz (15 g) margarine or butter
½ oz (15 g) fresh yeast
¾ pint (450 ml) tepid water

Granary Loaf
This wholesome wholewheat bread contains cracked wheat, wheat germ and malt which give the loaf its grainy texture and rich flavour.

In a large bowl mix 10 ounces (350 g) of wholewheat flour with 10 ounces (350 g) of strong white flour and 1 tablespoon (15 ml) of salt.

Add ½ ounce (15 g) of margarine or butter to the flour and rub it in. Add ¼ pound (100 g) of cracked wheat and 2 ounces (50 g) of wheat germ to the flour and mix well.

In a bowl blend ½ ounce (15 g) of fresh yeast with ¾ pint (450 ml) of tepid water and milk until the yeast has dissolved. Make a well in the flour and pour in the yeast liquid. Add 2 tablespoons (30 ml) of malt to the flour and mix to a soft dough.

Turn the dough out on to a floured surface and knead it well for 10 minutes, or until it becomes firm and elastic and is no longer sticky.

Lightly grease a large bowl. Put the dough into the bowl and cover with greased polythene. Leave the dough in a warm place to rise for 45 to 60 minutes, or until it has doubled in bulk.

When the dough has risen, knead it again for 2 to 3 minutes. Divide the dough in half and shape each half into a round loaf. Place the loaves on a greased baking sheet. Sprinkle 1 ounce (25 g) of cracked wheat over the loaves.

Preheat the oven to 425°F (220°C, Gas Mark 7).

Cover the baking sheet with greased polythene and leave the dough in a warm place to rise for 20 to 30 minutes, or until the dough has doubled in bulk.

Remove the polythene. Bake the loaves for 15 minutes. Lower the oven temperature to 375°F (190°C, Gas Mark 5) and continue baking for 20 to 25 minutes more.

Remove the loaves from the oven. Tap the base of each loaf. If they sound hollow the bread is ready. Cool the loaves on a wire rack.

INGREDIENTS TO MAKE TWO SMALL LOAVES:
10 oz (350 g) wholewheat flour
10 oz (350 g) strong white flour
1 tablespoon (15 ml) salt
½ oz (15 g) margarine or butter
5 oz (125 g) cracked wheat
2 oz (50 g) wheat germ
½ oz (15 g) fresh yeast
¾ pint (450 ml) tepid water and milk
2 tablespoons (30 ml) malt

Muffins

The muffin man was once a familiar sight in English streets, selling fresh muffins hot from the oven. Today muffins are less easy to buy, but fortunately these unsweetened, soft, round buns are simple to make at home. Serve the muffins hot and spread with butter, or split them in half and toast them.

Put 1 pound (500 g) of strong white flour into a mixing bowl with 1 teaspoon (5 ml) of salt. Blend ½ ounce (15 g) of fresh yeast with ½ pint (300 ml) of warm milk until the yeast has dissolved. Make a well in the centre of the flour and pour in the yeast liquid. Mix the ingredients together to form a soft dough.

Turn the dough out on to a floured surface and knead it well for 10 minutes, or until it becomes firm and elastic and is no longer sticky.

Lightly grease a large bowl. Put the dough into the bowl and cover with greased polythene. Leave the dough to rise in a warm place for 45 to 60 minutes, or until it has doubled in bulk.

When the dough has risen, knead it again for 2 to 3 minutes. Roll the dough out until it is about ½ inch (1 cm) thick. Cut 3-inch (8-cm) rounds out of the dough and put them on a floured baking sheet. Dust the rounds with flour and leave them to rise in a warm place for 20 to 30 minutes.

Cook the muffins gently on a griddle or in a large greased frying-pan for about 5 minutes on each side, or until they are golden brown. Alternatively, preheat the oven to 400°F (200°C, Gas Mark 6) and bake them for 15 to 20 minutes.

INGREDIENTS TO MAKE TWELVE MUFFINS:
1 lb (500 g) strong white flour
1 teaspoon (5 ml) salt
½ oz (15 g) fresh yeast
½ pint (300 ml) warm milk

Garlic Herb French Stick

Put 1½ pounds (750 g) of strong white flour into a large mixing bowl with 1 tablespoon (15 ml) of salt.

Blend ½ ounce (15 g) of fresh yeast with ¾ pint (450 ml) of tepid water until the yeast has dissolved. Make a well in the flour and pour in the yeast liquid. Mix the ingredients together to form a firm dough.

Turn the dough out on to a floured surface and knead it well for 10 minutes, or until the dough becomes firm and elastic and is no longer sticky.

Lightly grease a large bowl. Put the dough into the bowl and cover with greased polythene. Leave the dough to rise in a warm place for 45 to 60 minutes, or until it has doubled in bulk.

Meanwhile soften 4 ounces (100 g) of margarine or butter in a bowl. Add 3 or 4 finely chopped garlic cloves (depending on taste), 1 tablespoon (15 ml) of dried mixed herbs and 1 tablespoon (15 ml) of chopped parsley to the butter and mix well.

When the dough has risen, turn it out on to a floured surface and knead it again for 2 to 3 minutes. Divide the dough in two and roll each half out to form an oval as long as a baking sheet, about 14 by 10 inches (35 by 25 cm).

Spread half of the prepared butter mixture on each piece of dough, leaving a 1-inch (2-cm) margin all around the edges. Roll each oval up tightly lengthways and seal the edges.

Preheat the oven to 425°F (220°C, Gas Mark 7).

Place the loaves with the seams underneath on a well-greased baking sheet. Make diagonal slits into the top of the loaves at 2-inch (5-cm) intervals. Cover the baking sheet with greased polythene and leave the dough to rise in a warm place for 20 to 30 minutes.

Remove the polythene from the loaves. For a crisp crust, brush the loaves with 1 teaspoon (5 ml) of salt dissolved in 4 tablespoons (60 ml) of water.

Bake the loaves for 15 minutes, or until they are crisp and golden brown. Remove the loaves from the oven. Tap the base of each loaf. If they sound hollow the bread is ready. Serve the bread immediately or leave the loaves on a wire rack to cool.

INGREDIENTS TO MAKE TWO FRENCH STICKS:
1½ lb (750 g) strong white flour
salt
½ oz (15 g) fresh yeast
¾ pint (450 ml) tepid water
4 oz (100 g) margarine or butter
3 or 4 garlic cloves
1 tablespoon (15 ml) dried mixed herbs
1 tablespoon (15 ml) chopped parsley

ADDING FLAVOUR TO FRENCH LOAVES

Spread the filling over the dough and roll it up.

Franciscan Pizza

Put ½ pound (250 g) of strong white flour and 1 teaspoon (5 ml) of salt into a mixing bowl. Blend ¼ ounce (10 g) of fresh yeast with ¼ pint (150 ml) of tepid water until the yeast has dissolved. Make a well in the flour and pour in the yeast liquid. Mix the ingredients together until they form a firm dough.

Turn the dough out on to a floured surface and knead it well for 10 minutes, or until the dough becomes firm and elastic and is no longer sticky.

Lightly grease a large bowl. Put the dough into the bowl and cover with greased polythene. Leave the dough to rise in a warm place for 45 to 60 minutes, or until it has doubled in bulk.

Meanwhile, heat 1 tablespoon (15 ml) of corn oil in a frying-pan. Add ½ pound (250 g) of sliced onions to the pan and fry gently for 5 minutes, or until they are soft. Remove the onions from the pan, add a little more oil if necessary and fry 3 ounces (75 g) of sliced mushrooms for 2 minutes. Thinly slice 3 ounces (75 g) of salami, 2 blanched and peeled tomatoes and 2 ounces (50 g) of Bel Paese or Mozzarella cheese.

When the dough has risen, turn it out on to a lightly floured surface and knead it for 2 to 3 minutes. Roll out the dough to form a 9-inch (23-cm) round and put it on a greased baking sheet.

Preheat the oven to 425°F (220°C, Gas Mark 7).

Spread the cooked onions over the dough and arrange the slices of salami around the edge. Put the cooked mushrooms over the onions, cover them with the tomato slices and top the tomatoes with the cheese. Sprinkle with 1 teaspoon (5 ml) of dried oregano and freshly ground black pepper. Leave the pizza to rise for 15 minutes in a warm place.

Bake the pizza for 20 to 25 minutes, or until it has risen and is lightly browned around the edges.

INGREDIENTS TO MAKE ONE 9-INCH (23-CM) PIZZA:
½ lb (250 g) strong white flour
1 teaspoon (5 ml) salt
¼ ounce (10 g) fresh yeast
¼ pint (150 ml) tepid water
1 tablespoon (15 ml) corn oil
½ lb (250 g) onions
3 oz (75 g) mushrooms
3 oz (75 g) salami
2 tomatoes
2 oz (50 g) Bel Paese or Mozzarella cheese
1 teaspoon (5 ml) dried oregano
freshly ground black pepper

Orange Savarin

In a large bowl mix together 1 ounce (25 g) of white flour, ½ ounce (15 g) of fresh yeast and ¼ pint (150 ml) of warm milk. Leave the bowl in a warm place for about 20 minutes, or until the mixture has become puffed up and frothy.

Add ¼ pound (100 g) of white flour, ¼ teaspoon (1 ml) of salt, 1 tablespoon (15 ml) of castor sugar, 1 beaten egg and 1 ounce (25 g) of softened margarine or butter to the yeast mixture and beat for 3 minutes.

Preheat the oven to 400 F (200 C, Gas Mark 6).

Grease a 7-inch (18-cm) or 1½-pint (850-ml) ring mould and spoon the mixture into it. Cover the mould with greased polythene and leave the mixture to rise in a warm place for 20 to 30 minutes, or until it almost reaches the top of the tin. Remove the polythene.

Bake the savarin for 20 to 25 minutes, or until it is firm and golden brown.

Remove the savarin from the oven and allow it to cool for 5 minutes before turning it out on to a serving dish. Prick all over with a fork.

Add 2 tablespoons of rum to ¾ pint (450 ml) of orange juice and pour this mixture over the still warm savarin. Leave the savarin to cool.

Warm 3 tablespoons (45 ml) of honey and brush it over the savarin.

Peel and remove the pith from 3 oranges and cut the membrane away from the segments of fruit. Mix the orange segments with ½ pound (250 g) of seedless grapes and pile them into the centre of the savarin.

Prick the savarin then brush it with honey.

INGREDIENTS TO SERVE SIX :
5 oz (125 g) white flour
½ oz (15 g) fresh yeast
¼ pint (150 ml) warm milk
¼ teaspoon (1 ml) salt
1 tablespoon (15 ml) castor sugar
1 egg
1 oz (25 g) margarine or butter
2 tablespoons (30 ml) rum
¾ pint (450 ml) orange juice
3 tablespoons (45 ml) honey
3 oranges
½ lb (250 g) seedless grapes

Savoury Country Loaf

In a large bowl mix together ¾ pound (350 g) of strong white flour, ¾ pound (350 g) of wholewheat flour, 1 tablespoon (15 ml) of salt and a large pinch of pepper. Grate ¼ pound (100 g) of strong Cheddar cheese and mix 3 ounces (75 g) of it into the flour with ¼ pound (100 g) of chopped grilled bacon and 1 tablespoon (15 ml) of chopped sage.

Blend ½ ounce (15 g) of fresh yeast with ¾ pint (450 ml) of tepid water until the yeast has dissolved. Make a well in the dry ingredients and pour in the yeast liquid. Mix the ingredients together until they form a firm dough.

Turn the dough out on to a lightly floured surface and knead it well for 10 minutes, or until it is firm and elastic and is no longer sticky.

Put the dough into a lightly greased bowl and cover with greased polythene. Leave the dough to rise in a warm place for 45 to 60 minutes, or until it has doubled in bulk.

When the dough has risen, turn it out on to a lightly floured surface and knead it for 2 to 3 minutes.

Cut off a quarter of the dough. Shape the larger piece of dough into a ball and place it on a greased baking sheet. Shape the smaller piece of dough into a ball and place it on top of the larger ball. Flour the handle of a wooden spoon and push it through the centre of both balls, then pull it out again quickly.

Preheat the oven to 425°F (220°C, Gas Mark 7).

Cover the baking sheet with greased polythene and leave the dough to rise in a warm place for 20 to 30 minutes, or until it has doubled in bulk.

Sprinkle the loaf with the remaining grated cheese. Bake the loaf for 30 minutes, or until it is well risen, browned and sounds hollow when tapped underneath. Cool the loaf on a wire rack.

INGREDIENTS TO MAKE ONE LARGE LOAF :
¾ lb (350 g) strong white flour
¾ lb (350 g) wholewheat flour
1 tablespoon (15 ml) salt
pepper
¼ lb (100 g) strong Cheddar cheese
¼ lb (100 g) streaky bacon
1 tablespoon (15 ml) chopped sage
½ ounce (15 g) fresh yeast
¾ pint (450 ml) tepid water

Pitta Bread

Pitta is a traditional Middle Eastern bread with a soft white crust and a chewy centre that is ideal for absorbing sauces. The pitta must be baked in a hot oven, where it will puff up with a pocket of air inside. It is often slit in half and the pocket filled with hot kebabs, onions, tomatoes and coriander leaves.

Put 1 pound (500 g) of white flour into a mixing bowl with 1 teaspoon (5 ml) of salt. Dissolve ½ ounce (15 g) of fresh yeast in ½ pint (300 ml) of tepid water. Make a well in the flour and pour in the yeast liquid. Mix the ingredients together until they form a firm dough.

Turn the dough out on to a floured surface and knead it well for 10 minutes, or until the dough becomes firm and elastic and is no longer sticky.

Lightly grease a large bowl. Shape the dough into a ball and put it into the bowl. Brush the dough with oil to prevent it becoming crusty. Cover the bowl with polythene and leave the dough to rise in a warm place for 45 to 60 minutes, or until it has doubled in bulk.

Put 2 greased baking sheets in the oven and preheat the oven to 450°F (230°C, Gas Mark 8).

Turn the risen dough out on to a lightly floured surface and knead it for 2 to 3 minutes. Divide the dough into 6 pieces. Dust each piece with flour and roll it out to form an oval approximately 8 by 5 inches (20 by 13 cm) and ¼ inch (6 mm) thick. Put the pieces of dough on a floured board and dust them with flour.

Cover the dough with greased polythene and leave to rise in a warm place for 20 to 30 minutes.

Remove the polythene and transfer the pitta rapidly to the hot baking sheets. Bake for about 10 minutes, or until the pitta are just beginning to turn light brown. If the oven and baking sheets are not very hot, the pitta will not puff up as they should.

INGREDIENTS TO MAKE SIX PITTA :
1 lb (500 g) white flour
1 teaspoon (5 ml) salt
½ oz (15 g) fresh yeast
½ pint (300 ml) tepid water

Chelsea Buns

Traditionally these buns are placed so that they stick together when baked and have to be pulled apart for serving.

In a large bowl beat together 2 ounces (50 g) of strong white flour, ½ ounce (15 g) of fresh yeast and 4 fluid ounces (100 ml) of warm milk. Leave the bowl in a warm place for 20 to 30 minutes, or until the mixture becomes puffed up and frothy.

Meanwhile in another bowl mix 6 ounces (200 g) of strong white flour with ½ teaspoon (2·5 ml) of salt and ½ teaspoon (2·5 ml) of sugar. Add 1 ounce (25 g) of margarine or butter and rub it into the flour.

When the yeast batter is frothy, stir in 1 beaten egg and the flour mixture. Mix the ingredients well until they form a dough.

Turn the dough out on to a lightly floured surface and knead it well for 10 minutes, or until it becomes firm and elastic and is no longer sticky.

Put the dough into a lightly greased bowl and cover with greased polythene. Leave the dough to rise in a warm place for 45 to 60 minutes, or until it has doubled in bulk.

When the dough has risen, turn it out on to a floured surface and knead it again for 2 to 3 minutes. Roll the dough out to form an oblong about 12 by 9 inches (30 by 23 cm). Melt 1 ounce (25 g) of margarine or butter and brush it over the dough.

In a small bowl combine ¼ pound (100 g) of chopped mixed dried fruit, 2 ounces (50 g) of soft brown sugar and 1 teaspoon (5 ml) of ground mixed spice. Sprinkle this mixture evenly over the dough.

Roll the dough up lengthwise to form a neat long sausage. Cut the sausage into 9 equal pieces and lay them flat and close together on a greased baking sheet or in a greased cake tin.

Preheat the oven to 400°F (200°C, Gas Mark 6).

Cover the baking sheet with greased polythene and leave the dough to rise in a warm place for 20 to 30 minutes, or until it has doubled in bulk.

Remove the polythene. Bake the buns for 20 to 30 minutes, or until they have risen and are golden brown. Put the buns on a wire rack to cool.

INGREDIENTS TO MAKE NINE BUNS :
½ lb (250 g) strong white flour
½ oz (15 g) fresh yeast
4 fl oz (100 ml) warm milk
½ teaspoon (2.5 ml) salt
½ teaspoon (2.5 ml) sugar
2 oz (50 g) margarine or butter
1 egg
¼ lb (100 g) mixed dried fruit
2 oz (50 g) soft brown sugar
1 teaspoon (5 ml) ground mixed spice

Apple Cinnamon Braid

This attractive braid, filled with apples, sultanas and hazelnuts, can be served warm or cold.

In a large bowl beat together 2 ounces (50 g) of strong white flour, ½ ounce (15 g) of fresh yeast and 4 fluid ounces (100 ml) of warm milk. Put the bowl in a warm place for 20 to 30 minutes, or until the mixture has become puffed up and frothy.

In another bowl combine 6 ounces (200 g) of strong white flour with 2 teaspoons (10 ml) of ground cinnamon, ½ teaspoon (2·5 ml) of salt and 1 ounce (25 g) of castor sugar. Add 1 ounce (25 g) of margarine or butter and rub it into the flour mixture.

Stir 1 beaten egg and the flour mixture into the frothy yeast batter to form a dough.

Turn the dough out on to a lightly floured board and knead it well for 10 minutes, or until it becomes firm and elastic and is no longer sticky.

Lightly grease a bowl. Put the dough into the bowl and cover with greased polythene. Leave the dough to rise in a warm place for 45 to 60 minutes, or until it has doubled in bulk.

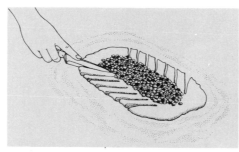

Make diagonal cuts along the sides of the dough.

Lift the short sides of the dough over the filling.

Braid the cut strips of dough over the filling.

Meanwhile peel, core and slice 1 pound (500 g) of cooking apples. Put the apple slices into a small saucepan. Add the grated rind and juice of ½ lemon, ¼ pound (100 g) of sultanas, 2 ounces (50 g) of soft brown sugar and 2 ounces (50 g) of coarsely chopped hazelnuts. Cover the pan and cook gently for 5 minutes, or until the apples are just tender. Remove the pan from the heat and allow the mixture to cool.

When the dough has risen, turn it out on to a floured board and knead it again for 2 to 3 minutes. Roll the dough out to form an oblong about 12 by 9 inches (30 by 23 cm).

Spread the prepared apple mixture down the centre of the dough not quite to the short ends, leaving a 3-inch (8-cm) margin of dough on each long side. With a sharp knife, make 2-inch (5-cm) diagonal cuts, 1 inch (2 cm) apart, into the longer margins. Lift the shorter sides and fold them over the filling. To make the braid start at one end, take a strip of dough from each side alternately and cross it over the filling. Continue along the sides until all the dough has been braided and the filling is just visible between the plaits.

Preheat the oven to 400°F (200°C, Gas Mark 6).

Put the braid on a greased baking sheet and cover with greased polythene. Leave the braid to rise in a warm place for 20 to 30 minutes, or until it has doubled in bulk.

Remove the polythene. Bake the braid for 30 minutes, or until it is golden brown. Remove the braid from the oven and tap the bottom. If it sounds hollow it is ready. Put the braid on a wire rack to cool.

INGREDIENTS TO MAKE ONE LARGE BRAID :
½ lb (250 g) strong white flour
½ oz (15 g) fresh yeast
4 fl oz (100 ml) warm milk
2 teaspoons (10 ml) ground cinnamon
½ teaspoon (2.5 ml) salt
1 oz (25 g) castor sugar
1 oz (25 g) margarine or butter
1 egg
1 lb (500 g) cooking apples
½ lemon
¼ lb (100 g) sultanas
2 oz (50 g) soft brown sugar
2 oz (50 g) hazelnuts

Kugelhopf

A Viennese speciality, kugelhopf is traditionally baked in a fluted ring mould so that the cake looks very dramatic when turned out, but it may be baked in any equivalent-sized cake tin.

Combine ½ pound (250 g) of white flour, ½ teaspoon (2·5 ml) of salt and 1 tablespoon (15 ml) of castor sugar in a mixing bowl.

Blend ½ ounce (15 g) of fresh yeast with ¼ pint (150 ml) of warm milk until the yeast has dissolved. Make a well in the flour and pour in the yeast liquid with 1 ounce (25 g) of melted margarine or butter and 2 egg yolks. Mix the ingredients well until they form a stiff batter.

Stir the grated rind and juice of 1 orange, ¼ pound (100 g) of raisins and 2 ounces (50 g) of split blanched almonds into the batter. In a small bowl whisk 2 egg whites until they are just stiff and fold them into the mixture.

Brush a 2-pint (1-litre) fluted ring mould with oil and spoon the prepared mixture into it until the mould is three-quarters full.

Preheat the oven to 375 F (190 C, Gas Mark 5).

Cover the mould with greased polythene and leave the mixture to rise in a warm place for 20 to 30 minutes, or until it has risen almost to the top of the mould.

Bake the kugelhopf for about 45 minutes, or until the top is browned.

Remove the cake from the oven and leave it to cool for a few minutes before turning it out on to a wire rack.

When the kugelhopf is cool, dust it with sifted icing sugar.

INGREDIENTS TO SERVE EIGHT:
½ lb (250 g) white flour
½ teaspoon (2.5 ml) salt
1 tablespoon (15 ml) castor sugar
½ oz (15 g) fresh yeast
¼ pint (150 ml) warm milk
1 oz (25 g) margarine or butter
2 eggs
1 orange
¼ lb (100 g) raisins
2 oz (50 g) split blanched almonds
icing sugar

Soda Bread

Bicarbonate of soda is used as the raising agent in this bread.

Preheat the oven to 400 F (200 C, Gas Mark 6).

In a large bowl mix 1 pound (500 g) of white flour with 1 teaspoon (5 ml) of salt, 1 teaspoon (5 ml) of bicarbonate of soda and 1 teaspoon (5 ml) of cream of tartar. Add 1 ounce (25 g) of margarine or butter and rub it into the flour. Make a well in the centre of the flour and pour in ½ pint (300 ml) of buttermilk or milk. Stir the ingredients together to form a soft, spongy dough.

Turn the dough out on to a floured surface and shape it into a large, round loaf or 2 smaller loaves about 2 inches (5 cm) thick. Place the loaf on a greased baking sheet and score the top of the loaf into quarters with a sharp knife.

Bake the loaf for 30 to 35 minutes, or until it is golden brown and sounds hollow when tapped underneath. Place the loaf on a wire rack to cool.

INGREDIENTS TO MAKE ONE LARGE OR TWO SMALL LOAVES:
1 lb (500 g) white flour
1 teaspoon (5 ml) salt
1 teaspoon (5 ml) bicarbonate of soda
1 teaspoon (5 ml) cream of tartar
1 oz (25 g) margarine or butter
½ pint (300 ml) buttermilk or milk

Wholewheat Apricot Plait

In a large bowl mix ½ pound (250 g) of wholewheat flour, ½ pound (250 g) of strong white flour, 1 teaspoon (5 ml) of salt, ¼ pound (100 g) of chopped dried apricots and the grated rind of 1 lemon.

In another bowl blend ½ ounce (15 g) of fresh yeast with ½ pint (300 ml) of warm milk until the yeast has dissolved. Make a well in the flour and pour in the yeast mixture, 2 tablespoons (30 ml) of honey and 2 ounces (50 g) of melted margarine or butter. Mix the ingredients together until they form a firm dough.

Turn the dough out on to a floured surface and knead it well for 10 minutes, or until it becomes firm and elastic and is no longer sticky.

Lightly grease a large bowl. Put the dough into the bowl and cover with greased polythene. Leave the dough to rise in a warm place for 45 to 60 minutes, or until it has doubled in bulk.

When the dough has risen, turn it out on to a lightly floured surface and knead it again for 2 to 3 minutes. Shape the dough into a sausage about 12 inches (30 cm) long. Cut it into 3 equal strands, leaving them joined at one end. Plait the strands of dough and pinch the ends together. Turn

the ends under the plait. Place the plait on a greased baking sheet.

Preheat the oven to 425 F (220 C, Gas Mark 7).

Cover the baking sheet with greased polythene and leave the plait to rise in a warm place for 20 to 30 minutes, or until it has doubled in bulk.

Brush the plait with milk and sprinkle it with 2 tablespoons (30 ml) of cracked wheat. Bake the plait for about 30 minutes, or until it is golden and sounds hollow when tapped underneath. Cool on a wire rack.

INGREDIENTS TO MAKE ONE LARGE PLAIT:
½ lb (250 g) wholewheat flour
½ lb (250 g) strong white flour
1 teaspoon (5 ml) salt
¼ lb (100 g) dried apricots
1 lemon
½ oz (15 g) fresh yeast
½ pint (300 ml) warm milk
2 tablespoons (30 ml) honey
2 oz (50 g) margarine or butter
2 tablespoons (30 ml) cracked wheat

MAKING A PLAIT

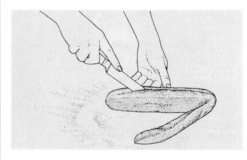

Cut the dough into three strands joined at one end.

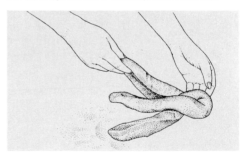

Cross the strands one over another alternately.

To make good pastry you require a light hand, a cool kitchen and cool ingredients (except for such pastry as suet crust, choux and hot-water crust) and the correct proportion of flour to fat to liquid.

Use fine white flour. If the flour is fine there is no need to sift it. Or try wholewheat flour or a mixture of wholewheat and white flours; the result will be heavier but tastier.

Use margarine or butter. Pastry made with soft fats, however, requires a different technique—see the recipe for pastry made with polyunsaturated margarine. Butter or margarine taken from the refrigerator will be too cold and hard to use, so leave it at room temperature for a few minutes until it is soft but still firm.

Ice-cold water is the liquid most commonly used to bind the dough, although milk or a mixture of milk and water, or egg and water is sometimes used. Once the dough is formed handle it as little as possible.

Other ingredients may be added to a basic pastry for flavour. Grated cheese, chopped herbs, ground spices and ground nuts may all be incorporated with the dry ingredients.

Cover the dough and chill it in the refrigerator for at least thirty minutes before rolling it out. This makes the pastry lighter and helps to prevent it from shrinking during baking.

Pastry dough may be refrigerated for up to two days; allow it to return to room temperature before using it. The dough may also be kept in the freezer for up to three months.

Roll the dough out on a smooth, clean, cool, lightly floured surface. Make light, short movements. And, finally, always preheat the oven to the required temperature.

Pastry dough is measured by the amount of flour used. Six ounces (150 g) of pastry, for example, refers to pastry made with that quantity of flour and not to the total weight of the pastry.

Shortcrust Pastry

The most popular pastry, and the easiest to make, is shortcrust. Traditionally the fat should consist of half butter and half lard but the pastry will have a particularly good flavour if made with butter, or margarine can be used instead. This quantity, 6 ounces (150 g), of pastry dough is sufficient to line a 7- to 8-inch (18- to 20-cm) flan ring or to cover a 1½-pint (850-ml) pie dish.

Put 6 ounces (150 g) of flour and ¼ teaspoon (1 ml) of salt into a mixing bowl. Add 3 ounces (75 g) of margarine or butter and cut it into small pieces with a round-bladed knife. Rub the pieces of fat into the flour with your fingertips until the mixture resembles fine breadcrumbs. Sprinkle 2 tablespoons (30 ml) of cold water over the flour and mix quickly with a knife until the ingredients form a stiff dough.

Turn the dough out on to a lightly floured board and knead it gently with the fingertips until it is smooth.

Cover and chill the dough until it is needed.

INGREDIENTS TO MAKE SIX OUNCES (150 G) OF PASTRY:

6 oz (150 g) flour
¼ teaspoon (1 ml) salt
3 oz (75 g) margarine or butter
2 tablespoons (30 ml) cold water

MAKING SHORTCRUST PASTRY

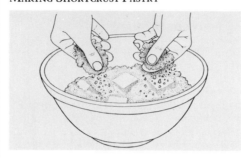

Rub the fat and flour lightly across your fingertips.

Sprinkle with cold water and mix quickly.

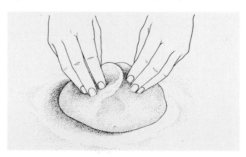

Knead gently with your fingertips to a smooth dough.

Lining a Flan Ring

A French quiche, or flan, is served in an open, free-standing pastry case. The case is formed in a metal flan ring, which is set on a baking sheet. When it is baked, slide the pastry case off the baking sheet and on to a wire rack. Remove the flan ring and leave to cool. A false-bottomed cake pan, 1 to 1½ inches (2 to 3 cm) deep, can be used instead of a flan ring.

Put a 7-inch (18-cm) flan ring on a baking sheet.

Roll out 6 ounces (150 g) of pastry dough on a lightly floured surface until it is about ⅛ inch (3 mm) thick and about 2 inches (5 cm) larger in diameter than the ring. Fold the dough in half and in half again to form a triangle. Lift the folded dough, lay it in the ring and unfold it. Alternatively, lift the dough up on the rolling pin and lay it over the ring.

Gently ease the dough into the ring. Use your knuckles, or roll a piece of dough into a ball and use that, to press the dough into the

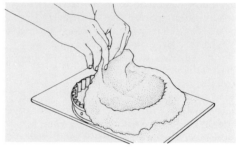

Lay the folded dough in the flan ring and unfold it,

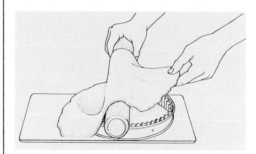

or roll the dough around the rolling pin to lift it.

Press the dough into the flan ring with your knuckles.

Trim the dough by rolling the pin over the flan ring.

ring, making sure no air is trapped between the dough and the ring. Trim off any excess dough with scissors or by running a sharp knife around the edge of the ring. If a fluted flan ring is being used, roll the rolling pin over the top of the ring to trim off any excess dough.

Baking Blind

Preheat the oven to 400°F (200°C, Gas Mark 7).

When the flan ring is lined, prick the dough all over with a fork. Line the dough with greaseproof paper or aluminium foil, then weight it down with dried beans, breadcrumbs or rice. (This is to prevent the pastry from rising during baking.)

Bake the pastry for 10 minutes then remove the greaseproof paper or foil and the beans, breadcrumbs or rice. Return the pastry to the oven for a further 5 minutes to dry out and colour slightly.

Remove the pastry from the oven and slide the ring off the baking sheet and on to a wire rack. Remove the ring and leave the pastry case to cool before filling.

Baked pastry cases can be frozen for up to 6 weeks.

PREPARING TO BAKE BLIND

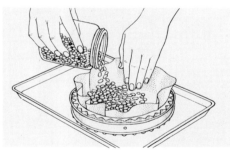

Weight the dough with beans to prevent it rising.

Sweet Flan Pastry

Although not as rich as *pâte sucrée*, the traditional French flan pastry, this rich shortcrust pastry is excellent for sweet flans and pies. Because this dough is slightly more sticky than ordinary shortcrust it must be chilled thoroughly before it is rolled out. For a spicier pastry add 1 tablespoon (15 ml) of ground mixed spice or cinnamon, or the grated rind of ½ lemon or orange to the flour.

Put 6 ounces (150 g) of flour into a mixing bowl. Add 3 ounces (75 g) of margarine or butter and cut it into small pieces with a round-bladed knife. Rub the fat into the flour with your fingertips until the mixture resembles fine bread-crumbs. Stir 1 ounce (25 g) of castor sugar into the mixture.

Beat 1 egg yolk with 1 tablespoon (15 ml) of cold water in a small bowl. Make a well in

the flour mixture and pour in the egg and water. Mix the ingredients until they form a firm dough.

Turn the dough out on to a lightly floured surface and knead it gently until it is smooth. Cover the dough and chill it.

Sweet flan pastry is baked in the same way as shortcrust pastry.

INGREDIENTS TO MAKE SIX OUNCES (150 G) OF PASTRY:

6 oz (150 g) flour
3 oz (75 g) margarine or butter
1 oz (25 g) castor sugar
1 egg yolk
1 tablespoon (15 ml) cold water

Shortcrust Pastry made with Polyunsaturated Margarine

Polyunsaturated and other soft margarines are too soft, even when refrigerated, to rub into flour easily. The following creamed method is best suited to soft margarines.

Put 3 ounces (75 g) of chilled soft margarine into a mixing bowl with 2 ounces (50 g) of flour and 2 tablespoons (30 ml) of cold water. Cream together with a fork until well mixed. Add ¼ pound (100 g) of flour and ¼ teaspoon (1 ml) of salt and mix to form a firm dough.

Turn the dough out on to a lightly floured surface and knead gently until smooth.

Cover and chill the dough until it is needed.

INGREDIENTS TO MAKE SIX OUNCES (150 G) OF PASTRY:

3 oz (75 g) polyunsaturated margarine
6 oz (150 g) flour
2 tablespoons (30 ml) cold water
¼ teaspoon (1 ml) salt

Choux Pastry

If polyunsaturated margarine is used in this recipe, it will produce a very light, crisp pastry.

Over low heat, melt 2 ounces (50 g) of margarine or butter in ¼ pint (150 ml) of water. Bring to the boil. Remove the pan from the heat immediately and pour in 2½ ounces (75 g) of white flour all at once. Stir vigorously with a wooden spoon until the mixture is smooth and comes away from the sides of the pan.

Allow the mixture to cool slightly. Beat in 2 eggs, one at a time, with a wooden spoon, until they are completely absorbed and the mixture is smooth and shiny.

It is best to use the dough at once. Preheat the oven to 425°F (220°C, Gas Mark 7). Thoroughly grease a large baking sheet.

Use either a piping bag or a spoon to shape the dough on to the baking sheet.

Bake for 20 minutes. Make a horizontal slit along the centre of each piece of pastry to allow the steam to escape. Lower the oven temperature to 375°F (190°C, Gas Mark 5) and continue baking for a further 10 minutes, or until the pastry is firm to the touch. Remove the pastry from the oven and leave on a wire rack to cool before filling.

INGREDIENTS TO MAKE TWO AND A HALF OUNCES (75 G) OF PASTRY:

2 oz (50 g) margarine or butter
2½ oz (75 g) white flour
2 eggs

Almond Pastry

The addition of ground almonds to a sweet shortcrust pastry gives it a rich biscuity texture. Other ground nuts such as walnuts and hazelnuts may be substituted.

Put ¼ pound (100 g) of flour into a mixing bowl. Add 3 ounces (75 g) of margarine or butter and cut it into small pieces with a round-bladed knife. Rub the fat into the flour with your fingertips until the mixture resembles breadcrumbs. Stir in 3 ounces (75 g) of ground almonds and 2 ounces (50 g) of castor sugar.

Beat 1 egg yolk with 2 teaspoons (10 ml) of cold water and 3 to 4 drops of almond essence in a small bowl. Make a well in the flour mixture and pour in the egg and water. Mix the ingredients until they form a soft dough.

Turn the dough out on to a lightly floured surface and knead it gently until it is smooth. Cover and chill the dough for at least 1 hour before using.

Almond pastry can be used instead of sweet flan pastry.

INGREDIENTS TO MAKE A QUARTER POUND (100 G) OF PASTRY:

¼ lb (100 g) flour
3 oz (75 g) margarine or butter
3 oz (75 g) ground almonds
2 oz (50 g) castor sugar
1 egg yolk
2 teaspoons (10 ml) cold water
3 to 4 drops almond essence

Gingerbread

Keep this gingerbread for 2 to 3 days before serving for its spicy flavour and moist texture to improve. Gingerbread will stay fresh for 2 weeks in an airtight container.

Preheat the oven to 300°F (150°C, Gas Mark 2). Grease a 7-inch (18-cm) square cake tin and line it with greaseproof paper. Grease the paper.

Put ¼ pound (100 g) of margarine or butter, 2 ounces (50 g) of soft brown sugar, 2 ounces (50 g) of black treacle and 6 ounces (150 g) of golden syrup into a saucepan. Stir over low heat until the butter has melted and the sugar has dissolved. Remove the pan from the heat and allow the mixture to cool slightly. Beat 2 eggs in a small bowl and add them to the pan with ¼ pint (150 ml) of yogurt. Stir the ingredients well.

Put ½ pound (250 g) of white flour, 1 tablespoon (15 ml) of ground ginger, 1 teaspoon (5 ml) of ground mixed spice and ½ teaspoon (2.5 ml) of bicarbonate of soda into a mixing bowl. Make a well in the flour and pour in the cooled butter-and-sugar mixture. Add 3 ounces (75 g) of chopped preserved ginger and mix well.

Pour the mixture into the prepared cake tin. Bake for 1½ hours, or until the cake has risen and is firm to the touch.

Remove the cake from the oven and allow it to cool slightly before turning it out of the tin on to a wire rack to cool completely.

INGREDIENTS TO MAKE ONE SMALL CAKE:
¼ lb (100 g) margarine or butter
2 oz (50 g) soft brown sugar
2 oz (50 g) black treacle
6 oz (150 g) golden syrup
2 eggs
¼ pint (150 ml) yogurt
½ lb (250 g) white flour
1 tablespoon (15 ml) ground ginger
1 teaspoon (5 ml) ground mixed spice
½ teaspoon (2.5 ml) bicarbonate of soda
3 oz (75 g) preserved ginger

Coffee Cheese Gâteau

Preheat the oven to 350°F (180°C, Gas Mark 4). Grease two 8-inch (20-cm) sandwich tins. Measure 6 ounces (150 g) of wholewheat flour into a bowl.

In a large bowl cream together 6 ounces (150 g) of margarine and 6 ounces (150 g) of castor sugar. Beat in 3 eggs alternately with 3 tablespoons (45 ml) of the flour. Mix 1½ teaspoons (7.5 ml) of baking powder with the remaining flour and fold into the mixture. Add 1 tablespoon (15 ml) of coffee essence. Stir until the ingredients are well blended.

Divide the batter between the prepared tins and level the surfaces. Bake the layers for 20 to 25 minutes, or until they are well

risen, brown and firm to the touch. Turn the layers out of the tins and cool them on wire racks.

Meanwhile, beat together ¾ pound (350 g) of curd cheese and ¼ pint (150 ml) of yogurt until smooth. Reserving a little for decoration, divide the mixture in half. Sandwich the layers together with one half of it. Stir 1 tablespoon (15 ml) of coffee essence into the other half of the cheese mixture and spread it over the top and sides of the cake.

Reserving a few for decoration, coarsely chop ¼ pound (100 g) of walnut halves. Press the chopped walnuts around the sides of the cake. Pipe whirls of the reserved cheese mixture on top of the cake and decorate with the reserved walnut halves.

INGREDIENTS TO MAKE ONE SMALL CAKE:
6 oz (150 g) wholewheat flour
6 oz (150 g) margarine
6 oz (150 g) castor sugar
3 eggs
1½ teaspoons (7.5 ml) baking powder
2 tablespoons (30 ml) coffee essence
¾ lb (350 g) curd cheese
¼ pint (150 ml) yogurt
¼ lb (100 g) walnut halves

Yogurt Wholewheat Scones

Yogurt is used to raise as well as to flavour these wedge-shaped scones.

Preheat the oven to 400°F (200°C, Gas Mark 6).

In a bowl mix ½ pound (250 g) of wholewheat flour with ½ teaspoon (2.5 ml) of salt and 2 teaspoons (10 ml) of baking powder. Add 1 ounce (25 g) of margarine or butter and rub it into the flour. Add ¼ pint (150 ml) of yogurt and stir until a soft dough is formed.

Turn the dough out on to a floured surface and knead it lightly. Roll the dough out to form a round about 1 inch (2 cm) thick. Cut the round into 8 wedges and place the wedges on a greased baking sheet. Bake the wedges for 10 to 15 minutes, or until they have risen and are golden brown.

Remove the wedges from the oven, split them and serve immediately with butter or cottage cheese.

INGREDIENTS TO MAKE EIGHT SCONES:
½ lb (250 g) wholewheat flour
½ teaspoon (2.5 ml) salt
2 teaspoons (10 ml) baking powder
1 oz (25 g) margarine or butter
¼ pint (150 ml) yogurt

Sunshine Fruit Cake

Preheat the oven to 350°F (180°C, Gas Mark 4). Grease a 2-pound (1-kg) loaf tin and line it with greaseproof paper. Grease the paper. Put ½ pound (250 g) of self-raising flour into a bowl.

In another large bowl cream together 6 ounces (150 g) of margarine and 6 ounces (150 g) of castor sugar until the mixture is pale and fluffy. Beat in 3 eggs alternately with 3 tablespoons (45 ml) of the flour. Fold in the remaining flour and ½ teaspoon (2.5 ml) of ground nutmeg. Grate the rind and squeeze the juice of 1 lemon and 1 orange and stir the rind and juice into the mixture.

Spoon the mixture into the prepared tin and level the surface. Bake the cake for 40 to 45 minutes, or until it is well risen, golden-brown and firm to the touch. Remove the cake from the tin and cool it on a wire rack.

Meanwhile, mash 2 large bananas in a bowl. Beat in ¼ pound (100 g) of curd cheese. Cut the cake into two layers. Spread half of the banana mixture on the bottom layer.

Peel and cut away the pith of 1 large grapefruit and 1 orange. Cut the membrane away from the segments of fruit and arrange half the segments on top of the filling. Put the top layer of the cake over the filling and cover it with the remaining banana mixture. Decorate with the remaining grapefruit and orange segments.

INGREDIENTS TO MAKE ONE SMALL CAKE:
½ lb (250 g) self-raising flour
6 oz (150 g) margarine
6 oz (150 g) castor sugar
3 eggs
½ teaspoon (2.5 ml) ground nutmeg
1 lemon
2 oranges
2 large bananas
¼ lb (100 g) curd cheese
1 grapefruit

Coconut Wheaties

Preheat the oven to 350°F (180°C, Gas Mark 4). Lightly grease 2 baking sheets.

Cream ¼ pound (100 g) of margarine or butter with ¼ pound (100 g) of soft brown sugar in a mixing bowl until light and fluffy. Beat in 1 egg. Mix in ½ pound (250 g) of wheatmeal flour, 1 teaspoon (5 ml) of baking powder and 2 ounces (50 g) of desiccated coconut to form a firm dough.

Turn the dough out on to a lightly floured board and knead gently until smooth. Roll the dough out to about ¼ inch (6 mm) thick. Stamp out round biscuits with a 2½-inch (6-cm) fluted cutter and place them on the prepared baking sheets. Sprinkle a pinch of desiccated coconut on the centre of each biscuit.

Bake the biscuits for 15 minutes, or until

they are lightly browned. Allow the biscuits to cool slightly then put them on a wire rack to cool completely.

INGREDIENTS TO MAKE TWENTY-FOUR BISCUITS:
¼ lb (100 g) margarine or butter
¼ lb (100 g) soft brown sugar
1 egg
½ lb (250 g) wheatmeal flour
1 teaspoon (5 ml) baking powder
3 oz (75 g) desiccated coconut

Lemon Wholewheat Shortbread

Use butter to give this rich, crisp, Scottish shortbread a particularly good flavour.

Preheat the oven to 300°F (150°C, Gas Mark 2). Lightly grease a 7-inch (18-cm) round sandwich tin.

Put ¼ pound (100 g) of wholewheat flour, 2 ounces (50 g) of rice flour, 2 ounces (50 g) of soft brown sugar and the grated rind of 1 lemon into a mixing bowl. Add ¼ pound (100 g) of butter and cut it into small pieces with a round-bladed knife. Rub the fat into the flour mixture to form a dough. Press the dough into the prepared tin with a spoon and level the surface. Alternatively, roll the dough out on a lightly floured surface to form a 7-inch (18-cm) round and carefully lift the round on to a lightly greased baking sheet.

Mark the top of the dough with a sharp knife, dividing it into 8 wedges. Prick the dough all over with a fork and crimp the edges. Bake the shortbread for 40 to 50 minutes, or until it is just coloured.

INGREDIENTS TO MAKE EIGHT BISCUITS:
¼ lb (100 g) wholewheat flour
2 oz (50 g) rice flour
2 oz (50 g) soft brown sugar
1 lemon
¼ lb (100 g) butter

Fruity Gingernuts

Preheat the oven to 350°F (180°C, Gas Mark 4). Lightly grease 2 baking sheets.

Put ¼ pound (100 g) of white flour, ½ teaspoon (2.5 ml) of bicarbonate of soda, 1 teaspoon (5 ml) of ground ginger and ½ teaspoon (2.5 ml) of ground cinnamon into a bowl. Mix in 2 ounces (50 g) of currants.

Melt 2 ounces (50 g) of margarine or butter with 3 tablespoons (45 ml) of golden syrup in a small saucepan over low heat. Make a well in the flour mixture and pour in the fat and syrup. Stir the ingredients well.

Take spoonfuls of the mixture and roll them into balls, the size of walnuts, between your hands. Put the balls well apart on the prepared baking sheets and flatten them slightly.

Bake the biscuits for 10 to 15 minutes, or until they are a deep golden brown. Allow the biscuits to cool and harden for 5 minutes. Put the biscuits on a wire rack to cool completely.

INGREDIENTS TO MAKE TWENTY TO TWENTY-FOUR BISCUITS:
¼ lb (100 g) white flour
½ teaspoon (2.5 ml) bicarbonate of soda
1 teaspoon (5 ml) ground ginger
½ teaspoon (2.5 ml) ground cinnamon
2 oz (50 g) currants
2 oz (50 g) margarine or butter
3 tablespoons (45 ml) golden syrup

Elizabethan Sandwich

Home-made lemon curd adds zest to this simple sandwich cake.

Preheat the oven to 350°F (180°C, Gas Mark 4). Grease an 8-inch (20-cm) round cake tin. Measure ¼ pound (100 g) of wholewheat flour into a bowl.

In a large mixing bowl cream ¼ pound (100 g) of margarine with ¼ pound (100 g) of soft brown sugar until the mixture is pale and creamy. Beat in 2 eggs alternately with 2 tablespoons (30 ml) of the flour, then fold in 1 teaspoon (5 ml) of baking powder and the remaining flour.

Pour into the prepared tin and level the surface. Bake for 20 to 25 minutes, or until the cake has risen and is brown and firm to the touch. Remove the cake from the tin and put it on a wire rack to cool.

Cut the cake into two layers. Spread ¼ pound (100 g) of lemon curd (see page 180) on one layer, then cover with the second layer.

INGREDIENTS TO MAKE ONE SMALL CAKE:
¼ lb (100 g) wholewheat flour
¼ lb (100 g) margarine
¼ lb (100 g) soft brown sugar
2 eggs
1 teaspoon (5 ml) baking powder
¼ lb (100 g) lemon curd (see page 180)

Halva Cake

Cut into slices and wrapped in foil, this moist cake will keep for up to 3 weeks.

Preheat the oven to 350°F (180°C, Gas Mark 4). Grease a 7-inch (18-cm) square cake tin, and line it with greaseproof paper so that the paper comes up well above the sides of the tin. Grease the paper. Put ¼ pound (100 g) of white flour into a bowl.

In a large bowl cream together 6 ounces (150 g) of margarine and 6 ounces (150 g) of castor sugar. Beat in 4 eggs alternately with 4 tablespoons (60 ml) of the flour. Fold the remaining flour, 2 teaspoons (10 ml) of ground cinnamon, ¼ pound (100 g) of semolina, 1 ounce (25 g) of desiccated coconut and the grated rind of 1 lemon into the creamed mixture.

Spoon the mixture into the prepared tin and level the surface. Sprinkle 1 tablespoon (15 ml) of poppy seeds over the top and press them in lightly. Bake the cake for 40 to 45 minutes, or until it is well risen, golden-brown and firm to the touch.

Meanwhile, in a small saucepan heat 2 tablespoons (30 ml) of clear honey with 1 tablespoon (15 ml) of lemon juice. Pour the honey and lemon juice over the cake immediately after it is taken from the oven. Cool the cake in the tin. Lift out carefully, remove the greaseproof paper and serve.

INGREDIENTS TO MAKE ONE SMALL CAKE:
¼ lb (100 g) white flour
6 oz (150 g) margarine
6 oz (150 g) castor sugar
4 eggs
2 teaspoons (10 ml) ground cinnamon
¼ lb (100 g) semolina
1 oz (25 g) desiccated coconut
1 lemon
1 tablespoon (15 ml) poppy seeds
2 tablespoons (30 ml) clear honey

TURNING OUT A MOIST CAKE

Gently lift the cake out by the paper.

Cottage Cheese Teabread is moist and fruity and is made with an unusual combination of ingredients, including cottage cheese, dates and walnuts.

Cottage Cheese Teabread

This is a light, moist teabread made with cottage cheese instead of butter.

Preheat the oven to 350°F (180°C, Gas Mark 4). Grease a 2-pound (1-kg) loaf tin and line it with greaseproof paper. Grease the paper.

Sieve ½ pound (250 g) of cottage cheese into a mixing bowl. Add 6 ounces (150 g) of soft brown sugar and beat until creamy. Add 3 eggs and beat them into the mixture.

Reserving a few for decoration, coarsely chop 2 ounces (50 g) of walnuts. Add the chopped walnuts to the creamed mixture with ¼ pound (100 g) of chopped, pitted dates. Fold ½ pound (250 g) of self-raising flour into the mixture.

Spoon the mixture into the loaf tin and level the surface. Press the reserved walnuts into the top of the teabread in a line down the centre.

Bake the teabread for 45 to 50 minutes, or until it is firm and golden brown. Turn the teabread out of the tin on to a wire rack to cool.

INGREDIENTS TO MAKE ONE TEABREAD :
½ **lb (250 g) cottage cheese**
6 oz (150 g) soft brown sugar
3 eggs
2 oz (50 g) walnuts
¼ **lb (100 g) pitted dates**
½ **lb (250 g) self-raising flour**

Farmhouse Fruit Cake

Wholewheat flour and brown sugar give this moist, crumbly fruit cake a rich dark colour. It will keep for at least a week in an airtight container.

Preheat the oven to 350°F (180°C, Gas Mark 4). Grease a 7-inch (18-cm) round cake tin and line it with greaseproof paper. Grease the paper.

Mix ¼ pound (100 g) of wholewheat flour, ¼ pound (100 g) of white flour, 2 teaspoons (10 ml) of baking powder and 1 teaspoon (5 ml) of ground nutmeg in a large bowl. Add 3 ounces (75 g) of margarine or butter. Cut it into small pieces with a round-bladed knife and rub it into the flour with your fingertips until the mixture resembles fine breadcrumbs.

Stir in 3 ounces (75 g) of soft brown sugar, 6 ounces (150 g) of sultanas, 2 ounces (50 g) of chopped mixed peel, 2 ounces (50 g) of chopped glacé cherries and the grated rind and juice of ½ lemon. Beat 2 eggs with ¼ pint (150 ml) of milk in a small bowl. Make a well in the flour-and-fruit mixture and pour in the beaten egg and milk. Stir the ingredients until they are thoroughly mixed.

Spoon the mixture into the prepared cake tin and level the surface. Arrange 2 ounces (50 g) of split blanched almonds on top.

Bake the cake for 1 to 1¼ hours, or until it is brown and firm to the touch. Allow the cake to cool slightly before turning it out of the tin on to a wire rack to cool completely.

INGREDIENTS TO MAKE ONE SMALL CAKE :
¼ **lb (100 g) wholewheat flour**
¼ **lb (100 g) white flour**
2 teaspoons (10 ml) baking powder
1 teaspoon (5 ml) ground nutmeg
3 oz (75 g) margarine or butter
3 oz (75 g) soft brown sugar
6 oz (150 g) sultanas
2 oz (50 g) mixed peel
2 oz (50 g) glacé cherries
½ **lemon**
2 eggs
¼ **pint (150 ml) milk**
2 oz (50 g) split blanched almonds

Macaroons

Macaroons are traditionally cooked on edible rice paper to prevent them sticking to the baking sheet. If rice paper is not available, use any non-stick baking paper.

Preheat the oven to 350°F (180°C, Gas Mark 4). Line baking sheets with rice paper or non-stick baking paper.

Whisk 1 egg white in a small bowl until it forms stiff peaks. Add 2 ounces (50 g) of ground almonds, 3 ounces (75 g) of castor sugar and ½ teaspoon (2.5 ml) of almond essence and fold them in gently to form a smooth, stiff mixture.

Put spoonfuls of the mixture on the prepared baking sheets, leaving room for the mixture to spread. Place a split almond in the centre of each biscuit.

Bake the biscuits for 15 to 20 minutes, or until they are just beginning to colour. Put the biscuits on a wire rack to cool.

INGREDIENTS TO MAKE TEN TO TWELVE BISCUITS :
1 egg white
2 oz (50 g) ground almonds
3 oz (75 g) castor sugar
½ **teaspoon (2.5 ml) almond essence**
split blanched almonds

Dutch Apple Cake

A layer of spiced apples tops this moist sponge cake. Baked in an oblong tin, it is cut into slices before serving.

Preheat the oven to 350°F (180°C, Gas Mark 4). Lightly grease a 2-pound (1-kg), 9- by 4-inches (23- by 10-cm) loaf tin.

Put ¼ pound (100 g) of margarine or butter into a mixing bowl with ¼ pound (100 g) of castor sugar. Beat the fat and sugar together until they become pale and creamy. Add 2 eggs, one at a time, beating the mixture well after each addition. Fold in 6 ounces (150 g) of self-raising flour. Add a little milk to give the mixture a soft dropping consistency. Spoon the mixture into the prepared baking tin.

Peel, core and thinly slice 1 pound (500 g) of cooking apples and arrange the slices on top of the cake mixture. In a bowl mix together the grated rind of ½ lemon, 2 teaspoons (10 ml) of ground ginger and 1 tablespoon (15 ml) of castor sugar and sprinkle this mixture over the apple slices.

Bake the cake for 30 minutes, or until it is golden brown and the apples are tender. Put the cake on a wire rack to cool.

INGREDIENTS TO MAKE ONE SMALL CAKE :
¼ **lb (100 g) margarine or butter**
¼ **lb (100 g) plus 1 tablespoon (15 ml) castor sugar**
2 eggs
6 oz (150 g) self-raising flour
milk
1 lb (500 g) cooking apples
½ **lemon**
2 teaspoons (10 ml) ground ginger

A selection of favourite cakes and biscuits; clockwise, Gingerbread, Fruity Gingernuts, Macaroons, Farmhouse Fruit Cake, Dutch Apple Cake and, for a special occasion, Coffee Cheese Gâteau.

Pancakes

Pancakes can be kept for up to 2 days in the refrigerator. Let them cool, then wrap them in foil and store them. Pancakes may be frozen for up to 2 months. Interleave the cooled pancakes with lightly oiled greaseproof paper or polythene so that single pancakes can be separated and defrosted. To defrost pancakes, leave them in their packaging at room temperature for 2 to 3 hours or in the refrigerator overnight. To reheat pancakes, preheat the oven to 375°F (190°C, Gas Mark 5) and put them, wrapped in aluminium foil, in the oven for 20 to 30 minutes. About 8 pancakes can be made from ½ pint (300 ml) of batter.

Make ½ pint (300 ml) of batter. Put ¼ pound (100 g) of white flour and ¼ teaspoon (1 ml) of salt into a mixing bowl. Make a well in the flour and pour in 1 egg and ¼ pint (150 ml) of milk. Stir the ingredients well with a wooden spoon until the batter is smooth. Beat in another ¼ pint (150 ml) of milk. This batter can be used immediately or left to stand for up to 2 hours.

Heat ½ teaspoon (2.5 ml) of sunflower oil in an 8-inch (20-cm) frying-pan, just enough to coat the bottom of the pan. Less oil will be needed if a non-stick frying-pan is used. When the oil is very hot, quickly pour enough batter into the pan to thinly coat the bottom. Tilt the pan so that the batter spreads evenly.

Cook until the top of the batter is set and the underside is golden brown. Turn or toss the pancake over and cook the other side. Slide the pancake on to a warm dish. Sprinkle with castor sugar and lemon juice. Roll up the pancake and serve immediately. Alternatively cover the pancake with an upturned bowl or wrap in a tea-towel to keep hot. Repeat, adding more oil to the pan if needed, until the batter is used up.

INGREDIENTS TO SERVE FOUR:
¼ lb (100 g) white flour
¼ teaspoon (1 ml) salt
1 egg
½ pint (300 ml) milk
sunflower oil
castor sugar
lemon juice

Savoury Pancake Stack

These pancakes are sure to satisfy the heartiest of appetites.

Melt 3 ounces (75 g) of margarine or butter in a saucepan. Add 1 chopped onion and 4 chopped sticks of celery and fry gently for 10 to 15 minutes, or until they are soft. Stir in 2 ounces (50 g) of flour. Gradually pour in ¾ pint (450 ml) of milk and continue stirring until the mixture begins to boil. Add ½ pound (250 g) of chopped cooked ham and 2 teaspoons (10 ml) of English mustard.

Spread a layer of filling over the cooked pancakes.

Stack the pancakes with filling between each one.

Season to taste with salt and pepper. Reduce the heat and simmer for 2 minutes. Remove the pan from the heat and set aside.

Put ¼ pound (100 g) of wholewheat flour and ¼ teaspoon (1 ml) of salt into a mixing bowl. Make a well in the flour and pour in 1 egg and ¼ pint (150 ml) of milk. Stir well with a wooden spoon until the batter is smooth. Beat in ¼ pint (150 ml) of water. Because wholewheat flour tends to make a a thick batter, add 2 to 3 tablespoons (30 to 45 ml) more of water if necessary.

Heat ½ teaspoon (2.5 ml) of sunflower oil in an 8-inch (20-cm) frying-pan. When the oil is very hot quickly pour enough batter into the pan to thinly coat the bottom. Tilt the pan so that the batter spreads evenly.

Cook until the top of the batter is set and the underside is golden brown. Turn or toss the pancake over and cook the other side.

Put the pancake on to a hot flameproof dish and spread with a layer of the prepared filling. Continue making the pancakes, stacking one above the other and spreading the filling between each layer, until the batter and the filling are used up. (This recipe should make 7 or 8 pancakes.)

Sprinkle the pile with 1 ounce (25 g) of grated Cheddar cheese. Put the dish under a hot grill until the cheese has melted. Alternatively, bake in a 400°F (200 C, Gas Mark 6) oven for 5 to 10 minutes.

Serve cut into wedges like a cake.

INGREDIENTS TO SERVE FOUR:
3 oz (75 g) margarine or butter
1 onion
4 celery sticks
2 oz (50 g) flour
1 pint (600 ml) milk
½ lb (250 g) cooked ham
2 teaspoons (10 ml) English mustard
salt
pepper
¼ lb (100 g) wholewheat flour
1 egg
sunflower oil
1 oz (25 g) Cheddar cheese

Mediterranean Pancakes

These pancakes are ideal to serve as a first course for a dinner party or as a main dish for lunch or supper.

Make ½ pint (300 ml) of batter and cook 8 pancakes. Put the pancakes on to a hot plate as they are cooked and cover with an upturned bowl or wrap in a tea-towel or aluminium foil to keep warm.

Preheat the oven to 375°F (190°C, Gas Mark 5).

Peel and slice 1 pound (500 g) of onions. Heat 1 ounce (25 g) of margarine or butter and 1 tablespoon (15 ml) of corn oil in a saucepan. Add the onions to the pan and fry gently for 5 minutes. Stir in 4 blanched, peeled and chopped ripe tomatoes, 2 ounces (50 g) of chopped anchovies, 3 tablespoons (45 ml) of tomato purée and 8 sliced stuffed olives. Season to taste with salt and pepper. Cover the pan and simmer gently for 20 minutes, stirring occasionally.

Spread each pancake with the mixture, roll them up and put them in an ovenproof dish. Cover and bake for 15 minutes.

Alternatively, allow the pancakes and filling to cool until they are needed. Fill the pancakes and bake for 25 minutes.

Garnish with stuffed olives and tomato slices and serve immediately.

INGREDIENTS TO SERVE EIGHT AS A STARTER:
½ pint (300 ml) pancake batter
1 lb (500 g) onions
1 oz (25 g) margarine or butter
1 tablespoon (15 ml) corn oil
6 ripe tomatoes
2 oz (50 g) anchovies
3 tablespoons (45 ml) tomato purée
16 stuffed olives
salt
pepper

Apple and Cottage Cheese Pancakes

Yogurt makes an excellent accompaniment for these cheese-filled pancakes.

Make ½ pint (300 ml) of pancake batter and cook 8 pancakes on one side only.

Peel, core and slice ¾ pound (350 g) of cooking apples. Put the apples into a saucepan with the grated rind and juice of ½ lemon, 1 tablespoon (15 ml) of water, 1 tablespoon (15 ml) of sugar, 1 ounce (25 g) of raisins and ½ teaspoon (2.5 ml) of ground mixed spice. Cover and, stirring occasionally, cook gently for 5 minutes, or until the apple slices are cooked but are still slightly crisp. Remove the pan from the heat and add ¼ pound (100 g) of cottage cheese. Mix the ingredients thoroughly.

Spread the apple and cheese mixture over the cooked side of each pancake. Roll the pancakes up, folding in the edges.

Heat 1 ounce (25 g) of margarine or butter with 1 tablespoon (15 ml) of corn oil in a frying-pan. Add the rolled pancakes and fry them until they are golden brown. Serve immediately.

INGREDIENTS TO SERVE FOUR:
½ **pint (300 ml) pancake batter**
¾ **lb (350 g) cooking apples**
½ **lemon**
1 **tablespoon (15 ml) sugar**
1 **oz (25 g) raisins**
½ **teaspoon (2.5 ml) ground mixed spice**
¼ **lb (100 g) cottage cheese**
1 **oz (25 g) margarine or butter**
1 **tablespoon (15 ml) corn oil**

FILLING ROLLED PANCAKES

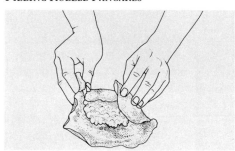

Roll the pancakes enclosing the filling.

Spicy Scotch Pancakes

These pancakes, also called drop scones, are served with butter or with clear honey.

Combine ¼ pound (100 g) of self-raising flour, 1 ounce (25 g) of castor sugar and 2 teaspoons (10 ml) of ground mixed spice in a mixing bowl. Beat 1 egg in a small bowl. Make a well in the flour mixture and pour in the beaten egg and ¼ pint (150 ml) of milk. Stir the ingredients well; the batter should have the consistency of thick cream.

Lightly grease a griddle or a heavy frying-pan and heat it gently. Drop 1 tablespoon (15 ml) of batter on to the hot griddle. Cook for 2 to 3 minutes, or until bubbles appear on the surface. Turn the pancake over using a palette knife and cook the other side until it is golden brown.

Remove the pancake from the pan and put it between the folds of a clean tea-towel to keep warm and moist. Continue to cook the pancakes until the batter is used up. Serve immediately.

INGREDIENTS TO MAKE TWELVE TO SIXTEEN PANCAKES:
¼ **lb (100 g) self-raising flour**
1 **oz (25 g) castor sugar**
2 **teaspoons (10 ml) ground mixed spice**
1 **egg**
¼ **pint (150 ml) milk**

Toad in the Hole

Meatballs cooked in a batter pudding look just like toads in holes when the batter puffs up around them.

Preheat the oven to 425°F (220°C, Gas Mark 7).

In a large bowl combine ¾ pound (350 g) of minced beef with 2 ounces (50 g) of fresh breadcrumbs, ½ teaspoon (2.5 ml) of dried mixed herbs and 1 grated onion. Season to taste with salt and pepper. Mix the ingredients thoroughly.

In a small bowl beat 1 egg and add just enough to the meat mixture to bind it. Divide the meat mixture into 8 pieces and shape each one into a ball.

Put 2 tablespoons (30 ml) of corn oil into a small roasting tin or a shallow ovenproof dish. Heat in the oven for 5 minutes. Add the meatballs to the hot oil and return the tin to the oven for 10 minutes.

Meanwhile, make up ½ pint (300 ml) of pancake batter. Pour it over the meatballs. Return the tin to the oven and cook for 30 to 40 minutes more, or until the batter is well risen, crisp and brown.

INGREDIENTS TO SERVE FOUR:
¾ **lb (350 g) minced beef**
2 **oz (50 g) fresh breadcrumbs**
½ **teaspoon (2.5 ml) dried mixed herbs**
1 **onion**
salt
pepper
1 **egg**
2 **tablespoons (30 ml) corn oil**
½ **pint (300 ml) pancake batter**

Grapefruit Crêpes

Put ¼ pound (100 g) of white flour and ¼ teaspoon (1 ml) of salt into a mixing bowl. Make a well in the flour and pour in 1 egg and ¼ pint (150 ml) of milk. Stir until the batter is smooth. Beat in ¼ pint (150 ml) of water. Cook 8 pancakes.

Squeeze the juice from 4 large oranges. Put the juice into a frying-pan, add 2 tablespoons 30 seconds. Remove the pan from the heat honey has dissolved. Simmer gently for 30 seconds. Remove the pan from the heat and stir in 2 tablespoons (30 ml) of Cointreau or Grand Marnier.

Peel and remove the pith from 1 grapefruit. Cut the membrane away from the segments of fruit. Fold each pancake in half, then in half again to form a triangle. Fill the pockets of the triangles with grapefruit segments.

Put the pancakes into the frying-pan and return to the heat. Simmer the pancakes for a few minutes, spooning the sauce over them several times, until they are heated through. Arrange the pancakes in a serving dish. Alternatively, preheat the oven to 375°F (190°C, Gas Mark 5) and put the pancakes into an ovenproof dish. Pour the sauce over them and bake for 15 minutes or until heated through.

In a small saucepan heat 2 tablespoons (30 ml) of brandy and pour it over the pancakes. Ignite the brandy and serve the pancakes flaming.

INGREDIENTS TO SERVE FOUR:
¼ **lb (100 g) white flour**
¼ **teaspoon (1 ml) salt**
1 **egg**
¼ **pint (150 ml) milk**
4 **large oranges**
2 **tablespoons (30 ml) honey**
2 **tablespoons (30 ml) Cointreau or Grand Marnier**
1 **grapefruit**
2 **tablespoons (30 ml) brandy**

FILLING FOLDED CRÊPES

Fill the pockets of the pancakes with fruit.

PASTA DOUGH IS MADE with flour and water and sometimes eggs. It is the base for a number of simple but superb dishes.

Although home-made pasta is traditionally made with white flour, wholewheat flour or a mixture of wholewheat and white flours may be used.

The dough may be stored, well wrapped in polythene, in the refrigerator for up to two days or in the freezer for up to two months.

When making pasta dough it is useful to have a large working surface, preferably of marble, and a long rolling pin.

Freshly-made pasta takes 5 minutes to cook; commercially-made, dried pasta takes 15 to 20 minutes to cook.

MAKING PASTA DOUGH

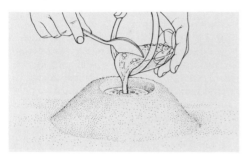

Make a well in the flour and pour in the liquid.

Draw the flour into the liquid to form a dough.

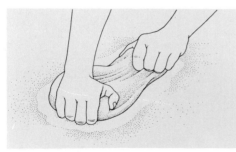

Knead well in the same way as bread dough.

Home-made Pasta

Put 1 pound (500 g) of flour mixed with 1 teaspoon (5 ml) of salt on to a large board or working surface. Beat 4 eggs with 2 tablespoons (30 ml) of water in a bowl. Make a well in the flour and pour in the beaten eggs and water. Using your hands, gradually draw the flour into the egg mixture until a stiff dough is formed, adding up to 2 tablespoons (30 ml) more of water if necessary.

Knead the dough in the same way as for bread, for 10 minutes, or until it is smooth and elastic.

INGREDIENTS TO MAKE ONE POUND (500 G) OF PASTA:
1 lb (500 g) flour
1 teaspoon (5 ml) salt
4 eggs

Spinach Pasta Dough

Spinach gives this pasta its attractive green colour and fine flavour.

Thoroughly wash ½ pound (250 g) of spinach in cold water. Drain well and put into a large saucepan. Add 1 teaspoon (5 ml) of salt, cover and cook for 10 minutes, or until tender. Drain well and chop roughly. Add 2 eggs and beat well.

Put 1 pound (500 g) of flour mixed with 2 teaspoons (10 ml) of salt on to a large board or working surface. Make a well in the flour and pour in the spinach and egg mixture. Using your hands, gradually draw the flour into the spinach and egg mixture until a stiff dough is formed.

Proceed as for home-made pasta.

INGREDIENTS TO MAKE ONE POUND (500 G) OF PASTA:
½ lb (250 g) spinach
1 teaspoon (5 ml) salt
2 eggs
1 lb (500 g) flour

Tagliatelle

After this pasta is cooked you may add such ingredients as sautéed mushrooms, crisply grilled chopped bacon, garlic, herbs or bolognese sauce.

Divide 1 pound (500 g) of pasta dough into a number of pieces. Roll each piece out very thinly on a lightly floured surface. Dust the dough and the working surface frequently with flour. Lift the rolled-out dough—it should be quite pliable and easy to handle without tearing—and spread it on a clean tea-towel over the back of a chair or on a table. Leave the dough to rest for 15 minutes.

Roll up each piece of dough loosely, Swiss-roll style, and cut it crossways at ¼-inch (6-mm) intervals. Unroll the strips and

leave them to dry for 10 minutes or longer —up to 24 hours.

Bring a large pan of salted water to the boil. Add the tagliatelle gradually so that the water does not stop boiling. Boil for 5 minutes, or until the tagliatelle is tender but still slightly firm—this is aptly described by the Italians as *al dente* (to the tooth).

Drain the tagliatelle. Put it into a serving bowl with ¼ pound (100 g) of butter or margarine and toss it quickly. Serve immediately with grated Parmesan cheese.

INGREDIENTS TO SERVE FOUR:
1 lb (500 g) pasta dough
salt
¼ lb (100 g) butter or margarine
grated Parmesan cheese

CUTTING PASTA

Roll the dough up gently, Swiss-roll style.

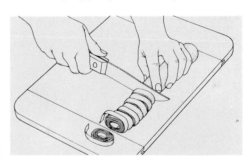

Slice the rolled pasta into noodles.

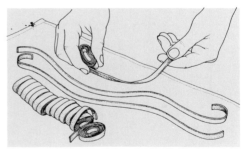

Unroll the noodles and leave to dry.

Baked Noodles with Cheese

Sustaining and tasty, this version of an old favourite calls for wholewheat pasta.

First, prepare, roll out and cut ½ pound (250 g) of pasta dough made with wholewheat flour (see tagliatelle).

Heat 2 ounces (50 g) of corn oil or butter in a saucepan. Add ¼ pound (100 g) of sliced button mushrooms and fry for 2 minutes. Stir in 1½ ounces (40 g) of flour. Gradually add 1 pint (550 ml) of milk, stirring constantly, and bring to the boil. Continue boiling and stirring until the mixture thickens. Stir in ¼ pound (100 g) of chopped cooked ham, 3 ounces (75 g) of peanuts and 3 ounces (75 g) of grated strong Cheddar cheese. Season to taste with salt and pepper. Remove the pan from the heat.

Bring a large pan of salted water to the boil. Add the pasta and cook it for 5 minutes, or until it is just tender. Drain and fold the pasta into the hot sauce. Put it into a greased ovenproof dish and sprinkle 1 ounce (25 g) of grated strong Cheddar cheese over the top.

Put the dish under a hot grill until the sauce is bubbling and golden brown on top. Alternatively, bake at 400°F (200°C, Gas Mark 6) for 20 to 30 minutes.

Serve immediately.

INGREDIENTS TO SERVE FOUR:
½ lb (250 g) pasta dough made with wholewheat flour (see tagliatelle)
2 oz (50 g) corn oil or butter
¼ lb (100 g) button mushrooms
1½ oz (40 g) flour
1 pint (550 ml) milk
¼ lb (100 g) cooked ham
3 oz (75 g) peanuts
¼ lb (100 g) strong Cheddar cheese
salt
pepper

Lasagne Verdi al Forno

This rich and satisfying dish requires no accompaniment other than a crisp green salad.

Divide ½ pound (250 g) of spinach pasta dough into 2 pieces. Roll each piece out very thinly and leave the dough to rest (see tagliatelle).

Meanwhile, finely chop 2 ounces (50 g) of streaky bacon, 1 medium-sized onion, 1 stick of celery and 1 carrot. Heat 1 tablespoon (15 ml) of corn oil in a saucepan. Add the chopped bacon and vegetables and fry for 5 minutes.

Add ¾ pound (350 g) of minced beef and continue frying for 3 minutes. Stir in 1 ounce (25 g) of flour. Add ½ pint (300 ml) of beef stock, 2 tablespoons (30 ml) of tomato purée and ½ teaspoon (2.5 ml) of dried oregano, season to taste with salt and pepper and bring to the boil, stirring frequently. Cover the pan,

reduce the heat and simmer gently for 30 minutes.

Preheat the oven to 400°F (200°C, Gas Mark 6).

Meanwhile, make a béchamel sauce. Halve 1 medium-sized onion and put it into a saucepan with ¾ pint (450 ml) of milk, 2 parsley sprigs and 1 bay leaf and bring to the boil. Remove the pan from the heat and leave to infuse for 10 minutes.

Melt 1 ounce (25 g) of margarine or butter in another saucepan. Stir in 1 ounce (25 g) of flour. Strain the milk and add it to the pan gradually, stirring continually. Bring to the boil and continue to cook for 1 minute, stirring. Season to taste with salt and pepper and ¼ teaspoon (1 ml) of ground nutmeg. Remove the pan from the heat and set aside.

Cut the pieces of pasta dough into 2-inch (5-cm) wide strips and leave the dough to dry for 10 minutes.

Bring a large pan of salted water to the boil. Add the lasagne strips gradually and boil for 5 minutes, or until they are just tender. Drain the lasagne and immediately immerse in cold water. Drain again and spread the lasagne on a clean tea-towel to dry.

Grease an ovenproof dish and spoon a thin layer of meat sauce on the bottom. Cover completely with a layer of béchamel sauce, then put a layer of lasagne on top. Repeat these layers until the dish is full, finishing with a layer of béchamel sauce. Sprinkle 1 tablespoon (15 ml) of grated Parmesan cheese over the top.

Bake the lasagne for 20 to 30 minutes, or until it is bubbling and golden brown on top.

INGREDIENTS TO SERVE FOUR:
½ lb (250 g) spinach pasta dough (see tagliatelle)
2 oz (50 g) streaky bacon
2 medium-sized onions
1 celery stick
1 carrot
1 tablespoon (15 ml) corn oil
¾ lb (350 g) minced beef
2 oz (50 g) flour
½ pint (300 ml) beef stock
2 tablespoons (30 ml) tomato purée
½ teaspoon (2.5 ml) dried oregano
salt
pepper
¾ pint (450 ml) milk
2 parsley sprigs
1 bay leaf
1 oz (25 g) margarine or butter
¼ teaspoon (1 ml) ground nutmeg
1 tablespoon (15 ml) grated Parmesan cheese

Chicken Cannelloni

Divide ½ pound (250 g) of pasta dough into 2 pieces. Roll each piece out very thinly (see tagliatelle) and leave the dough to rest.

Preheat the oven to 400°F (200°C, Gas Mark 6).

Heat 1 tablespoon (15 ml) of corn oil in a small saucepan. Add 1 chopped onion and fry for 3 minutes. Mince or finely chop ½ pound (250 g) of cooked chicken meat. Add the chicken and 2 ounces (50 g) of fresh breadcrumbs, 2 tablespoons (30 ml) of chopped parsley and the grated rind of ½ lemon to the onion. Season to taste with salt and pepper and stir until well mixed. Beat 1 egg in a small bowl and add just enough to bind the chicken mixture.

Cut the pieces of pasta dough into 8 rectangles about 4 by 3 inches (10 by 8 cm) and leave to dry for 10 minutes.

Bring a large pan of salted water to the boil, gradually add the cannelloni and boil for 5 minutes, or until it is just tender. Drain the cannelloni and immerse it in cold water. Drain again and separate the cannelloni on a clean cloth.

Divide the stuffing mixture into 8 sausage-shaped pieces. Put one on each piece of cannelloni and roll tightly to form tubes.

Put the tubes into a greased ovenproof dish. Pour ½ pint (300 ml) of tomato sauce (see page 108) over the tubes. Bake the cannelloni for 20 to 30 minutes, or until the sauce is bubbling.

Serve immediately with a bowl of grated Parmesan cheese.

INGREDIENTS TO SERVE FOUR:
½ lb (250 g) pasta dough (see tagliatelle)
1 tablespoon (15 ml) corn oil
1 onion
½ lb (250 g) cooked chicken meat
2 oz (50 g) fresh breadcrumbs
2 tablespoons (30 ml) chopped parsley
½ lemon
salt
pepper
1 egg
½ pint (300 ml) tomato sauce (see page 108)
grated Parmesan cheese

Ravioli with Ricotta

Freshly made, these delicate little "cushions" of pasta are superb. Curd cheese may be substituted for ricotta.

Put $\frac{1}{2}$ pound (250 g) of pasta dough (see page 42) on a lightly floured surface and divide it into two. Roll each half out very thinly to form a rectangle about 14 by 12 inches (35 by 30 cm). Leave the dough to rest for 15 minutes.

Meanwhile, put $\frac{1}{2}$ pound (250 g) of ricotta cheese with 1 ounce (25 g) of grated Parmesan cheese, $\frac{1}{4}$ teaspoon (1 ml) of dried marjoram, $\frac{1}{4}$ teaspoon (1 ml) of ground nutmeg, 1 beaten egg and a pinch of salt and pepper into a large bowl and mix thoroughly.

Brush one half of the pasta with water. At 2-inch (5-cm) intervals put 1 teaspoon (5 ml) of the ricotta mixture. Cover with the other half of the pasta and seal by pressing along the edges and between the mounds of ricotta filling. Using a 2-inch (5-cm) fluted pastry cutter, cut round each mound or cut into squares (about 28). Leave the ravioli to dry for 10 minutes before cooking it.

Add the ravioli to a large pan of boiling salted water and cook for 5 minutes, or until

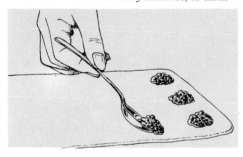

Put spoonfuls of filling at intervals on the pasta.

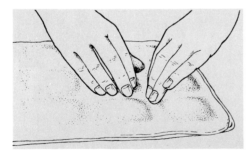

Cover with pasta and seal around the filling.

Cut around the mounds of filling.

it is just tender. Drain the ravioli and put it into a hot serving dish. Sprinkle with 1 ounce (25 g) of grated Parmesan cheese and 1 tablespoon (15 ml) of chopped parsley and serve immediately.

INGREDIENTS TO SERVE FOUR:
$\frac{1}{2}$ lb (250 g) pasta dough (see page 42)
$\frac{1}{2}$ lb (250 g) ricotta cheese
2 oz (50 g) Parmesan cheese
$\frac{1}{4}$ teaspoon (1 ml) dried marjoram
$\frac{1}{4}$ teaspoon (1 ml) ground nutmeg
1 egg
salt
pepper
1 tablespoon (15 ml) chopped parsley

Aubergine and Pasta Casserole

In this dish the vegetables are layered with the pasta and then topped with yogurt, which sets on the top like cheese. Macaroni, spaghetti or noodles may be used.

Cook $\frac{1}{2}$ pound (250 g) of pasta (see page 42) in a large pan of salted boiling water until it is just tender. Drain well.

Preheat the oven to 375°F (190°C, Gas Mark 5).

Cut 1 large aubergine into thin slices. Spread the slices on a plate and sprinkle them liberally with salt. Leave for at least 30 minutes. Wash the slices and drain well.

Slice $\frac{1}{2}$ pound (250 g) of tomatoes. Finely chop 1 small onion and mix it with 1 crushed garlic clove in a small bowl.

In a casserole arrange layers of aubergine, tomato and cooked pasta, sprinkling each layer with a little of the onion and garlic and salt and pepper. Finish with a layer of overlapping aubergine slices.

Spread $\frac{1}{4}$ pint (150 ml) of yogurt over the top. Sprinkle with 2 tablespoons (30 ml) of grated Parmesan cheese.

Bake for 40 to 45 minutes, or until the aubergine is cooked and the top is golden brown.

INGREDIENTS TO SERVE FOUR:
$\frac{1}{2}$ lb (250 g) pasta (see page 42)
1 large aubergine
$\frac{1}{2}$ lb (250 g) tomatoes
1 small onion
1 garlic clove
salt
pepper
$\frac{1}{4}$ pint (150 ml) yogurt
2 tablespoons (30 ml) grated Parmesan cheese

Pasta al Pesto

This dish may be made with any pasta, although the thin, string-like varieties are best. If you are making your own pasta follow the instructions for rolling and cutting given in the recipe for tagliatelle. The pesto sauce is mixed in at the table.

Remove the stalks from a large bunch of basil and put the leaves, about 2 ounces (50 g), into a mortar or small mixing bowl with 1 crushed garlic clove, 1 ounce (25 g) of walnuts, 2 ounces (50 g) of grated Parmesan cheese and a little salt. Pound the ingredients with a pestle until they form a thick purée.

Beat in 3 tablespoons (45 ml) of olive oil, a little at a time, until the sauce is well blended and thick like creamed butter. Alternatively, put all the ingredients, except the oil, into a liquidizer and blend to form a purée. Slowly add the oil and blend at high speed until the sauce is smooth.

Add $\frac{1}{2}$ pound (250 g) of freshly made pasta (see page 42) to a large pan of boiling salted water and cook for 5 minutes, or until it is just tender. Drain the pasta and pile it into a hot serving dish. Spoon the sauce over the pasta and top with a knob of butter or margarine.

Serve immediately with a bowl of grated Parmesan cheese.

INGREDIENTS TO SERVE FOUR:
1 large basil bunch
1 garlic clove
1 oz (25 g) walnuts
6 oz (150 g) Parmesan cheese
salt
3 tablespoons (45 ml) olive oil
$\frac{1}{2}$ lb (250 g) freshly made pasta (see page 42)
butter or margarine

Tomato Gnocchi

Pour 1 pint (600 ml) of milk into a saucepan with 1 small onion, cut in half, 1 bay leaf and 1 pinch each of ground nutmeg, salt and pepper. Bring to the boil. Remove the pan from the heat and discard the bay leaf and the onion.

Sprinkle $\frac{1}{4}$ pound (100 g) of semolina into the milk. Cook over very low heat, stirring constantly, until the mixture is very thick. Remove the pan from the heat and beat in 2 eggs, $\frac{1}{2}$ teaspoon (2.5 ml) of French mustard and 2 ounces (50 g) of grated Parmesan cheese.

Turn the mixture into a greased shallow dish and spread to a thickness of $\frac{1}{2}$ inch (1 cm). Set the dish aside until the mixture is cool, preferably overnight.

Preheat the oven to 400°F (200°C, Gas Mark 6). Grease a shallow ovenproof dish.

Slice 4 tomatoes thinly. Put the tomato slices into the prepared dish. Cut the semolina gnocchi into $1\frac{1}{2}$-inch (3-cm) squares. Arrange the squares on the tomatoes, letting them overlap slightly. Sprinkle the top with 1 ounce (25 g) of grated Parmesan cheese.

Bake the dish for 15 minutes, or until the top is crisp and brown.

INGREDIENTS TO SERVE FOUR:
1 pint (600 ml) milk
1 small onion
1 bay leaf
ground nutmeg
salt
pepper
¼ lb (100 g) semolina
2 eggs
½ teaspoon (2.5 ml) French mustard
3 oz (75 g) Parmesan cheese
4 tomatoes

PREPARING TOMATO GNOCCHI

Cut the set gnocchi into squares.

Arrange the squares on the tomato slices.

Singapore Noodles

Cook ½ pound (250 g) of noodles or spaghetti in a large saucepan of boiling salted water until tender. Drain well.

Meanwhile, finely chop or crush 1 large garlic clove, slice ¼ pound (100 g) of mushrooms and peel and finely chop ¼-inch (6-mm) slice of root ginger. Finely shred ¼ pound (100 g) of cooked pork and cook and peel ¼ pound (100 g) of prawns.

Heat 1 tablespoon (15 ml) of peanut oil in a large saucepan. Add the garlic, mushrooms and ginger and fry for 2 minutes. Add the pork and prawns and stir-fry for 1 minute.

Stir in ¼ pint (150 ml) of chicken stock and 2 tablespoons (30 ml) of dry sherry or 1

tablespoon (15 ml) of soy sauce. Add ¼ pound (100 g) of shredded cabbage and 2 chopped spring onions and bring to the boil.

Add the drained noodles and stir-fry for 3 to 5 minutes, or until the noodles are heated through and are lightly browned.

Garnish with chopped coriander or parsley and serve immediately.

INGREDIENTS TO SERVE FOUR TO SIX:
½ lb (250 g) of noodles or spaghetti
1 large garlic clove
¼ lb (100 g) mushrooms
root ginger
¼ lb (100 g) cooked pork
¼ lb (100 g) prawns
1 tablespoon (15 ml) peanut oil
¼ pint (150 ml) chicken stock
2 tablespoons (30 ml) dry sherry or 1 tablespoon (15 ml) soy sauce
¼ lb (100 g) shredded cabbage
2 spring onions
chopped coriander or parsley

Spaghetti with Tuna Sauce

Cook ½ pound (250 g) of spaghetti in a large pan of boiling salted water until tender.

Meanwhile, prepare the sauce. Heat 1 tablespoon (15 ml) of corn oil in a saucepan. Add 1 chopped large onion and 1 crushed garlic clove and fry for 3 minutes, or until the onions are tender but not brown.

Add ½ pint (300 ml) of chicken or fish stock and 3 tablespoons (45 ml) of dry white wine or vermouth to the pan. Bring to the boil and cook for 2 minutes, or until the stock has reduced slightly.

Flake 6 ounces (150 g) of tuna fish into the pan and simmer for 2 to 3 minutes. Season to taste with salt and pepper.

Drain the pasta well and arrange it in a serving dish. Pour the hot sauce over the pasta and sprinkle with 2 tablespoons (30 ml) of chopped parsley.

INGREDIENTS TO SERVE FOUR:
½ lb (250 g) spaghetti
salt
1 tablespoon (15 ml) corn oil
1 large onion
1 garlic clove
½ pint (300 ml) chicken or fish stock
3 tablespoons (45 ml) dry white wine or vermouth
6 oz (150 g) tuna fish
pepper
2 tablespoons (30 ml) chopped parsley

Noodle Soup

For a lighter soup the chicken may be left out of this recipe.

Put 2 pints (1 litre) of well-seasoned chicken stock into a large saucepan and bring to the boil.

Finely slice 1 stick of celery and add to the stock. Reduce the heat and simmer for 5 minutes.

Slice 4 spring onions and add to the stock with ¼ pound (100 g) of vermicelli and ¼ pound (100 g) of bean sprouts. Add ¼ pound (100 g) of shredded cooked chicken meat.

Simmer the soup for 5 minutes, or until the noodles are tender but the vegetables are still crisp. Serve immediately.

INGREDIENTS TO SERVE FOUR TO SIX:
2 pints (1 litre) chicken stock
1 celery stick
4 spring onions
¼ lb (100 g) vermicelli
¼ lb (100 g) bean sprouts
¼ lb (100 g) cooked chicken meat

Orange Macaroni Pudding

A sharp, sweet sauce complements the bland pasta in this unusual macaroni pudding.

Melt 1 ounce (25 g) of margarine or butter in a saucepan. Stir in 1 ounce (25 g) of flour. Add ½ pint (300 ml) of milk and bring to the boil, stirring constantly. Continue boiling and stirring the mixture until the sauce thickens.

Reduce the heat to simmering point and add the grated rind and juice of 2 oranges, 2 tablespoons (30 ml) of castor sugar, ¼ pound (100 g) of sultanas and ½ teaspoon (2.5 ml) of ground cinnamon. Stir the ingredients well and continue to simmer for 2 minutes.

Add 6 ounces (150 g) of macaroni shells to a large pan of boiling water and cook for 10 to 15 minutes, or until the shells are just tender. Drain the macaroni shells and fold into the hot sauce.

Serve the pudding immediately.

INGREDIENTS TO SERVE FOUR:
1 oz (25 g) margarine or butter
1 oz (25 g) flour
½ pint (300 ml) milk
2 oranges
2 tablespoons (30 ml) castor sugar
¼ lb (100 g) sultanas
½ teaspoon (2.5 ml) ground cinnamon
6 oz (150 g) macaroni shells

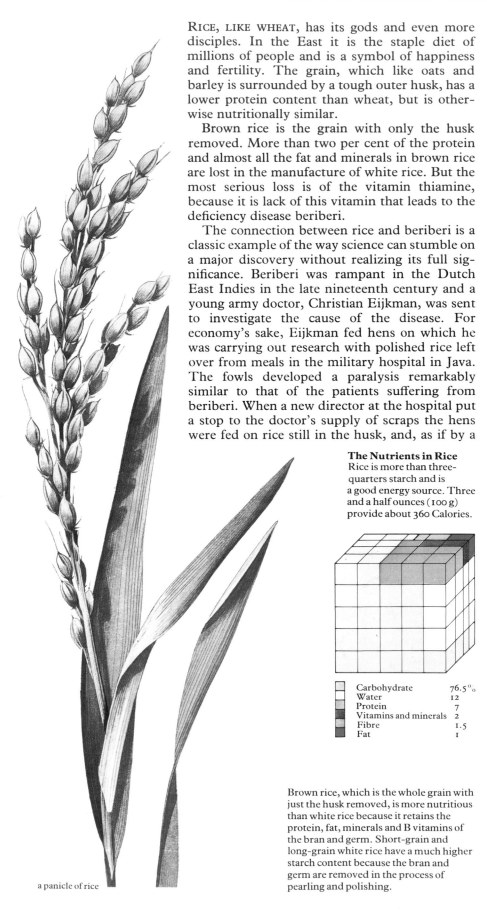

RICE, LIKE WHEAT, has its gods and even more disciples. In the East it is the staple diet of millions of people and is a symbol of happiness and fertility. The grain, which like oats and barley is surrounded by a tough outer husk, has a lower protein content than wheat, but is otherwise nutritionally similar.

Brown rice is the grain with only the husk removed. More than two per cent of the protein and almost all the fat and minerals in brown rice are lost in the manufacture of white rice. But the most serious loss is of the vitamin thiamine, because it is lack of this vitamin that leads to the deficiency disease beriberi.

The connection between rice and beriberi is a classic example of the way science can stumble on a major discovery without realizing its full significance. Beriberi was rampant in the Dutch East Indies in the late nineteenth century and a young army doctor, Christian Eijkman, was sent to investigate the cause of the disease. For economy's sake, Eijkman fed hens on which he was carrying out research with polished rice left over from meals in the military hospital in Java. The fowls developed a paralysis remarkably similar to that of the patients suffering from beriberi. When a new director at the hospital put a stop to the doctor's supply of scraps the hens were fed on rice still in the husk, and, as if by a

miracle, they recovered. It took almost half a century of investigation, however, before the full significance of thiamine in preventing beriberi became known.

The loss of thiamine in milled rice is minimized by a process known as parboiling, and it is estimated that in India more than half the rice is treated in this way. The method is to steep the unmilled rice in warm water for several days, then to steam-heat it and finally dry it. Thiamine and other valuable vitamins and minerals in the husk and bran dissolve in the warm water and are carried into the endosperm, which makes up three-quarters of the grain, so that they are not lost in milling. The grain, which is milled after this treatment, is not so strikingly white, but it contains more than twice as much thiamine as untreated milled grain.

Most of the world's rice is produced in the tropics, where, since it is an aquatic plant, it is usually grown in standing water—the vast paddies with labourers bent double over the plants provide the universal image of rice-growing. But the rice grown in warm temperate zones is more likely to be grown on dry land.

India was probably the birthplace of rice, but the first clear evidence of its cultivation comes from China in about 3000 BC. For more than the four thousand years of Imperial China the

The Nutrients in Rice
Rice is more than three-quarters starch and is a good energy source. Three and a half ounces (100 g) provide about 360 Calories.

Carbohydrate	76.5%
Water	12
Protein	7
Vitamins and minerals	2
Fibre	1.5
Fat	1

Brown rice, which is the whole grain with just the husk removed, is more nutritious than white rice because it retains the protein, fat, minerals and B vitamins of the bran and germ. Short-grain and long-grain white rice have a much higher starch content because the bran and germ are removed in the process of pearling and polishing.

a panicle of rice

Most rice is grown in the monsoon belt where heavy rains and irrigation methods, like these terraces in Sri Lanka, provide the conditions required by many varieties of the grain.

Emperor, and other members of the hierarchy, took part in an annual symbolic ceremony of ploughing a rice field. The Arabs introduced the cultivation of rice to Spain, and it spread to Italy in the fifteenth century. Rice reached America in 1700, and South Carolina, where it was first cultivated, was for a long time the country's most important rice-growing region.

There are several thousand varieties of rice, but the basic distinction in cooking is between three main types—long, medium and short grains. The long grains of Patna and Basmati rice are fluffy and separate when cooked and are therefore best used for savoury rice dishes and for plain boiled rice. Medium- and short-grain rices, such as Java, Italian and Carolina, are stickier and more moist grains, which are used to make moulds and stuffings and rice pudding.

Rice has an important role in sophisticated cuisines both of the East and the West. Many national rice dishes, or corruptions of them, have become almost universal. Pilav, basically a mixture of rice, meat and vegetables, is a national peasant dish in Turkey, but it turns up as plov in Russia, pilaw in Poland and pilaf in most of western Europe. For this dish, under whatever name, long-grained rice is essential.

Risotto, of Italian origin, is creamy and thick, and is best made with short-grained rice, preferably the Piedmontese variety, which does not go soggy with slow cooking. Like missionaries, Italian restaurateurs have spread the dish throughout the West. Spanish paella, yet another rice dish, was most probably the progenitor of jambalaya, a dish popular in the United States.

In all these dishes other ingredients, such as poultry, fish and vegetables, are integral parts, but rice provides the foundation. For real appreciation of rice, however, one has to turn to Chinese and Japanese cooking. There rice is a vital part of a meal, rather than part of a dish. In Japan the three main meals are called morning rice, afternoon rice and evening rice, and the test of a good cook is in the immaculate quality of the rice. To the Chinese gourmet there is nothing to surpass the sweet natural flavour (*hsien*) of perfectly cooked rice.

Rice has its other uses, too. Cooked under pressure at very high temperatures it is converted into a breakfast cereal. The Swedes, Norwegians, Danes and Belgians make rice porridge, and all their recipes have in common a sprinkling of cinnamon. Norwegians serve it with a drink of raspberry cordial and Danes eat it with melted butter and non-alcoholic beer.

Inevitably, like other grains, rice is made into an alcoholic drink. The Japanese brew is sake and the Chinese samshu. Little wonder that the most respectful Japanese name for rice is *gohan*, meaning "honourable food".

In a gesture to please the rice gods the Balinese display charms, like the figure made of coins above, at harvest festivals. Such symbols are common in some countries of Asia, where millions of peoples' lives depend on the success of the rice crop.

Boiled White Rice

Of the many methods of cooking rice this is the most nutritious because any nutrient that is lost into the cooking water is reabsorbed into the rice.

Cold cooked rice may be stored, covered, in the refrigerator for up to 1 week.

Put the rice and the water into a saucepan in the proportions of 1 to 2. This may be 1 bowl of rice to 2 bowls of water, or ½ pound (250 g) of rice to 1 pint (600 ml) of water. Add ½ teaspoon (2.5 ml) of salt and bring to the boil.

Cover the pan, reduce the heat and simmer gently for 15 to 20 minutes, or until the rice is tender, there is no hard core in the centre of the grains and all the water has been absorbed.

INGREDIENTS TO SERVE FOUR :
½ lb (250 g) white rice
1 pint (600 ml) water
½ teaspoon (2.5 ml) salt

Boiled Brown Rice

Brown rice is the whole unpolished grains of rice with only the inedible husk removed. It is more nutritious than white rice because it contains more fibre and more vitamin B. It takes about twice as long to cook as white rice and has a chewy texture and nutty flavour.

Put ½ pound (250 g) of brown rice into a large saucepan with 1 pint (600 ml) of water. Add ½ teaspoon (2.5 ml) of salt and bring to the boil.

Cover the pan, reduce the heat and simmer for 30 to 40 minutes, or until the rice is chewy but tender and all the liquid has been absorbed.

INGREDIENTS TO SERVE FOUR :
½ lb (250 g) brown rice
1 pint (600 ml) water
½ teaspoon (2.5 ml) salt

Oven-cooked Rice

This method of cooking rice can also be used to reheat cold cooked rice. Put the rice in an ovenproof dish, cover and bake for 10 to 15 minutes.

Preheat the oven to 350°F (180°C, Gas Mark 4).

Put ½ pound (250 g) of rice into an ovenproof dish. Add 1 pint (600 ml) of boiling water (twice as much water as rice) and ½ teaspoon (2.5 ml) of salt.

Cover and put into the oven. Cook brown rice for 60 to 80 minutes and white rice for 30 to 40 minutes, or until the rice is tender and all the water has been absorbed.

INGREDIENTS TO SERVE FOUR :
½ lb (250 g) rice
1 pint (600 ml) boiling water
½ teaspoon (2.5 ml) salt

Rice Minestrone

Heat 1 tablespoon (15 ml) of safflower oil in a large saucepan. Add 1 chopped onion and 1 diced carrot, 1 chopped stick of celery and 1 crushed garlic clove. Fry for 3 minutes, stirring frequently. Stir in 2 pints (1 litre) of well-seasoned chicken or vegetable stock and bring to the boil. Lower the heat and simmer for 20 minutes.

Add 3 ounces (75 g) of rice with 2 blanched, peeled, chopped medium-sized tomatoes, ¼ of a small cabbage, shredded, 2 ounces (50 g) of sliced green beans and 2 ounces (50 g) of shelled peas. Simmer for 15 minutes or until the rice is tender and the vegetables are cooked.

Sprinkle with grated Parmesan cheese and serve immediately.

INGREDIENTS TO SERVE FOUR :
1 tablespoon (15 ml) safflower oil
1 onion
1 carrot
1 celery stick
1 garlic clove
2 pints (1 litre) chicken or vegetable stock
3 oz (75 g) rice
2 medium-sized tomatoes
¼ small cabbage
2 oz (50 g) green beans
2 oz (50 g) shelled peas
grated Parmesan cheese

Paella

Cut 1 small chicken into 8 pieces. Slice 1 onion. Chop 2 ounces of bacon. Remove the seeds and pith from 1 small green pepper. Chop the pepper.

Heat 3 tablespoons (45 ml) of corn oil in a large, heavy frying-pan. Add the onion and bacon and fry for 3 minutes. Add the chicken pieces and cook until they are lightly browned. Add 1 crushed garlic clove, the chopped green pepper and ½ pound (250 g) of long-grain rice. Continue to cook the mixture for 1 minute, stirring constantly.

Blend 2 pinches of powdered saffron with 1½ pints (850 ml) of well-seasoned chicken stock and stir into the rice mixture. Bring to the boil, stirring occasionally.

Shell ½ pound (250 g) of prawns. Beard and scrub ½ pint (300 ml) of mussels. Add the mussels and prawns to the rice mixture. Cover the pan, reduce the heat and simmer gently for 15 minutes.

Add ¼ pound (100 g) of shelled peas to the pan and continue to simmer for 5 minutes more, or until the rice and chicken are tender, the stock has been absorbed and the mussels have opened.

Discard any mussels which remain closed. Serve immediately.

INGREDIENTS TO SERVE FOUR :
1 small chicken
1 onion
2 oz (50 g) bacon
1 small green pepper
3 tablespoons (45 ml) corn oil
1 garlic clove
½ lb (250 g) long-grain rice
powdered saffron
1½ pints (850 ml) chicken stock
½ lb (250 g) prawns
½ pint (300 ml) mussels
¼ lb (100 g) shelled peas

PREPARING SHELLFISH

Scrape any beard off mussels with a sharp knife.

Remove the head and shell and devein prawns.

Savoury Brown Rice

Put ½ pound (250 g) of brown rice into a saucepan with 1 pint (600 ml) of water or vegetable stock. Bring to the boil, cover, lower the heat and simmer for 30 minutes.

Add ¼ pound (100 g) of sweetcorn kernels with 4 chopped spring onions and ¼ pound (100 g) of peanuts to the rice. Simmer for a further 5 to 10 minutes, or until the rice and corn are tender, adding more water if necessary. Season to taste with salt and pepper. Serve immediately.

INGREDIENTS TO SERVE FOUR:
½ lb (250 g) brown rice
1 pint (600 ml) water or vegetable stock
¼ lb (100 g) sweetcorn kernels
4 spring onions
¼ lb (100 g) peanuts
salt
pepper

Persian Rice with Herbs

A delicious accompaniment to fish, this rice dish is traditionally served at New Year in Iran because its greenness is believed to ensure happiness in the year ahead.

Any fresh herbs may be added, although if dried herbs are substituted add only half the quantity given because they have a much stronger flavour.

Put ½ pound (250 g) of Basmati or long-grain rice into a saucepan. Cover with 1 pint (600 ml) of water and bring to the boil. Lower the heat and simmer for 5 minutes.

Add 1 tablespoon (15 ml) of chopped chives, 1 tablespoon (15 ml) of chopped parsley and 2 tablespoons (30 ml) of chopped mixed herbs such as tarragon, thyme, marjoram and basil to the rice. Stir in the grated rind of ½ lemon and season with salt and pepper. Mix well, cover the pan and simmer gently for 10 minutes, or until the rice is tender and the water has been absorbed.

INGREDIENTS TO SERVE FOUR:
½ lb (250 g) Basmati or long-grain rice
1 tablespoon (15 ml) chopped chives
1 tablespoon (15 ml) chopped parsley
2 tablespoons (30 ml) chopped mixed herbs
½ lemon
salt
pepper

Chinese Fried Rice

This rice dish is a good accompaniment to many savoury foods, but cooked meat, fish and vegetables may be added.

In a small bowl beat 2 eggs and season with salt and pepper. Heat 1 tablespoon (15 ml) of peanut oil in a *wok* or a large, heavy frying-pan. Pour the eggs into the pan and cook as an omelette until they are almost set. Slide the omelette on to a plate and chop it coarsely.

Add another tablespoon (15 ml) of peanut oil to the pan with 2 ounces (50 g) of chopped bacon and 1 chopped onion. Stirring frequently, fry for 3 to 5 minutes, or until the bacon is cooked and the onion tender. Add ½ pound (250 g) of cold cooked rice with 2 ounces (50 g) of cooked peas, 4 coarsely chopped spring onions and the chopped omelette. Stir continuously and continue frying for 2 to 3 minutes, or until the ingredients are heated through. Stir in 1 tablespoon (15 ml) of soy sauce and serve immediately.

INGREDIENTS TO SERVE FOUR:
2 eggs
salt
pepper
2 tablespoons (30 ml) peanut oil
2 oz (50 g) bacon
1 onion
½ lb (250 g) cold cooked rice
2 oz (50 g) cooked peas
4 spring onions
1 tablespoon (15 ml) soy sauce

STIR-FRYING

Heat the rice mixture in a pan and stir continuously.

Nasi Goreng

Chopped chillies may be added to this spicy Indonesian dish, but take care because they are very hot.

Heat 2 tablespoons (30 ml) of corn oil in a large frying-pan. Add 1 chopped onion and 1 crushed garlic clove and fry for 3 minutes, stirring constantly. Add ½ teaspoon (2.5 ml) of chilli powder, ¼ teaspoon (1 ml) of ground coriander and ¼ teaspoon (1 ml) of ground cumin and fry for 1 minute, stirring constantly.

Add ½ pound (250 g) of cold cooked rice with 3 ounces (75 g) of chopped cooked ham, 2 ounces (50 g) of cooked peeled prawns, 2 ounces (50 g) of peanuts and a 1 inch (2.5-cm) piece of cucumber, diced. Fry for 5 minutes, stirring constantly, or until the ingredients are heated through. Serve immediately.

INGREDIENTS TO SERVE FOUR:
2 tablespoons (30 ml) corn oil
1 onion
1 garlic clove
½ teaspoon (2.5 ml) chilli powder
¼ teaspoon (1 ml) ground coriander
¼ teaspoon (1 ml) ground cumin
½ lb (250 g) cold cooked rice
3 oz (75 g) cooked ham
2 oz (50 g) cooked peeled prawns
2 oz (50 g) peanuts
1-inch (2.5-cm) piece cucumber

Pilau

This Middle Eastern rice dish is often served with kebabs.

Heat 2 tablespoons (30 ml) of corn oil in a saucepan. Add 1 chopped onion and fry, stirring frequently, for 5 minutes, or until the onion is lightly browned.

Add ½ pound (250 g) of Basmati or long-grain rice, 2 ounces (50 g) of raisins, 2 ounces (50 g) of chopped dried apricots and 2 ounces (50 g) of chopped walnuts.

Pour 1 pint (600 ml) of chicken or vegetable stock over the rice mixture. Stir in ½ teaspoon (2.5 ml) of ground cinnamon and season to taste with salt and pepper. Bring to the boil, stirring occasionally. Lower the heat, cover and simmer for 15 minutes, or until the rice is tender and the stock has been absorbed.

INGREDIENTS TO SERVE FOUR:
2 tablespoons (30 ml) corn oil
1 onion
½ lb (250 g) Basmati or long-grain rice
2 oz (50 g) raisins
2 oz (50 g) dried apricots
2 oz (50 g) walnuts
1 pint (600 ml) chicken or vegetable stock
½ teaspoon (2.5 ml) ground cinnamon
salt
pepper

Kedgeree

Put ¾ pound (350 g) of smoked haddock fillets into a saucepan with 1 pint (600 ml) of water, 2 peppercorns, 1 bay leaf, 2 parsley sprigs and the grated rind and juice of ½ lemon. Bring to the boil. Cover the pan, reduce the heat and simmer gently for 10 minutes, or until the haddock is tender. Drain the fish. Strain and reserve the liquor.

Add water if necessary to make the fish liquor up to 1 pint (600 ml). Put the liquor and ½ pound (250 g) of long-grain white rice into a saucepan. Bring to the boil. Cover, lower the heat and simmer for 15 to 20 minutes, or until the rice is tender and all the liquor has been absorbed.

Coarsely chop 2 hard-boiled eggs. Flake the haddock and add it with the eggs to the rice. Stirring constantly, heat gently for 3 to 5 minutes, or until the ingredients are hot.

Garnish with 1 sliced hard-boiled egg and 1 tablespoon (15 ml) of chopped parsley. Serve immediately.

INGREDIENTS TO SERVE FOUR:
¾ lb (350 g) smoked haddock fillets
2 peppercorns
1 bay leaf
2 parsley sprigs
½ lemon
½ lb (250 g) long-grain white rice
3 eggs
1 tablespoon (15 ml) chopped parsley

POACHING AND SKINNING FISH

Simmer fillets of fish in acidulated water.

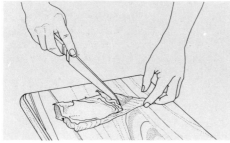

Scrape towards the head to skin poached fish.

Spinach and Chestnut Rice

Preheat the oven to 350°F (180°C, Gas Mark 4).

Put ½ pound (250 g) of rice and 1 pint (600 ml) of water into a large saucepan. Add ½ teaspoon (2.5 ml) of salt and bring to the boil. Cover the pan, reduce the heat and simmer for 15 to 20 minutes, or until the rice is tender and all the water has been absorbed.

Meanwhile, thoroughly wash 1 pound (500 g) of spinach in cold water and put it into a large saucepan. Add 1 teaspoon (5 ml) of salt, cover the pan and cook for 10 minutes, or until the spinach is tender. Drain the spinach well and chop it coarsely.

Make two cuts through the shells of ½ pound (250 g) of chestnuts. Put them into a saucepan with enough water to cover. Bring to the boil and cook until the shells split. Drain the chestnuts and peel off the shells and inner skins while they are still warm.

Combine the rice, spinach and chestnuts in a mixing bowl and season to taste with salt and pepper. Transfer the mixture to an ovenproof dish. Sprinkle with ¼ pound (100 g) of fresh breadcrumbs. Flake 2 ounces (50 g) of margarine or butter over the dish.

Bake for 35 minutes, or until the top is crisp and golden.

INGREDIENTS TO SERVE FOUR:
½ lb (250 g) rice
salt
1 lb (500 g) spinach
½ lb (250 g) chestnuts
pepper
¼ lb (100 g) fresh breadcrumbs
2 oz (50 g) margarine or butter

Risotto Milanese

This is an extremely versatile dish and any leftover meats or vegetables may be added to make a substantial main-course dish.

Heat 1 ounce (25 g) of margarine or butter with 1 tablespoon (15 ml) of corn oil in a large saucepan. Add 1 chopped medium-sized onion and 3 ounces (75 g) of chopped bacon and fry for 5 minutes, stirring frequently, until the onion is beginning to brown. Add ¼ pound (100 g) of sliced mushrooms and ½ pound (250 g) of rice to the pan and fry for 1 minute, stirring constantly.

Add 1 pint (600 ml) of chicken or vegetable stock to the rice and season to taste with salt and pepper. Continue stirring and bring to the boil. Cover, reduce the heat and simmer gently for 15 to 20 minutes or until the rice is cooked, adding more stock if necessary, and the stock has been absorbed.

Grate ¼ pound (100 g) of Cheddar cheese and add half to the rice mixture. Stir the rice until the cheese has melted.

Turn the mixture into a warm serving

dish. Sprinkle with the remaining grated cheese and serve.

INGREDIENTS TO SERVE FOUR:
1 oz (25 g) margarine or butter
1 tablespoon (15 ml) corn oil
1 medium-sized onion
3 oz (15 g) bacon
¼ lb (100 g) mushrooms
½ pound (250 g) rice
1 pint (600 ml) chicken or vegetable stock
salt
pepper
¼ lb (100 g) Cheddar cheese

Spanish Rice Casserole

This colourful rice dish makes an excellent accompaniment to chicken.

Heat 1 tablespoon (15 ml) of corn oil in a saucepan. Add 4 rashers of chopped streaky bacon and 1 chopped onion and fry, stirring frequently, for 5 minutes. Cut 1 green pepper into strips and add to the pan with ½ pound (250 g) of long-grain rice. Fry, stirring constantly, for 1 minute.

Blanch, peel and chop 4 ripe, medium-sized tomatoes. Stir ¾ pint (450 ml) of chicken or vegetable stock and the tomatoes into the rice mixture. Add ¼ teaspoon (1 ml) of dried mixed herbs. Season to taste with salt and pepper. Bring to the boil and cover. Lower the heat and simmer gently for 15 minutes, or until the rice is tender and the liquid has been absorbed.

Alternatively, put in an ovenproof casserole, cover and bake at 375°F (190°C, Gas Mark 5) for 20 to 30 minutes.

INGREDIENTS TO SERVE FOUR:
1 tablespoon (15 ml) corn oil
4 rashers streaky bacon
1 onion
1 green pepper
½ lb (250 g) long-grain rice
4 ripe medium-sized tomatoes
¾ pint (450 ml) chicken or vegetable stock
¼ teaspoon (1 ml) dried mixed herbs
salt
pepper

Apricot Lamb Polo

Preheat the oven to 350°F (180°C, Gas Mark 4).

Heat 1 tablespoon (15 ml) of corn oil in a large saucepan. Add 1 chopped large onion and fry for 5 minutes, stirring frequently, until the onion is lightly browned. Cut 1 pound (500 g) of lean boned neck or leg of lamb into 1-inch (2-cm) cubes. Add to the pan and fry until the meat is brown.

Add ½ teaspoon (2.5 ml) of ground cinnamon, salt and pepper to taste, 1 pint (600 ml) of water and 1 tablespoon (15 ml) of lemon juice to the pan. Mix well.

Bring to the boil, stirring constantly. Stir in 6 ounces (150 g) of dried apricots. Cover, reduce the heat and simmer for 1 to 1½ hours, or until the meat and the apricots are tender. If there is still quite a lot of liquid in the lamb stew, boil it rapidly, uncovered, until the liquid has reduced but the stew is still moist.

Meanwhile, put 1 pint (600 ml) of water into a large saucepan. Add ½ pound (250 g) of long-grain white rice and 1 teaspoon (5 ml) of salt. Bring to the boil. Cover, reduce the heat and simmer for 10 minutes. Drain the rice.

Put a layer of the parboiled rice into an ovenproof dish, then put in a layer of the meat mixture. Continue making layers, finishing with a layer of rice.

Cover the dish and bake for 20 minutes. Serve immediately.

INGREDIENTS TO SERVE FOUR:
1 tablespoon (15 ml) corn oil
1 large onion
1 lb (500 g) lean boned neck or leg of lamb
½ teaspoon (2.5 ml) ground cinnamon
salt
pepper
1 tablespoon (15 ml) lemon juice
6 oz (150 g) dried apricots
½ lb (250 g) long-grain white rice

Orange Rice Salad

Prepare the dressing, pour 3 tablespoons (45 ml) of wine vinegar into a small bowl and add 5 tablespoons (75 ml) of sunflower oil, 1 tablespoon (15 ml) at a time, beating the mixture vigorously with a fork after each addition. Add the juice of 1 orange and 1 tablespoon (15 ml) of chopped mixed herbs and beat again.

Put ½ pound (250 g) of warm cooked rice into a large mixing bowl. Add 3 fluid ounces (100 ml) of the dressing and mix well. Warm rice will absorb the dressing better.

Peel and remove the pith from 2 oranges. Cut away the membrane from the segments of fruit. Add the segments to the rice with 1 chopped stick of celery, 2 ounces (50 g) of sultanas and 2 ounces (50 g) of chopped walnuts. Mix well. Cover and chill.

INGREDIENTS TO SERVE FOUR TO SIX:
3 tablespoons (45 ml) wine vinegar
5 tablespoons (75 ml) sunflower oil
3 oranges
1 tablespoon (15 ml) chopped mixed herbs
½ lb (250 g) warm cooked rice
1 celery stick
2 oz (50 g) sultanas
2 oz (50 g) walnuts

Rice and Nut Ring

An elegant way to serve rice for a dinner party, this rice ring can be prepared in advance and kept chilled for up to 2 days before reheating. The pale-green pistachio nuts are an attractive addition.

Preheat the oven to 350°F (180°C, Gas Mark 4). Lightly grease a 1½-pint (850-ml), 7- to 8-inch (18- to 20-cm) ring mould.

Heat 1 ounce (25 g) of margarine or butter with 1 tablespoon (15 ml) of corn oil in a

Spoon nuts into the lightly greased mould.

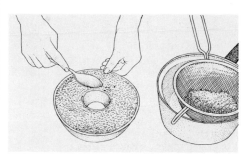

Cover with cooked rice and press into the mould.

Turn the mould out on to a plate and serve.

saucepan. Add 2 ounces (50 g) of coarsely chopped blanched almonds, 1 ounce (25 g) of chopped walnuts and ½ ounce (15 g) of peeled and split pistachio nuts. Fry, stirring constantly, for 30 seconds, or until the nuts are golden brown. Spoon the nuts into the prepared mould.

Put ½ pound (250 g) of cold cooked rice into the mould on top of the nuts, pressing it down firmly with the back of a spoon.

Bake the mould for 15 minutes. Cover the mould with a plate, invert and carefully remove the mould.

Serve immediately.

INGREDIENTS TO SERVE FOUR:
1 oz (25 g) margarine or butter
1 tablespoon (15 ml) corn oil
2 oz (50 g) blanched almonds
1 oz (25 g) walnuts
½ oz (15 g) peeled, split pistachio nuts
½ lb (250 g) cold cooked rice

Braised Rice and Onions

Preheat the oven to 350°F (180°C, Gas Mark 4).

Peel and thinly slice 1 pound (500 g) of onions. Separate the slices into rings and put half of them into an ovenproof dish.

Sprinkle the onion rings with ¼ pound (100 g) of long-grain white rice, 4 sage leaves, 1 bay leaf, salt and pepper. Cover with the remaining onion. Pour in ½ pint (300 ml) of water.

Cover and bake for 1 hour, or until the rice and onions are tender and the water has been absorbed. Stir once or twice during cooking to mix the rice with the onions.

Serve hot.

INGREDIENTS TO SERVE FOUR:
1 lb (500 g) onions
¼ lb (100 g) long-grain white rice
4 sage leaves
1 bay leaf
salt
pepper

Cherry Rice Pudding

Preheat the oven to 350°F (180°C, Gas Mark 4).

Put 3 ounces (75 g) of short-grain rice and 1 pint (600 ml) of milk into a saucepan. Add 2 tablespoons (30 ml) of castor sugar, the grated rind of ½ lemon, ½ teaspoon (2.5 ml) of grated nutmeg and 2 ounces (50 g) of raisins and mix well. Bring to the boil. Reduce the heat and simmer, stirring occasionally, for 15 minutes, or until the rice has swollen and the mixture is creamy.

Stir 2 egg yolks into the rice. Whisk 2 egg whites until stiff and fold into the rice. Stone ½ pound (250 g) of cherries and put them into an ovenproof dish. Pour the rice mixture over the cherries.

Bake the pudding for 20 to 30 minutes, or until the top is puffed up and brown.

INGREDIENTS TO SERVE FOUR:
3 oz (75 g) short-grain rice
1 pint (600 ml) milk
2 tablespoons (30 ml) castor sugar
½ lemon
½ teaspoon (2.5 ml) grated nutmeg
2 oz (50 g) raisins
2 eggs
½ lb (250 g) cherries

TWO GRAINS—RYE AND OATS—which probably made their first appearance as weeds in wheat fields are now among the world's noteworthy cereals. They also have in common great hardiness in cold climates, an ability to thrive in poor soil and a more pronounced flavour than wheat, rice or maize. They differ from each other in that rye can be made into bread and is eaten by humans, while most of the world's oat crop is fed to animals. Human beings thus deprive themselves of one of the cereals which is rich in protein and fat and which is also well endowed with the B vitamins.

The original home of rye is believed to have been Asia Minor. By the Iron Age it was grown farther north and by the Middle Ages it was established as a major crop in central and northern Europe. From there it was taken to America, where it was used to make an alcoholic drink as well as to provide food.

The production and popularity of rye is greatest in a broad belt running south from the Arctic Circle through Scandinavia and Russia and into northeastern Europe, Germany and parts of France. In Finland, for example, the harvest is celebrated with a rye porridge, which is sometimes served with stewed pork.

Rye has never been a popular grain in England, where people have always hankered for as white a loaf of bread as they could get. Nevertheless, until the eighteenth century all but the wealthy English had to be content with bread made from maslin, a flour milled from a mixture of wheat and rye, or even from barley and rye.

Perhaps it was because the English mixed rye with other grains that they escaped the disastrous outbreaks of poisoning, caused by eating rye bread, that periodically swept through Europe. The first serious outbreak was in AD 857, when thousands of people died in the Rhine Valley. The last was in 1951 in the Rhône Valley, where hundreds of people appeared to go mad overnight.

These disasters are now known to have been caused by a virulent fungus, called ergot, which can infect the ripe heads of rye. The fungus contains several poisonous alkaloids, one of which is closely allied to LSD. Any further outbreaks of ergotism seem unlikely because strict precautions are now taken to ensure that infected rye is not milled.

The protein value of rye bread is considerably lower than that of wheaten bread. There is also no comparison in the flavour or texture. The readiness with which rye ferments gives the bread its

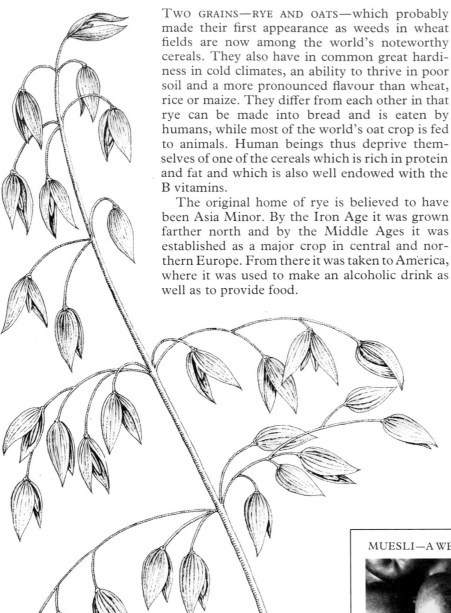

a panicle of oats

The Nutrients in Oats
As a cereal oats are very high in fat and are also rich in protein and three and a half ounces (100 g) provide almost 400 Calories.

Carbohydrate	66 %
Protein	11.5
Water	10
Fat	9
Vitamins and minerals	2
Fibre	1.5

MUESLI—A WELL-BALANCED MEAL

There are few more nutritious dishes than muesli, whose basic ingredients —rolled oats, raw apple, lemon juice, hazelnuts and milk—make a perfectly balanced meal. Muesli was devised early in the twentieth century by the Swiss physician Dr Bircher-Benner, at his famous clinic. Different ingredients may be added, but all muesli recipes are based on the traditional raw goodness that the doctor revered.

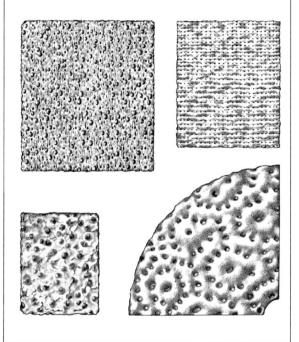

THE CRISPBREAD MYTH
The popularity of crispbread owes much to its image as a slimming aid. Rye flour is usually the main ingredient because it is the most filling cereal. Although slice for slice crispbread provides fewer calories than bread, weight for weight crispbread is more fattening: it is crispbread's slim slice that achieves the calorie saving. Crispbread can only aid slimming as an integral part of a calorie-controlled diet.

distinctive sour flavour—and this flavour you may either like or dislike. The Poles, Scandinavians, Germans, French and also many Americans are among those who enjoy it.

In England rye bread has never managed to shake off its association with poverty. Rye crispbread, on the other hand, has a following among British as well as American slimmers, who seem to believe that it is endowed with magical properties. Manufacturers, however, are not permitted to make extravagant slimming claims for it and may only recommend it as an aid to weight loss.

There is as great a variety of rye breads as of those made from wheat. Depending on the rate of extraction the flour will vary from pale to rich and dark. But because of the grain's low gluten content, all rye breads have a dense texture. The heaviest and blackest rye bread is the German pumpernickel, which is made from coarsely ground rye. Mixing wheat flour, which is richer in gluten, with rye flour gives a more open texture to the otherwise solid loaf.

Among the milled grains there is no flavour to compare with the nutty sweetness of oats. In spite of this oats are one of the least popular of cereals, except in Ireland and in Scotland where

the addiction to oats has long been a source of jibes by English writers. In the eighteenth century, Dr Johnson, in his *Dictionary of the English Language*, defined the oat as "a grain, which in England is generally given to horses, but in Scotland supports the people". In the early nineteenth century the satirist Sydney Smith described Scotland as "that knuckle end of England—that land of Calvin, oatcakes and sulphur".

The fearsome names of some of the oat-based Scottish and Irish dishes could have come straight out of Tolkien's *Lord of the Rings*. There is brose, a Scottish porridgy soup, and brotchán, an Irish version; crowdie, a Scottish dish made with oatmeal and buttermilk, and the Irish–Scottish sowans, a fermented gruel that is probably made more palatable when taken, as at Christmas, with whisky. Haggis, which is basically a mixture of offal and oatmeal, was known to the Romans, but it is now as Scottish as the tartan. The Irish make an oatmeal-based sausage called white pudding, while the Scottish version is mealie pudding, or, more enticingly, skirlie. A hodgils is a Scottish oatmeal dumpling, and so is the mysteriously named fitless cock.

Generally, the consumption of oatmeal was, until recently, largely in the form of real porridge, but this has now lost much of its breakfast-time supremacy to convenience foods made mainly from maize, wheat and rice. These are ready-to-serve, while the coarse oatmeal, that makes the best porridge, needs long, slow cooking and constant stirring. And, according to a tradition that goes back to the Druids, porridge must always be stirred to the right.

Oatmeal is lacking in gluten and cannot be made into bread, but it does make delicious oatcakes. Here again the Scots excel with their bannocks and broonies. Parkin, a sticky cake of oatmeal and treacle, has its devotees. In the north of England it is traditionally eaten around the bonfires on Guy Fawkes's night. And in the United States oatmeal is made into delicious, raisin-studded biscuits.

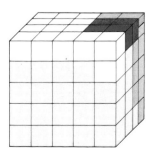

The Nutrients in Rye
Rye is the only cereal, other than wheat, with a high enough gluten content to make bread and it has the same calorific content as wheat.

Carbohydrate	72	%
Water	15	
Protein	7.5	
Vitamins and minerals	2	
Fat	2	
Fibre	1.5	

a head of rye

Pumpernickel

Of German origin, this recipe makes a firm black bread. Because rye has little gluten it will not rise as much as bread made from a strong wheat flour.

In a large bowl mix 1½ pounds (750 g) of rye flour with 1 tablespoon (15 ml) of salt. Add 2 ounces (50 g) of margarine. Cut the fat into small pieces with a round-bladed knife and rub it into the flour.

Put 2 tablespoons (30 ml) of black treacle into a small saucepan with ½ pint (300 ml) of milk. Cook over very low heat until the treacle has dissolved and the milk is lukewarm.

Blend ¾ ounce (20 g) of fresh yeast with ¼ pint (150 ml) of tepid water until the yeast has dissolved. Make a well in the flour mixture and pour in the yeast liquid and the warm milk and treacle. Mix until a sticky dough has formed.

Turn the dough out on to a floured surface and knead it well for 10 minutes, or until the dough is firm and no longer sticky. Add more flour if necessary.

Put the dough into a lightly greased bowl and cover with greased polythene, or put it into a large greased polythene bag. Leave the dough to rise in a warm place for 45 to 60 minutes, or until it has doubled in bulk.

Preheat the oven to 400°F (200°C, Gas Mark 6).

When the dough has risen turn it out on to a lightly floured surface and knead it again for 2 to 3 minutes. Divide the dough into halves, shape each half into an oval and put them on a lightly greased baking sheet. Alternatively, put the dough into two 1-pound (½-kg) loaf tins. Sprinkle 1 tablespoon (15 g) of caraway seeds over the loaves and press the seeds lightly into the dough. Cover the dough and leave it to rise in a warm place until it has doubled in bulk, or risen to the top of the tins.

Bake for 45 minutes, or until the loaves are dark brown and sound hollow when tapped underneath. Cool on a wire rack.

INGREDIENTS TO MAKE TWO SMALL LOAVES:
1½ lb (750 g) rye flour
1 tablespoon (15 ml) salt
2 oz (50 g) margarine
2 tablespoons (30 ml) black treacle
½ pint (300 ml) milk
¾ oz (20 g) fresh yeast
¼ pint (150 ml) tepid water
1 tablespoon (15 ml) caraway seeds

Sour Dough Rye Bread

Heat ¾ pint (450 ml) of milk until it is lukewarm. Put ½ ounce (15 g) of fresh yeast into a large mixing bowl, pour in a little of the milk and stir until the yeast has dissolved. Stir in the remaining milk and ½ pound (250 g) of rye flour. Cover and leave in a warm place for at least 12 hours, until the mixture smells sour.

Stir ¼ pound (100 g) more of rye flour, ½ pound (250 g) of strong white flour and 1 tablespoon (15 ml) of salt into the mixture to make a firm dough. Turn the dough out on to a floured surface. Knead it for 10 minutes, adding more flour if necessary, until the dough has become firm and elastic. Put the dough into a lightly greased bowl. Cover with greased polythene and leave it in a warm place for about 1 hour, or until the dough has risen and doubled in bulk.

When the dough has risen, turn it out on to a lightly floured surface and knead again for 2 to 3 minutes. Divide the dough into halves and shape into 2 loaves. Put the loaves on a greased baking sheet or into two 1-pound (½-kg) loaf tins. Cover with greased polythene and leave to rise in a warm place for 20 to 30 minutes, or until the dough has doubled in bulk, or reached the top of the tins.

Preheat the oven to 425°F (220°C, Gas Mark 7).

Bake the loaves for 15 minutes, then reduce the oven temperature to 375°F (190°C, Gas Mark 5) and bake for 20 to 25 minutes more, or until the loaves are brown and sound hollow when tapped underneath. Leave to cool on a wire rack before storing or serving.

INGREDIENTS TO MAKE TWO SMALL LOAVES:
¾ pint (450 ml) milk
½ oz (15 g) fresh yeast
¾ lb (350 g) rye flour
½ lb (250 g) strong white flour
1 tablespoon (15 ml) salt

Peasant Bread

In a large mixing bowl combine 1 pound (500 g) of wholewheat flour, ¼ pound (100 g) of rye flour, ¼ pound (100 g) of cornmeal and 1 tablespoon (15 ml) of salt. Mix well. Into a small saucepan pour ½ pint (300 ml) of milk, ¼ pint (150 ml) of water and 2 tablespoons (30 ml) of molasses or treacle. Cook over low heat until the molasses has dissolved and the mixture is warm enough to hold your finger in without discomfort.

Put ½ ounce (15 g) of fresh yeast into a bowl. Stirring, gradually add the warm milk mixture. Mix until well blended.

Pour the yeast liquid on to the dry ingredients. Mix until a sticky dough is formed. Turn the dough out on to a floured surface and knead it, adding more flour if

necessary, for 10 minutes, or until the dough is firm and no longer sticky.

Put the dough into a lightly greased bowl, cover with greased polythene and leave in a warm place for about 1 hour, or until the dough has risen and doubled in bulk.

Preheat the oven to 400°F (200°C, Gas Mark 6).

When the dough has risen turn it out of the bowl and knead it again for a few minutes. Divide the dough into halves and shape into 2 oval loaves.

Put the loaves on a greased baking sheet, or into two 1-pound (½-kg) loaf tins. Make 3 diagonal cuts in the top of each loaf. Cover with greased polythene and leave to rise until the dough has doubled in bulk or reached the top of the tins.

Bake for 35 minutes, or until the loaves are dark brown, firm to the touch and sound hollow when tapped underneath. Cool on a wire rack.

INGREDIENTS TO MAKE TWO SMALL LOAVES:
1 lb (500 g) wholewheat flour
¼ lb (100 g) rye flour
¼ lb (100 g) cornmeal
1 tablespoon (15 ml) salt
½ pint (300 ml) milk
2 tablespoons (30 ml) molasses or treacle
½ oz (15 g) fresh yeast

SHAPING BREAD

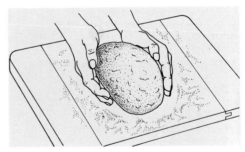

Mould the dough into loaves with your hands.

Old-fashioned Parkin

This Scottish oatcake may be stored for 2 to 3 weeks in an airtight container. It improves with keeping.

Preheat the oven to 325°F (170°C, Gas Mark 3). Grease a 10- by 8- by 2-inch (28- by 20- by 5-cm) cake tin and line it with greaseproof paper. Grease the paper.

Put ¼ pound (100 g) of margarine or butter into a saucepan with 2 ounces (50 g) of soft brown sugar, ¼ pound (100 g) of black treacle and ¼ pound (100 g) of golden syrup. Heat gently until the fat has melted and the sugar has dissolved. Set aside until cool.

Beat 2 eggs with ¼ pint (150 ml) of milk and stir into the cooled melted ingredients.

In a large bowl mix together ½ pound (250 g) of wheatmeal flour, 6 ounces (150 g) of medium oatmeal, ½ teaspoon (2.5 ml) of bicarbonate of soda and 2 teaspoons (10 ml) of ground ginger.

Make a well in the flour mixture and pour in the melted ingredients. Stir until well mixed. Spread the mixture in the prepared tin. Bake for 1 to 1¼ hours, or until the cake is firm to the touch. Cool on a wire rack.

Wrap the cake in foil and keep it for at least 1 day before serving.

INGREDIENTS TO MAKE ONE LARGE CAKE:
¼ lb (100 g) margarine or butter
2 oz (50 g) soft brown sugar
¼ lb (100 g) black treacle
¼ lb (100 g) golden syrup
2 eggs
¼ pint (150 ml) milk
½ lb (250 g) wheatmeal flour
6 oz (150 g) medium oatmeal
½ teaspoon (2.5 ml) bicarbonate of soda
2 teaspoons (10 ml) ground ginger

Harvest Oatcake

This golden country cake is made with oats, wholewheat flour and wheatgerm, and is flavoured with oranges and honey. It is very easy to make; everything is mixed together in one bowl.

Preheat the oven to 350°F (180°C, Gas Mark 4). Grease a 7-inch (18-cm) square cake tin.

In a large mixing bowl blend together 1 egg, 4 tablespoons (60 ml) of corn oil, 6 tablespoons (90 ml) of honey and 1 teaspoon (5 ml) of vanilla essence. Grate the rind of 1 orange into the bowl. Squeeze the juice from 3 oranges and stir it into the mixture.

Blend in 2 teaspoons (10 ml) of baking powder, ¼ pound (100 g) of wholewheat flour, ½ pound (250 g) of rolled oats and ¼ pound (100 g) of wheatgerm. Mix well.

Turn the batter into the prepared cake tin. Level the surface and bake for 40 to 45 minutes, or until the cake has risen and the top is golden. Cool slightly before removing from the tin.

INGREDIENTS TO MAKE ONE SMALL CAKE:
1 egg
4 tablespoons (60 ml) corn oil
6 tablespoons (90 ml) honey
1 teaspoon (5 ml) vanilla essence
3 oranges
2 teaspoons (10 ml) baking powder
¼ lb (100 g) wholewheat flour
½ lb (250 g) rolled oats
¼ lb (100 g) wheatgerm

Oatwheels

Preheat the oven to 350°F (180°C, Gas Mark 4).

In a large mixing bowl cream together ¼ pound (100 g) of margarine with ¼ pound (100 g) soft brown sugar until the mixture is pale and fluffy. Mix 1 teaspoon (5 ml) of baking powder with ¼ pound (100 g) of wheatmeal flour and stir into the creamed mixture with ¼ pound (100 g) of rolled oats and the grated rind and juice of ½ lemon.

Press the mixture together with your hands. Carefully roll the mixture out on a floured surface to ¼ inch (6 mm) thick. Using a 3½-inch (9-cm) fluted cutter stamp out 12 to 15 biscuits, rerolling the dough as necessary. Carefully lift the biscuits on to a lightly greased baking sheet.

Bake for 10 to 15 minutes, or until the biscuits are just beginning to colour at the edges. Allow the biscuits to cool slightly before transferring them to a wire rack.

INGREDIENTS TO MAKE TWELVE TO FIFTEEN BISCUITS:
¼ lb (100 g) margarine
¼ lb (100 g) soft brown sugar
1 teaspoon (5 ml) baking powder
¼ lb (100 g) wheatmeal flour
¼ lb (100 g) rolled oats
½ lemon

Scottish Oatcakes

Traditionally called farls in Scotland, these oatcakes may be served warm or cold with butter or jam.

Preheat the oven to 400°F (200°C, Gas Mark 6).

Put ¼ pound (100 g) of medium oatmeal into a mixing bowl. Stir in a pinch of salt, ¼ teaspoon (1 ml) of bicarbonate of soda and ¼ teaspoon (1 ml) of ground cinnamon. Put 1 ounce (25 g) of margarine into a small saucepan with 1 tablespoon (15 ml) of water and heat slowly until the margarine has melted. Bring to the boil, then pour into the oatmeal mixture. Stir to a soft dough.

Bind the dough together with your hands, then turn it out on to a floured surface and knead lightly. Roll the dough out thinly to form an 8-inch (20-cm) round. Cut the round into 8 wedges.

Carefully lift the wedges on to a greased baking sheet. Bake for 15 to 20 minutes, or until the oatcakes are crisp, lightly browned and the edges are beginning to curl up.

INGREDIENTS TO MAKE EIGHT OATCAKES:
¼ lb (100 g) medium oatmeal
salt
¼ teaspoon (1 ml) bicarbonate of soda
¼ teaspoon (1 ml) ground cinnamon
1 oz (25 g) margarine

Herb Rye Crispbread

This wafer-thin crispbread can be eaten as a savoury biscuit or as a substitute for bread.

Preheat oven to 400°F (200°C, Gas Mark 6).

Put ½ pound (250 g) of rye flour into a mixing bowl and rub in 2 ounces (50 g) of margarine. Mix in 1 teaspoon (5 ml) of dried mixed herbs and ½ teaspoon (2.5 ml) of salt. Stir in 4 tablespoons (60 ml) of milk or water and mix until the ingredients are thoroughly blended and the dough is firm.

Divide the dough into halves. Knead each half lightly on a floured surface. Roll each piece of dough out thinly to about 9 inches (23 cm) square. Cut into 3-inch (8-cm) squares. Put the squares on to lightly greased baking sheets. Prick each square well with a fork to prevent it from rising and bubbling during baking.

Bake the crispbread for 10 to 15 minutes, or until the edges just begin to colour, but do not let them brown. Cool the crispbreads slightly on baking sheets, then transfer them to wire racks.

INGREDIENTS TO MAKE EIGHTEEN CRISPBREADS:
½ lb (250 g) rye flour
2 oz (50 g) margarine
1 teaspoon (5 ml) dried mixed herbs
½ teaspoon (2.5 ml) salt
4 tablespoons (60 ml) milk or water

MAKING CRISPBREAD

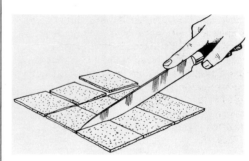

Roll the dough out thinly and cut into squares.

Prick the squares well to prevent them rising.

55

Flapjacks

These crunchy, sticky bars will keep well for up to 2 weeks if they are stored in an airtight container.

Preheat the oven to 375 °F (190 °C, Gas Mark 5). Grease a 7- to 8-inch (18- to 20-cm) square cake tin.

Put 3 ounces (75 g) of margarine or butter into a saucepan with 2 ounces (50 g) of soft brown sugar and 2 tablespoons (30 ml) of golden syrup. Heat gently until the sugar has dissolved. Remove from the heat and stir in 6 ounces (150 g) of rolled oats. Mix well.

Press the mixture into the prepared tin and level the surface. Bake for 20 minutes, or until golden brown and firm to the touch.

Cut into 12 bars while still in the tin. Cool in the tin until the bars are hard, then put on a wire rack.

INGREDIENTS TO MAKE TWELVE BARS:
3 oz (75 g) margarine or butter
2 oz (50 g) soft brown sugar
2 tablespoons (30 ml) golden syrup
6 oz (150 g) rolled oats

MAKING FLAPJACKS

Press the mixture into a tin with a knife.

Cut into bars and cool in the tin.

Muesli

This nutritious cereal is not only a delicious breakfast dish but served with fresh fruit makes an excellent dessert. It can be stored in an airtight container for up to 1 month. To serve muesli spoon it into serving bowls, add milk, yogurt or fresh orange juice and mix to a creamy consistency.

Combine ½ pound (250 g) of rolled oats with 2 ounces (50 g) of wheatgerm and 4 tablespoons (60 ml) of soft brown sugar. Add ½ pound (250 g) of mixed dried fruit such as sultanas, currants, raisins, apricots, apples, figs, dates or prunes and ¼ pound (100 g) of chopped almonds, walnuts or hazelnuts. Mix well.

INGREDIENTS TO MAKE ONE AND A HALF POUNDS (700 G) OF MUESLI:
½ lb (250 g) rolled oats
2 oz (50 g) wheatgerm
4 tablespoons (60 ml) soft brown sugar
½ lb (250 g) mixed dried fruit
¼ lb (100 g) nuts

Almond Crunch Granola

This crunchy breakfast cereal, made from toasted oats, nuts and honey, is more delicious than any you can buy. Serve it with milk and fresh or dried fruit.

Preheat the oven to 350 °F (180 °C, Gas Mark 4).

Mix 1 pound (500 g) of rolled oats with ½ pound (250 g) of coarsely chopped blanched almonds or a mixture of nuts. Stir in 8 tablespoons (120 ml) of clear honey, 2 tablespoons (30 ml) of safflower oil and 1 teaspoon (5 ml) of vanilla essence. Mix well. Spread the mixture thinly on 2 lightly greased baking sheets.

Bake for 20 to 25 minutes, turning occasionally so that the oats are evenly and lightly browned.

Cool. Store in sealed jars or containers for up to 1 month.

INGREDIENTS TO MAKE ONE AND A HALF POUNDS (750 G) OF CEREAL:
1 lb (500 g) rolled oats
½ lb (250 g) blanched almonds
8 tablespoons (120 ml) clear honey
2 tablespoons (30 ml) safflower oil
1 teaspoon (5 ml) vanilla essence

Porridge

This traditional Scottish breakfast dish can be made from coarse, medium or fine oatmeal or from rolled oats. For a good flavour and creamy texture, soak the oats in the milk, preferably overnight.

Put 2 pints (1 litre) of milk or water into a saucepan and bring to the boil. Remove the pan from the heat and stir in ¼ pound (100 g) of oatmeal or rolled oats. Leave to soak, overnight if possible.

Return the pan to the heat and bring to the boil. Reduce the heat and simmer, stirring continuously, until the oats are swollen and tender. Simmer fine oatmeal and rolled oats for 5 minutes, medium oatmeal for 15 minutes and coarse oatmeal for longer.

Add salt to taste and water if a thinner consistency is preferred. Serve immediately.

INGREDIENTS TO SERVE FOUR TO SIX:
2 pints (1 litre) milk or water
¼ lb (100 g) oatmeal or rolled oats
salt

Oats and Rye Raisin Bread

Preheat the oven to 400 °F (200 °C, Gas Mark 6). Grease a 2-pound (1-kg) loaf tin.

Combine ½ pound (250 g) of wholewheat flour with ¼ pound (100 g) of rye flour and ¼ pound (100 g) of oatmeal or rolled oats in a large mixing bowl. Add 1 teaspoon (5 ml) of bicarbonate of soda, 1 teaspoon (5 ml) of baking powder, 1 teaspoon (5 ml) of salt and 2 tablespoons (30 ml) of soft brown sugar. Add ¼ pound (100 g) of raisins and mix well.

Stir ½ pint (300 ml) of yogurt into the flour mixture and mix to a soft dough.

Turn the dough out on to a lightly floured board and knead it until it becomes smooth. Shape the dough into a loaf and put it into the prepared tin or on a greased baking sheet.

Bake for 40 to 45 minutes, or until the loaf has risen, is brown on top and sounds hollow when tapped underneath.

INGREDIENTS TO MAKE 1 LARGE LOAF:
½ lb (250 g) wholewheat flour
¼ lb (100 g) rye flour
¼ lb (100 g) oatmeal or rolled oats
1 teaspoon (5 ml) bicarbonate of soda
1 teaspoon (5 ml) baking powder
1 teaspoon (5 ml) salt
2 tablespoons (30 ml) soft brown sugar
¼ lb (100 g) raisins
½ pint (300 ml) yogurt

Delicious Date Bars

Preheat the oven to 375°F (190°C, Gas Mark 5).

In a large bowl mix 6 ounces (150 g) of rolled oats with ¼ pound (100 g) of wholewheat flour. Rub in ¼ pound (100 g) of margarine or butter until it is well mixed. Mould the mixture together with your hands until it forms a firm dough. Press half of the dough into a greased 7-inch (18-cm) square cake tin.

Coarsely chop ½ pound (250 g) of pitted dates. Add 1 tablespoon (15 ml) of honey and 2 tablespoons (30 ml) of lemon juice to the dates and mix well. Spread the date mixture over the layer of dough. Spread the remaining dough over the date mixture, pressing down well so that some of the dates show through.

Bake for 30 to 40 minutes, or until the top is golden brown. Cut into bars while still warm and let them cool in the tin.

INGREDIENTS TO MAKE TWELVE BARS:
6 oz (150 g) rolled oats
¼ lb (100 g) wholewheat flour
¼ lb (100 g) margarine or butter
½ lb (250 g) pitted dates
1 tablespoon (15 ml) honey
2 tablespoons (30 ml) lemon juice

MAKING DATE BARS

Cover the dough in the tin with the date mixture.

Press the remaining dough on top with your fingers.

Brown Oatmeal Bread

In a large bowl mix together 1 pound (500 g) of wholewheat flour, 10 ounces (300 g) of medium oatmeal or rolled oats, 1 tablespoon (15 ml) of salt and 1 tablespoon (15 ml) of soft brown sugar.

Add ½ ounce (15 g) of margarine and rub it into the flour.

Blend ½ ounce (15 g) of fresh yeast with ¾ pint (450 ml) of tepid water until the yeast has dissolved. Make a well in the flour and pour in the yeast liquid. Mix to a soft dough that is traditionally used to stuff herrings.

Turn the dough out on to a lightly floured surface and knead well for 10 minutes, or until the dough is firm and elastic and no longer sticky.

Shape the dough into a ball and put it into a lightly greased bowl. Cover the bowl with greased polythene. Leave the dough to rise in a warm place for about 1 hour, or until it has doubled in bulk.

Preheat the oven to 425°F (210°C, Gas Mark 7).

When the dough has risen, knead it again for 2 to 3 minutes. Divide the dough into halves and shape each half into an oval loaf. Put the loaves on a greased baking sheet and make 3 diagonal cuts across the top of each loaf. Cover with greased polythene and leave to rise in a warm place for 30 minutes, or until the loaves have doubled in bulk.

Bake for 30 to 40 minutes, or until the loaves are lightly browned and sound hollow when tapped underneath.

INGREDIENTS TO MAKE 2 SMALL LOAVES:
1 lb (500 g) wholewheat flour
10 oz (300 g) medium oatmeal or rolled oats
1 tablespoon (15 ml) salt
1 tablespoon (15 ml) soft brown sugar
½ oz (15 g) margarine
½ oz (15 g) fresh yeast
¾ pint (450 ml) tepid water

Oatmeal Stuffing

This is a piquant version of a Scottish recipe that is traditionally used to stuff herrings.

Combine ¼ pound (100 g) of rolled oats with 1 tablespoon (15 ml) of grated onion, 1 tablespoon (15 ml) of chopped thyme, 2 tablespoons (30 ml) of chopped parsley, the grated rind of 1 lemon, salt and pepper. Add 1 beaten egg with 2 tablespoons (30 ml) of milk and 1 teaspoon (5 ml) of lemon juice. Mix well.

INGREDIENTS TO STUFF FOUR MEDIUM-SIZED HERRINGS:
¼ lb (100 g) rolled oats
1 tablespoon (15 ml) grated onion
1 tablespoon (15 ml) chopped thyme
2 tablespoons (30 ml) chopped parsley
1 lemon
salt
pepper
1 egg
2 tablespoons (30 ml) milk
1 teaspoon (5 ml) lemon juice

Apple Oat Crumble

Preheat the oven to 375°F (190°C, Gas Mark 5).

Peel and core 1 pound (500 g) of tart apples. Cut the apples into thin slices. Put the apple slices into a 1½-pint (850-ml) pie dish or ovenproof dish and sprinkle with 2 ounces (50 g) of soft brown sugar. Scatter 6 cloves over the apples.

Melt 1½ ounces (35 g) of margarine or butter in a large saucepan. Add 2 ounces (50 g) of soft brown sugar and cook over low heat, stirring constantly, until the sugar has dissolved. Remove the pan from the heat and stir in ¼ pound (100 g) of rolled oats. Mix well.

Spoon the oat mixture over the apples and level the surface. Bake for 30 to 40 minutes, or until the crumble is golden brown.

INGREDIENTS TO SERVE FOUR:
1 lb (500 g) tart apples
¼ lb (100 g) soft brown sugar
6 cloves
1½ oz (35 g) margarine or butter
¼ lb (100 g) rolled oats

Danish Holecake

These crispbreads were stored and eaten all through the winter by Danish peasants, who threaded them together by the holes cut in them and hung them from the rafters of their cottages.

Preheat the oven to 450°F (230°C, Gas Mark 8). Grease 2 large baking sheets.

Put 1 pound (500 g) of rye flour and 1 teaspoon of salt into a mixing bowl. Make a well in the flour and pour in ½ pint (300 ml) of tepid water. Mix to a dough.

Put the dough on to a lightly floured board and roll it out very thinly. Cut 4 large rounds out of the dough using a dinner plate as a guide. Using a pastry cutter, cut a hole near the edge of each round.

Transfer the rounds to the baking sheets and bake for 10 minutes.

INGREDIENTS TO MAKE 4 LARGE CRISPBREADS:
1 lb (500 g) rye flour
1 teaspoon (5 ml) salt
½ pint (300 ml) tepid water

MORE MAIZE IS PRODUCED than any other cereal except wheat, but most of it is eaten by animals. Known as corn in the United States, it is the one cereal of American origin and the inhabitants of the middle Americas were growing maize three thousand years before Christopher Columbus brought it back to Spain from the Caribbean in 1496. It is now also grown in the warmer parts of Europe, and in Africa, Asia and Australia.

Maize is nutritionally inferior to wheat, largely because it contains less protein, and the protein it does have is of lower biological value since it has inadequate amounts of the amino acids tryptophan and lysine. Tryptophan is needed for conversion within the body to the vitamin niacin, a shortage of which may cause pellagra, a disease which may be prevalent in places where maize is the staple food. During the past three

a panicle of sorghum

an ear of dent type maize used for flour

In Africa where maize is the staple diet the people often suffer from pellagra, a disease caused by a deficiency of the B vitamin niacin. Maize contains niacin, but in a form the human body cannot make use of. There is no pellagra in Mexico, however, even though tortillas are the basis of most meals. These spicy pancakes are made of maize mixed with lime water which produces an alkaline condition that frees the niacin.

decades, however, plant breeders have produced mutants with more protein and a better balance of amino acids.

The other drawback to maize is that it does not contain sufficient gluten to produce a dough that will rise. Cornbread, therefore, bears no resemblance to a wheaten loaf. "Breads" made from cornmeal are popular in the United States, Latin America and in parts of southwest France. Coarsely ground cornmeal is made into a porridge in the southern United States, where it is called hominy grits, and in Italy, where it is known as polenta.

But maize turns up in many other forms. It can be pulverized to make cornflour, which is used to thicken sauces and soups (especially in Chinese cookery) and, mixed with wheat flour, to lighten cakes. Maize can also be exploded to make popcorn, hydrolysed to make corn syrup and crushed to extract the excellent polyunsaturated corn oil.

For many people all over the world the introduction to maize was effected in childhood through the American Kellogg brothers and their cornflakes. In the modern large-scale manufacture of cornflakes the broken grains, or grits, are steamed, flavoured with salt, malt and sugar,

an ear of common millet

a head of barley

a stem of buckwheat

fortified with thiamine, riboflavin and niacin, dried, rested for a day or two, flattened into flakes between rollers, toasted in rotary ovens, cooled and, finally, packed.

Grains that in one part of the world are a staple food may elsewhere provide only beer or bird-seed. The most notable and most ancient are barley and the millet group of grains.

Barley may well be the oldest cultivated grain. In Neolithic times it was eaten as a paste, and it was still popular with the Ancient Greeks. In Tibet a concoction of toasted barley flour, black tea and yak butter has survived into the twentieth century. In India, Japan and the Baltic States it is still an important food and in the Near East it is a staple. Barley meal is used in parts of Europe for porridge and malt breads. But in the United States and western Europe the grain is eaten mainly as pot barley or pearl barley. Pot barley is the whole grain minus the outer husk. It tastes nuttier than pearl barley, which lacks most of the bran and germ, as well as the husk. These barleys give a delicious flavour and smoothness to soups.

More than half of the world's barley crop is used as animal fodder and most of the rest is turned into beer and whisky. Barley has been used for making beer since time immemorial. Barley wine was being brewed in Babylon in 2800 BC.

The other grains are sorghum, millet and buck-wheat. Although sorghum is mainly used for animal feed, it is nutritionally comparable to maize and is a basic food in many parts of Africa and Asia. Millet, which has a higher protein content than maize, barley or sorghum, is a staple in parts of Africa and India, where it is made into such foods as porridge, and unleavened bread, or chapatis. Buckwheat is a staple in Russia and Poland, where it is often served and cooked like rice. In the United States buckwheat flour is used to make griddle cakes.

MALT EXTRACT

Usually made from malted barley, malt extract has been given to children for more than a hundred years. The advertisement (right) shows a Victorian child eagerly stretching for it. The malt was often mixed with cod liver oil (high in vitamins A and D) whose taste children loathed. This advertisement also recommended malt extract to nursing mothers and consumptives, implying that bouncing health was but a spoonful away. What it didn't say is that malt extract is only a good energy source because it is fifty per cent sugars.

The Nutrients in Barley
Barley is a good source of B vitamins, especially niacin, and three and a half ounces (100 g) provide about 350 Calories.

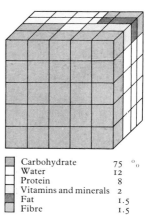

	Carbohydrate	75 %
	Water	12
	Protein	8
	Vitamins and minerals	2
	Fat	1.5
	Fibre	1.5

The Nutrients in Millet and Maize
Millet is high in protein and, like maize, has a high fat content. Both calorie counts are similar to barley.

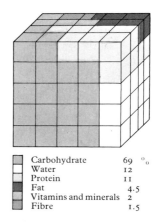

	Carbohydrate	69 %
	Water	12
	Protein	11
	Fat	4.5
	Vitamins and minerals	2
	Fibre	1.5

Corn Muffins

Preheat the oven to 425°F (220°C, Gas Mark 7).

Put 5 ounces (125 g) of cornmeal into a mixing bowl with 3 ounces (75 g) of flour, 1 tablespoon (15 ml) of baking powder and 1 tablespoon (15 ml) of sugar. Mix well.

Lightly beat 1 egg in a mixing bowl. Beat in 8 fluid ounces (250 ml) of milk and 2 tablespoons (30 ml) of corn oil. Pour the liquid into the dry ingredients and mix well.

Spoon the batter into 15 greased deep bun tins, filling each three-quarters full. Sprinkle each one with ¼ teaspoon (1 ml) of grated Parmesan cheese.

Bake for 15 to 20 minutes, or until the muffins have risen and are golden brown. Remove the muffins from the tins and cool them on a wire rack.

INGREDIENTS TO MAKE FIFTEEN MUFFINS:
5 oz (125 g) cornmeal
3 oz (75 g) flour
1 tablespoon (15 ml) baking powder
1 tablespoon (15 ml) sugar
1 egg
8 fl oz (250 ml) milk
2 tablespoons (30 ml) corn oil
1 tablespoon (15 ml) grated Parmesan cheese

MAKING MUFFINS

Spoon or pour the batter into muffin tins.

Mixed Grain Bread

In a large bowl mix ½ pound (250 g) of strong white flour with ½ pound (250 g) of barley or rye flour, ¼ pound (100 g) of cornmeal, ¼ pound (100 g) of rolled oats and 1 tablespoon (15 ml) of salt.

Blend ½ ounce (15 g) of fresh yeast with ¾ pint (400 ml) of tepid water. Mix until the yeast is dissolved. Make a well in the flour mixture and pour in the yeast liquid. Mix to a firm dough.

Turn the dough out on to a lightly floured surface and knead well for 10 minutes, or until the dough is firm and elastic and is no longer sticky.

Put the dough into a lightly greased bowl and cover with greased polythene, or put the bowl into a large greased polythene bag.

Leave the dough to rise in a warm place for 45 to 60 minutes, or until it has risen and doubled in bulk. When the dough has risen turn it out on to a lightly floured surface and knead again for 2 to 3 minutes.

Preheat the oven to 425°F (220°C, Gas Mark 7).

Divide the dough into halves. Shape each half into an oval and place it on a greased baking sheet. The dough may, alternatively, be put into two greased 1-pound (½-kg) loaf tins. Make diagonal cuts across the top of the loaves. Cover and leave to rise in a warm place until the dough has risen almost to the top of the tins and has doubled in bulk.

Bake in the centre of the oven for 30 to 40 minutes, or until the loaves are golden brown and sound hollow when tapped underneath. Cool on a wire rack.

INGREDIENTS TO MAKE TWO SMALL LOAVES:
½ lb (250 g) strong white flour
½ lb (250 g) barley or rye flour
¼ lb (100 g) cornmeal
¼ lb (100 g) rolled oats
1 tablespoon (15 ml) salt
½ oz (15 g) fresh yeast
¾ pint (400 ml) tepid water

Spoonbread

Preheat the oven to 400°F (200°C, Gas Mark 6).

Pour 1 pint (600 ml) of milk into a saucepan and bring to the boil. Stir in 3 ounces (75 g) of cornmeal and 1 teaspoon (5 ml) of salt. Reduce the heat and simmer gently, stirring continuously, for about 5 minutes, or until the mixture thickens. Remove the pan from the heat and allow to cool until the mixture is lukewarm.

Add 4 egg yolks to the mixture, stirring until well blended.

Whisk 4 egg whites until stiff and then fold them into the mixture. Pour into a 3-pint (1½-litre) soufflé dish.

Bake for 40 to 45 minutes, or until the mixture is well risen and golden brown. Serve immediately.

INGREDIENTS TO SERVE FOUR:
1 pint (600 ml) milk
3 oz (75 g) cornmeal
1 teaspoon (5 ml) salt
4 eggs

Wholewheat Cornbread

Preheat the oven to 400°F (200°C, Gas Mark 6).

Mix ¼ pound (100 g) of cornmeal with ¼ pound (100 g) of wholewheat flour, 1 tablespoon (15 ml) of baking powder, 1 teaspoon (5 ml) of salt and 1 tablespoon (15 ml) of sugar.

In a mixing bowl lightly beat 1 egg. Stir in ½ pint (300 ml) of buttermilk or milk. Pour the mixture on to the dry ingredients. Stir well until blended.

Pour the batter into a greased 7-inch (18-cm) square cake tin. Bake for 30 to 35 minutes, or until the cornbread has risen, is lightly browned and firm to the touch.

Allow to cool for a few minutes in the tin before turning out on to a wire rack.

INGREDIENTS TO MAKE ONE SMALL LOAF:
¼ lb (100 g) cornmeal
¼ lb (100 g) wholewheat flour
1 tablespoon (15 ml) baking powder
1 teaspoon (5 ml) salt
1 tablespoon (15 ml) sugar
1 egg
½ pint (300 ml) buttermilk or milk

Banana Malt Loaf

Malt gives this easy-to-make teabread a particularly rich flavour.

Combine 3 tablespoons (45 ml) of malt extract in a small saucepan with 2 ounces (50 g) of soft brown sugar, 1 ounce (25 g) of margarine and ¼ pint (150 ml) of milk. Cook over very low heat until the sugar has dissolved.

In a large bowl mix together ½ pound (250 g) of wholewheat flour, 2 teaspoons (10 ml) of baking powder and ¼ teaspoon (1 ml) of salt. Add the malt mixture and stir well to blend.

Stir in 2 finely chopped or mashed bananas and 3 ounces (75 g) of sultanas and mix well.

Preheat the oven to 325°F (170°C, Gas Mark 3).

Spoon the batter into a greased 2-pound (1-kg) loaf tin and level the surface. Bake for 1 to 1¼ hours, or until the loaf is golden brown and firm to the touch. Turn the loaf out of the tin and cool on a wire rack.

INGREDIENTS TO MAKE ONE LARGE LOAF:
3 tablespoons (45 ml) malt extract
2 oz (50 g) soft brown sugar
1 oz (25 g) margarine
¼ pint (150 ml) milk
½ lb (250 g) wholewheat flour
2 teaspoons (10 ml) baking powder
¼ teaspoon (1 ml) salt
2 bananas
3 oz (75 g) sultanas

Polenta Baked with Mushrooms

Preheat the oven to 400°F (200°C, Gas Mark 6).

Put 2 pints (1 litre) of water into a large saucepan with 1 teaspoon (5 ml) of salt and bring to the boil.

Stir in ½ pound (250 g) of cornmeal. Simmer gently for 20 minutes, stirring occasionally, until the polenta is thick, smooth and soft. Stir in 2 ounces (50 g) of grated Parmesan cheese, ¼ teaspoon (1 ml) of grated nutmeg and salt and pepper to taste.

Slice 6 ounces (150 g) of mushrooms. Poach them in boiling water for 5 minutes and then drain them.

Spread a third of the polenta in an ovenproof dish. Cover the polenta with half of the poached mushrooms. Spread another third of the polenta over the mushrooms in the dish. Sprinkle the remaining mushrooms on top and cover with the remaining polenta. Sprinkle 1 ounce (25 g) of grated Parmesan cheese over the polenta.

Bake for 30 minutes, or until the polenta is browned on top.

INGREDIENTS TO SERVE FOUR TO SIX:
salt
½ lb (250 g) cornmeal
3 oz (75 g) grated Parmesan cheese
¼ teaspoon (1 ml) grated nutmeg
pepper
6 oz (150 g) mushrooms

Tortillas

Serve these Mexican corn pancakes in a napkin to keep them warm and moist. Tortillas may be reheated in an ungreased frying-pan.

Mix ½ pound (250 g) of masa harina (flour made from maize) with 1 teaspoon (5 ml) of salt in a mixing bowl.

Make a well in the flour and pour in ½ pint (300 ml) of water. Mix to a soft dough. Turn the dough out on to a lightly floured surface and knead it, adding a little more flour if necessary, until the dough no longer sticks to your fingers.

Divide the dough into 12 pieces, roll each piece into a ball and flatten it slightly. Put the pieces of dough between 2 sheets of greaseproof paper, one at a time, and roll them out very thinly to 5-inch (13-cm) rounds. Add more flour if the dough sticks to the paper.

Cook the tortillas in an ungreased frying-pan for 1 minute on each side, or until they are lightly browned. Put the tortillas in aluminium foil in a warm oven while the remainder are being cooked.

INGREDIENTS TO MAKE TWELVE TORTILLAS:
½ lb (250 g) masa harina
1 teaspoon (5 ml) salt

Chicken Enchiladas

Make 1 pint (600 ml) of tomato sauce (see page 108). Add 2 ounces (50 g) of diced chillies or 1 teaspoon (5 ml) of chilli powder and 1 tablespoon (15 ml) of chopped oregano or basil and mix well.

Preheat the oven to 350°F (180°C, Gas Mark 4).

Cut ½ pound (250 g) of cooked chicken meat into small pieces. Beat ¼ pound (100 g) of curd cheese with 4 tablespoons (60 ml) of milk until smooth and creamy. Finely slice 4 small black olives and 2 spring onions and add them to the cheese mixture with 1 tablespoon (15 ml) of chopped parsley. Stir in the chopped chicken and season to taste with salt and pepper.

Make 12 tortillas. Heat the tomato sauce in a large saucepan. Dip the tortillas, one at a time, into the sauce until the tortilla is heated through. Remove the tortilla and put some of the cheese and chicken filling in the centre of the sauce-covered side. Roll the tortilla up to form a cylinder. Repeat until all the tortillas have been filled and rolled.

Place the enchiladas in a baking dish. Pour the remaining tomato sauce over the enchiladas and sprinkle with 2 tablespoons (30 ml) of grated Parmesan cheese.

Bake for 20 minutes, or until the enchiladas are heated through and lightly browned on top.

INGREDIENTS TO SERVE SIX:
1 pint (600 ml) tomato sauce (see page 108)
2 oz (50 g) chillies or 1 teaspoon (5 ml) chilli powder
1 tablespoon (15 ml) chopped oregano or basil
½ lb (250 g) cooked chicken meat
¼ lb (100 g) curd cheese
4 tablespoons (60 ml) milk
4 small black olives
2 spring onions
1 tablespoon (15 ml) chopped parsley
salt
pepper
12 tortillas
2 tablespoons (30 ml) grated Parmesan cheese

Barley and Mushroom Pilaf

It is best to begin to prepare this dish the day before serving so that the barley can soak overnight in the stock.

Heat 2 tablespoons (30 ml) of corn oil in a frying-pan. Add 1 chopped large onion and cook, stirring frequently, for 3 minutes. Slice ¼ pound (100 g) of mushrooms. Add them to the onion in the pan and fry for 1 minute, stirring constantly. Add 6 ounces (150 g) of pearl barley and fry for 1 minute more, stirring occasionally.

Transfer the barley mixture to an ovenproof dish. Pour in ¾ pint (450 ml) of chicken stock. Season to taste with salt and freshly ground black pepper. Put 1 bay leaf on top. Cover the dish and refrigerate for at least 2 hours but preferably overnight.

Preheat the oven to 375°F (190°C, Gas Mark 5). Bake the casserole, covered, for 1 hour, or until the stock is absorbed and the barley is tender and slightly chewy.

Serve immediately sprinkled with 1 ounce (25 g) of grated Cheddar cheese.

INGREDIENTS TO SERVE FOUR:
2 tablespoons (30 ml) corn oil
1 large onion
¼ lb (100 g) mushrooms
6 oz (150 g) pearl barley
¾ pint (450 ml) chicken stock
salt
freshly ground black pepper
1 bay leaf
1 oz (25 g) grated Cheddar cheese

Barley Yogurt Soup

Soak 3 ounces (75 g) of pearl barley in enough water to cover for at least 12 hours.

Heat 1 tablespoon (15 ml) of corn oil in a large saucepan. Add 1 chopped large onion and fry over low heat, stirring frequently, for 5 minutes, or until the onion is soft and translucent. Add 2 pints (1 litre) of chicken stock and bring to the boil. Add 1 bay leaf and the drained barley. Season to taste with salt and pepper. Cover, lower the heat and simmer gently for 50 to 60 minutes, or until the barley is tender and swollen. Remove the pan from the heat and stir in 2 tablespoons (30 ml) of chopped parsley. Adjust the seasoning.

Just before serving, beat ½ pint (300 ml) of yogurt in a small mixing bowl until it is smooth. Stir a little of the hot soup into the yogurt, then pour the yogurt mixture into the pan, whisking well. Reheat the soup, but do not allow it to boil or the yogurt will curdle.

Serve immediately, sprinkled with chopped mint.

INGREDIENTS TO SERVE FOUR TO SIX:
3 oz (75 g) pearl barley
1 tablespoon (15 ml) corn oil
1 large onion
2 pints (1 litre) chicken stock
1 bay leaf
salt
pepper
2 tablespoons (30 ml) chopped parsley
½ pint (300 ml) yogurt
mint

The Nutrients in White Fish

White fish have excellent protein and little fat and three and a half ounces (100g) provide about 70 Calories.

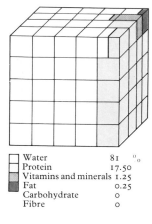

Water	81	%
Protein	17.50	
Vitamins and minerals	1.25	
Fat	0.25	
Carbohydrate	0	
Fibre	0	

FRESHLY CAUGHT FISH is one of the most wholesome, nutritious and delicious foods you could hope for.

Unfortunately, fish has one failing—it rapidly putrifies; so it is dried, salted, smoked and canned. But all these processes turn fresh fish into something different, however appetizing. The only way to retain some of the freshness of the fish caught in distant fishing grounds is to freeze it. The modern method of quick-freezing on board ship ensures that fish remains "fresh" for three to eight months. The nutritional value is not greatly diminished, but no one can pretend that the flavour and texture are the same. The vast quantities of fish caught nearer home, landed quickly and sold fresh are more likely to taste as fish should.

The edible part of fish can be from fifteen to more than twenty per cent protein. And the protein is of good quality because, like poultry and meat protein, it contains most of the essential amino acids. Its fat is polyunsaturated—a great plus mark over meat. Percentages of fat, however, vary widely according to the type of fish and the time of year it is caught. Such fat fish as herrings and mackerel, which grow fat on plankton near the surface of the sea, are about twenty per cent fat in summer, when plankton is plentiful, but by the end of winter they are less than half that

turbot

lemon sole

halibut

amount. Such fish as cod, haddock and flat fish that live on the sea bed are low in fat. Plaice, for example, has only two per cent, while halibut has four per cent fat. Shellfish are also low in fat, but they contain almost twice as much cholesterol as fish, poultry and game.

The small flat fish include the firm-fleshed sole, found at its best in Britain, Norway and Denmark, and the softer-fleshed lemon soles, dabs and flounders. (The American sole is, in fact, a flounder, but it is superior to European flounders.) Of the large flat fish the giant is halibut, which flourishes off the Canadian Pacific coast, and in that stretch of the North Sea between Scotland and Norway. Others include the even more delicious and moist turbot of the English Channel, the French Atlantic coast and the Baltic and the smaller brill. Both turbot and brill are not to be found in American waters.

Other worthwhile non-fat fish are sea bass, sea bream, the hideous-looking catfish, cod, haddock, hake, John Dory, the fish reputedly caught by Saint Peter in the Sea of Galilee but at its best in the Mediterranean, monkfish, or angler fish, fearsome to look at but firm and sweet to eat, grey and red mullets, pompano, one compelling reason for visiting New Orleans, and whiting, if in childhood all the bones did not, sadly, put you off it for life.

Among fat fish there is nothing to approach the flavour of salmon, especially when it is eaten in its prime in early spring. Although the salmon spends most of its time at sea it is caught in fresh water. The most delicious fat fish of the sea is a

oysters

crab

scallops

lobster

shrimps

mussels

Shellfish (above) are high in first-class protein, as well as in iron, calcium, riboflavin and niacin. They also contain up to three per cent fat and, unlike fish, have a small amount of carbohydrate. Scallops, for example, are about four per cent carbohydrate and oysters five per cent. But shellfish are very high in cholesterol. Lobster has twice as much cholesterol as meat; oysters have even more.

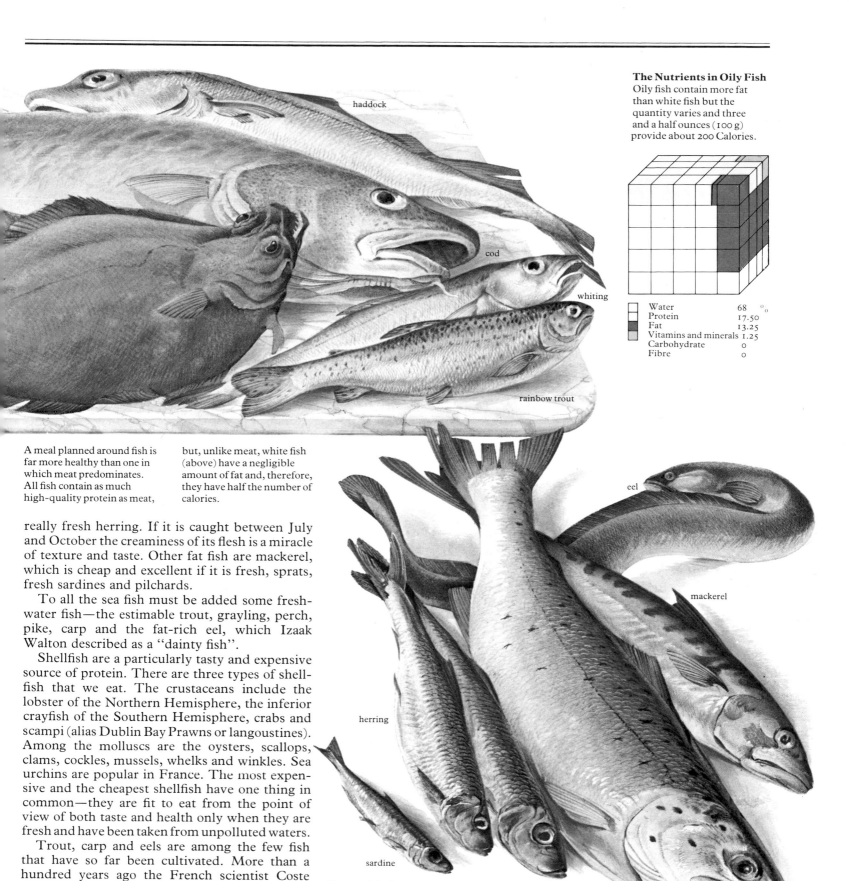

haddock

cod

whiting

rainbow trout

eel

mackerel

herring

sardine

salmon

A meal planned around fish is
far more healthy than one in
which meat predominates.
All fish contain as much
high-quality protein as meat,
but, unlike meat, white fish
(above) have a negligible
amount of fat and, therefore,
they have half the number of
calories.

really fresh herring. If it is caught between July
and October the creaminess of its flesh is a miracle
of texture and taste. Other fat fish are mackerel,
which is cheap and excellent if it is fresh, sprats,
fresh sardines and pilchards.

To all the sea fish must be added some fresh-
water fish—the estimable trout, grayling, perch,
pike, carp and the fat-rich eel, which Izaak
Walton described as a "dainty fish".

Shellfish are a particularly tasty and expensive
source of protein. There are three types of shellfish that we eat. The crustaceans include the
lobster of the Northern Hemisphere, the inferior
crayfish of the Southern Hemisphere, crabs and
scampi (alias Dublin Bay Prawns or langoustines).
Among the molluscs are the oysters, scallops,
clams, cockles, mussels, whelks and winkles. Sea
urchins are popular in France. The most expensive and the cheapest shellfish have one thing in
common—they are fit to eat from the point of
view of both taste and health only when they are
fresh and have been taken from unpolluted waters.

Trout, carp and eels are among the few fish
that have so far been cultivated. More than a
hundred years ago the French scientist Coste
foresaw the time when the seas and rivers would
be thoroughly farmed, and there would be
plentiful cheap supplies not only of oysters but of
salmon, trout and lobsters as well.

The exquisite flavour of the
oily fish (above) is matched
by their excellent food value.
Fortunately, the fat in oily
fish is polyunsaturated. They
also contain less cholesterol
than either meat or shellfish
and provide niacin and
vitamin D that are absent
from white fish.

Poached Fish

Poaching is the simplest way to cook fish to retain its full flavour. It is suitable for fillets, steaks and whole fish.

First prepare a court bouillon. Pour 2 pints (1 litre) of water, or a mixture of dry white wine and water, into a saucepan. Slice 1 carrot, 1 onion and 1 stick of celery and add them to the pan. Grate in the rind of ½ lemon and squeeze in the juice. Add a few parsley sprigs, 1 bay leaf, 2 peppercorns and salt. Bring to the boil, cover the pan, reduce the heat and simmer for 20 minutes. Strain the liquid and let it cool until it is lukewarm.

Put the fish into a pan. Pour in the court bouillon. (The fish may be tied loosely in muslin for easy removal.) Cover the pan and cook over very low heat. The bouillon should barely bubble. Cooking time will vary according to the thickness of the fish, but allow 8 to 10 minutes for every pound (500 g).

The fish may also be poached in an oven preheated to 350°F (180°C, Gas Mark 4). A small whole fish or fish steaks will take 15 to 20 minutes to poach in the oven.

INGREDIENTS TO SERVE FOUR:
2 pints (1 litre) water or a mixture of dry white wine and water
1 carrot
1 onion
1 celery stick
½ lemon
parsley sprigs
1 bay leaf
2 peppercorns
salt
4 small whole fish, fillets or steaks or 1 large whole fish

POACHING FISH

Tie the fish loosely in muslin for easy removal.

Fish Chowder

This fish soup makes a substantial meal. Any firm white fish, including cod, halibut, bass, turbot and hake, can be used.

Put ½ pound (250 g) of fish fillets into a saucepan. Cover with 1 pint (600 ml) of water and add the grated rind and juice of ½ lemon, salt, pepper and 1 bouquet garni, consisting of 1 bay leaf and sprigs of parsley and thyme tied together. Bring to simmering point and poach the fish gently for 10 to 15 minutes, or until it is tender.

Remove the fish from the pan with a perforated spoon. Discard the skin and flake the fish. Remove the bouquet garni from the cooking liquor.

Peel ½ pound (250 g) of potatoes and cut into small dice. Add the potatoes to the fish liquor with 1 medium-sized leek, thinly sliced, 1 ounce (25 g) of rice and ¼ teaspoon (1 ml) of ground nutmeg. Cover the pan and simmer for 15 minutes, or until the potatoes and rice are tender.

Stir in the flaked fish and ½ pint (300 ml) of milk. Adjust the seasoning, reheat and serve.

INGREDIENTS TO SERVE FOUR TO SIX:
½ lb (250 g) fillets of firm white fish
½ lemon
salt
pepper
1 bouquet garni, consisting of 1 bay leaf and parsley and thyme sprigs
½ lb (250 g) potatoes
1 medium-sized leek
1 oz (25 g) rice
¼ teaspoon (1 ml) ground nutmeg
½ pint (300 ml) milk

Baked Salmon Steaks

Preheat the oven to 350°F (180°C, Gas Mark 4). Lightly grease an ovenproof dish.

Put 4 salmon steaks into the dish. Sprinkle them with salt, pepper and the juice of ½ lemon. Put 1 sprig of parsley or dill on each steak.

Cover the dish with foil and bake for about 20 minutes, or until the steaks are cooked.

Serve hot with yogurt hollandaise sauce (see page 93) or hot cucumber sauce (see page 109).

INGREDIENTS TO SERVE FOUR:
4 salmon steaks
salt
pepper
½ lemon
4 parsley or dill sprigs
yogurt hollandaise sauce (see page 93) or hot cucumber sauce (see page 109)

Mackerel Baked in Cider

Preheat the oven to 350°F (180°C, Gas Mark 4).

Heat 1 tablespoon (15 ml) of corn oil in a frying-pan. Slice 1 large onion and fry for 3 minutes, or until it is lightly browned. Peel and core 1 large cooking apple, about ½ pound (250 g), and slice it into the pan. Fry gently for 2 minutes. Pour in ⅓ pint (200 ml) of dry cider, add 2 ounces (50 g) of sultanas and bring to the boil. Season to taste with salt and pepper.

Pour the cider mixture into a shallow ovenproof dish. Roll up 8 medium-sized fillets of mackerel so that the skin is on the outside. Secure the rolls with cocktail sticks.

Put the mackerel rolls into the dish. Bake for 25 to 30 minutes, basting occasionally with the sauce, until the mackerel is tender and the skin is browned on the top.

INGREDIENTS TO SERVE FOUR:
1 tablespoon (15 ml) corn oil
1 large onion
1 large cooking apple
⅓ pint (200 ml) dry cider
2 oz (50 g) sultanas
salt
pepper
8 medium-sized mackerel fillets

Chinese Baked Snappers

Preheat the oven to 375°F (190°C, Gas Mark 5).

Scrape the scales off 4 medium-sized red snappers. (Scrape with the back of a knife from the tail towards the head.) Cut off the fins. Gut the fish and wash well.

Shred 1 pound (500 g) of cabbage and put it into a large ovenproof dish. Put ¼ pound (100 g) of bean sprouts on top. Add salt and pepper to taste, 1 tablespoon (15 ml) of soy sauce and 1 tablespoon (15 ml) of lemon juice.

Put the snappers on top of the vegetables with 4 sprigs of coriander.

Cover the dish with foil and bake for 15 to 20 minutes, or until fish and vegetables are tender.

INGREDIENTS TO SERVE FOUR:
4 medium-sized red snappers
1 lb (500 g) cabbage
¼ lb (100 g) bean sprouts
salt
pepper
1 tablespoon (15 ml) soy sauce
1 tablespoon (15 ml) lemon juice
4 coriander sprigs

Fish en Papillotte with Herbs

Enclosing whole fish in foil parcels is a delicious way to cook and serve them. The flavour is sealed in and the fish cook in their own juices. If red mullet is not available, mackerel, bluefish or snappers may be substituted.

Scrape the scales from 4 medium-sized red mullets, using the back of a knife and scraping from the tail towards the head. Cut off the fins but leave on the heads and tails. In each fish make a slit from underneath the head to halfway along towards the tail and remove the guts.

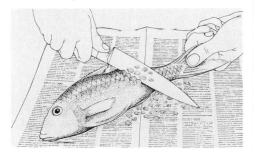

Scrape fish from tail to head with the back of a knife.

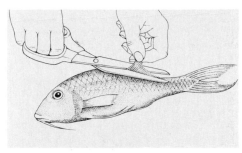

Cut the fins off with scissors, leaving the tail.

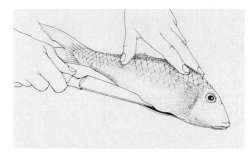

Slit the fish for half its length and gut it.

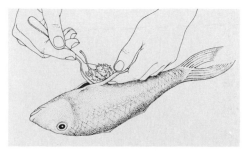

Spoon the stuffing into the cavity of the fish.

Preheat the oven to 375°F (190°C, Gas Mark 5).

Stuff each fish with 1 slice of onion, 1 sprig of thyme, 1 sprig of parsley and 1 bay leaf. Sprinkle each fish with salt and pepper and put a slice of lemon on top.

Put each stuffed fish on a lightly greased square of foil or greaseproof paper and fold it into a neat parcel. Put the parcels on a baking sheet and bake for 15 to 20 minutes, or until the fish is tender.

Serve the mullets in their parcels.

INGREDIENTS TO SERVE FOUR:
4 medium-sized red mullets
1 small onion
4 thyme sprigs
4 parsley sprigs
4 bay leaves
salt
pepper
4 lemon slices

Plaki

This is the Greek method of baking a whole fish with onions, tomatoes, olives and herbs.

Remove the fins and guts from 1 whole large oily fish such as grey mullet, bream or brill, and scrape away the scales if necessary. Wash well.

Preheat the oven to 350°F (180°C, Gas Mark 4).

Slice ½ pound (250 g) of onions. Spread half of them on the bottom of a shallow ovenproof dish, large enough to hold the fish. Slice ½ pound (250 g) of tomatoes and arrange half of them on top of the sliced onions. Sprinkle with 2 tablespoons (30 ml) of chopped parsley, salt and pepper.

Put the fish on top with the remaining onions and tomatoes. Put 8 pitted black olives around it. Slice 1 lemon and arrange the slices down the centre of the fish. Top with 1 sprig of rosemary.

Pour ¼ pint (150 ml) of white wine over the fish. Cover the dish with foil and bake for 40 to 45 minutes, or until the fish and vegetables are tender.

INGREDIENTS TO SERVE FOUR:
2½- to 3-lb (1¼- to 1½-kg) whole oily fish
½ lb (250 g) onions
½ lb (250 g) tomatoes
2 tablespoons (30 ml) chopped parsley
salt
pepper
8 pitted black olives
1 lemon
1 rosemary sprig
¼ pint (150 ml) white wine

Fish Salad

This refreshing fish and prawn salad can be served as a first course or as a luncheon dish. Halibut or turbot may be used instead of cod.

First make a court bouillon. Pour 2 pints (1 litre) of water into a saucepan. Add 1 bay leaf, 2 peppercorns, 2 parsley sprigs, 1 small onion stuck with 1 clove, 2 teaspoons (10 ml) of vinegar and ½ teaspoon (2.5 ml) of salt. Bring to the boil. Cover the pan, reduce the heat and simmer for 15 minutes. Strain the court bouillon.

Put 1 pound (500 g) of cod fillets into a saucepan and add enough of the court bouillon to barely cover them. Cook over very low heat for 8 minutes, or until the cod is tender. Drain the fish and leave it to cool, then flake it coarsely into a mixing bowl.

Remove the seeds and pith from 1 small green pepper. Cut the pepper into thin strips. Thinly slice 1 small onion. Chop 2 sticks of celery. Add the pepper, onion and celery to the flaked fish with ¼ pound (100 g) of peeled cooked prawns.

For the dressing, beat together 5 tablespoons (75 ml) of tomato juice, 1 tablespoon (15 ml) of lemon juice and 1 tablespoon (15 ml) of Worcestershire sauce. Add salt and pepper to taste. Spoon the dressing over the fish mixture. Refrigerate for at least 30 minutes before serving.

To serve, put 1 lettuce leaf in the bottoms of 4 individual bowls. Divide the fish mixture between the bowls and garnish with lemon slices.

INGREDIENTS TO SERVE FOUR:
1 bay leaf
2 peppercorns
2 parsley sprigs
2 small onions
1 clove
2 teaspoons (10 ml) vinegar
salt
1 lb (500 g) cod fillets
1 small green pepper
2 celery sticks
¼ lb (100 g) peeled cooked prawns
5 tablespoons (75 ml) tomato juice
1 tablespoon (15 ml) lemon juice plus ½ lemon
1 tablespoon (15 ml) Worcestershire sauce
pepper
4 lettuce leaves

Trout Baked with Grapefruit and Hazelnuts

Preheat the oven to 350°F (180°C, Gas Mark 4).

Put ¼ pound (100 g) of hazelnuts under a hot grill for 1 to 2 minutes, or until they brown. (Watch them carefully because they burn easily.) Remove the thin brown skins by rubbing the nuts together in a clean tea-towel or a paper bag. Discard the skins.

Fill the cavities of 4 cleaned, medium-sized trout with the hazelnuts. Put the fish into a lightly greased, shallow ovenproof dish and sprinkle them with salt and pepper.

Cut the peel and white pith from 2 grapefruits. Working over the fish so that any juice pours over them, cut the membrane away from the segments of fruit. Put the grapefruit segments around the fish.

Bake uncovered for 20 to 30 minutes, or until the trout are tender.

INGREDIENTS TO SERVE FOUR:
¼ lb (100 g) shelled hazelnuts
4 medium-sized trout
salt
pepper
2 grapefruits

Delicious and sophisticated, Trout Baked with Grapefruit and Hazelnuts makes an excellent main-course dish.

Stuffed Fish Rolls

This recipe brings out the delicate flavour of white fish. Lemon sole, Dover sole, plaice or haddock may be used. The cucumber sauce may be poured over the fish rolls or served separately in a sauce boat.

Preheat the oven to 350°F (180°C, Gas Mark 4).

For the stuffing, finely chop or grate 1 small onion. Cut a 4-inch (10-cm) piece of cucumber into small dice. Heat ½ ounce (15 g) of margarine in a saucepan. Add the onion and the cucumber to the pan and fry gently for 5 minutes.

Remove the pan from the heat and stir in 2 ounces (50 g) of fresh breadcrumbs, 1 ounce (25 g) of chopped walnuts, the grated rind of 1 lemon and 2 tablespoons (30 ml) of chopped parsley. Lightly beat 1 egg and stir it into the stuffing mixture. Season to taste with salt and pepper.

Spread the stuffing on 4 large fillets of white fish. Roll the fillets up from the tail end. Secure each roll with a cocktail stick. Put the fish rolls into a shallow ovenproof dish.

Cover the dish and bake for 20 minutes, or until the fish is cooked.

For the sauce, cut a 2-inch (5-cm) piece of cucumber into small dice. Stir the cucumber into ¼ pint (150 ml) of warm yogurt. Season to taste. Serve the fish hot, garnished with cucumber slices and walnut halves.

INGREDIENTS TO SERVE FOUR:
½ oz (15 g) margarine
1 small onion
7-inch (18-cm) piece cucumber
2 oz (50 g) fresh breadcrumbs
1 oz (25 g) chopped walnuts
1 lemon
2 tablespoons (30 ml) chopped parsley
1 egg
salt
pepper
4 large white fish fillets
¼ pint (150 ml) warm yogurt
1 oz (25 g) walnut halves

Mediterranean Fish and Tomato Casserole

Chop 2 rashers of streaky bacon. Finely chop 1 large onion. Remove the seeds and pith from 1 small green pepper and chop it finely. Blanch, peel and coarsely chop 5 ripe medium-sized tomatoes. Cut 1 pound (500 g) of skinned fillets of firm white fish (cod, halibut, bass, Dover sole or lemon sole) into pieces.

In a large, heavy frying-pan, over low heat, fry the chopped bacon until the fat runs. Add the chopped onion and green pepper to the pan with 1 crushed garlic clove and fry for 2 minutes, or until the onion is soft.

Stir in 1 tablespoon (15 ml) of flour. Stirring constantly, gradually pour in ¼ pint (150 ml) of dry white wine and ¼ pint (150 ml) of water. Add the chopped tomatoes, ½ teaspoon of dried basil, salt and pepper.

Still stirring, boil the sauce until it thickens. Add the fish. Cover the pan, reduce the heat and simmer gently for 10 to 15 minutes, or until the fish is cooked.

Serve hot, garnished with 2 tablespoons (30 ml) of chopped parsley and 1 ounce (25 g) of chopped roasted peanuts.

INGREDIENTS TO SERVE FOUR:
2 streaky bacon rashers
1 large onion
1 small green pepper
5 ripe medium-sized tomatoes
1 lb (500 g) firm white fish fillets
1 garlic clove
1 tablespoon (15 ml) flour
¼ pint (150 ml) dry white wine
½ teaspoon (2.5 ml) dried basil
salt
pepper
2 tablespoons (30 ml) chopped parsley
1 oz (25 g) chopped roasted peanuts

Fish Steaks with Fennel

Preheat the oven to 350 F (180 C, Gas Mark 4).

Heat 1 tablespoon (15 ml) of corn oil in a saucepan. Add 1 thinly sliced large fennel bulb to the pan. Fry the fennel for 3 minutes, or until it is lightly coloured. Stir in ½ pound of ripe tomatoes, which have been blanched, peeled and chopped, the grated rind and juice of ½ lemon, 1 tablespoon (15 ml) of chopped parsley, ½ teaspoon (2.5 ml) of ground coriander, salt and pepper. Stirring frequently, bring to the boil. Cover the pan, reduce the heat and simmer for 10 minutes, stirring occasionally.

Transfer the sauce to a shallow ovenproof dish. Arrange 4 haddock or halibut steaks on top. Cover the dish and bake for 20 to 25 minutes, or until the fish is cooked.

INGREDIENTS TO SERVE FOUR:
1 tablespoon (15 ml) corn oil
1 large fennel bulb
½ lb (250 g) ripe tomatoes
½ lemon
1 tablespoon (15 ml) chopped parsley
½ teaspoon (2.5 ml) ground coriander
salt
pepper
4 haddock or halibut steaks

Soused Herrings are a favourite with Scandinavians, who know all there is to know about cooking herrings. Serve with toast as a tasty first course.

Soused Herrings

This dish can be made in advance. Make double the quantity and pack the fish into a jar. Pour in the cooking liquor and seal the jar. The herrings will keep for up to 1 week.

Preheat the oven to 350 F (180 C, Gas Mark 4).

Remove the heads, fins and guts from 4 herrings. Clean the fish and remove the backbones without removing the tails. Season the herrings with salt and pepper, then roll each fish up towards the tail. Put the rolled herrings into a shallow ovenproof dish with the tails pointing upwards.

Thinly slice 1 medium-sized carrot and 1 medium-sized onion and scatter the slices over and around the fish with 6 peppercorns and 2 bay leaves. Pour in ¼ pint (150 ml) of water and ¼ pint (150 ml) of wine vinegar.

Cover the dish and bake for 30 minutes. Allow to cool and serve.

INGREDIENTS TO SERVE FOUR:
4 herrings
salt
pepper
1 medium-sized carrot
1 medium-sized onion
6 peppercorns
2 bay leaves
¼ pint (150 ml) wine vinegar

Orange Capered Skate

Steaks of any firm white fish, such as cod, halibut or turbot may be substituted for the skate.

Cut a 1½- to 2-pound (750- to 1-kg) wing of skate into 4 pieces and wash well. Put into a large saucepan or deep frying-pan and barely cover with water. Add 1 tablespoon (15 ml) of vinegar, 1 teaspoon (5 ml) of salt, 1 bay leaf and 1 sprig of parsley. Bring to simmering point and poach the skate gently for 15 to 20 minutes, or until it is tender. Carefully lift out the skate with a fish slice. Remove the skin, put the fish on a warm serving dish and keep it hot.

Heat 1 tablespoon (15 ml) of corn oil in a small saucepan. Add 1 finely chopped small onion and fry it for 3 minutes, or until it is lightly browned. Stir in the juice of 2 oranges, 1 tablespoon (15 ml) of capers, salt and pepper. Bring to the boil, stirring constantly. Reduce the heat and simmer for 30 seconds. Pour the sauce over the skate and serve immediately, garnished with parsley.

INGREDIENTS TO SERVE FOUR:
1½- to 2-lb (750- to 1-kg) wing of skate
1 tablespoon (15 ml) vinegar
salt
1 bay leaf
parsley sprigs
1 tablespoon (15 ml) corn oil
1 small onion
2 oranges
1 tablespoon (15 ml) capers
pepper

Baked Cod Steaks

Preheat the oven to 350 F (180 C, Gas Mark 4).

Wash ½ pound (250 g) of button mushrooms and put them into a shallow ovenproof dish. (Leave small mushrooms whole and halve or quarter larger mushrooms.) Sprinkle the mushrooms with salt and pepper. Put 4 cod steaks on top.

Beat ½ pint (300 ml) of yogurt until it is smooth, then spread it over the cod steaks. Sprinkle 2 tablespoons (30 ml) of chopped parsley over the top.

Cover the dish with foil and bake for 20 to 30 minutes, or until the fish is tender.

Serve garnished with sprigs of parsley.

INGREDIENTS TO SERVE FOUR:
½ lb (250 g) button mushrooms
salt
pepper
4 cod steaks
½ pint (300 ml) yogurt
2 tablespoons (30 ml) chopped parsley
parsley sprigs

Watercress and Lemon Rolled Sole

Remove the skin from 4 large fillets of Dover or lemon sole. Preheat the oven to 350°F (180°C, Gas Mark 4).

Make the stuffing. Put 2 ounces (50 g) of fresh breadcrumbs into a mixing bowl. Reserving a few sprigs for garnish, remove the coarse stalks from 1 small bunch of watercress. Chop the leaves and tender stalks. Add to the breadcrumbs. Grate in the rind of 1 lemon, then add 1 tablespoon (15 ml) of lemon juice. Lightly beat 1 small egg and stir it in. Season with salt and pepper.

Spread the stuffing on the skinned sides of the fish fillets. Roll the fillets up from the tail end and secure with cocktail sticks.

Put the fish rolls into a lightly greased, shallow ovenproof dish, cover and bake for 15 to 20 minutes, or until the fish is tender.

Serve hot, garnished with the reserved watercress and twists of lemon.

INGREDIENTS TO SERVE FOUR:
4 large Dover or lemon sole fillets
2 oz (50 g) fresh breadcrumbs
1 watercress bunch
1½ lemons
1 small egg
salt
pepper

PREPARING FISH ROLLS

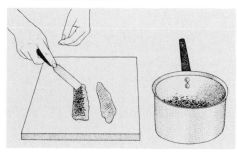

Spread stuffing over the skinned side of fillets.

Secure the rolled fillets with cocktail sticks.

Indonesian Grilled Spiced Fish

Clean 4 whole medium-sized fish such as red mullets or snappers. Put the fish on a large plate. Make diagonal cuts along the sides of the fish to allow the marinade to penetrate.

For the marinade, crush 1 garlic clove and grate 1 small onion into a small bowl. Add 2 tablespoons (30 ml) of lemon juice, 1 teaspoon (5 ml) of soy sauce, ½ teaspoon (2.5 ml) of chilli powder, ¼ teaspoon (1 ml) of ground coriander, salt and pepper. Mix well. Pour the marinade over the fish. Marinate the fish for about 45 minutes, turning and basting them occasionally.

Cook the fish under a moderately hot grill, basting them occasionally and turning them once, for about 15 minutes, or until the fish is cooked and the skin is crisp and browned.

INGREDIENTS TO SERVE FOUR:
4 medium-sized red mullets or snappers
1 garlic clove
1 small onion
2 tablespoons (30 ml) lemon juice
1 teaspoon (5 ml) soy sauce
½ teaspoon (2.5 ml) chilli powder
¼ teaspoon (1 ml) ground coriander
salt
pepper

Steamed Mussels

This is the simplest and most delicious way to cook mussels.

Wash 3 pints (1½ litres) of mussels under cold running water. Scrub each mussel well with a small, stiff brush. Using a knife scrape off any weed that is clinging to the shells. Discard any mussels that remain open. Put the mussels into a colander and wash them again under cold running water.

Put the mussels into a large saucepan. Finely chop 1 small onion and add it to the pan with 1 crushed garlic clove, salt and pepper. Pour in ¼ pint (150 ml) of dry white wine and ¼ pint (150 ml) of water.

Cover the pan, bring to the boil and cook for 5 minutes. Remove the mussels, take off the top shells and arrange the mussels in individual serving bowls. Discard any mussels that have not opened.

Stir 1 tablespoon (15 ml) of chopped parsley into the cooking liquor, adjust the seasoning and pour it over the mussels. Serve at once.

INGREDIENTS TO SERVE FOUR:
3 pints (1½ litres) mussels
1 small onion
1 garlic clove
salt
pepper
¼ pint (150 ml) dry white wine
1 tablespoon (15 ml) chopped parsley

Prawn-filled Avocadoes

First make the filling. Put ¼ pint (150 ml) of yogurt into a mixing bowl. Add 1 teaspoon (5 ml) of chopped parsley, 1 teaspoon (5 ml) of chopped mint, 1 teaspoon (5 ml) of chopped chives and 1 teaspoon (5 ml) of chopped lemon balm if it is available. Stir in the juice of ½ small lemon. Season with salt and pepper. Mix well.

Stir in ¼ pound (100 g) of cooked peeled prawns and leave to marinate for at least 30 minutes.

Just before serving, cut 2 avocadoes into halves lengthways. Remove the stones and

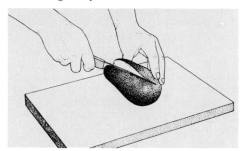

Use a sharp knife to cut avocadoes in half.

Lever out the stone with the point of a knife.

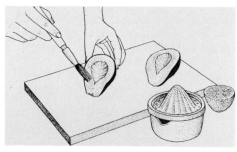

Brush with lemon juice to prevent browning.

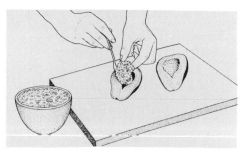

Spoon filling into the cavities in the avocadoes.

rub the cut surfaces with lemon juice to prevent them turning brown.

Divide the filling between the avocado halves and serve.

INGREDIENTS TO SERVE FOUR:
¼ pint (150 ml) yogurt
1 teaspoon (5 ml) chopped parsley
1 teaspoon (5 ml) chopped mint
1 teaspoon (5 ml) chopped chives
1 teaspoon (5 ml) chopped lemon balm
1 small lemon
salt
pepper
¼ lb (100 g) cooked peeled prawns
2 avocadoes

Prawns Provençal

Chop 1 small onion and 1 small green pepper. Blanch and peel ½ pound (250 g) of tomatoes. Cut them into halves and remove the seeds. Coarsely chop the tomatoes.

Heat 1 tablespoon (15 ml) of corn oil in a saucepan. Add the onion and green pepper and fry over low heat for 5 minutes. Add the tomatoes to the pan with ¼ pint (150 ml) of dry white wine, 1 tablespoon (15 ml) of chopped basil or oregano, salt and pepper. Cover the pan, reduce the heat and simmer gently for 15 minutes.

Add ¾ pound (350 g) of peeled prawns and cook for 5 minutes more.

Serve immediately, sprinkled with 1 tablespoon (15 ml) of chopped parsley.

INGREDIENTS TO SERVE FOUR:
1 small onion
1 small green pepper
½ lb (250 g) tomatoes
1 tablespoon (15 ml) corn oil
¼ pint (150 ml) dry white wine
1 tablespoon (15 ml) chopped basil or oregano
salt
pepper
¾ lb (350 g) peeled prawns
1 tablespoon (15 ml) chopped parsley

Taramasalata

This Greek fish pâté made from smoked cod's roe is delicious as a starter or as a dip for raw vegetables. Traditionally it is made with lots of olive oil, but this recipe substitutes yogurt, which gives a more refreshing flavour. Serve it with toast or a selection of raw vegetables. It will keep up to 5 days in the refrigerator.

Pour boiling water over ½ pound (250 g) of smoked cod's roe, then peel off the skin. Put the roe into a mixing bowl.

Trim the crusts from 2 thick slices of bread and soak the bread in 2 tablespoons (30 ml) of milk or water for 2 to 3 minutes. Drain well by squeezing the liquid from the bread. Add the bread to the roe. Beat in ¼ pint (150 ml) of yogurt, 1 crushed garlic clove and the juice of 1 lemon. Beat well until the mixture is smooth or put all the ingredients into a liquidizer and blend until smooth. Season to taste with salt and pepper.

Spoon the taramasalata into a serving dish, cover and chill in the refrigerator for several hours before serving.

Sprinkle with 1 tablespoon (15 ml) of chopped parsley and serve.

INGREDIENTS TO SERVE FOUR:
½ lb (250 g) smoked cod's roe
2 bread slices
2 tablespoons (30 ml) milk or water
¼ pint (150 ml) yogurt
1 garlic clove
1 lemon
salt
pepper
1 tablespoon (15 ml) chopped parsley

Smoked Haddock Mousse

Thinly slice 1 small onion and 1 carrot and put them into a saucepan with ¼ pint (150 ml) of water, salt, pepper, 1 bay leaf, 3 parsley sprigs and the grated rind of ½ lemon. Bring to the boil, reduce the heat and simmer gently for 10 minutes.

Add 1 pound (500 g) of smoked haddock fillets to the pan. Simmer for 10 minutes, or until the haddock is cooked. Remove the fish from the pan. Skin it and flake it into a mixing bowl.

Reduce the fish liquor by boiling until 4 tablespoons (60 ml) remain in the pan. Remove the pan from the heat and sprinkle in ½ ounce (15 g) of powdered gelatine. Soak the gelatine for 2 minutes then cook over low heat, stirring, until the gelatine has dissolved.

Add ½ pint (300 ml) of yogurt to the flaked fish. Beat until smooth. Add the juice of ½ lemon and salt and pepper to taste. Pour in the dissolved gelatine and mix well.

Pour the mousse into 4 individual dishes or 1 large dish or mould. Chill in the refrigerator for at least 4 hours before serving.

INGREDIENTS TO SERVE FOUR:
1 small onion
1 carrot
salt
pepper
1 bay leaf
3 parsley sprigs
1½ lemons
1 lb (500 g) smoked haddock fillets
½ oz (15 g) powdered gelatine
½ pint (300 ml) yogurt

Kipper Pâté Lemons

This pâté can be stored in the refrigerator for up to 1 week or frozen for as long as 1 month.

Cook ½ pound (250 g) of kippers under a low grill for 4 minutes on each side. Remove the skins and flake the kippers into a mixing bowl.

Cut 2 large lemons into halves. Using a grapefruit knife scoop out the fruit. Reserve the lemon skins. Using a sharp knife cut the fruit away from the membrane. Work over a bowl to catch the juice. Coarsely chop the lemon and add it with the juice to the flaked kippers. Add ¼ pound (100 g) of curd or cream cheese. Beat until the ingredients are well blended. Season to taste with salt and pepper.

Cut a small piece off the bottom of each lemon skin so it will stand. Spoon the pâté into the lemon rinds. Serve with toast.

INGREDIENTS TO SERVE FOUR:
½ lb (250 g) kippers
2 large lemons
¼ lb (100 g) curd cheese or cream cheese
salt
pepper
4 slices toasted wholewheat bread

PREPARING LEMON CUPS

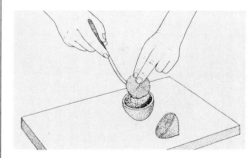

Cut the fruit from a lemon with a grapefruit knife.

Trim the bottoms to make the cups stand upright.

THE CHICKEN, which has travelled far since the domestication in prehistoric times of its ancestor, the Indian jungle fowl, is now the world's ubiquitous culinary bird. When it is alive it is a bird of many images, from the scrawny barnyard fowl, which has to scratch for its living, to the pampered castrato known as a capon. When it is cooked the chicken appears in hundreds of guises. But however the flavour of the chicken and the way it is cooked varies the flesh remains high in protein, low in fat and is easily digested.

The youngest table chicken, eaten at three weeks old, is the tasteless *petit poussin*. When the bird is slightly older and weighs about one and a half pounds, it becomes a *poussin*, and, although tender, it is still fairly tasteless. The American counterpart is the somewhat heavier broiler. The spring chicken, or *poulet*, is up to three months old, weighs about three pounds (1½ kg) and has much more flavour if it is not overcooked. A roasting chicken is up to eight months old and weighs four to five pounds (2 to 2½ kg). A neutered hen, or *poularde*, has firm white flesh and is five and a half pounds (2½ kg), while a castrated cockerel, or capon, can weigh almost twice as much.

The Roman consul Fannius must be thanked for unwittingly introducing the capon to the world. Worried that the gluttonous Romans were eating hens almost to extinction he forbade his subjects to eat them. But the Fannius Law forgot to mention cocks. The ingenious Romans, well aware of the physical changes that overcame eunuchs, began castrating the cock. The bird, its

aggression lost, not only grew larger than the prohibited hen, but acquired the excellent culinary reputation that it still has today.

At the other extreme is the ovenready bird, wretched in life and insipid in death. Nonetheless it is largely responsible for the great increase in the eating of chicken over the last two decades. Today, on average the British each eat about twenty pounds (9 kg) of chicken a year, more than two and a half times as much as in the 1930s.

Turkeys and ducks have suffered less than chickens from intensive farming and industrial technology, and so far geese have escaped it.

The huge turkeys that star in Dickens's novels are now out of favour and the British and Americans are turning to smaller birds, which are also the favourites of the Italians and Spanish. The large birds are now mainly for such ceremonial occasions as Christmas and Thanksgiving Day.

The Nutrients in Chicken and Turkey
These birds contain first-class protein and three and a half ounces (100 g) provide about 220 Calories.

Water	63%
Protein	20
Fat	16
Vitamins and minerals	1
Carbohydrate	0
Fibre	0

THE OVENREADY CHICKEN

The ovenready chicken is likely to have led a life that is nasty, hygienic and short. It will live in a shed along with five or ten thousand others, scratching around in a deep layer of wood shavings, often dosed to keep it healthy until it is fat enough to die at twelve to sixteen weeks. Carried along a conveyor track it is stunned, killed, bled, scalded, plucked by a sequence of rubber fingers and flails, eviscerated, decapitated, plunged into ice water, trussed, packed into a plastic bag and quick-frozen. To enhance its minimal flavour it may be dusted, sprayed or injected with the inevitable monosodium glutamate. Despite all that its nutritional value, if not its flavour content, is still high.

While chicken and turkey are high in protein and low in fat, the domestic duck and goose are rich in fat and flavour. They are birds of antiquity; in ancient Egypt both were sacrificed to the gods and the goose had a role in the myths of creation.

The best English table duck is the white Aylesbury; the best American breed is the Long Island, which is descended from nine Peking ducks imported in the late nineteenth century; and the best French ducks are the Rouen and Nantes duck. Unlike most other breeds French ducks are very lean and have a gamy flavour.

Goose is no longer popular in Great Britain or in the United States, but remains so in Germany, Sweden, Norway, Denmark, Holland and Hungary. The large white goose is the one generally preferred. A goose will live to a ripe old age, but if it is to be eaten it should not be allowed to live more than two years. Wild geese are beautiful to watch, difficult to shoot and unappetizing to eat.

To this rather limited choice of poultry, or domesticated birds, can be added the neglected guinea-fowl, or guinea-hen. This is a West African bird, still found wild, but which is greatly superior as the domesticated version. Its flavour is reminiscent of the American Bronze turkey, with a slight hint of gamyness. But its size is that of the pheasant, to which it is related.

Pheasant, partridge and the minute quail are game birds that have succumbed to a certain amount of domestication. If pheasant is not eaten on the day it is killed it must be hung from four to ten days to give it taste and make it tender again. A young plump partridge is at its delicately flavoured best when hung for only three to five days. Quail, which are related to partridge, should be eaten at the latest the day after they have been killed.

The Nutrients in Duck and Goose
Both birds are high in fat as well as protein and three and a half ounces (100 g) have about 340 Calories.

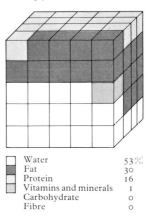

☐ Water	53%
☐ Fat	30
☐ Protein	16
☐ Vitamins and minerals	1
Carbohydrate	0
Fibre	0

Chicken, whether fresh or frozen, is an excellent source of protein, B vitamins and iron. Nevertheless, free-range chickens undoubtedly have the better flavour. Turkey (top, far left) is equally as nutritious as chicken. Unfortunately, both contain some cholesterol. West African guinea-fowl (top left) are related to the pheasant and have a slightly gamy flavour. Geese (bottom left) and ducks (centre left) have almost twice as much saturated fat as chicken and turkey. They are also moderately high in cholesterol.

Boiled Chicken

Boiling, or more accurately poaching, is an excellent way to cook a chicken. The meat is succulent and the useful stock is rich. A boiling fowl or a roasting chicken may be cooked this way. A boiling fowl, however, should be barely covered with water and simmered for 2 to 3 hours.

Remove the giblets and any excess fat from inside a 2½-pound (1.20-kg) roasting chicken. Put the chicken, breast upwards, into a large saucepan. Add the giblets. Pour in enough water to come halfway up the chicken breast.

Add the grated rind and juice of 1 lemon, salt, 6 peppercorns, 1 blade of mace and 1 bay leaf. Peel and quarter 1 onion, thickly slice 1 carrot and 1 stick of celery and add to the pan with 1 sprig of thyme and 2 sprigs of parsley.

Cover the pan and bring to the boil. Reduce the heat and simmer gently for about 1 hour, or until the chicken is tender. Transfer the chicken to a serving dish, strain the stock into a bowl and leave to cool. Then skim off the fat.

The chicken may be served hot, with a sauce or gravy made from the stock, or cold. For a recipe requiring cooked chicken meat, let the chicken cool, remove the skin and cut the meat from the bones. This should give 1 pound (500 g) of cooked chicken meat.

INGREDIENTS TO SERVE FOUR :
2½-lb (1.20-kg) roasting chicken
1 lemon
salt
6 peppercorns
1 mace blade
1 bay leaf
1 onion
1 carrot
1 celery stick
1 thyme sprig
2 parsley sprigs

Chicken and Noodles

Cut 1 small chicken, about 2 pounds (950 g), into quarters. Blanch, skin and coarsely chop 4 ripe medium-sized tomatoes. Coarsely chop ½ pound (250 g) of onions. Put the chicken pieces into an ovenproof dish with the chopped tomatoes and onions and ⅔ pint (400 ml) of water, 1 crushed garlic clove, ½ teaspoon (2.5 ml) of dried oregano and salt. Cover and simmer gently for 45 minutes.

Take the chicken pieces from the pan. Remove the skin and cut the meat off the bones. Cut the chicken meat into pieces.

Add ½ pound (250 g) of spinach noodles (see tagliatelle, page 42) to the liquid in the pan and cook for 5 minutes, or until the pasta is just tender. Add the chicken meat and cook for 5 minutes, or until the chicken is heated through.

Serve immediately sprinkled with grated Parmesan cheese.

INGREDIENTS TO SERVE FOUR :
1 small chicken
4 ripe medium-sized tomatoes
½ lb (250 g) onions
1 garlic clove
½ teaspoon (2.5 ml) dried oregano
salt
½ lb (250 g) spinach noodles (see tagliatelle, page 42)
grated Parmesan cheese

PREPARING CHICKEN QUARTERS

Lay the chicken on its back and cut it in half.

Lay each half flat and cut into two pieces.

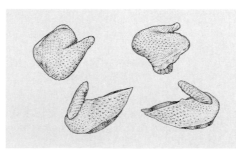

Each quarter will serve one person.

Lemon and Herb Baked Chicken

Preheat the oven to 350°F (180°C, Gas Mark 4).

Put 4 chicken breasts into an ovenproof dish or small roasting tin and bake, uncovered, for 30 minutes.

Meanwhile, finely chop 2 medium-sized onions. Put the onion into a mixing bowl with the grated rind and juice of 1 large lemon.

Add 4 tablespoons (60 ml) of chopped parsley, 1 tablespoon (15 ml) of chopped thyme, 1 tablespoon (15 ml) of chopped sage and 1 tablespoon (15 ml) of chopped mint. Mix well. Season to taste with salt and pepper.

Remove the chicken from the oven and pour off any fat that is in the pan. Pour ¼ pint (150 ml) of well-seasoned chicken stock over the chicken. Press the herb mixture on top of the chicken breasts. Return the chicken to the oven and bake for 15 to 20 minutes, or until the herb topping is crisp and lightly browned. Serve hot or cold.

INGREDIENTS TO SERVE FOUR :
4 chicken breasts
2 medium-sized onions
1 large lemon
4 tablespoons (60 ml) chopped parsley
1 tablespoon (15 ml) chopped thyme
1 tablespoon (15 ml) chopped sage
1 tablespoon (15 ml) chopped mint
salt
pepper
¼ pint (150 ml) chicken stock

Chicken Jerusalem

Heat 1 tablespoon (15 ml) of corn oil in a large saucepan. Add 4 chicken quarters and fry them until they are brown. Remove the chicken from the pan. Add 2 chopped medium-sized onions and fry gently for 3 minutes. Add ½ pint (300 ml) of chicken stock with the grated rind and juice of ½ lemon, 4 sprigs of thyme, salt and pepper.

Peel 1 pound (500 g) of Jerusalem artichokes. Coarsely dice the artichokes and add them to the pan. Bring to the boil and add the chicken pieces. Cover, reduce the heat and simmer gently for 30 minutes.

Slice 6 ounces (150 g) of button mushrooms and add them to the pan. Cover and continue cooking for 10 to 15 minutes, or until the chicken is tender.

Remove the chicken pieces to a warm serving dish. Garnish with a few of the sliced mushrooms and diced artichokes. Put the remaining vegetables and the stock into a liquidizer and blend to a smooth purée.

Pour the purée over the chicken, garnish with sprigs of watercress and serve.

INGREDIENTS TO SERVE FOUR :
1 tablespoon (15 ml) corn oil
4 chicken quarters
2 medium-sized onions
½ pint (300 ml) chicken stock
½ lemon
4 sprigs thyme
salt
pepper
1 lb (500 g) Jerusalem artichokes
6 oz (150 g) button mushrooms
watercress sprigs

Chicken à la Grecque

A marvellous dish for a buffet, this cold chicken dish should be made 1 day in advance.

Coarsely chop 1 large onion. Thinly slice 1 large carrot. Heat 2 tablespoons (30 ml) of olive oil in a saucepan. Add the onion and the carrot to the pan and fry over low heat until the onion is soft but not coloured. Add 1 crushed garlic clove, ¼ pint (150 ml) of dry white wine and 1 bouquet garni, made with 1 bay leaf and sprigs of parsley and thyme. Season with salt and pepper.

Blanch and peel ½ pound (250 g) of tomatoes. Cut the tomatoes into quarters and remove the seeds. Add the tomatoes to the pan with ½ pound (250 g) of button mushrooms. Bring to the boil, reduce the heat and simmer gently, uncovered, for 15 minutes.

Remove the bouquet garni from the pan and add 1 pound (500 g) of cooked chicken meat, coarsely chopped, and 1 thinly sliced red pepper. Stir well. Marinate in the refrigerator for 12 hours.

Sprinkle with 2 tablespoons of chopped parsley before serving.

INGREDIENTS TO SERVE FOUR:
1 large onion
1 large carrot
2 tablespoons (30 ml) olive oil
1 garlic clove
¼ pint (150 ml) dry white wine
1 bouquet garni, made with 1 bay leaf and parsley and thyme sprigs
salt
pepper
½ lb (250 g) tomatoes
½ lb (250 g) button mushrooms
1 lb (500 g) cooked chicken meat
1 red pepper
2 tablespoons (30 ml) chopped parsley

Devilled Chicken Legs

For the marinade, combine in a small mixing bowl 2 tablespoons (30 ml) of corn oil, 2 tablespoons (30 ml) of tarragon or wine vinegar, 2 tablespoons (30 ml) of water, 1 tablespoon (15 ml) of French mustard, 1 tablespoon (15 ml) of chopped sweet mango chutney, 1 grated onion, ½ teaspoon (2.5 ml) of curry powder, ½ teaspoon (2.5 ml) of ground ginger, salt and pepper. Mix well.

Score 4 chicken legs, or 8 drumsticks, with a sharp knife to allow the marinade to penetrate the meat. Put the chicken in a large bowl and pour in the marinade. Marinate for at least 12 hours in the refrigerator or 4 hours at room temperature, turning the chicken pieces occasionally.

Remove the chicken from the marinade and put on a grill pan under a hot grill. Grill the chicken for 15 minutes, or until the pieces are crisp and golden brown, turning once and basting frequently with the marinade.

Serve hot or cold, garnished with sprigs of watercress.

INGREDIENTS TO SERVE FOUR:
2 tablespoons (30 ml) corn oil
2 tablespoons (30 ml) tarragon or wine vinegar
1 tablespoon (15 ml) French mustard
1 tablespoon (15 ml) sweet mango chutney
1 onion
½ teaspoon (2.5 ml) curry powder
½ teaspoon (2.5 ml) ground ginger
salt
pepper
4 chicken legs or 8 drumsticks
watercress sprigs

Chicken Tandoori

This is a famous Indian dish. Its name comes from the *tandur*, the very hot charcoal oven in which it is traditionally cooked.

First make the marinade. Put ½ pint (300 ml) of yogurt into a mixing bowl. Add 1 grated small onion, 1 crushed garlic clove, the grated rind and juice of 1 small lemon and 1 tablespoon (15 ml) of tomato purée. Add 2 teaspoons (10 ml) of chilli powder, 2 teaspoons (10 ml) of paprika, ½ teaspoon (2.5 ml) of ground ginger, salt and pepper. Mix well.

Remove the skin from 4 chicken quarters. Put the chicken pieces in a dish and pour the marinade over them. Cover and marinate in the refrigerator for 24 hours. Baste the chicken occasionally.

Remove the chicken pieces from the marinade and put them under a hot grill. Cook for 15 to 20 minutes, turning frequently and basting with the marinade, until the chicken is cooked through. Alternatively, the chicken may be baked in a very hot oven for 20 to 30 minutes, basting frequently.

Serve immediately.

INGREDIENTS TO SERVE FOUR:
½ pint (300 ml) yogurt
1 small onion
1 garlic clove
1 small lemon
1 tablespoon (15 ml) tomato purée
2 teaspoons (10 ml) chilli powder
2 teaspoons (10 ml) paprika
½ teaspoon (2.5 ml) ground ginger
salt
pepper
4 chicken quarters

Chicken Véronique with Yogurt

Chicken pieces cooked with grapes and ginger and served with a creamy yogurt sauce make this a light and refreshing dish for a summer dinner.

Preheat the oven to 350°F (180°C, Gas Mark 4).

Put 4 chicken quarters into an ovenproof casserole and sprinkle with 1½ teaspoons (7.5 ml) of ground ginger, salt and pepper. Cut ½ pound (250 g) of green grapes into halves and remove the seeds. Scatter the grapes over the chicken. Add ½ pint (300 ml) of water, cover the casserole and bake for 1 hour, or until the chicken is tender.

Remove the chicken and the grapes to a warm serving dish.

Pour ½ pint (150 ml) of yogurt into a mixing bowl and stir in 1 tablespoon (15 ml) of cornflour. Slowly pour the liquid from the casserole into the yogurt, whisking well. Return the yogurt mixture to the pan and cook over very low heat, stirring constantly, until the sauce is thickened. Season the sauce to taste and pour it over the chicken. Sprinkle 2 ounces (50 g) of browned flaked almonds on top and serve immediately.

INGREDIENTS TO SERVE FOUR:
4 chicken quarters
1½ teaspoons (7.5 ml) ground ginger
salt
pepper
½ lb (250 g) green grapes
½ pint (300 ml) yogurt
1 tablespoon (15 ml) cornflour
2 oz (50 g) browned flaked almonds

French Chicken Casserole

Preheat the oven to 350°F (180°C, Gas Mark 4).

Arrange 4 chicken quarters in an ovenproof casserole with ½ pound (250 g) of small onions, 2 sliced sticks of celery, 4 sprigs of rosemary and 6 blanched, peeled and chopped ripe medium-sized tomatoes. Season to taste with salt and pepper. Pour over ¼ pint (150 ml) of water.

Cover and bake for 30 minutes. Stir in 12 stuffed olives and cook for 30 minutes more, or until the chicken is tender.

Serve hot.

INGREDIENTS TO SERVE FOUR:
4 chicken quarters
½ lb (250 g) small onions
2 celery sticks
4 rosemary sprigs
6 ripe medium-sized tomatoes
salt
pepper
12 stuffed olives

Cherry and Orange Duck

For this dish the duck is first roasted to
brown the skin and to melt away some of the
fat and is then braised with cherries and
orange juice.

Preheat the oven to 400 F (200 C, Gas
Mark 6).

Put 1 halved onion into the cavity of a
4-pound (1.80-kg) duck. Put the duck on a
rack in a roasting tin. Prick the skin all over
with a fork to allow the fat to run out. Rub
the skin with salt. Roast the duck for 1 hour.

Pit 1 pound (500 g) of cherries. Put the
pitted cherries into a bowl. Add the grated
rind of 1 orange and the juice of 2 oranges
to the cherries.

When the duck has cooked for 1 hour,
drain off the fat that has collected in the
roasting tin. Remove the rack and put the
duck back into the tin. Pour the cherries and
orange juice around the duck with ¼ pint
(150 ml) of chicken stock. Cover the tin with
foil and roast for 30 minutes more.

Remove the duck to a warm serving dish.
Drain half of the cherries, put them around
the duck and keep warm.

For the sauce, liquidize the remaining
cherries with the cooking liquor. Reheat the
sauce, season to taste with salt and pepper
and serve with the duck.

INGREDIENTS TO SERVE FOUR:
1 onion
4-lb (1.80-kg) duck
salt
1 lb (500 g) cherries
2 oranges
¼ pint (150 ml) chicken stock
pepper

Chicken with Ginger and Bean Sprouts

Coarsely chop 2 rashers of streaky bacon.
Peel and coarsely chop 1 medium-sized onion.
Cut 2 thin slices of root ginger. Peel off the
skin and cut the ginger into thin strips. Cut
the meat from 4 chicken breasts, about
1½ pounds (700 g), and slice it into strips.
Slice ¼ pound (100 g) of button mushrooms.

Heat 1 tablespoon (15 ml) of peanut oil in a
large, heavy frying-pan. Add the bacon to
the pan and fry over high heat, stirring
constantly, for 1 minute. Add the chopped
onion and 1 crushed garlic clove and fry,
still stirring, until the onion is tender. Add
the ginger and the chicken and fry for
3 minutes, stirring all the time. Add the
sliced mushrooms and ¼ pound (100 g) of
bean sprouts and stir-fry for 1 minute.

Blend 1 teaspoon (5 ml) of cornflour with
¼ pint (150 ml) of chicken stock and
1 teaspoon (5 ml) of soy sauce and add it
to the chicken mixture. Season to taste with
salt and pepper. Continue to stir-fry for a

further 2 minutes, or until the chicken is
cooked.

Garnish with sprigs of parsley or coriander
and serve immediately.

INGREDIENTS TO SERVE FOUR:
2 streaky bacon rashers
1 medium-sized onion
root ginger
4 chicken breasts
¼ lb (100 g) button mushrooms
1 tablespoon (15 ml) peanut oil
1 garlic clove
¼ lb (100 g) bean sprouts
1 teaspoon (5 ml) cornflour
¼ pint (150 ml) chicken stock
1 teaspoon (5 ml) soy sauce
salt
pepper
parsley or coriander sprigs

Orange Chicken Parcels

Preheat the oven to 400 F (200 C, Gas
Mark 6). Cut 4 pieces of foil, each large
enough to enclose a portion of chicken.

Rub 4 chicken quarters with ½ teaspoon
(2.5 ml) of salt. Slice 1 medium-sized onion.
Divide the onion slices between the pieces of
foil and put 1 chicken quarter on top of each
piece.

Peel and remove the pith from 1 orange.
Cut away the membrane from the segments
of fruit. Put the orange segments on top of the
chicken pieces. Grate the rind from another
orange and sprinkle over the chicken.
Squeeze the juice from the orange, mix it with
1 tablespoon (15 ml) of Worcestershire sauce
and pour it over the chicken. Lightly fold the
foil around the chicken pieces. Put the parcels
on a baking sheet. Bake for 45 minutes, or
until the chicken is tender.

To serve, remove the chicken from the foil
and garnish with sprigs of watercress.

INGREDIENTS TO SERVE FOUR:
4 chicken quarters
½ teaspoon (2.5 ml) salt
1 medium-sized onion
2 oranges
**1 tablespoon (15 ml) Worcestershire
  sauce**
watercress sprigs

well-seasoned chicken stock. Add the strips of chicken meat to the stock with 1 bay leaf and the grated rind and juice of 1 lemon. Half-cover the pan, reduce the heat and simmer gently for 30 minutes.

Remove the stones from 8 black olives. Cut each olive into quarters and add to the pan. Adjust the seasoning, adding salt or pepper if necessary. Cook for a further 15 minutes, or until the stock is absorbed and the rice is cooked.

Garnish with lemon slices and serve immediately.

INGREDIENTS TO SERVE FOUR:
1 small chicken
2 tablespoons (30 ml) corn oil
2 medium-sized onions
½ lb (250 g) brown rice
1½ pints (850 ml) chicken stock
1 bay leaf
1½ lemons
8 black olives
salt
pepper

Cocky-Leeky

This Scottish chicken and leek soup is traditionally made with prunes, which give it a rich flavour.

Put 1 small chicken, about 1½ pounds (700 g), or 2 large chicken quarters, into a large saucepan with 2 pints (1 litre) of water. Add ¼ pound (100 g) of stoned prunes and 1 bouquet garni made with 1 bay leaf and sprigs of parsley and thyme. Season to taste with salt and pepper. Bring to the boil. Cover the pan, reduce the heat and simmer gently for 1 hour.

Remove the chicken from the pan. Add 1 pound (500 g) of sliced leeks to the soup and continue to simmer, covered, for 15 minutes. Meanwhile, skin the chicken and cut the meat from the bones. Coarsely chop the chicken meat. Add the chopped chicken to the soup with 2 tablespoons (30 ml) of chopped parsley and simmer for 5 minutes longer. Adjust the seasoning. Serve immediately.

INGREDIENTS TO SERVE FOUR TO SIX:
1 small chicken
¼ lb (100 g) stoned prunes
1 bouquet garni, made with 1 bay leaf and parsley and thyme sprigs
salt
pepper
1 lb (500 g) leeks
2 tablespoons (30 ml) chopped parsley

Poultry is extremely versatile and is the basis of many marvellous dishes, such as Cherry and Orange Duck, left, and Chinese Chicken with Ginger and Bean Sprouts, right.

Chicken Liver with Mange-tout and Orange

This dish makes a delicious and unusual starter.

Cut ½ pound (250 g) of chicken livers into ½-inch (1-cm) slices. Put 1 teaspoon (5 ml) of cornflour into a mixing bowl and stir in 1 tablespoon (15 ml) of soy sauce and the grated rind and juice of 1 orange. Add the sliced chicken livers and marinate for at least 10 minutes.

Meanwhile, remove the tops and strings from ½ pound (250 g) of mange-tout. Blanch in boiling water for 2 minutes, or until tender but still crisp. Drain.

Heat 1 tablespoon (15 ml) of peanut oil in a heavy frying-pan. Add 2 chopped spring onions and fry over high heat, stirring constantly, for 30 seconds. Add the liver and marinade and fry, stirring, for 2 to 3 minutes, or until the liver is cooked and lightly browned. Add the blanched mange-tout and

cook, stirring constantly, for 2 minutes.

Serve immediately in warmed individual serving dishes, garnished with thin slices of orange.

INGREDIENTS TO SERVE FOUR AS A STARTER:
½ lb (250 g) chicken livers
1 teaspoon (5 ml) cornflour
1 tablespoon (15 ml) soy sauce
1½ oranges
½ lb (250 g) mange-tout
1 tablespoon (15 ml) peanut oil
2 spring onions

Moroccan Chicken Rice

Cut the meat from 1 small chicken, about 2 pounds (1 kg). Slice the meat into strips. (The skin and bones can be used to make chicken stock.)

Heat 2 tablespoons (30 ml) of corn oil in a large saucepan. Add 2 chopped medium-sized onions and fry, over high heat, stirring frequently, for 5 minutes, or until the onions have browned. Stir in ½ pound (250 g) of brown rice and then add 1½ pints (850 ml) of

Congo Chicken

This African-style dish may be served hot or cold.

Preheat the oven to 350°F (180°C, Gas Mark 4).

Put 4 chicken quarters into an ovenproof dish or a small roasting tin and bake uncovered for 30 minutes, or until the chicken is lightly browned.

Meanwhile, remove the seeds and pith from 1 green pepper. Cut the pepper into strips. Plunge the pepper strips into boiling water for 1 minute and then rinse in cold water.

Chop ½ pound (250 g) of roasted salted peanuts and put them into a mixing bowl. Stir in ¼ pint (150 ml) of yogurt, 4 tablespoons (60 ml) of chopped parsley and salt and pepper to taste.

Remove the chicken from the oven and spread the pieces with the peanut mixture. Arrange the strips of pepper around the chicken and return it to the oven for 15 minutes, or until the chicken is tender and the topping is crisp and lightly browned.

INGREDIENTS TO SERVE FOUR:
4 chicken quarters
1 green pepper
½ lb (250 g) roasted salted peanuts
¼ pint (150 ml) yogurt
4 tablespoons (60 ml) chopped parsley
salt
pepper

Chicken and Thyme Pie

Boil a 2½- to 3-pound (1.20- to 1.40-kg) chicken (see boiled chicken, page 72). Reserve the chicken liver. Allow the chicken to cool. Strain and reserve ½ pint (250 ml) of the cooking liquid.

Make ¾ pound (350 g) of shortcrust pastry with wholewheat flour (see page 34). Reserving one-third of the pastry for the lid, roll the rest out on a lightly floured surface and line an 11- by 4- by 2½-inch (28- by 10- by 6-cm) rectangular tin. Let the excess pastry overlap the edges of the tin.

Preheat the oven to 400°F (200°C, Gas Mark 6).

Cut the chicken into pieces, remove and discard the skin and cut the meat from the bones. Coarsely chop the meat and put it into a mixing bowl.

Coarsely chop ¼ pound (100 g) of streaky bacon and the chicken liver. Add the bacon and liver to the chicken meat with the grated rind and juice of ½ lemon, 2 tablespoons (30 ml) of chopped parsley, 1 tablespoon (15 ml) of chopped thyme, salt and freshly ground black pepper. Mix well.

Spoon half of the chicken mixture into the pastry case. Arrange ½ pound (250 g) of sliced cooked ham on top then spoon in the

remainder of the chicken mixture. Fold the edges of the pastry case over the filling.

Put the reserved pastry on to a lightly floured surface and roll it out large enough to cover the pie. Dampen the edges of the pastry case and the edges of the lid with water. Lift the lid carefully on to the pastry case. Trim the lid to fit the pie and seal the edges well by pressing them with a fork. Cut a hole in the centre of the lid.

Reroll any pastry trimmings and make leaves and a tassel for decoration. Fit the tassel into the hole in the lid and arrange the leaves at either end of the pie.

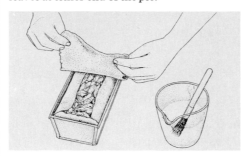

Cover the pie with rolled out pastry to form a lid.

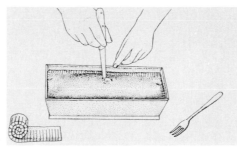

Cut a hole in the lid and make a pastry tassel.

Decorate the pie with leaves cut from pastry.

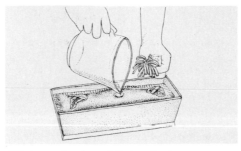

Lift the tassel and pour jelly into the pie.

Brush the top of the pie with a glaze of beaten egg. Bake the pie for 1 hour. If the top of the pie browns too quickly cover it with aluminium foil. Cool the pie in the tin.

Meanwhile, in a small saucepan, stir ½ ounce (15 g) of powdered gelatine into the reserved chicken stock. Heat gently until the gelatine has dissolved. When the stock is just beginning to set, remove the pastry tassel from the lid of the pie and pour in the jellied stock. Replace the tassel. Refrigerate the pie overnight.

INGREDIENTS TO SERVE EIGHT:
2½- to 3-lb (1.20- to 1.40-kg) boiled chicken (see page 72)
1 chicken liver
¾ lb (350 g) shortcrust pastry made with wholewheat flour (see page 34)
¼ lb (100 g) streaky bacon
½ lemon
2 tablespoons (30 ml) chopped parsley
1 tablespoon (15 ml) chopped thyme
salt
freshly ground black pepper
½ lb (250 g) cooked ham
1 egg
½ oz (15 g) powdered gelatine

Turkey and Cranberry Casserole

Preheat the oven to 350°F (180°C, Gas Mark 4).

Wash ½ pound (250 g) of leeks and cut them into thick slices. Scrape ½ pound (250 g) of carrots and cut them into thick slices. Peel and quarter ½ pound (250 g) of potatoes, ½ pound (250 g) of turnips and ½ pound (250 g) of medium-sized onions.

Stick 2 cloves into one of the onion quarters. Put it into the cavity of a 7- to 10-pound (3- to 4.50-kg) turkey with a thick slice of lemon and a few sprigs of parsley.

Put half of the prepared vegetables into an ovenproof casserole or a roasting tin. Put the turkey on top of the vegetables. Mix the remaining vegetables with ¼ pound (100 g) of cranberries and arrange them around the turkey.

Wash the turkey giblets and add them to the casserole with 1 bouquet garni, consisting of 1 bay leaf and sprigs of parsley and thyme. Add 2 pints (1 litre) of turkey or chicken stock and salt and pepper.

Cover the casserole and bake for 2½ to 3 hours. Uncover and cook for 20 minutes more, or until the turkey is tender and brown.

Transfer the turkey to a serving dish and arrange the vegetables around it. Discard the bouquet garni and giblets. Serve some of the stock with the turkey.

Pour the remaining stock into a bowl and chill it until the next day. Skim any fat from the top and pour the stock into a saucepan. Chop any left-over turkey and vegetables and add to the stock with 2 ounces (50 g) of rice. Simmer for 15 minutes, or until the rice is cooked. Serve as a hot soup.

INGREDIENTS TO SERVE EIGHT TO TWELVE:
½ lb (250 g) leeks
½ lb (250 g) carrots
½ lb (250 g) potatoes
½ lb (250 g) turnips
½ lb (250 g) medium-sized onions
3 cloves
7- to 10-lb (3- to 4.50-kg) turkey and
    giblets
1 thick lemon slice
parsley sprigs
¼ lb (100 g) cranberries
1 bouquet garni consisting of 1 bay leaf
    and parsley and thyme sprigs
2 pints (1 litre) turkey or chicken stock
salt
pepper
2 oz (50 g) rice

SKIMMING POULTRY STOCK

Skim any fat from the top of the chilled stock.

Chicken with Celery and Cheese

This is an old English recipe, braised chicken with celery covered in cheese sauce.

Heat 2 tablespoons (30 ml) of corn oil in a large flameproof casserole. Add 4 chicken quarters and fry them until they are brown. Remove the chicken pieces from the casserole. Add 2 sliced onions and fry them for 3 minutes.

Wash 1 head of celery and cut off the leaves. Cut the stalks into sticks about ½ by 2 inches (1 by 5 cm) and add them to the casserole. Reserve the best celery leaves for garnish and add the rest to the casserole with ¼ pint (150 ml) of chicken stock and the browned chicken pieces. Cover the casserole and simmer over low heat for 45 minutes. Alternatively, bake at 350 F (180 C, Gas Mark 4) for 1 hour.

Remove the chicken pieces to a warm serving dish. Grate ¼ pound (100 g) of Cheddar cheese and add it to the celery sauce. Heat gently, stirring, until the cheese has melted and thickened the sauce. Pour the sauce over the chicken, garnish with the reserved celery leaves and serve.

INGREDIENTS TO SERVE FOUR:
2 tablespoons (30 ml) corn oil
4 chicken quarters
2 onions
1 celery head
¼ pint (150 ml) chicken stock
¼ lb (100 g) Cheddar cheese

Chicken and Pork Adobo

Cut 1 pound (500 g) of boned shoulder or neck fillet of pork into 2-inch (5-cm) cubes. Put them into a large saucepan. Cut 1 small chicken into quarters and add them to the pan.

Slice 2 onions and add them to the pan with 1 crushed garlic clove, 1 bay leaf, salt and pepper. Add ½ pint (300 ml) of water, 5 tablespoons (75 ml) of cider vinegar or wine vinegar and 1 tablespoon (15 ml) of soy sauce. Bring to the boil. Cover the pan, reduce the heat and simmer for 1 hour, or until the meat is tender.

Mix in ¼ pound (100 g) of button mushrooms. Continue to cook, uncovered, for about 10 minutes, or until the mushrooms are cooked and the sauce has reduced and thickened.

Sprinkle with 1 tablespoon (15 ml) of chopped parsley and serve immediately.

INGREDIENTS TO SERVE FOUR:
1 lb (500 g) boned shoulder or neck fillet
    of pork
1 small chicken
2 onions
1 garlic clove
1 bay leaf
salt
pepper
5 tablespoons (75 ml) cider vinegar or
    wine vinegar
1 tablespoon (15 ml) soy sauce
¼ lb (100 g) button mushrooms
1 tablespoon (15 ml) chopped parsley

Normandy Pheasant

The pheasant is first roasted to brown the skin and then braised in cider with apples and raisins to make a well-flavoured and succulent dish.

Preheat the oven to 425 F (220 C, Gas Mark 7).

Put 1 cock pheasant or 2 hen pheasants into a roasting tin and roast for 30 minutes, or until lightly browned.

Add to the pan 2 sliced medium-sized onions, 2 large cooking apples, sliced, and 2 ounces (50 g) of seedless raisins. Pour ½ pint (300 ml) of dry cider over the pheasant and sprinkle with salt and pepper.

Cover the tin with foil. Lower the oven temperature to 375 F (190 C, Gas Mark 5)

and cook the pheasant for a further 30 to 40 minutes.

Remove the pheasant from the roasting tin and cut into individual portions. Put the pheasant portions on a warm serving dish with some of the apples, onions and raisins. Keep warm.

Pour the liquid and the remaining vegetables into a saucepan. Add 1 tablespoon (15 ml) of red currant jelly and bring to the boil, stirring. Reduce the heat and simmer gently for 5 minutes, or until the sauce has thickened slightly and the jelly has melted.

Pour the sauce over the pheasant, garnish with sprigs of watercress and serve.

INGREDIENTS TO SERVE FOUR:
1 cock or 2 hen pheasants
2 medium-sized onions
2 large cooking apples
2 oz (50 g) seedless raisins
½ pint (300 ml) dry cider
salt
pepper
1 tablespoon (15 ml) red currant jelly
watercress sprigs

Chicken with Prunes

Rabbit can be substituted for chicken in this tasty casserole.

Soak ½ pound (250 g) of stoned prunes overnight.

Cut 4 rashers of streaky bacon into 1-inch (2-cm) pieces and fry over low heat in a large saucepan for 3 minutes, or until the fat runs. Add ½ pound (250 g) of sliced onions, or whole small onions if available, and fry them until they are lightly browned.

Cut 1 large chicken into quarters and coat them in 1 tablespoon (15 ml) of seasoned flour. Add the chicken pieces to the pan and brown lightly. Then add ½ pint (300 ml) of chicken stock, 1 tablespoon (15 ml) of wine vinegar, salt and pepper. Drain the prunes and add them to the pan.

Cover the pan and simmer gently for 1 hour, or until the chicken is tender.

INGREDIENTS TO SERVE FOUR:
½ lb (250 g) stoned prunes
4 streaky bacon rashers
½ lb (250 g) onions
1 large chicken
1 tablespoon (15 ml) seasoned flour
½ pint (300 ml) chicken stock
1 tablespoon (15 ml) wine vinegar
salt
pepper

MEAT /A Little Goes a Long Way

The Nutrients in Meat
Meat is high in protein and in fat and three and a half ounces (100 g) of beef steak, for example, provide about 250 Calories.

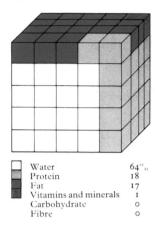

Water	64%
Protein	18
Fat	17
Vitamins and minerals	1
Carbohydrate	0
Fibre	0

To some people the eating of flesh is abhorrent; to others a diet without meat is unthinkable. Both meat and meatless diets can be perfectly healthy. Vegetarians must make sure that their non-animal proteins are balanced to provide all the essential amino acids. Lovers of meat should be careful not to be seduced by its succulence into eating too much—a common failing in Western diets.

Much of the reputation of meat rests on its being such a good source of protein, and well balanced in amino acids. There are other things in its favour too. It is rich in B vitamins—thiamine (especially in pork), niacin and B_{12}, and it is a good source of iron, phosphorus, potassium, sodium and magnesium. It is also digested slowly, thus delaying the return of hunger soon after a meal. And its smell when it is cooked is a remarkably effective and agreeable stimulus to the digestive juices.

The aroma and flavour of meat are intimately connected, as you can discover by eating with your nose held tightly closed. So far science has been unable to explain exactly either smell or flavour. About one hundred and eighty substances have been tracked down in the odour of cooking beef, and separately some of them smell quite unpleasant. The cooked fat appears to account for the difference of flavour between such meats as beef, lamb and pork, but there are, in fact, many variables that decide the flavour of meat. These include the breed, the sex and the age of the animal, the food it ate and the way the meat was stored after slaughter. The difference that age makes is obvious in comparing veal with beef and lamb with mutton. The flavour of lamb also reveals where the lamb has grazed: lamb from the mountains is herby and sweet; from the marshes it has a tang of salt; and from the chalk downs it is spicy. These subtle and distinctive flavours can be lost if the lamb is fattened on roots or concentrates. Pork is liable to taste of fish if the pig was reared on large amounts of fish products. The beef from an intensively raised cow is more tender, more tasteless and fattier than that from a free-range cow.

Newly killed meat is insipid, but the flavour improves during the next twenty-four hours. Thereafter, the meat should be hung for about ten days to allow the action of enzymes to make it more tender.

There is no meat that is the universal favourite. The English, Americans, French and Dutch like beef. The English, however, have never been fond of veal, but it is popular in the United States and on the Continent. The best veal is reckoned to be that from a calf two and a half to three months old which has been fed only on milk. The Italians like it even younger, while veal in Spain is more likely to be one- to two-year-old baby beef; it is at least

better than Spanish beef, which may well be vanquished bull.

Pork is the most popular meat in Germany, and it is increasingly being eaten throughout the West. It is the basic meat of the Chinese, but it is rejected by both Muslims and Jews. They are happy, however, to eat the flesh of sheep; lamb and mutton have, indeed, escaped most meat taboos.

Strictly speaking, lamb is from a sheep under a year old and thereafter it becomes mutton. But the English often give the courtesy title of lamb to anything reasonably tender. A certain austerity produces the sweetest flavour as in the lamb reared in Iceland, Norway, the highlands of Britain and in Greece, and it limits the amount of fat.

The goat has a certain following, but only when a kid, for it becomes inedible if it is more than three months old, which may explain why the ancients so willingly sacrificed goats to the gods.

Beef, lamb and pork contribute high-quality protein, B vitamins and iron to the diet. Unfortunately, these meats, and particularly pork, also contain a high proportion of saturated fat as well as a moderate amount of cholesterol. They should, therefore, be eaten in moderation. Deposits of fat, or "marbling", between the muscle fibres is even greater in the meat of intensively reared animals than that of free-grazing herds. Organ meats, such as liver and kidney, have the advantage of being lower in fat than muscle meat. They are equal in protein value and higher in iron and vitamins A, thiamine and riboflavin. But they have more than twice the amount of cholesterol.

Although there are more wild than domesticated animals their contribution to Western diets is relatively small. Furred game, to distinguish it from feathered game, includes rabbit, hare, deer, boar and bear—all of which have lean meat.

Meat, like fish, rapidly putrifies. The salting of meat is one of the oldest and most effective ways of preserving it for the winter. Today meat is salted, and also smoked, predominantly to make bacon and ham, because we enjoy the taste. There is little to choose between the energy and protein values of bacon and fresh pork, but some of the vitamins thiamine and niacin are lost in the salting.

By comparison with salting, canning is an infant in the history of preservation, dating only from the end of the eighteenth century. Some of the early canned meats were revolting—coarse meat and lumps of fat in a thin gravy. The British Navy had a macabre name for them—"Sweet Fanny Adams", after a woman whose body had been hacked to pieces by her murderer. Since then canned meat has become more spuriously palatable, but even further removed from the wholesome original.

Hamburgers and beefburgers are in the tradition of the cooked or easy-to-cook meats that have been around for several thousand years. The Greeks and Romans were as fond of sausages as are present-day Americans, who manage to consume an average of eighty hot dogs per head every year. There were cooked-meat shops in London as far back as the Middle Ages and William Cobbett, in the early nineteenth century, fulminated against the laziness of the rural labouring classes for patronizing them instead of cooking wholesome food at home. The taste for "convenience" meats was not confined to the working classes. One of England's most famous Prime Ministers, William Pitt the younger, is reputed to have said on his death bed: "I think I could eat one of Bellamy's veal pies."

Lancashire Hot Pot

Preheat the oven to 350°F (180°C, Gas Mark 4).

Cut any excess fat from 8 middle or best end of neck lamb chops. Put the chops into an ovenproof casserole. Peel and remove the central core of 2 lamb kidneys. Slice the kidneys and add them to the casserole with ½ pound (250 g) of sliced onions and 1 sliced large carrot. Sprinkle with 2 tablespoons (30 ml) of chopped mint and salt and pepper to taste.

Peel and thinly slice 1 pound (500 g) of potatoes. Overlapping the potato slices, arrange them on top of the lamb and the vegetables. Pour in ½ pint (300 ml) of well-seasoned lamb or beef stock. Brush the potatoes lightly with corn oil.

Cover the casserole and bake for 1½ hours, or until the meat is tender. Uncover and cook until the potatoes are golden brown.

INGREDIENTS TO SERVE FOUR:
8 middle or best end of neck lamb chops
2 lamb kidneys
½ lb (250 g) onions
1 large carrot
2 tablespoons (30 ml) chopped mint
salt
pepper
1 lb (500 g) potatoes
½ pint (300 ml) lamb or beef stock
corn oil

PREPARING LANCASHIRE HOT POT

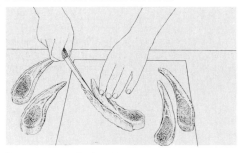

Trim any excess fat from lamb chops.

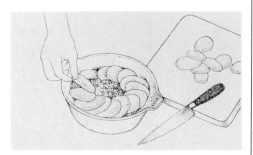

Cover the meat and vegetables with potato slices.

Lamb Curry

Heat 3 tablespoons (45 ml) of corn oil in a large saucepan. Add 2 finely chopped onions and fry, stirring, for 3 minutes. Peel and finely chop a 1-inch (2-cm) piece of root ginger and add it to the pan with 2 crushed garlic cloves and 1 finely chopped, seeded green chilli and continue frying.

In a small bowl mix 1 teaspoon (5 ml) of turmeric, 2 teaspoons (10 ml) of ground coriander, 1 teaspoon (5 ml) of ground cumin, ½ teaspoon (2.5 ml) of cayenne pepper and 1 teaspoon (5 ml) of ground paprika with enough cold water to make a paste. Add the paste to the pan and fry, stirring, for 5 minutes. Stir in 1 to 2 teaspoons (15 to 30 ml) of water if the mixture gets too dry.

Cut 2 pounds (1 kg) of lean boned shoulder or leg of lamb into 1-inch (2-cm) cubes. Add the cubes to the pan and fry, stirring, for 5 minutes.

Pour in 1 pint (600 ml) of chicken stock. Stir to mix, season to taste with salt and pepper and bring to the boil. Cover the pan, reduce the heat and simmer gently for 40 minutes.

Add ½-inch (1-cm) slice of creamed coconut to the pan and stir until it has completely dissolved. Continue simmering for 20 minutes more, or until the lamb is tender.

INGREDIENTS TO SERVE FOUR TO SIX:
3 tablespoons (45 ml) corn oil
2 onions
root ginger
2 garlic cloves
1 green chilli
1 teaspoon (5 ml) turmeric
2 teaspoons (10 ml) ground coriander
1 teaspoon (5 ml) ground cumin
½ teaspoon (2.5 ml) cayenne pepper
1 teaspoon (5 ml) ground paprika
2 lb (1 kg) lean boned shoulder or leg of lamb
1 pint (600 ml) chicken stock
salt
pepper
creamed coconut

Moussaka

This adaptation of a popular Greek dish uses a yogurt sauce rather than the traditional béchamel.

Preheat the oven to 350°F (180°C, Gas Mark 4).

Cut 3 medium-sized aubergines into ¼-inch (6-mm) slices. Put the slices into a colander set over a bowl. Sprinkle the aubergines generously with salt to draw out the juice, which can be bitter. Leave for at least 30 minutes to drain. Rinse the aubergines and pat them dry with absorbent kitchen paper.

Brush the slices lightly with corn oil and put them on a lightly greased baking sheet. Cook under a hot grill for 5 minutes, turning the slices over once, or until they are golden brown.

Heat 1 tablespoon (15 ml) of corn oil in a large saucepan. Add 1 chopped large onion and fry for 3 minutes. Add 1 pound (500 g) of minced lamb and fry for a further 5 minutes stirring constantly, or until the meat is no longer red.

Stir in 1 tablespoon (15 ml) of tomato purée and ¼ pint (150 ml) of lamb or beef stock. Season to taste with salt and freshly ground black pepper. Bring to the boil. Cover the pan, reduce the heat and simmer for 15 to 20 minutes, or until the meat is cooked.

Put a layer of aubergine slices into an ovenproof dish. Pour over half of the meat mixture. Add another layer of the aubergines, followed by the other half of the meat mixture. Arrange the last of the aubergine slices on top.

To make the sauce, beat 2 eggs in a bowl. Beat in ½ pint (300 ml) of yogurt, 1 ounce (25 g) of flour, salt and pepper. Pour the sauce over the aubergines and meat. Sprinkle 2 ounces (50 g) of grated Cheddar cheese over the top.

Bake for 30 minutes, or until the sauce is set and brown on top.

INGREDIENTS TO SERVE FOUR:
3 medium-sized aubergines
salt
corn oil
1 large onion
1 lb (500 g) minced lamb
1 tablespoon (15 ml) tomato purée
¼ pint (150 ml) lamb or beef stock
freshly ground black pepper
2 eggs
½ pint (300 ml) yogurt
1 oz (25 g) flour
2 oz (50 g) grated Cheddar cheese

Navarin of Lamb

The meat and vegetables in this French lamb dish are cooked together in a casserole making a complete and satisfying meal.

Put 2 ounces (50 g) of haricot beans and 2 ounces (50 g) of pearl barley into a bowl. Cover with cold water and leave to soak overnight.

Cut any excess fat off of 2 pounds (1 kg) of best end of neck or shoulder of lamb and then cut the meat into 8 pieces.

Heat 1 tablespoon (15 ml) of corn oil in a large saucepan. Add the meat and fry until it is brown on all sides. Remove the meat and put it on absorbent kitchen paper to drain off the fat. Put the meat into a large casserole.

Pour off all but 1 tablespoon (15 ml) of the oil from the pan. Add 1 chopped large onion and fry for 3 minutes, or until the onion is golden brown. Stir in 1 tablespoon (15 ml) of flour. Stirring continuously, gradually add 1 pint (600 ml) of lamb or beef stock. When all the stock has been added stir in 1 tablespoon (15 ml) of tomato purée. Season to taste with salt and pepper.

Bring to the boil. Reduce the heat and simmer for 1 minute. Drain the beans and barley and add them to the meat in the casserole. Pour the stock into the casserole and add 1 bouquet garni, consisting of 1 bay leaf and sprigs of parsley and thyme tied together. Bring to the boil and cover the casserole. Reduce the heat and simmer for 1 hour. Alternatively, bake in the oven at 350°F (180°C, Gas Mark 4) for 1 hour.

Remove the bouquet garni from the casserole. Add 8 small button onions, 4 sliced medium-sized carrots and 2 small turnips, cut into quarters. Cover the casserole again and continue to cook for 30 to 45 minutes, or until the vegetables are tender.

Sprinkle with 2 tablespoons (30 ml) of chopped parsley and serve immediately.

INGREDIENTS TO SERVE FOUR:
2 oz (50 g) haricot beans
2 oz (50 g) pearl barley
2 lb (1 kg) best end of neck or shoulder
of lamb
1 tablespoon (15 ml) corn oil
1 large onion
1 tablespoon (15 ml) flour
1 pint (600 ml) lamb or beef stock
1 tablespoon (15 ml) tomato purée
salt
pepper
1 bouquet garni, consisting of 1 bay leaf
and sprigs of parsley and thyme
8 small button onions
4 medium-sized carrots
2 small turnips
2 tablespoons (30 ml) chopped parsley

Noisettes à la Provençale

Noisettes are slices cut from boned and trimmed best end of neck of lamb. The meat is tightly rolled up and tied at 1½-inch (3-cm) intervals with string. The rolled meat is then sliced between the strings to make lean and succulent portions.

Cut 1 garlic clove in half. Rub both sides of 4 noisettes of lamb with the cut garlic. Sprinkle the noisettes with salt and pepper and put them into a bowl. Pour in ¼ pint (150 ml) of dry vermouth or dry white wine. Add 4 sprigs of rosemary. Marinate the noisettes for at least 1 hour, turning them occasionally.

Remove the noisettes from the marinade and put on the grill pan under a hot grill.

Cut the bones from the meat.

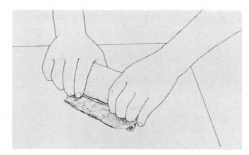

Roll the meat up tightly and tie with string.

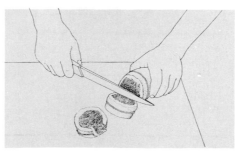

Slice the meat between the strings.

Grill for about 5 minutes, turning them once, until both sides are brown.

Meanwhile, prepare the sauce. Put the marinade into a saucepan. Blanch and peel 1½ pounds (700 g) of tomatoes. Cut the tomatoes in half and remove the seeds. Remove the pith and seeds from 1 green pepper and cut it into thin strips. Add the tomatoes and pepper to the pan. Bring to the

boil. Cover the pan, reduce the heat and simmer gently for 5 minutes, or until the tomatoes have reduced to a pulp.

When the noisettes are brown, drain off any excess fat and add the noisettes to the sauce in the pan. Spoon the sauce over the noisettes, cover the pan and simmer gently for 10 minutes, or until the noisettes are tender.

Transfer the noisettes to a warm serving dish. If the sauce is too liquid, boil uncovered for 2 minutes, then pour it over the meat. Serve immediately, garnished with sprigs of watercress.

INGREDIENTS TO SERVE FOUR:
1 garlic clove
4 noisettes of lamb
salt
pepper
¼ pint (150 ml) dry vermouth or dry
white wine
4 rosemary sprigs
1½ lb (700 g) tomatoes
1 green pepper
watercress sprigs

Lamb Chops Tartare

Preheat the oven to 375°F (190°C, Gas Mark 5).

Pour ½ pint (300 ml) of yogurt into a bowl and add 1 tablespoon (15 ml) of chopped gherkins, 1 tablespoon (15 ml) of capers, 2 tablespoons (30 ml) of chopped parsley and 4 chopped stuffed olives. Mix well. Season to taste with salt and pepper. Put 4 lamb chops into a shallow ovenproof casserole or dish. Pour the yogurt mixture over the chops.

Bake for 1 hour, or until the lamb is tender and the yogurt has set.

Garnish with slices of stuffed olive and parsley sprigs and serve immediately.

INGREDIENTS TO SERVE FOUR:
½ pint (300 ml) yogurt
1 tablespoon (15 ml) chopped gherkins
1 tablespoon (15 ml) capers
parsley sprigs
stuffed olives
salt
pepper
4 lamb chops

81

Beef in Yogurt Sauce

This is a delicious, less rich, version of the classic Beef Stroganoff.

Cut 1 pound (500 g) of lean steak (fillet, rump or sirloin) into strips about 2 by ½ inch (5 by 1 cm).

Peel and slice 1 large onion. Wash and slice 6 ounces (150 g) of mushrooms. Blanch and peel 2 ripe medium-sized tomatoes. Cut them in half and remove the seeds. Chop the tomatoes coarsely.

Heat 2 tablespoons (30 ml) of corn oil in a large, heavy frying-pan. Add the onions and fry them for 2 minutes, stirring frequently. Add the mushrooms and fry for 2 minutes more. Using a slotted spoon remove the onions and mushrooms from the pan.

Add the strips of beef to the pan and, stirring constantly, fry quickly until they are no longer red.

Return the onions and mushrooms to the pan with the chopped tomatoes. Season well with salt and pepper. Cook over low heat, stirring constantly, for two minutes.

Stir in ¼ pint (150 ml) of yogurt and heat gently. Do not allow the sauce to boil or the yogurt may curdle.

Serve immediately, sprinkled with 1 tablespoon (15 ml) of chopped parsley.

INGREDIENTS TO SERVE FOUR:
**1 lb (500 g) lean fillet, rump or sirloin
  steak
1 large onion
6 oz (150 g) mushrooms
2 ripe medium-sized tomatoes
2 tablespoons (30 ml) corn oil
salt
pepper
¼ pint (150 ml) yogurt
1 tablespoon (15 ml) chopped parsley**

Pot au Feu

This classic French dish is actually two dishes—a delicious beef broth and a main course of tender boiled beef and vegetables. Several different kinds of meat—beef, pork, veal and chicken—are often used as well as bones or an oxtail for extra flavour.

Roll a 4-pound (2-kg) piece of brisket of beef and tie it securely with string. Put ¼ pound (100 g) of ox liver into a large pan and put the brisket on top of it. Sprinkle with salt and pour in enough cold water to cover the meat.

Add to the pan 3 sticks of celery cut into quarters, 1 onion studded with 2 cloves, 1 bouquet garni, consisting of 2 bay leaves and sprigs of parsley and thyme, 3 peppercorns and 2 garlic cloves. Bring to the boil over moderate heat, skimming off the scum that rises to the surface. Reduce the heat to very low and simmer gently for 2 hours.

Peel and quarter 4 carrots, 4 turnips, 4 parsnips and 4 onions and add them to the pan. Cover the pan and continue to simmer over very low heat for 1 hour more.

Cut 1 medium-sized cabbage into wedges. Cut 2 leeks into quarters. Add the cabbage and the leeks to the beef with 3 tablespoons (45 ml) of drained capers. Cook the stew for 30 minutes more, or until the beef is tender.

Drain the beef. Cut and discard the string. Put the beef on a large, hot serving dish. Drain the vegetables and arrange them around the meat. Strain the cooking stock, skim off any fat and serve some of the stock with the beef.

Serve the remaining stock as a clear soup the following day.

INGREDIENTS TO SERVE EIGHT TO TEN:
**4 lb (2 kg) beef brisket
¼ lb (100 g) ox liver
salt
3 celery sticks
5 onions
2 cloves
1 bouquet garni, consisting of 2 bay
  leaves and parsley and thyme sprigs
3 peppercorns
2 garlic cloves
4 carrots
4 turnips
4 parsnips
1 medium-sized cabbage
2 leeks
3 tablespoons (45 ml) drained capers**

ROLLING BRISKET OF BEEF

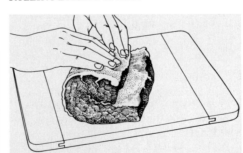

Roll a piece of brisket of beef up tightly.

Tie the rolled meat securely at intervals with string.

Steak with Mushrooms and Red Wine

Cut 1½ pounds (700 g) of lean rump or fillet of beef into 4 steaks. Rub the steaks with 1 cut garlic clove.

Pour ¼ pint (150 ml) of dry red wine into a bowl. Mix in 1 bay leaf, 4 sprigs of thyme, a little salt and freshly ground black pepper. Put the steaks into the marinade. Baste them well then leave to marinate for at least 30 minutes.

Take the steaks from the marinade and put on a grill pan under a hot grill. The timing will depend on the thickness of the steaks and how rare or well done you like them.

Meanwhile, prepare the sauce. Wash 6 ounces (150 g) of mushrooms. Slice them and put them into a large saucepan. Add the wine marinade and ¼ pint (150 ml) of beef stock. Cover the pan and bring to the boil. Then reduce the heat and simmer for 2 minutes. Add the grilled steaks to the pan, baste them with the sauce, cover the pan and simmer gently for 1 minute.

Put the steaks on a warm serving dish. Boil the sauce for 1 minute, then pour it over the steaks.

Serve immediately sprinkled with 2 tablespoons (30 ml) of chopped parsley.

INGREDIENTS TO SERVE FOUR:
**1½ lb (700 g) rump or fillet of beef
1 garlic clove
¼ pint (150 ml) dry red wine
1 bay leaf
4 thyme sprigs
salt
freshly ground black pepper
6 oz (150 g) mushrooms
¼ pint (150 ml) beef stock
2 tablespoons (30 ml) chopped parsley**

Stuffed Beef Rolls

Preheat the oven to 350°F (180°C, Gas Mark 4).

Cut 1½ pounds (700 g) of rump steak into 4 thin slices. Lay the slices, one at a time, between 2 sheets of greaseproof paper. Beat the steak with a rolling pin to flatten them.

For the stuffing, heat 1 ounce (25 g) of margarine in a saucepan. Add 1 chopped onion and fry for 3 minutes, stirring frequently. Coarsely chop ¼ pound (100 g) of mushrooms and add them to the pan. Fry for 2 minutes. Remove the pan from the heat and stir in 2 ounces (50 g) of fresh breadcrumbs, 1 tablespoon (15 ml) of chopped parsley, 1 teaspoon (5 ml) of chopped thyme, the grated rind of 1 lemon, salt and pepper.

Spread the stuffing on the slices of steak. Roll the slices up neatly and secure them with string or cocktail sticks. Arrange the beef rolls in a shallow ovenproof dish.

Blanch and peel ½ pound (250 g) of tomatoes. Cut the tomatoes into quarters and remove the seeds. Put the tomatoes around the beef rolls with 2 bay leaves. Pour in ½ pint (300 ml) of well-seasoned beef stock or dry red wine.

Cover the dish and bake for 1 hour, or until the beef rolls are tender.

INGREDIENTS TO SERVE FOUR:
1½ lb (700 g) rump steak
1 oz (25 g) margarine
1 onion
¼ lb (100 g) mushrooms
2 oz (50 g) fresh breadcrumbs
1 tablespoon (15 ml) chopped parsley
1 teaspoon (5 ml) chopped thyme
1 lemon
salt
pepper
½ lb (250 g) tomatoes
2 bay leaves
½ pint (300 ml) beef stock or dry red wine

PREPARING BEEF ROLLS

Flatten slices of steak with a rolling pin.

Spread the slices with stuffing and roll them up.

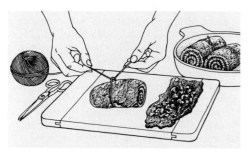

Tie the rolls and put them into an ovenproof dish.

Bobatie

Preheat the oven to 350°F (180°C, Gas Mark 4).

Heat 1 tablespoon (15 ml) of corn oil in a large saucepan. Add ½ pound (250 g) of sliced onions to the pan and fry for 3 minutes, or until the onions are just beginning to brown. Add 1½ pounds (700 g) of minced beef with 1 chopped small cooking apple and fry, stirring constantly, for 3 minutes.

Add 1 tablespoon (15 ml) of curry powder, 2 ounces (50 g) of raisins, 2 ounces (50 g) of peanuts, the juice of 1 small lemon, salt and pepper. Mix well. Cook over very low heat for 5 minutes.

Transfer the beef mixture to an ovenproof dish or casserole. Press 2 bay leaves into the top, cover and bake for 45 minutes.

Beat 1 egg with ¼ pint (150 ml) of milk. Remove the cover from the dish, discard the bay leaves and pour the egg and milk mixture over the meat. Return the dish to the oven and bake for 15 to 20 minutes more, or until the topping has set.

INGREDIENTS TO SERVE FOUR:
1 tablespoon (15 ml) corn oil
½ lb (250 g) sliced onions
1½ lb (700 g) minced beef
1 small cooking apple
1 tablespoon (15 ml) curry powder
2 oz (50 g) raisins
2 oz (50 g) peanuts
1 small lemon
salt
pepper
2 bay leaves
1 egg
¼ pint (150 ml) milk

Cassoulet

Wash ½ pound (250 g) of haricot beans under cold running water. Put the beans into a bowl, cover with cold water and leave them to soak for at least 12 hours.

Preheat the oven to 325°F (170°C, Gas Mark 3).

Chop ¼ pound (100 g) of streaky bacon and put it into an ovenproof casserole. Add 1 pound (500 g) of pork belly, cut into 1-inch (2-cm) cubes, 4 small chicken or rabbit quarters and ½ pound (250 g) of garlic sausage cut into ½-inch (1-cm) cubes.

Drain the beans and add them to the casserole with 1½ pints (850 ml) of chicken stock and ½ pound (250 g) of blanched, peeled and coarsely chopped tomatoes. Add 1 bouquet garni, consisting of 1 bay leaf and sprigs of parsley and thyme tied together. Season with salt and pepper. Mix well. Cover the casserole and bake for 1½ hours.

Discard the bouquet garni. If the mixture looks dry add a little more stock. Sprinkle ¼ pound (100 g) of fresh breadcrumbs over

the top and continue to bake the casserole, uncovered, for 1 hour more.

INGREDIENTS TO SERVE FOUR TO SIX:
½ lb (250 g) haricot beans
¼ lb (100 g) streaky bacon
1 lb (500 g) pork belly
4 small chicken or rabbit quarters
½ lb (250 g) garlic sausage
1½ pints (850 ml) chicken stock
½ lb (250 g) tomatoes
1 bouquet garni, consisting of 1 bay leaf and parsley and thyme sprigs
salt
pepper
¼ lb (100 g) fresh breadcrumbs

Pork and Cabbage Soup

For this Chinese soup all the ingredients are cut into small pieces so that they cook very quickly.

Cut ½ pound (250 g) of pork fillet or boned pork chops into thin strips. Put them into a large saucepan.

Thinly slice 2 ounces (50 g) of button mushrooms. Finely shred ½ pound (250 g) of cabbage. Finely chop 1 spring onion. Add the mushrooms, cabbage and spring onion to the pan.

Cut a ¼-inch (6-mm) slice of root ginger. Peel off and discard the skin. Chop the ginger finely. Add it to the pan. Pour in 1½ pints (850 ml) of well-seasoned chicken stock.

Bring to the boil. Reduce the heat and simmer for 10 minutes, or until the pork is cooked. Season with salt and pepper. Serve immediately.

INGREDIENTS TO SERVE FOUR:
½ lb (250 g) pork fillet or boned pork chops
2 oz (50 g) button mushrooms
½ lb (250 g) cabbage
1 spring onion
root ginger
1½ pints (850 ml) chicken stock
salt
pepper

Pork Goulash

Slice $\frac{3}{4}$ pound (350 g) of onions. Cut
1 pound (500 g) of lean boned shoulder or
fillet of pork into 2-inch (5-cm) cubes.
Blanch, peel and quarter 2 tomatoes.

Heat 1 tablespoon (15 ml) of corn oil in a
large saucepan. Add the onions to the pan
and fry them for 3 minutes, stirring
frequently. Add the pork to the pan and fry
until the cubes are well browned. Stir in
1 tablespoon (15 ml) of paprika and
1 tablespoon (15 ml) of flour and cook for
1 minute, stirring constantly.

Add 1 pint (600 ml) of well-seasoned
chicken stock, the quartered tomatoes,
2 tablespoons (30 ml) of tomato purée, the
grated rind of 1 lemon, salt and pepper.
Bring to the boil, stirring constantly. Cover
the pan, reduce the heat and simmer gently
for 1 to 1½ hours, or until the meat is tender.

Add $\frac{1}{4}$ pound (100 g) of button mushrooms
to the goulash and continue to cook for
10 minutes.

Just before serving put $\frac{1}{4}$ pint (150 ml) of
yogurt into a small saucepan. Warm the
yogurt over very low heat, do not allow it
to boil. Mix the warmed yogurt into the
goulash. Sprinkle with a little paprika and
serve.

INGREDIENTS TO SERVE FOUR:
$\frac{3}{4}$ **lb (350 g) onions**
**1 lb (500 g) boned shoulder or fillet of
    pork**
2 tomatoes
1 tablespoon (15 ml) corn oil
paprika
1 tablespoon (15 ml) flour
1 pint (600 ml) chicken stock
2 tablespoons (30 ml) tomato purée
1 lemon
salt
pepper
$\frac{1}{4}$ **lb (100 g) button mushrooms**
$\frac{1}{4}$ **pint (150 ml) yogurt**

Pâté de Campagne

Line the bottom and sides of a 2-pound (1-kg)
loaf tin or terrine with $\frac{1}{2}$ pound (250 g) of
sliced streaky bacon, laying the rashers
crossways in the tin. If any bacon is left over
chop it finely.

Put 1 pound (500 g) of minced pork and
1 pound (500 g) of minced veal into a mixing
bowl with the chopped bacon. Finely chop or
mince $\frac{1}{2}$ pound (250 g) of pig's liver and add
it to the bowl. Crush 2 garlic cloves and add
them to the bowl with 2 teaspoons (10 ml) of
salt and freshly ground black pepper to taste.

Grate in the rind of 1 orange. Squeeze the
juice of the orange and add it to the bowl
with 2 tablespoons (30 ml) of brandy.

Add 1 tablespoon (15 ml) of chopped sage
and 1 tablespoon (15 ml) of chopped thyme

to the bowl and mix thoroughly.
Refrigerate for 2 hours.

Preheat the oven to 325°F (170°C, Gas
Mark 3).

Press the meat mixture into the
bacon-lined tin. Level the top and press in
2 bay leaves and 4 sage leaves. Cover the tin
and put it into a roasting tin. Half fill the
roasting tin with water. Bake for 1½ hours.

Let the pâté cool slightly, cover it and put
a weight on top until it has cooled completely.
Cover and refrigerate for at least 4 hours
before serving.

Serve the pâté from the terrine or turn it
out of the tin on to a plate and cut it into
slices.

INGREDIENTS TO SERVE SIX TO EIGHT:
$\frac{1}{2}$ **lb (250 g) streaky bacon rashers**
1 lb (500 g) minced pork
1 lb (500 g) minced veal
$\frac{1}{2}$ **lb (250 g) pig's liver**
2 garlic cloves
2 teaspoons (10 ml) salt
freshly ground black pepper
1 orange
2 tablespoons (30 ml) brandy
sage sprigs
1 tablespoon (15 ml) chopped thyme
2 bay leaves

MAKING PATE

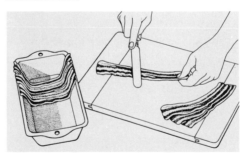

Line a tin with stretched rashers of bacon.

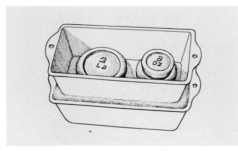

Weight the pâté while it is cooling.

Somerset Stuffed Pork

Preheat the oven to 350°F (180°C, Gas
Mark 4).

Finely chop or grind 3 ounces (75 g) of
toasted hazelnuts. Put them into a mixing
bowl with salt and pepper. Peel and core
1 small cooking apple and grate half of it into
the bowl. Add just enough beaten egg to bind
the ingredients. Mix well.

Trim any fat off 1 large or 2 small fillets of
pork, 1 to 1½ pounds (500 to 700 g). Cut
halfway through the fillets lengthways. Open
out the fillets. Put them, one at a time,
between 2 pieces of greaseproof paper and
flatten them with a rolling pin or a mallet.
Spread the stuffing mixture down the centre
of the fillets and roll them up tightly
lengthways. Secure the rolls with string.

Slice $\frac{1}{2}$ pound (250 g) of onions and put
them into a roasting tin or ovenproof dish.
Slice the remaining $\frac{1}{2}$ apple and arrange the
slices on top of the onions. Put the stuffed
pork on top of the apple and onions. Sprinkle
1 ounce (25 g) of whole toasted hazelnuts
around the pork. Pour in $\frac{1}{2}$ pint (300 ml) of
cider. Season with salt and pepper.

Cover and bake for 45 minutes, then
uncover and cook, basting occasionally, for
20 to 30 minutes more, or until the pork is
brown.

INGREDIENTS TO SERVE FOUR:
$\frac{1}{4}$ **lb (100 g) toasted hazelnuts**
salt
pepper
1 small cooking apple
1 egg
1 to 1½ lb (500 to 700 g) pork fillet
$\frac{1}{2}$ **lb (250 g) onions**
$\frac{1}{2}$ **pint (300 ml) cider**

Stuffed Veal

Have a 3½-pound (1.65-kg) shoulder, best
end or breast of veal boned and flattened.

Preheat the oven to 375°F (190°C, Gas
Mark 5).

Put the veal, boned side up, on a board.
Sprinkle it with salt and pepper.

Arrange 4 thin slices of Parma ham, or
cooked ham, about 2 ounces (50 g), on top of
the veal. Put 4 thin slices of Gruyère cheese,
about 3 ounces (75 g), on top of the ham.
Sprinkle with 8 sage leaves. Roll the veal up
neatly and tie it with string. Put the veal roll
into a roasting tin. Pour in $\frac{1}{4}$ pint (150 ml) of
chicken stock and $\frac{1}{4}$ pint (150 ml) of dry
white wine.

Cover the tin with aluminium foil and
bake for 1 hour. Remove the foil and baste the
meat. Continue to cook for 30 minutes more,
or until the veal is brown. Lift it out on to a
warm serving dish and keep hot.

Mix 2 teaspoons (10 ml) of cornflour with
2 tablespoons (30 ml) of cold water. Put the

roasting tin over low heat. Stir the cornflour mixture into the cooking liquor. Stirring constantly, bring to the boil. Continue to boil and stir the sauce until it has thickened. Season to taste with salt and pepper.

Garnish the veal with sage leaves and serve with the sauce in a sauce boat.

INGREDIENTS TO SERVE SIX:
3½-lb (1.65-kg) shoulder, best end or breast of veal
salt
pepper
4 thin slices of Parma ham or cooked ham
4 thin slices Gruyère cheese
sage leaves
¼ pint (150 ml) chicken stock
¼ pint (150 ml) dry white wine
2 teaspoons (10 ml) cornflour

Veal Escalopes with Orange

Cut 1 pound (500 g) of veal into 4 escalopes. Put the escalopes, one at a time, between two pieces of greaseproof paper. Flatten them with a rolling pin until they are ¼ inch (6 mm) thick.

Heat 2 tablespoons (30 ml) of sunflower oil in a frying-pan. Add the escalopes to the pan and fry over high heat until they are brown on both sides. Lift the escalopes out of the pan and keep them warm.

Finely chop 1 medium-sized onion and add it to the pan. Stirring frequently, fry the onion for 5 minutes, or until it is soft and translucent. Stir in 1 tablespoon (15 ml) of flour. Stirring constantly, gradually add ½ pint (300 ml) of chicken stock.

Add the grated rind and juice of 1 orange. Peel and remove the pith from another orange. Cut the membrane away from the segments of fruit. Add the segments to the pan with 3 tablespoons (45 ml) of Madeira and salt and pepper to taste. Bring to the boil. Reduce the heat and simmer for 1 minute.

Return the escalopes to the pan. Cover and simmer gently for 10 minutes.

Transfer the escalopes to a warm serving dish, pour the sauce over them, garnish with sprigs of watercress and serve immediately.

INGREDIENTS TO SERVE FOUR:
1 lb (500 g) veal
2 tablespoons (30 ml) sunflower oil
1 medium-sized onion
1 tablespoon (15 ml) flour
½ pint (300 ml) chicken stock
2 oranges
3 tablespoons (45 ml) Madeira
salt
pepper
watercress sprigs

Kidneys and Mushrooms in Wine

Slice 1 onion. Remove the skins from 1 pound (500 g) of lambs' kidneys. Cut the kidneys in half and remove the cores.

Heat 1 tablespoon (15 ml) of corn oil in a large, heavy frying-pan. Add the onion and fry for 3 minutes. Add the kidneys to the pan with ¼ pound (100 g) of button mushrooms. Continue to fry, stirring occasionally, until the mushrooms are tender.

Stir in 1 tablespoon (15 ml) of flour. Stirring constantly, gradually add ¼ pint (150 ml) of red wine and bring to the boil. Add 1 bouquet garni, consisting of 1 bay leaf and sprigs of parsley and thyme. Cover the pan, reduce the heat and simmer gently for 10 minutes, or until the kidneys are cooked. (Overcooking will toughen them.)

Remove the bouquet garni. Season to taste with salt and pepper. Sprinkle with 1 tablespoon (15 ml) of chopped parsley and serve immediately.

INGREDIENTS TO SERVE FOUR:
1 onion
1 lb (500 g) lambs' kidneys
1 tablespoon (15 ml) corn oil
¼ lb (100 g) button mushrooms
1 tablespoon (15 ml) flour
¼ pint (150 ml) red wine
1 bouquet garni, consisting of 1 bay leaf and parsley and thyme sprigs
salt
pepper
1 tablespoon (15 ml) chopped parsley

PREPARING KIDNEYS

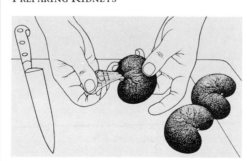

Pierce and remove the fine outer skin of kidneys.

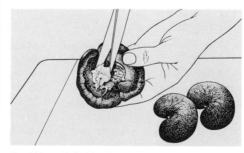

Cut kidneys in half and remove the cores.

Chicken Liver Pâté

Put ½ pound (250 g) of chicken livers in a saucepan with 2 ounces (50 g) of chopped streaky bacon. Add 1 chopped small onion, 1 crushed garlic clove, 1 bay leaf, 1 sprig of thyme, salt, pepper and 4 tablespoons (60 ml) of chicken stock.

Cover the pan and cook over low heat, stirring occasionally, for 15 minutes. Remove the bay leaf. Pour the mixture into a liquidizer. Add 1 tablespoon (15 ml) of brandy. Blend to a smooth paste.

Transfer the pâté to a serving dish. Chill for at least 2 hours before serving.

INGREDIENTS TO SERVE FOUR:
½ lb (250 g) chicken livers
2 oz (50 g) streaky bacon
1 small onion
1 garlic clove
1 bay leaf
1 thyme sprig
salt
pepper
4 tablespoons (60 ml) chicken stock
1 tablespoon (15 ml) brandy

Braised Liver and Vegetables

Preheat the oven to 350 F (180 C, Gas Mark 4).

Thinly slice 1 medium-sized onion, separate the slices into rings and put them into an ovenproof casserole or dish.

Thinly slice 1 pound (500 g) of courgettes and put the slices on top of the onions. Sprinkle with 1 tablespoon (15 ml) of chopped thyme, salt and pepper.

Arrange 1 pound (500 g) of sliced lamb's liver on top of the courgettes. Sprinkle with salt and pepper. Pour in ¼ pint (150 ml) of tomato juice.

Cover the casserole and bake for 40 to 45 minutes, or until the liver and vegetables are cooked.

INGREDIENTS TO SERVE FOUR:
1 medium-sized onion
1 lb (500 g) courgettes
1 tablespoon (15 ml) chopped thyme
salt
pepper
1 lb (500 g) lamb's liver
¼ pint (150 ml) tomato juice

No prizes for guessing whether brown or white eggs are best—they are equally nutritious, rich in proteins that have all the essential amino acids. It is the breed of hen that determines shell colour. And the grim battery system can produce as fine an egg as the free-range run. But no egg is perfect, for a high cholesterol content mars the magnificence of the golden yolk.

FEW PEOPLE NOW BELIEVE that the universe was created out of one great Mother Egg, or that witches use the shells as boats—although they may think it safer to smash the empty shells in the egg cups. But most English people—and most Bostonians—persist in believing that brown eggs are better than white, while New Yorkers believe the opposite. It is far more difficult to sort egg facts from egg fallacies than it is to separate yolks from whites.

One estimate is that more than two hundred thousand million eggs are eaten throughout the world every year, and most of them are hen's eggs. Among the wild birds' eggs, those of the quail are most popular, the once much-prized plovers' eggs now being rightly protected. The original jungle fowl from which the modern hen is descended might lay about twenty eggs a year; her intensively reared descendant must lay at the rate of at least two hundred and fifty eggs a year if she is to go on living.

The laying hen is the prime victim of factory farming, whether kept on deep litter or in batteries. Under the battery system the hens, which by nature are scratching, scavenging birds, are hatched in electric incubators, reared indoors in their hundreds for five months and then caged in twos or threes in batteries of wire cages. There they spend nearly a year laying an egg almost every day. Feeding, with processed feedstuffs, watering, collecting of eggs and removal of droppings is likely to be entirely automated, making it possible for one person to be in charge of about ten thousand birds.

In the West, the vast majority of eggs are produced in this way. In Britain fewer than eight per cent of hens are now kept out-of-doors, their number being quite incapable of laying all the eggs offered for sale as "free range". It is not easy to distinguish battery eggs from other eggs, although if they have faint black lines almost circling the shell, they are most certainly from

batteries, for these lines are caused by the eggs rolling along the wire base of the cage.

You may well object to hens being incarcerated, but if they have been properly fed their eggs will have the same nutritional value as free-range eggs, and, again, with the right diet, there need be no difference in flavour. The colour of the shell, which depends on the breed of the hen, bears no relationship to the nutritional value of the egg. The colour of the yolk, from pale yellow to vivid orange, can be manipulated through the hen's diet. Free range or battery, the egg is twelve per cent protein, twelve per cent fat (almost all of it in the yolk) and seventy-four per cent water, giving a Calorie value of about ninety for a two-ounce egg. It is also a good source of iron and vitamins A and D.

To describe an egg as free range is either true or false, but to describe it as fresh is meaningless. It is impossible to buy a really fresh egg in a shop; to get that you will have to keep your own hens.

An egg will stay fresh for twelve days at ordinary room temperature, three weeks in a domestic refrigerator and up to nine months in commercial cold storage. The freshness affects nutritional value little, but flavour and, above all, texture will deteriorate as the egg gets older. The white of an egg boiled on the day it is laid will stay milky; it cannot be beaten successfully, that is until it is stiff, before it is about three days old, and it will not set firmly when it is hard-boiled until the end of a week or more.

The rate at which an egg declines into staleness depends on how well it is stored. It should be kept cool and in the dark, to cut down loss of moisture through the shell, and pointed end downwards so that the air space within the broad end of the egg remains at the top.

Even within its shell an egg cannot hide its age if you put it in water. A fresh egg sinks, an ageing egg floats. When you break open an egg the yolk of a fresh one sits firmly in the centre of the white; that of an ageing egg breaks as it emerges from the shell.

Eggs remain an eminently wholesome food, even when they are produced under intensive conditions. They can be vexatious at times, cracking while they boil, turning into scrambled rubber when your back is turned and, as Mr Mantalini said in Dickens's *Nicholas Nickleby* when he was complaining about them being messy to eat, "yolk runs down the waistcoat, and yolk of egg does not match any waistcoat but a yellow waistcoat, dammit".

Science accuses the egg of a more serious fault. The yolk is rich in cholesterol, which is suspected of promoting atherosclerosis. Some experiments suggest that the danger is lessened if the fowls are fed unsaturated fatty acids in, for example, sunflower seed oil.

The Nutrients in Eggs
Eggs are particularly high in protein, fat, iron and vitamins A and D. A two-ounce (57 g) egg has about 90 Calories.

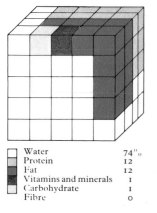

Water	74%
Protein	12
Fat	12
Vitamins and minerals	1
Carbohydrate	1
Fibre	0

IF CHICKENS EVER STOPPED LAYING...
All birds' eggs are edible, although many people might baulk at a three-and-a-half-pound ostrich egg that takes forty minutes to boil. Of the domesticated birds, the egg of a duck is richer in fat than a hen's egg, and is also rather more likely to carry organisms that cause food poisoning. Turkey and guinea-fowl eggs are delicately flavoured, but a goose egg, which weighs about half a pound is stronger tasting. Egg sizes are compared below.

guinea-fowl egg

duck egg

chicken egg

turkey egg

goose egg

Eggs are exceptionally versatile as well as nutritious. At the end of the eighteenth century the Irish poet Thomas Moore conceded that whatever the faults of the French, one could not "help loving the land who has taught us six hundred and eighty ways to dress eggs". And besides the immense number of dishes in which an egg remains recognizably an egg, there are many more in which the egg submerges its identity for the betterment of another food.

Until recently it might have been said with confidence that the whole art of cake-making could not exist without eggs. But no longer, thanks to man's diabolical ingenuity. Fish and skimmed milk are now treated to provide substitutes for eggs in commercial baking, and animal blood plasma is used in place of egg whites. Fortunately, no one has yet produced a totally artificial egg, complete with white and yolk in a shell, although doubtless someone, somewhere, is trying hard to make hens redundant.

Egg White Omelette with Herbs

This fluffy omelette is good for those on a low-cholesterol diet and is an excellent way to use up extra egg whites.

Beat 2 egg whites in a bowl until they are stiff. Fold in 1 tablespoon (15 ml) of yogurt, a pinch of chopped mixed herbs and salt and pepper to taste.

Lightly grease a small non-stick frying-pan and put it over moderate heat. Pour in the egg mixture and spread it to cover the bottom of the pan. Cook gently until it is brown underneath.

Sprinkle with 1 teaspoon (5 ml) of grated Parmesan cheese. Put the pan under a moderate grill until the top of the omelette is set and golden brown.

Fold the omelette in half, garnish with parsley sprigs and serve immediately.

INGREDIENTS TO SERVE ONE:
2 egg whites
1 tablespoon (15 ml) yogurt
mixed herbs
salt
pepper
1 teaspoon (5 ml) grated Parmesan cheese
parsley sprigs

SEPARATING EGGS

Working over a bowl crack the egg in half.

Drain the white keeping the yolk in the shell.

Spanish Pepper Omelette

Serve this large, flat omelette cut into wedges and straight from the pan in which it is cooked.

Heat 2 tablespoons (30 ml) of olive oil in a large frying-pan. Add 1 thinly sliced onion and 1 thinly sliced green pepper and fry gently for 3 minutes, or until the onion is soft and translucent.

Add 2 blanched, skinned, seeded and chopped tomatoes and a ½ garlic clove crushed. Season to taste with salt and pepper. Cook for 2 minutes more.

Lightly beat 6 eggs, season with salt and pepper and pour over the vegetables. Cook, stirring occasionally from the outside to the centre. When the omelette is almost set, lower the heat and stop stirring.

When the omelette is just set and lightly brown underneath remove the pan from the heat. Sprinkle the omelette with 1 tablespoon (15 ml) of chopped parsley or mixed herbs and serve immediately.

INGREDIENTS TO SERVE FOUR:
2 tablespoons (30 ml) olive oil
1 onion
1 green pepper
2 tomatoes
½ garlic clove
salt
pepper
6 eggs
1 tablespoon (15 ml) chopped parsley or mixed herbs

Mushrooms and Eggs en Cocotte

Preheat the oven to 375°F (190°C, Gas Mark 5).

Heat 1 tablespoon (15 ml) of corn oil in a saucepan. Add 1 chopped small onion and fry for 3 minutes, stirring occasionally. Add ¼ pound (100 g) of chopped mushrooms and fry for 2 minutes more. Season to taste with salt and pepper.

Spoon the mixture into 4 cocottes or individual ovenproof dishes. Break 1 egg into each dish and sprinkle with salt and pepper.

Bake the cocottes for 5 to 10 minutes, or until the whites of the eggs are set but the yolks are still soft. Serve immediately.

INGREDIENTS TO SERVE FOUR:
1 tablespoon (15 ml) corn oil
1 small onion
¼ lb (100 g) mushrooms
salt
pepper
4 eggs

Leek Eggah

Cut into slices or squares, this Arabic dish can be eaten hot or cold, as an hors d'oeuvre or as a light lunch or supper dish.

Preheat the oven to 350°F (180°C, Gas Mark 4). Lightly grease a rectangular ovenproof dish.

Thinly slice 1 pound (500 g) of young leeks. Put them into ¼ pint (150 ml) of boiling salted water to which the juice of ½ lemon has been added. Reduce the heat and simmer for 5 to 10 minutes, or until the leeks are just tender. Drain the leeks and put them into the prepared dish.

Beat 6 eggs with 4 tablespoons (60 ml) of milk. Season to taste with salt and pepper. Pour the egg mixture over the leeks.

Bake for 30 to 35 minutes, or until the mixture is firm and golden brown.

INGREDIENTS TO SERVE FOUR:
1 lb (500 g) young leeks
salt
½ lemon
6 eggs
4 tablespoons (60 ml) milk
pepper

Onion Quiche

Preheat the oven to 400°F (200°C, Gas Mark 6).

Make 6 ounces (100 g) of cheese pastry with wholewheat flour (see quiche lorraine) and line an 8-inch (20-cm) flan ring or dish. Bake blind for 15 minutes. Remove the paper and beans and bake for 5 minutes more.

Peel and thinly slice 1 pound (500 g) of onions. Heat 2 tablespoons (30 ml) of corn oil in a frying-pan. Add the onions to the pan, cover, and cook over moderate heat for 10 minutes, or until the onions are soft and translucent. Remove the lid and continue to fry until the onions are lightly browned. Season with salt, pepper and a pinch of grated nutmeg. Arrange the cooked onions in the flan case.

Beat 2 eggs with ¼ pint (150 ml) of milk or single cream. Pour the mixture over the onions.

Bake for 30 to 35 minutes, or until the filling is set. Serve hot or cold.

INGREDIENTS TO SERVE FOUR TO SIX:
6 oz (150 g) cheese pastry made with wholewheat flour (see quiche lorraine)
1 lb (500 g) onions
2 tablespoons (30 ml) corn oil
salt
pepper
grated nutmeg
2 eggs
¼ pint (150 ml) milk or single cream

Quiche Lorraine

Cheese pastry is not traditionally used for this popular French dish, but it makes a pleasant change from plain shortcrust pastry.

Preheat the oven to 400°F (200°C, Gas Mark 6). Put an 8-inch (20-cm) flan ring on a baking sheet.

Combine 6 ounces (150 g) of flour, ¼ teaspoon (1 ml) of salt and a pinch of pepper in a mixing bowl. Add 3 ounces (75 g) of margarine or butter and cut it into small pieces with a round-bladed knife. Rub the fat into the flour with your fingertips until the mixture resembles fine breadcrumbs. Stir in 3 ounces (75 g) of finely grated mature Cheddar cheese.

In a small bowl beat 1 egg yolk with 1 tablespoon (15 ml) of cold water. Make a well in the flour mixture and pour in the egg and water. Mix quickly with a knife and then with your fingertips to form a firm dough.

Turn the dough out on to a lightly floured surface and knead it gently until it is smooth.

Roll the pastry out and line the flan ring (see page 34). Line the pastry with greaseproof paper, weight it down with dried beans and bake for 15 minutes. Remove the paper and beans and bake for 5 to 10 minutes more, or until the pastry is just beginning to brown. Take it out of the oven.

Lower the oven temperature to 350°F (180°C, Gas Mark 4).

Chop ¼ pound (100 g) of streaky bacon and fry for 2 minutes. Add 1 ounce (25 g) of chopped onion and ¼ pound (100 g) of sliced button mushrooms and fry for 2 minutes more, or until the onion is soft. Pour off the fat and spoon the bacon, onions and mushrooms into the pastry case.

Beat together 2 eggs and ¼ pint (150 ml) of single cream or milk. Season to taste with salt and pepper. Pour the egg mixture into the pastry case and sprinkle 1 ounce (25 g) of grated Cheddar cheese over the top.

Bake the quiche for 25 to 30 minutes, or until the custard is set and lightly browned.

INGREDIENTS TO SERVE FOUR TO SIX:
6 oz (150 g) flour
salt
pepper
3 oz (75 g) margarine or butter
¼ lb (100 g) mature Cheddar cheese
1 egg yolk plus 2 eggs
¼ lb (100 g) streaky bacon
1 oz (25 g) chopped onion
¼ lb (100 g) button mushrooms
¼ pint (150 ml) single cream or milk

Egg and Gherkin Mousse

Put ½ pint (300 ml) of milk into a saucepan with 1 small onion, cut into quarters, 2 sprigs of parsley and 1 bay leaf and bring to the boil. Remove the pan from the heat. Season to taste with salt and pepper and leave the milk to infuse for 10 minutes, then strain it.

Melt 1 ounce (25 g) of margarine in a saucepan. Stir in 1 ounce (25 g) of flour. Stirring constantly, gradually add the strained milk and bring to the boil. Reduce the heat and simmer for 1 minute. Adjust the seasoning. Cover the pan and set aside.

When the milk mixture is cool, stir in

Dissolve gelatine in a cup, stood in hot water.

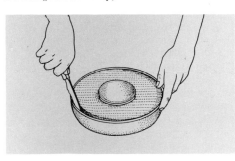

Run a knife around between the mould and mousse.

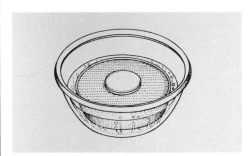

Stand the mould up to its rim in hot water.

Cover with a plate, invert and remove the mould.

¼ pound (100 g) of cottage cheese, ¼ pint (150 ml) of yogurt, 4 finely chopped hard-boiled eggs, 2 tablespoons (30 ml) of finely chopped gherkins and 1 tablespoon (15 ml) of Worcestershire sauce.

Dissolve ½ ounce (15 g) of gelatine in 2 tablespoons (30 ml) of water in a cup set in a pan of hot water. Mix the gelatine into the other ingredients.

Pour the mousse into a dampened 1½-pint (850-ml) ring mould. Cover and put into the refrigerator for about 6 hours, or until set.

To turn out, loosen the edges of the mousse with a knife and dip the mould into a bowl of hot water for a few seconds. Cover the mould with a plate and invert. Fill the centre of the mould with sprigs of watercress.

INGREDIENTS TO SERVE FOUR:
½ pint (300 ml) milk
1 small onion
2 parsley sprigs
1 bay leaf
salt
pepper
1 oz (25 g) margarine
1 oz (25 g) flour
¼ lb (100 g) cottage cheese
¼ pint (150 ml) yogurt
4 hard-boiled eggs
2 tablespoons (30 ml) chopped gherkins
1 tablespoon (15 ml) Worcestershire sauce
½ oz (15 g) powdered gelatine
watercress sprigs

Cottage Scramble

Cut the rind from ¼ pound (100 g) of streaky bacon. Chop the bacon coarsely and fry it in a small saucepan for 3 minutes, or until it is cooked.

Lightly beat 6 eggs. Season with salt and pepper and pour over the bacon. Cook gently, stirring occasionally, until the egg is scrambled. Stir in ½ pound (250 g) of cottage cheese and continue to cook over low heat until the cheese is heated through.

Meanwhile, toast 4 slices of wholewheat bread. Divide the scrambled eggs among the pieces of toast. Garnish with sprigs of watercress and serve immediately.

INGREDIENTS TO SERVE FOUR:
¼ lb (100 g) streaky bacon
6 eggs
salt
pepper
½ lb (250 g) cottage cheese
4 slices wholewheat bread
watercress sprigs

Eggs Florentine

A perfect combination, poached eggs on a bed of spinach and topped with cheese sauce makes a delicious lunch or supper dish.

Thoroughly wash 1 pound (500 g) of spinach in cold water, drain it and put it into a large saucepan. Add 1 teaspoon (5 ml) of salt, cover the pan and cook for 10 minutes, or until the spinach is tender. Drain the spinach well and chop it coarsely. Put the spinach into a flameproof dish and keep it hot.

In a small saucepan combine $\frac{1}{2}$ pint (300 ml) of yogurt with 1 egg yolk, 1 tablespoon (15 ml) of flour, 1 teaspoon (5 ml) of French mustard and 2 tablespoons (30 ml) of grated Parmesan cheese. Season to taste with grated nutmeg, salt and pepper. Heat gently, stirring constantly, until the sauce boils and thickens. Remove from the heat immediately.

Poach 4 eggs and put them on top of the spinach. Pour the cheese sauce over the eggs and sprinkle with 1 tablespoon (15 ml) of grated Parmesan cheese.

Put the dish under a hot grill until the sauce is lightly browned and bubbling. Serve immediately.

INGREDIENTS TO SERVE FOUR:
1 lb (500 g) spinach
salt
$\frac{1}{2}$ pint (300 ml) yogurt
1 egg yolk
1 tablespoon (15 ml) flour
1 teaspoon (5 ml) French mustard
3 tablespoons (45 ml) grated Parmesan cheese
grated nutmeg
pepper
4 eggs

POACHING EGGS

Poach eggs in gently simmering acidulated water.

Egg and Beef Loaf

This beef loaf can be served hot or cold as a main-course dish.

Preheat the oven to 350°F (180°C, Gas Mark 4). Grease a 2-pound (1-kg) loaf tin.

Put $\frac{3}{4}$ pound (350 g) of minced beef into a large mixing bowl with $\frac{1}{4}$ pound (100 g) of sausage meat and $\frac{1}{4}$ pound (100 g) of fresh breadcrumbs. Finely chop 2 sticks of celery and add them to the bowl with 1 grated onion, 1 grated carrot, 1 tablespoon (15 ml) of chopped parsley and $\frac{1}{2}$ teaspoon (2.5 ml) of dried mixed herbs. Season well with salt and pepper. Mix until the ingredients are blended.

In a small bowl lightly beat 1 egg with 2 tablespoons (30 ml) of tomato purée. Stir into the meat mixture. Put half of the meat mixture into the prepared loaf tin and press it well down with the back of a spoon. Put 2 hard-boiled eggs in the centre and cover them with the remaining meat mixture. Put 1 bay leaf on top and cover the tin with aluminium foil.

Bake for 1 to $1\frac{1}{4}$ hours, or until the meat is tender and has shrunk slightly away from the sides of the tin.

Allow the loaf to cool in the tin or turn it out of the tin and serve immediately.

INGREDIENTS TO SERVE FOUR TO SIX:
$\frac{3}{4}$ lb (350 g) minced beef
$\frac{1}{4}$ lb (100 g) sausage meat
$\frac{1}{4}$ lb (100 g) fresh breadcrumbs
2 celery sticks
1 onion
1 carrot
1 tablespoon (15 ml) chopped parsley
$\frac{1}{2}$ teaspoon (2.5 ml) dried mixed herbs
salt
pepper
1 egg
2 tablespoons (30 ml) tomato purée
2 hard-boiled eggs
1 bay leaf

Curried Eggs

Coarsely chop 1 large onion. Peel, core and chop $\frac{1}{2}$ cooking apple. Heat 2 tablespoons (30 ml) of corn oil in a saucepan. Add the onion and fry for 3 minutes.

Add the apple to the onion. Stir in 2 teaspoons (10 ml) of curry powder with 1 tablespoon (15 ml) of flour. Cook for 1 minute, stirring constantly.

Add $\frac{1}{2}$ pint (300 ml) of chicken or vegetable stock and bring to the boil, stirring constantly, until the sauce is thick and smooth. Add 1 bay leaf, 1 sprig of thyme and salt and pepper to taste. Cover the pan, reduce the heat and simmer gently for 30 minutes.

Hard boil 6 eggs, remove the shells and cut the eggs into halves lengthways. Arrange the eggs in a serving dish. Pour the curry sauce over the eggs.

Serve at once or reheat in the oven at 400°F (200°C, Gas Mark 6) for 20 minutes.

INGREDIENTS TO SERVE FOUR:
1 large onion
$\frac{1}{2}$ cooking apple
2 tablespoons (30 ml) corn oil
2 teaspoons (10 ml) curry powder
1 tablespoon (15 ml) flour
$\frac{1}{2}$ pint (300 ml) chicken or vegetable stock
6 eggs
1 bay leaf
1 thyme sprig
salt
pepper

Eggs and Chicken in Aspic

Pour $\frac{3}{4}$ pint (450 ml) of well-seasoned chicken stock into a saucepan and bring to the boil. Skim any fat and scum from the surface of the stock. Allow the stock to cool slightly and strain through a muslin cloth.

Return the stock to the saucepan. Stir in $\frac{1}{4}$ pint (150 ml) of dry white wine, 1 tablespoon (15 ml) of lemon juice and $\frac{1}{2}$ ounce (15 g) of powdered gelatine. Heat gently, stirring occasionally, until the gelatine has dissolved. Bring to the boil and remove the pan from the heat. Strain the aspic into a jug.

Dampen a $1\frac{1}{2}$-pint (850-ml) jelly mould with cold water and pour in a layer of the aspic. Chill the mould for 10 to 15 minutes, or until the aspic is firm. Stand the jug in a bowl of hot water to keep the remaining aspic soft.

Meanwhile, chop $\frac{1}{2}$ pound (250 g) of cooked chicken meat and slice 4 hard-boiled eggs. Put a layer of chicken meat and egg slices over the aspic in the mould. Cover with more of the soft aspic and chill again.

Repeat the layers, finishing with a layer of aspic, until all the chicken, eggs and aspic have been used up. Chill each layer of aspic.

Chill until the aspic has set completely. Dip the mould in hot water for a few seconds. Cover with a plate and invert. Surround the mould with sprigs of watercress and serve.

INGREDIENTS TO SERVE FOUR:
$\frac{3}{4}$ pint (450 ml) chicken stock
$\frac{1}{4}$ pint (150 ml) dry white wine
1 tablespoon (15 ml) lemon juice
$\frac{1}{2}$ oz (15 g) powdered gelatine
$\frac{1}{2}$ lb (250 g) cooked chicken meat
4 hard-boiled eggs
watercress sprigs

Eggs Mornay

Immerse 6 eggs in simmering water for 10 minutes. Transfer the eggs to a bowl of cold water.

For the sauce, heat 1 ounce (25 g) of margarine in a saucepan. Stir in 1 ounce (25 g) of flour. Beat in ½ pint (300 ml) of milk. Bring to the boil, stirring constantly, until the sauce is thick and smooth. Remove from the heat and stir in 2 ounces (50 g) of grated strong Cheddar cheese, a pinch of mustard, salt and pepper.

Remove the shells from the cooled hard-boiled eggs. Slice the eggs and arrange them in an ovenproof dish. Pour the hot sauce over the eggs.

Sprinkle 1 ounce (25 g) of grated Cheddar cheese over the top. Put the dish under a hot grill for 3 to 4 minutes, or until the sauce is bubbling and lightly browned on top.

Garnish with sprigs of parsley and serve immediately.

INGREDIENTS TO SERVE FOUR:
6 eggs
1 oz (25 g) margarine
1 oz (25 g) flour
½ pint (300 ml) milk
3 oz (75 g) strong Cheddar cheese
mustard
salt
pepper
parsley sprigs

Dill Stuffed Eggs

Immerse 6 eggs in simmering water for 10 minutes. Transfer the eggs to a bowl of cold water.

For the stuffing, cream ¼ pound (100 g) of curd cheese with 4 tablespoons (60 ml) of yogurt. Add 4 tablespoons (60 ml) of chopped dill, ½ teaspoon (2.5 ml) of lemon juice and salt and pepper to taste.

When the eggs are cold, remove their shells and cut the eggs into halves lengthways. Carefully scoop out the yolks and rub them through a sieve into the stuffing mixture. Beat the stuffing until it is smooth and well blended.

Pipe or spoon the stuffing into the hollow centres of each of the egg whites. Chill in the refrigerator until needed.

INGREDIENTS TO SERVE FOUR TO SIX:
6 eggs
¼ lb (100 g) curd cheese
4 tablespoons (60 ml) yogurt
4 tablespoons (60 ml) chopped dill
½ teaspoon (2.5 ml) lemon juice
salt
pepper

Egg Flower Soup

This is a Chinese soup into which beaten eggs are stirred, forming strands resembling a flower.

Bring 2 pints (1 litre) of well-seasoned chicken stock to the boil. Add 1 tablespoon (15 ml) of soy sauce, 1 teaspoon (5 ml) of lemon juice and ¼-inch (6-mm) slice of root ginger, peeled and finely chopped or grated.

Just before serving beat 4 eggs with a little salt and pepper. Pour the eggs slowly into the boiling soup; the eggs should form threads and float. Remove the soup from the heat.

Sprinkle 2 finely sliced spring onions and 1 tablespoon (15 ml) of chopped parsley over the soup and serve immediately.

INGREDIENTS TO SERVE FOUR TO SIX:
2 pints (1 litre) chicken stock
1 tablespoon (15 ml) soy sauce
1 teaspoon (5 ml) lemon juice
root ginger
4 eggs
salt
pepper
2 spring onions
1 tablespoon (15 ml) chopped parsley

Spinach and Egg Roulade

Preheat the oven to 400°F (200°C, Gas Mark 6). Line a shallow 13- by 9-inch (32- by 23-cm) baking tin with greaseproof paper. Brush the paper with oil.

Thoroughly wash ¾ pound (350 g) of spinach in cold water, drain it and put it into a large saucepan. Add 1 teaspoon (5 ml) of salt, cover the pan and cook for 10 minutes, or until the spinach is tender. Drain the spinach well and chop it coarsely.

Put the spinach into a large mixing bowl. Beat in 4 egg yolks and ¼ pint (150 ml) of soured cream. Season to taste with salt and pepper. Whisk 4 egg whites until stiff and fold them into the mixture.

Pour the roulade mixture into the prepared tin and level the surface. Bake for 10 to 15 minutes, or until the roulade is well risen, firm and just beginning to turn brown.

Meanwhile, prepare the filling. In a small saucepan combine ½ pint (300 ml) of milk, 1 small onion, quartered, 1 bay leaf and 2 stalks of parsley. Bring to the boil. Remove the pan from the heat. Season the milk to taste with salt and pepper and leave it to infuse for 10 minutes. Strain it.

Melt 1 ounce (25 g) of margarine in a saucepan. Stir in 1 ounce (25 g) of flour. Stirring constantly, gradually add the strained milk. Bring to the boil, reduce the heat and simmer for 1 minute. Adjust the seasoning and leave to cool.

Hard boil 4 eggs, remove the shells and chop coarsely. Stir into the filling.

Sprinkle 1 tablespoon (15 ml) of grated Parmesan cheese over a large piece of greaseproof paper. Turn the roulade out on to the paper. Peel off the greaseproof paper on which it was baked. Spread the egg sauce over the roulade, leaving a 1-inch (2-cm) margin all around. Roll the roulade like a Swiss roll by gently lifting the greaseproof paper so that the roulade folds over. Carefully lift it on to a serving dish.

Serve immediately.

INGREDIENTS TO SERVE FOUR:
¾ lb (350 g) spinach
salt
8 eggs
¼ pint (150 ml) soured cream
pepper
½ pint (300 ml) milk
1 small onion
1 bay leaf
2 parsley stalks
1 oz (25 g) margarine
1 oz (25 g) flour
1 tablespoon (15 ml) grated Parmesan cheese

MAKING A ROULADE

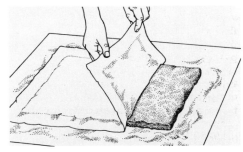

Turn the roulade out and remove the baking paper.

Spread the roulade with filling.

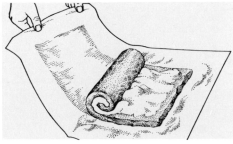

Lift the paper so that the roulade folds into a roll.

Baked Eggs

Preheat the oven to 400°F (200°C, Gas Mark 6). Grease a 1½-pint (850-ml) ovenproof dish.

Scrub and thickly slice 1½ pounds (700 g) of potatoes. Put the potatoes into a saucepan, cover with salted water and bring to the boil. Cover the pan, reduce the heat and simmer for 15 minutes, or until the potatoes are tender.

Finely chop 1 large onion. Heat 1 tablespoon (15 ml) of corn oil in a frying-pan. Add the onion and fry until it is soft and translucent. Spread the onion in the prepared dish.

Drain the potatoes and mash them with salt, pepper and ground nutmeg to taste. Add 2 tablespoons (30 ml) of milk to the potato and beat it well in with a fork.

Spoon the mashed potato over the onions and level the surface. Make 4 hollows in the potato with the back of a spoon and crack 1 egg into each hollow.

Grate ¼ pound (100 g) of mature Cheddar cheese over the eggs and potato and bake for 20 minutes, or until the eggs have set and the cheese is golden brown on top.

INGREDIENTS TO SERVE FOUR:
1½ lb (700 g) potatoes
salt
1 large onion
1 tablespoon (15 ml) corn oil
pepper
ground nutmeg
2 tablespoons (30 ml) milk
4 eggs
¼ lb (100 g) mature Cheddar cheese

Macaroni Carbonara

Cook ½ pound (250 g) of macaroni in a large pan of salted boiling water until tender. Drain well.

In a large pan heat 1 ounce (25 g) of margarine. Add ¼ pound (100 g) of chopped bacon or cooked ham and fry. Add the drained pasta to the pan and toss lightly to mix.

In a bowl beat 4 eggs with salt and pepper and pour over the pasta. Stir gently over low heat until the eggs begin to thicken.

Stir in 2 ounces (50 g) of grated Parmesan cheese and season to taste with salt and pepper.

Serve immediately.

INGREDIENTS TO SERVE FOUR:
½ lb (250 g) macaroni
1 oz (25 g) margarine
¼ lb (100 g) bacon or cooked ham
4 eggs
salt
pepper
2 oz (50 g) grated Parmesan cheese

Oeufs Provençal

Preheat the oven to 375°F (190°C, Gas Mark 5).

Heat 1 tablespoon (15 ml) of corn oil in a saucepan. Add 1 chopped large onion and 1 crushed garlic clove and fry for 3 minutes.

Blanch and peel 1 pound (500 g) of tomatoes. Coarsely chop the tomatoes and add them to the pan. Add 1 bay leaf, 1 teaspoon (5 ml) of chopped oregano, 1 teaspoon (5 ml) of chopped basil and salt and pepper to taste. Cover the pan and cook over low heat for 15 to 20 minutes, or until the tomatoes are reduced to a purée.

Divide the purée between 4 ramekins or individual ovenproof dishes and make a hollow in the centre of each. Break 1 egg into each ramekin and sprinkle with salt and pepper.

Bake for 10 minutes, or until the eggs are set. Serve immediately.

INGREDIENTS TO SERVE FOUR:
1 tablespoon (15 ml) corn oil
1 large onion
1 garlic clove
1 lb (500 g) tomatoes
1 bay leaf
1 teaspoon (5 ml) chopped oregano
1 teaspoon (5 ml) chopped basil
salt
pepper
4 eggs

Eggs and Courgettes

Preheat the oven to 350°F (180°C, Gas Mark 4). Grease a 1½-pint (850-ml) ovenproof dish.

Heat 2 tablespoons (30 ml) of corn oil in a large deep frying-pan. Add 1 crushed garlic clove and fry over low heat for 1 minute. Add 1½ pounds (700 g) of sliced courgettes and continue to fry, stirring occasionally, until they are well browned.

Thinly slice 1 large onion and add it to the pan with 1 teaspoon (5 ml) of chopped tarragon and salt and pepper to taste. Continue to cook until the onions are soft.

Meanwhile, beat 4 eggs with 4 tablespoons (60 ml) of yogurt. Transfer the courgette mixture to the prepared dish and pour in the eggs and yogurt.

Bake for 20 minutes, or until the eggs and yogurt have set and are golden brown on top.

INGREDIENTS TO SERVE FOUR:
2 tablespoons (30 ml) corn oil
1 garlic clove
1½ lb (700 g) courgettes
1 large onion
1 teaspoon (5 ml) chopped tarragon
salt
pepper
4 eggs
4 tablespoons (60 ml) yogurt

Hazelnut and Coffee Soufflé

Tie a double strip of greaseproof paper around a 1¼-pint (750-ml), 5- to 6-inch (13- to 15-cm) soufflé dish. The paper should form a collar that stands 3 inches (8 cm) above the rim of the dish.

Put 3 egg yolks into a mixing bowl with 2 ounces (50 g) of castor sugar. Put the bowl over a pan of simmering water and beat until the mixture is thick and creamy. Remove the bowl from the heat and continue beating until the mixture has cooled. Stir in ¼ pint (150 ml) of yogurt.

Dissolve 2 teaspoons (10 ml) of powdered gelatine in ¼ pint (150 ml) of strong black coffee, in a cup set in a pan of hot water.

Reserving a few for decoration, chop ¼ pound (100 g) of toasted whole hazelnuts. Reserve 3 tablespoons (45 ml) of the chopped hazelnuts and stir the remainder into the soufflé mixture with the coffee and gelatine.

Beat 3 egg whites until they are stiff and fold them into the soufflé. Pour into the prepared dish. Chill for about 6 hours, or until set.

Remove the paper from the dish and coat the sides of the soufflé with the reserved chopped nuts. Decorate the top with the reserved whole hazelnuts.

INGREDIENTS TO SERVE FOUR TO SIX:
3 eggs
2 oz (50 g) castor sugar
¼ pint (150 ml) yogurt
2 teaspoons (10 ml) powdered gelatine
¼ pint (150 ml) strong black coffee
¼ lb (100 g) toasted whole hazelnuts

PREPARING A SOUFFLE DISH

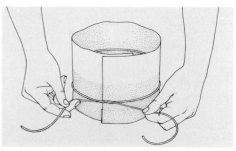

Tie a strip of greaseproof paper around the dish.

Plum and Orange Custards

Preheat the oven to 350°F (180°C, Gas Mark 4).

Halve and stone ½ pound (250 g) of dessert plums. Divide the plums among 4 individual soufflé or ovenproof dishes. Peel and remove the pith from 1 orange and cut the membrane away from the segments of fruit. Divide the segments among the dishes.

To make the custard, beat together ½ pint (300 ml) of yogurt, 2 eggs and 1 tablespoon (15 ml) of castor sugar. Add the grated rind of ½ orange. Pour the custard into the dishes.

Put the dishes into a roasting tin. Pour in enough hot water to reach halfway up the sides of the dishes. Bake for 20 minutes, or until the custard is set and firm to the touch.

Serve immediately.

INGREDIENTS TO SERVE FOUR:
½ lb (250 g) dessert plums
1½ oranges
½ pint (300 ml) yogurt
2 eggs
1 tablespoon (15 ml) castor sugar

BAKING IN A BAIN-MARIE

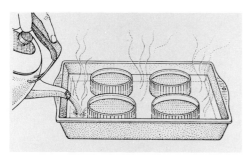

Bake dishes in a tin half-filled with hot water.

Candied Bread and Butter Pudding

This is a spicy version of a favourite English pudding.

Remove the crusts from 6 thin slices of wholewheat bread. Spread thinly with 2 ounces (50 g) of margarine or butter. Line the bottom of a 2-pint (1-litre) greased ovenproof dish with 3 slices of the bread.

Mix ¼ pound (100 g) of candied peel with 2 tablespoons (30 ml) of castor sugar in a bowl. Sprinkle half of the peel and sugar mixture over the bread. Arrange the remaining bread slices on top and sprinkle with the rest of the peel and sugar.

Beat 3 eggs with 1 pint (600 ml) of milk in a bowl. Strain over the bread. Leave to stand for 30 minutes to allow the custard to soak into the bread.

Meanwhile, preheat the oven to 350°F (180°C, Gas Mark 4).

Bake the pudding for 30 to 40 minutes, or until the custard is set and the top is crisp and golden brown.

INGREDIENTS TO SERVE FOUR:
6 thin slices wholewheat bread
2 oz (50 g) margarine or butter
¼ lb (100 g) candied peel
2 tablespoons (30 ml) castor sugar
3 eggs
1 pint (600 ml) milk

Confectioner's Custard

This custard has a smooth texture and may be served with fresh fruits instead of cream.

Pour ¼ pint (150 ml) of milk into a small saucepan and heat to just below boiling point.

Whisk 1 egg in a bowl with 1 tablespoon (15 ml) of cornflour, 1 tablespoon (15 ml) of castor sugar and ¼ teaspoon (1 ml) of vanilla essence.

Add the hot milk to the bowl and mix well. Pour the mixture back into the pan and slowly bring to the boil, stirring constantly, until the custard thickens.

Leave to cool, stirring occasionally to prevent a skin forming.

Whisk 5 tablespoons (75 ml) of yogurt into the mixture and serve.

INGREDIENTS TO MAKE A QUARTER OF A PINT (150 ML) OF CUSTARD:
¼ pint (150 ml) milk
1 egg
1 tablespoon (15 ml) cornflour
1 tablespoon (15 ml) castor sugar
¼ teaspoon (1 ml) vanilla essence
5 tablespoons (75 ml) yogurt

White Mayonnaise

This light and foamy mayonnaise is made from only the white of an egg. It will remain frothy for up to 1 week if stored in the refrigerator.

In a mixing bowl whisk 1 egg white until it is thick but not too stiff. Add ¼ pint (150 ml) of corn, olive or sunflower oil a little at a time, beating well after each addition.

Beat in 1 tablespoon (15 ml) of lemon juice, ½ teaspoon (2.5 ml) of mustard, ¼ teaspoon (1 ml) of salt and freshly ground black pepper. Chill until required.

INGREDIENTS TO DRESS A SALAD TO SERVE FOUR:
1 egg white
¼ pint (150 ml) corn, olive or sunflower oil
1 tablespoon (15 ml) lemon juice
½ teaspoon (2.5 ml) mustard
¼ teaspoon (1 ml) salt
freshly ground black pepper

Mayonnaise

This mayonnaise requires only half the amount of oil used in a traditional mayonnaise.

Put 1 egg yolk, ½ teaspoon (2.5 ml) of French mustard, ¼ teaspoon (1 ml) of salt and freshly ground black pepper into a mixing bowl. Whisk the ingredients to mix them. Add 4 tablespoons (60 ml) of corn, olive or sunflower oil, a few drops at a time, whisking constantly until the mayonnaise has thickened.

Stir in 2 tablespoons (30 ml) of yogurt and 2 teaspoons (10 ml) of lemon juice and whisk again. Whisk 1 egg white until it is stiff and fold it into the mayonnaise. Serve immediately.

INGREDIENTS TO DRESS A SALAD TO SERVE FOUR:
1 egg
½ teaspoon (2.5 ml) French mustard
¼ teaspoon (1 ml) salt
freshly ground black pepper
4 tablespoons (60 ml) corn, olive or sunflower oil
2 tablespoons (30 ml) yogurt
2 teaspoons (10 ml) lemon juice

Yogurt Hollandaise Sauce

This is a lighter version of a true hollandaise. Serve it with fish and vegetable dishes.

In a small saucepan combine 3 tablespoons (45 ml) of wine vinegar, 5 peppercorns, 1 bay leaf and 1 mace blade and bring to the boil. Continue boiling until the liquid has reduced to 2 teaspoons (10 ml).

Beat 3 egg yolks in a small mixing bowl. Strain the vinegar into them. Put the bowl over a pan of hot water and heat gently, stirring constantly, until the yolks are thick.

Add ¼ pint (150 ml) of yogurt and continue stirring until the sauce is thick enough to coat the back of a spoon. Be careful not to overheat or the sauce will curdle.

Serve lukewarm.

INGREDIENTS TO MAKE A QUARTER PINT (150 ML) OF SAUCE:
3 tablespoons (45 ml) wine vinegar
5 peppercorns
1 bay leaf
1 mace blade
3 egg yolks
¼ pint (150 ml) yogurt

A BREAST-FED INFANT and a suckled calf are both getting their perfect food—mother's milk. If the child is switched to cows' milk, however, it will be given something which is less than perfect. Although the milk of all mammals has the same constituents, the proportions of the constituents differ. Human milk contains far less protein and more carbohydrate than cow's milk.

But even though it cannot be described as "perfect", milk is still one of the most valuable of all foods in the human diet. Its quality will vary according to the breed of the cow, the quality of its fodder, and the season. In the summer, for example, milk is of the best quality and three glasses a day will provide an adult with twenty-five to thirty per cent of the protein he needs (including most of the essential amino acids), at least ten per cent of the calories, more than the daily requirement of calcium, fifty per cent of the riboflavin, thirty per cent of the vitamin A and seventeen per cent of the thiamine he requires.

It is thanks to Pasteur, the great nineteenth-century French chemist, that milk is now a safe as well as a nutritious food. The process of pasteurization named after him involves heating the milk to destroy disease-carrying organisms and bacteria that make it sour quickly. Pasteurization destroys some of the thiamine and vitamin C, but far less than is destroyed if you boil milk at home. The flavour of milk is also changed by pasteurization, but it is a deprivation in the cause of health that we learn to live with.

To many people pasteurized milk tastes less unpleasant than sterilized milk, which has been subjected to far greater heat to make it stay "fresh" for at least a week, even when not in a refrigerator. Half the thiamine and vitamin C is lost by sterilization. UHT (ultra high temperature) milk, which is heated to 275°F (135°C) for one or two seconds, will keep for several months in sealed cartons without refrigeration. Vitamin losses in UHT milk are lower than in sterilized milk.

There are other processes that make milk even less perishable, but at the same time even further removed from the original wholefood. Evaporated milk has had its water content reduced from about eighty-six to seventy-four per cent. The sticky sweet condensed milk is part evaporated milk with a lot of added sugar.

It is the nature of fresh milk to go sour because the bacteria in the milk convert the milk sugar, called lactose, into lactic acid. This accounts for the sharpness of sour-milk products, but the particular flavour of the product depends on which bacteria have been at work. Souring is commonly produced by *Lactobacillus acidophilus*, but it is *Lactobacillus bulgaricus* that is responsible for the special flavour of yogurt.

When the souring milk reaches a certain level

IN PRAISE OF YOGURT

There is no proven recipe for longevity, but yogurt is one food that has long been associated with the attainment of great age. Like most Bulgarians, the centenarian above eats yogurt every day. The Bulgarians, however, are extremely health conscious and their diet is very well balanced. Certainly, yogurt contains more protein and riboflavin than milk itself and is also more easily digested, but it can't by itself work miracles of rejuvenation.

of acidity the protein, which was in solution in the milk, changes into a curd, which floats in the clear liquid, the whey, that remains. The curds can be eaten as they are or made into cheesecake, but their main role is in the making of cheese, a "natural" convenience food with a recorded history of six thousand years. Most cheese is richer in protein than meat, fish or poultry. It is a good source of the vitamins A, D, E and riboflavin and it is rich in phosphorus and calcium.

Whole curd is the basis of all cheese, but several thousand different types are made from it. The texture and flavour of the cheese will vary according to the type of milk used, the bacteria involved and the manufacturing process. Cows' milk is now most widely used in cheese-making, but goats' milk is popular in many parts of Europe. Ewes' milk, the richest milk of the three, is less popular for cheese-making, although it does produce the famous Roquefort.

Whatever the milk the starting point of cheese is the curd. The simplest process is the one used to make what the French call *fromage blanc*. The curd of soured skimmed milk is hung in a muslin bag through which the whey drips.

The manufacture of the world-famous cheeses is far more complicated. It may involve not only the use of rennin, an enzyme usually obtained from a calf's stomach, which (as in the making of junket) coagulates milk without souring it, but also the heating of the curd and, to produce the blue-veined cheeses, inoculating it with moulds.

Cheese is an excellent source of protein and also of calcium, riboflavin and vitamin A. But, with the exception of such low-fat cheeses as cottage cheese, it is also high in saturated fat and cholesterol. Above, left to right, front row: Brie, cottage cheese and Ricotta; centre: a natural Tomme, Roquefort and Parmesan; back row: Edam and English Cheddar.

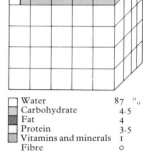

The Nutrients in Milk
Milk is a well-balanced food containing first-class protein and three and a half ounces (100 g) provide about 65 Calories.

Water	87 %
Carbohydrate	4.5
Fat	4
Protein	3.5
Vitamins and minerals	1
Fibre	0

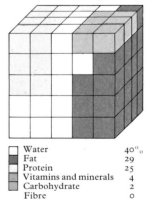

The Nutrients in Cheese
Cheese is rich in protein, fat and calcium and three and a half ounces (100 g) of Cheddar, for example, provide about 400 Calories.

Water	40 %
Fat	29
Protein	25
Vitamins and minerals	4
Carbohydrate	2
Fibre	0

Roquefort is a prime example of what can be involved in the making of a cheese. It is made during the lambing season from the unskimmed milk of ewes, and is a mixture of morning and evening milkings; the morning milk is richer in fat. Rennin from a lamb's stomach is added and the whey is drained from the resulting curd. The curd is then placed between layers of breadcrumbs on which the mould *Penicillium glaucum roqueforti* has been grown. The pressed cheese is then stored in the damp and cool limestone caves of Roquefort in the French Massif Central.

Fermented curds can also be made into such soft cheeses as Brie and Camembert, or into such hard cheese as Cheshire, Wensleydale, Edam, Stilton and Gorgonzola.

There is also processed cheese. This is the twentieth-century invention of two Swiss scientists and consists of several types of cheese which have been heated and emulsified and packaged. Its only claim to virtue is that it keeps well—and it is indeed best kept and not eaten.

Home-made Cottage Cheese

Any type of milk may be used to make cottage cheese, but skimmed milk contains less fat. Use commercial skimmed milk or 3 ounces (75 g) of skimmed milk powder to 1 pint (600 ml) of water. For extra flavour, yogurt, herbs or spices may be added.

In a saucepan heat 1 pint (600 ml) of milk until it is just tepid. Add 1½ teaspoons (7.5 ml) of rennet and mix well. Pour the milk into a bowl. Leave in a warm place for 15 minutes, or until the milk has set and curds have formed.

Put the bowl over a saucepan of hot water. Gently heat to a temperature of 110°F (43°C), cool enough to hold your finger in without discomfort. Continue stirring until the curds and the whey separate. Put a sieve over a bowl and line it with muslin. Pour in the curds and whey. Tie the corners of the muslin together to form a bag and suspend the bag over the bowl for 12 to 24 hours to drain. If, however, the bag is squeezed gently from time to time, the cheese should be drained in 2 to 3 hours.

Put the drained curds in a bowl, mash them with a fork and season to taste with salt and pepper. Cover and store in the refrigerator. It will keep for up to 1 week.

INGREDIENTS TO MAKE A QUARTER-POUND (100 g) OF CHEESE:
1 pint (600 ml) milk
1½ teaspoons (7.5 ml) rennet
salt
pepper

MAKING COTTAGE CHEESE

Tie the curds and whey in muslin and drain.

Cheese and Onion Pie

Preheat the oven to 400°F (200°C, Gas Mark 6).

Peel and thinly slice 1½ pounds (700 g) of onions. Put into a saucepan with ½ pint (300 ml) of water. Cover the pan, bring to the boil and simmer for 10 minutes, or until the onions are soft. Drain the onions and allow them to cool.

Cut ½ pound (250 g) of mature Cheddar cheese into ½-inch (1-cm) cubes.

Put half of the onions into a 1½-pint (850-ml) pie dish. Scatter the cubes of cheese and 1 ounce (25 g) of sultanas over the onions. Sprinkle with salt, pepper and a generous pinch of grated nutmeg.

Arrange the remaining onions on top and sprinkle with more seasoning.

Make 6 ounces (150 g) of shortcrust pastry with wholewheat flour (see page 34) and roll it out a little bigger than the pie dish. Cut a ½-inch (1-cm) strip from around the edge of the pastry and press it on to the dampened rim of the pie dish. Brush the strip of pastry lightly with water, then cover the pie with the remaining pastry. Press the edges of the pastry together to seal them. Trim off any excess pastry. Flute the edges of the pastry and decorate the pie with leaves cut from the pastry trimmings.

Brush the pie with beaten egg or milk. Bake for 45 minutes, or until the pastry is crisp and brown.

Serve immediately.

INGREDIENTS TO SERVE 4:
1½ lb (700 g) onions
½ lb (250 g) mature Cheddar cheese
1 oz (25 g) sultanas
salt
pepper
grated nutmeg
6 oz (150 g) shortcrust pastry made with
**   wholewheat flour (see page 34)**
1 egg or milk

Tartare Party Dip

Serve this dip with pieces of celery, carrot, green pepper, cauliflower and mushrooms.

Put ½ pound (250 g) of cottage cheese and ¼ pint (150 ml) of yogurt into a mixing bowl. Add 1 grated small onion, 1 tablespoon (15 ml) of chopped gherkins, 1 tablespoon (15 ml) of finely chopped celery, 1 tablespoon (15 ml) of finely chopped green pepper, 1 tablespoon (15 ml) of chopped parsley and the grated rind of ½ lemon. Mix well. Season to taste with salt and pepper.

Chill. Serve sprinkled with ground paprika.

INGREDIENTS TO SERVE FOUR TO SIX:
½ lb (250 g) cottage cheese
¼ pint (150 ml) yogurt
1 small onion
1 tablespoon (15 ml) chopped gherkins
1 tablespoon (15 ml) chopped celery
1 tablespoon (15 ml) chopped green
**   pepper**
1 tablespoon (15 ml) chopped parsley
½ lemon
salt
pepper
ground paprika

Cottage Cheese and Tuna Cocottes

Preheat the oven to 400°F (200°C, Gas Mark 6).

Lightly brush 4 individual ovenproof dishes with oil. Put them on a baking sheet.

Put ½ pound (250 g) of cottage cheese into a mixing bowl. Add 2 eggs and beat well. Flake in 6 ounces (150 g) of tuna fish. Add the grated rind and the juice of ½ lemon and 1 tablespoon (15 ml) of chopped parsley. Mix well. Season to taste with salt and pepper. Spoon the mixture into the prepared dishes.

Bake for 10 to 15 minutes, or until the mixture is lightly set and golden brown on top. Garnish with sprigs of parsley and serve immediately.

INGREDIENTS TO SERVE FOUR:
½ lb (250 g) cottage cheese
2 eggs
6 oz (150 g) tuna fish
½ lemon
1 tablespoon (15 ml) chopped parsley
salt
pepper
parsley sprigs

Coeur à la Crème

Serve this version of a traditional French dessert with fresh berries or a fruit purée.

Sieve ½ pound (250 g) of cottage cheese into a mixing bowl. Stir in ¼ pint (150 ml) of double cream and ¼ pint (150 ml) of soured cream. Add 2 tablespoons (30 ml) of castor sugar and mix well. Beat 2 egg whites until they are stiff, then fold them into the cheese mixture.

Press the mixture into 6 individual heart-shaped moulds that have holes in the bottom for the mixture to drain. Put the moulds on to a deep plate. Alternatively, line a sieve with muslin and put it over a bowl. Press the mixture into the sieve. Put the moulds or the sieve in the refrigerator overnight to drain and chill. Turn out on to a plate and serve.

INGREDIENTS TO SERVE SIX:
½ lb (250 g) cottage cheese
¼ pint (150 ml) double cream
¼ pint (150 ml) soured cream
2 tablespoons (30 ml) castor sugar
2 egg whites

Pashka

This traditional Russian Easter dish can be eaten as a dessert or spread on cakes and breads.

Sieve ½ pound (250 g) of cottage cheese into a mixing bowl. Beat in ¼ pint (150 ml) of soured cream. Add 1 ounce (25 g) of chopped blanched almonds, 1 ounce (25 g) of chopped mixed candied peel, 2 ounces (50 g) of raisins and the grated rind of ½ lemon. Mix well.

Line a sieve with muslin and put the sieve over a bowl. Spoon the mixture into the sieve. Leave it in the refrigerator for 12 to 24 hours to drain. When the pashka is solid, turn it out on to a serving dish.

INGREDIENTS TO SERVE FOUR:
½ lb (250 g) cottage cheese
¼ pint (150 ml) soured cream
1 oz (25 g) blanched almonds
1 oz (25 g) mixed candied peel
2 oz (50 g) raisins
½ lemon

Orange Cheese Puffs

Preheat the oven to 400°F (200°C, Gas Mark 6). Grease a large baking sheet.

Make 2½ ounces (75 g) of choux pastry (see page 35). Use either a piping bag or a spoon to shape small rounds of dough on to the baking sheet. Bake for 20 minutes. Slit each puffed-up round, lower the oven temperature to 350°F (180°C, Gas Mark 4) and bake the puffs for 10 minutes more. Put them on a wire rack to cool.

To make the filling, sieve ¾ pound (350 g) of cottage cheese into a mixing bowl. Add the grated rind and juice of 1 orange and 2 to 3 tablespoons (30 to 45 ml) of milk. Stir the ingredients well, the mixture should have a creamy consistency. Stir in 1 tablespoon (15 ml) of castor sugar.

To make the sauce, in a small saucepan blend 2 teaspoons (10 ml) of cornflour with ¼ pint (150 ml) of water. Stir in 4 tablespoons (60 ml) of orange marmalade and the juice of ½ lemon. Stirring constantly, bring the mixture to the boil. Lower the heat and simmer for 5 minutes, stirring frequently.

Fill the puffs with the cheese filling. Pile them into a serving dish and pour the hot sauce over them. Serve immediately.

INGREDIENTS TO SERVE FOUR TO SIX:
2½ oz (75 g) choux pastry (see page 35)
¾ lb (350 g) cottage cheese
1 orange
2 to 3 tablespoons (30 to 45 ml) milk
1 tablespoon (15 ml) castor sugar
2 teaspoons (10 ml) cornflour
4 tablespoons (60 ml) orange marmalade
½ lemon

Orange and Lemon Cheesecake

If you do not have a loose-bottomed cake tin, first put the cheesecake mixture into a regular cake tin and chill it until it is set. Then press the biscuit crust lightly on top of the cheesecake and chill again. Cover the tin with a plate, invert, remove the tin and serve.

Grease a 7- to 8-inch (18- to 20-cm) loose-bottomed cake tin. Put 6 ounces (150 g) of digestive biscuits into a polythene bag and crush them with a rolling pin. The biscuits may be crushed in a liquidizer.

Melt 3 ounces (75 g) of margarine or butter in a saucepan. Add the crushed biscuits and stir until they are well mixed.

Crush biscuits in a bag with a rolling pin.

Press the crumb and butter mixture into a tin.

Spoon the biscuit mixture into the prepared cake tin and press it down with the back of a spoon. Put the tin into the refrigerator for 30 minutes.

Meanwhile, in a mixing bowl beat 2 egg yolks with 2 ounces (50 g) of castor sugar until the mixture is thick and creamy. Stir in the grated rind and juice of 1 orange and 1 lemon. Put the bowl over a pan of hot water and cook over low heat, stirring constantly, until the mixture is thick enough to coat the back of a spoon.

In a cup set in a pan of hot water, dissolve ½ ounce (15 g) of powdered gelatine in 2 tablespoons (30 ml) of water. Stir into the egg mixture. Allow to cool slightly. Sieve ¾ pound (350 g) of cottage cheese into the bowl. Add ¼ pint (150 ml) of soured cream and mix well.

Beat 2 egg whites until stiff and fold them into the mixture. Pour the cheesecake mixture over the biscuit crust. Chill in the refrigerator until the mixture has set.

Run a knife around the edge of the cheesecake and remove it from the tin. Decorate the top with orange and lemon slices.

INGREDIENTS TO SERVE SIX TO EIGHT:
6 oz (150 g) digestive biscuits
3 oz (75 g) margarine or butter
2 eggs
2 oz (50 g) castor sugar
2 oranges
2 lemons
½ oz (15 g) powdered gelatine
¾ lb (350 g) cottage cheese
¼ pint (150 ml) soured cream

Baked Curd Cheesecake

This rich-tasting cheesecake can be made with a plain shortcrust, rich shortcrust, spiced or almond pastry, or without the pastry if you are counting calories.

Preheat the oven to 400°F (200°C, Gas Mark 6).

Make ¼ pound (100 g) of shortcrust pastry (see page 34). Roll out the pastry and line the bottom of a 7- to 8-inch (18- to 20-cm) loose-bottomed cake tin. Line the pastry with foil or greaseproof paper, weight it down with dried beans and bake it for 15 minutes. Remove the paper and beans and bake for 5 minutes more, or until the pastry is just beginning to brown. Allow the pastry case to cool.

Reduce the oven temperature to 350°F (180°C, Gas Mark 4).

Meanwhile, make the filling. Put ½ pound (250 g) of curd cheese into a large mixing bowl and stir in ¼ pint (150 ml) of yogurt. Add 2 ounces (50 g) of castor sugar, 1 ounce (25 g) of cornflour, 3 ounces (75 g) of sultanas and the grated rind and juice of 1 lemon. Stir until well mixed. Stir in 2 egg yolks.

Beat 2 egg whites until they are stiff. Fold them into the cheese mixture.

Pour the cheesecake mixture into the tin. Bake for 30 to 35 minutes, or until it is set and the top is golden brown. Cool before serving.

INGREDIENTS TO SERVE SIX TO EIGHT:
¼ lb (100 g) shortcrust pastry (see page 34)
½ lb (250 g) curd cheese
¼ pint (150 ml) yogurt
2 oz (50 g) castor sugar
1 oz (25 g) cornflour
3 oz (75 g) sultanas
1 lemon
2 eggs

Cottage Cheese and Salami Flan

This savoury flan with its unusual combination of flavours will not brown when it is cooked. If it is overcooked, however, the filling will split so remove it from the oven as soon as it is set.

Preheat the oven to 400°F (200°C, Gas Mark 6).

Roll out 6 ounces (150 g) of shortcrust pastry (see page 34) and use to line an 8-inch (20-cm) flan dish. Line the pastry with greaseproof paper weighed down with dried beans and bake it for 15 minutes. Remove the paper and beans and bake the pastry for 5 to 10 minutes more, or until it is just beginning to brown. Remove from the oven and allow to cool.

Reduce the oven temperature to 350°F (180°C, Gas Mark 4).

Remove the skin from ¼ pound (100 g) of thinly sliced salami. Reserving 3 slices for garnish, arrange the salami on the bottom of the pastry case.

In a mixing bowl lightly beat 2 eggs. Stir in ½ pound (250 g) of cottage cheese, 1 grated small onion, ½ teaspoon (2.5 ml) of dried mixed herbs and a pinch of salt and of pepper. Mix well. Spoon the mixture into the flan case. Bake the flan for 25 to 30 minutes, or until the filling has set.

Allow the flan to cool slightly. Garnish it with the reserved salami and serve.

INGREDIENTS TO SERVE FOUR TO SIX :
6 oz (150 g) shortcrust pastry (see page 34)
¼ lb (100 g) salami
2 eggs
½ lb (250 g) cottage cheese
1 small onion
½ teaspoon (2.5 ml) dried mixed herbs
salt
pepper

Chilled Watercress Soup

Melt 1 ounce (25 g) of margarine in a large saucepan. Add 1 chopped onion and fry over low heat for 5 minutes, or until the onion is soft but not browned.

Add 1 pint (600 ml) of chicken stock, the grated rind and juice of ½ lemon, salt and pepper. Dice ½ pound (250 g) of peeled potatoes and add them to the pan. Bring to the boil. Cover the pan, reduce the heat and simmer gently for 15 to 20 minutes, or until the potatoes are cooked.

Thoroughly wash 2 bunches of watercress, about 6 ounces (150 g). Reserve a few sprigs for garnish. Remove the coarse stalks. Coarsely chop the watercress and add it to the pan. Simmer the soup for 2 minutes more. Pour the soup into a liquidizer and blend it.

Pour the soup into a tureen. Allow it to cool slightly and then beat in ½ pint (300 ml) of yogurt. Chill it thoroughly. Garnish with the reserved sprigs of watercress and serve.

INGREDIENTS TO SERVE FOUR TO SIX :
1 oz (35 g) margarine
1 onion
1 pint (600 ml) chicken stock
½ lemon
salt
pepper
½ lb (250 g) peeled potatoes
2 watercress bunches
½ pint (300 ml) yogurt

Raspberry Cheese Mousse

Sieve ½ pound (250 g) of raspberries into a mixing bowl, or purée them in a liquidizer and then sieve them. Stir in ½ pound (250 g) of sieved cottage cheese. Add ¼ pint (150 ml) of yogurt and the grated rind and juice of ½ lemon. Mix well.

Dissolve ½ ounce (15 g) of powdered gelatine in 3 tablespoons (45 ml) of water in a cup set in a pan of hot water. Stir the gelatine into the raspberry mixture.

Beat 2 egg whites until they are stiff and fold them into the mixture. Fold in 1 tablespoon (15 ml) of castor sugar.

Pour the mixture into a 2-pint (1.20-litre) ring mould or a 7-inch (18-cm) cake tin. Chill in the refrigerator until set.

To turn out, dip the mould in hot water for 10 seconds. Cover the mould with a plate and invert.

To decorate, blanch, peel and slice 3 peaches. Dip the slices into 1 tablespoon (15 ml) of lemon juice to prevent them from browning. Pile the peach slices in the centre of the ring or arrange them on top of the mousse.

INGREDIENTS TO SERVE SIX TO EIGHT:
½ lb (250 g) raspberries
½ lb (250 g) cottage cheese
¼ pint (150 ml) yogurt
½ lemon, plus 1 tablespoon (15 ml) lemon juice
½ oz (15 g) powdered gelatine
2 egg whites
1 tablespoon (15 ml) castor sugar
3 peaches

Blue Cheese Dip

In a mixing bowl, mash ½ pound (250 g) of a blue cheese, such as Stilton or Roquefort. Sieve ¼ pound (100 g) of cottage cheese into the bowl. Add ¼ pint (150 ml) of yogurt. Mix until well blended.

Store in the refrigerator for up to 2 days. Allow the dip to return to room temperature before serving.

INGREDIENTS TO SERVE FOUR TO SIX:
½ lb (250 g) Stilton or Roquefort cheese
¼ lb (100 g) cottage cheese
¼ pint (150 ml) yogurt

Cheese and Tomato Soufflé

A mixture of eggs, milk, cheese and air, the perfect soufflé should be firm on the outside but creamy in the middle.

Preheat the oven to 375°F (190°C, Gas Mark 5).

Melt 1 ounce (25 g) of margarine in a large saucepan and stir in 1 ounce (25 g) of flour. Stirring constantly, gradually add ¼ pint (150 ml) of milk. Bring to the boil, reduce the heat and cook gently for 1 minute. Remove the pan from the heat.

Add ¼ pound (100 g) of grated mature Cheddar cheese and stir until melted. Stir in 1 tablespoon (15 ml) of tomato purée and ½ teaspoon (2.5 ml) of dried basil. Season to taste with salt and pepper.

Add 4 blanched, peeled and coarsely chopped medium-sized tomatoes and 4 egg yolks. Beat well.

Beat 4 egg whites until they are stiff. Add 2 tablespoons (30 ml) of the egg whites to the cheese mixture and stir well. Carefully fold in the remainder of the egg whites.

Pour the mixture into a 2-pint (1-litre) soufflé dish and bake for 35 to 40 minutes, or until the soufflé is well risen and the top is golden brown. Serve immediately.

INGREDIENTS TO SERVE FOUR:
1 oz (25 g) margarine
1 oz (25 g) flour
¼ pint (150 ml) milk
¼ lb (100 g) mature Cheddar cheese
1 tablespoon (15 ml) tomato purée
½ teaspoon (2.5 ml) dried basil
salt
pepper
4 medium-sized tomatoes
4 eggs

Milk, yogurt and cheese make refreshing and exciting fare for summer buffets: from left to right, Chilled Watercress Soup, Cottage Cheese and Salami Flan and Blue Cheese Dip.

Cheese and Apple Rarebit

Grate ½ pound (250 g) of Cheddar cheese into a mixing bowl. Peel and core 2 dessert apples and grate them into the bowl. Add 1 teaspoon (5 ml) of French mustard and 2 tablespoons (30 ml) of milk. Mix well. Season to taste with salt and pepper.

Core 1 dessert apple and cut it into 4 rings. Toss the rings in 1 tablespoon (15 ml) of lemon juice.

Toast 4 slices of wholewheat bread. Pile the cheese and apple mixture on to each slice. Cook under a moderate grill for 3 minutes, or until the top is golden brown and bubbling.

Garnish each rarebit with an apple ring and a sprig of watercress. Serve immediately.

INGREDIENTS TO SERVE FOUR:
½ lb (250 g) Cheddar cheese
3 dessert apples
1 teaspoon (5 ml) French mustard
2 tablespoons (30 ml) milk
salt
pepper
1 tablespoon (15 ml) lemon juice
4 slices wholewheat bread
4 watercress sprigs

Cheese and Bacon Pudding

Preheat the oven to 400°F (200°C, Gas Mark 6).

Cut 6 ounces (150 g) of bread into small cubes, about ½ inch (1 cm) square, and put them into a lightly greased 2-pint (1-litre) ovenproof dish.

In a mixing bowl beat together 3 eggs and ¾ pint (450 ml) of milk. Add ¼ pound (100 g) of grated strong Cheddar cheese. Season to taste with salt and pepper. Mix well. Pour the cheese mixture over the bread cubes. Let the cubes stand for 15 minutes to allow the cheese mixture to soak into the bread.

Put 4 rashers of bacon on top. Bake for 30 to 40 minutes, or until the bacon is cooked and the custard is well risen, golden brown and set. Pour off the excess fat from the bacon and serve at once.

INGREDIENTS TO SERVE FOUR:
6 oz (150 g) bread
3 eggs
¾ pint (450 ml) milk
¼ lb (100 g) strong Cheddar cheese
salt
pepper
4 bacon rashers

Home-made Yogurt

The taste of home-made yogurt is very different and far superior to commercial varieties. Easy to make, it can be prepared from whole milk or skimmed milk. Special machines that keep the yogurt at a constant warm temperature are available, but are not necessary to produce good results. For yogurt to set properly and quickly it requires a temperature of about 85° to 90°F (29° to 32°C). The back of an old-fashioned Aga cooker, the oven of an electric cooker at its lowest setting or a vacuum flask are ideal.

Pour 1 pint (600 ml) of milk into a saucepan and bring to the boil. Cover the pan, remove it from the heat and allow the milk to cool to a temperature of 110°F (43°C), cool enough to hold your finger in without discomfort.

Add 3 tablespoons (45 ml) of yogurt to the cooled milk and mix well. Pour the milk and yogurt mixture into a warm, wide-necked vacuum flask. Seal the flask and leave undisturbed for 10 hours or overnight to set.

Alternatively, pour the milk and yogurt mixture into a bowl and leave it in an 85° to 90°F (29° to 32°C) oven overnight.

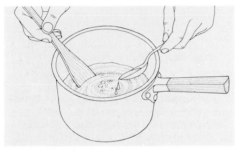

Bring the milk to the boil, cool and stir in yogurt.

Seal in a warm vacuum flask overnight.

Chill the set yogurt in a covered container.

The longer the yogurt is left to incubate, the thicker and more acidic in taste it will become.

When the yogurt has set, put it in a covered container and chill in the refrigerator for up to 1 week.

INGREDIENTS TO MAKE ONE PINT (600 ML) OF YOGURT:
1 pint (600 ml) milk or skimmed milk
3 tablespoons (45 ml) yogurt

Black Currant Yogurt Sorbet

Put ½ pound (250 g) of black currants and 2 to 3 tablespoons (30 to 45 ml) of water into a saucepan. Cook gently for 5 minutes, or until the fruit is tender. Reserve 2 tablespoons (30 ml) of the black currants and purée the remainder through a sieve. Stir the reserved black currants, ½ pint (300 ml) of yogurt and the juice of ½ lemon into the purée.

Dissolve 2 teaspoons (10 ml) of powdered gelatine in 2 tablespoons (30 ml) of water in a small bowl set in a pan of hot water. Add to the purée with sugar to taste and mix well. Chill until the mixture just begins to set.

Whisk 2 egg whites until they are stiff and fold them into the purée. Spoon into an ice tray or other container and freeze until firm.

INGREDIENTS TO SERVE FOUR:
½ lb (250 g) black currants
½ pint (300 ml) yogurt
½ lemon
2 teaspoons (10 ml) powdered gelatine
sugar
2 egg whites

Cucumber Raita Salad

This cool Indian salad makes a marvellous accompaniment to hot, spicy dishes.

Peel and thinly slice 1 large cucumber. Put the cucumber slices into a sieve, sprinkle them with ½ teaspoon (2.5 ml) of salt and leave to drain for 30 minutes.

Put ½ pint (300 ml) of yogurt into a serving dish with 1 tablespoon (15 ml) of chopped mint. Add the cucumber, season with freshly ground black pepper and stir well.

Chill until needed. Garnish with 1 tablespoon (15 ml) of chopped mint and serve.

INGREDIENTS TO SERVE FOUR:
1 large cucumber
½ teaspoon (2.5 ml) salt
½ pint (300 ml) yogurt
2 tablespoons (30 ml) chopped mint
freshly ground black pepper

Yogurt Cheese

Vary the fresh sharp flavour of yogurt cheese by beating in chopped chives, crushed garlic or other herbs.

In a bowl mix ½ pint (300 ml) of yogurt with ¼ teaspoon (1 ml) of salt. Put a sieve over another bowl and line it with muslin. Pour in the yogurt mixture and leave it to drain for 3 hours. Much of the liquid will drain out, leaving a smooth "creamy" cheese.

INGREDIENTS TO MAKE A QUARTER POUND (100 G) OF CHEESE:
½ pint (300 ml) yogurt
¼ teaspoon (1 ml) salt

Mint Yogurt Dressing

Wash 1 sprig of fresh mint and remove the leaves from the stalk. Chop the leaves finely and put into a mixing bowl. Add salt and pepper and ¼ pint (150 ml) of yogurt. Mix well.

Alternatively, put all the ingredients into a liquidizer and blend.

INGREDIENTS TO DRESS A SALAD TO SERVE FOUR:
1 mint sprig
salt
pepper
¼ pint (150 ml) yogurt

Ginger Junket

Rennet is used to coagulate the milk in this light, finely flavoured dessert.

Gently heat 1 pint (600 ml) of milk in a saucepan until it reaches blood heat (just warm to the touch). Add 1 tablespoon (15 ml) of castor sugar and stir until it has dissolved.

Finely chop 2 pieces of preserved ginger. Stir it into the warm milk with 1 teaspoon (5 ml) of rennet.

Pour the mixture into 4 individual serving dishes or glasses immediately and leave at room temperature to set.

Sprinkle with ground ginger and serve.

INGREDIENTS TO SERVE FOUR:
1 pint (600 ml) milk
1 tablespoon (15 ml) castor sugar
2 preserved ginger pieces
1 teaspoon (5 ml) rennet
ground ginger

Brown Bread Ice-cream

This ice-cream is not too rich and has an unusual and pleasant flavour. Toast the breadcrumbs to give a crunchy texture.

Beat ¼ pint (150 ml) of double cream until it is thick. Fold in ¼ pint (150 ml) of yogurt and 2 egg yolks. Stir 2 ounces (50 g) of fresh wholewheat breadcrumbs and 1 tablespoon (15 ml) of sherry or rum into the cream mixture.

Beat 2 egg whites until they are stiff. Beat in 1 ounce (25 g) of icing sugar.

Fold the whisked egg whites into the cream mixture and pour into a freezing tray or polythene container and freeze.

For a smoother ice-cream, when the mixture is half-frozen turn it out into a bowl and whisk for 2 minutes. Return to the freezing tray and freeze until firm.

INGREDIENTS TO SERVE FOUR:
¼ pint (150 ml) double cream
¼ pint (150 ml) yogurt
2 eggs
2 oz (50 g) fresh wholewheat
   breadcrumbs
1 tablespoon (15 ml) sherry or rum
1 oz (25 g) icing sugar

Yogurt Cream

Serve this cream with fresh summer fruits.

Whisk ¼ pint (150 ml) of double cream in a bowl until thick. Fold in ¼ pint (150 ml) of yogurt.

Spoon the cream and yogurt mixture into a serving dish and sprinkle with 1 tablespoon (15 ml) of soft brown sugar. Chill overnight to allow the sugar to seep into the mixture.

INGREDIENTS TO SERVE FOUR:
¼ pint (150 ml) double cream
¼ pint (150 ml) yogurt
1 tablespoon (15 ml) soft brown sugar

Syllabub

This smooth, creamy dessert with just a hint of tartness makes a perfect complement to a rich meal.

Grate the rind and squeeze the juice of 1 large lemon into a large mixing bowl. Add 5 tablespoons (75 ml) of white wine, 1 tablespoon (15 ml) of brandy, 2 ounces (50 g) of castor sugar and ½ pint (300 ml) of double cream and whisk until the mixture stands in soft peaks. Add ¼ pint (150 ml) of yogurt and whisk again until thick.

Spoon the mixture into individual serving dishes or glasses. Serve at once or chill in the refrigerator for several hours.

Decorate with lemon slices.

INGREDIENTS TO SERVE FOUR TO SIX:
1 large lemon
5 tablespoons (75 ml) white wine
1 tablespoon (15 ml) brandy
2 oz (50 g) castor sugar
½ pint (300 ml) double cream
¼ pint (150 ml) yogurt
lemon slices

Apricot Yogurt Whip

If you wish to make this light, frothy dessert in advance, set it lightly with 2 teaspoons (10 ml) of powdered gelatine dissolved in 2 tablespoons (30 ml) of water.

Put ¼ pound (100 g) of dried apricots into a bowl and cover with ½ pint (150 ml) of water. Leave to soak overnight.

Put the apricots and water into a small saucepan and simmer for 20 to 25 minutes, or until tender. Liquidize, sieve or mash the apricots to a purée. Stir in ¾ pint (450 ml) of yogurt and 1 tablespoon (15 ml) of castor sugar. Whisk 2 egg whites in a bowl until stiff and fold into the purée.

Spoon into 4 sundae glasses, decorate with 1 ounce (25 g) of toasted hazelnuts and serve immediately.

INGREDIENTS TO SERVE FOUR:
¼ lb (100 g) dried apricots
¾ pint (450 g) yogurt
1 tablespoon (15 ml) castor sugar
2 egg whites
1 oz (25 g) toasted hazelnuts

Chilled Yogurt and Tomato Soup

This attractive cold soup is ideal on hot summer days.

Whisk together 1 pint (600 ml) of yogurt and 1 pint (600 ml) of tomato juice in a bowl. Add the grated rind and juice of 1 lemon and mix well.

Peel 1 small cucumber. Reserving a 1-inch (2-cm) piece for garnish, cut the cucumber into ¼-inch (6-mm) cubes. Stir the cubes into the yogurt mixture. Season to taste with salt and pepper. Chill in the refrigerator until needed.

Before serving thinly slice the reserved piece of cucumber and ½ lemon. Garnish the soup with the slices of cucumber and lemon and 1 tablespoon (15 ml) of chopped chives.

INGREDIENTS TO SERVE FOUR TO SIX:
1 pint (600 ml) yogurt
1 pint (600 ml) tomato juice
1½ lemons
1 small cucumber
salt
pepper
1 tablespoon (15 ml) chopped chives

Ranch-style Dressing

To vary the flavour of this piquant American salad dressing, add finely chopped herbs or green pepper. It will keep for up to 1 week in the refrigerator.

Beat together ¼ pint (150 ml) of buttermilk with ¼ pint (150 ml) of yogurt in a bowl.

Stir in 1 teaspoon (5 ml) of grated onion and ¼ teaspoon (1 ml) of crushed garlic. Season to taste with salt and pepper.

Cover the bowl and refrigerate.

INGREDIENTS TO DRESS A SALAD TO SERVE FOUR:
¼ pint (150 ml) buttermilk
¼ pint (150 ml) yogurt
1 teaspoon (5 ml) grated onion
¼ teaspoon (1 ml) crushed garlic
salt
pepper

Orange Egg Flip

This nourishing breakfast drink is ideal for people in a hurry.

Beat together 1 egg, ¼ pint (150 ml) of yogurt and the juice of 1 orange. Drink immediately.

INGREDIENTS TO SERVE ONE:
1 egg
¼ pint (150 ml) yogurt
1 orange

FOR A VEGETABLE WHICH WAS, according to a Turkish myth, the devil's creation, the onion has been credited with some remarkable virtues, both magical and medical. It has been said that if a man sleeps with an onion under his pillow he will dream of his future wife, or if he rubs onion juice on his bald head his hair will rapidly grow again. It has been claimed that onions cure boils, restore bad eyesight, reduce blood pressure, increase lust, clean out the bowels and induce sleep. There is no end to the claims made for them and none of them has been substantiated. It is much the same for other members of the onion family. Garlic has been reputed to make peasants work harder and Roman soldiers fight more stubbornly and roses smell more sweetly if it is planted among them. Leeks, according to the Roman emperor Nero, ensure that you are in good voice.

But does all this add up to the greatest vegetable confidence trick of all time? What are the qualities that make the onion the most universally used and apparently the most indispensable vegetable? They are insignificant as a source of energy—one pound ($\frac{1}{2}$ kg) of boiled onions provides only 60 Calories. On the other hand, a quarter of a pound of fried onions provide about 350 Calories. Pyramid-building was hard work, and the slaves who built them required a large number of calories each day. They must have eaten a lot of bread and drunk copious amounts of beer with their supposedly staple diet of onions. Onions provide no carotene or vitamin D and their vitamin C content is far behind that of the brassicas. Their contribution to our mineral needs is not outstanding. Even in sulphur, which is their strong point, they are no better than cabbage, and Brussels sprouts leave them far behind.

Whatever their virtue, however, there is no denying their attraction; the English eat about a quarter of a million tons of onions a year. Most of them are imported, and when imports were stopped during the Second World War the deprivation felt was greater than could be accounted for simply by the loss of flavour. Whatever the nutritional analysis shows perhaps there is something magical in an onion. On the other hand, there may be a danger in eating them to excess, because they contain an alkaloid that has been shown to cause anaemia in dogs and may do the same in humans.

Onions can be eaten raw or cooked in a host of ways—boiled, fried, baked, made into soups and sauces, used in stews and other savoury dishes and pickled.

They vary in the intensity of their flavour—some are more pungent, others sweeter. While all need the sun to ripen them, the greater the heat the milder the onion will taste. The mild varieties are usually sold as Spanish onions. Red-coloured varieties have a stronger flavour. Those grown in cooler climates are smaller, stronger and keep

better. But wet weather produces large, soft-fleshed bulbs which soon rot.

Onions are available in the shops all the year round, because crops ripen at different times in various parts of the world. But to provide a year-round supply from your own garden is difficult, because stored onions will sprout or rot before the new crop is ready.

Leeks, which can be harvested during the autumn, winter and spring, are a better alternative as a garden crop. Because they are hardy they can stay in the ground during the winter and can be dug up as you need them and eaten fresh, when they taste their best. Leeks have a far more subtle taste than onions, and they are more nutritious both in vitamins (notably carotene and vitamin C in the leaves) and minerals (including twice as much sulphur, potassium and calcium). They are popular throughout Europe, but less so in the United States.

Onions and leeks are the two members of the

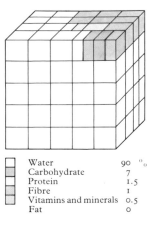

The Nutrients in Onions
Onions are high in sulphur, and unless fried they are low in calories. Three and a half ounces (100 g) provide about 30 Calories.

Water	90 %
Carbohydrate	7
Protein	1.5
Fibre	1
Vitamins and minerals	0.5
Fat	0

Members of the onion family have little nutritional value, but their wide range of flavours are indispensable. The most delicately flavoured white onion is the shallot. The large Spanish onions are so sweet that they are delicious eaten raw. The "ordinary onion" is more pungent and ideal for flavouring cooked dishes. Garlic is also strong, but develops a sweetness when cooked. Of the green onions, chives and "spring" onions are best eaten in salads. Leeks have the sweetest flavour of all. Below, clockwise: shallots (in the box), pots of chives, leeks, garlic and spring onions surrounding Spanish and "ordinary onions". Onions are best stored on strings (right).

THE MEDICINAL ONION

Although the onion has little nutritional value, for centuries it has been widely revered as a food. Possibly this is because it is known to stimulate the contractions of the intestine and to improve the circulation of the blood. It has now been discovered that onions reduce serum cholesterol, thus helping to lessen the likelihood of coronary heart disease. It is doubtful, however, that onions, when fried, can do more than ameliorate the effect of the fat in which they are cooked. But pickled onions would stand a good chance of becoming one of the health foods of the future were it not for their unfortunate effect on the breath.

onion family used as vegetables—the others are used for flavouring. Shallots are a smaller, somewhat less pungent version of the onion with the merest hint of garlic. Introduced into Europe in the Middle Ages, supposedly one of the spoils of war of the returning Crusaders, shallots achieved particular esteem in French cookery.

Chives, the smallest and most subtle of the onions, were being used by the Chinese five thousand years ago. By having a pot of them indoors for use in winter and spring and by planting them in window-boxes or in a corner of the garden, you can be assured of a supply of chives all year. The bulbs are left in the soil to produce more leaves.

Home-grown Welsh onions are useful as a winter substitute for "spring", or salad, onions, which, although available all year, are expensive. Garlic has an onion flavour with a difference. It is best treated with a certain discretion, although there are some dishes—aioli, the Provençal mayonnaise, and gazpacho, Spanish cold vegetable soup, for example—in which garlic is used with abandon for a throat-tingling effect. Dishes containing garlic are not suitable for deep-freezing for in the process they often develop an unpleasant flavour.

In the Middle Ages it was thought that garlic warded off werewolves and vampires. Today health food literature still frequently gives the impression that garlic will cure all ills. But even ignoring such extravagant claims, garlic is worth growing, especially since cloves for planting are cheap and easily cultivated.

Leek and Bacon Quiche

Preheat the oven to 400°F (200°C, Gas Mark 6).

Make 6 ounces (100 g) of shortcrust pastry with wholewheat flour (see page 34). Roll it out and line an 8-inch (20-cm) flan ring or dish. Bake blind for 15 minutes. Remove the baking paper and the beans and bake for 5 minutes more.

Reduce the oven temperature to 375°F (190°C, Gas Mark 5).

Make the filling. Trim 1 pound (500 g) of leeks. Slice them crossways, wash thoroughly and drain well.

Chop ¼ pound (100 g) of bacon. Fry it gently in a large saucepan until the fat runs. Add the leeks, cover the pan and cook over very low heat, stirring occasionally, for 10 minutes, or until the leeks are tender.

Using a slotted spoon, transfer the leeks and bacon to the flan case.

Beat 2 eggs with ¼ pint (150 ml) of milk. Season to taste with salt and pepper. Pour over the leeks. Sprinkle with 1 tablespoon (15 ml) of grated Parmesan cheese.

Bake for 30 minutes, or until the filling is set and lightly browned on top.

INGREDIENTS TO SERVE FOUR TO SIX:
6 oz (100 g) shortcrust pastry made with wholewheat flour (see page 34)
1 lb (500 g) leeks
¼ lb (100 g) bacon
2 eggs
¼ pint (150 ml) milk
salt
pepper
1 tablespoon (15 ml) grated Parmesan cheese

Leek and Tomato Casserole

Preheat the oven to 350°F (180°C, Gas Mark 4).

Slice 1 pound (500 g) of leeks. Wash them thoroughly. Put half of the leeks into a casserole or ovenproof dish.

Slice ½ pound (250 g) of tomatoes and put them in a layer over the leeks, sprinkling them with salt, pepper, the juice of ½ lemon and 1 crushed garlic clove.

Put the remaining leeks on top of the tomatoes. Sprinkle them with the juice of ½ lemon and salt and pepper.

Cover and bake for 30 to 40 minutes, or until the leeks are just tender. Serve hot or cold.

INGREDIENTS TO SERVE FOUR:
1 lb (500 g) leeks
½ lb (250 g) tomatoes
salt
pepper
1 lemon
1 garlic clove

Leeks Vinaigrette

Trim 12 young leeks and cut them lengthways almost to the root end. Wash them thoroughly. Tie them together neatly.

In a large saucepan bring ½ pint (300 ml) of salted water to the boil. Add the leeks, cover the pan, reduce the heat and simmer gently for 15 minutes, or until the leeks are tender. Drain the leeks. Put them in a bowl to cool. Untie them.

In a small bowl mix together 1 teaspoon (5 ml) of French mustard, salt, pepper, 1 teaspoon (5 ml) of lemon juice and 2 tablespoons (30 ml) of corn oil.

Pour the dressing over the leeks. Marinate them for at least 2 hours. Serve them chilled.

INGREDIENTS TO SERVE FOUR:
12 young leeks
salt
1 teaspoon (5 ml) French mustard
pepper
1 teaspoon (5 ml) lemon juice
2 tablespoons (30 ml) corn oil

PREPARING LEEKS

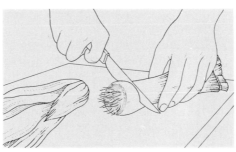

Trim the roots and leaves.

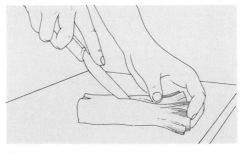

Slit the leeks lengthways almost to the root end.

Rinse thoroughly under cold running water.

Garlic Sauce

Serve this sauce with lamb or a strongly flavoured oily fish, such as mackerel.

Peel 1 large bulb of garlic, about 16 cloves. Put them in a saucepan. Add 1 sprig of rosemary, 1 ounce (25 g) of fresh breadcrumbs, salt and pepper. Pour in ½ pint (300 ml) of beef stock and ¼ pint (150 ml) of milk. Bring to the boil. Cover the pan, reduce the heat and simmer for 30 minutes, stirring occasionally.

Sieve the sauce or liquidize it to a purée. Pour it back into the pan, adjust the seasoning and reheat.

INGREDIENTS TO SERVE FOUR:
1 large garlic bulb
1 rosemary sprig
1 oz (25 g) fresh breadcrumbs
salt
pepper
½ pint (300 ml) beef stock
¼ pint (150 ml) milk

Garlic Soup

Peel 8 large garlic cloves and put them into a saucepan. Peel ½ pound (250 g) of potatoes, cut them into ½-inch (1-cm) dice and add them to the pan.

Pour in 1½ pints (850 ml) of water. Add 1 bay leaf, 1 sprig of thyme, 1 sage leaf, 1 basil leaf, salt and pepper.

Bring to the boil, cover the pan, reduce the heat and simmer for 30 minutes.

Pour the soup into a liquidizer and blend it well. Return the soup to the pan, reheat and adjust the seasoning. Serve hot.

INGREDIENTS TO SERVE FOUR:
8 large garlic cloves
½ lb (250 g) potatoes
1 bay leaf
1 thyme sprig
1 sage leaf
1 basil leaf
salt
pepper

French Onion Soup

Peel and thinly slice 1 pound (500 g) of onions. Melt 1 ounce (25 g) of butter in a large saucepan with 1 tablespoon (15 ml) of corn oil. Add the onions to the pan. Cover the pan and cook the onions over moderate heat, stirring occasionally, for about 15 minutes, or until they are soft and translucent.

Raise the heat to moderately high and stir in 1 teaspoon (5 ml) of salt and ½ teaspoon (2.5 ml) of sugar. Cook the onions, stirring frequently, for about 30 minutes, or until they are a deep golden brown.

Stir in 1½ pints (850 ml) of beef stock,

½ pint (300 ml) of red wine, 1 bay leaf and
½ teaspoon (2.5 ml) of dried sage. Cover the
pan, reduce the heat and simmer gently for
30 to 40 minutes. Add salt and pepper to taste.

Serve hot with slices of toasted French
bread sprinkled with grated Parmesan cheese.

INGREDIENTS TO SERVE FOUR:
1 lb (500 g) onions
1 oz (25 g) butter
1 tablespoon (15 ml) corn oil
salt
½ teaspoon (2.5 ml) sugar
1½ pints (850 ml) beef stock
½ pint (300 ml) red wine
1 bay leaf
½ teaspoon (2.5 ml) dried sage
pepper
French bread
grated Parmesan cheese

Braised Onions

Peel 1 pound (500 g) of medium-sized onions.
Cut them into quarters and put them into a
saucepan. Add ¼ pint (150 ml) of water,
2 tablespoons (30 ml) of wine vinegar,
¼ pound (100 g) of sultanas, 2 ounces (50 g) of
walnuts, 1 crushed garlic clove, 2 sprigs of
thyme, 1 bay leaf, salt and pepper.

Bring to the boil, cover the pan, reduce the
heat and simmer, stirring occasionally, for
15 to 20 minutes, or until the onions are just
tender and the water has evaporated. If the
water has not completely evaporated during
cooking continue to cook uncovered for a
few minutes.

Serve hot.

INGREDIENTS TO SERVE FOUR:
1 lb (500 g) onions
2 tablespoons (30 ml) wine vinegar
¼ lb (100 g) sultanas
2 oz (50 g) shelled walnuts
1 garlic clove
2 thyme sprigs
1 bay leaf
salt
pepper

CRUSHING GARLIC

Crush finely chopped garlic with the flat of a knife blade.

Onion and Sage Stuffing

Onion and sage stuffing is traditionally served
with pork. Use this to stuff a boned, rolled
joint of pork or a 2- to 3-pound (1- to 1.50-kg)
chicken.

Peel and chop 2 large onions. Put them into
a saucepan and cover with cold water. Bring
to the boil, reduce the heat and simmer for
5 minutes, or until the onions are tender.

Chop 2 ounces (50 g) of bacon. Put it into a
frying-pan and fry until the fat runs. Remove
the pan from the heat and stir in ¼ pound
(100 g) of fresh breadcrumbs.

Peel, core and finely chop ¼ pound (100 g)
of cooking apples. Add the apple to the
breadcrumbs with 2 tablespoons (30 ml) of
chopped sage, or 2 teaspoons (10 ml) of dried
sage, salt and pepper.

Drain the onion, add it to the stuffing and
mix well.

INGREDIENTS TO SERVE FOUR:
2 large onions
2 oz (50 g) streaky bacon
¼ lb (100 g) fresh breadcrumbs
¼ lb (100 g) cooking apples
2 tablespoons (30 ml) chopped sage or
** 2 teaspoons (10 ml) dried sage**
salt
pepper

Onion and Caper Sauce

This creamy onion sauce, flavoured with
mustard and capers, is particularly good with
lamb or beef.

Peel and finely chop 2 onions. Heat
1 ounce (25 g) of margarine with 1 tablespoon
(15 ml) of corn oil. Add the onions and fry
over low heat for 5 minutes, or until they are
soft but not coloured.

Stir in 2 tablespoons (30 ml) of flour. Still
stirring, gradually add ¾ pint (450 ml) of milk
and bring to the boil. Continue to boil,
stirring constantly, until the sauce thickens.

Reduce the heat and stir in 1 teaspoon
(5 ml) of prepared mustard, 1 tablespoon
(15 ml) of capers and salt and pepper to taste.
Simmer for 5 minutes, stirring occasionally.

Serve hot.

INGREDIENTS TO SERVE FOUR:
2 onions
1 oz (25 g) margarine
1 tablespoon (15 ml) corn oil
2 tablespoons (30 ml) flour
¾ pint (450 ml) milk
1 teaspoon (5 ml) prepared mustard
1 tablespoon (15 ml) capers
salt
pepper

Raw Onion Salad

Peel and thinly slice 3 medium-sized onions.
Put them into a serving bowl. Thinly slice
3 tomatoes and ½ cucumber and add to the
onions.

Cut 2 green chillies in half and discard the
seeds. Chop the chillies and sprinkle over the
salad with 1 tablespoon (15 ml) of chopped
coriander leaves. If you find chillies too hot
use ½ green pepper instead.

In a small bowl combine 1 tablespoon
(15 ml) of wine vinegar, 4 tablespoons
(60 ml) of corn oil and salt and pepper to
taste.

Pour the dressing over the salad and toss
lightly. Put in the refrigerator to marinate for
at least 30 minutes.

Serve chilled.

INGREDIENTS TO SERVE FOUR TO SIX:
3 medium-sized onions
3 tomatoes
½ cucumber
2 green chillies or ½ green pepper
1 tablespoon (15 ml) chopped
** coriander leaves**
1 tablespoon (15 ml) wine vinegar
4 tablespoons (60 ml) corn oil
salt
pepper

SLICING AND CHOPPING ONIONS

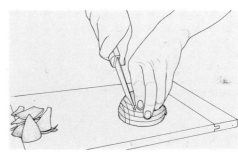

To chop onion slice vertically and then horizontally.

To cut onion rings, slice the onion horizontally.

VEGETABLE FRUITS /The Exotics of the Vegetable World

YOU ARE UNLIKELY to grow fat on vegetable fruits. All except one are more than ninety per cent water and contain only the merest trace of fat and precious little carbohydrate. The exception is the avocado pear, which stands out among vegetables (or fruits) because it contains about seventeen per cent fat. But obesity brought about by a surfeit of avocados must be rare.

Some vegetable fruits have nutritionally little merit except the negative virtue of being non-fattening, but our diet would be the poorer without them. Cucumbers may be ninety-seven per cent water, but what deliciously flavoured water. And the equally moist vegetable marrow certainly serves as a tasty and convenient container for stuffing.

The vegetable fruit that excels all others in flavour is the tomato. Eaten raw it is also a good source of carotene and vitamin C, and is low in calories; half a pound ($\frac{1}{4}$ kg) of raw tomatoes provides only 35 Calories. As vegetables go the tomato is a comparative newcomer. Its original home was Mexico and Peru and it was introduced into Europe only in the mid-sixteenth century, first into Italy and then spreading northwards through France. When it reached England the tomato was admired for its decorativeness but mistrusted as food, possibly because of its association with other members of its family—the then still suspect potato, the tobacco plant, the poisonous mandrake and the deadly nightshade.

Depending on the variety and where they are grown there are great differences in the flavour and the degree of sweetness or acidity of tomatoes. Under a hot sun they grow large and sweet—the sweet Italian tomatoes are outstanding; they are, indeed, the only canned vegetable worth eating.

Unhappily, as tomatoes have become more popular over the past thirty years they have deteriorated in flavour because, for commercial reasons, the sole aim of growers is to obtain heavy yields of tomatoes with tough skins so that they travel well. It is not even easy to find the older varieties to grow yourself, but it is worth trying. Eating a tomato when it is freshly picked from the garden, the greenhouse or even from a window box is an experience that can never be obtained from one bought in a shop. With such a poor choice of good tomatoes it is unfortunate that there is a prejudice against yellow tomatoes, the skins of which are softer and the flesh sweeter.

The more you enjoy a food the more perfection you demand. In honesty it has to be admitted that there are tomatoes, eaten raw, that are disappointing. Happily the tomato is versatile when it is cooked—in soups, sauces, stews, soufflés or stuffed in endless ways. It must be remembered, however, that if they are fried, the cooking oil may increase the calorific value of the tomatoes by as much as five times.

For many thousands of years the world has been divided into cucumber-eaters and cucumber-haters. The case against cucumbers was summed up by the erudite third-century writer on food Athenaeus: "The cucumber is hard to digest and to purge from the system; moreover it causes chilliness, provokes bile and inhibits coition." With care these dangers—at least about indigestibility—can be avoided. If you grow your own cucumbers you can choose the new variety of the easily cultivated ridge cucumber, which has the self-explanatory name of Burpless, or the white cucumber, which is popular in Europe. The cucumbers usually sold are the larger frame cucumbers, grown in the steamy heat of green-

Vegetable fruits are full of flavour, and, with the exception of avocados, they are low in calories. Clockwise below: a golden pumpkin to cook in a pie or casserole; tomatoes, a good source of vitamins A and C; hot chillies for flavouring; avocados, a useful source of B vitamins; green peppers, packed with vitamin C; courgettes, the most flavourful of the marrows; refreshing cucumbers; and aubergines, only low in calories if they are not cooked in oil.

houses. If these are to be eaten raw they can be made less indigestible by thinly slicing the unpeeled cucumber, sprinkling it with salt and then after about an hour pouring off the resulting liquid. Only then do you add dressing, preferably a sharp one to contrast with the clean sweetness of the cucumber.

The herbalists set great store by the health-giving properties of cucumber, but we scarcely eat enough for them to be regarded as nutritionally important. Even their vitamin C is often wasted through peeling. But the cucumber, raw or cooked, has a unique flavour.

Sweet peppers are the only other popular vegetable fruit that can be enjoyed both raw and cooked; marrows, squashes, pumpkins and aubergines are totally unpalatable when they are raw. The peppers used as a vegetable are the milder varieties of *Capsicum annuum*, they are eaten immature and green or when they have ripened to a striking redness and taste sweeter and less pungent.

Varieties of *Capsicum annuum*, some mild, some hot, are dried and ground to make paprika, especially in Hungary and Spain. The small, hot, red peppers, or chillies, which are the fruits of *Capsicum frutescens*, are used not as a vegetable but for flavouring or making into red, or cayenne, pepper. None of the capsicums have any connection with the plant *Piper nigrum* that provides us with black and white pepper.

Mature marrows are best thought of as nutritionally harmless containers in which to stuff and cook more interesting food, for they have but little nourishment or flavour of their own. But picked in their infancy as courgettes and gently fried they are a most subtle-tasting vegetable. Pumpkins are more nourishing than marrows, but in pumpkin pie their simple health-giving qualities get rather lost among the pastry, eggs, sugar and spices.

Aubergines are more potentially treacherous, because of the insatiable way in which they soak up the olive oil or butter in which they are cooked. The dish known as Imam Bayildi requires vast amounts of oil and serves as a warning. The story goes that when the *imam*, or priest, married a girl who was unrivalled in cooking aubergines he asked for her dowry to be given in twelve large jars of olive oil to cook them in. In the first eleven nights of their marriage the aubergines had used up all the dowry. On being told the news the imam fainted. He could have suffered a worse fate—saturation with saturated fat.

The Nutrients in Vegetable Fruits
Vegetable fruits are largely water and three and a half ounces (100 g) of tomatoes provide about 15 Calories.

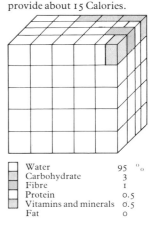

Water	95 %
Carbohydrate	3
Fibre	1
Protein	0.5
Vitamins and minerals	0.5
Fat	0

Sweet peppers (left) are red when ripe, green when less mature. An exceptionally good source of vitamin C, they contain about six times as much as tomatoes. Peppers add a pleasant smoky pungency to stews and casseroles and can be stuffed, but they are better nutritionally eaten raw in salads, so that none of the water-soluble vitamin C is lost in cooking.

Tomato and Rosemary Soup

This delicious hot soup may be made from tomatoes that are too ripe and soft to use for a salad.

Put 1 pound (500 g) of very ripe tomatoes into a saucepan. Add 1 chopped large onion and ¾ pound (350 g) of potatoes, peeled and diced. Grate in the rind of ½ lemon and then squeeze in the juice. Pour in 1 pint (600 ml) of well-seasoned chicken or vegetable stock with 4 rosemary sprigs and salt and pepper to taste. Cover the pan and simmer the soup gently for 30 minutes, or until the tomatoes are very soft.

Sieve the soup or liquidize it and then sieve it to remove the tomato seeds.

Return the pureed soup to the pan, adjust the seasoning to taste and reheat.

INGREDIENTS TO SERVE FOUR:
1 lb (500 g) ripe tomatoes
1 large onion
¾ lb (350 g) potatoes
½ lemon
**1 pint (600 ml) chicken or vegetable
 stock**
4 rosemary sprigs
salt
pepper

Tomato Sauce

Heat 1 tablespoon (15 ml) of corn oil in a saucepan. Add 1 chopped rasher of bacon, 1 chopped small onion, 1 chopped small carrot and ½ stick of celery, chopped. Fry over low heat for 5 minutes, stirring frequently, until the vegetables have softened but are not coloured.

Cut 1 pound (500 g) of ripe tomatoes into halves. Add the tomatoes to the pan with ½ pint (300 ml) of well-seasoned beef or vegetable stock, the grated rind of ½ lemon, 1 bay leaf and salt and pepper to taste. Cover the pan and simmer over very low heat for 30 minutes.

Sieve the vegetables and stock or liquidize and then sieve them.

Return the purée to the pan. Adjust the seasoning to taste and reheat.

INGREDIENTS TO MAKE ONE PINT (600 ML) OF
SAUCE:
1 tablespoon (15 ml) corn oil
1 bacon rasher
1 small onion
1 small carrot
½ celery stick
1 lb (500 g) ripe tomatoes
½ pint (300 ml) beef or vegetable stock
½ lemon
1 bay leaf
salt
pepper

Tomato and Mint Water Ice

Tomato water ice, flavoured with lemon and mint, makes a refreshing and unusual start to a meal.

Cut 1½ pounds (700 g) of ripe tomatoes into quarters. Put them into a saucepan with 1 chopped small onion and the grated rind and juice of ½ lemon. Add 4 large sprigs of mint, 2 teaspoons (10 ml) of Worcestershire sauce and salt and pepper. Cover the pan and cook over very low heat for 10 minutes, or until the tomatoes are soft.

Liquidize the mixture until it is smooth, then sieve it to remove the tomato skins and seeds. Adjust the seasoning. Leave to cool. Pour the tomato mixture into a rigid container, cover it tightly and freeze until solid.

Remove the water ice from the freezer and leave it at room temperature for 15 minutes to soften slightly so that the ice can be spooned out or crushed. Pile the ice into individual bowls, garnish with sprigs of mint and serve at once.

INGREDIENTS TO SERVE FOUR:
1½ lb (700 g) ripe tomatoes
1 small onion
½ lemon
mint sprigs
**2 teaspoons (10 ml) Worcestershire
 sauce**
salt
pepper

PREPARING TOMATOES

Blanch tomatoes in boiling water and peel.

Cut the tomatoes in half and scoop out the seeds.

Baked Stuffed Aubergines

First make the stuffing. Heat 1 tablespoon (15 ml) of olive oil in a large saucepan. Chop 2 large onions, about ¾ pound (350 g), and fry them, stirring frequently, for 5 minutes, or until they are soft and translucent.

Blanch and peel ½ pound (250 g) of tomatoes. Cut the tomatoes into halves and remove the seeds. Coarsely chop the tomatoes and add them to the pan.

Preheat the oven to 350°F (180°C, Gas Mark 4).

Cut 2 large aubergines into halves lengthways. Scoop out the flesh, chop it and add it to the pan reserving the shells. Simmer over low heat for 10 minutes, then stir in 1 tablespoon (15 ml) of chopped parsley and salt and pepper to taste.

Divide the filling between the 4 aubergine shells. Put the aubergines into a lightly greased ovenproof dish. Cover with foil and bake them for 40 minutes. Serve immediately.

INGREDIENTS TO SERVE FOUR:
1 tablespoon (15 ml) olive oil
2 large onions
½ lb (250 g) tomatoes
2 large aubergines
1 tablespoon (15 ml) chopped parsley
salt
pepper

Courgettes with Lemon and Herbs

Preheat the oven to 350°F (180°C, Gas Mark 4).

Wash and thickly slice 1½ pounds (300 g) of courgettes. In a small bowl mix together the grated rind of ½ lemon, 1 tablespoon (15 ml) of chopped parsley, 1 tablespoon (15 ml) of chopped thyme, salt and pepper.

Arrange the courgette slices in an ovenproof dish, sprinkling each layer with the herb mixture.

Squeeze the juice of the ½ lemon into a small bowl and add 5 tablespoons (75 ml) of chicken or vegetable stock. Pour the liquid over the courgettes.

Cover and bake for 30 minutes, until the courgettes are just tender but not soft. Alternatively, put all the ingredients into a saucepan and cook covered for 10 minutes, or until the courgettes are tender.

INGREDIENTS TO SERVE FOUR:
1½ lb (700 g) courgettes
½ lemon
1 tablespoon (15 ml) chopped parsley
1 tablespoon (15 ml) chopped thyme
salt
pepper
**5 tablespoons (75 ml) chicken or
 vegetable stock**

Ratatouille

This delicious vegetable stew is usually cooked in lots of oil. In this recipe, however, the vegetables cook in their own juices for a more concentrated flavour. It may be served hot or cold.

Chop 1 large onion and put it into a large saucepan with 1 crushed garlic clove.

Wash and slice 1 pound (500 g) of courgettes and add them to the pan. Cut 1 pound (500 g) of aubergines into slices and then cut the slices into quarters and add them to the pan.

Cut 1 green pepper into quarters lengthways. Remove the white pith and the seeds. Cut the pepper into eighths and add it to the pan.

Blanch and peel 1 pound (500 g) of tomatoes. Cut them into quarters and remove the seeds. Add the tomatoes to the pan with 1 tablespoon (15 ml) of dried oregano. Season to taste with salt and pepper.

Cover the pan and cook over very low heat, stirring occasionally, for 30 minutes, or until the vegetables are tender.

INGREDIENTS TO SERVE FOUR:
1 large onion
1 garlic clove
1 lb (500 g) courgettes
1 lb (500 g) aubergines
1 green pepper
1 lb (500 g) tomatoes
1 teaspoon (5 ml) dried oregano
salt
pepper

PREPARING PEPPERS FOR STUFFING

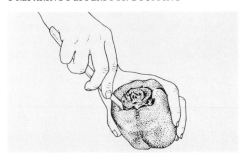

Carefully cut a lid from the top of the pepper.

Scoop out the pith and the seeds.

Iced Cucumber and Mint Soup

Cut about 2 inches (5 cm) from 1 large cucumber and reserve it for garnish. Cut the rest of the cucumber into ½-inch (1-cm) cubes. Put the cucumber into a saucepan. Peel and chop 1 small onion and 1 small potato and add to the cucumber in the pan.

Add 1 pint (600 ml) of chicken or vegetable stock, the grated rind and juice of 1 large lemon, 2 tablespoons (30 ml) of chopped mint and salt and pepper. Cover the pan and simmer over low heat for 15 to 20 minutes, or until the cucumber and potato are tender.

Sieve or liquidize the soup then let it cool. Stir in ¼ pint (150 ml) of yogurt and adjust the seasoning.

Serve the soup well chilled, garnished with thin slices of the reserved cucumber and sprigs of mint.

INGREDIENTS TO SERVE FOUR:
1 large cucumber
1 small onion
1 small potato
1 pint (600 ml) chicken or vegetable stock
1 large lemon
1 small mint sprig
salt
pepper
¼ pint (150 ml) yogurt

Hot Cucumber Sauce

Serve this sauce with fish.

Melt 1 ounce (25 g) of margarine in a saucepan. Finely chop 1 small onion. Fry it over low heat for 3 minutes, stirring frequently, until it is soft and translucent.

Peel ½ large cucumber. Cut the cucumber into ¼-inch (6-mm) slices and then dice it. Add the diced cucumber to the onion in the pan. Cover and cook over very low heat for 5 minutes.

Stir in 1 ounce (25 g) of flour. Still stirring, gradually pour in ½ pint (300 ml) of milk. Then add 1 tablespoon (15 ml) of chopped mint and salt and pepper. Bring the sauce to the boil, stirring. Reduce the heat and then simmer for 1 minute.

Serve hot.

INGREDIENTS TO SERVE FOUR:
1 oz (25 g) margarine
1 small onion
½ large cucumber
1 oz (25 g) flour
½ pint (150 ml) milk
1 tablespoon (15 ml) chopped mint
salt
pepper

Chilled Avocado Soup

Cut 2 large, ripe avocadoes into halves and remove the stones. Scoop the flesh from the avocado skins and put it into the liquidizer with the juice of ½ lemon, 1 pint (600 ml) of well-seasoned chicken stock and ¼ pint (150 ml) of yogurt. Season to taste with salt and pepper. Blend until the ingredients are smooth.

Pour the soup into a bowl or a tureen. Cover and chill well before serving. To prevent the soup discolouring, add the avocado stones and remove them just before serving.

Serve the soup cold, garnished with 2 tablespoons (30 ml) of chopped chives.

INGREDIENTS TO SERVE FOUR:
2 large ripe avocadoes
½ lemon
1 pint (600 ml) chicken stock
¼ pint (150 ml) yogurt
salt
pepper
2 tablespoons (30 ml) chopped chives

Avocado Mousse

This smooth, pale-green mousse makes an appetizing start to a meal.

Pour ½ pint (300 ml) of strong, well-seasoned chicken stock into the liquidizer. Add ¼ pint (150 ml) of yogurt, ¼ lb (100 g) of curd cheese, the grated rind and juice of ½ lemon and ½ small onion.

Cut 2 ripe large avocadoes into halves and remove the stones. Scoop the flesh from the skins and add it to the other ingredients.

Blend until the mixture is smooth.

Dissolve ½ ounce (15 g) of powdered gelatine in 2 tablespoons (30 ml) of cold water in a cup set in a pan of hot water. Pour the dissolved gelatine into the mousse. Blend for 10 seconds more.

Pour the mousse into a 1½-pint (850-ml) soufflé dish or mould. Chill in the refrigerator until set. Serve in the dish or unmould just before serving.

INGREDIENTS TO SERVE FOUR:
½ pint (300 ml) strong chicken stock
¼ pint (150 ml) yogurt
¼ lb (100 g) curd cheese
½ lemon
½ small onion
2 ripe large avocadoes
½ oz (15 g) powdered gelatine
2 tablespoons (30 ml) cold water

Marrow and Tomato Casserole

Preheat the oven to 350°F (180°C, Gas Mark 4).

Peel a small marrow, about 2 pounds (1 kg). Cut it in half and scoop out the seeds from the centre. Cut the marrow into cubes, about 1 inch (2 cm) square. Blanch, peel and quarter 6 tomatoes. Chop 1 medium-sized onion.

Arrange layers of marrow, tomato and onion in a casserole, sprinkling each layer with salt and pepper. Top with 2 ounces (50 g) of grated Gruyère cheese.

Cover the casserole and bake for 20 minutes. Uncover the casserole and bake for 15 minutes more.

INGREDIENTS TO SERVE FOUR:
1 small marrow
6 tomatoes
1 medium-sized onion
salt
pepper
2 oz (50 g) grated Gruyère cheese

Pumpkin Ring

Fill the centre of this unusual vegetable dish with cooked peas, small onions or mushrooms.

Preheat the oven to 350°F (180°C, Gas Mark 4).

Cut a 3-pound (1.50-kg) pumpkin into halves. Remove the seeds, the stringy portion and the outside shell. Cut the pumpkin into small pieces and put them into a saucepan. Add boiling water to cover and cook, covered, for 20 minutes, or until the pumpkin is tender. Drain the pumpkin and mash it well.

Served with diced cucumber, tomato and green pepper, Gazpacho is a delicious cold soup to serve on a hot day.

Beat in 4 tablespoons (60 ml) of melted margarine or butter, 2 fluid ounces (50 ml) of milk and 1 ounce (25 g) of fresh breadcrumbs. Beat 3 eggs and add them to the pumpkin. Grate 1 small onion and add it with salt and pepper to taste. Mix well.

Put the mixture into a buttered 1-quart (1-litre) ring mould. Put the mould into a roasting tin half-filled with hot water. Bake for 45 minutes, or until the pumpkin is firm.

Turn out on to a serving dish.

INGREDIENTS TO SERVE SIX TO EIGHT:
3-lb (1.50-kg) pumpkin
4 tablespoons (60 ml) margarine or butter
2 fl oz (50 ml) milk
1 oz (25 g) fresh breadcrumbs
3 eggs
1 small onion
salt
pepper

Peperonata

Heat 1 tablespoon (15 ml) of olive oil in a large, heavy frying-pan. Slice 1 large onion. Add it to the pan and cook over low heat for 3 minutes.

Cut 4 medium-sized green peppers into halves lengthways. Remove the seeds and pith. Cut the peppers into long narrow strips and add them to the pan. Cover and cook gently for 10 minutes, stirring occasionally.

Blanch and peel 8 tomatoes, about ¾ pound (350 g). Cut the tomatoes into quarters and add them to the pan. Cover and simmer gently for 20 minutes, or until the tomatoes have reduced to a purée. Add salt and pepper to taste. Serve hot or cold.

INGREDIENTS TO SERVE FOUR:
1 tablespoon (15 ml) olive oil
1 large onion
4 medium-sized green peppers
8 tomatoes
salt
pepper

Gazpacho

Blanch and peel 1 pound (500 g) of ripe tomatoes. Cut the tomatoes into halves and remove the seeds. Reserve 1 tomato half and put the remainder into the liquidizer.

Chop 1 small onion and add it to the tomatoes with 1 crushed garlic clove.

Cut 1 large green pepper into halves, remove the pith and the seeds. Reserve a quarter of the pepper and coarsely chop the rest. Add to the liquidizer.

Reserve 1 inch (2 cm) of ¼ large cucumber. Slice the rest and add it to the other ingredients with 1 tablespoon (15 ml) of wine vinegar and the grated rind and juice of

1 small lemon. Blend all the ingredients until the mixture is smooth. Pour the soup into a tureen or bowl and stir in enough cold water to give a "creamy" consistency. Chill well.

Finely dice the reserved tomato, cucumber and green pepper. Add ice cubes to the soup and serve with the diced vegetables.

INGREDIENTS TO SERVE FOUR:
1 lb (500 g) ripe tomatoes
1 small onion
1 garlic clove
1 large green pepper
¼ large cucumber
1 tablespoon (15 ml) wine vinegar
1 small lemon

Stuffed Peppers

Preheat the oven to 375°F (190°C, Gas Mark 5).

First prepare the filling. Cook 6 ounces (150 g) of brown rice in ½ pint (300 ml) of water for 30 minutes, or until the rice is tender and the water has been absorbed.

Blanch and peel 4 medium-sized tomatoes. Cut them into halves and remove the seeds. Chop the tomatoes and put them into a mixing bowl with the cooked rice.

Add ¼ pound (100 g) of cooked and peeled prawns, 1 large onion, finely chopped or grated, 2 ounces (50 g) of anchovy fillets and 1 crushed garlic clove. Add 1 tablespoon (15 ml) of chopped parsley, 1 tablespoon (15 ml) of chopped thyme, 8 sliced stuffed olives and salt and pepper. Mix well.

Cut a slice off the tops of 4 green peppers. Remove the white pith and the seeds. Stand the peppers upright, cutting a small slice off the bottom if necessary, in an ovenproof dish or small roasting tin. Divide the filling among the peppers.

Pour 5 tablespoons (75 ml) of chicken stock into the dish or tin. Cover with foil. Bake for 30 to 40 minutes, or until the peppers are tender.

Serve hot or cold.

INGREDIENTS TO SERVE FOUR:
6 oz (150 g) brown rice
4 medium-sized tomatoes
¼ lb (100 g) cooked peeled prawns
1 large onion
2 oz (50 g) anchovy fillets
1 garlic clove
1 tablespoon (15 ml) chopped parsley
1 tablespoon (15 ml) chopped thyme
8 stuffed olives
salt
pepper
4 green peppers
5 tablespoons (75 ml) chicken stock

A rich stuffing, varied in flavour and texture, baked in crisp green peppers, makes Stuffed Peppers a tasty dish for lunch or supper.

THERE MAY BE more nutritious vegetables than the stalks and shoots we eat, but few are as delicious. They come from many plant families. Asparagus, for example, is a lily, globe artichokes and cardoons are thistles and various chards are from the beet family. Their flavours are just as diverse as their classification.

Celery, now one of the most flavoursome of these vegetables, was used in the Middle Ages mainly as medicine, since at that time it was appropriately bitter and evil-smelling. Then Italian gardeners took it in hand and developed it into an acceptable vegetable, which became popular throughout Europe in the seventeenth and eighteenth centuries. It was the Italians who began the technique of blanching, which involves earthing up the soil to cover the celery stalks as they grow so that they become sweet and crisp. Celeriac is the version of celery grown as a root, but the stalks can be cooked and eaten like those of seakale. Neither celery nor celeriac rates high in the nutritional charts.

Asparagus, however, contains a considerable amount of protein, a fair amount of ascorbic acid and is exceptionally rich in folic acid (although much of both vitamins are lost in cooking). There are cheaper ways of satisfying these nutritional requirements, but there is no other way of enjoying the flavour of asparagus. What we eat are the immature shoots, which appear in the spring, and if they are not picked grow into ferns.

Self-sufficiency enthusiasts could use the young shoots of elder, or even of hops, in the same way. A far more rewarding substitute for asparagus was grown in English cottage gardens for centuries, but is not now widely cultivated. The early colonists took it to America, but it is now neglected there, too. Among the many names of this plant are Poor Man's Asparagus and Good King Henry. (Henry VIII was supposed to have eaten it to bring relief to his painful legs.) The young blanched shoots can be used as asparagus substitutes, the leaves as spinach and the flower buds as themselves. Their nutritional distinction is

SUCCULENT BAMBOO SHOOTS

The edible shoots of bamboo are cut soon after they emerge through the soil, but usually when they are longer than asparagus spears and three inches (8 cm) or more in diameter. Their flavour makes up for their nutritional value, for they have little except small amounts of vitamin C. The tender winter shoots, which taste rather like globe artichokes, are considered to have the best flavour. Unfortunately, since bamboo shoots are grown mainly in Southeast Asia, people in the West are unlikely to taste them fresh and must be content to eat those which have been canned.

The young shoots, or spears, of asparagus are richer in protein and flavour than are most stalks and shoots. In Britain and America, where green-tipped asparagus are preferred, the spears are allowed to grow several inches above ground (right) before being cut. The French and Germans, however, like white asparagus, so they cut the spears just as the tips emerge through the soil.

that, for vegetables, they are rich in iron.

Globe artichokes were introduced into England in the seventeenth century but never became popular. They are expensive to buy and harder to grow in the English climate than in southern Europe and in California, where they flourish with the abandon of weeds. As an inconvenience food the artichoke is outstanding. Each scale of the many layered "globe" has to be broken off, dipped in a sauce to enhance the flavour and sucked to extract what little flesh there is inside it. That done, you are confronted with the centre, or choke, of tightly packed stamens, which have to be removed cleanly with a sharp knife. Beneath the choke is the really delectable heart.

Globe artichokes, like many other plants, can be used to produce chards, a name confusingly applied not only to forced, blanched shoots, but also to the midribs of leaves of seakale beet, which is also known as Swiss chard. The succulent white shoots of seakale are most likely to be encountered in shops in Britain, because seakale is not popular on the Continent or in the United States. Raw or boiled, it is a delicious winter vegetable.

The nutty-tasting cardoon, a close relative of the artichoke, also provides forced stalks in winter, but they are more likely to be found on the Continent than in Britain or in the United States. Their flavour vaguely suggests both artichoke and celery. To enjoy the chards of young stems of salsify and scorzonera you may have to grow these root vegetables yourself; it is quite easy to do so.

The bulbous stem base of Florence fennel has a sweet aniseed flavour and is milder and even sweeter when cooked as a vegetable than when used as flavouring or eaten raw in salads. The Greeks believed it made them slim, courageous and long-lived. Pliny saw another virtue in it; since the stems are light, they made excellent walking sticks for the aged.

The fruits of many plants are used as vegetables, but rhubarb is a vegetable which is usually used as a fruit. The Poles, however, mix rhubarb and potatoes as a vegetable dish.

The Nutrients in Stalks and Shoots
These are low in calories. Three and a half ounces (100 g) of celery, for example, provide 15 Calories.

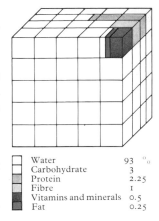

Water	93 %
Carbohydrate	3
Protein	2.25
Fibre	1
Vitamins and minerals	0.5
Fat	0.25

Delicious low-calorie vegetables, stalks and shoots such as celery (far left) and Florence fennel (left) also add crunch and flavour to salads. Asparagus (far left) and globe artichokes (left) must be cooked.

Rhubarb, although a vegetable, is eaten as a fruit. It is a pity that the oxalic acid in the stalks makes rhubarb so sour, because if it could be eaten without sugar it would contain only one Calorie per ounce.

Fennel Braised with Tomato

Wash 2 fennel bulbs, then cut them into quarters lengthways. Put the fennel into a saucepan with 4 blanched, peeled and chopped large tomatoes and 4 tablespoons (60 ml) of water. Grate in the rind of 1 lemon, then add the squeezed juice, 1 teaspoon (5 ml) of dried oregano and salt and pepper to taste.

Bring to the boil, cover the pan, reduce the heat and simmer gently, stirring occasionally, for about 30 minutes, or until the fennel is tender.

Stir in 1 tablespoon (15 ml) of chopped mint. Serve hot.

INGREDIENTS TO SERVE FOUR:
2 fennel bulbs
4 large tomatoes
1 lemon
1 teaspoon (5 ml) dried oregano
salt
pepper
1 tablespoon (15 ml) chopped mint

Fennel Braised with Apple

Preheat the oven to 350°F (180°C, Gas Mark 4).

Wash 2 large fennel bulbs and cut them into quarters lengthways. Put the fennel into a casserole or ovenproof dish.

Peel and core 1 large cooking apple. Cut the apple into slices and put the slices into the casserole with ¼ pint (150 ml) of chicken stock, 1 tablespoon (15 ml) of lemon juice and salt and pepper to taste.

Fennel Braised with Apple makes an ideal accompaniment to pork or fish.

Cover and bake for 30 minutes, or until the fennel is tender, but not soft.

Drain the stock into a saucepan and boil for about 3 minutes, or until it is reduced to 3 tablespoons (45 ml). Pour the sauce over the fennel, sprinkle with 1 tablespoon (15 ml) of chopped parsley and serve.

INGREDIENTS TO SERVE FOUR:
2 large fennel bulbs
1 large cooking apple
¼ pint (150 ml) chicken stock
1 tablespoon (15 ml) lemon juice
salt
pepper
1 tablespoon (15 ml) chopped parsley

Fennel Salad

Pour ¼ pint (150 ml) of yogurt into a large salad bowl. Stir in 1 tablespoon (15 ml) of lemon juice and salt and pepper to taste.

Wash 2 medium-sized fennel bulbs and cut them into thin slices. Put the fennel slices into the salad bowl with the yogurt mixture. Slice 4 medium-sized tomatoes and add them to the fennel. Cut a 2-inch (5-cm) piece of cucumber into slices and then into quarters and add to the salad.

Toss well, until all the ingredients are coated with the yogurt dressing.

INGREDIENTS TO SERVE FOUR:
¼ pint (150 ml) yogurt
1 tablespoon (15 ml) lemon juice
salt
pepper
2 medium-sized fennel bulbs
4 medium-sized tomatoes
2-inch (5-cm) cucumber piece

Asparagus

To appreciate the real flavour of asparagus it is best to cook it very gently and then serve it simply with melted margarine or butter or a yogurt hollandaise sauce.

Wash 2 pounds (1 kg), about 24 spears, of asparagus carefully. Using a knife or vegetable peeler, scrape the lower part of the stems. Trim the stalks so that they are all the same length, cutting off any tough woody parts at the bottom.

Tie the asparagus together, at the base and just below the tips, in bundles of about 12 spears.

The best way to cook asparagus is in a special asparagus steamer—a tall, narrow saucepan which contains a basket in which the stalks cook in boiling water while the tips cook in the steam. You can, however, easily improvise by putting the bundles of asparagus upright into a jar and covering them with perforated aluminium foil. Immerse the jar in a pan of simmering water for 20 to 30 minutes, or until the stalks and tips are tender, but not limp.

When the asparagus is cooked, remove the bundles from the pan, drain them, put them on serving dishes and remove the strings.

Serve the asparagus hot with individual bowls of melted margarine or butter flavoured with lemon juice, chopped parsley and salt and pepper or with a yogurt hollandaise sauce (see page 93). Asparagus may also be served cold with a basic vinaigrette dressing (see page 153).

INGREDIENTS TO SERVE FOUR:
2 lb (1 kg) asparagus
6 oz (150 g) margarine or butter,
lemon juice, parsley, salt and pepper
or ¼ pint (150 ml) yogurt hollandaise
sauce (see page 93)
or ¼ pint (150 ml) basic vinaigrette
dressing (see page 153)

Cream of Asparagus Soup

Wash and scrape the woody stalks of 1 pound (500 g) of asparagus. Cut off some of the tips and reserve for garnish. Chop the remaining asparagus.

Melt 1 ounce (25 g) of margarine in a large saucepan. Add 1 chopped medium-sized onion to the pan and fry for 3 minutes, or until it is soft and translucent. Then stir in 1 ounce (25 g) of flour. Stirring constantly, gradually add 1½ pints (850 ml) of chicken or vegetable stock and bring to the boil. Add the chopped asparagus. Cover the pan, reduce the heat and simmer for 20 minutes, or until the asparagus is tender.

Meanwhile, cook the reserved asparagus tips separately in a little simmering water for 5 to 10 minutes, or until they are just tender. Drain the tips.

A truly gourmet dish: Asparagus served with Yogurt Hollandaise Sauce.

When the asparagus is cooked, sieve or liquidize the soup and then return it to the pan. Stir in ¼ pint (150 ml) of milk, 1 teaspoon (5 ml) of lemon juice and salt and pepper to taste. Reheat the soup, but do not let it boil.

Serve hot or cold, garnished with the asparagus tips.

INGREDIENTS TO SERVE FOUR TO SIX:
1 lb (500 g) asparagus
1 oz (25 g) margarine
1 medium-sized onion
1 oz (25 g) flour
1½ pints (850 ml) chicken or vegetable stock
¼ pint (150 ml) milk
1 teaspoon (5 ml) lemon juice
salt
pepper

Asparagus Flan

This flan may be served hot or cold, but it is probably at its best about 1 hour after it is baked when it is still warm.

Preheat the oven to 400°F (200°C, Gas Mark 6).

Make 6 ounces (150 g) of shortcrust pastry with wholewheat flour (see page 34). Line an 8-inch (20-cm) flan ring or dish with the pastry. Bake the flan case blind for 15 minutes. Remove the greaseproof paper and the beans and bake for another 5 minutes.

Reduce the oven temperature to 350°F (180°C, Gas Mark 4).

Meanwhile, cook 8 large or 12 small spears of asparagus until they are just tender. Drain them well. Arrange the asparagus in the pastry case with the spears radiating out from the centre like spokes of a wheel. Trim the asparagus stalks if necessary and reserve.

For the custard, beat together 2 eggs, ¼ pint (150 g) of single cream or milk, the grated rind of ½ lemon and salt and pepper to taste. Finely chop the reserved asparagus stalks and add them to the custard. Pour the custard over the asparagus, then sprinkle it with 1 tablespoon (15 ml) of grated Parmesan cheese.

Bake for 25 to 30 minutes, or until the custard is set.

Garnish the centre of the flan where the stalks meet with 2 twisted slices of lemon.

INGREDIENTS TO SERVE FOUR TO SIX:
6 oz (150 g) shortcrust pastry made with wholewheat flour (see page 34)
8 large or 12 small asparagus spears
2 eggs
¼ pint (150 ml) single cream or milk
1 lemon
salt
pepper
1 tablespoon (15 ml) grated Parmesan cheese

Asparagus au Gratin

Cook 1 pound (500 g) of asparagus until just tender. Drain the asparagus, reserving the cooking liquor for the sauce. Put the asparagus into a flameproof dish with ¼ pound (100 g) of diced cooked ham and ¼ pound (100 g) of mushrooms, sliced and lightly poached and drained.

For the sauce, melt 1 ounce (25 g) of margarine in a small saucepan. Stir in 1 ounce (25 g) of flour. Stirring constantly, gradually add ½ pint (300 ml) of milk and 4 tablespoons (60 ml) of the reserved cooking liquor. Bring to the boil, stirring constantly, until the sauce is smooth and has thickened. Add 1 teaspoon (5 ml) of lemon juice and salt and pepper to taste. Simmer for 1 minute, then pour it over the ham and vegetables.

Sprinkle 2 tablespoons (30 ml) of grated Parmesan cheese over the asparagus. Put the dish under a hot grill for 5 minutes, until the sauce is brown and bubbling, and serve.

INGREDIENTS TO SERVE FOUR:
1 lb (500 g) asparagus
¼ lb (100 g) cooked ham
¼ lb (100 g) mushrooms
1 oz (25 g) margarine
1 oz (25 g) flour
½ pint (300 ml) milk
1 teaspoon (5 ml) lemon juice
salt
pepper
2 tablespoons (30 ml) grated Parmesan cheese

COOKING ASPARAGUS

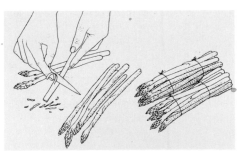

Scrape, trim and tie asparagus stalks in bundles.

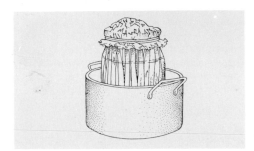

You can improvise if you do not have an asparagus pan.

Celery Soup

Separate the sticks of 1 head of celery. Wash them well. Reserve some of the leaves for garnish and coarsely chop the rest with the sticks.

Put the chopped celery into a saucepan with 1 chopped large onion and ½ pound (250 g) of potatoes which have been peeled and coarsely chopped. Add 1 pint (600 ml) of well-seasoned chicken or vegetable stock, the grated rind of ½ lemon and salt and pepper to taste.

Bring to the boil, cover, reduce the heat and simmer for 30 minutes, or until the celery and potatoes are soft. Liquidize or sieve the vegetables to a purée.

Return the soup to the pan. Stir in ½ pint (300 ml) of milk. Reheat, but do not boil. Adjust the seasoning. Serve sprinkled with 1 ounce (25 g) of grated Cheddar cheese and the reserved celery leaves.

INGREDIENTS TO SERVE FOUR:
1 celery head
1 large onion
½ lb (250 g) potatoes
1 pint (600 ml) chicken or vegetable stock
½ lemon
salt
pepper
½ pint (300 ml) milk
1 oz (25 g) grated Cheddar cheese

Celery Provençal

Wash 1 large head of celery. Drain it well and cut it into 2-inch (5-cm) lengths. Blanch, peel and coarsely chop 6 ripe medium-sized tomatoes. Finely chop 8 anchovy fillets.

Put the celery, tomatoes and anchovies into a saucepan with 8 pitted black olives and ¼ pint (150 ml) of water.

Cover the pan and simmer over low heat for 20 minutes, or until the celery is cooked but still crisp. Uncover the pan and simmer for 5 minutes to reduce the sauce.

Serve hot.

INGREDIENTS TO SERVE FOUR:
1 large celery head
6 ripe medium-sized tomatoes
8 anchovy fillets
8 pitted black olives

Celery Salad

Separate the sticks from ½ large celery head or from 1 small celery head. Wash and drain them. Slice the celery sticks and put them into a salad bowl with 2 ounces (50 g) of sultanas and 1 ounce (25 g) of chopped walnuts.

Squeeze 1 tablespoon (15 ml) of lemon juice into a bowl.

Cut 1 large dessert apple into quarters and remove the core. Chop the apple coarsely. Toss the chopped apple in the lemon juice to prevent it from browning, then add the apple to the salad.

For the dressing, whisk together any remaining lemon juice with the grated rind and juice of 1 orange, 3 tablespoons (45 ml) of corn oil and salt and pepper to taste.

Pour the dressing over the salad and toss well.

INGREDIENTS TO SERVE FOUR:
½ large or 1 small celery head
2 oz (50 g) sultanas
1 oz (25 g) chopped walnuts
1 tablespoon (15 ml) lemon juice
1 large dessert apple
1 orange
3 tablespoons (45 ml) corn oil
salt
pepper

Rhubarb Crumble

The crumble topping for this dish is made with rolled oats instead of flour.

Preheat the oven to 375 F (190 C, Gas Mark 5).

Wash 1 pound (500 g) of rhubarb and cut it into 1-inch (2-cm) lengths.

Put the rhubarb into a 1½-pint (850-ml) pie dish or ovenproof dish. Add 2 tablespoons (30 ml) of sugar and the juice of ½ orange.

For the crumble, put ¼ pound (100 g) of rolled oats into a mixing bowl. Add 2 ounces (50 g) of margarine or butter, 2 ounces (50 g) of soft brown sugar and 1 teaspoon (5 ml) of ground cinnamon. Rub these ingredients together with the fingers until well mixed. Spoon the crumble on top of the rhubarb.

Bake for 30 to 40 minutes, or until the crumble is golden brown.

INGREDIENTS TO SERVE FOUR:
1 lb (500 g) rhubarb
2 tablespoons (30 ml) sugar
½ orange
¼ lb (100 g) rolled oats
2 oz (50 g) margarine or butter
2 oz (50 g) soft brown sugar
1 teaspoon (5 ml) ground cinnamon

Artichokes

Wash 4 artichokes in salted water. Cut off the stalks at the base of the leaves and pull off any of the outer leaves that are dried or discoloured. Using scissors trim off the points of the outer leaves. Rub the cut surfaces with lemon juice.

The hairy chokes may be removed before or after cooking. If they are removed before cooking, the artichokes will take less time to cook. To remove the choke, spread the top leaves apart, pull out the small inside leaves to reveal the choke. Scrape away the choke with a teaspoon leaving the heart exposed.

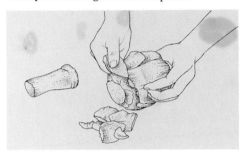

Trim artichoke stalks and remove the outer leaves.

Trim the tops and the leaves of the artichoke.

To remove the choke, pull out the inner leaves.

Scoop out the choke and rub cut areas with lemon.

Cook the artichokes, uncovered, in a large pan of boiling salted water until the leaves pull out easily. This will take 20 to 40 minutes, depending on the size and age of the artichokes. Remove the artichokes from the pan and put them upside down on a plate to drain thoroughly.

Serve the artichokes hot with a little melted butter or yogurt hollandaise sauce (see page 93), or cold with mayonnaise (see page 93) or basic vinaigrette dressing (see page 153).

INGREDIENTS TO SERVE FOUR:
**4 artichokes
salt
lemon juice
6 oz (150 g) margarine or butter
   or ¼ pint (150 ml) yogurt hollandaise
   sauce (see page 93)
   or ¼ pint (150 ml) mayonnaise (see
   page 93)
   or ¼ pint (150 ml) basic vinaigrette
   dressing (see page 153)**

Artichoke Heart Salad

Prepare and cook 4 large artichokes. Pull off and discard all the artichoke leaves. Scrape off the choke until you are left with just the artichoke heart.

The hearts may be removed from the rest of the artichoke before cooking, rubbed with lemon juice to prevent browning and then simmered in water to which a few drops of lemon juice have been added for 15 to 20 minutes, or until they are tender.

After the artichoke hearts have cooled, arrange them on lettuce leaves on a serving dish or on individual dishes.

In a mixing bowl, combine 4 tablespoons (60 ml) of yogurt, 1 teaspoon (5 ml) of lemon juice, 1 tablespoon (15 ml) of chopped chives and salt and pepper. Add ¼ pound (100 g) of cooked peeled prawns and mix well. Spoon the dressing over the artichoke hearts and serve.

INGREDIENTS TO SERVE FOUR:
**4 large artichokes
lettuce leaves
4 tablespoons (60 ml) yogurt
1 teaspoon (5 ml) lemon juice
1 tablespoon (15 ml) chopped chives
salt
pepper
¼ lb (100 g) peeled cooked prawns**

Stuffed Artichokes

Cut the stalks off 4 large artichokes and trim the leaves. Cook the artichokes in boiling salted water for 20 to 40 minutes, or until the leaves pull off easily. Drain and remove the choke and some of the inner leaves.

Preheat the oven to 375°F (190°C, Gas Mark 5).

For the stuffing, finely chop 3 ounces (75 g) of streaky bacon and cook in a saucepan until the fat runs. Chop 1 large onion and add it to the bacon. Fry for 5 minutes, stirring frequently, until the onion is soft and translucent. Take the pan from the heat and stir in 3 ounces (75 g) of breadcrumbs, the grated rind and juice of 1 lemon, 1 tablespoon (15 ml) of chopped parsley and salt and pepper to taste. Mix well. Divide the stuffing between the artichokes.

Put the artichokes into an ovenproof dish or roasting tin. Pour ½ pint (300 ml) of chicken stock around them. Cover the dish with foil and bake for 20 minutes.

Serve hot.

INGREDIENTS TO SERVE FOUR:
**4 large artichokes
salt
3 oz (75 g) streaky bacon
1 large onion
3 oz (75 g) breadcrumbs
1 lemon
1 tablespoon (15 ml) chopped parsley
pepper
½ pint (300 ml) chicken stock**

Braised Artichokes with Mushrooms

Cut the stems off 2 artichokes and trim off the tops of the leaves so that the artichokes are about 2 inches (5 cm) high. Cut the artichokes into quarters and remove the choke from each quarter.

Preheat the oven to 350°F (180°C, Gas Mark 4).

Fill a saucepan with salted water. Bring the water to the boil and drop in the artichoke quarters. Simmer for 10 minutes. Drain well.

Put the drained artichokes into a casserole with ½ pint (300 ml) of chicken stock and 2 tablespoons (30 ml) of lemon juice. Cover and bake for 20 minutes.

Wash ¼ pound (100 g) of button mushrooms and cut them into quarters. Add the mushrooms to the casserole, stirring them into the liquid. Bake for 10 minutes longer, or until the mushrooms are cooked.

If there is too much liquid, drain it off into a saucepan and boil it for a few minutes until it is reduced. Then pour over the artichokes.

Serve hot or cold sprinkled with 2 tablespoons (30 ml) of chopped parsley.

INGREDIENTS TO SERVE FOUR:
**2 artichokes
salt
½ pint (300 ml) chicken stock
2 tablespoons (30 ml) lemon juice
¼ lb (100 g) button mushrooms
2 tablespoons (30 ml) chopped parsley**

The Nutrients in Brassicas
These vegetables are high in vitamins and three and a half ounces (100 g) of broccoli, for example, provide only 35 Calories.

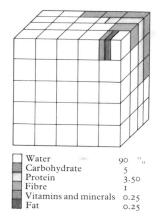

Water	90 %
Carbohydrate	5
Protein	3.50
Fibre	I
Vitamins and minerals	0.25
Fat	0.25

IF WE ATE TO PEOPLE'S HEALTH instead of drinking to it the toasts might appropriately be consumed in turnip tops—a daunting thought. It is one of the sadnesses of life that what is particularly good for you is not necessarily desirable, for turnip tops are among the most nutritious but the least palatable of all the eminently worthy green vegetables. Fortunately, there are far more acceptable leaf vegetables and brassicas that contain a wealth of vitamins and minerals.

Some of the carotene in vegetables can be converted into vitamin A in the human body. In the analysis of vegetables, therefore, it is the carotene content that is given rather than the vitamin A value. The amount of carotene in the leaves of vegetables is more or less related to how much of the green pigment chlorophyll they contain. The dark green and tougher outer leaves of cabbage, for example, may have fifty times as much carotene as the white, and more tender, heart.

On most nutritional counts boiled spinach would be the most desirable green vegetable to eat. It has about five grams of protein per hundred grams, five hundred and ninety-five milligrams of calcium, four milligrams of iron, six milligrams of carotene and twenty-five milligrams of vitamin C, or ascorbic acid. But, unfortunately, spinach also contains a considerable amount of oxalic acid and that locks up the calcium and iron, making them unavailable to the body. It is, of course, still a valuable source of carotene and vitamin C.

One hundred grams of boiled broccoli tops contain about one hundred and sixty milligrams of calcium, one and a half milligrams of iron and forty milligrams of vitamin C. Above all, they taste good, especially the variety known as calabrese. Calabrese is available much of the year fresh, and all year round frozen. The coarser white and purple sprouting broccoli are excellent standbys for winter and early spring. Smaller sprigs with thin stalks are more tender, and for best eating the flower buds should be tightly closed.

Kale should probably come next on the list—it is strong in carotene and ascorbic acid and has the ability to survive through bitter winters—but few people enjoy it. Its main role is as animal feed.

There are other brassicas that may be eaten—and enjoyed—just as well raw as cooked, and as a result their vitamin C content will be much higher. Cauliflower can be chewed after it has been broken into small florets, but cabbage and Brussels sprouts need shredding, and that means losing about one-fifth of the vitamin C through exposure to the air. This, however, is not as bad as the loss brought about by boiling, for vitamin C dissolves in water. When they are boiled their vitamin C content falls by half. Raw cauliflower has seventy milligrams of ascorbic acid in one hundred grams, and only half of that when it

ANATOMY OF A
BRUSSELS SPROUT

Brussels sprouts, like all the brassicas, are high in sulphur—hence their characteristic smell. They are also high in vitamin C —eaten raw there are about eighty milligrams in one hundred grams. Although the heart (see section below) makes enjoyable eating, it is the darker green outer leaves that contain the most carotene. So discard these sparingly.

Spinach (above) and such brassicas as cauliflower, cabbage, Chinese cabbage and broccoli (below) are all nutritious vegetables. They contain a wealth of vitamins and minerals and also contribute some protein to the diet. With the exception of spinach, they are important sources of calcium and iron and they all provide valuable amounts of vitamins C, K and carotene and the B vitamins, folic acid and riboflavin.

is boiled. Cabbage suffers an even worse loss when it is cooked. Raw it has about fifty milligrams of ascorbic acid and three-quarters of this is lost when it is cooked. Winter cabbage and savoys are higher in calcium than cauliflowers or sprouts and all four are rich in potassium.

The most subtle-tasting and least sulphurous brassica is the Chinese cabbage, although it, too, becomes strong in sulphur when it is old and huge. The Chinese have used this vegetable for fifteen centuries, but it is only now beginning to be appreciated in the West. It is equally good raw or briefly cooked, as in pan-frying, to retain its crispness.

The Chinese cabbage is not the only brassica that can suffer at the hands of an unfeeling cook, ending up as a soggy mess of leaves or a mush of curds. Not only are their flavour and texture annihilated, but their nutritional worth is sacrificed. What is needed is a code of conduct for the cooking of cabbage, cauliflower and all of the other brassicas.

The wealth of vitamins and minerals in these vegetables is all too easily lost in preparing them for cooking. Leave their preparation until the last possible moment because vitamin C is lost through oxidation and cutting up the vegetable exposes a greater surface to the air and greatly increases vitamin C losses. Above all, never leave cut vegetables standing in water. All you need do is briskly wash off any possible traces of insecticides. The reason is simple: vitamin C is readily soluble in water and will be leached out and minerals may also be lost.

Never put bicarbonate of soda in the water in which vegetables are to be cooked. Although the bicarbonate may make them stay green, all their vitamin C will be lost in the alkaline water.

Cook vegetables in a minimum of boiling, not cold water. If cold water is used the enzymes which cause oxidation and vitamin loss become very destructive as the temperature rises. Boiling water immediately inactivates these enzymes.

Cover the pan when cooking vegetables in order to cut down on cooking time. Drain them while they still have some bite and as much of their flavour and food value as is possible. There is no danger that they will be indigestible, since most of them are perfectly digestible raw.

Even when you have done everything you can to minimize the loss of vitamins, by the time you serve the vegetables you will probably still have lost up to a half of their vitamin C content and up to forty per cent of their thiamine, riboflavin and niacin content. You will lose still more vitamin C if you do not eat them immediately, but leave them to keep warm on the stove.

For the sake of your taste buds and the good of your health it is worthwhile taking a little extra care in preparing these valuable vegetables.

Brussels Sprouts with Chestnuts

Make a small cut through the shells of
½ pound (250 g) of chestnuts. Put them into a
large saucepan with enough water to cover.
Bring to the boil and cook until the shells
split. Alternatively, the chestnuts may be put
on a baking sheet in the top of a hot oven and
roasted for 5 to 10 minutes, or until the
shells crack.

Drain the chestnuts and peel off the shell
and the inner skin while they are still warm.

Chop ¼ pound (100 g) of bacon and put it
into a large saucepan. Fry for 2 minutes, or
until the fat runs. Add the peeled chestnuts
and fry, stirring constantly, for 3 minutes, or
until they are lightly browned.

Pour in ¼ pint (150 ml) of chicken or
turkey stock. Reduce the heat, cover the pan
and simmer gently for 20 minutes.

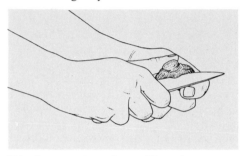

Trim the stem and outer leaves of Brussels sprouts.

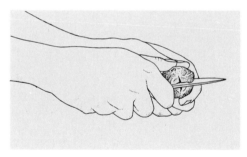

Cut a cross in the stem to ensure even cooking.

Trim and wash 1 pound (500 g) of Brussels
sprouts and add them to the pan. Cover the
pan and continue to simmer over low heat
for 5 to 10 minutes, or until the chestnuts and
sprouts are just tender. (Add more stock if
necessary.) Serve immediately.

INGREDIENTS TO SERVE FOUR TO SIX:
½ lb (250 g) chestnuts
¼ lb (100 g) bacon
¼ pint (150 ml) chicken or turkey stock
1 lb (500 g) Brussels sprouts

Brussels Sprouts and Green Grapes

Trim the outer leaves off 1 pound (500 g) of
Brussels sprouts and wash them thoroughly.
Steam them in about 1 inch (2 cm) of boiling
water for 10 to 12 minutes, or until they are
just done. Season with salt and pepper.

When the sprouts are tender, add ½ pound
(250 g) of seedless green grapes. Cook just
until the grapes look plump and are hot.

Drain the sprouts and grapes well and put
them into a serving bowl. Add 2 tablespoons
(30 ml) of margarine or butter. Toss lightly
until the fat has melted. Serve immediately.

INGREDIENTS TO SERVE FOUR:
1 pound (500 g) Brussels sprouts
salt
pepper
½ pound (250 g) seedless green grapes
**2 tablespoons (30 ml) margarine or
  butter**

Brussels Salad

Trim and wash 1 pound (500 g) of Brussels
sprouts. Put them into a large saucepan with a
little boiling salted water and cook for
5 minutes, or until they are tender but still
crisp. Drain and cool.

Core and slice 2 dessert apples. Toss the
slices immediately in 1 tablespoon (15 ml) of
lemon juice to prevent them from turning
brown. Add to the sprouts.

Chop 2 ounces (50 g) of walnuts and add to
the sprouts.

In a small bowl combine 1 tablespoon
(15 ml) of wine vinegar with 4 tablespoons
(60 ml) of corn oil, salt and freshly ground
black pepper. Pour the dressing over the
salad and toss well.

INGREDIENTS TO SERVE FOUR:
1 lb (500 g) Brussels sprouts
salt
2 dessert apples
1 tablespoon (15 ml) lemon juice
2 oz (50 g) walnuts
1 tablespoon (15 ml) wine vinegar
4 tablespoons (60 ml) corn oil
freshly ground black pepper

Spinach Flan

Preheat the oven to 400°F (200°C, Gas
Mark 6).

Make 6 ounces (150 g) of shortcrust pastry
with wholewheat flour (see page 34). Roll it
out and line an 8-inch (20-cm) flan ring or
dish. Bake the pastry blind for 15 minutes.
Remove the greaseproof paper and the beans
and bake for 5 to 10 minutes more, or until the
pastry is slightly coloured.

Reduce the oven temperature to 350°F
(180°C, Gas Mark 4).

Meanwhile, prepare the filling. Remove
and discard the coarse stalks from 1 pound
(500 g) of spinach. Wash the spinach
thoroughly and put it into a large saucepan

with only the water that clings to the leaves
after washing. Cover the pan and cook over
low heat for 10 minutes, or until the spinach is
tender. Drain the spinach, pressing it down
well with the back of a wooden spoon to
squeeze out all the liquid. Finely chop the
spinach.

Put the chopped spinach into a mixing
bowl with the juice of ½ lemon, ¼ teaspoon
(1 ml) of grated nutmeg, salt and pepper.

In a small bowl beat 2 eggs with
4 tablespoons (60 ml) of yogurt. Stir the egg
mixture into the spinach. Add ½ pound
(250 g) of sieved cottage cheese and
2 tablespoons (30 ml) of grated Parmesan
cheese. Mix well.

Spoon the filling into the pastry case and
level the surface. Bake for 30 minutes, or
until the filling is set and the top is lightly
browned.

INGREDIENTS TO SERVE FOUR TO SIX:
**6 oz (150 g) shortcrust pastry made with
  wholewheat flour (see page 34)**
1 lb (500 g) spinach
½ lemon
¼ teaspoon (1 ml) grated nutmeg
salt
pepper
2 eggs
4 tablespoons (60 ml) yogurt
½ lb (250 g) cottage cheese
**2 tablespoons (30 ml) grated Parmesan
  cheese**

Baked Spinach Parmesan

Preheat the oven to 375°F (190°C, Gas
Mark 5).

Remove the coarse stalks from 1 pound
(500 g) of spinach. Coarsely chop the larger
leaves. Wash the spinach well and put it into
a large saucepan. Cover the pan and cook for
3 minutes, stirring occasionally, until the
spinach is just tender. Drain the spinach
well.

In a mixing bowl beat 3 eggs, then stir in
2 ounces (50 g) of grated Parmesan cheese,
salt and pepper. Stir in the drained spinach.
Spoon the spinach mixture into a shallow
ovenproof dish. Sprinkle with 1 ounce (25 g)
of grated Parmesan cheese. Bake for 10 to
15 minutes, or until the eggs are set.

Serve at once.

INGREDIENTS TO SERVE FOUR:
1 lb (500 g) spinach
3 eggs
3 oz (75 g) grated Parmesan cheese
salt
pepper

Spinach with Bacon and Coconut

Chop ¼ pound (100 g) of streaky bacon. Chop 1 small onion. Remove and discard the coarse stalks from 1 pound (500 g) of spinach. Coarsely chop the large leaves. Wash and drain the spinach thoroughly.

Heat 1 tablespoon (15 ml) of corn oil in a large saucepan. Add the bacon and the onion to the pan and fry over very low heat, stirring frequently, for 5 minutes. Add 2 ounces (50 g) of desiccated coconut. Fry for 1 minute, or until the coconut is beginning to brown. Add the spinach to the pan with 1 tablespoon (15 ml) of lemon juice. Fry over very low heat, stirring frequently, for 3 to 5 minutes, until the spinach is just tender but still bright green. Season to taste with salt and pepper.

Serve immediately.

INGREDIENTS TO SERVE FOUR:
¼ lb (100 g) streaky bacon
1 small onion
1 lb (500 g) spinach
1 tablespoon (15 ml) corn oil
2 oz (50 g) desiccated coconut
1 tablespoon (15 ml) lemon juice
salt
pepper

Spinach Soup

Wash and drain 1 pound (500 g) of spinach. Remove any coarse stalks. Coarsely chop the spinach. Put it into a large saucepan with 1 chopped onion, salt, pepper and ½ teaspoon (2.5 ml) of grated nutmeg. Grate in the rind of ½ lemon then squeeze in the juice. Pour in 1 pint (600 ml) of well-seasoned chicken or vegetable stock. Cover the pan and simmer over low heat for 10 minutes.

Pour the contents of the pan into a liquidizer. Blend until smooth. Return the soup to the pan. Stir in ¼ pint (150 ml) of yogurt. Adjust the seasoning. Reheat, but do not allow the soup to boil or the yogurt might curdle.

Serve the soup hot or chilled, garnished with 4 thin slices of lemon.

INGREDIENTS TO SERVE FOUR:
1 lb (500 g) spinach
1 onion
salt
pepper
½ teaspoon (2.5 ml) grated nutmeg
1 lemon
1 pint (600 ml) chicken or vegetable
    stock
¼ pint (150 ml) yogurt

Raw Spinach Salad

Wash ½ pound (250 g) of young small spinach leaves thoroughly and drain them well. Put them into a salad bowl.

Cut a 3-inch (8-cm) piece of cucumber into thin slices and add them to the spinach.

To make the dressing, heat 2 tablespoons (30 ml) of corn oil in a frying-pan. Add ¼ pound (100 g) of chopped streaky bacon. Fry until the bacon is well done and very crisp. Add the juice of 1 lemon, salt and pepper to the pan. Let the dressing cool slightly, then pour it over the spinach.

Toss the salad well. It may be kept in the refrigerator, covered, for several hours before serving.

INGREDIENTS TO SERVE FOUR:
½ lb (250 g) young small spinach leaves
3-inch (8-cm) piece cucumber
2 tablespoons (30 ml) corn oil
¼ lb (100 g) streaky bacon
1 lemon
salt
pepper

Baked Cabbage

Preheat the oven to 400°F (200°C, Gas Mark 6).

Shred ¾ pound (350 g) of green cabbage. Put half of it into an ovenproof casserole or dish. Spread 5 tablespoons (75 ml) of yogurt over the cabbage. Sprinkle with 2 ounces (50 g) of sultanas, 2 ounces (50 g) of peanuts, salt and pepper.

Put the remaining cabbage into the casserole and cover it with 5 tablespoons (75 ml) more of yogurt.

Sprinkle 2 ounces (50 g) of grated Cheddar cheese and a little grated nutmeg over the top.

Bake for 15 to 20 minutes, or until the top is lightly browned. Serve immediately.

INGREDIENTS TO SERVE FOUR:
¾ lb (350 g) green cabbage
¼ pint (150 ml) yogurt
2 oz (50 g) sultanas
2 oz (50 g) peanuts
salt
pepper
2 oz (50 g) grated Cheddar cheese
grated nutmeg

Stuffed Cabbage Leaves

Preheat the oven to 375°F (190°C, Gas Mark 5).

Take 8 leaves from the outside of a large cabbage and blanch them in boiling salted water for 2 minutes. This should soften the cabbage leaves sufficiently so that they can easily be rolled up around the stuffing.

For the stuffing, heat 1 tablespoon (15 ml) of corn oil in a pan. Add 1 chopped onion and fry gently for 5 minutes. Add ¾ pound (350 g) of minced beef and fry, stirring frequently, until it is brown.

Blanch and peel 4 tomatoes. Cut them into halves and remove the seeds. Coarsely chop the tomatoes and add them to the meat with 1 tablespoon (15 ml) of chopped parsley, a pinch of dried mixed herbs, salt and pepper. Cover the pan, reduce the heat and simmer gently for 15 minutes, stirring occasionally. If the mixture is too liquid, boil, uncovered, for 2 minutes, stirring constantly.

Divide the stuffing between the blanched cabbage leaves. Roll up the leaves around the stuffing, folding in the edges.

Put the stuffed cabbage leaves into a shallow ovenproof dish. Cover the dish and bake for 20 minutes.

Serve immediately with hot tomato sauce (see page 108).

INGREDIENTS TO SERVE FOUR:
8 large cabbage leaves
salt
1 tablespoon (15 ml) corn oil
1 onion
¾ lb (350 g) minced beef
4 tomatoes
1 tablespoon (15 ml) chopped parsley
dried mixed herbs
pepper
tomato sauce (see page 108)

STUFFING CABBAGE LEAVES

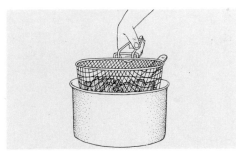

Blanch the leaves in boiling water to soften them.

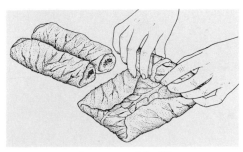

Roll the cabbage leaves around the filling.

Coleslaw

Put ¼ pint (150 ml) of yogurt into a large mixing bowl. Season to taste with salt and pepper.

Finely shred ½ pound (250 g) of white cabbage into the mixing bowl. Grate 2 large carrots and add them to the cabbage.

Cut 2 firm green apples into quarters, core them and cut them into thin slices. Put them into a small bowl with the juice of ½ lemon. Lightly toss the apple in the lemon juice and add to the cabbage with ¼ pound (100 g) of seedless green grapes, 2 ounces (50 g) of coarsely chopped pecan nuts and 2 tablespoons (30 ml) of chopped chives.

Toss well so that all the ingredients are coated with the yogurt.

INGREDIENTS TO SERVE SIX:
¼ pint (150 ml) yogurt
salt
pepper
½ lb (250 g) white cabbage
2 large carrots
2 green apples
½ lemon
¼ lb (100 g) seedless green grapes
2 oz (50 g) pecan nuts
2 tablespoons (30 ml) chopped chives

Cabbage and Apple Soup

Shred ½ pound (250 g) of cabbage and put it into a large saucepan.

Chop 1 large onion and add it to the pan with 1 crushed garlic clove. Peel, core and coarsely chop 1 large tart apple. Add the apple to the pan.

Cut a ¼-inch (6-mm) slice from a piece of root ginger. Peel and finely chop the ginger and add it to the pan. If root ginger is not available, ¼ teaspoon (1 ml) of ground ginger may be substituted.

Pour in 1½ pints (850 ml) of well-seasoned chicken or vegetable stock.

Bring to the boil, cover the pan, reduce the heat and simmer for 10 minutes, or until the cabbage and apple are tender. Liquidize the soup to a purée.

Reheat and serve.

INGREDIENTS TO SERVE FOUR:
½ lb (250 g) cabbage
1 large onion
1 garlic clove
1 large tart apple
root ginger or ¼ teaspoon (1 ml) ground ginger
1½ pints (850 ml) chicken or vegetable stock
salt
pepper

Crisp vegetables and sweet fruit tossed with yogurt, chives and pecans make Coleslaw a winter treat.

Cabbage Casserole

Preheat the oven to 375°F (190°C, Gas Mark 5).

Cut ½ medium-sized white cabbage, about 1 pound (500 g), into 4 to 6 wedges. Put them into a casserole or ovenproof dish.

Thinly slice 1 large carrot and add it to the cabbage with 1 finely chopped onion. Peel, core and slice 1 cooking apple and add it to the casserole. Season with salt and pepper, then pour in ¼ pint (150 ml) of vegetable or chicken stock and 1 tablespoon (15 ml) of wine vinegar.

Cover the casserole and bake for 30 to 40 minutes, or until the cabbage is just tender.

INGREDIENTS TO SERVE FOUR:
½ medium-sized white cabbage
1 large carrot
1 onion
1 cooking apple
salt
pepper
¼ pint (150 ml) vegetable or chicken stock
1 tablespoon (15 ml) wine vinegar

Chinese Cabbage with Bean Sprouts

Chop 1 large onion. Shred 1 pound (500 g) of Chinese cabbage. Blanch and peel 2 tomatoes and cut them into quarters.

Heat 1 tablespoon (15 ml) of peanut oil in a large, heavy frying-pan. Add the chopped onion and fry over high heat, stirring constantly, for 2 minutes.

Add the Chinese cabbage to the pan and stir-fry for 2 minutes. Add the tomatoes, ¼ pound (100 g) of bean sprouts, 1 tablespoon (15 ml) of soy sauce and pepper to taste.

Braised Broccoli with Brazil nuts and anchovies is an unusual and appetizing vegetable dish.

Stir-fry for 2 minutes more, or until the cabbage is just tender, but still crisp.

Serve immediately.

INGREDIENTS TO SERVE FOUR:
1 large onion
1 lb (500 g) Chinese cabbage
2 tomatoes
1 tablespoon (15 ml) peanut oil
¼ lb (100 g) bean sprouts
1 tablespoon (15 ml) soy sauce
pepper

Braised Broccoli

Divide 1½ pounds (700 g) of broccoli into spears. Wash them well and put into a large saucepan.

Add 2 ounces (50 g) of anchovy fillets to the broccoli. Cut 2 ounces (50 g) of shelled Brazil nuts into ¼-inch (6-mm) slices and add them to the pan with 8 stuffed olives. Pour in ¼ pint (150 ml) of chicken or vegetable stock.

Bring to the boil. Reduce the heat, cover the pan and simmer gently for 5 to 10 minutes, or until the broccoli is just tender.

Lift out the broccoli and arrange it on a warm serving dish. Boil the stock rapidly for a couple of minutes to reduce it and then pour it over the broccoli.

Serve immediately.

INGREDIENTS TO SERVE FOUR:
1½ lb (700 g) broccoli
2 oz (50 g) anchovy fillets
2 oz (50 g) shelled Brazil nuts
8 stuffed olives
¼ pint (150 ml) chicken or vegetable stock

Baked Broccoli

Preheat the oven to 375°F (190°C, Gas Mark 5).

Divide 1½ pounds (700 g) of broccoli into spears, or florets, wash well and put into a large saucepan. Pour in ¼ pint (150 ml) of water and sprinkle with salt and pepper. Bring to the boil. Cover the pan, reduce the heat and simmer gently for 5 to 10 minutes, or until the broccoli is tender but still crisp.

Drain the broccoli and arrange it in an ovenproof dish.

Mix ¼ pint (150 ml) of yogurt with 1 beaten egg, 1 tablespoon (15 ml) of grated Parmesan cheese, salt and pepper. Pour the yogurt sauce over the broccoli and sprinkle with 1 tablespoon (15 ml) more of grated Parmesan cheese.

Bake for 15 to 20 minutes, or until the sauce is bubbling and lightly browned on top.

INGREDIENTS TO SERVE FOUR:
1½ lb (700 g) broccoli
salt
pepper
¼ pint (150 ml) yogurt
1 egg
**2 tablespoons (30 ml) grated Parmesan
  cheese**

Roman Broccoli

Cauliflower may also be cooked in this way.

Chop 1 large onion. Heat 1 tablespoon (15 ml) of olive oil in a large saucepan. Add the onion with 1 crushed garlic clove to the pan and fry for 3 minutes.

Blanch and peel ½ pound (250 g) of tomatoes. Slice the tomatoes and add to the onions. Pour ¼ pint (150 ml) of well-seasoned chicken or vegetable stock into the pan. Add 1 tablespoon (15 ml) of chopped oregano, marjoram or basil. Bring to the boil and simmer for 2 minutes. Stir in 8 stuffed olives.

Divide 1 medium-sized broccoli head into large florets, wash well and add to the pan. Cover the pan and simmer for 5 to 10 minutes, or until the broccoli is tender.

Sprinkle with 1 tablespoon (15 ml) of chopped parsley and serve immediately.

INGREDIENTS TO SERVE FOUR:
1 large onion
1 tablespoon (15 ml) olive oil
1 garlic clove
½ lb (250 g) tomatoes
**¼ pint (150 ml) chicken or vegetable
  stock**
**1 tablespoon (15 ml) chopped oregano,
  marjoram or basil**
8 stuffed olives
1 medium-sized broccoli head
1 tablespoon (15 ml) chopped parsley

Cauliflower au Gratin

Divide 1 medium-sized cauliflower into large florets, wash well and put them into a saucepan. Pour in ½ pint (300 ml) of water and season with salt and pepper. Bring to the boil. Cover the pan, reduce the heat and simmer for 5 to 10 minutes, or until the cauliflower is tender but still crisp.

Drain the cauliflower, reserving the liquor. Arrange the cauliflower in a warm ovenproof dish and keep hot. Add enough milk to the cooking liquor to bring it up to ½ pint (300 ml).

For the sauce, chop 2 ounces (50 g) of bacon. Heat 1 ounce (25 g) of margarine in a saucepan. Add the bacon and 1 chopped small onion to the pan and fry for 3 minutes. Add 1 ounce (25 g) of split blanched almonds and continue to fry until the almonds are lightly browned. Stir in 2 tablespoons (30 ml) of flour. Still stirring, gradually add the reserved liquor and milk. Bring to the boil, stirring constantly, and continue to cook until the sauce is thick and smooth. Add 2 ounces (50 g) of grated mature Cheddar cheese. Remove the pan from the heat and stir until the cheese has melted.

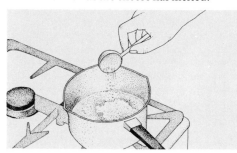

Stir flour rapidly into the melted fat.

Stirring briskly gradually add the liquid.

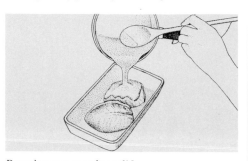

Pour the sauce over the cauliflower.

Season the sauce with salt and pepper. Pour it over the cauliflower. Sprinkle with 1 ounce (25 g) more of grated mature Cheddar cheese.

Put the dish under a hot grill for 2 to 3 minutes, or until the sauce is bubbling and golden brown on top.

INGREDIENTS TO SERVE FOUR:
1 medium-sized cauliflower
salt
pepper
milk
2 oz (50 g) bacon
1 oz (25 g) margarine
1 small onion
1 oz (25 g) split blanched almonds
2 tablespoons (30 ml) flour
**3 oz (75 g) grated mature Cheddar
  cheese**

Cream of Cauliflower Soup

Discard the outside leaves and the base of the stalk of 1 small cauliflower. Cut and coarsely chop the remaining stalk and leaves. Divide the cauliflower into small florets and put them into a saucepan with the chopped leaves and stalk. Pour in 1 pint (600 ml) of well-seasoned chicken or vegetable stock and ½ pint (300 ml) of milk. Grate in the rind of ½ lemon and squeeze in the juice. Add a pinch of grated nutmeg and salt and pepper to taste.

Bring to the boil. Cover the pan, reduce the heat and simmer for 10 to 15 minutes, or until the cauliflower is tender. Reserving a few cauliflower florets for garnish, pour the rest into a liquidizer and blend to a smooth purée. Return the soup to the pan and reheat.

Garnish with 1 tablespoon (15 ml) of chopped parsley and the reserved cauliflower florets. Serve hot.

INGREDIENTS TO SERVE FOUR:
1 small cauliflower
**1 pint (600 ml) chicken or vegetable
  stock**
½ pint (300 ml) milk
½ lemon
grated nutmeg
salt
pepper
1 tablespoon (15 ml) chopped parsley

Cauliflower, Mushroom and Ham Salad

This crisp salad with a mustard dressing may be served as a light main dish or as an hors d'oeuvre.

Divide 1 small cauliflower into small florets. Wash well and drain.

Slice 2 ounces (50 g) of button mushrooms and put them into a bowl with the drained cauliflower. Chop ¼ pound (100 g) of cooked sliced ham and add it to the cauliflower.

For the dressing, whisk 2 tablespoons (30 ml) of wine vinegar with 5 tablespoons (75 ml) of corn oil and 2 teaspoons (10 ml) of French mustard. Stir in 1 tablespoon (15 ml) of finely chopped chives. Season to taste with salt and freshly ground black pepper. Pour the dressing over the salad.

Toss the salad and leave to marinate for at least 30 minutes before serving.

INGREDIENTS TO SERVE FOUR :
1 small cauliflower
2 oz (50 g) button mushrooms
¼ lb (100 g) cooked sliced ham
2 tablespoons (30 ml) wine vinegar
5 tablespoons (75 ml) corn oil
2 teaspoons (10 ml) French mustard
1 tablespoon (15 ml) chopped chives
salt
freshly ground black pepper

Gado Gado

This mixed vegetable salad is an Indonesian speciality. The lightly cooked vegetables are served cold with a peanut sauce.

Cook the following vegetables separately in a little water, until they are tender but still crisp : ½ pound (250 g) of chopped white cabbage, ½ pound (250 g) of spinach, ½ pound (250 g) of cauliflower florets, ½ pound (250 g) of sliced carrots. Drain the vegetables and leave them to cool.

Hard boil 2 eggs. Let them cool. Peel and slice them.

Put a layer of each vegetable into a salad bowl. Top with 2 ounces (50 g) of bean sprouts and then put the hard-boiled egg slices on top. Pour over ½ pint (300 ml) of peanut sauce (see pork saté, page 200). Sprinkle with 1 ounce (25 g) of desiccated coconut.

INGREDIENTS TO SERVE FOUR TO SIX :
½ lb (250 g) white cabbage
½ lb (250 g) spinach
½ lb (250 g) cauliflower florets
½ lb (250 g) carrots
2 eggs
2 oz (50 g) bean sprouts
½ pint (300 ml) peanut sauce (see pork saté, page 200)
1 oz (25 g) desiccated coconut

Pickled Cauliflower and Cabbage

A good accompaniment to cold meats, this cauliflower and cabbage pickle will keep for up to 1 month.

Cut 1 medium-sized cauliflower into small florets and wash well. Coarsely shred ½ pound (250 g) of red cabbage.

Fill two 2-pound (1-kg) kilner jars with layers of cauliflower florets, red cabbage and the leaves of 8 sticks of celery. Sprinkle 2 teaspoons (10 ml) of salt into each jar. Pour ¼ pint (150 ml) of wine vinegar into each jar. Fill up the jars with water.

Seal the jars and leave at room temperature for 1 week to mature.

INGREDIENTS TO MAKE FOUR POUNDS (2 KG) OF PICKLE :
1 medium-sized cauliflower
½ lb (250 g) red cabbage
celery leaves
4 teaspoons (20 ml) salt
½ pint (300 ml) wine vinegar

PREPARING CAULIFLOWER AND CABBAGE

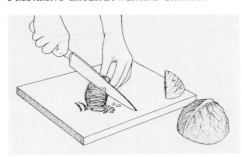

Coarsely shred cabbage using a sharp knife.

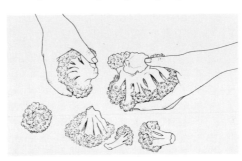

Divide cauliflower into florets.

Lemon and Herb Cauliflower

Remove and coarsely chop the leaves from 1 medium-sized cauliflower. Divide the cauliflower into large florets.

Put the florets and the chopped leaves into a large saucepan. Pour in ¼ pint (150 ml) of boiling water and 1 tablespoon (15 ml) of lemon juice. Sprinkle with salt and pepper.

Cover the pan and simmer over low heat for 5 to 8 minutes or until the cauliflower is tender but still crisp.

Remove the cauliflower to a warm serving dish and keep hot. Boil the cooking liquor rapidly for 2 minutes, or until it is reduced to 4 tablespoons (60 ml). Stir in 1 tablespoon (15 ml) of chopped parsley and 1 tablespoon (15 ml) of chopped chives. Pour the liquor over the cauliflower.

Serve immediately.

INGREDIENTS TO SERVE FOUR :
1 medium-sized cauliflower
1 tablespoon (15 ml) lemon juice
salt
pepper
1 tablespoon (15 ml) chopped parsley
1 tablespoon (15 ml) chopped chives

Cauliflower in Cider

Divide 1 medium-sized cauliflower into large florets. Wash the florets and put them into a saucepan. Pour ½ pint (300 ml) of dry cider over the florets and sprinkle them with salt and pepper. Bring to the boil, cover the pan and simmer for 5 to 10 minutes, or until the cauliflower is tender.

Drain the florets, reserving the cooking cider and arrange them in a warm ovenproof dish. Keep hot.

For the sauce, chop 2 ounces (50 g) of bacon. Put 1 ounce (25 g) of margarine into a saucepan with the bacon and fry until the bacon is crisp. Stir in 2 tablespoons (30 ml) of flour. Bring the cooking cider up to ½ pint (300 ml) with more cider or milk and add it to the saucepan.

Bring to the boil, stirring constantly. Continue to cook, stirring, until the sauce is thick and smooth. Season to taste with salt, pepper and grated nutmeg.

Pour the sauce over the cauliflower and serve immediately.

INGREDIENTS TO SERVE FOUR :
1 medium-sized cauliflower
dry cider
salt
pepper
2 oz (50 g) bacon
1 oz (25 g) margarine
2 tablespoons (30 ml) flour
grated nutmeg

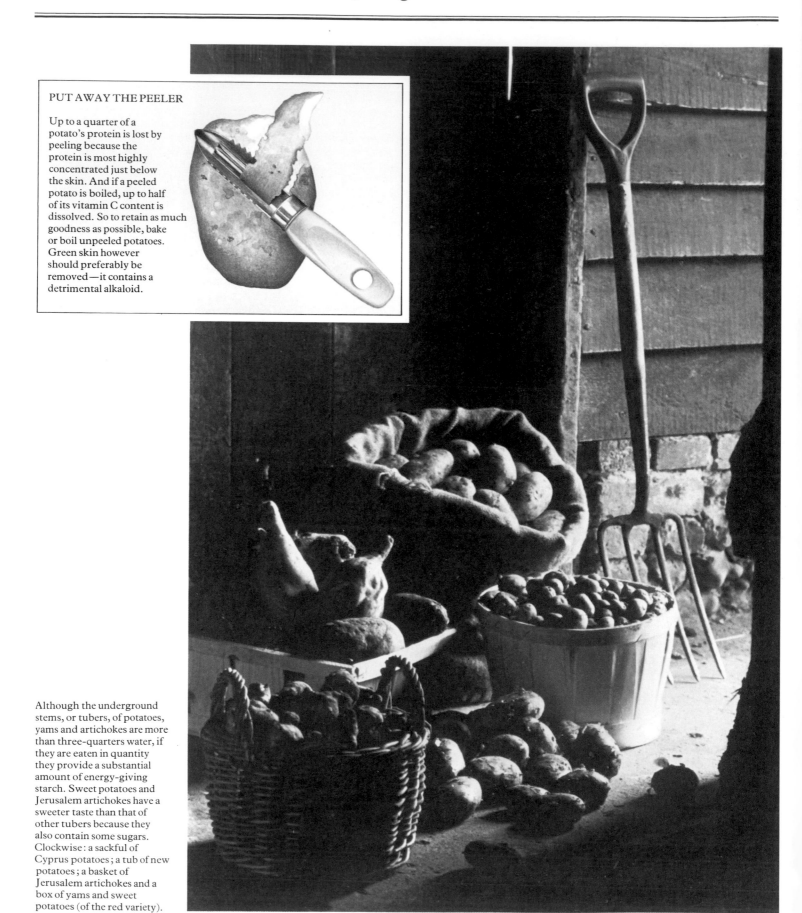

PUT AWAY THE PEELER

Up to a quarter of a potato's protein is lost by peeling because the protein is most highly concentrated just below the skin. And if a peeled potato is boiled, up to half of its vitamin C content is dissolved. So to retain as much goodness as possible, bake or boil unpeeled potatoes. Green skin however should preferably be removed—it contains a detrimental alkaloid.

Although the underground stems, or tubers, of potatoes, yams and artichokes are more than three-quarters water, if they are eaten in quantity they provide a substantial amount of energy-giving starch. Sweet potatoes and Jerusalem artichokes have a sweeter taste than that of other tubers because they also contain some sugars. Clockwise: a sackful of Cyprus potatoes; a tub of new potatoes; a basket of Jerusalem artichokes and a box of yams and sweet potatoes (of the red variety).

THE POTATO, having gone through a period of nutritional disgrace, has been rehabilitated. It is now bread, which has three times as many calories, that is taking the blame for putting extra inches on our waistlines.

Although the potato has been a familiar food since the first century AD, wherever it has been introduced it has taken a long time to become accepted. It was brought to Europe from its original home in South America by Spanish conquerors in the second half of the sixteenth century. But more than a century passed before it became widely eaten in the British Isles; the Scots and Irish at first rejected it because it was not mentioned in the Bible. By the end of the eighteenth century, however, it had become one of the major crops not only of Ireland but of continental Europe.

Poverty and the potato have often gone together, and as standards of living have risen people have turned to other foods. But in wartime when food is scarce, potatoes have always come into their own. Today, even in the midst of peaceful affluence the potato, which is a valuable source of vitamin C, is an important part of the diet.

Like many other foods the potato has been assailed by technology. It has been washed and prepacked mechanically, canned, turned into crisps, frozen chips and instant mash (for which credit, if that is the word, is claimed by the Eastern Research Center of the United States Agriculture Department at Wyndmoor, Pennsylvania).

Potatoes have suffered even more at the hands of farmers. Of the hundred or so varieties that are theoretically available in England, ten provide almost all of the commercial crop, and excellence of flavour is generally the least of the farmer's reasons for growing them.

One of the most widely grown varieties is Majestic, which has been around for sixty-six years. It crops well and keeps satisfactorily, and little else can be said for it. The tubers are given to cracking, their texture is soapy, their flavour insipid and they tend to go black when boiled. Newer varieties have recently been challenging Majestic, but they taste little better, while many established varieties with superior texture and flavour have gone out of commercial cultivation altogether because they crop less profitably.

To the drawback of poor flavour of the potatoes you buy must be added the damage done by mechanical harvesting. One potato in every five is damaged, according to a British survey. The potatoes get a further battering when they are washed and prepacked. Buying the "convenience" of prepacked potatoes is folly—their bruises turn black and have to be cut away and in the humid atmosphere inside the plastic bag the potatoes quickly go bad and the skins become green and

toxic as the result of exposure to the light.

The English and the Irish prefer starchy, floury potatoes, while the French like them waxy. The preferences are related not to nationality, but to different methods of cooking, whether it is done in fat or oil or in water. The English traditionally bake potatoes in their jackets, or mash or boil them (the French call boiled potatoes Pommes à l'anglaise) and for this they need floury potatoes. But the French are fonder of potatoes cooked in oil or butter, and for this waxy potatoes are best. That is the simple choice, but shoppers are often denied it. Vegetable gardeners do, however, have a choice, and as they cook so should they grow. A few varieties—floury, waxy, early and maincrop—would be adequate for the five hundred or so ways potatoes can be cooked.

The sweet potato, which is the tuberous root of a tropical vine, is unrelated to the common potato and is altogether different. Its flesh is yellow, sweet and faintly scented. Nutritionally it is useful for its carotene and vitamin C content, but amounts of these vary considerably. The sweet potato arrived in Europe in the sixteenth century and the buccaneering Sir Francis Drake, who brought it to Britain, thought it more delicious than the sweetest apple. In spite of such sponsorship it never became popular in Britain, although the West Indian immigrants have been more successful in reintroducing it. In France, where sweet potatoes had Louis XV and the Empress Josephine as royal patrons, they have fared a little better, although not as well as in Spain. They are popular in America, especially in the South, and in Creole cookery.

Some tubers which are sold as yams in the United States are in fact a variety of sweet potatoes. The true yams, which are an important food in parts of West Africa, Vietnam and Cambodia, are the tubers of a family of climbing plants which are grouped together on the basis that some species twine anti-clockwise when climbing and some twine clockwise. One way or the other their nutritional value is similar to other tubers; they are starchy vegetables that contain little protein but useful amounts of carotene and vitamin C.

There are two other tubers that are somewhat alike in flavour and texture although they come from opposite ends of the world. One is the Jerusalem artichoke, which is not an artichoke and which comes from North America, and the other is the Chinese (or Japanese) artichoke, which although also not an artichoke does come from China. Jerusalem artichokes look like tormented potatoes and Chinese artichokes have been described as looking like petrified worms. In spite of their shape they have a pleasantly sweet flavour, which in winter is a reminder of the flavour of the globe artichokes of summer.

The Nutrients in Potatoes
Potatoes provide useful amounts of starch, vitamin C, thiamine and niacin, and three and a half ounces (100 g) provide about 80 Calories.

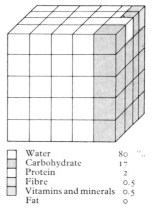

Water	80	"₀
Carbohydrate	17	
Protein	2	
Fibre	0.5	
Vitamins and minerals	0.5	
Fat	0	

Herb Baked New Potatoes

Preheat the oven to 400°F (200°C, Gas Mark 6).

Scrub 1½ pounds (700 g) of new potatoes, but do not peel them.

Grease a sheet of aluminium foil large enough to enclose the potatoes. Put the potatoes into the centre and sprinkle them with salt and freshly ground black pepper. Put 4 mint sprigs and 4 parsley sprigs among the potatoes. Fold the foil around the potatoes and seal the edges.

Bake for 30 to 45 minutes, depending on the size of the potatoes, or until they are tender.

Remove the potatoes from the foil and put them in a serving dish. Sprinkle with 1 tablespoon (15 ml) of chopped mint and 1 tablespoon (15 ml) of parsley.

INGREDIENTS TO SERVE FOUR:
1½ lb (700 g) new potatoes
salt
freshly ground black pepper
1 small mint bunch
1 small parsley bunch

Piquant New Potato Salad

Scrub but do not peel 1½ pounds (700 g) of small new potatoes. Cook them in boiling salted water until they are just tender.

Meanwhile make the dressing. In a small mixing bowl combine 4 tablespoons (60 ml) of corn oil with 1 tablespoon (15 ml) of wine vinegar. Add 1 tablespoon (15 ml) of capers, 1 tablespoon (15 ml) of chopped gherkins, 1 tablespoon (15 ml) of chopped parsley and salt and pepper to taste. Mix well.

Drain the potatoes and put them into a salad bowl. Cut the larger potatoes into halves or quarters. Pour the dressing over the potatoes while they are still hot. Toss lightly but well.

Grill 2 ounces (50 g) of bacon until it is very crisp. Let the bacon cool, then crumble it over the potatoes.

Serve the salad warm or cold.

INGREDIENTS TO SERVE FOUR:
1½ lb (700 g) new potatoes
salt
4 tablespoons (60 ml) corn oil
1 tablespoon (15 ml) wine vinegar
1 tablespoon (15 ml) capers
1 tablespoon (15 ml) chopped gherkins
1 tablespoon (15 ml) chopped parsley
pepper
2 oz (50 g) bacon

Potato and Tuna Salad

This tasty dish can be served as a starter or as a main dish.

Scrub 1 pound (500 g) of potatoes. Put them into a saucepan with 1 pint (600 ml) of boiling salted water and cook them until they are just tender. Drain well. Let the potatoes cool, then slice them thickly into a salad bowl.

Coarsely flake 8 ounces (250 g) of tuna fish and add to the potatoes. Wash and thinly slice 2 ounces (50 g) of mushrooms and add them to the salad with 8 sliced stuffed olives.

For the dressing, mix ¼ pint (150 ml) of yogurt with the grated rind and juice of 1 lemon, 1 tablespoon (15 ml) of chopped parsley, salt and pepper. Pour over the salad and toss lightly.

INGREDIENTS TO SERVE FOUR TO SIX:
1 lb (500 g) potatoes
8 oz (250 g) tuna fish
2 oz (50 g) mushrooms
8 stuffed olives
¼ pint (150 ml) yogurt
1 lemon
1 tablespoon (15 ml) chopped parsley
salt
pepper

Potatoes Baked with Salami

Preheat the oven to 375°F (190°C, Gas Mark 5).

Peel 1½ pounds (700 g) of potatoes and cut them into thin slices. Slice ½ pound (250 g) of tomatoes. Thinly slice ¼ pound (100 g) of salami.

In a casserole or ovenproof dish arrange the potatoes in layers with the tomatoes and salami. Season each layer with salt and pepper.

Cover and bake for 1 hour, or until the potatoes are tender.

Serve hot.

INGREDIENTS TO SERVE FOUR:
1½ lb (700 g) potatoes
½ lb (250 g) tomatoes
¼ lb (100 g) salami
salt
pepper

Scalloped Potatoes with Yogurt

Preheat the oven to 400°F (200°C, Gas Mark 6).

Peel and thinly slice 1½ pounds (700 g) of potatoes.

Finely chop or grate 1 small onion. In a small bowl mix the onion with salt, pepper and ½ pint (300 ml) of yogurt.

Layer the potato slices in a casserole, spreading each layer with the yogurt mixture.

Arrange the top layer of potatoes attractively in overlapping circles, then spread with the remaining yogurt.

Cover and bake for 30 minutes. Uncover and bake for 30 minutes more, or until the potatoes are cooked and the top is crisp and brown.

Serve hot.

INGREDIENTS TO SERVE FOUR:
1½ lb (700 g) potatoes
1 small onion
salt
pepper
½ pint (300 ml) yogurt

Potato and Carrot Boulangère

Preheat the oven to 400°F (200°C, Gas Mark 6).

Peel and thinly slice 1 pound (500 g) of potatoes. Wash and thinly slice ½ pound (250 g) of carrots. Thinly slice 1 small onion and divide the slices into rings. Finely chop 2 ounces (50 g) of streaky bacon.

In a casserole arrange the potatoes, carrots, onion, bacon and 3 ounces (75 g) of grated or sliced Gruyère cheese, salt and pepper in alternate layers. Finish with a layer of potato.

Pour in ½ pint (300 ml) of well-seasoned chicken stock. Cover and bake for 30 minutes. Uncover, brush the top with corn oil and bake for 30 minutes more, or until the potatoes are cooked and brown on top.

Serve hot.

INGREDIENTS TO SERVE FOUR:
1 lb (500 g) potatoes
½ lb (250 g) carrots
1 small onion
2 oz (50 g) streaky bacon
3 oz (75 g) Gruyère cheese
salt
pepper
½ pint (300 ml) chicken stock
corn oil

Potatoes à l'Orange

Preheat the oven to 375°F (190°C, Gas Mark 5).

Peel 1½ pounds (700 g) of potatoes and cut them into thin slices. Arrange half of the potatoes in a casserole or ovenproof dish.

Grate the rind of 1 orange over the potatoes, then squeeze in the juice. Cut the peel and pith from another orange and, working over the casserole to catch any juice, cut the membrane away from the segments of fruit. Arrange the orange segments on top of the potatoes. Sprinkle with 1 ounce (25 g) of blanched almonds, 1 chopped spring onion, salt and pepper.

Arrange the remaining potato slices on top.

Sprinkle with 1 ounce (25 g) of blanched almonds, 1 chopped spring onion, salt and pepper. Squeeze in the juice of 1 more orange.

Cover and bake for 1 hour, or until the potatoes are tender.

INGREDIENTS TO SERVE FOUR:
1½ lb (700 g) potatoes
3 oranges
2 oz (50 g) blanched almonds
2 spring onions
salt
pepper

Duchesse Potatoes with Parsnips

These whirls of creamed potato and parsnip may be made in advance and reheated just before serving. The parsnips add sweetness to the potatoes, but the dish may be made only with potatoes.

Peel and thickly slice ¾ pound (350 g) of potatoes. Peel and thickly slice ¾ pound (350 g) of parsnips. Put the potatoes and the parsnips into a saucepan with ½ pint (300 ml) of salted water. Cover the pan and bring to the boil. Reduce the heat and simmer for about 20 minutes, or until the potatoes and parsnips are tender.

Preheat the oven to 400 F (200 C, Gas Mark 6).

Drain the vegetables well, then mash them to a smooth purée.

In a small bowl beat 1 egg with salt and pepper. Add to the potato and parsnip purée and beat well.

Let the purée cool slightly, then spoon it into a piping bag fitted with a large star nozzle. Pipe whirls of potato on to a lightly greased baking sheet. Top each whirl with a blanched almond.

Bake for 10 to 15 minutes until heated through and golden brown. Alternatively the potatoes may be made in advance, piped and then stored until needed.

INGREDIENTS TO SERVE FOUR:
¾ lb (350 g) potatoes
¾ lb (350 g) parsnips
1 egg
salt
pepper
blanched almonds

Baked Cheese Soufflé Potatoes

Preheat the oven to 400 F (200 C, Gas Mark 6).

Scrub 2 very large potatoes, or 4 smaller potatoes, about 1½ pounds (700 g). Bake for 1 to 1½ hours, depending on the size, or until the potatoes are cooked and soft when pressed.

Cut large potatoes in half or cut a slice off the top of smaller potatoes. Scoop the cooked potato out of the centres leaving shells about ¼ inch (6 mm) thick. Mash the potato.

Separate 2 eggs into 2 mixing bowls. Beat the egg yolks slightly then stir in the mashed potato, 2 ounces (50 g) of grated strong Cheddar cheese, 2 chopped spring onions, a pinch of grated nutmeg, salt and pepper.

Whisk the egg whites until they are stiff and fold into the cheese and potato mixture. Spoon the mixture back into the potato skins. Put the stuffed potatoes on a lightly greased baking sheet. Bake for 15 to 20 minutes, or until the filling has risen and is golden brown on top. Serve at once.

INGREDIENTS TO SERVE FOUR:
2 large or 4 smaller potatoes
2 eggs
2 oz (50 g) strong Cheddar cheese
2 spring onions
grated nutmeg
salt
pepper

STUFFING POTATOES

Scoop the cooked potato from the skin.

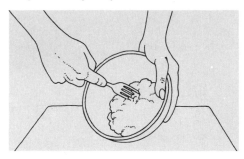

Mash the potato well.

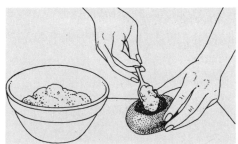

Spoon the filling back into the potato skin.

Potatoes Braised in Red Wine

Preheat the oven to 375 F (190 C, Gas Mark 5).

Peel 1½ pounds (700 g) of potatoes and cut them into ¼-inch (6-mm) slices. Put the potatoes into a casserole or ovenproof dish and pour in ½ pint (300 ml) of dry red wine.

Sprinkle with 2 tablespoons (30 ml) of chopped thyme, 2 tablespoons (30 ml) of chopped parsley, salt and pepper. Mix lightly so that all the potatoes are coated with wine and herbs.

Cover and bake for about 1 hour, or until the potatoes are tender and almost all the wine has been absorbed. The potatoes will be a delicate pink colour on the outside but still white inside.

Serve hot.

INGREDIENTS TO SERVE FOUR:
1½ lb (700 g) potatoes
½ pint (300 ml) dry red wine
2 tablespoons (30 ml) chopped thyme
2 tablespoons (30 ml) chopped parsley
salt
pepper

Aubergine and Potato Casserole

Cut 2 medium-sized aubergines into thin slices. Spread the slices on a plate and sprinkle them liberally with salt. Leave for at least 30 minutes. Wash the slices and drain them well.

Preheat the oven to 375 F (190 C, Gas Mark 5).

Peel 1 pound (500 g) of potatoes and cut them into thin slices. Grate 1 small onion. Grate ¼ pound (100 g) of Gruyère cheese.

In an ovenproof casserole arrange layers of the potato and aubergine slices, sprinkling each layer with a little of the grated onion, Gruyère cheese and salt and pepper. Arrange the top layer so that there are alternate slices of potato and aubergine overlapping in a circle.

Pour in ¼ pint (150 ml) of chicken or vegetable stock.

Brush the top with 1 tablespoon (15 ml) of corn oil.

Bake the casserole for 1 hour, or until the vegetables are tender and the top is brown.

INGREDIENTS TO SERVE FOUR:
2 medium-sized aubergines
salt
1 lb (500 g) potatoes
1 small onion
¼ lb (100 g) Gruyère cheese
pepper
¼ pint (150 ml) chicken or vegetable stock
1 tablespoon (15 ml) corn oil

Irish Potato Cakes

Preheat the oven to 425°F (220°C, Gas Mark 7). Lightly grease a baking sheet.

Peel and slice 1 pound (500 g) of potatoes. Put them into a saucepan with boiling salted water to cover. Simmer for 15 minutes, or until the potatoes are tender. Drain the potatoes and mash them well.

Add to the mashed potatoes 2 teaspoons (10 ml) of chopped sage, 2 chopped spring onions, 1 teaspoon (5 ml) of salt and freshly ground black pepper. Stir in ¼ pound (100 g) of self-raising flour. Mix well. Add a little more flour if necessary to make a soft dough that will roll out.

On a lightly floured surface roll out the potato dough to a 7-inch (18-cm) round. Cut it into 8 wedges and put them on the baking sheet.

Bake for 20 minutes, or until the cakes have risen and are crisp and golden brown. Alternatively, the cakes may be fried in a lightly greased pan until they are brown on both sides. Serve hot.

INGREDIENTS TO SERVE FOUR:
1 lb (500 g) potatoes
salt
2 teaspoons (10 ml) chopped sage
2 spring onions
freshly ground black pepper
¼ lb (100 g) self-raising flour

Shepherd's Pie

This recipe specifies raw minced beef, but lean chopped or sliced left-over beef or lamb may be used. The pie can be prepared in advance and baked just before serving.

Put 2 chopped rashers of streaky bacon into a saucepan and fry over low heat until the fat runs. Add 1 chopped onion and ½ pound (250 g) of thinly sliced carrots to the pan. Continue to fry gently, stirring occasionally, for 3 minutes. Add ¼ pound (100 g) of sliced mushrooms and cook for 2 minutes more. Add 1 pound (500 g) of minced beef and fry, stirring constantly, until the meat has browned.

Stir in 1 tablespoon (15 ml) of flour. Stirring constantly, add 1 tablespoon (15 ml) of tomato purée and gradually pour in ¼ pint (150 ml) of beef stock and bring to the boil.

Reduce the heat and simmer gently for 20 to 30 minutes, or until the meat is tender. Season to taste with salt and pepper. Transfer the meat mixture to an ovenproof dish.

Preheat the oven to 375°F (190°C, Gas Mark 5).

Meanwhile, peel and coarsely chop 1½ pounds (700 g) of potatoes. Put the potatoes into a saucepan with enough cold salted water to cover. Bring to the boil and cook for 15 to 20 minutes, or until the potatoes are tender. Drain the potatoes. Add a little milk, margarine, salt and pepper and mash them well.

Spread the mashed potatoes over the meat mixture and level the surface with a fork. Bake for 25 to 30 minutes, or until the potato is crisp and brown on top.

INGREDIENTS TO SERVE FOUR:
2 streaky bacon rashers
1 onion
½ lb (250 g) carrots
¼ lb (100 g) mushrooms
1 lb (500 g) minced beef
1 tablespoon (15 ml) flour
1 tablespoon (15 ml) tomato purée
¼ pint (150 ml) beef stock
salt
pepper
1½ lb (700 g) potatoes
milk
margarine

Potato Soup

Peel 1 pound (500 g) of potatoes, slice them and put them into a large saucepan. Chop 1 large onion and add it to the pan with 2 sprigs of thyme, ¼ teaspoon (1 ml) of grated nutmeg and salt and pepper.

Pour in 1½ pints (850 ml) of well-seasoned beef stock. Cover the pan and bring to the boil. Reduce the heat and simmer for 30 minutes, or until the potatos are tender. Liquidize or sieve the soup to a purée. Return the soup to the pan, reheat and adjust the seasoning.

Serve hot, sprinkled with 2 tablespoons

Press cooked vegetables through a sieve to purée.

(30 ml) of grated Parmesan cheese and 1 tablespoon (15 ml) of chopped chives.

INGREDIENTS TO SERVE FOUR:
1 lb (500 g) potatoes
1 large onion
2 thyme sprigs
¼ teaspoon (1 ml) grated nutmeg
salt
pepper
1½ pints (850 ml) beef stock
2 tablespoons (30 ml) grated Parmesan cheese
1 tablespoon (15 ml) chopped chives

Vichysoisse

Peel and chop ½ pound (250 g) of onions and put them into a large saucepan. Trim 1 pound (500 g) of leeks. Cut them into thin slices. Wash them thoroughly and add them to the pan. Peel and dice 1 pound (500 g) of potatoes and add them to the pan.

Pour in 2 pints (1 litre) of well-seasoned chicken stock, the grated rind and juice of ½ lemon and salt and pepper to taste. Bring to the boil, cover the pan, reduce the heat and simmer for 30 minutes, or until the vegetables are tender.

Liquidize the soup or sieve it to a purée. Stir in ¼ pint (150 ml) of milk or single cream. Adjust the seasoning.

Chill well before serving.

INGREDIENTS TO SERVE SIX:
½ lb (250 g) onions
1 lb (500 g) leeks
1 lb (500 g) potatoes
2 pints (1 litre) chicken stock
½ lemon
salt
pepper
¼ pint (150 ml) milk or single cream

Stuffed Jacket Potatoes

Preheat the oven to 400°F (200°C, Gas Mark 5).

Scrub 4 large potatoes. With a sharp knife score them around the middle lengthways. Bake the potatoes for 50 to 60 minutes, or until they are cooked.

Cut the potatoes into halves lengthways and carefully scoop the potato out of the skins into a mixing bowl. Reserve the skins. Mash the potato well.

Grill or fry 2 ounces (50 g) of bacon until crisp. Drain well and then crumble the bacon into the mashed potato. Stir ½ pound (250 g) of cottage cheese, 2 tablespoons (30 ml) of chopped chives or spring onions, 1 tablespoon (15 ml) of chopped parsley, salt and pepper into the potatoes. Add enough milk to bind the ingredients together and mix well.

Spoon the stuffing back into the reserved potato skins and sprinkle 2 ounces (50 g) of grated Cheddar cheese over them.

Return the stuffed potatoes to the oven for 10 to 15 minutes, or until brown on top.

INGREDIENTS TO SERVE FOUR:
4 large potatoes
2 oz (50 g) bacon
½ lb (250 g) cottage cheese
2 tablespoons (30 ml) chopped chives or spring onions
1 tablespoon (15 ml) chopped parsley
salt
pepper
milk
2 oz (50 g) Cheddar cheese

Normandy Sweet Potatoes

This sweet potato dish is particularly good served with pork.

Preheat the oven to 350°F (180°C, Gas Mark 4).

Peel and thinly slice 1 pound (500 g) of sweet potatoes. Peel, core and thickly slice 1 large cooking apple.

In a small bowl mix 1 ounce (25 g) of sultanas with the juice and grated rind of 1 lemon and salt and pepper to taste.

In a casserole or ovenproof dish arrange layers of the sweet potato and apple slices. Sprinkle each layer with the sultana mixture. Pour in ¼ pint (150 ml) of chicken stock.

Cover and bake for 45 minutes, or until the potatoes are tender.

Serve hot.

INGREDIENTS TO SERVE FOUR:
1 lb (500 g) sweet potatoes
1 large cooking apple
1 oz (25 g) sultanas
1 lemon
salt
pepper
¼ pint (150 ml) chicken stock

Sweet Potato and Avocado Casserole

Preheat the oven to 375°F (190°C, Gas Mark 5).

Scrub 8 sweet potatoes. Put them into a large saucepan with enough boiling water to cover. Cover the pan, bring to the boil and cook for 25 minutes, or until the potatoes are tender. When the potatoes are cool enough to handle, peel and mash them or purée them in a liquidizer.

Peel 1 medium-sized avocado. Mash it well, then beat it into the puréed sweet potatoes. Grate in the rind of 1 orange, then squeeze in the juice. Season with salt, pepper and a large pinch of grated nutmeg.

Spoon the mixture into a lightly greased ovenproof dish. Bake for 20 to 30 minutes, or until it is brown on top.

Serve hot.

INGREDIENTS TO SERVE FOUR:
8 sweet potatoes
1 medium-sized avocado
1 orange
salt
pepper
grated nutmeg

Creamed Mixed Potatoes

Peel and slice ¾ pound (350 g) of sweet potatoes and ¾ pound (350 g) of white potatoes. Put them into a saucepan with boiling salted water to cover. Simmer for about 20 minutes, or until the potatoes are tender. Drain well.

Mash the potatoes until they are smooth. Beat in 4 tablespoons (60 ml) of milk and 1 ounce (50 g) of margarine. Add more milk if necessary for a creamy consistency. Season to taste with salt and pepper.

Serve hot, sprinkled with a large pinch of grated nutmeg.

INGREDIENTS TO SERVE FOUR TO SIX:
¾ lb (350 g) sweet potatoes
¾ lb (350 g) white potatoes
salt
4 tablespoons (60 ml) milk
1 oz (50 g) margarine
pepper
grated nutmeg

Braised Jerusalem Artichokes

Peel 1½ pounds (700 g) of Jerusalem artichokes. Cut them into ¼-inch (6-mm) slices. Put them into a saucepan with the grated rind and juice of 1 lemon, 2 tablespoons (30 ml) of chopped thyme and salt and pepper to taste. Pour in ¼ pint (150 ml) of water.

Cover the pan and bring to the boil. Reduce the heat and simmer for about 10 minutes, or until the artichokes are tender and almost all the water has evaporated.

Serve hot or cold, sprinkled with 1 tablespoon (15 ml) of chopped parsley.

INGREDIENTS TO SERVE FOUR:
1½ lb (700 g) Jerusalem artichokes
1 lemon
2 tablespoons (30 ml) chopped thyme
salt
pepper
1 tablespoon (15 ml) chopped parsley

Jerusalem Artichoke and Ham Soufflé

Preheat the oven to 375°F (190°C, Gas Mark 5).

Peel 1 pound (500 g) of Jerusalem artichokes. (If the artichokes are very knobbly and difficult to peel, cook them first and then the skins can be peeled off easily.) Simmer the artichokes in a saucepan in a little salted water for about 20 minutes, or until they are tender.

In a large mixing bowl, mash the artichokes well. Stir in ¼ pint (150 ml) of yogurt and salt and pepper to taste. Alternatively, put the artichokes into a liquidizer with the yogurt, salt and pepper and blend to a smooth

purée. Chop ¼ pound (100 g) of sliced cooked ham and mix it into the purée.

Separate 3 large eggs. Stir the yolks into the purée. Whisk the whites until they are stiff. Fold them in.

Pour the mixture into a 3-pint (1½-litre) soufflé dish. Bake for 40 to 45 minutes, or until the soufflé is well risen, firm to the touch and golden brown.

Serve at once.

INGREDIENTS TO SERVE FOUR:
1 lb (500 g) Jerusalem artichokes
¼ pint (150 ml) yogurt
salt
pepper
¼ lb (100 g) cooked sliced ham
3 large eggs

PREPARING JERUSALEM ARTICHOKES

Cook knobbly artichokes before peeling.

Jerusalem Artichoke Soup

Peel and coarsely chop 1 pound (500 g) of Jerusalem artichokes. Peel and chop 1 medium-sized onion. Put the artichokes and the onion into a large saucepan with 1 pint (600 ml) of well-seasoned chicken stock, ½ pint (300 ml) of milk, salt and pepper. Cover the pan and bring to the boil. Reduce the heat and simmer for 20 minutes, or until the artichokes are tender.

Sieve the soup or liquidize it to a smooth purée. Return the soup to the pan, reheat and adjust the seasoning.

Serve hot, garnished with 2 tablespoons (30 ml) of chopped parsley.

INGREDIENTS TO SERVE FOUR TO SIX:
1 lb (500 g) Jerusalem artichokes
1 medium-sized onion
1 pint (600 ml) chicken stock
½ pint (300 ml) milk
salt
pepper
2 tablespoons (30 ml) chopped parsley

EVEN IN PREHISTORIC TIMES when man was still a hunter his diet was not all meat. What evidence there is at least establishes this fact. Many writers have shown great imagination in conjuring up the details of the likely scene—the women scouring the countryside for anything edible while their men were away on the chase. In the spring and summer they would pick young shoots and leaves and in autumn they would gather berries and nuts. Then in the bleak midwinter the women would be reduced to scrabbling in the earth for the wild roots that would help avert starvation until spring came again.

This scenario, however accurate, is hard to associate with, for example, the celebrated French dish Carottes Vichy, in which tender young carrots are cooked in butter, sugar and Vichy water, then glazed and sprinkled with parsley. Nonetheless, although people and their roots have changed considerably since prehistoric times, it is difficult to dispel the air of impoverishment that hangs over the roots we usually eat. The fault is ours, for we, like our prehistoric ancestors, tend to eat roots in winter because there is little else to choose. We are therefore eating them when they are at their worst. Not only are they old, woody or stringy, but they become less and less nutritious every week they are stored. There obviously is a place for roots in a winter diet, but the time to enjoy them is in late spring or summer when they are young and small, tender and sweet. Among roots, with one exception, small really is beautiful. Celeriac alone is better larger and is worth saving as a winter choice.

Carrots are undoubtedly the most useful of all roots. Teeth permitting, they are good to chew raw and in a dish of crudités they are usually the first to disappear. When young, carrots are delicious grated in salads or gently cooked in butter. In winter they are invaluable in stews, for they do not lose their colour or their shape in long cooking. Carotene, which is converted into vitamin A in the body, is the major nutritional reason for eating carrots. To ensure that this vitamin is not squandered, the carrots should not be scraped or peeled, for the greatest concentration is in the skin or just beneath it.

Other roots, such as beets, turnips, swedes and parsnips, contain either no carotene or the merest trace. Some have a moderate amount of vitamin C. Kohlrabi, for example, contains as much vitamin C as oranges.

The main positive virtue of most roots lies in their mineral content, but they also have the negative virtue of being reasonably low in calories, so that they fill without fattening. There is also the likelihood that you will at least enjoy some of them, if not all, for their flavour.

The most subtle of the root vegetable flavours is that of the raw, very young, white turnip, but

The Nutrients in Roots
A high water content makes starchy roots low in calories and three and a half ounces (100 g) of carrots, for example, provide about 20 Calories.

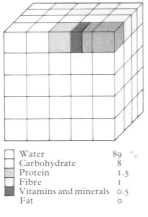

☐ Water	89	%
Carbohydrate	8	
Protein	1.5	
Fibre	1	
Vitamins and minerals	0.5	
Fat	0	

Many roots are valued for their low-calorie bulk. Radishes and beetroot, for example, contribute not more than 30 Calories per hundred grams. Carrots have the additional merit of being very rich in carotene, which the body converts into vitamin A. In the basket (right) next to the carrots is scorzonera, or black salsify, and grouped on the ground are turnips, swedes, parsnips, beetroots and radishes.

UNUSUAL ROOTS

Staple foods in some tropical countries, cassava (right) and arrowroot (far right) are roots with an unusually high starch content. Tapioca flour, made from cassava, and powdered arrowroot, which is used to thicken sauces, may be eighty-five per cent starch and provide as many as 350 Calories in one hundred grams. Horseradish (centre) is only slightly higher in starch than most roots, but it is outstandingly high in vitamin C, providing one hundred and twenty milligrams of this vitamin in one hundred grams. But no one could eat so much, and should not, since horseradish is poisonous in large quantities.

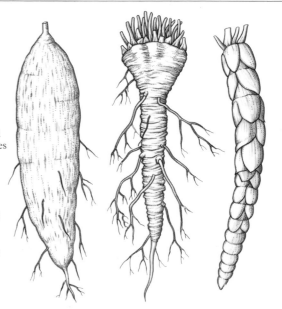

even then its skin is likely to be tough and must be peeled. As an older vegetable the turnip is useful in stews, for it has the valuable property of absorbing the rich flavours of whatever is cooked with it. The yellow-fleshed swede, or rutabaga, is more domineering, and is best used alone. It can be boiled, mashed and then chastened with a little butter, cream and pepper. Above all, swedes must be eaten young and small.

Kohlrabi is woody and flavourless when it is old and large, but when the vegetable is young it has a somewhat nutty turnip flavour.

The sweetest-tasting roots are the creamy-fleshed parsnips, which because of their extreme hardiness are a reliable winter vegetable, and the red-fleshed beets. Beetroot is available much of the year, but is at its best in early summer—again when young and small.

Celeriac is the most distinctively flavoured root, and the ugliest, but it must not be missed if you like the taste of celery. It is best to choose roots about six inches (15 cm) in diameter and it is essential to peel them. They can be grated raw for salads or cooked. There is a hint of celeriac in the flavour of the root of Hamburg parsley, but in shape it resembles a parsnip.

A curiously large number of roots have lost their one-time popularity. The delicately flavoured salsify, or so-called oyster plant, was popular until Victorian times, but has now almost been forgotten. So, too, has its black-skinned version, scorzonera. The sweet-potato flavour of skirret, a great favourite in the Tudor period, is now no longer appreciated. Neither are the turnip-flavoured rampion and the turnip-rooted chervil, which tastes of aniseed.

Salsify au Gratin

The delicate flavour of salsify is complemented by a lemon and herb sauce and grated cheese in this dish.

Pour ½ pint (300 ml) of water into a saucepan. Add the grated rind and juice of 1 lemon.

Peel 1½ pounds (700 g) of salsify, about 8 large roots. Cut into 2-inch (5-cm) pieces and drop immediately into the saucepan. This prevents the salsify from turning brown. Add 1 large sprig of thyme, the stalks from 1 small bunch of parsley, salt and pepper.

Cover the pan and bring to the boil. Reduce the heat and simmer gently for 10 minutes, or until the salsify is just tender. Transfer the salsify to a flameproof serving dish and keep warm. Reserve the cooking liquor.

Melt 1 ounce (25 g) of margarine or butter in a saucepan, then stir in 1 ounce (25 g) of flour to make a roux. Add milk to make the cooking liquor up to ½ pint (300 ml) and, stirring constantly, gradually add it to the roux. Bring to the boil, stirring, and cook until the sauce has thickened. Reduce the heat, stir in 2 tablespoons (30 ml) of chopped parsley, salt and pepper and simmer gently for 2 minutes.

Pour the sauce over the salsify, then sprinkle with 2 tablespoons (30 ml) of grated Parmesan cheese. Place under a hot grill for 2 to 3 minutes, until the top is brown and bubbling.

Serve hot.

INGREDIENTS TO SERVE FOUR:
1 lemon
1½ lb (700 g) salsify
1 thyme sprig
1 small bunch parsley
salt
pepper
1 oz (25 g) margarine or butter
1 oz (25 g) flour
milk
2 tablespoons (30 ml) chopped parsley
2 tablespoons (30 ml) grated Parmesan cheese

Sweet and Sour Carrots

Chop 2 ounces (50 g) of bacon. Cut a ¼-inch (6-mm) slice of root ginger. Peel and finely chop it. Scrub 1½ pounds (700 g) of carrots and thinly slice them. Chop 4 spring onions.

In a large, heavy frying-pan fry the bacon until the fat runs. Add the ginger and 1 crushed garlic clove and fry for 1 minute.

Add the carrots and the spring onions to the pan and fry over moderate heat, stirring constantly, for 3 minutes.

Add 6 tablespoons (90 ml) of water mixed with 2 tablespoons (30 ml) of wine vinegar, 1 tablespoon (15 ml) of soy sauce, and 1 tablespoon (15 ml) of soft brown sugar and

salt and pepper to taste. Cover the pan, reduce the heat and simmer for 10 minutes. Uncover and simmer for a further 3 to 5 minutes, or until the liquid has reduced and the carrots are tender but still a little crunchy.

Serve sprinkled with 1 tablespoon (15 ml) of chopped coriander or parsley sprigs.

INGREDIENTS TO SERVE FOUR:
2 oz (50 g) bacon
root ginger
1½ lb (700 g) carrots
4 spring onions
1 garlic clove
2 tablespoons (30 ml) wine vinegar
1 tablespoon (15 ml) soy sauce
1 tablespoon (15 ml) soft brown sugar
salt
pepper
1 tablespoon (15 ml) chopped coriander or parsley sprigs

PREPARING ROOT GINGER

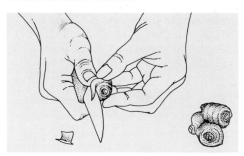

Thinly peel root ginger using a sharp knife.

Chop the ginger very finely before cooking.

Spiced Carrot Cake

Grated carrots give a delicious moistness to this spiced, orange-flavoured cake.

Preheat the oven to 350°F (180°C, Gas Mark 4). Grease an 8-inch (20-cm) round cake tin and line it with greaseproof paper. Grease the paper. Put ¼ pound (100 g) of self-raising flour into a mixing bowl.

In a bowl cream ¼ pound (100 g) of soft margarine and ¼ pound (100 g) of soft brown sugar until the mixture is pale and fluffy.

Beat in 2 eggs, one at a time, alternately with 2 tablespoons of the flour. Scrub ¼ pound (100 g) of carrots and

coarsely grate them into the batter. Add the grated rind and juice of ½ orange. Add 2 ounces (50 g) of ground almonds. Beat until well mixed.

Mix ½ teaspoon (2.5 ml) of ground ginger and ½ teaspoon (2.5 ml) of ground cinnamon with the remaining flour. Fold it into the batter.

Spoon the batter into the prepared cake tin. Bake for 45 to 55 minutes, or until the cake is well risen, golden brown and firm to the touch.

INGREDIENTS TO MAKE ONE SMALL CAKE:
¼ lb (100 g) self-raising flour
¼ lb (100 g) soft margarine
¼ lb (100 g) soft brown sugar
2 eggs
¼ lb (100 g) carrots
½ orange
2 oz (50 g) ground almonds
½ teaspoon (2.5 ml) ground ginger
½ teaspoon (2.5 ml) ground cinnamon

Glazed Carrots

Scrub 1½ pounds (700 g) of young carrots. Leave the small carrots whole, cut larger ones into halves lengthways. Put them into a saucepan with the grated rind and juice of ½ lemon, ½ pint (300 ml) of chicken stock and salt and pepper to taste.

Bring to the boil, cover the pan, reduce the heat and simmer for 10 to 15 minutes, or until the carrots are just tender. Transfer the carrots to a serving dish and keep warm.

Boil the cooking liquor rapidly until it is reduced to about 6 tablespoons (90 ml). Remove the pan from the heat, stir in 2 tablespoons (30 ml) of chopped chives or parsley. Pour the sauce over the carrots and serve.

INGREDIENTS TO SERVE FOUR:
1½ lb (700 g) young carrots
½ lemon
½ pint (300 ml) chicken stock
salt
pepper
2 tablespoons (30 ml) chopped chives or parsley

Sherried Carrots

Preheat the oven to 350°F (180°C, Gas Mark 4).

Scrub 1½ pounds (700 g) of carrots. Quarter them and cut them into sticks about 3 inches (8 cm) long. Put the carrots into a casserole with 2 ounces (50 g) of blanched almonds, ¼ pint (150 ml) of medium or sweet sherry and ¼ pint (150 ml) of water. Season with salt and pepper.

Cover and bake for 1 hour, or until the carrots are just tender and most of the liquid has been absorbed.

Serve hot, garnished with 1 tablespoon (15 ml) of chopped parsley.

INGREDIENTS TO SERVE FOUR:
1½ lb (700 g) carrots
2 oz (50 g) blanched almonds
¼ pint (150 ml) medium or sweet sherry
salt
pepper
1 tablespoon (15 ml) chopped parsley

Cream of Winter Soup

Peel and coarsely chop ½ pound (250 g) of potatoes. Scrub ½ pound (250 g) of carrots and cut into thick slices. Peel and coarsely chop ½ pound (250 g) of parsnips, swedes or turnips. Slice 2 sticks of celery.

Put all the vegetables into a large saucepan with 2 pints (1 litre) of well-seasoned chicken stock, 4 sage leaves, 1 bay leaf, 1 parsley sprig, salt and pepper.

Cover the pan and bring to the boil. Reduce the heat and simmer for 40 minutes, or until the vegetables are tender.

Sieve or liquidize the soup to a purée. Return the soup to the pan and reheat. Adjust the seasoning. Serve hot.

INGREDIENTS TO SERVE SIX:
½ lb (250 g) potatoes
½ lb (250 g) carrots
½ lb (250 g) parsnips, swedes or turnips
2 celery sticks
2 pints (1 litre) chicken stock
4 sage leaves
1 bay leaf
1 parsley sprig
salt
pepper

Chilled Carrot and Orange Soup

Scrub and coarsely chop 1 pound (500 g) of carrots. Put them into a large saucepan with 1 chopped onion and 1½ pints (850 ml) of well-seasoned chicken stock. Add the grated rind and juice of 2 oranges. Season with salt and pepper.

Cover the pan and bring to the boil. Reduce the heat and simmer for 30 minutes, or until

the carrots are tender.

Liquidize or sieve the soup to a purée. Let it cool. Adjust the seasoning.

Chill the soup. Serve garnished with 1 tablespoon (15 ml) of chopped chives.

INGREDIENTS TO SERVE FOUR:
1 lb (500 g) carrots
1 onion
1½ pints (850 ml) chicken stock
2 oranges
salt
pepper
1 tablespoon (15 ml) chopped chives

Carrot and Orange Salad

First make the dressing. In a salad bowl whisk 4 tablespoons (60 ml) of corn oil with the grated rind and juice of 1 orange, the juice of 1 lemon, salt and pepper. Add 2 ounces (50 g) of sultanas and leave to soak for at least 1 hour so that the raisins will swell up and absorb the orange flavour.

Scrub 1 pound (500 g) of carrots. Coarsely grate them into the salad bowl. Add 2 ounces (50 g) of bean sprouts. Toss well to coat the carrots and bean sprouts with the dressing.

INGREDIENTS TO SERVE FOUR:
4 tablespoons (60 ml) corn oil
1 orange
1 lemon
salt
pepper
2 oz (50 g) sultanas
1 lb (500 g) carrots
2 oz (50 g) bean sprouts

Carrots Braised with Apples

Preheat the oven to 350°F (180°C, Gas Mark 4).

Scrub and slice 1 pound (500 g) of carrots. Put them into a casserole or ovenproof dish.

Peel, core and thickly slice 1 cooking apple. Put the slices on top of the carrots. Grate in the rind of ½ lemon, then squeeze in the juice. Pour in ¼ pint (50 ml) of water. Season with salt and pepper. Sprinkle with 2 ounces (50 g) of sultanas.

Cover and bake for 1 hour, or until the carrots are just tender.

INGREDIENTS TO SERVE FOUR:
1 lb (500 g) carrots
1 cooking apple
½ lemon
salt
pepper
2 oz (50 g) sultanas

Swedes with Lemon and Carrots

Peel 1 pound (500 g) of swedes and cut them into ½-inch (1-cm) cubes. Scrub ½ pound (250 g) of carrots and cut them into ½-inch (1-cm) cubes.

Put the swedes and carrots into a saucepan with the grated rind and juice of ½ lemon, ¼ pint (150 ml) of chicken stock and salt and pepper.

Cover the pan and bring to the boil. Reduce the heat and simmer for 10 minutes, or until the vegetables are just tender and most of the stock has been absorbed.

Transfer to a serving dish, garnish with 1 tablespoon (15 ml) of chopped chives or parsley and serve.

INGREDIENTS TO SERVE FOUR:
1 lb (500 g) swedes
½ lb (250 g) carrots
½ lemon
¼ pint (150 ml) chicken stock
salt
pepper
1 tablespoon (15 ml) chopped chives or parsley

CUBING SWEDE

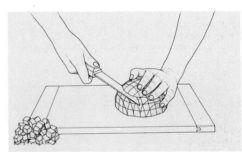

Slice peeled swede in three directions to cube it.

Orange Glazed Turnips

Peel 1½ pounds (700 g) of turnips. Slice them thinly and put them into a saucepan.

Grate in the rind of 1 orange and then add the squeezed juice from 2 large oranges. Season with salt and pepper.

Cover the pan and bring to the boil. Reduce the heat and simmer gently for 10 to 15 minutes, or until the turnips are just tender.

Transfer the turnips to a warm serving dish, sprinkle with 2 tablespoons (30 ml) of chopped parsley and serve.

INGREDIENTS TO SERVE FOUR:
1½ lb (700 g) turnips
2 large oranges
salt
pepper
2 tablespoons (30 ml) chopped parsley

Turnips Braised with Bacon and Sage

Chop ¼ pound (100 g) of bacon. Chop 1 small onion. Put the bacon into a large saucepan and fry over low heat until the fat runs. Add the onion to the pan and fry for 3 minutes.

Peel 1½ pounds (700 g) of turnips and cut them into quarters, or sixths if they are large.

Add the turnips to the pan with ½ pint (300 ml) of beef stock, 1 tablespoon (15 ml) of chopped sage, salt and pepper.

Cover the pan and bring to the boil. Reduce the heat and simmer for 15 minutes, or until the turnips are just tender. Transfer the turnips to a serving dish and keep warm.

Reduce the cooking liquor to 5 tablespoons (75 ml) by boiling rapidly. Pour over the turnips and serve immediately.

INGREDIENTS TO SERVE FOUR:
¼ lb (100 g) bacon
1 small onion
1½ lb (700 g) turnips
½ pint (300 ml) beef stock
1 tablespoon (15 ml) chopped sage
salt
pepper

Roast Parsnips and Bacon

This is one of the most delicious ways to cook parsnips. Don't peel them because the skin will get crisp while the inside will remain sweet and tender and become flavoured by the bacon. Serve with roast meat.

Preheat the oven to 400°F (200°C, Gas Mark 6).

Scrub 1 pound (500 g) of parsnips. Trim off the root ends. Cut into quarters lengthways, or sixths if the parsnips are very large. Put the parsnips into a small roasting tin or ovenproof dish. Put ¼ pound (100 g) of bacon rashers over the top.

Bake uncovered for 30 minutes, or until the bacon is crisp and the parsnips are tender. Serve hot.

INGREDIENTS TO SERVE FOUR:
1 lb (500 g) parsnips
¼ lb (100 g) bacon rashers

Parsnip, Tomato and Cheese Casserole

This is a delicious vegetable casserole for a light lunch or supper dish. Serve it with boiled rice.

Preheat the oven to 375°F (190°C, Gas Mark 5).

Scrub 1½ pounds (700 g) of parsnips and cut them into thin slices. Slice ½ pound (250 g) of tomatoes. Grate ¼ pound (100 g) of Gruyère cheese and reserve 2 tablespoons (30 ml).

Put a layer of the sliced parsnips into a casserole or ovenproof dish. Cover with a layer of tomato slices. Sprinkle with some of the grated cheese and salt and pepper.

Repeat the layers, finishing with a layer of parsnips. Spread ¼ pint (150 ml) of yogurt over the top and sprinkle with the reserved cheese.

Cover the dish and bake for 40 to 45 minutes, or until the parsnips are almost tender. Uncover the dish and continue to bake for 10 to 15 minutes more, or until the top is crisp and browned.

Serve hot.

INGREDIENTS TO SERVE FOUR AS A MAIN DISH:
1½ lb (700 g) parsnips
½ lb (250 g) tomatoes
¼ lb (100 g) Gruyère cheese
salt
pepper
¼ pint (150 ml) yogurt

PREPARING PARSNIPS

Cut the tops off the parsnips.

Scrub the parsnips with a stiff brush.

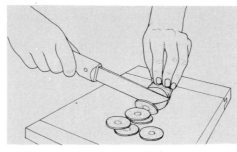

Cut them into thin slices.

Citrus Braised Parsnips

Scrub 1½ pounds (700 g) of young parsnips. Quarter them and cut them into sticks about 3 inches (8 cm) long.

Put the parsnips into a saucepan with the grated rind and juice of 1 orange and 1 lemon. Sprinkle with a pinch of grated nutmeg. Season with salt and pepper.

Pour in ¼ pint (150 ml) of chicken stock. Cover the pan and bring to the boil. Reduce the heat and simmer for 10 minutes, or until the parsnips are just tender.

Transfer the parsnips to a serving dish and keep warm. Reduce the cooking liquor to about 6 tablespoons (90 ml) by boiling rapidly for a few minutes. Pour over the parsnips and serve.

INGREDIENTS TO SERVE FOUR TO SIX:
1½ lb (700 g) parsnips
1 orange
1 lemon
grated nutmeg
salt
pepper
¼ pint (150 ml) chicken stock

Bortsch

Thinly peel 1 pound (500 g) of raw beetroot and shred them into a large saucepan. Chop 1 large onion and shred ¼ pound (100 g) of cabbage. Add the onion and the cabbage to the saucepan with the grated rind and juice of 1 small lemon, 2 tablespoons (30 ml) of tomato purée and 2 bay leaves. Pour in 2 pints (1 litre) of beef stock. Season with salt and pepper.

Cover the pan and bring to the boil. Reduce the heat and simmer for 45 minutes, or until the vegetables are tender.

Before serving add soured cream to taste.

INGREDIENTS TO SERVE FOUR TO SIX:
1 lb (500 g) raw beetroot
1 large onion
¼ lb (100 g) cabbage
1 small lemon
2 tablespoons (30 ml) tomato purée
2 bay leaves
2 pints (1 litre) beef stock
salt
pepper
soured cream

Beetroot and Yogurt Salad

Serve this tangy salad with cold meats.

Thinly peel 1 pound (500 g) of cooked beetroot. Slice the beetroot and cut the slices into ¼-inch (6-mm) sticks. Put them into a mixing bowl.

Thinly slice 1 large stick of celery. Core and chop 1 dessert apple. Add the celery and apple to the beetroot.

For the dressing stir the grated rind and juice of ½ lemon into ¼ pint (150 ml) of yogurt. Season with salt and pepper. Pour the dressing over the beetroot mixture and toss lightly until well mixed.

Transfer to a serving bowl. Chill before serving.

INGREDIENTS TO SERVE FOUR:
1 lb (500 g) cooked beetroot
1 large celery stick
1 dessert apple
½ lemon
¼ pint (150 ml) yogurt
salt
pepper

Beetroot Ragoût

This sweet and sour beetroot stew makes a good accompaniment to roast or grilled meat, particularly pork.

Peel ½ pound (250 g) of potatoes and cut them into ½-inch (1-cm) cubes. Put the potatoes into a saucepan with ½ pint (300 ml) of beef stock, salt and pepper. Cover the pan and bring to the boil. Reduce the heat and simmer for 5 minutes.

Thinly peel 1 pound (500 g) of cooked beetroot. Thickly slice them and then cut the slices into halves or quarters, depending on how large the beetroots are. Peel, core and thinly slice 1 cooking apple.

Add the beetroot and apple slices to the saucepan with 2 ounces (50 g) of sultanas, 2 tablespoons (30 ml) of wine vinegar, 1 bay leaf and salt and pepper to taste.

Cover the pan and simmer gently for 10 minutes, or until the potato is cooked. Serve hot.

INGREDIENTS TO SERVE FOUR:
½ lb (250 g) potatoes
½ pint (300 ml) beef stock
salt
pepper
1 lb (500 g) cooked beetroot
1 cooking apple
2 oz (50 g) sultanas
2 tablespoons (30 ml) wine vinegar
1 bay leaf

Beetroot with Orange

Steam 1½ pounds (700 g) of beetroot or boil them in a small amount of water.

Thinly peel the beetroot, then slice them.

Put the beetroot slices into a saucepan with the grated rind and juice of 3 oranges. Season with salt and pepper.

Cover the pan and heat gently for 5 minutes, or until the beetroot is hot and most of the orange juice has been absorbed.

Serve hot or cold.

INGREDIENTS TO SERVE FOUR:
1½ lb (700 g) beetroot
3 oranges
salt
pepper

Celeriac and Salami Salad

Peel ¾ pound (350 g) of celeriac and cut into julienne sticks. Blanch the celeriac for 1 minute in boiling salted water to which the juice of ½ lemon has been added. Drain and cool.

For the dressing, put ¼ pint (150 ml) of

Peel the rough skin off the celeriac.

Slice the celeriac into very thin sticks.

Blanch the celeriac sticks in boiling salted water.

yogurt into a mixing bowl. Stir in 1 to 2 teaspoons (5 to 10 ml) of French mustard, salt and pepper.

Reserve 4 slices from ¼ pound (100 g) of sliced salami and cut the rest into quarters.

Add the celeriac and salami to the dressing and mix well.

Arrange the leaves from 1 small lettuce on a serving dish or individual plates. Spoon the salad on top and garnish with the reserved salami.

INGREDIENTS TO SERVE FOUR:
¾ lb (350 g) celeriac
½ lemon
¼ pint (150 ml) yogurt
1 to 2 teaspoons (5 to 10 ml) French mustard
salt
pepper
¼ lb (100 g) salami
1 small lettuce

Radish Salad

Top and tail about 30 large radishes. Wash the radishes well and cut them into thin slices. Put the sliced radishes into a salad bowl.

For the dressing, pour ¼ pint (150 ml) of yogurt into a mixing bowl. Add 1 tablespoon (15 ml) of chopped parsley, 1 tablespoon (15 ml) of chopped chives, 1 tablespoon (15 ml) of chopped tarragon or chervil, 1 tablespoon (15 ml) of lemon juice and salt and pepper to taste. Stir until well mixed and pour over the radishes.

Chill thoroughly before serving.

INGREDIENTS TO SERVE FOUR:
30 large radishes
¼ pint (150 ml) yogurt
1 tablespoon (15 ml) chopped parsley
1 tablespoon (15 ml) chopped chives
1 tablespoon (15 ml) chopped tarragon or chervil
1 tablespoon (15 ml) lemon juice
salt
pepper

Horseradish Sauce

Serve this sauce with roast beef.

Put 3 tablespoons (45 ml) of grated horseradish into a mixing bowl. Stir in ¼ pint (150 ml) of yogurt, salt and pepper.

Set aside for at least 1 hour before serving to allow the flavour to develop.

INGREDIENTS TO SERVE FOUR:
3 tablespoons (45 ml) grated horseradish
¼ pint (150 ml) yogurt
salt
pepper

HIGH IN FOOD VALUE and fine in flavour, peas and beans come as near to the perfect vegetable as is possible. Whether fresh or dried, they provide more energy and protein than either root or green vegetables. They are a good source of B vitamins and fresh and frozen peas and broad beans contain a reasonable amount of vitamin C. They are valuable in any diet and invaluable to vegetarians.

Nevertheless, during their long history—possibly as long as nine thousand years—the popularity of these vegetables has waxed and waned. The ancient Egyptians connected beans with death and in medieval Europe dried peas and beans were associated with famine, when there was little else to eat, and with Lent, when so many other foods were forbidden. But any danger that these vegetables might fall so much out of favour as to slide into oblivion, in the way vegetables do, was eliminated when they began to be eaten fresh rather than dried.

From its ancient home in Central and South America the French bean (alias green bean, haricot vert, snap bean and string bean) was brought to Europe early in the sixteenth century. A hundred years later the runner bean followed, but it was first grown for its flowers rather than for its pods. Today the runner bean is most popular in Britain and the countries of the eastern Mediterranean, but generally the smaller French bean is preferred on the Continent. Nutritionally there is little to choose between French beans and runner beans when they are boiled, but if they are eaten raw runner beans have twice as much vitamin C.

The eating of fresh peas spread northwards from Italy in the sixteenth century. In Britain they were made fashionable by Charles II and in France by Louis XIV, who almost stuffed himself to death with them. The popularity of peas was given further boosts when they became the first vegetable to be canned and then the first to be frozen. But in canning, fresh peas lose most of their vitamin C and so much of their colour that green dye has to be added to them. Peas do not lose their vitamin C when they are frozen.

As rich in protein as meat, and strong in B vitamins and iron, pulses would seem to be worthy of a prominent place in the diet. Unfortunately, before they can be eaten, dried peas and beans must be soaked and cooked. When this is done their water content increases from about twelve per cent to seventy per cent and in lentils, for example, the protein content falls to a quarter, and the energy value falls from almost 300 Calories to about 95 in one hundred grams. In the basket (left) clockwise: orange lentils, chick-peas, kidney beans, soya beans, green split peas, yellow split peas in the small basket, green lentils and mung beans. On the ground are haricot beans and black-eyed peas are in the bowl.

SOME PODS AND SEEDS

The amount of protein in the seeds of legumes and of the cereal maize ranges from about one per cent in runner beans to more than thirty per cent in soya beans. But eaten in quantity even runner beans make a useful protein contribution to the diet. Sweetcorn and kidney beans are also high in carbohydrate and are a good source of energy.

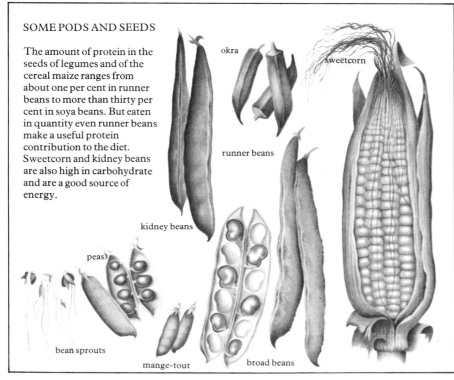

okra

sweetcorn

runner beans

kidney beans

peas

broad beans

bean sprouts

mange-tout

Once—and not so many years ago—"fresh" peas and beans belonged to summer, but today, when frozen, they are vegetables for all seasons. Peas are the most successful of all frozen vegetables, monotonously so, for if food is predictably and uniformly acceptable you escape disappointment by sacrificing any peak of excellence. Moreover, those people who eat frozen peas all the year round miss that impatient expectancy the rest of us enjoy while waiting for the first crops of early summer and the heightened enjoyment when they arrive.

For centuries, dried peas and beans and other pulses were the staple winter diet and their canned and frozen rivals have only partly ousted them. In the Middle Ages the dried beans were broad beans, but haricot beans have since taken their place. Haricot beans can be eaten on their own as a vegetable, as baked beans, in stews or as the basis of savoury dishes.

There are many other beans to choose from as well. The pale green lima beans, also known as butter beans, which are especially popular in the United States, have a delicate flavour. The dark red kidney beans are extremely good when they are baked. There are also black-eyed beans, rose cocoa beans and dappled pink pintos, or frijoles. The small, round and red adzuki beans from Japan and China are particularly sweet. On the other hand, the most nutritious bean, the soya, has a bitter aftertaste unless it is heavily disguised by other flavours.

Dried beans and peas are bursting with protein —about twenty per cent. It puts them on a par with meat. The same is true of chick-peas and other pulses such as lentils, whether the small orange Egyptian variety or the more flavoursome French green or brown lentils.

Dried pulses lack vitamin C, but by sprouting them they can be made rich in both C and B vitamins. The small green mung beans are the most widely used for sprouting, but soya beans, lentils and chick-peas will also do as long as they have not been split.

The Nutrients in Peas
Peas are a useful source of B vitamins, vitamin C and carotene and three and a half ounces (100 g) provide about 70 Calories.

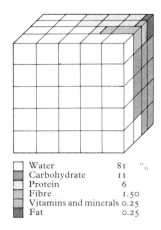

Water	81	%
Carbohydrate	11	
Protein	6	
Fibre	1.50	
Vitamins and minerals	0.25	
Fat	0.25	

The Nutrients in Kidney Beans
These beans are as high in protein as meat and three and a half ounces (100 g) provide about 330 Calories.

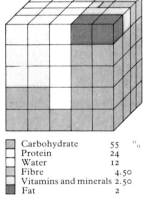

Carbohydrate	55	%
Protein	24	
Water	12	
Fibre	4.50	
Vitamins and minerals	2.50	
Fat	2	

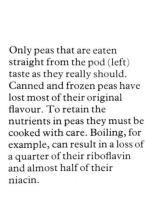

Only peas that are eaten straight from the pod (left) taste as they really should. Canned and frozen peas have lost most of their original flavour. To retain the nutrients in peas they must be cooked with care. Boiling, for example, can result in a loss of a quarter of their riboflavin and almost half of their niacin.

Runner Beans with Mushrooms and Yogurt

Top and tail 1 pound (500 g) of runner beans and string them if necessary. Slice the beans thinly into a saucepan.

Thinly slice ¼ pound (100 g) of button mushrooms and add them to the pan with the grated rind and juice of ½ lemon, ¼ pint (150 ml) of water, salt and pepper. Cover the pan and bring to the boil. Reduce the heat and simmer gently for 5 to 8 minutes, or until the beans and mushrooms are just tender.

Stir in ¼ pint (150 ml) of yogurt. Cook gently to heat the yogurt through, but do not boil or it may curdle.

Serve immediately.

INGREDIENTS TO SERVE FOUR:
1 lb (500 g) runner beans
¼ lb (100 g) button mushrooms
½ lemon
salt
pepper
¼ pint (150 ml) yogurt

Runner Beans with Garlic and Sage

Top and tail 1 pound (500 g) of runner beans and string them if necessary. Cut the beans into diagonal slices about 1 inch (2 cm) long.

Heat 1 tablespoon (15 ml) of corn oil in a saucepan. Add 2 crushed garlic cloves and fry gently for 1 minute, or until lightly browned.

Stir in 1 tablespoon (15 ml) of chopped sage. Add the beans, ¼ pint (150 ml) of water and salt and pepper.

Cover the pan and bring to the boil. Reduce the heat and simmer for about 5 minutes, or until the beans are tender, but still slightly crisp.

Serve hot or cold, sprinkled with 1 tablespoon (15 ml) of chopped parsley.

INGREDIENTS TO SERVE FOUR:
1 lb (500 g) runner beans
1 tablespoon (15 ml) corn oil
2 garlic cloves
1 tablespoon (15 ml) chopped sage
salt
pepper
1 tablespoon (15 ml) chopped parsley

French Beans Provençal

This dish may be served hot as a vegetable accompaniment or cold as a starter.

Slice ½ pound (250 g) of onions. Blanch and peel ½ pound (250 g) of tomatoes. Cut them into halves and remove the seeds. Cut 1 small green pepper into halves. Remove the seeds and cut away the white pith. Chop the pepper. Top and tail 1 pound (500 g) of French beans.

Heat 2 tablespoons (30 ml) of corn oil in a saucepan. Add the onions and 1 crushed garlic clove and fry for 3 minutes, stirring frequently.

Add the tomatoes and pepper to the pan with 1 tablespoon (15 ml) of chopped oregano and salt and pepper to taste. Cover the pan and simmer gently for 5 minutes, or until the tomatoes are reduced to a pulp.

Slice the French beans into the pan and simmer, stirring occasionally, for 5 to 10 minutes, or until the beans are tender but still crisp. Serve hot or cold.

INGREDIENTS TO SERVE FOUR:
½ lb (250 g) onions
½ lb (250 g) tomatoes
1 small green pepper
1 lb (500 g) French beans
2 tablespoons (30 ml) corn oil
1 garlic clove
1 tablespoon (15 ml) chopped oregano
salt
pepper

PREPARING GREEN BEANS

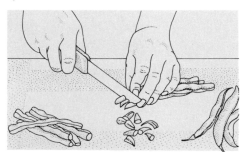

Cut the tops and ends off green beans.

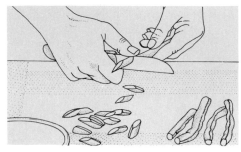

String the beans if necessary and slice them.

French Beans with Grapes

Top and tail 1 pound (500 g) of French beans and put them into a saucepan.

Cut 6 ounces (150 g) green grapes into halves and remove the seeds. Add the grapes to the pan with the grated rind and juice of ½ lemon, ¼ pint (150 ml) of water and salt and pepper.

Chop 1 ounce (25 g) of blanched almonds and sprinkle them over the beans.

Cover the pan and bring to the boil. Reduce the heat and simmer for 10 minutes, or until the beans are tender but still crisp and most of the water has evaporated. Boil uncovered for 2 to 3 minutes more, or until the cooking liquor is reduced to about 4 tablespoons (60 ml).

Serve immediately.

INGREDIENTS TO SERVE FOUR:
1 lb (500 g) French beans
6 oz (150 g) green grapes
½ lemon
salt
pepper
1 oz (25 g) blanched almonds

Salad Niçoise

Top and tail ½ pound (250 g) of French beans. Cook them, covered, in a small amount of boiling salted water until they are barely tender. Drain the beans, rinse them in cold water and put them into a salad bowl.

Cut 1 small green pepper into narrow strips, discarding the pith and seeds. Cut 3 tomatoes into small wedges and add to the beans with the green pepper strips.

Flake 6 ounces (150 g) of tuna fish and arrange in the bowl with 2 hard-boiled eggs, cut into quarters.

Garnish with 8 anchovy fillets, cut into halves, and 10 pitted black olives.

Just before serving add ¼ pint (150 ml) of basic vinaigrette dressing (see page 153) flavoured with ½ garlic clove, crushed.

INGREDIENTS TO SERVE FOUR:
½ lb (250 g) French beans
1 small green pepper
3 tomatoes
6 oz (150 g) tuna fish
2 hard-boiled eggs
8 anchovy fillets
10 black olives
basic vinaigrette dressing (see page 153)
½ garlic clove

French Bean, Lemon and Almond Salad

Top and tail 1 pound (500 g) of French beans. Cook them, covered, in a small amount of boiling salted water for 3 to 5 minutes, or until barely tender. Drain the beans and rinse them in cold water to cool them. Put them into a salad bowl.

For the dressing, heat 2 tablespoons (30 ml) of corn oil in a saucepan. Add 2 ounces (50 g) of split blanched almonds and fry gently for about 3 minutes, or until the almonds are lightly browned. Remove the pan from the heat and stir in 1 tablespoon (15 ml) of lemon juice, 1 tablespoon (15 ml) of chopped parsley, salt and pepper. Pour immediately over the beans and toss well to coat all the beans in the lemon dressing.

Chill before serving.

INGREDIENTS TO SERVE FOUR TO SIX:
1 lb (500 g) French beans
2 tablespoons (30 ml) corn oil
2 oz (50 g) split blanched almonds
1 tablespoon (15 ml) lemon juice
1 tablespoon (15 ml) chopped parsley
salt
pepper

Mange-tout with Bacon and Lemon

In this dish the mange-tout are stir-fried in the Chinese style, so that they cook quickly and retain their crispness.

Wash 1 pound (500 g) of mange-tout. Top and tail them and string them if necessary. Chop 2 ounces (50 g) of bacon and put it into a *wok* or a large frying-pan with 1 tablespoon (15 ml) of corn oil. Fry for 2 minutes, stirring constantly.

Add the mange-tout and fry, stirring constantly, for 1 minute.

Add 5 tablespoons (75 ml) of chicken stock, the juice of 1 small lemon and salt and pepper. Cook over moderate heat, stirring constantly, for about 5 minutes, or until the mange-tout are tender but still crisp and most of the stock has evaporated.

Serve immediately.

INGREDIENTS TO SERVE FOUR:
1 lb (500 g) mange-tout
2 oz (50 g) bacon
1 tablespoon (15 ml) corn oil
5 tablespoons (75 ml) chicken stock
1 small lemon
salt
pepper

Peas with Grapefruit and Mint

Shell 2 pounds (1 kg) of peas and put them into a saucepan with the grated rind and juice of 1 grapefruit.

Cut the peel and pith from another grapefruit. Working over the pan, cut the membrane away from the segments of fruit. Add the grapefruit segments to the peas with 1 tablespoon (15 ml) of chopped mint, salt and pepper.

Cover the pan and bring to the boil slowly. Reduce the heat and simmer gently for 15 minutes, or until the peas are just tender and almost all the juice has been absorbed.

Serve hot, garnished with sprigs of mint.

INGREDIENTS TO SERVE FOUR:
2 lb (1 kg) peas
2 grapefruit
1 small bunch mint
salt
pepper

Pea Purée

Shell 2 pounds (1 kg) of peas. Put them into a saucepan with 4 tablespoons (60 ml) of chicken stock, salt and pepper. Chop 1 small onion and add it to the peas.

Cover the pan and bring to the boil slowly. Reduce the heat and simmer gently, stirring occasionally, for 15 minutes, or until the peas are tender and all the stock has been absorbed. Add more stock if necessary.

Put the peas into a liquidizer with 4 tablespoons (60 ml) of yogurt. Blend to a smooth purée.

Return the purée to the pan and reheat, stirring vigorously, but do not boil. Adjust the seasoning. Serve hot or cold garnished with 1 tablespoon (15 ml) of chopped parsley.

INGREDIENTS TO SERVE FOUR TO SIX:
2 lb (1 kg) peas
4 tablespoons (60 ml) chicken stock
salt
pepper
1 small onion
4 tablespoons (60 ml) yogurt
1 tablespoon (15 ml) chopped parsley

SHELLING PEAS

Open the pod and push the peas out.

Green Pea Soup

Shell 1 pound (500 g) of peas and put them into a large saucepan. Shred ½ lettuce and add to the peas.

Chop 1 small onion and add it to the pan with 1 sprig of rosemary, salt and pepper.

Pour in 1½ pints (850 ml) of chicken stock. Grate in the rind of ½ lemon then squeeze in the juice.

Cover the pan and bring to the boil. Reduce the heat and simmer for 30 minutes. Liquidize or sieve the soup to a purée.

Return the puréed soup to the pan, adjust the seasoning and reheat.

INGREDIENTS TO SERVE FOUR:
1 lb (500 g) peas
½ lettuce
1 small onion
1 sprig rosemary
salt
pepper
1½ pints (850 ml) chicken stock
½ lemon

Peas with Rice and Tomatoes

This vegetable risotto makes a substantial lunch or supper dish.

Chop 2 ounces (50 g) of bacon. Chop 1 large onion. Blanch and peel 4 medium-sized tomatoes, cut them into quarters and remove the seeds.

Heat 1 tablespoon (15 ml) of corn oil in a saucepan. Add the bacon and the onion and fry for 3 minutes, stirring frequently. Add the tomatoes to the pan, cover and cook for 2 minutes.

Add ½ pound (250 g) of brown rice to the pan with 1 pint (600 ml) of chicken stock and salt and pepper to taste. Cover the pan and simmer for 20 minutes.

Shell 1 pound (500 g) of peas. Add the peas to the pan and continue to cook, covered, for 20 minutes more, or until the rice is tender but still a little chewy, the peas are cooked and all the stock has been absorbed.

Serve hot, sprinkled with 2 tablespoons (30 ml) of grated Parmesan cheese and 1 tablespoon (15 ml) of chopped parsley.

INGREDIENTS TO SERVE FOUR:
2 oz (50 g) bacon
1 large onion
4 medium-sized tomatoes
1 tablespoon (15 ml) corn oil
½ lb (250 g) brown rice
1 pint (600 ml) chicken stock
salt
pepper
1 lb (500 g) peas
2 tablespoons (30 ml) grated Parmesan cheese
1 tablespoon (15 ml) chopped parsley

141

Pois à la Française

This French method of cooking peas with lettuce and spring onions is delicious.

Wash but do not drain the leaves of 1 round lettuce. Put the large outside leaves into a saucepan.

Shell 2 pounds (1 kg) of peas and put them on top of the lettuce.

Chop 4 spring onions and add them to the pan with 1 tablespoon (15 ml) of chopped mint, salt and pepper. Shred the remaining lettuce and put it on top of the peas. Add 4 tablespoons (60 ml) of water.

Cover the pan, bring slowly to the boil, then reduce the heat and simmer gently for 15 minutes, or until the peas are tender.

Transfer to a serving dish, with the cooking liquid, garnish with sprigs of mint and serve.

INGREDIENTS TO SERVE FOUR TO SIX:
1 round lettuce
2 lb (1 kg) peas
4 spring onions
1 small bunch mint
salt
pepper

Baby Broad Beans in the Pod

When broad beans are very young they are delicious eaten in the pod like mange-tout.

Top and tail 1 pound (500 g) of baby broad beans. Cut them diagonally into pieces about 2 inches (5 cm) long and put them into a saucepan.

Add ¼ pint (150 ml) of chicken stock or water, the juice of 1 small lemon, salt and pepper.

Cover the pan and bring to the boil. Reduce the heat and simmer, stirring occasionally, for 5 to 10 minutes, or until the beans are just tender but still a little crisp. All the liquid should have evaporated by the time the beans are cooked.

Serve at once, sprinkled with 1 tablespoon (15 ml) of chopped parsley.

INGREDIENTS TO SERVE FOUR:
1 lb (500 g) baby broad beans
¼ pint (150 ml) chicken stock or water
1 small lemon
salt
pepper
1 tablespoon (15 ml) chopped parsley

Broad Beans in Yogurt Parsley Sauce

Shell 2 pounds (1 kg) of broad beans. Put them into a saucepan with ¼ pint (150 ml) of water, salt and pepper.

Cover the pan and bring to the boil. Reduce the heat and simmer for 5 to 10 minutes, depending on the size and age of the beans, until just tender.

Drain the beans and return them to the pan.

For the sauce, pour ¼ pint (150 ml) of yogurt into a mixing bowl. Stir in 2 tablespoons (30 ml) of chopped parsley and 2 tablespoons (30 ml) of chopped chives or spring onions, salt and pepper.

Pour the yogurt sauce over the beans and reheat, but do not boil or the yogurt may curdle.

Serve hot or cold.

INGREDIENTS TO SERVE FOUR:
2 lb (1 kg) broad beans
salt
pepper
¼ pint (150 ml) yogurt
2 tablespoons (30 ml) chopped parsley
2 tablespoons (30 ml) chopped chives or spring onions

SHELLING BROAD BEANS

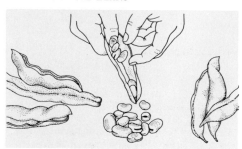

Open the pod and push the beans out with your thumb.

Broad Beans Creole

Shell 2 pounds (1 kg) of young broad beans. Put the beans into a saucepan with a small amount of boiling salted water, cover the pan and boil rapidly for 5 to 10 minutes, or until the beans are tender. Drain the beans.

Chop 1 medium-sized onion. Cut 1 small green pepper in half and remove the seeds and the white pith. Chop the pepper. Blanch and peel 6 ripe medium-sized tomatoes. Cut them into halves and remove the seeds.

Fry two slices of bacon in a saucepan until crisp. Remove from the pan with a slotted spoon. Add the chopped onion and pepper to the pan and fry, stirring frequently, for 5 minutes, or until tender but not brown. Add the tomatoes, cover the pan and cook, stirring occasionally, for 15 minutes.

Add the beans and season to taste with salt and pepper. Cook for 3 minutes more and then transfer to a serving dish. Crumble the bacon over the vegetables. Serve hot.

INGREDIENTS TO SERVE FOUR:
2 pounds (1 kg) young broad beans
salt
1 medium-sized onion
1 small green pepper
6 ripe medium-sized tomatoes
2 bacon slices
pepper

Okra Stew

Wash 1 pound (500 g) of young, tender okra pods. Cut off the stems without cutting into the pods. Chop 1 medium-sized onion. Blanch, peel and quarter ½ pound (250 g) of tomatoes.

Heat 1 tablespoon (15 ml) of corn oil in a saucepan. Add the chopped onion to the pan with 1 crushed garlic clove. Fry, stirring frequently, for 3 minutes.

Add the tomatoes to the pan with ½ teaspoon (2.5 ml) of ground coriander, the grated rind and juice of ½ lemon, salt and pepper. Cover the pan and cook over low heat for 5 minutes, or until the tomatoes are reduced to a pulp.

Add the okra to the pan, cover and continue to cook for 8 to 10 minutes, or until the okra is tender. Serve hot or cold.

INGREDIENTS TO SERVE FOUR:
1 pound (500 g) young okra
1 medium-sized onion
½ pound (250 g) tomatoes
1 tablespoon (15 ml) corn oil
1 garlic clove
½ teaspoon (2.5 ml) ground coriander
½ lemon
salt
pepper

PREPARING OKRA

Trim the stems of okra, leaving the pods intact.

Chinese Bean Sprouts

Chop 2 ounces (50 g) of bacon and 4 spring onions. Peel and finely chop ¼-inch (6-mm) slice of root ginger. Thinly slice 4 sticks of celery. Slice ¼ pound (100 g) of mushrooms.

Heat 1 tablespoon (15 ml) of peanut oil in a large frying-pan or a *wok*. Add the bacon, spring onions, celery and ginger to the pan and fry over high heat, stirring constantly, for 3 minutes. Add the mushrooms and stir-fry for 1 minute.

Add 1 pound (500 g) of bean sprouts, 5 tablespoons (75 ml) of chicken stock and 1 tablespoon (15 ml) of soy sauce. Continue to stir-fry for 2 to 3 minutes, or until the bean sprouts are hot and well coated in the sauce but are still crisp.

INGREDIENTS TO SERVE FOUR TO SIX:
2 ounces (50 g) bacon
4 spring onions
root ginger
4 celery sticks
¼ pound (100 g) mushrooms
1 tablespoon (15 ml) peanut oil
1 pound (500 g) bean sprouts
5 tablespoons (75 ml) chicken stock
1 tablespoon (15 ml) soy sauce

Corn on the Cob

For corn kernels, cook the whole ears of corn first. Then cut the kernels off the cob with a sharp knife. A medium-sized ear gives about ¼ pound (100 g) of kernels.

Remove the husks and silk from 4 medium-sized ears of corn. Line a large saucepan with the husks. Add 1 inch of boiling water. Drop the ears into the pan one by one so that the temperature of the water does not drop. Cover the pan and boil for 4 to 10 minutes, depending on the age of the corn.

Drain and serve with margarine or butter, salt and freshly ground black pepper.

INGREDIENTS TO SERVE FOUR:
4 medium-sized ears of corn
margarine or butter
salt
freshly ground black pepper

Corn Chowder

Chop 1 large onion and ¼ pound (100 g) of streaky bacon. Heat 1 tablespoon (15 ml) of corn oil in a large saucepan. Add the onion and bacon to the pan and fry, stirring frequently, for 3 minutes.

Peel 1 pound (500 g) of potatoes and cut them into ½-inch (1-cm) cubes. Add the potatoes to the pan with ¾ pint (450 ml) of water and salt and pepper to taste. Bring to the boil, cover the pan, reduce the heat and simmer for 15 minutes, or until the potatoes are tender.

Add ½ pound (250 g) of cooked sweetcorn kernels. Stir in ½ pint (300 ml) of milk and continue to simmer for 5 minutes. Adjust the seasoning. Serve hot, sprinkled with 2 ounces (50 g) of grated Cheddar cheese and 1 tablespoon (15 ml) of chopped parsley.

INGREDIENTS TO SERVE FOUR TO SIX:
1 large onion
¼ lb (100 g) streaky bacon
1 tablespoon (15 ml) corn oil
1 lb (500 g) potatoes
salt
pepper
½ lb (250 g) cooked sweetcorn kernels
½ pint (300 ml) milk
2 oz (50 g) Cheddar cheese
1 tablespoon (15 ml) chopped parsley

Sweetcorn Flan

Preheat the oven to 400°F (200°C, Gas Mark 6).

Make 6 ounces (150 g) of shortcrust pastry (see page 34) and line an 8-inch (20-cm) flan ring or dish. Bake blind for 15 minutes. Remove the baking paper and beans and bake for a further 5 to 10 minutes, or until the pastry is just beginning to colour.

Reduce the oven temperature to 350°F (180°C, Gas Mark 4).

Spread ½ pound (250 g) of cooked sweetcorn kernels and ¼ pound (100 g) of chopped cooked ham in the pastry case.

Beat 2 eggs with ¼ pint (150 ml) of milk. Grate in 1 small onion. Season with salt and pepper.

Pour the mixture into the pastry case and bake for 25 minutes, or until set.

INGREDIENTS TO SERVE FOUR TO SIX:
6 oz (150 g) shortcrust pastry (see page 34)
½ lb (250 g) cooked sweetcorn kernels
¼ lb (100 g) cooked ham
2 eggs
¼ pint (150 g) milk
1 small onion
salt
pepper

Mealie Bread

Preheat the oven to 375°F (190°C, Gas Mark 5). Grease a 1-pound (500-g) loaf tin.

Put 2 eggs and ¾ pound (350 g) of cooked sweetcorn kernels in a liquidizer and blend for 1 minute. Add 1 tablespoon (15 ml) of softened margarine or butter, 1 tablespoon (15 ml) of sugar, 1 teaspoon (5 ml) of baking powder and 1 teaspoon (5 ml) of salt and blend to a smooth purée. Alternatively, the sweetcorn may be mashed in a bowl and the remaining ingredients beaten in.

Transfer the purée to the prepared loaf tin and cover with foil. Bake for 1 hour.

Turn the loaf out on to a wire rack to cool.

INGREDIENTS TO MAKE 1 SMALL LOAF:
2 eggs
¾ lb (350 g) cooked sweetcorn kernels
1 tablespoon (15 ml) margarine or butter
1 tablespoon (15 ml) sugar
1 teaspoon (5 ml) baking powder
1 teaspoon (5 ml) salt

Chilli con Carne

This is a moderately hot version of the famous Mexican dish. More chilli powder or finely chopped chillies may be added with caution.

Soak ½ pound (250 g) of red kidney beans in cold water overnight. Blanch, peel and coarsely chop 1 pound (500 g) of ripe tomatoes.

Heat 2 tablespoons (30 ml) of corn oil in a large saucepan. Add 2 sliced onions with 1 crushed garlic clove. Fry for 3 minutes, stirring frequently.

Cut any excess fat from 1 pound (500 g) of chuck steak. Cut the beef into small cubes. Add the meat to the pan and fry, stirring constantly, until it is brown.

Stir in 1 tablespoon (15 ml) of flour and 2 teaspoons (10 ml) of chilli powder. Drain the kidney beans well and add them to the pan with the tomatoes, ½ pint (300 ml) water, salt and pepper. Cover the pan, reduce the heat and simmer for 1 hour, or until the beans are cooked. Stir occasionally during cooking and add a little water if the mixture becomes too dry.

Adjust the seasoning and serve immediately.

INGREDIENTS TO SERVE FOUR:
½ lb (250 g) red kidney beans
1 lb (500 g) ripe tomatoes
2 tablespoons (30 ml) corn oil
2 onions
1 garlic clove
1 lb (500 g) chuck steak
1 tablespoon (15 ml) flour
2 teaspoons (10 ml) chilli powder
salt
pepper

BEFORE DRIED PULSES CAN BE COOKED they must be soaked. This can be done in one of three ways, depending on the time available. Dried pulses should be soaked in the proportion of ½ pound (250 g) of dried pulses to 1 pint (600 ml) of water. The pulses absorb a lot of water and after soaking they should have doubled in size and weight.

SOAKING OVERNIGHT
Put ½ pound (250 g) of dried pulses into a bowl. Pour in 1 pint (600 ml) of cold water. Soak the pulses for 8 to 12 hours.

SOAKING FOR TWO HOURS
Put ½ pound (250 g) of dried pulses into a bowl. Pour in 1 pint (600 ml) of boiling water. Soak the pulses for 2 hours.

SOAKING FOR ONE HOUR
Put ½ pound (250 g) of dried pulses into a saucepan with 1 pint (600 ml) of cold water. Bring to the boil and cook the pulses for 2 minutes. Remove the pan from the heat and leave the pulses to soak for 1 hour.

Bean Soup

Soak ½ pound (250 g) of dried butter beans in 1 pint (600 ml) of water.

Drain the butter beans and reserve the water. Put the beans into a large saucepan with 1 chopped onion, 2 chopped celery sticks, 1 sliced large carrot, the grated rind and juice of ½ lemon and 1 bay leaf. Add 1 to 1½ pints (600 to 900 ml) of beef stock to the soaking liquid to make it up to 2 pints (1 litre). Pour it over the beans and vegetables. Season with salt and pepper.

Cover the pan and bring to the boil. Reduce the heat and simmer gently for 2 hours, or until the beans are tender.

Liquidize or sieve the soup. Return the soup to the pan and reheat. Adjust the seasoning and add more stock if necessary.

INGREDIENTS TO SERVE FOUR:
½ lb (250 g) dried butter beans
1 onion
2 celery sticks
1 large carrot
½ lemon
1 bay leaf
1 to 1½ pints (600 to 900 ml) beef stock
salt
pepper

Butter Beans Hors d'Oeuvre

Butter beans cooked with garlic and herbs make a delicious and unusual starter.

Soak ½ pound (250 g) of dried butter beans in 1 pint (600 ml) of water.

Drain the beans and reserve the water. Put the beans into a saucepan with 1 chopped large onion, 1 or 2 large garlic cloves, crushed, 2 tablespoons (30 ml) of chopped parsley, 1 tablespoon (15 ml) of chopped thyme and 1 tablespoon (15 ml) of chopped marjoram or oregano. Add the grated rind and juice of 1 small lemon, 1 bay leaf and salt and pepper. Add water to bring the soaking water up to 1 pint (600 ml) and pour it into the saucepan.

Cover the pan and bring to the boil. Reduce the heat and simmer for about 2 hours, or until the beans are tender.

Drain the beans. Reserve the cooking liquor. Put the beans into a bowl. Return the cooking liquor to the pan and boil rapidly until it is reduced to about ¼ pint (150 ml), then pour it over the beans.

Serve cold, sprinkled with 1 tablespoon (15 ml) of chopped parsley.

INGREDIENTS TO SERVE FOUR AS A STARTER:
½ lb (250 g) dried butter beans
1 large onion
1 or 2 large garlic cloves
3 tablespoons (45 ml) chopped parsley
1 tablespoon (15 ml) chopped thyme
1 tablespoon (15 ml) chopped marjoram or oregano
1 small lemon
1 bay leaf
salt
pepper

Butter Beans Provençal

Soak ½ pound (250 g) of dried butter beans in 1 pint (600 ml) of water.

Drain the beans, reserving the soaking water, and put them into a saucepan. Add more water to bring the soaking water up to 1 pint (600 ml). Pour it over the beans. Cover the pan and bring to the boil. Reduce the heat and simmer for 45 to 60 minutes, or until the beans are almost tender. Drain the beans and reserve the cooking liquor.

For the sauce, chop 2 ounces (50 g) of bacon. Chop ½ pound (250 g) of onions and 1 garlic clove. Blanch and peel ¾ pound (350 g) of tomatoes, then cut them into quarters. Cut 1 small green pepper into strips, discarding the seeds and the pith.

Heat 1 tablespoon (15 ml) of corn oil in a saucepan. Add the chopped bacon, onions and garlic. Fry for 3 minutes, stirring frequently, until the onions are lightly browned.

Add the tomatoes and green pepper and ¼ pint (150 ml) of the strained cooking liquor.

Season with salt and pepper. Bring to the boil. Add the butter beans and 12 halved stuffed olives.

Cover the pan, reduce the heat and simmer, stirring occasionally, for 45 to 60 minutes, or until the beans are tender.

Serve hot or cold.

INGREDIENTS TO SERVE FOUR:
½ lb (250 g) dried butter beans
2 oz (50 g) bacon
½ lb (250 g) onions
1 garlic clove
¾ lb (350 g) tomatoes
1 small pepper
1 tablespoon (15 ml) corn oil
salt
pepper
12 stuffed olives

Butter Bean Goulash

Soak ½ pound (250 g) of dried butter beans in 1 pint (600 ml) of water. Drain the beans and reserve the soaking water.

Chop ¼ pound (100 g) of bacon. Slice ½ pound (250 g) of onions and 2 celery sticks. Blanch and peel ½ pound (250 g) of tomatoes and cut them into quarters.

Over low heat, fry the bacon in a saucepan until the fat runs. Add the chopped onions and celery and fry, stirring frequently, for 3 minutes, or until lightly browned. Stir in 1 tablespoon (15 ml) of paprika and cook for 1 minute. Add the tomatoes to the pan.

Add water to bring the soaking water up to 1 pint (600 ml). Add to the pan with the grated rind and juice of ½ lemon, salt and pepper. Bring to the boil. Add the butter beans. Cover the pan and simmer for 2 hours, or until the beans are tender.

Add ¼ pound (100 g) of sliced mushrooms. Cover the pan and cook for 10 to 15 minutes more, or until the mushrooms are cooked.

Serve hot.

INGREDIENTS TO SERVE FOUR:
½ lb (250 g) dried butter beans
¼ lb (100 g) bacon
½ lb (250 g) onions
2 celery sticks
½ lb (250 g) tomatoes
1 tablespoon (15 ml) paprika
½ lemon
salt
pepper
¼ lb (100 g) mushrooms

Curried Soya Beans

Soak ½ pound (250 g) of dried soya beans in 1 pint (600 ml) of water.

Drain the soya beans, reserving the water, and put them into a saucepan. Add water to bring the soaking water up to 2 pints (1 litre) and pour it over the beans. Cover the pan and bring to the boil. Reduce the heat and simmer for 2 to 3 hours, or until the beans are tender.

Drain the beans, reserving the cooking water.

Grind spices in a mortar to mix a curry powder.

Meanwhile, heat 2 tablespoons (30 ml) of corn oil in a saucepan. Add 1 chopped large onion and 1 crushed large garlic clove and fry for 3 minutes, stirring frequently. Peel and finely chop 1-inch (2-cm) slice of root ginger and add it to the pan with 1 finely chopped seeded green chilli and continue frying.

In a mortar grind together 1 teaspoon (5 ml) of turmeric, 2 teaspoons (10 ml) of ground coriander, 1 teaspoon (5 ml) of ground cumin, ½ teaspoon (2.5 ml) of chilli powder and 1 teaspoon (5 ml) of ground paprika. Add enough cold water to make a paste.

Add the paste to the onion mixture and fry, stirring constantly, for 5 minutes. Stir in 1 to 2 tablespoons (5 to 10 ml) of the reserved bean stock if the mixture gets too dry.

Pour in 1 pint (600 ml) of bean stock and mix well. Season to taste with salt. Bring to the boil, stirring occasionally, then add the soya beans. Cover the pan and simmer for 1 hour, or until the beans are tender and have absorbed the flavour of the curry. Alternatively, cook covered in the oven, at 350°F (180°C, Gas Mark 4), for 1 hour.

INGREDIENTS TO SERVE FOUR:
½ lb (250 g) dried soya beans
2 tablespoons (30 ml) corn oil
1 large onion
1 large garlic clove
root ginger
1 green chilli
1 teaspoon (5 ml) turmeric
2 teaspoons (10 ml) ground coriander
1 teaspoon (5 ml) ground cumin
½ teaspoon (2.5 ml) chilli powder
1 teaspoon (5 ml) ground paprika
salt

Soya Bean Casserole

Soya beans baked with onions, tomatoes and cheese make a substantial main course dish.

Soak ½ pound (250 g) of dried soya beans in 1 pint (600 ml) of water.

Drain the beans, reserving the soaking water, and put them into a saucepan. Add water to bring the soaking water up to 2 pints (1 litre) and pour it over the beans. Cover the pan and bring to the boil. Reduce the heat and simmer for 2 to 3 hours, or until the beans are tender. Drain the beans and reserve the cooking water.

Preheat the oven to 350°F (180°C, Gas Mark 4).

Thinly slice 1 large onion and ¾ pound (350 g) of tomatoes.

In a small bowl combine 1 tablespoon (15 ml) of grated Parmesan cheese, 1 tablespoon (15 ml) of chopped parsley, 1 tablespoon (15 ml) of chopped mixed herbs and salt and pepper.

Put half of the drained beans into a casserole or ovenproof dish. Arrange half of the onions and tomatoes on top and sprinkle with the cheese mixture. Put the remaining beans and the onions and tomatoes on top. Pour in ½ pint (300 ml) of bean cooking water or beef stock. Sprinkle with 1 tablespoon (15 ml) of grated Parmesan cheese.

Cover the dish and bake for 40 minutes. Uncover the dish and bake for 20 minutes more, or until brown on top.

INGREDIENTS TO SERVE FOUR:
½ lb (250 g) dried soya beans
1 large onion
¾ lb (350 g) tomatoes
2 tablespoons (30 ml) grated Parmesan cheese
1 tablespoon (15 ml) chopped parsley
1 tablespoon (15 ml) chopped mixed herbs
salt
pepper
½ pint (300 ml) beef stock

Baked Soya Bean Cakes

These onion- and cheese-flavoured soya bean cakes may be served hot with tomato sauce, or cold.

Soak ½ lb (250 g) of dried soya beans in 1 pint (600 ml) of water. Drain the beans, reserving the soaking water, and put them into a saucepan. Add water to bring the soaking water up to 2 pints (1 litre) and pour it over the beans. Cover the pan and bring to the boil. Reduce the heat and simmer for about 3 hours, or until the beans are soft enough to mash. Drain the beans.

Preheat the oven to 425°F (220°C, Gas Mark 7).

Mash the soya beans well. Add 1 grated small onion, 2 ounces (50 g) of grated strong Cheddar cheese, 2 tablespoons (30 ml) of chopped parsley, salt and pepper. Mix well. Beat 1 egg and stir it into the mixture.

Divide the mixture into 8 pieces and shape each piece into a round cake. Put the cakes on a greased baking sheet and bake for 20 to 30 minutes, or until they are brown and crisp.

INGREDIENTS TO SERVE FOUR:
½ lb (250 g) dried soya beans
1 small onion
2 oz (50 g) strong Cheddar cheese
2 tablespoons (30 ml) chopped parsley
salt
pepper
1 egg

Bean Cassoulet

Soak ½ pound (250 g) of dried haricot beans in 1 pint (600 ml) of water.

Drain the beans, reserving the water, and put them into a saucepan. Add water to bring the soaking water up to 1 pint (600 ml) again. Pour into the saucepan. Cover the pan and bring to the boil. Reduce the heat and simmer for 1 hour, or until the beans are just tender. Drain the beans.

Preheat the oven to 350°F (180°C, Gas Mark 4).

Slice ½ pound (250 g) of onions. Scrub ½ pound (250 g) of carrots and slice them thinly. Slice 2 celery sticks. Cut ¼ pound (100 g) of sliced salami into halves. Slice ¼ pound (100 g) of garlic sausage, then cut the slices into halves. Blanch, peel and coarsely chop 1 pound (500 g) of ripe tomatoes.

Layer the haricot beans in a casserole or ovenproof dish with the onions, carrots, celery, salami and garlic sausage. Put the chopped tomatoes on top, pour over ¼ pint (150 ml) of water and sprinkle with salt and pepper. Put 1 bay leaf on top.

Bake, covered, for 1½ hours, stirring occasionally.

INGREDIENTS TO SERVE FOUR:
½ lb (250 g) dried haricot beans
½ lb (250 g) onions
½ lb (250 g) carrots
2 celery sticks
¼ lb (100 g) sliced salami
¼ lb (100 g) garlic sausage
1 lb (500 g) ripe tomatoes
salt
pepper
1 bay leaf

Baked Beans

Soak $\frac{1}{2}$ pound (250 g) of dried haricot beans in 1 pint (600 ml) of water.

Drain the beans, reserving the soaking water, and put them into a saucepan. Add water to bring the soaking water up to 1 pint (600 ml) and pour it over the beans. Cover the pan and bring to the boil. Reduce the heat and simmer for 1 hour, or until the beans are tender, adding more water if necessary. Drain the beans and reserve the cooking liquor.

Preheat the oven to 350°F (180°C, Gas Mark 4).

In a bowl combine $\frac{1}{2}$ pint (300 ml) of the cooking liquor, 1 chopped onion, 1 tablespoon (15 ml) of dark molasses, 2 tablespoons (30 ml) of tomato purée, 2 teaspoons (10 ml) of dried mustard, 2 teaspoons (10 ml) of Worcestershire sauce and 1 teaspoon (5 ml) of salt.

Put the beans into a casserole or ovenproof dish. Pour in the spicy liquid and mix well. Arrange $\frac{1}{2}$ pound (250 g) of thickly sliced bacon or salt pork on top.

Cover the casserole and bake for $1\frac{1}{2}$ hours. Uncover and bake for 30 minutes more. Alternatively, the beans may be cooked in a very slow oven for about 5 hours, uncovering the casserole for the last hour. Add a little more cooking liquor if the beans become dry during cooking.

Serve hot.

INGREDIENTS TO SERVE FOUR:
$\frac{1}{2}$ lb (250 g) dried haricot beans
1 onion
1 tablespoon (15 ml) dark molasses
2 tablespoons (30 ml) tomato purée
2 teaspoons (10 ml) dried mustard
2 teaspoons (10 ml) Worcestershire sauce
1 teaspoon (5 ml) salt
$\frac{1}{2}$ lb (250 g) thickly sliced bacon or salt pork

Haricots Bourguignonne

Soak $\frac{1}{2}$ pound (250 g) of dried haricot beans in 1 pint (600 ml) of water. Add water to bring the soaking water up to 1 pint (600 ml) again. Put the beans and the water into a saucepan and bring to the boil. Cover the pan, reduce the heat and simmer for 1 hour, or until the beans are almost tender. Drain the beans and reserve the cooking liquor.

For the sauce, chop $\frac{1}{4}$ pound (100 g) of bacon. Chop 1 large onion. Slice $\frac{1}{4}$ pound (100 g) of mushrooms.

Fry the bacon gently in a saucepan until the fat runs. Add the chopped onion and fry for 3 minutes, stirring frequently. Add the mushrooms to the pan and fry for 2 minutes.

Pour $\frac{1}{4}$ pint (150 ml) of the cooking liquor and $\frac{1}{2}$ pint (300 ml) of red wine into the pan. Season with salt and pepper and bring to the boil. Add the drained beans, cover the pan, reduce the heat and simmer gently for 45 to 60 minutes, or until the beans are cooked and the wine sauce has reduced and thickened slightly.

Serve hot, sprinkled with 1 tablespoon (15 ml) of chopped parsley.

INGREDIENTS TO SERVE FOUR:
$\frac{1}{2}$ lb (250 g) dried haricot beans
$\frac{1}{4}$ lb (100 g) bacon
1 large onion
$\frac{1}{4}$ lb (100 g) mushrooms
$\frac{1}{2}$ pint (300 ml) red wine
salt
pepper
1 tablespoon (15 ml) chopped parsley

Haricot and Tuna Salad

This piquant Italian dish from Tuscany makes a substantial starter.

Soak $\frac{1}{2}$ pound (250 g) of dried haricot beans in 1 pint (600 ml) of water.

Drain the soaked beans, reserving the water, and put them into a saucepan. Add water to bring the soaking water up to 1 pint (600 ml) and pour it into the pan. Add $\frac{1}{2}$ teaspoon (2.5 ml) of salt. Cover the pan and bring to the boil. Reduce the heat and simmer for 45 to 60 minutes, or until the beans are tender. Drain the beans and set aside to cool.

Put the cooled beans into a bowl. Flake 6 ounces (150 g) of tuna fish and add it to the beans with 1 finely chopped small onion, 4 tablespoons (60 ml) of chopped parsley and the grated rind of 1 lemon.

Pour in $\frac{1}{2}$ pint (300 ml) of basic vinaigrette dressing (see page 153). Toss well. Marinate in the refrigerator for at least 2 hours before serving, toss again, then sprinkle with 1 tablespoon (15 ml) of chopped parsley.

INGREDIENTS TO SERVE SIX AS A STARTER:
$\frac{1}{2}$ lb (250 g) dried haricot beans
$\frac{1}{2}$ teaspoon (2.5 ml) salt
6 oz (150 g) tuna fish
1 small onion
5 tablespoons (75 ml) chopped parsley
1 lemon
$\frac{1}{2}$ pint (300 ml) basic vinaigrette dressing (see page 153)

Sweet and Sour Beans

Soak $\frac{1}{2}$ pound (250 g) of dried haricot beans in 1 pint (600 ml) of water.

Put the beans into a saucepan. Add water to bring the soaking water up to 1 pint (600 ml). Pour it into the saucepan. Cook the beans, covered, for 1 hour, or until tender. Drain the beans and reserve the cooking liquor.

Chop $\frac{1}{4}$ pound (100 g) of bacon. Chop 1 small onion. Scrub $\frac{1}{2}$ pound (250 g) of carrots and cut into $\frac{1}{2}$-inch (1-cm) dice. Peel and core 1 tart large apple and slice it thickly. Shred $\frac{1}{2}$ pound (250 g) white cabbage.

Put the bacon into a large saucepan and fry over low heat until the fat runs. Add the onion, and fry, stirring frequently, for 3 minutes.

Add the diced carrots, the sliced apple, 2 ounces (50 g) of sultanas and the drained beans to the pan. Add water to make the cooking liquor up to 1 pint (600 ml) and add it to the pan with 1 tablespoon (15 ml) of wine vinegar and salt and pepper to taste. Simmer, covered, for 20 minutes. Add the cabbage and continue to cook, covered, for 5 to 10 minutes, or until the vegetables are cooked. Serve hot.

INGREDIENTS TO SERVE FOUR TO SIX:
$\frac{1}{2}$ lb (250 g) dried haricot beans
$\frac{1}{4}$ lb (100 g) bacon
1 small onion
$\frac{1}{2}$ lb (250 g) carrots
1 tart large apple
$\frac{1}{2}$ lb (250 g) white cabbage
2 oz (50 g) sultanas
1 tablespoon (15 ml) wine vinegar
salt
pepper

Mexican Kidney Beans

Soak $\frac{1}{2}$ pound (250 g) of dried kidney beans in $1\frac{1}{2}$ pints (850 ml) of water. Drain the beans.

Slice $\frac{1}{2}$ pound (250 g) of onions. Cut 1 green pepper into strips, discarding the seeds and pith. Blanch, peel and coarsely chop 1 pound (500 g) of ripe tomatoes.

Heat 2 tablespoons (30 ml) of corn oil in a saucepan. Add the sliced onions and 1 large clove of garlic, crushed, and fry for 3 minutes, stirring frequently. Stir in $\frac{1}{2}$ teaspoon (2.5 ml) of chilli powder with the green pepper and fry for 1 minute.

Add the tomatoes, $1\frac{1}{4}$ pints (750 ml) of water and salt and pepper. Bring to the boil, stirring occasionally, then add the drained kidney beans.

Cover the pan, reduce the heat and simmer for $1\frac{1}{2}$ hours, or until the beans are tender. Stir in 2 ounces (50 g) of peanuts and cook for 10 minutes more. Serve hot.

INGREDIENTS TO SERVE FOUR:
$\frac{1}{2}$ lb (250 g) dried kidney beans
$\frac{1}{2}$ lb (250 g) onions
1 green pepper
1 lb (500 g) ripe tomatoes
2 tablespoons (30 ml) corn oil
1 large garlic clove
$\frac{1}{2}$ teaspoon (2.5 ml) chilli powder
salt
pepper
2 oz (50 g) peanuts

Hopping John

This recipe from the United States is a mixture of black-eyed peas, rice and tomatoes.

Soak ½ pound (250 g) of dried black-eyed peas in 1 pint (600 ml) of water.

Drain the peas, reserving the soaking water, and put them into a saucepan. Add water to bring the soaking water up to 1 pint (600 ml) and pour it over the peas. Cover the pan and bring to the boil. Reduce the heat and simmer for 1 hour, or until the beans are tender.

Blanch and peel ½ pound (250 g) of ripe tomatoes. Cut them into halves and remove the seeds. Coarsely chop the tomatoes and add to the peas with ¼ pound (100 g) of brown rice.

Cover the pan and continue to simmer, stirring occasionally, for about 40 minutes adding a little more water during cooking if necessary, or until the peas and rice are cooked and all the water has been absorbed.

Season to taste with salt and pepper and serve sprinkled with 2 tablespoons (30 ml) of chopped parsley.

INGREDIENTS TO SERVE FOUR:
½ lb (250 g) dried black-eyed peas
½ lb (250 g) ripe tomatoes
¼ lb (100 g) brown rice
salt
pepper
2 tablespoons (30 ml) chopped parsley

Pease Pudding

This old English pudding of dried peas is traditionally served with pork.

Soak ½ pound (250 g) of dried peas in 1 pint (600 ml) of water.

Put the soaked peas and the soaking water into a saucepan with 1 sprig of mint, 1 sprig of parsley and 1 sprig of thyme. Cover the pan and bring to the boil. Reduce the heat and simmer for 1 hour, or until the peas are soft. Stir occasionally and add a little more water if necessary.

Preheat the oven to 350°F (180°C, Gas Mark 4).

Drain the peas, then liquidize or sieve them. Beat 1 egg, then stir it into the pea purée. Season with salt and pepper.

Lightly grease an ovenproof dish. Spoon the pea mixture into it and level the surface. Bake for 30 minutes.

Serve hot.

INGREDIENTS TO SERVE FOUR:
½ lb (250 g) dried peas
1 mint sprig
1 parsley sprig
1 thyme sprig
1 egg
salt
pepper

Lentil and Nut Rissoles

Put 6 ounces (150 g) of split red lentils into a saucepan. Chop 1 small onion and add it to the pan. Pour in ¾ pint (450 ml) of water. Cover the pan and bring to the boil. Reduce the heat and simmer gently, stirring occasionally, for 40 to 45 minutes, or until the lentils are soft and all the water has been absorbed.

Preheat the oven to 400°F (200°C, Gas Mark 6). Chop ¼ pound (100 g) of almonds and put them on a board.

Let the lentil purée cool, then beat in ¼ pound (100 g) of curd cheese, 2 ounces (50 g) of fresh breadcrumbs, 2 tablespoons (30 ml) of chopped parsley and salt and pepper.

Divide the mixture into 8 and shape into rolls. Coat them with the chopped almonds.

Put the rolls on a greased baking sheet and bake for 20 to 30 minutes, or until they are golden brown.

Serve hot or cold.

INGREDIENTS TO SERVE FOUR:
6 oz (150 g) split red lentils
1 small onion
¼ lb (100 g) almonds
salt
pepper
¼ lb (100 g) curd cheese
2 oz (50 g) fresh breadcrumbs
2 tablespoons (30 ml) chopped parsley

PREPARING LENTIL AND NUT RISSOLES

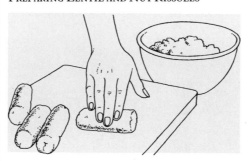

Shape the lentil mixture into rolls.

Roll the lentil rissoles in chopped nuts.

Lentil and Ham Soup

Put ¼ pound (100 g) of split red lentils into a large saucepan.

Chop 1 large onion. Slice 1 large carrot. Finely slice 2 sticks of celery. Add the onion, carrot and celery to the pan with ¼ pound (100 g) of chopped cooked ham. Pour in 2 pints (1 litre) of well-seasoned beef stock.

Cover the pan and bring to the boil. Reduce the heat and simmer, stirring occasionally, for 45 to 60 minutes, or until the lentils have cooked and have thickened the soup.

Season to taste with salt and pepper and serve hot.

INGREDIENTS TO SERVE FOUR TO SIX:
¼ lb (100 g) split red lentils
1 large onion
1 large carrot
2 celery sticks
¼ lb (100 g) cooked ham
2 pints (1 litre) beef stock
salt
pepper

Hummus

This Middle Eastern purée of chick peas can be eaten as a spread or a dip.

Soak ½ pound (250 g) of chick peas in 1 pint (600 ml) of water.

Put the chick peas and soaking water into a saucepan with 1 crushed clove of garlic. Cover the pan and bring to the boil. Reduce the heat and simmer for 30 to 40 minutes, or until the chick peas are tender, adding more water if necessary.

Drain the chick peas if necessary. Mash them to a purée, then stir in ¼ pint (150 ml) of yogurt, the juice of ½ lemon, salt and pepper. Beat until smooth. Alternatively, put all the ingredients into a liquidizer and blend until smooth.

Sprinkle with paprika and serve hot or cold.

INGREDIENTS TO SERVE FOUR:
½ lb (250 g) chick peas
1 garlic clove
¼ pint (150 ml) yogurt
½ lemon
salt
pepper
paprika

SALAD LEAVES /Filling Without Fattening

THE SIMPLEST SALAD is made with raw green leaves. It may be of one type of leaf, usually lettuce, or a mixture of several types. Either way it is called a green salad. The English and French eat it with meat, fish and poultry, while in the United States a green salad is usually served as a separate course, often at the start of a meal. The American way is nutritionally more sensible; you are likely to eat more health-promoting salad when you are hungry than when you are satiated with other food, particularly meat.

The image of the "simple salad" is of cool, crisp, tender greenness; the reality on the plate is too often a pile of badly savaged lettuce doused in oil and vinegar. If you are able to grow your own salad vegetables, and grow them well, nothing should go wrong. The most important quality of a salad is freshness, for without that there can be no crispness.

The lettuce is the most popular salad plant. Grown either outdoors or under glass it is available all year round, and yet one seldom tires of it. The soft, round cabbage or butterhead type has the tenderest leaves, but they soon wilt. The large cabbage types of summer have dense hearts, which will keep crisp in the salad compartment of a refrigerator. The inner leaves of the elongated Cos lettuce are tender and sweet, but the dark green outside leaves can be tough.

We are always being encouraged to eat the outer leaves of lettuce because they are richer in vitamin C. But some common sense compromise is needed here. The outer leaves of lettuces bought in a shop are those most likely to have been exposed to pesticides when they were growing, and to have wilted in marketing. The outer leaves of lettuces grown in our own gardens have probably suffered the attentions of slugs and the

The Nutrients in Salad Leaves
Salad leaves have few calories. Three and a half ounces (100 g) of lettuce, for example, provide less than 20.

All the crisp, green salad vegetables, right, are very low in calories and they are also filling. In the bowl, clockwise from the front are: mustard and cress, chicory, Cos lettuce and Webb's lettuce, surrounding a soft-hearted, cabbage-type lettuce. These salad plants are all a reasonably good source of vitamin C, but cress is particularly rich in it, as well as being high in carotene.

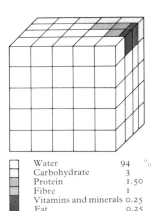

Water	94	%
Carbohydrate	3	
Protein	1.50	
Fibre	1	
Vitamins and minerals	0.25	
Fat	0.25	

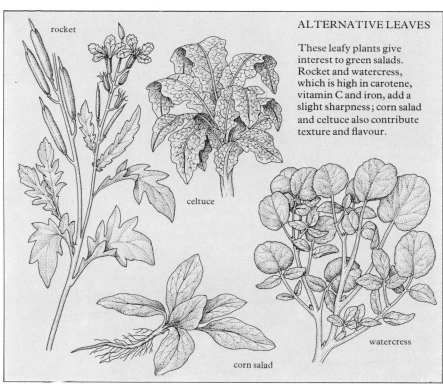

rocket

celtuce

corn salad

watercress

ALTERNATIVE LEAVES

These leafy plants give interest to green salads. Rocket and watercress, which is high in carotene, vitamin C and iron, add a slight sharpness; corn salad and celtuce also contribute texture and flavour.

Nutritionally exceptional, salad alfalfa (above) has the added virtue of needing only a jam jar and water to sprout. Full of protein and vitamins, particularly vitamin C, and such minerals as calcium, iron and phosphorus, salad alfalfa is ready to eat in three to four days. It has a crunchy texture and a taste reminiscent of fresh, sweet garden peas. But unlike the peas it can be grown with next to no effort all year round.

neighbours' pets. The solution is to discard the outer leaves and eat more of the heart, which is, anyway, so much more enjoyable. There is no danger of obesity from eating a lot of lettuce because it is so low in calories. On the contrary, the bulkiness of salad, and the time taken to eat it, are likely to lessen your intake of more fattening food.

In a simple green salad other leaves may be substituted for lettuce. The most likely alternatives are curly endive and the broad-leaved endive. The leaves of the growing plant have to be blanched by the exclusion of light or they are unacceptably bitter.

Chicory, sometimes called Belgian endive, is another variant. What we eat are the forced blanched chicons; if these tightly packed bundles of leaves are exposed to the light they soon become flabby and bitter. Celtuce, a lettuce on a stem, is seldom available in shops, but it is quite easy to grow. Although not primarily a salad plant, shredded Chinese cabbage makes beautifully crisp eating. It is less chewy than finely shredded white cabbage, which is also commonly used in salads.

The cresses—watercress, the comparable American cress, and the cress usually found in partnership with mustard—introduce a variety of warm to hot tastes to salads. Dandelion leaves and corn salad provide other sharp tastes. Both grow wild, but there are more succulent cultivated varieties.

Any salad, particularly a green salad, may be improved or ruined by a dressing. A little salt seems natural, since the word for salad in many languages is derived from *sal*, the Latin word for salt. But oil, vinegar or lemon juice will change the texture and flavour. If that is what you want there is no harm in it; lemon juice will give added vitamin C and you can substitute such polyunsaturated oils as corn oil or safflower oil for olive oil, whatever food snobs say.

You may also enjoy tossing salads as a gastronomic performance. The washed leaves must be dried in a towel, cotton bag or wire basket. The softer the leaves the greater the care that must be taken to keep them from becoming sodden with dressing. How much oil to use is largely a matter of taste, but even a large salad will not need more than a tablespoonful. Then toss the salad to spread the oil over the leaves. The method is to lift them about six inches (15 cm) in the air with a large wooden salad fork and spoon, and then give them a whirl as you let them fall back into the bowl. When the leaves are reasonably well coated, add the lemon juice and vinegar (preferably wine or cider vinegar) and the salt and pepper, and toss them again.

Salads can also be eaten with only salt and a pinch of ground black pepper. Dressers and tossers may find them surprisingly good and different. Thousand Island, Russian and similar dressings, which are souped up with tabasco or ketchup, let alone bottled salad cream, should certainly be avoided with green salads and preferably altogether.

Endive Salad with Mushrooms and Ham

Cut the stalk from 1 head of endive, separate the leaves, wash and drain them well.

Wash 2 ounces (50 g) of mushrooms. Cut them into thin slices and put them into a salad bowl. Add 6 tablespoons (90 ml) of basic vinaigrette dressing or tomato dressing (see page 153) and toss until all the mushrooms are coated. Marinate the mushrooms for 30 minutes.

Cut $\frac{1}{2}$ pound (250 g) piece of cooked ham into strips about 1 by $\frac{1}{4}$ inch (2 cm by 6 mm) and add them to the mushrooms.

Wash and thinly slice 1 small bulb of fennel and add it to the bowl with 2 tomatoes cut into wedges. Add the endive. Toss well before serving.

INGREDIENTS TO SERVE FOUR:
1 endive head
2 oz (50 g) mushrooms
6 tablespoons (90 ml) basic vinaigrette or tomato juice dressing (see page 153)
$\frac{1}{2}$ lb (250 g) cooked ham
1 small fennel bulb
2 tomatoes

Chicory, Watercress and Orange Salad

Separate the leaves from 2 large heads of chicory. Wash and dry them. Put the larger leaves around the edge of a salad bowl with the leaves pointing upwards. Slice the remaining chicory and put it in the centre.

Remove the coarse stalks from 1 large bunch of watercress. Wash and drain the watercress and add half to the chicory in the centre and reserve the rest.

Cut the peel and pith from 3 oranges. Cut the fruit into thin slices and arrange them in the centre of the bowl. Put the remaining watercress in a ring between the oranges and chicory.

Pour over 6 tablespoons (90 ml) of basic vinaigrette dressing made with lemon juice (see page 153).

Chop 1 ounce (25 g) of walnuts and sprinkle over the top.

Serve immediately.

INGREDIENTS TO SERVE FOUR:
2 large chicory heads
1 large watercress bunch
3 oranges
6 tablespoons (90 ml) basic vinaigrette dressing made with lemon juice (see page 153)
1 oz (25 g) walnuts

This tempting display of crisp salads includes, clockwise, Chicory, Watercress and Orange Salad, Tossed Salad, Caesar Salad, Cress and Egg Salad and Endive Salad with Mushrooms and Ham.

Cress and Egg Salad

Hard boil and cool 4 eggs. Wash and dry
1 small lettuce and arrange the leaves in
1 large or 4 individual salad bowls.

Peel the eggs, cut them into halves
lengthways and arrange them on the lettuce
leaves. Pour $\frac{1}{4}$ pint (150 ml) of watercress
yogurt dressing (see page 153) over the eggs.

Thinly slice 8 red or white radishes and
arrange them around the eggs.

Garnish the salad generously with mustard
and cress or watercress.

INGREDIENTS TO SERVE FOUR:
4 large eggs
1 small lettuce
$\frac{1}{4}$ pint (150 ml) watercress yogurt
dressing (see page 153)
8 red or white radishes
mustard and cress or watercress

Tossed Salad

Wash 1 medium-sized cos lettuce and a
variety of other greens, including chicory,
endive, escarole, watercress and young
spinach leaves and leave to drain.

Rub the inside of a large salad bowl with
$\frac{1}{2}$ garlic clove. Discard the garlic. Tear the
greens into fairly large pieces and put them
into the bowl. Cut 2 ripe medium-sized
tomatoes into wedges and add them to the
salad. Peel and slice $\frac{1}{2}$ cucumber and add it to
the bowl with 2 coarsely chopped spring
onions. Separate and wash 1 small bunch of
seedless green grapes. Slice 4 crisp red
radishes and add with the grapes to the bowl.
Sprinkle with 2 tablespoons (30 ml) of
crumbled Roquefort or Stilton cheese and
2 ounces (50 g) of anchovies rolled with
capers.

Toss the salad lightly. Add 4 tablespoons
(60 ml) of olive oil or corn oil, $1\frac{1}{2}$ tablespoons
(22 ml) of wine vinegar, and salt and pepper
to taste. Toss well and serve immediately.

INGREDIENTS TO SERVE FOUR TO SIX:
1 medium-sized cos lettuce
other greens as available
$\frac{1}{2}$ garlic clove
2 ripe medium-sized tomatoes
$\frac{1}{2}$ cucumber
2 spring onions
1 small bunch seedless green grapes
4 crisp red radishes
2 tablespoons (30 ml) crumbled
Roquefort or Stilton cheese
2 oz (50 g) of anchovies, preferably
rolled with capers
4 tablespoons (60 ml) olive oil or corn oil
$1\frac{1}{2}$ tablespoons (22 ml) wine vinegar
salt
pepper

Caesar Salad

Preheat the oven to 325 F (170 C, Gas Mark 3).

Cut 2 slices of bread into cubes. Put them on a baking sheet and bake them, turning them occasionally, for 15 to 20 minutes, or until they are crisp and lightly browned. Cook 1 egg in simmering water for 1 minute. Coarsely chop 8 anchovy fillets.

Put 1 teaspoon (5 ml) of salt in the bottom of a large salad bowl. Crush 1 garlic clove into the salt. Add freshly ground black pepper.

Wash 1 large cos lettuce and drain the leaves well. Tear the lettuce leaves into

Drain washed salad leaves in a salad basket.

bite-sized pieces and add to the salad bowl with the bread croûtons and anchovy fillets. Add 6 tablespoons (90 ml) of olive oil or corn oil and 2 tablespoons (30 ml) of lemon juice and toss well. Sprinkle with 2 tablespoons (30 ml) of grated Parmesan cheese. Break the coddled egg into the bowl and toss thoroughly. Sprinkle with 1 tablespoon (15 ml) of Parmesan cheese and serve immediately.

INGREDIENTS TO SERVE FOUR:
2 slices of bread
1 egg
8 anchovy fillets
1 teaspoon (5 ml) salt
1 garlic clove
freshly ground black pepper
1 large cos lettuce
6 tablespoons (90 ml) olive oil or corn oil
2 tablespoons (30 ml) lemon juice
3 tablespoons (45 ml) grated Parmesan cheese

Lettuce Soup

Lettuce makes a soup with a surprisingly strong flavour. It is an ideal way to use lettuce that is not quite crisp enough to use in a salad.

Wash 1 large lettuce. Shred it and put it into a saucepan. Grate 1 medium-sized onion and add to the lettuce. Grate in the rind of ½ lemon, then squeeze in the juice. Add ¼ teaspoon (1 ml) of grated nutmeg and 1 pint (600 ml) of well-seasoned chicken stock and salt and pepper to taste.

Bring to the boil, cover the pan, reduce the heat and simmer for 15 minutes. Sieve or liquidize the soup. Return it to the pan and pour in ¾ pint (450 ml) of milk.

Reheat and serve hot.

INGREDIENTS TO SERVE FOUR:
1 large lettuce
1 medium-sized onion
½ lemon
¼ teaspoon (1 ml) grated nutmeg
1 pint (600 ml) chicken stock
salt
pepper
¾ pint (450 ml) milk

Baked Stuffed Lettuce

Preheat the oven to 350 F (180 C, Gas Mark 4).

Keeping them whole wash and dry 2 round lettuces.

For the stuffing, flake 8 ounces (250 g) of tuna fish into a mixing bowl. Add 2 ounces (50 g) of fresh breadcrumbs, 1 tablespoon (15 ml) of chopped parsley and 8 black olives, that have been pitted and chopped. Stir in 1 tablespoon (15 ml) of lemon juice, 1 crushed garlic clove and salt and pepper. Mix well.

Spread open the centre of the lettuces and spoon in the stuffing.

Pour 5 tablespoons (75 ml) of water into a casserole, then put in the stuffed lettuces.

Cover the casserole and bake for 15 minutes.

Serve at once.

INGREDIENTS TO SERVE FOUR:
2 round lettuces
8 oz (250 g) tuna fish
2 oz (50 g) fresh breadcrumbs
1 tablespoon (15 ml) chopped parsley
8 black olives
1 tablespoon (15 ml) lemon juice
1 garlic clove
salt
pepper

STUFFING LETTUCE

Open the leaves and stuff the lettuce.

Seafood, Avocado and Grape Salad

Wash 1 cos lettuce and drain the leaves well. Tear the leaves into bite-sized pieces and put them into a large salad bowl. Add ½ pound (250 g) of cooked crab meat, ½ pound (250 g) of shelled cooked prawns and ¼ pound (100 g) of seedless green grapes.

Peel and remove the stone from 1 medium-sized avocado. Dice the avocado into a small bowl. Lightly toss the avocado with 1 tablespoon (15 ml) of lemon juice then add it to the salad bowl.

Pour in 6 tablespoons (90 ml) special salad dressing. Toss well and serve.

INGREDIENTS TO SERVE FOUR:
1 cos lettuce
½ lb (250 g) cooked crab meat
½ pound (250 g) shelled cooked prawns
¼ lb (100 g) seedless green grapes
1 medium-sized avocado
1 tablespoon (15 ml) lemon juice
6 tablespoons (90 ml) special salad dressing

Watercress and Grapefruit Salad

Wash and drain 2 large bunches of watercress. Remove the coarse stalks and put the watercress into a salad bowl.

Thinly slice a 2-inch (5-cm) length of cucumber. Cut the slices into quarters and add them to the watercress.

Toast 2 ounces (50 g) of shelled hazelnuts under a hot grill for 1 to 2 minutes or on the top shelf of a hot oven for 5 to 10 minutes. (Watch them carefully because they burn easily.) Remove the thin brown skins by rubbing the nuts together in a clean tea-towel or a paper bag. Discard the skins and put the hazelnuts into the salad bowl.

Cut the peel and pith from 1 grapefruit. Working over the salad bowl to catch any juice, cut the membrane away from the segments of fruit. Add the segments to the bowl. Squeeze the juice from another ½ grapefruit over the salad. Season with salt and pepper to taste and toss lightly.

INGREDIENTS TO SERVE FOUR:
2 large watercress bunches
2-inch (5-cm) cucumber length
2 oz (50 g) shelled hazelnuts
1½ grapefruits
salt
pepper

Chicory Salad

Wash and drain 1 bunch of watercress. Remove and discard the coarse stalks. Put the watercress into a salad bowl.

Cut 4 heads of chicory into halves lengthways. Wash and drain well, then break them into bite-sized pieces and put into the salad bowl.

In a small bowl combine 4 fluid ounces (120 ml) of corn oil, 3 tablespoons (45 ml) of wine vinegar and 1 tablespoon (15 ml) of chopped chives. Add a pinch of paprika, season to taste with salt and pepper and mix well.

Just before serving pour the dressing over the watercress and chicory and toss lightly.

INGREDIENTS TO SERVE FOUR:
1 watercress bunch
4 chicory heads
4 fluid ounces (120 ml) corn oil
3 tablespoons (45 ml) wine vinegar
1 tablespoon (30 ml) chopped chives
paprika
salt
pepper

Braised Chicory

Preheat the oven to 350 F (180 C, Gas Mark 4).

Cut 4 heads of chicory into halves lengthways. Wash and drain them. Put them into a casserole or an ovenproof dish.

Pour in ¼ pint (150 ml) of chicken stock mixed with the juice of 1 orange, salt, pepper and a pinch of grated nutmeg.

Cover and bake for 15 to 20 minutes, or until the chicory is tender but is still crisp.

Drain the chicory. Pour the stock into a saucepan. Return the chicory to the casserole.

Boil the stock for a few minutes until it has reduced to about 4 tablespoons (60 ml), then pour it over the chicory. Serve at once.

INGREDIENTS TO SERVE FOUR:
4 large chicory heads
¼ pint (150 ml) chicken stock
1 orange
salt
pepper
grated nutmeg

PREPARING CHICORY

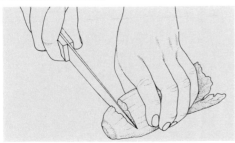

With a sharp knife trim the base of the chicory.

Watercress Yogurt Dressing

Wash 1 small bunch of watercress and remove the coarse stalks. Chop the watercress finely and put it into a mixing bowl with 1 teaspoon (5 ml) of lemon juice, ¼ pint (150 ml) of yogurt, salt and pepper. Mix well. Alternatively put all the ingredients into a liquidizer and blend well.

INGREDIENTS TO DRESS A SALAD TO SERVE FOUR:
1 small watercress bunch
1 teaspoon (5 ml) lemon juice
¼ pint (150 ml) yogurt
salt
pepper

Piquant Yogurt Dressing

Mix ¼ pint (150 ml) of yogurt with the grated rind of ½ lemon, 1 tablespoon (15 ml) of chopped parsley, 1 tablespoon (15 ml) of chopped chives or spring onions and 1 teaspoon (5 ml) of chopped gherkins. Season to taste with salt and freshly ground black pepper and mix well.

INGREDIENTS TO DRESS A SALAD TO SERVE FOUR:
¼ pint (150 ml) yogurt
½ lemon
1 tablespoon (15 ml) chopped parsley
1 tablespoon (15 ml) chopped chives
  or spring onions
1 teaspoon (5 ml) chopped gherkins
salt
freshly ground black pepper

Tomato Juice Dressing

Whisk together 4 tablespoons (60 ml) of tomato juice with 2 tablespoons (30 ml) of lemon juice. Stir in 1 tablespoon (15 ml) of chopped parsley, chives or mint. Season to taste with salt and freshly ground black pepper. Mix well.

INGREDIENTS TO DRESS A SALAD TO SERVE FOUR:
4 tablespoons (60 ml) tomato juice
2 tablespoons (30 ml) lemon juice
1 tablespoon (15 ml) chopped parsley,
  chives or mint
salt
freshly ground black pepper

Special Salad Dressing

In a small bowl mix together 1 crushed garlic clove, 4 tablespoons (60 ml) of corn oil or olive oil, 1 tablespoon (15 ml) of wine vinegar, 1 teaspoon (5 ml) of French mustard and 1 tablespoon (15 ml) of yogurt or single cream. Stir until well blended.

INGREDIENTS TO DRESS A SALAD TO SERVE FOUR:
1 garlic clove
4 tablespoons (60 ml) corn oil or olive oil
1 tablespoon (15 ml) wine vinegar
1 teaspoon (5 ml) French mustard
1 tablespoon (15 ml) yogurt or single
  cream

Basic Vinaigrette Dressing

One tablespoon (15 ml) of chopped herbs, such as parsley, chives, mint, tarragon, oregano or basil, may be added to this dressing.

Put 2 tablespoons (30 ml) of wine vinegar or lemon juice into a small bowl with 5 to 6 tablespoons (75 to 90 ml) or corn oil or olive oil. Add a pinch of dried mustard and salt and freshly ground black pepper to taste. Whisk until well blended and the ingredients have formed a smooth emulsion.

INGREDIENTS TO DRESS A SALAD TO SERVE FOUR:
2 tablespoons (30 ml) wine vinegar or
  lemon juice
5 to 6 tablespoons (75 to 90 ml) corn oil,
  olive oil or sunflower oil
dried mustard
salt
freshly ground black pepper

CHOPPING HERBS

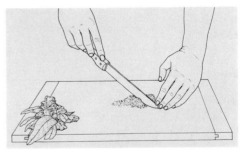

Chop herbs with a sharp knife on a board,

or with a curved blade in a wooden bowl.

The word mushroom has various meanings. It is sometimes used to denote all club-shaped fungi in the class Basidiomycetes or, more specifically, any edible species belonging to the Agaricaceae family. It can also mean any umbrella-shaped edible fungus. More often, however, the word is used to mean all edible fungi including truffles and morels.

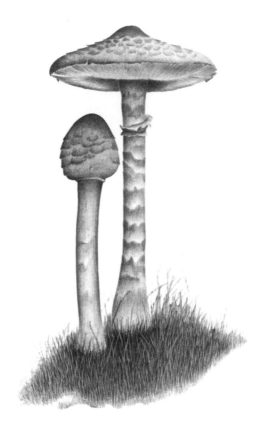

The parasol mushroom (*Lepiota procera*, right) is delicately flavoured with a large cap up to about six inches (15 cm) across, covered with brown scales, and a long mottled brown stem. It is found during the summer and autumn, often growing near, but not under, trees.

MOST PEOPLE IN BRITAIN are afraid to eat any mushrooms except supermarket mushrooms—guaranteed safe if not satisfying. In fact, few mushrooms are dangerous to eat, but many are not worth the effort and some are indeed deadly.

The mystery of mushrooms has fascinated men since the beginning of history; their life style is so different from other plants. Like the other members of the fungi group they do not contain chlorophyll, and instead of converting inorganic substances into organic, as green plants do, they have, like animals, to feed on organic material. Furthermore, unlike most plants, mushrooms do not flower but reproduce themselves by spores, not by seeds.

In most parts of Europe numerous varieties of wild mushrooms are eaten, and it would be considered almost criminal not to do so. People grow up with a taste for them, and acquire a knowledge of which are safe to pick and which are dangerous. Anyone without such experience who is planning to eat wild mushrooms should buy and study well a first-rate field guide that includes the poisonous species. After that, if in doubt throw out.

"Mushroom" has increasingly come to mean only the common field mushroom and the mass-produced cultivated mushroom, which has been derived from it. The cultivated mushroom is invaluable if only because it is available all year. But to neglect the wild species involves the loss of

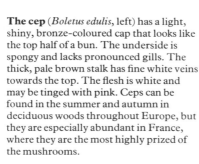

The chanterelle (*Cantharellus cibarius*, left) has an unmistakable shape, colour and odour. The cap looks like a fluted funnel with the gills clearly visible. Both the cap and the short stem are yellow, and the aroma is faintly reminiscent of apricots. The delicately flavoured flesh is firmer than that of other mushrooms and needs to be cooked slightly longer. It is common in deciduous woods in the summer and autumn.

The cep (*Boletus edulis*, left) has a light, shiny, bronze-coloured cap that looks like the top half of a bun. The underside is spongy and lacks pronounced gills. The thick, pale brown stalk has fine white veins towards the top. The flesh is white and may be tinged with pink. Ceps can be found in the summer and autumn in deciduous woods throughout Europe, but they are especially abundant in France, where they are the most highly prized of the mushrooms.

The field mushroom (*Agaricus campestris*, above) looks like the familiar cultivated mushroom. The cap is white and the gills turn pink and then dark brown. It is most likely to be found in the early autumn in fields that are permanently used as pasture. The deadly destroying angel (*Amanita virosa*) has a similar shape to the field mushroom but grows in woods. Fortunately it is uncommon, and differs from a field mushroom in being totally white. The highly poisonous death cap (*Amanita phalloides*) is sometimes confused with the field mushroom, but its cap has an olive tinge and the white gills and stem may also be slightly tinged with green. It appears in deciduous woods or adjoining fields in summer and early autumn.

some incomparable flavours. It is for flavour rather than nutritional value that mushrooms are eaten, but even for that they are not to be scorned. Many wild mushrooms have appreciable amounts of vitamin D, which is not found in green vegetables. And both wild and cultivated mushrooms are good sources of niacin as well as potassium and phosphorus.

Seaweeds, which are a kind of algae, are almost as mysterious as mushrooms, but they are far more nutritious. They are rich in minerals—the gamut runs from aluminium to zinc, with a particular abundance of calcium, potassium and sodium. Iodine is also present and is a strong selling point. Some health-food enthusiasts make the most extravagant claims for the virtues of seaweed. It certainly is nutritionally valuable, but in anything like their natural state most species taste like salt with the consistency of rubber. Even so, more than seventy species serve Man directly as food and concerted efforts are being made to make seaweeds more palatable.

The Celts, Japanese and Chinese share a taste for seaweeds, but in general in the West they are not popular. Most of us eat more seaweed than we realize, however, in the form of vegetable gelatines, in ice-cream, salad dressing, soups and sauces and as sausage skins. Seaweeds are also used to manufacture the harmless indigestible substances that are used as fillers in slimming aids.

EDIBLE SEAWEED

An excellent source of vitamins and minerals, red seaweed can be eaten as a vegetable. Laver (*Porphyra umbilicalis*, top right), once a traditional breakfast accompaniment to bacon and eggs in South Wales, can be bought already boiled and minced, smelling like cabbage and looking like brown spinach. It is then rolled in oatmeal and fried. Laver can also be grilled and eaten on toast. Although many of the larger brown seaweeds are inedible, the common bladder wrack (*Fucus vesiculosus*, below right), which makes a popping sound when it is trodden on, contains useful nutrients. It is usually eaten in the form of pills which are available from health food shops.

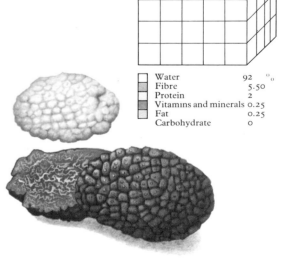

In Japan, brown seaweed, or kelp, gathered from the sea shore, is laid out to dry (left) before being fried or made into soup. The Japanese, who consume large quantities of seaweed, also use kelp as a seasoning or as a garnish for rice.

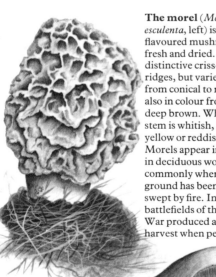

The morel (*Morchella esculenta*, left) is a richly flavoured mushroom, both fresh and dried. The cap has a distinctive criss-cross of ridges, but varies in shape from conical to round and also in colour from ochre to deep brown. When young the stem is whitish, but it turns yellow or reddish as it ages. Morels appear in the spring in deciduous woods, most commonly wherever the ground has been disturbed or swept by fire. In France the battlefields of the First World War produced a great morel harvest when peace came.

The bluet, or blewit, (*Tricholoma personatum*, right) is an edible mushroom popular in parts of England. The cap is grey or pale brown tinged with lilac and the stem is streaked with blue. It is found in pastureland in the autumn.

Truffles are the aristocrats among fungi. Because these woodland plants grow underground all year round most people are unlikely to encounter any except in cans and bottles. They have more aroma than flavour and a little goes a long way in cooking. The most sought after is the Périgord truffle (*Tuber melanosporum*, bottom right). The white flesh of the young truffle gradually turns grey and then almost violet-black. The so-called white truffle of Italy (top right) has a somewhat peppery flavour.

The Nutrients in Mushrooms
Mushrooms are a useful source of B vitamins and three and a half ounces (100 g) provide about 10 Calories.

☐ Water	92	%
☐ Fibre	5.50	
☐ Protein	2	
☐ Vitamins and minerals	0.25	
☐ Fat	0.25	
☐ Carbohydrate	0	

Mushroom Armenienne

Slice 1 large onion, 1 large carrot and 1 stick of celery. Blanch and peel ½ pound (250 g) of tomatoes. Cut the tomatoes into quarters and remove the seeds.

Heat 2 tablespoons (30 ml) of olive oil in a large saucepan. Add the sliced onion, carrot and celery and fry for 3 minutes, stirring frequently. Crush 1 large garlic clove, add it to the pan and fry for 1 minute more

Add ¼ pint (150 ml) of red wine, 1 bouquet garni, consisting of sprigs of thyme and parsley and 1 bay leaf, and salt and pepper to taste. Stir in the tomatoes and 1 pound (500 g) of washed, whole button mushrooms.

Bring to the boil, then reduce the heat and simmer gently for 15 minutes.

Leave the mixture to cool, remove the herbs and chill for at least 1 hour before serving.

Serve sprinkled with 2 tablespoons (30 ml) of chopped parsley.

INGREDIENTS TO SERVE FOUR:
**1 large onion
1 large carrot
1 celery stick
½ lb (250 g) tomatoes
2 tablespoons (30 ml) olive oil
1 garlic clove
¼ pint (150 ml) red wine
1 bouquet garni, consisting of sprigs of
    thyme and parsley and 1 bay leaf
salt
pepper
1 lb (500 g) button mushrooms
2 tablespoons (30 ml) chopped parsley**

Stuffed Mushrooms

Preheat the oven to 375 F (190 C, Gas Mark 5).

Wash 8 large flat mushrooms but do not peel them. Cut off and reserve the stalks. Put the mushroom caps into a lightly greased ovenproof dish.

Finely chop ¼ pound (100 g) of bacon. Finely chop 1 medium-sized onion. Put the bacon into a saucepan and fry over low heat until the fat runs. Add the onion and 1 crushed garlic clove and fry with the bacon, stirring frequently, for about 3 minutes. Finely chop the reserved mushroom stalks, add them to the pan and fry for 2 minutes more.

Remove the pan from the heat and stir in the grated rind of 1 lemon, 2 tablespoons (30 ml) of chopped parsley, salt, pepper and a pinch of grated nutmeg.

Add 3 ounces (75 g) of fresh breadcrumbs and 2 tablespoons (30 ml) of dry sherry and mix well.

Divide the filling between the mushroom caps. Sprinkle them with grated Parmesan cheese.

Bake for 20 minutes, or until the

mushrooms are tender and the stuffing is lightly browned on top. Serve immediately.

INGREDIENTS TO SERVE FOUR:
**8 large flat mushrooms
¼ lb (100 g) bacon
1 medium-sized onion
1 garlic clove
1 lemon
2 tablespoons (30 ml) chopped parsley
salt
pepper
nutmeg
3 oz (75 g) fresh breadcrumbs
2 tablespoons (30 ml) dry sherry
grated Parmesan cheese**

STUFFING MUSHROOMS

Wash and trim the stalks from large flat mushrooms.

Spoon the filling onto the mushrooms.

Mushroom Flan

Preheat the oven to 400 F (200 C, Gas Mark 6).

Make 6 ounces (150 g) of shortcrust pastry with wholewheat flour (see page 34) and line an 8-inch (20-cm) flan ring or pie dish. Bake for 15 minutes. Remove the baking paper and beans and bake for 5 minutes more.

Reduce the oven temperature to 350 F (180°C, Gas Mark 4).

Wash and slice ½ pound (250 g) of button mushrooms. Put them into a saucepan with the grated rind and juice of ½ lemon, 2 sprigs of thyme, salt and pepper. Cover the pan and heat gently for 5 minutes, or until the mushrooms are tender.

Strain the mushrooms and reserve the juice. Put the mushrooms into the flan case.

Beat 2 eggs with ¼ pint (150 ml) of milk and

the reserved mushroom juice. Season with salt and pepper. Pour over the mushrooms
Bake for 30 minutes, or until the custard is set.

Serve warm or cold.

INGREDIENTS TO SERVE FOUR TO SIX:
**6 oz (150 g) shortcrust pastry made with
    wholewheat flour (see page 34)
½ lb (250 g) button mushrooms
½ lemon
2 thyme sprigs
salt
pepper
2 eggs
¼ pint (150 ml) milk**

Mushroom Duxelles

This thick concentrated mushroom sauce is very versatile. It can be used as a sauce or flavouring for many dishes. Duxelles can be stored in the refrigerator, in a tightly covered jar, for 1 week.

Finely chop 1 medium-sized onion. Finely chop ½ pound (250 g) of flat mushrooms including the stalks.

Heat 2 tablespoons (30 ml) of corn oil in a saucepan. Add the onion and fry, stirring frequently, for 3 minutes.

Add the mushrooms and fry for 3 minutes. Stir in ¼ teaspoon (1 ml) of dried mixed herbs and ¼ teaspoon (1 ml) of paprika and cook for 1 minute more.

Add ¼ pint (150 ml) of dry white wine, ¼ pint (150 ml) of beef stock and 1 teaspoon (5 ml) of lemon juice. Simmer, uncovered, until the liquid has reduced and the sauce is thick. Season to taste with salt and pepper.

INGREDIENTS TO MAKE ONE PINT (600 ML) OF SAUCE:
**1 medium-sized onion
½ lb (250 g) flat mushrooms
2 tablespoons (30 ml) corn oil
¼ teaspoon (1 ml) dried mixed herbs
¼ teaspoon (1 ml) paprika
¼ pint (150 ml) dry white wine
¼ pint (150 ml) beef stock
1 teaspoon (5 ml) lemon juice
salt
pepper**

Mushrooms Poached with Lemon and Herbs

Trim the stalks and wash 1 pound (500 g) of mushrooms. Cut large mushrooms into halves or quarters and leave the small ones whole.

Put the mushrooms into a saucepan with the grated rind and juice of 1 lemon, salt, pepper, 4 sprigs of thyme and 1 large sprig of parsley.

Cover the pan and cook over very low heat for about 2 minutes, to draw out the juices. Then raise the heat and simmer gently for 5 minutes, or until the mushrooms are tender. (Overcooking will toughen the mushrooms.)

Serve hot or cold.

INGREDIENTS TO SERVE FOUR:
1 lb (500 g) mushrooms
1 lemon
salt
pepper
4 thyme sprigs
1 large parsley sprig

Mushroom Soup

Wash and slice ½ pound (250 g) of mushrooms and put them into a saucepan with 1 chopped medium-sized onion and the grated rind and juice of ½ lemon.

Pour in 1 pint (600 ml) of chicken stock and ½ pint (300 ml) of milk. Add 1 sprig of thyme and salt and pepper to taste.

Cover the pan and bring to the boil. Reduce the heat and simmer for 5 minutes. Remove a few sliced mushrooms for garnish and simmer the soup for 10 minutes.

Liquidize the soup and pour it back into the pan. Reheat and adjust the seasoning.

Serve hot garnished with the reserved mushrooms.

INGREDIENTS TO SERVE FOUR TO SIX:
½ lb (250 g) mushrooms
1 medium-sized onion
½ lemon
1 pint (600 ml) chicken stock
½ pint (300 ml) milk
1 thyme sprig
salt
pepper

Makizushi

For this Japanese hors d'oeuvre, vinegared rice, or *sushi*, and tuna fish are wrapped in thin sheets of *nori*, dried laver seaweed. Short-grained rice should be used in this dish because it sticks together. Serve cold with drinks or as a first course.

Put ½ pound (250 g) of short-grained rice into a saucepan. Add 1 pint (600 ml) of water and a little salt. Cover the pan and bring to the boil. Reduce the heat and simmer the rice for about 15 minutes, or until the rice is tender and all the water has been absorbed. Remove the pan from the heat and leave covered for 5 minutes.

Transfer the cooked rice to a mixing bowl. Add 4 tablespoons (60 ml) of white wine vinegar and mix well. Let the rice cool slightly.

Pass 6 sheets of dried *nori* quickly over a

gas flame. This turns the *nori* from black to green and improves the flavour.

Lay the sheets of *nori* on a flat surface. Spread the rice over the seaweed leaving a margin of 2 inches (5 cm) along one of the short sides on each sheet. Flake 8 ounces (250 g) of tuna fish. Put the fish in a strip along the centre of the *nori* sheets.

Tightly roll up the *nori* towards the uncovered edge like a Swiss roll, sealing the join. Leave to stand for 5 minutes then cut the rolls into 1-inch (2-cm) slices, trimming off the ends if necessary.

INGREDIENTS TO SERVE SIX TO EIGHT:
½ lb (250 g) short-grained rice
salt
4 tablespoons (60 ml) white wine vinegar
6 sheets dried nori seaweed
8 oz (250 g) tuna fish

MAKING MAKIZUSHI

Pass sheets of dried seaweed rapidly over a flame.

Cover with filling and roll the dried seaweed up.

Slice the makizushi.

Seaweed Baked Fish

Cod, haddock or halibut steaks or a whole round fish, such as mackerel, can be substituted for the fillets in this recipe and baked on the seaweed.

Preheat the oven to 350°F (180°C, Gas Mark 4).

Put 2 ounces (50 g) of dried wakame seaweed into an ovenproof dish. Pour in ½ pint (300 ml) of water and toss the seaweed.

Cover the dish and bake for 30 minutes, or until the seaweed has softened, it will absorb the water and become plump. Stir the seaweed once or twice during cooking to prevent the top from becoming dry. Alternatively, the seaweed may be cooked in a saucepan for about 20 minutes.

When the seaweed is tender put 4 rolled fillets of white fish on top. Add a little more water if the seaweed looks dry.

Cover the dish and bake for 20 to 30 minutes, depending on the size of the fish.

Serve hot, garnished with wedges of lemon.

INGREDIENTS TO SERVE FOUR:
2 oz (50 g) dried wakame seaweed
4 white fish fillets
1 lemon

Irish Moss Ginger Mould

Irish moss or carrageen seaweed can be used for setting foods instead of gelatine. Agar agar, which is powdered dried seaweed, can be substituted.

Measure ½ ounce (15 g) of carrageen. Rinse off the salt, which is used to preserve it, by stirring it briskly in hot water and then removing it immediately.

Put the carrageen into a saucepan with 1½ pints (850 ml) of milk and the grated rind of 1 lemon and 1 orange. Peel and coarsely chop 1 ounce (25 g) of root ginger and add it to the milk.

Bring to the boil, reduce the heat and simmer gently, stirring occasionally, for 15 minutes, or until the mixture thickens and coats the back of the spoon.

Wet a 1½-pint (850-ml) ring mould and pour the mixture into it. Refrigerate the mould for at least 3 hours before serving.

To serve, turn the mould out on to a plate and fill the centre with sliced oranges or bananas.

INGREDIENTS TO SERVE FOUR TO SIX:
½ oz (15 g) carrageen seaweed
1½ pints (850 ml) milk
1 lemon
1 orange
1 oz (25 g) root ginger
orange or banana slices

IN RECENT YEARS it has become fashionable to rhapsodize about the bounty of Nature and to moan about our neglect of it. Books written in the rosy glow of enthusiasm make us feel that the Garden of Eden is still there for the picking, or at least in a medieval version, for the Middle Ages have a particular fascination for the wild-fooders.

But there are several things to bear in mind before you set off in the car in search of, for example, Billy Buttons, Rags and Tatters, Chucky Cheeses, Goodnight-at-Moon, Flibberty Gibbets, or any other of the folksy names given to the mallow (*Malva sylvestris*), in order, with the help of an electric blender, to make a passable imitation of Melokhia, the supposedly aphrodisiac Arab peasant soup. In the first place, although the Ancient Romans liked mallows, medieval peasants had already come to regard them as famine fare. More important, in the Middle Ages there was far more countryside and there were far fewer people, and no automobiles. If the two-car families of the industrialized nations seriously took to hunting for wild food what countryside remains would quickly be ravaged.

Furthermore where would you search—banks, hedgerows and roadside verges polluted by the exhaust of cars or sprayed with labour-saving herbicides, or on farm land, trampling on cultivated crops on which your existence depends? Or would you crowd on to commons, wiping out the already diminishing number of species?

There is another consideration. Some of these supposedly desirable wayside plants have gone out of favour simply because the cultivated varieties are so much better. This applies particularly to roots, of which the wild specimens are miserably small and bitter. Many leaves are also not only bitter but tough, because we pick them when we happen to be in the country and not at the exact moment when they are young, tender and succulent.

You are more likely to catch them at that stage if you have a weed-ridden garden of your own. Then, for most of the year, the leaves of wild dandelions will provide you with a sharp addition to salads, or they can be cooked like spinach. If you manured them and drew soil around the leaves you would have a substitute for chicory. Their roots, roasted and ground, are a substitute for coffee, and wine can be made from the flowers. Chickweed is a very persistent garden weed, and

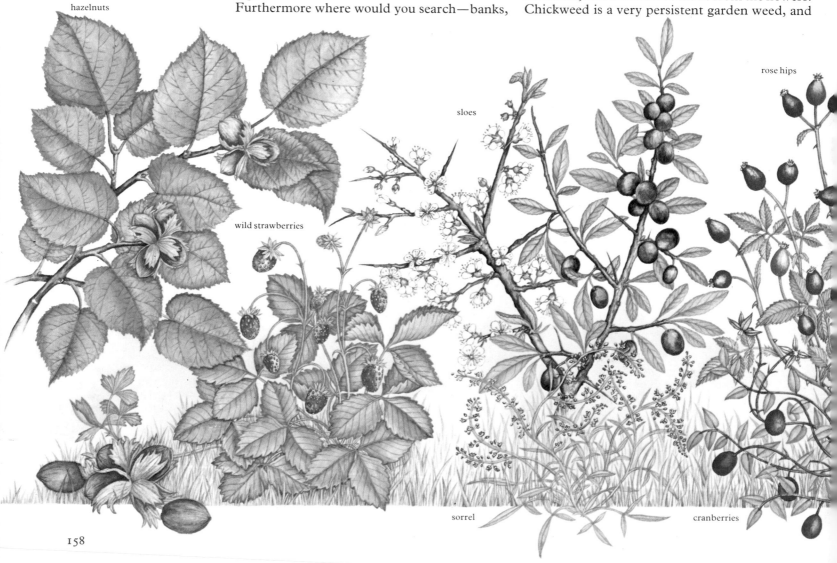

hazelnuts

wild strawberries

sloes

rose hips

sorrel

cranberries

it is worthwhile stewing it in butter as a change from putting it on the compost heap. Since ground elder (or bishop's weed, according to one's ecclesiastical prejudices) is virtually impossible to get rid of, it is worth eating as a substitute for spinach. Yet another spinach substitute is the inevitable nettle. It should be picked only in the early springtime of its youth, for in summer it becomes horribly bitter and undesirably laxative.

The real countryside, when you find it, undoubtedly does offer some beautiful flavours. While roots have been improved by cultivation, many fruits have suffered. Tiny wild strawberries, wild raspberries and blackberries have flavours which cannot be matched by garden varieties. It is, however, politic to curb your greed and leave some of these berries for the birds so that they may scatter the remaining good seed on the land and thereby provide more fruit in the coming years.

There are other plentiful berries that make excellent jellies. Rose hips, mixed with a few crab apples so that they set, make an excellent jelly to go with game. A good jelly can be made with the haws of hawthorn if they, too, are mixed with crab apples. Elderberries are better used with blackberries than on their own. If you can get them before the birds do, the beautiful scarlet berries of the rowan, or mountain ash, make a smoky marmaladey jelly. Dark blue sloes are the tartest of all berries, totally inedible until they have matured for a few months in gin, although it is actually for the refreshingly flavoured gin that you go to this trouble. Sloes also make a very brightly coloured jelly.

The best jelly of all is made from another sour fruit—the wild crab apple, the jelly of which may be anything from a delicate yellow to a deep pink.

After berries, nuts are the most desirable wayside food, but even if you are lucky enough to live near a nut-bearing wayside, your choice will be quite restricted, and will depend on the climate.

If you do go foraging, pick with restraint. Do not strip plants of their leaves or berries or nuts; take a little here and there. Do not snap off branches to reach berries or nuts that are out of arm's reach. Do not wrench mushrooms or other fungi out of the ground, merely twist the stalks. Do not pull up roots. There is then a better chance that something will be left for the following year, both for you and for the wild life that depends far more than humans do on this food.

blackberries

crab apples

sweet chestnuts

bilberries

dandelions

Nettle Soup

Nettles make a delicious soup in spring and early summer when the nettles are young and tender. Cut off the shoots from the top of the nettles, taking off about the top 2 inches (5 cm), including the stalk and the leaves. Cut them with scissors or wear gloves to prevent the nettles from stinging you.

Chop 1 large onion and put it into a large saucepan. Peel and chop ½ pound (250 g) of potatoes. Put the potatoes into the pan. Add 2 sprigs of mint, 1½ pints (850 ml) of chicken stock, salt, pepper and the juice of ½ lemon.

Cover the pan and bring to the boil. Reduce the heat and simmer for 20 minutes.

Wash about 30 nettle tops and add to the soup. Simmer gently for 1 minute. Liquidize and then sieve the soup.

Return the soup to the pan and reheat. Adjust the seasoning, adding a little more stock or milk if a thinner consistency is required. Serve hot or chilled.

INGREDIENTS TO SERVE FOUR TO SIX:
1 large onion
½ lb (250 g) potatoes
2 mint sprigs
1½ pints (850 ml) chicken stock
salt
pepper
½ lemon
30 nettle tops

Dandelion Greens with Bacon

Chop ¼ pound (100 g) of bacon. Put the bacon into a saucepan and fry over low heat until the fat runs.

Wash ½ pound (250 g) of dandelion leaves, about 4 handfuls, and add to the bacon. Fry, stirring constantly, for 1 minute.

Add 5 tablespoons (75 ml) of water, salt and pepper. Cover the pan and cook over low heat for about 2 minutes, or until the leaves are tender but still a bright green colour.

Serve hot.

INGREDIENTS TO SERVE FOUR:
¼ lb (100 g) bacon
½ lb (250 g) dandelion leaves
salt
pepper

Sorrel Purée

Sorrel cooks to a purée in the same way as spinach, but sorrel has a hint of lemon in its flavour, which makes it a delicious accompaniment to egg dishes as well as to fish, poultry and veal. The purée may be liquidized to make a smooth sauce.

Remove the stalks and wash 1 pound (500 g) of sorrel leaves. Put the leaves into a saucepan without draining them.

Cover the pan and cook over low heat, stirring occasionally, for 2 to 3 minutes or until the sorrel wilts. Stir in salt and pepper and a pinch of grated nutmeg.

Serve hot.

INGREDIENTS TO SERVE FOUR:
1 lb (500 g) sorrel leaves
salt
pepper
grated nutmeg

Hazelnut Torte

Preheat the oven to 350°F (180°C, Gas Mark 4). Lightly grease two 8-inch (20-cm) sandwich tins and line them with greaseproof paper. Grease the paper.

Separate 4 eggs into 2 mixing bowls. Whisk the egg whites until stiff. Do not wash the whisk.

Add ¼ pound (100 g) of soft brown sugar to the egg yolks and whisk with the same whisk until the mixture is thick and creamy.

Grind ¼ pound (100 g) of hazelnuts. (Leave the thin brown skins on the hazelnuts because this gives a better flavour.)

Fold the egg whites, the ground hazelnuts and the grated rind of 1 lemon into the whisked egg yolks until well blended.

Divide the mixture between the prepared sandwich tins.

Bake for 25 to 30 minutes, or until the layers have risen, are lightly browned and springy to the touch.

Leave the layers to cool in the tins until they shrink away from the sides, then turn out.

When the layers are completely cool sandwich them together using ½ pound (250 g) of crushed strawberries, raspberries or apricot purée for the filling.

INGREDIENTS TO SERVE SIX:
4 eggs
¼ lb (100 g) soft brown sugar
¼ lb (100 g) shelled hazelnuts
1 lemon
½ lb (250 g) strawberries, raspberries or apricot purée

Crab Apple Compote

These small tart apples, which are usually made into jelly or jam, are also delicious cooked in a spicy syrup.

For the syrup, pour 1 pint (600 ml) of water into a saucepan. Add ¼ pound (100 g) of sugar, the thinly pared rind and juice of ½ lemon, 1 cinnamon stick and 2 cloves.

Cook over low heat until the sugar has dissolved, then bring to the boil. Reduce the heat and simmer for 5 minutes.

Wash and core 1½ pounds (700 g) of crab apples. Add the apples to the syrup. Simmer gently for 15 to 20 minutes, or until the apples are tender. Do not overcook or they will burst.

Using a slotted spoon transfer the apples to a serving bowl. Boil the syrup for about 5 minutes, or until it has reduced and thickened slightly. Strain the syrup over the apples.

Serve hot or cold.

INGREDIENTS TO SERVE FOUR TO SIX:
¼ lb (100 g) sugar
½ lemon
1 cinnamon stick
2 cloves
1½ lb (700 g) crab apples

Rose Hip Soup

This Scandinavian fruit soup is really a purée of rose hips that can be served as a dessert.

Trim the ends from 1 pound (500 g) of rose hips. Wash the rose hips well and put them into a saucepan with 1 pint (600 ml) of water. Cover the pan and bring to the boil. Reduce the heat and simmer for 20 to 30 minutes, or until the rose hips are tender.

Liquidize the rose hips with the water and then sieve the purée into a saucepan.

Blend 2 tablespoons (30 ml) of arrowroot with a little of the purée, then stir into the fruit purée in the pan.

Bring to the boil, stirring constantly, and boil until the soup thickens. Sweeten to taste with a little honey and simmer for 2 minutes more.

Pour into 4 individual serving dishes or 1 large dish and leave to cool.

Serve chilled, sprinkled with 1 ounce (25 g) of flaked almonds.

INGREDIENTS TO SERVE FOUR:
1 lb (500 g) rose hips
2 tablespoons (30 ml) arrowroot
honey
1 ounce (25 g) flaked almonds

Roast Chestnuts

This is one of the most enjoyable ways to eat chestnuts and the simplest method of preparing them for a number of other dishes.

Preheat the oven to 400°F (200°C, Gas Mark 6).

Cut 2 slits in the skins of 2 pounds (1 kg) of chestnuts using a sharp knife. Put the chestnuts on a baking sheet in the top of the oven and roast them for 10 to 15 minutes, or until the skins split.

Pile the chestnuts on to a plate and serve immediately. Peel off both layers of skin while the chestnuts are still warm.

INGREDIENTS TO SERVE FOUR TO SIX:
2 lb (1 kg) chestnuts

Chestnut Stuffing

Prepare and peel 1 pound (500 g) of chestnuts. Chop 2 ounces (50 g) of bacon. Chop 1 large onion.

Over low heat fry the bacon in a saucepan until the fat runs.

Add the onion to the pan and fry for 3 minutes. Remove the pan from the heat and stir in ¼ pound (100 g) of fresh wholewheat breadcrumbs, the grated rind of 1 lemon and 1 tablespoon (15 ml) of chopped parsley.

Put the peeled chestnuts into a saucepan, cover with water and bring to the boil. Simmer for 30 minutes, or until the chestnuts are tender. Drain the chestnuts and either chop them for a coarse stuffing, or liquidize them or sieve them for a smoother stuffing.

Add the chopped or puréed chestnuts to the breadcrumb mixture. Mix well and season with salt, pepper and grated nutmeg. Add 1 tablespoon (15 ml) of brandy if desired. Beat 1 egg and stir it into the stuffing.

INGREDIENTS TO STUFF ONE TWELVE-POUND (6-KG) TURKEY:
1 lb (500 g) chestnuts
2 oz (50 g) bacon
1 large onion
¼ lb (100 g) fresh wholewheat breadcrumbs
1 lemon
1 tablespoon (15 ml) chopped parsley
salt
pepper
grated nutmeg
1 tablespoon (15 ml) brandy
1 egg

Mont Blanc

This famous puréed chestnut dessert is made much lighter by using yogurt instead of cream and by the addition of a whisked egg white.

Prepare and peel 1 pound (500 g) of chestnuts.

Put the chestnuts into a saucepan with 1 vanilla pod. Add water to cover. Bring to the boil, then reduce the heat and simmer for 20 to 30 minutes, or until the chestnuts are tender.

Remove and discard the vanilla pod and drain the chestnuts. Liquidize or sieve them to a purée.

Put the purée into a mixing bowl and stir in ¼ pint (150 ml) of yogurt and 1 tablespoon (15 ml) of brandy or lemon juice. Add 1 to 2 tablespoons (15 to 30 ml) of soft brown sugar.

Whisk 1 egg white until just stiff, then fold into the chestnut purée.

Carefully pile the chestnut mixture on to a serving dish. Spoon 2 tablespoons (30 ml) of yogurt on the top to cap the mountain with snow.

Serve chilled.

INGREDIENTS TO SERVE FOUR:
1 lb (500 g) chestnuts
1 vanilla pod
¼ pint plus 2 tablespoons (180 ml) yogurt
1 tablespoon (15 ml) brandy or lemon juice
1 to 2 tablespoons (15 to 30 ml) soft brown sugar
1 egg white

Elderflower Water

Elderflowers make a refreshing summer drink that may be stored in a cool place for several weeks.

Cut enough elderflower florets to give about 1 pint (600 ml) of tightly packed flowers. Put them into a large bowl with the grated rind and juice of 2 lemons and ½ pound (250 g) of sugar.

Pour in 3 pints (1.60 litres) of boiling water and stir until the sugar has dissolved.

Cover the bowl and leave to stand overnight. Strain the liquid and pour it into bottles. Serve chilled.

INGREDIENTS TO MAKE THREE PINTS (1.60 LITRES) OF ELDERFLOWER WATER:
1 pint (600 ml) elderflowers
2 lemons
½ lb (250 g) sugar

Sloe Gin

Made in autumn when sloes are ripe, this unusual liqueur matures in time for Christmas. Properly sealed it will keep indefinitely. Serve the sloes with the gin or separately as a dessert, or add a few to fruit pies or trifles.

Remove the stalks from 1 pound (500 g) of sloes. Wash the sloes and prick them well with a large needle. This allows the gin to permeate the sloes.

Put the sloes into a large kilner jar. Add ¼ pound (100 g) of sugar. Pour 1½ pints (850 ml) of gin into the jar.

Seal the jar and store in a cool dark place for 2 to 3 months, shaking the bottle occasionally.

Serve the liqueur with 1 or 2 sloes in the glass. The sloes will have lost their bitterness.

INGREDIENTS TO MAKE 1½ PINTS (850 ML) OF LIQUEUR:
1 lb (500 g) sloe berries
¼ lb (100 g) sugar
1½ pints (850 ml) gin

MAKING SLOE GIN

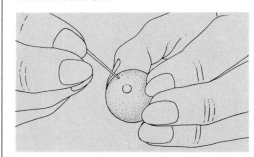

Prick the sloe skins well with a needle.

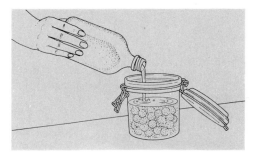

Put into a jar, add sugar and gin to cover.

Seal the jar and store, shaking occasionally.

IT HAS NEVER BEEN VERY CLEAR what it is in the daily apple that is supposed to keep the doctor away. There are many other popular fruits and vegetables that are far better sources of vitamins and minerals. But the popular trust in apples may be more justified than nutritional charts suggest.

Consider, for example, our estimated requirements of vitamin C and the quantity an apple provides—and an apple is not a fruit which is associated with vitamin C. It is generally accepted that ten milligrams of ascorbic acid a day will prevent scurvy. But recommended intakes are always far more generous to allow for individual variation and increased utilization of vitamin C in times of stress. In Britain the recommended intake of vitamin C for an adult male is thirty milligrams a day.

An average-sized, three-and-a-half-ounce (100 mg) raw apple is estimated to contain five milligrams of vitamin C. And if its health-giving virtue lies in its vitamin C content it would take six apples a day to keep an English doctor away.

The vitamin and mineral content of an apple varies, however, according to its variety, the kind of soil in which it was grown, how ripe it is and how long it has been stored. The amount of vitamin C in an apple increases as it ripens and falls as it is stored. But the most striking differences in the amounts of vitamin C depend, it appears, on the variety. The range is from less than three milligrams to more than thirty milligrams in a medium-sized apple.

It is a comforting thought that some of the most nutritious apples are also the best flavoured. At the top of the vitamin C league is the ancient French variety Calville Blanche d'Hiver, arguably the most delicious of all apples. Not far behind is the venerable English Ribston Pippin. Of the

The Nutrients in Apples, Pears and Quinces
These are quite high in fibre and three and a half ounces (100 g) of pears, for example, provide about 60 Calories.

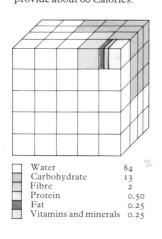

Water	84 %
Carbohydrate	13
Fibre	2
Protein	0.50
Fat	0.25
Vitamins and minerals	0.25

American apples, the richest in vitamin C is Northern Spy with almost eighteen milligrams. The ubiquitous Golden Delicious, however, has only eight milligrams. All apples contain fructose and glucose to give you energy—a medium-sized apple provides about sixty Calories—and they are a valuable source of roughage.

Apples have been cultivated for more than three thousand years, since they were developed from the wild crab apple, *Malus pumila*. The most popular English dessert apple is still Cox's Orange Pippin, which is spicy and soft, but crisp. A best-selling son of Cox is Laxton's Superb. Blenheim Orange, both an eater and a cooker, has a nutty flavour that connoisseurs say goes well with port, and many people enjoy James Grieve for its acid sweetness.

The image of an apple is crunchiness, but cooking it provides other beautiful flavours and textures—tart in sauce, sweet in pies and uniquely

EXTRACTING APPLE JUICE

Sweet-tasting apple juice is not the easiest of juices to squeeze out, so most people buy it bottled. The cider press (left) is no longer used, but more modern presses play a part in making both unfermented apple juice and fermented cider. The fruit is first ground into a pulp or pomace, then fed into the press which converts it into "cheeses". Wrapped in open-meshed cloths, layers of these cheeses lie on slatted wooden racks while the juice drips through. To make cider, the juice is then fermented, usually with the natural yeasts on apples, but to stop apple juice fermenting it is pasteurized. To prevent the juice oxidizing, extra vitamin C is often added.

Apples are the fruit that many people turn to for instant goodness. They provide energy because they are relatively high in sugar and three and a half ounces (100 g) provide about 60 Calories. They add roughage to the diet and are a good source of minerals and vitamin C, although the amount of vitamin C depends on how ripe the apple is and how long it has been stored. Pears (in the smaller basket, centre) are similar to apples in their nutritional potential, as are the less familiar quinces (inset).

frothy when baked. Crab apples provide a jelly that is beautiful in colour and flavour.

Apples are the major fruit crop of temperate climates, and indeed in the world as a whole they are beaten only by grapes, oranges and bananas. We eat far fewer pears—only a third of the apple consumption. This is understandable, for while the apple is a very dependable fruit, the pear is infuriatingly unreliable. One day it is hard, and then, almost while your back is turned, it has become mealy. It is also deceitful, fooling you by turning rotten from the inside instead of from the outside. But caught at just the right moment of ripeness, all its failings are forgiven. Even if its mouth-watering succulence can be embarrassing, it is perfection. And pears, like apples, provide energy, vitamins, minerals and roughage.

As with apples, there are thousands of varieties of pears, and a few of the best have been cultivated for centuries. The three outstanding pears are

Conference, an English pear of the late nineteenth century, Doyenné du Comice and Williams Bon Chrétien, known in the United States as Bartlett.

These and other dessert pears are far better for cooking than the so-called cooking pears, which need long slow cooking to make them soft. Just as apples are used to make cider, there are bitter pears that are rich in tannin which have been used for more than twenty-five hundred years to make pear cider, or perry.

Quinces have an equally long history and the trees themselves can live a century or more. They are now not widely grown—a pity, for a quince tree when it is covered in white or pink blossoms is a beautiful sight. The fruit, however, even when it is left on the tree until November, is hard and acid, and impossible to eat raw. But quinces do have a honey-like aroma, and they make excellent pies, jams and jellies. They are made into a sweet pâté in Spain, Germany and France.

French Apple Flan

Preheat the oven to 400°F (200°C, Gas Mark 6).

Make 6 ounces (150 g) of almond pastry (see page 35). Roll it out on a floured surface and line an 8-inch (20-cm) fluted flan ring or dish.

Bake blind for 15 minutes. Remove the baking beans and paper and bake for 5 minutes more.

Lower the oven temperature to 375°F (190°C, Gas Mark 5).

Peel and core 2 pounds (1 kg) of tart apples. Slice the apples thinly into a bowl. Add the juice of 1 lemon and 1 tablespoon (15 ml) of sugar and toss lightly.

Arrange the apple slices neatly in overlapping circles in the pastry case.

For the glaze, put 2 tablespoons (30 ml) of apricot jam into a saucepan with 2 tablespoons (30 ml) of water and the lemon juice remaining from the apples. Cook over very low heat until the jam has dissolved, then, stirring constantly, bring to the boil.

Brush half of the glaze over the apples. Bake for 30 minutes, or until the apples are tender and lightly browned.

Remove the flan from the oven. Reheat the remaining glaze and brush it over the apples.

Serve hot or cold.

INGREDIENTS TO SERVE FOUR TO SIX :
6 oz (150 g) almond pastry (see page 35)
2 lb (1 kg) tart apples
1 lemon
1 tablespoon (15 ml) sugar
2 tablespoons (30 ml) apricot jam

PREPARING FRENCH APPLE FLAN

Overlap apple slices in circles in the pastry case.

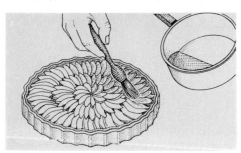

Brush the apple slices with apricot jam glaze.

Apple and Mint Sauce

Serve this sauce with lamb, pork or poultry.

Peel and core 1 pound (500 g) of tart apples. Slice the apples and put them into a saucepan with 2 tablespoons (30 ml) of lemon juice, 4 tablespoons (60 ml) of water and 2 tablespoons (30 ml) of chopped mint.

Cover the pan and cook over low heat for 10 to 15 minutes, or until the apples are reduced to a pulp.

Liquidize or sieve the apples to a smooth purée. Return the purée to the pan and reheat, adding sugar to taste.

INGREDIENTS TO SERVE FOUR TO SIX :
1 lb (500 g) tart apples
2 tablespoons (30 ml) lemon juice
2 tablespoons (30 ml) chopped mint
sugar

Baked Apple Custard

Preheat the oven to 350°F (180°C, Gas Mark 4).

Peel and core 1½ pounds (700 g) of tart apples. Slice the apples and put them into a saucepan with 2 tablespoons (30 ml) of rum or lemon juice, 1 to 2 tablespoons (15 to 30 ml) of sugar and ¼ teaspoon (1 ml) of ground cinnamon. Cover the pan and cook over low heat, stirring occasionally, for 10 to 15 minutes, or until the apples are reduced to a pulp. Sieve or liquidize the apples to a smooth purée.

Beat 4 eggs with ¼ pint (150 ml) of milk. Beat the mixture into the apple purée.

Pour the apple mixture into a 1½-pint (850-ml) ring mould. Put the ring mould into a roasting tin half-filled with water.

Bake for 1 hour, or until the custard is set and firm to the touch.

To serve the custard hot, leave it in the mould for 5 minutes before turning out. To serve cold leave it in the mould until it is cold, then turn it out.

Core and slice 1 red dessert apple and arrange the slices in the centre of the mould.

INGREDIENTS TO SERVE FOUR :
1½ lb (700 g) tart apples
2 tablespoons (30 ml) rum or lemon juice
1 to 2 tablespoons (15 to 30 ml) sugar
¼ teaspoon (1 ml) ground cinnamon
4 eggs
¼ pint (150 ml) milk
1 red dessert apple

Apple and Red Currant Snow

Peel and core 1½ pounds (700 g) of tart apples. Slice the apples and put them into a saucepan with 3 tablespoons (45 ml) of red currant jelly and the juice of ½ lemon. Cover the pan and cook over low heat, stirring occasionally, for 15 minutes, or until the apples are reduced to a pulp.

Sieve or liquidize the apples to a smooth purée. Let the apple purée cool, then stir in ¼ pint (150 ml) of yogurt.

Whisk 2 egg whites until stiff and fold into the apple and yogurt mixture.

Spoon into 1 serving bowl or 4 individual dishes or glasses.

Over low heat, cook 1 tablespoon (15 ml) of red currant jelly in a saucepan with 1 tablespoon (15 ml) of water until the jelly has dissolved. Add 2 ounces (50 g) of flaked almonds to the pan. Stir gently until the almonds are glazed. Turn out on to a plate or a piece of foil and allow to cool. Arrange the glazed almonds on top of the apple snow.

INGREDIENTS TO SERVE FOUR :
1½ lb (700 g) tart apples
4 tablespoons (60 ml) red currant jelly
½ lemon
¼ pint (150 ml) yogurt
2 egg whites
2 oz (50 g) flaked almonds

Orange Candied Apples

Peel and core 2 pounds (1 kg) of tart apples. Slice the apples. Put them into a saucepan with the grated rind and juice of 2 oranges, 2 ounces (50 g) of chopped candied orange peel, 2 ounces (50 g) of currants and 1 tablespoon (15 ml) of honey, if desired.

Cover the pan and cook over low heat for 10 to 15 minutes, or until the apples are tender but still in whole slices.

Serve hot or cold.

INGREDIENTS TO SERVE FOUR TO SIX :
2 lb (1 kg) tart apples
2 oranges
2 oz (50 g) candied orange peel
2 oz (50 g) currants
1 tablespoon (15 ml) honey

Apple Roulade

Peel and core 1 pound (500 g) of tart apples. Slice them and put them into a saucepan with the grated rind and juice of 1 lemon and 2 tablespoons (30 ml) of icing sugar.

Cover the pan and cook over low heat, stirring occasionally, for 15 minutes, or until the apples are reduced to a pulp. Sieve or liquidize the apples to a smooth purée. Put the purée into a bowl and stir in 2 ounces (50 g) of ground almonds. Allow to cool.

Preheat the oven to 400°F (200°C, Gas Mark 6).

Separate 4 eggs, beating the yolks into the cool apple purée and putting the whites into a separate bowl. Whisk the egg whites until stiff then fold lightly into the apple purée.

Line a 13- by 9-inch (32- by 22-cm) swiss-roll pan or a baking sheet with a raised rim with greaseproof paper and brush the paper lightly with oil. Spread the apple mixture in the tin.

Bake for 10 to 15 minutes, or until firm and just beginning to brown lightly.

Dust a large sheet of greaseproof paper with 1 tablespoon (15 ml) of sugar. Turn the roulade out on to the prepared paper and peel off the baking paper.

Spread ½ pound (250 g) of raspberries over the roulade to within 1 inch (2 cm) of the edges. Roll up, like a swiss roll, by lifting up the greaseproof paper so that the roulade turns into a roll.

Carefully lift the roulade on to a serving dish. Serve hot or cold.

INGREDIENTS TO SERVE FOUR TO SIX:
1 lb (500 g) tart apples
1 lemon
3 tablespoons (45 ml) icing sugar
2 oz (50 g) ground almonds
4 eggs
½ lb (250 g) raspberries

Apples Baked in Cider

Preheat the oven to 350°F (180°C, Gas Mark 4).

Peel and core 2 pounds (1 kg) of dessert apples. Slice the apples and put them into an ovenproof dish with ¼ pound (100 g) of sultanas and ½ pint (300 ml) of sweet cider.

Cover the dish and bake for 20 minutes. Uncover the dish, baste the apples with the cider and bake for 10 minutes more.

Serve hot or cold.

INGREDIENTS TO SERVE SIX:
2 lb (1 kg) dessert apples
¼ lb (100 g) sultanas
½ pint (300 ml) sweet cider

Baked Apples

Coarsely chop ¼ pound (100 g) of dried apricots. Put them into a bowl with 2 tablespoons (30 ml) of brandy. Soak the apricots for several hours or, preferably, overnight.

Preheat the oven to 350°F (180°C, Gas Mark 4).

Core 4 tart large apples. Make a shallow cut through the skin around the centre of each apple to prevent the skins from bursting during cooking.

Put the apples into an ovenproof dish. Spoon 1 teaspoon (5 ml) of soft brown sugar into the centre of each apple. Press the apricots into the centre.

Spoon 4 tablespoons (60 ml) of water around the apples and bake for 45 minutes, or until the apples are tender.

Serve hot with the juice from the dish. Top each apple with yogurt.

INGREDIENTS TO SERVE FOUR:
¼ lb (100 g) dried apricots
2 tablespoons (30 ml) brandy
4 tart large apples
4 teaspoons (20 ml) soft brown sugar
yogurt

PREPARING BAKED APPLES

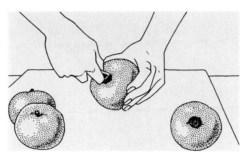

Use a corer or sharp knife to core apples.

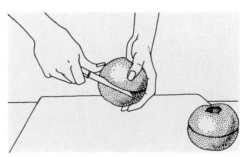

Slit the skin around the middle of each apple.

Fill the hollow centres of the apples.

Apple Layer Pudding

Preheat the oven to 350°F (180°C, Gas Mark 4). Grease an 8-inch (20-cm) spring-form cake tin.

Peel and core 2 pounds (1 kg) of tart apples and put them into a saucepan. Add 1 tablespoon (15 ml) of water, 6 cloves and 1 ounce (25 g) of soft brown sugar. Heat gently, stirring continuously, until the apples are tender.

Sieve the apples into a bowl. Stir in 1 ounce (25 g) of melted butter and the grated rind of 1 lemon. Set aside to cool slightly.

Meanwhile, mix 6 ounces (150 g) of dry wholewheat breadcrumbs with 2 ounces (50 g) of soft brown sugar and 1 teaspoon (5 ml) of ground cinnamon.

Beat 2 eggs into the apple mixture and spoon one-third of it into the prepared tin. Level the surface. Cover with a layer of the breadcrumb mixture. Repeat the layers twice more, ending with a layer of breadcrumbs.

Bake the pudding for 20 minutes, or until the top is golden brown.

Beat ¼ pint (150 ml) of yogurt and spread it over the top of the pudding. Remove the sides of the tin and serve immediately.

INGREDIENTS TO SERVE SIX TO EIGHT:
2 lb (1 kg) tart apples
6 cloves
3 oz (75 g) soft brown sugar
1 oz (25 g) melted butter
1 lemon
6 oz (150 g) dry wholewheat breadcrumbs
1 teaspoon (5 ml) ground cinnamon
2 eggs
¼ pint (150 ml) yogurt

Apple Crème

Preheat the oven to 350°F (180°C, Gas Mark 4).

Peel and core 1½ pounds (700 g) of tart apples. Slice the apples thickly. Heat 1 ounce (25 g) of butter in a saucepan. Add the apples, ¼ teaspoon (1 ml) of ground cinnamon and 6 cloves to the saucepan and cook them gently for 10 minutes, stirring constantly. Transfer the apples to a greased ovenproof dish.

Beat 2 eggs with ½ pint (300 ml) of warm milk and 1 tablespoon (15 ml) of sugar. Pour it over the apples.

Bake for 40 to 45 minutes. Serve hot or cold.

INGREDIENTS TO SERVE FOUR:
1½ lb (700 g) tart apples
1 oz (25 g) butter
¼ teaspoon (1 ml) ground cinnamon
6 cloves
2 eggs
½ pint (300 ml) warm milk
1 tablespoon (15 ml) sugar

Apple and Ginger Mousse

Put the grated rind and juice of 1 lemon into a saucepan.

Peel, core and slice 2 pounds (1 kg) of tart apples and add to the saucepan. Toss lightly to coat the apples with the lemon juice. Add 1 tablespoon (15 ml) of honey. Cover the pan and cook over low heat, stirring occasionally, for about 15 minutes, or until the apples are reduced to a pulp.

Liquidize or sieve the apples to a smooth purée. Put the purée into a large bowl.

Separate 2 eggs, adding the yolks to the apple purée and putting the whites in a separate bowl. Beat the yolks into the apple purée with ½ pint (300 ml) of yogurt. Finely chop 1 piece of preserved ginger and stir it into the purée with 1 tablespoon (15 ml) of the ginger syrup.

In a cup set in a pan of hot water dissolve ½ ounce (15 g) of powdered gelatine in 2 tablespoons (30 ml) of water. Stir the gelatine into the apple mixture.

When the apple mixture is just beginning to thicken, whisk the 2 egg whites until they are stiff and fold them in.

Around the top of a 1½-pint (850-ml) soufflé dish tie a strip of greaseproof paper to form a collar 2 inches (5 cm) above the rim. Pour the mousse into the dish.

Refrigerate for 2 to 3 hours before serving.

To serve, carefully remove the paper collar or unmould and decorate the top of the mousse with slices of preserved ginger or yogurt cheese (see page 100).

INGREDIENTS TO SERVE FOUR TO SIX:
**1 lemon
2 lb (1 kg) tart apples
1 tablespoon (15 ml) honey
2 eggs
½ pint (150 ml) yogurt
preserved ginger in syrup
½ oz (15 g) powdered gelatine
yogurt cheese (see page 100)**

Spiced Apple and Hazelnut Pie

Preheat the oven to 400°F (200°C, Gas Mark 6).

Put the grated rind and juice of 1 lemon into a large mixing bowl. Add ¼ teaspoon (1 ml) of ground ginger, ¼ teaspoon (1 ml) of ground cinnamon, ¼ teaspoon (1 ml) of grated nutmeg and 1 to 2 tablespoons (15 to 30 ml) of soft brown sugar. Add 2 ounces (50 g) of sultanas. Mix well.

Peel and core 1½ pounds (700 g) of tart apples. Slice them into the bowl. Toss lightly to coat the apple slices in the spice mixture.

Familiar fruits, apples and pears make wonderful desserts. From left to right; Apple and Ginger Mousse, Spiced Apple and Hazelnut Pie and Pears in Red Wine.

Arrange the apples in a 1½-pint (850-ml) pie dish.

Make 6 ounces (150 g) of shortcrust pastry with wholewheat flour (see page 34) adding 2 ounces (50 g) of chopped roasted hazelnuts. On a floured surface roll the pastry out to a round a little larger than the top of the pie dish. Cut a ½-inch (1-cm) strip of pastry from around the edge and press it on to the dampened rim of the pie dish. Dampen the strip of pastry and put the remaining pastry on top. Seal the edges together and flute them. Cut the pastry trimmings into leaves and decorate the top of the pie with them. Brush the pastry with beaten egg or milk.

Bake for 15 minutes. If the pastry is getting too brown, lower the oven temperature to 350°F (180°C, Gas Mark 4) and bake for 15 to 20 minutes more, or until the pastry is crisp and brown.

INGREDIENTS TO SERVE SIX
**1 lemon
¼ teaspoon (1 ml) ground ginger
¼ teaspoon (1 ml) ground cinnamon
¼ teaspoon (1 ml) grated nutmeg
1 to 2 tablespoons (15 to 30 ml) soft brown sugar
2 oz (50 g) sultanas
1½ lb (700 g) tart apples
6 oz (150 g) shortcrust pastry made with wholewheat flour (see page 34)
2 oz (50 g) chopped roasted hazelnuts
1 egg or milk**

Pears in Red Wine

Put $\frac{1}{2}$ pint (300 ml) of red wine and $\frac{1}{2}$ pint (300 ml) of water into a large saucepan with 3 strips of lemon rind, 2 ounces (50 g) of sugar, 2 tablespoons (30 ml) of red currant jelly and 1 cinnamon stick. Cook over very low heat until the sugar and jelly have dissolved.

Peel 4 to 6 ripe pears, preferably with stalks, leaving the pears whole and the stalks attached. Put the pears into the pan, submerging them as much as possible in the wine mixture.

Cover the pan and cook the pears over low heat for about 20 minutes, or until tender.

Carefully lift out the pears and put them into a serving bowl.

Strain the wine sauce and return it to the pan. Blend 1 tablespoon (15 ml) of arrowroot with a little cold water, then pour it into the pan. Bring to the boil, stirring constantly, until the sauce is slightly thickened, then reduce the heat and simmer for 2 minutes.

Pour the wine sauce over the pears.

Serve cold.

INGREDIENTS TO SERVE FOUR TO SIX:
½ pint (300 ml) red wine
1 lemon
2 oz (50 g) sugar
2 tablespoons (30 ml) red currant jelly
1 cinnamon stick
4 to 6 ripe pears
1 tablespoon (15 ml) arrowroot

Pear and Yogurt Custard Flan

Preheat the oven to 400°F (200°C, Gas Mark 6).

Make 6 ounces (150 g) of sweet flan pastry using wholewheat flour and ground cinnamon (see page 35). Roll out the pastry on a floured surface and line an 8-inch (20-cm) flan ring or dish. Bake blind for 15 minutes. Remove the baking paper and beans and bake for a further 10 minutes.

Reduce the oven temperature to 350°F (180°C, Gas Mark 4).

Cut 3 pears into halves, remove the cores and peel thinly. Put the pear halves into a saucepan with 1 tablespoon (15 ml) of water and the juice of $\frac{1}{2}$ lemon. Cover the pan and poach gently for 5 minutes, or until the pears are just tender. Remove the pears from the pan with a slotted spoon and drain well.

For the custard, beat 2 eggs in a mixing bowl, then whisk in $\frac{1}{2}$ pint (300 ml) of yogurt with 1 tablespoon (15 ml) of castor sugar. Spoon half of the custard into the flan case and bake for 20 minutes.

Arrange the pear halves on top of the custard, cut-side downwards. Spoon the remaining custard around the pears and bake for 10 to 15 minutes, or until the custard is just set.

INGREDIENTS TO SERVE SIX:
6 oz (150 g) sweet flan pastry using wholewheat flour and ground cinnamon (see page 35)
3 pears
½ lemon
2 eggs
½ pint (300 ml) yogurt
1 tablespoon (15 ml) castor sugar

Pear and Stilton Savoury

A delicious savoury, with which to either start or end a meal.

Cut 4 pears into quarters and remove the cores. Slice each pear into an individual flameproof dish.

Cut $\frac{1}{2}$ pound (250 g) of Stilton cheese into thin slices and arrange them on top of the pear slices.

Put under a hot grill for 3 to 5 minutes, until the cheese is bubbling and brown on top. Alternatively, bake in a hot oven for 10 minutes.

Serve at once.

INGREDIENTS TO SERVE FOUR:
4 pears
½ lb (250 g) Stilton cheese

Pear and Honey Sorbet

Cut 2 pounds (1 kg) of pears into quarters. Remove the cores and peel. Slice the pears into a saucepan. Add the grated rind and juice of 1 lemon and 2 to 3 tablespoons (30 to 45 ml) of honey.

Cover the pan and cook over low heat for 15 minutes, or until the pears are tender.

Sieve or liquidize the pears to a smooth purée.

Pour the pear purée into a plastic container and put it into the freezer for 1 hour, or until the purée is half-frozen.

When the purée is half-frozen, remove it from the freezer and beat it well. Whisk 1 egg white until stiff and fold it into the purée.

Return to the freezer until solid, then cover tightly. The sorbet may be stored in the freezer for up to 3 months.

To serve, let the sorbet soften slightly in the refrigerator or at room temperature, then spoon into individual serving dishes.

INGREDIENTS TO SERVE FOUR TO SIX:
2 lb (1 kg) pears
1 lemon
2 to 3 tablespoons (30 to 45 ml) honey
1 egg white

Pear, Cucumber and Mint Cocktail

Cut 4 pears into quarters. Remove the cores. Slice the pears and put them into a bowl.

Cut a 3-inch (8-cm) length of cucumber into slices, then cut the slices into quarters and add to the pears.

For the dressing, whisk together 2 tablespoons (30 ml) of lemon juice, 2 tablespoons (30 ml) of salad oil and 1 tablespoon (15 ml) of chopped mint. Pour the dressing over the pears and cucumber and toss lightly but well.

Marinate in the refrigerator for at least 2 hours before serving.

Serve in individual dishes garnished with sprigs of mint.

INGREDIENTS TO SERVE FOUR TO SIX:
4 pears
3-inch (8-cm) cucumber length
2 tablespoons (30 ml) lemon juice
2 tablespoons (30 ml) salad oil
1 small mint bunch

Pear and Ginger Fool

Cut 4 large pears into quarters. Peel them, remove the cores and slice them into a saucepan.

Add the grated rind and juice of ½ lemon, ¼ teaspoon (1 ml) of ground ginger and 1 tablespoon (15 ml) of the syrup from a jar of preserved ginger.

Cover the pan and cook over low heat,

stirring occasionally, for 10 to 15 minutes, or until the pears are tender.

Sieve the pears to a smooth purée. Stir in ¼ pint (150 ml) of yogurt. Alternatively, put the cooked pears into the jar of a liquidizer with the yogurt and blend to a smooth purée.

Pour into 4 individual serving dishes. Chill in the refrigerator.

Serve decorated with slices of preserved ginger.

INGREDIENTS TO SERVE FOUR:
4 large pears
½ lemon
¼ teaspoon (1 ml) ground ginger
preserved ginger in syrup
¼ pint (150 ml) yogurt

PREPARING PEARS

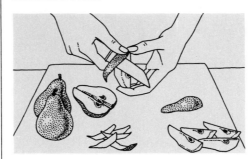

Cut pears into quarters and peel them.

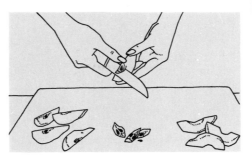

Cut out the cores with a sharp knife.

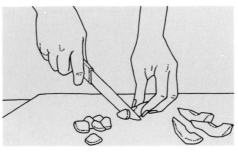

Thinly slice the quartered pears.

Stuffed Pears

Preheat the oven to 350°F (180°C, Gas Mark 4).

Cut a thin slice from the base of 4 large ripe pears so that they stand upright. Peel the pears and slice a 1-inch (2-cm) piece off the top of each one to make a lid. Scoop the cores out with a teaspoon.

Mix 2 ounces (50 g) of chopped pitted dates with 2 ounces (50 g) flaked blanched almonds and 2 tablespoons (30 ml) of honey. Spoon the mixture into the hollow pears. Cover with the lids.

Stand the pears in a greased ovenproof dish and pour in ¼ pint (150 ml) of white wine. Bake for 30 minutes, or until the pears are tender.

Serve immediately.

INGREDIENTS TO SERVE FOUR:
4 large ripe pears
2 oz (50 g) pitted dates
2 oz (50 g) flaked blanched almonds
2 tablespoons (30 ml) honey
¼ pint (150 ml) white wine

Pears with Beans

Peel and core 1 pound (500 g) of firm pears. Chop the pears into large chunks and put them into a saucepan. Add ¾ pint (450 ml) of dry white wine and the peeled rind of 1 lemon. Simmer gently over low heat for 10 minutes.

Top and tail 1 pound (500 g) of French beans. Wash the beans, slice them and add them to the pears. Continue to simmer until the beans are tender.

Meanwhile, make ¼ pint (150 ml) of yogurt hollandaise sauce (see page 93). Drain the pears and beans and put them into a serving dish.

Spoon the sauce over the pears and beans or serve it separately in a sauce boat. Serve immediately.

INGREDIENTS TO SERVE FOUR:
1 lb (500 g) firm pears
¾ pint (250 ml) dry white wine
1 lemon
1 lb (500 g) French beans
¼ pint (150 ml) yogurt hollandaise sauce (see page 93)

Autumn Pudding

Preheat the oven to 350°F (180°C, Gas Mark 4). Lightly grease a 1½-pint (850-ml) deep ovenproof dish.

Cut the crust from 1 small loaf of wholewheat bread. Thinly slice the bread.

Dip the bread slices into 3 ounces (75 g) of melted margarine or butter. Line the dish with the bread slices, overlapping them slightly so that they completely cover the inside of the dish.

Peel, core and thinly slice 1 pound (500 g) of tart apples. Wash and hull ¾ pound (375 g) of blackberries. Put the apples and blackberries into a saucepan with 2 ounces (50 g) of sugar, the grated rind and juice of ½ lemon and 2 tablespoons (30 ml) of water. Cover the pan and slowly bring to the boil. Reduce the heat and simmer for 1 minute.

Spoon the fruit mixture into the bread-lined dish. Cover the fruit with overlapping slices of bread. Put an ovenproof dish or plate on top of the pudding and weight it.

Bake for 40 to 45 minutes.

Turn the pudding out on to a plate and serve immediately or chill and serve cold.

INGREDIENTS TO SERVE FOUR TO SIX:
1 small wholewheat loaf
3 oz (75 g) margarine or butter
1 lb (500 g) tart apples
¾ lb (375 g) blackberries
2 oz (50 g) sugar
½ lemon

Apple, Date and Celery Salad

Separate the stalks from 1 medium-sized head of celery. Wash well and chop into ½-inch (1-cm) pieces. Thinly slice ¼ pound (100 g) of pitted dates. Wash and core ½ pound (250 g) of tart apples. Cut the apples into ½-inch (1-cm) cubes. Put the celery, dates and apples into a salad bowl.

In a small bowl combine 2 tablespoons (30 ml) of honey, ½ pint (300 ml) of yogurt and 1 tablespoon (15 ml) of finely chopped mint.

Pour the yogurt mixture over the celery and fruit and toss gently. Serve chilled, sprinkled with 1 ounce (25 g) of chopped pistachio nuts.

INGREDIENTS TO SERVE FOUR:
1 medium-sized celery head
¼ lb (100 g) pitted dates
½ lb (250 g) tart apples
2 tablespoons (30 ml) honey
½ pint (300 ml) yogurt
1 tablespoon (15 ml) chopped mint
1 oz (25 g) pistachio nuts

Apple Chutney

Serve this delicious fruit chutney with cold pork or ham. Stored in sealed jars, it will keep for 2 to 3 weeks.

Wash 1 pound (500 g) of cooking apples and grate them coarsely into a large mixing bowl. Discard the cores. Peel and coarsely grate ½ pound (250 g) of onions and add them to the apples.

Cut 1 large green pepper into halves and remove the seeds and pith. Finely chop the pepper and 2 ounces (50 g) of pitted dates. Add the pepper and dates to the bowl with ¼ pound (100 g) of sultanas and 1 ounce (25 g) of finely chopped crystallized ginger.

In a bowl mix 2 tablespoons (30 ml) of white wine vinegar with 1 teaspoon (5 ml) of salt and 1 teaspoon (5 ml) of sugar. Pour over the chopped fruit and onions and mix well.

Spoon the chutney into sterilized jars, seal and store.

INGREDIENTS TO MAKE TWO AND A QUARTER POUNDS (1 KG) OF CHUTNEY:
1 lb (500 g) cooking apples
½ lb (250 g) onions
1 large green pepper
2 oz (50 g) pitted dates
¼ lb (100 g) sultanas
1 oz (25 g) crystallized ginger
2 tablespoons (30 ml) white wine vinegar
1 teaspoon (5 ml) salt
1 teaspoon (5 ml) sugar

Spiced Apple Drink

Wash 2 pounds (1 kg) of apples and grate them coarsely into a clean 1-gallon (4-litre) wide-necked container, such as a plastic bucket or bowl. Add the cores and 1 gallon (4 litres) of cold water. Put in a cool place for 1 week and stir once a day.

Add 1 pound (500 g) of sugar, 2 tablespoons (30 ml) of ground ginger, 2 tablespoons (30 ml) of ground cinnamon, 1 tablespoon (15 ml) of cloves and 1 tablespoon (15 ml) of allspice. Stir the liquid until the sugar has dissolved. Leave to stand for 1 day more, then strain the liquid through a muslin cloth. Siphon or pour the liquid into clean bottles.

Lightly cork the bottles and leave them in a cool place for 1 week before drinking.

INGREDIENTS TO MAKE ONE GALLON (4 LITRES) OF DRINK:
2 lb (1 kg) apples
1 lb (500 g) sugar
2 tablespoons (30 ml) ground ginger
2 tablespoons (30 ml) ground cinnamon
1 tablespoon (15 ml) cloves
1 tablespoon (15 ml) allspice

Quince Cheese

The strong flavour of quince makes it ideal for preserving into this thick pulpy jam. Serve it with cold or hot meat, poultry or game.

Wash 3 pounds (1.40 kg) of quinces. Chop them coarsely, including the cores, and put them into a large saucepan.

Coarsely chop 1 unpeeled orange and add it to the pan. Pour in enough water to just cover the quinces. Simmer gently for 30 to 40 minutes, or until the fruit is very soft.

Sieve the quince pulp and weigh the purée. Return the purée to the pan and stir in ¾ pound (350 g) of sugar for every pound (500 g) of purée.

Cook over low heat, stirring constantly, until the sugar has dissolved, the cheese is thick and a firm line can be drawn through it with a wooden spoon.

Lightly grease the inside of 4 clean, warm, wide necked 1 pound (500 g) jars so that the cheese can be turned out easily, as it sets quite solid. Pour the cheese into the jars.

Cover the cheese with waxed discs, waxed side down. Wipe cellophane discs with a clean damp cloth and put them on top of the jars. Secure with rubber bands. Label the jars and store in a cool dark place.

It is best to leave the cheese to mature for 3 months.

To serve, turn the cheese out of the jars and cut into slices.

INGREDIENTS TO MAKE FOUR POUNDS (2 KG) OF CHEESE:
3 lb (1.40 kg) quinces
1 orange
sugar

TESTING QUINCE CHEESE FOR SETTING

When the cheese is ready it will retain a clear line.

greengage plums

Victoria plums

River's Early plums

Coe's Golden Drops

Napoleon cherries

Black Morello cherries

All the luscious fruits illustrated above are species of the genus *Prunus*. They are valued more for their flavour and succulence than their nutritional value. But they do contain small amounts of vitamin C, and their yellow flesh is a clue to their carotene content, which is particularly high in nectarines, apricots and peaches. They all contain useful minerals.

THAT "ABSENCE MAKES THE HEART GROW FONDER", is just as true of the stomach as of the heart. Some of the enjoyment of apples is lost because they are there for the biting all the year round; there is nothing to look forward to. Not so with the more fleeting cherries, plums, apricots, peaches and nectarines. There are months of pleasurable anticipation, and then the brief spell of luscious, gluttonous plenty.

By a wise dispensation the most succulent of these orchard fruits—the nectarine, a smooth-skinned form of peach—is the most nutritious, brimming with vitamin C, carotene and thiamine, as well as juice. Apricots have somewhat less vitamin C, but provide more carotene and a good contribution of riboflavin. Peaches are more variable nutritionally, depending on the variety. The yellow-fleshed types contain more carotene

than the white-fleshed varieties, but the white flesh is very often judged to have a more delicate flavour.

There are more than two thousand varieties of peach, and not only do they differ in the colour of their flesh but their skin ranges from greenish-yellow to predominantly crimson and varies in degree of velvetyness. The stones also are different: in the free-stone varieties the soft flesh parts easily from the stone, but in cling-stone peaches the firm flesh is hard to pull away.

About two thousand years ago the popularity of the peach spread westwards from China through Asia to Europe. The early Spanish explorers took them to America, where half of the world's peaches are now grown. Unfortunately, many of them are put into cans, from which they emerge with their taste and texture remarkably altered. They bear even less similarity to the original when they are dried.

Nectarines and peaches are even more difficult to catch at their prime than are pears, because they will not ripen satisfactorily off the tree. The lucky connoisseur who grows his own nectarines and peaches can seek out a likely victim early in the morning and if he has chosen rightly it will fall into his palm at the lightest touch.

Apricots, like peaches, come from China, but have a much longer history. They have also travelled farther, for American astronauts took them to the moon as a pleasantly rich source of minerals, especially potassium and magnesium.

Nutritionally, cherries lag somewhat behind peaches and apricots, but they are by no means inferior in flavour. There are two species of cherries: the sour one is used in cooking, and the

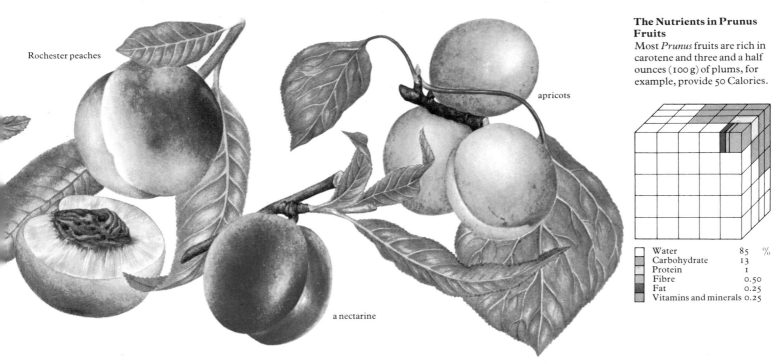

Rochester peaches

apricots

a nectarine

The Nutrients in Prunus Fruits
Most *Prunus* fruits are rich in carotene and three and a half ounces (100 g) of plums, for example, provide 50 Calories.

Water	85	%
Carbohydrate	13	
Protein	1	
Fibre	0.50	
Fat	0.25	
Vitamins and minerals	0.25	

sweet one is eaten as dessert. Cherries grow wild in many parts of Europe, perhaps as a result of the Roman soldier's habit of eating them while on the march and spitting out the stones.

The main sour varieties are the black Morellos and red Amarelles. The important sweet groups are the firm-fleshed and sweet bigarreau varieties, such as Black hearts and White hearts, and the softer-fleshed juicy guignes such as Tartarian. Hybrids of the sour and sweet species are known as Dukes or Royals. Each variety has its proper role, eaten raw, stewed, in pies, jams or as a flavouring for brandy and gin.

Plums do not have the aura of luxury that still surrounds peaches, even though now more peaches than plums are being grown. But the right variety, grown in favourable conditions, and picked when fully ripe, is out of this world.

Wild species of plums still survive in the Northern Hemisphere along with their cultivated descendants. The wild plum of western Europe is the blackthorn, or sloe, and the wild plum of western Asia is the cherry plum. These are the progenitors of European plums. Many of the dessert plums grown in the United States and Australia are, however, descended from the so-called Japanese plum, which hails from China. The flavour is generally inferior to that of the best European plums.

For aroma and sweetness there is nothing to beat a ripe gage—christened after Sir Thomas Gage, who brought it to England from the Continent in the eighteenth century. The gage is a round plum, with pale green or yellow flesh and a ripe sensuous smell. It also makes excellent jam and preserves. The most succulent varieties are

Early Transparent, and two of American up-bringing—Jefferson and Denniston's Superb.

The Victoria, which is ripe around late August, is the most popular dessert plum; it also jams and bottles successfully. Of the later varieties the best are Kirke's Blue, a beautiful, rich-tasting purple plum, and Coe's Golden Drop. Cooking plums are less juicy and not so rich in flavour. The most popular are River's Early Prolific, Czar and Marjorie's Seedling, all of which are purple.

Damsons are the least popular of plums, because they are small and usually sour, but nevertheless they make excellent preserves. And if the wind has not blown them off the trees by November they become surprisingly sweet.

As if the fruit of apricot, peach, cherry and plum was not prize enough their blossom is one of the great joys of spring.

Fruits can be stored and preserved in many different ways and *Prunus* fruits are particularly versatile. Plums, for example, can be canned, bottled and used to make jam or preserves. They can be frozen whole or as a purée. For centuries they have been dried to make prunes. The Chinese preserve them in salt. Below, left to right, back row: canned plums, plum jam, plum purée and plum preserve. Front row: salted plums, bottled plums and fresh plums, prunes.

Apricot Ring

Cut 1½ pounds (700 g) of apricots into halves and remove the stones. Put the apricots into a saucepan with ½ pint (300 ml) of water. Bring to the boil then reduce the heat and simmer gently for 10 to 15 minutes, or until the apricots are tender.

Drain the apricots and reserve about one-third of them.

Put the remaining apricots into a liquidizer with ½ pint (300 ml) of yogurt. Blend until smooth. Sweeten to taste with sugar.

In a cup set in a pan of hot water, dissolve 2 teaspoons (10 ml) of powdered gelatine in the juice of 1 lemon. Stir the dissolved gelatine into the apricot purée.

Pour into a 1½-pint (850-ml) ring mould. Refrigerate for at least 3 hours before serving.

To serve, turn the ring out by running a knife around the edge and dipping the mould into hot water for a few seconds. Then invert on to a serving plate. Fill the centre of the ring with the reserved apricots.

INGREDIENTS TO SERVE FOUR TO SIX:
1½ lb (700 g) apricots
½ pint (300 ml) yogurt
2 teaspoons (10 ml) powdered gelatine
1 lemon

PREPARING APRICOTS

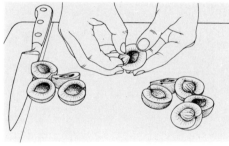

Cut apricots into halves and remove the stones.

Apricot and Almond Tart

Preheat the oven to 400°F (200°C, Gas Mark 6).

Make 6 ounces (150 g) of almond pastry (see page 35) and line an 8-inch (20-cm) flan ring or dish. Bake blind for 15 minutes.

Remove the baking paper and beans and bake for 5 minutes more.

Reduce the oven temperature to 350°F (180°C, Gas Mark 4).

Cut 1 pound (500 g) of apricots into halves and remove the stones. Arrange the apricots in the flan case. Sprinkle with 1 tablespoon (15 ml) of soft brown sugar and 1 ounce (25 g) of split blanched almonds.

Bake for 20 to 30 minutes, or until the apricots are tender.

Put 4 tablespoons (60 ml) of apricot jam into a small saucepan. Add the juice of ½ lemon and cook over very low heat until the jam has melted.

Spoon the hot apricot glaze over the baked tart.

Serve hot or cold.

INGREDIENTS TO SERVE FOUR TO SIX:
6 oz (150 g) almond pastry (see page 35)
1 lb (500 g) apricots
1 tablespoon (15 ml) soft brown sugar
1 oz (25 g) split blanched almonds
4 tablespoons (60 ml) apricot jam
½ lemon

Apricot and Hazelnut Trifle

Cut 1 pound (500 g) apricots into halves and remove the stones. Put the apricots into a saucepan with ¼ pint (150 ml) of water and 2 tablespoons (30 ml) of soft brown sugar.

Bring to the boil slowly, then reduce the heat and simmer gently for 5 minutes. Stir in 2 tablespoons (30 ml) of brandy. Let the apricots cool in the syrup.

Put ½ pound (250 g) of ratafia biscuits into the bottom of a serving bowl, preferably a glass bowl so that the layers can be seen. Pour the apricots and the syrup over the biscuits.

Make ½ pint (300 ml) of confectioner's custard using 2 egg yolks (see page 93). Whisk ¼ pint (150 ml) of yogurt into the custard and pour it over the apricots.

Whisk 2 egg whites until stiff, then fold in ½ pint (300 ml) of yogurt. Pile on top of the custard and sprinkle with 1 ounce (25 g) of toasted hazelnuts.

INGREDIENTS TO SERVE SIX:
1 lb (500 g) apricots
2 tablespoons (30 ml) soft brown sugar
2 tablespoons (30 ml) brandy
½ lb (250 g) ratafia biscuits
½ pint (300 ml) confectioner's custard (see page 93)
¾ pint (450 ml) yogurt
2 eggs
1 oz (25 g) toasted hazelnuts

Apricot Crème

Preheat the oven to 250°F (180°C, Gas Mark 4).

Pour 1 pint (600 ml) of milk into a saucepan and cook over low heat until it is hot, but not boiling.

Put 4 eggs into a mixing bowl. Add 1 tablespoon (15 ml) of castor sugar and ½ teaspoon (2.5 ml) of vanilla essence and beat well.

Pour in the hot milk and stir well. Strain the custard into a 1½-pint (850-ml) soufflé dish or cake tin.

Put the soufflé dish into a roasting tin half-filled with hot water. Bake for 45 to 50 minutes, or until the custard is set.

Let the custard cool in the soufflé dish and refrigerate, preferably overnight.

To turn the custard out, run a knife around the edge and invert on to a serving dish.

For the sauce, remove the stones from ½ pound (250 g) of apricots. Put the apricots into a saucepan with the juice of 1 large orange. Cover the pan and simmer over low heat for 5 minutes, or until the apricots are very tender. Liquidize or sieve the apricots with the orange juice. Add sugar to taste. Let the sauce cool, then pour it over the unmoulded custard.

INGREDIENTS TO SERVE FOUR TO SIX:
1 pint (600 ml) milk
4 eggs
1 tablespoon (15 ml) castor sugar
½ teaspoon (2.5 ml) vanilla essence
½ lb (250 g) apricots
1 large orange
sugar

Cheese and Apricot Salad

Remove the stones from ½ pound (250 g) of apricots. Cut the apricots into ½-inch (6-mm) cubes.

Blend ½ pound (250 g) of ricotta cheese with ¼ pint (150 ml) of yogurt. Fold in the apricots and 2 ounces (50 g) of shelled pistachio nuts. Chill for at least 1 hour.

Remove the coarse stalks from 1 large bunch of watercress. Wash and drain the watercress thoroughly. Line 4 individual serving dishes with the watercress.

Spoon the cheese and fruit mixture on to the watercress and serve immediately.

INGREDIENTS TO SERVE FOUR:
½ lb (250 g) apricots
½ lb (250 g) ricotta cheese
¼ pint (150 ml) yogurt
2 oz (50 g) shelled pistachio nuts
1 large watercress bunch

Cherry Clafouti

Preheat the oven to 425°F (220°C, Gas Mark 7).

Put 1 ounce (25 g) of margarine or butter into an ovenproof dish. Heat the dish in the oven until the fat has melted and is bubbling.

Meanwhile, put ¼ pound (100 g) of white flour and ¼ teaspoon (1 ml) of salt into a mixing bowl. Beat 1 egg with ¼ pint (150 ml) of milk. Make a well in the flour and pour in the egg and milk. Mix to a smooth batter. Beat in another ¼ pint (150 ml) of milk.

Put ¾ pound (350 g) of stoned cherries into the hot dish. Pour the batter over the cherries.

Bake for 35 to 40 minutes, or until the clafouti is well risen and brown.

Serve hot or warm.

INGREDIENTS TO SERVE FOUR:
1 oz (25 g) margarine or butter
¼ lb (100 g) white flour
¼ teaspoon (1 ml) salt
1 egg
½ pint (300 ml) milk
¾ lb (350 g) stoned cherries

Spiced Cherries in Wine

Remove the stones from 1½ pounds (700 g) of cherries.

Pour ½ pint (300 ml) of red wine into a saucepan. Add 2 tablespoons (30 ml) of red currant jelly, 2 tablespoons (30 ml) of sugar and 1 stick of cinnamon. Cook over very low heat until the sugar and jelly have dissolved, then bring to the boil.

Add the cherries to the pan, reduce the heat and simmer gently for 5 minutes, or until the cherries are tender but not wrinkled.

Using a slotted spoon, remove the cherries and put them into a serving bowl. Boil the wine syrup for a couple of minutes to reduce and thicken it slightly. Remove the cinnamon stick then pour the syrup over the cherries.

Chill before serving.

INGREDIENTS TO SERVE FOUR TO SIX:
1½ lb (700 g) cherries
½ pint (300 ml) red wine
2 tablespoons (30 ml) red currant jelly
2 tablespoons (30 ml) sugar
1 cinnamon stick

Cherry and Almond Snow

Remove the stones from 1 pound (500 g) of cherries. Liquidize the cherries or chop them finely. Put the cherries into a mixing bowl with 2 ounces (50 g) of ground almonds, 1 tablespoon (15 ml) of soft brown sugar, the grated rind of 1 lemon, ¼ teaspoon (1 ml) of ground cinnamon and ¼ pint (150 ml) of yogurt. Mix well.

Whisk 2 egg whites until stiff, then fold into the cherry mixture.

Spoon into 4 individual glasses or dishes and chill.

INGREDIENTS TO SERVE FOUR:
1 lb (500 g) cherries
2 oz (50 g) ground almonds
1 tablespoon (15 ml) soft brown sugar
1 lemon
¼ teaspoon (1 ml) ground cinnamon
¼ pint (150 ml) yogurt
2 egg whites

STONING CHERRIES

A special cherry stoner is easy to use.

Summer Salad

Remove the stones from 2 large ripe peaches. Core 2 large firm apples. Thinly slice the peaches and the apples and 2 bananas. Stone ¼ pound (100 g) of black cherries. Remove the pips from ¼ pound (100 g) of green grapes. Hull ¼ pound (100 g) of strawberries and cut the strawberries into halves.

Squeeze the juice from 1 lemon into a large serving bowl. Add the fruit and toss well in the lemon juice.

Squeeze the juice from 2 large oranges into a bowl. Stir in 2 tablespoons (30 ml) of Cointreau and pour over the fruit. Chill well.

INGREDIENTS TO SERVE SIX:
2 large peaches
2 large firm apples
2 bananas
¼ lb (100 g) black cherries
¼ lb (100 g) green grapes
¼ lb (100 g) strawberries
1 lemon
2 large oranges
2 tablespoons (30 ml) Cointreau

Spiced Damson Charlotte

Preheat the oven to 375°F (190°C, Gas Mark 5).

Remove the stones from 1½ pounds (700 g) of damsons. Put half into an ovenproof dish.

Put 6 ounces (150 g) of fresh wholewheat breadcrumbs into a mixing bowl with the grated rind of 1 lemon, 2 ounces (50 g) of soft brown sugar and 1 teaspoon of ground cinnamon or ginger. Mix well. Arrange half of the crumb mixture on top of the damsons in the dish.

Repeat the layers once more.

Bake for 30 to 40 minutes, or until the topping is crisp and brown.

Serve hot.

INGREDIENTS TO SERVE FOUR TO SIX:
1½ lb (700 g) damsons
6 oz (150 g) fresh wholewheat breadcrumbs
1 lemon
2 oz (50 g) soft brown sugar
1 teaspoon (5 ml) ground cinnamon or ginger

Plum and Apple Mould

Wash and remove the stones and any stalks from ½ pound (250 g) of plums. Peel, core and thinly slice ½ pound (250 g) of tart apples.

Melt 2 ounces (50 g) of butter in a large saucepan. Stir in 2 tablespoons (30 ml) of cold water. Add the prepared fruit and simmer gently, stirring occasionally, until tender.

Purée the fruit by sieving or liquidizing it. Return the purée to the pan and add sugar to taste. Continue to cook over low heat, stirring constantly, until the purée has thickened.

Remove the pan from the heat and beat in 2 eggs. Return the pan to the heat and stir constantly until the mixture thickens. Set aside to cool.

Beat ¼ pint (150 ml) of yogurt and stir it into the mixture. Spoon into a serving bowl or mould and chill for at least 1 hour. Dip the mould or bowl into hot water for 10 seconds and then invert on to a serving plate.

INGREDIENTS TO SERVE FOUR:
½ lb (250 g) plums
½ lb (250 g) tart apples
2 oz (50 g) butter
sugar
2 eggs
¼ pint (150 ml) yogurt

Plums Poached with Oranges

Preheat the oven to 350°F (180°C, Gas Mark 4).

Wash 1 pound (500 g) of Victoria plums and put them into an ovenproof dish.

Grate the rind of ½ orange over the plums then pour in the juice of 2 oranges. Cut the peel and pith from 1 orange. Working over the dish, cut the membrane away from the segments of fruit. Add the orange segments to the plums. Spoon 2 tablespoons (30 ml) of honey over the fruit.

Cover the dish and bake for 20 to 30 minutes, or until the plums are tender.

Serve hot or cold.

INGREDIENTS TO SERVE FOUR:
1 lb (500 g) Victoria plums
3 oranges
2 tablespoons (30 ml) honey

Plum and Red Currant Flan

Preheat the oven to 400°F (200°C, Gas Mark 6).

Make 6 ounces (150 g) of sweet flan pastry with wholewheat flour and add cinnamon (see page 35). Line an 8-inch (20-cm) flan ring or dish. Bake blind for 15 minutes. Remove the baking paper and beans and bake for 5 to 10 minutes more, or until the pastry has coloured slightly.

For the custard filling, make ½ pint (300 ml) of confectioner's custard (see page 93). Then beat in ¼ pint (150 ml) of yogurt and 1 tablespoon (15 ml) of sherry. Let the custard cool, then spoon it into the cooled flan case and level the surface.

Cut 1 pound (500 g) of cooking plums into halves and remove the stones.

Put 4 tablespoons (60 ml) of red currant jelly into a large saucepan and cook over very

low heat until the jelly has melted. Put the plums into the pan, cut sides down. Cover the pan and bring to the boil. Reduce the heat and simmer gently for 5 to 10 minutes, or until the plums are tender.

Arrange the plums on top of the custard, with the cut sides upwards. Pour the syrup from the pan over the plums.

Serve cold.

INGREDIENTS TO SERVE FOUR TO SIX:
6 oz (150 g) sweet flan pastry made with wholewheat flour and cinnamon (see page 35)
½ pint (300 ml) confectioner's custard (see page 93)
¼ pint (150 ml) yogurt
1 tablespoon (15 ml) sherry
1 lb (500 g) cooking plums
4 tablespoons (60 ml) red currant jelly

Cheese and Yogurt Peach Pie

A refreshing summer dessert, this flan may be made with other fruits such as raspberries, strawberries, apricots or oranges.

Make 6 ounces (150 g) of biscuit crust (see orange and lemon cheesecake, page 97) and use to line a 7- to 8-inch (18- to 20-cm) loose-bottomed cake tin. Chill the crust for 30 minutes.

Meanwhile, in a bowl, beat ½ pound (250 g) of curd cheese with ½ pint (300 ml) of yogurt.

Reserving a few for decoration, roughly chop 2 ounces (50 g) of walnut halves. Remove the stones and roughly chop 2 ounces (50 g) of dates. Stir 2 ounces (50 g) of soft brown sugar into the cheese and yogurt mixture with the chopped walnuts and dates.

Thinly slice 4 ripe large peaches. Reserving a few for decoration, arrange the peach slices on the biscuit crust. Spoon the cheese and

yogurt mixture over the peaches. Arrange the reserved peach slices and walnut halves on top of the mixture. Chill, preferably overnight.

INGREDIENTS TO SERVE SIX:
6 oz (150 g) biscuit crust (see orange and lemon cheesecake, page 97)
½ lb (250 g) curd cheese
½ pint (300 ml) yogurt
2 oz (50 g) walnut halves
2 oz (50 g) dates
2 oz (50 g) soft brown sugar
4 ripe large peaches

Frozen Peach Yogurt

Peaches that are overripe may be used for this lovely dessert.

Blanch, peel and stone 4 ripe large peaches. Put the peaches into a mixing bowl with the grated rind of 1 lemon and the juice of 1 lemon and 1 orange. Mash well then beat in ¼ pint (150 ml) of yogurt. Alternatively, all the ingredients may be blended in a liquidizer. Add sugar to taste.

Pour the peach mixture into a rigid container. Freeze until almost solid, then remove from the freezer and whisk well. Return to the freezer until firm. Cover, seal and store in the freezer until required.

INGREDIENTS TO SERVE FOUR:
4 ripe large peaches
1 lemon
1 orange
¼ pint (150 ml) yogurt
sugar

Baked Stuffed Peaches

Preheat the oven to 350°F (180°C, Gas Mark 4).

Cut 4 large peaches into halves. Remove and reserve the stones. Scoop out and reserve some of the peach flesh to make more room for the filling.

Beat 1 egg in a mixing bowl. Stir in 1 ounce (25 g) of ground almonds, 1 ounce (25 g) of flaked almonds and the reserved peach pulp. Add 2 ounces (50 g) of raspberries and toss lightly but well. Crack open the peach stones and blanch and peel the kernels. Chop them and add to the filling.

Spoon the filling into the peach halves. Put the peaches into an ovenproof dish.

In a small saucepan, over very low heat, dissolve 2 ounces (50 g) of sugar in ¼ pint (150 ml) of white wine or water. Pour the syrup over the peaches.

Plum and Red Currant Flan is a mouthwatering dessert of ripe plums on custard, glazed with red currant jelly.

Bake for 20 to 30 minutes, or until the peaches are heated through and tender. Serve hot.

INGREDIENTS TO SERVE FOUR:
4 large peaches
1 egg
1 oz (25 g) ground almonds
1 oz (25 g) flaked almonds
2 oz (50 g) raspberries
2 oz (50 g) sugar
¼ pint (150 ml) white wine or water

A sophisticated dessert such as Baked Stuffed Peaches can be simply achieved by combining subtle flavours and textures.

Spiced Brandied Peaches
Preheat the oven to 350°F (180°C, Gas Mark 4).

Cut 4 large peaches into halves and remove and reserve the stones. Put the peaches into an ovenproof dish.

Put the juice of 2 oranges into a small saucepan with 2 tablespoons (30 ml) of red currant jelly, 1 stick of cinnamon and 2 cloves. Cook over very low heat until the jelly melts, then bring to the boil. Pour the syrup over the peaches.

Cover the dish and bake, basting occasionally, for 15 minutes, or until the peaches are heated through and just tender. (Alternatively, the peaches may be poached in the syrup in a saucepan for 5 to 10 minutes.)

Meanwhile, crack open the peach stones. Blanch and peel the kernels. Then chop them. Scatter the chopped kernels over the peaches when they come out of the oven.

Warm 4 tablespoons (60 ml) of brandy, pour over the hot peaches and ignite. Serve hot or cold.

INGREDIENTS TO SERVE FOUR:
4 large peaches
2 oranges
2 tablespoons (30 ml) red currant jelly
1 cinnamon stick
2 cloves
4 tablespoons (60 ml) brandy

UNLESS THE "GOLDEN APPLE" of Greek mythology was an orange, as some insist, this most popular of citrus fruits is a comparative newcomer in the West. Most of the citrus family come from China, where references to them date from as early as 2000 BC. But it was only when vitamin C became one of the gods of the twentieth century that almost magical qualities were attributed to them.

Citrus fruits certainly are rich in vitamin C, but there are richer sources. And while some fruits contain more vitamin C when they are ripe, the riper an orange is the less vitamin C it has.

Assuming that an orange weighing three and a half ounces (100 g) contains about fifty milligrams of ascorbic acid, the same weight of black currants, with a content of two hundred milligrams, is way ahead. You would even do better eating raw cabbage or cauliflower, although perhaps they would be less appetizing. Nor are oranges generally the most important source of vitamin C. In some parts of the Western World that honour belongs to potatoes. Nevertheless the orange deserves a high rank among the good ingredients for it is refreshing and although it is sweet it is reasonably low in calories—a medium-

The charm of citrus fruits is that they provide a readily available source of vitamin C. Although they are not in fact as rich in vitamin C as, for example, black currants or green peppers, they do make a valuable contribution to health, either eaten whole or squeezed for their juice. On the hamper (right) are blood oranges, whose nutritional value is the same as ordinary oranges—their colour is due to a red pigment. Below them are clockwise: Jaffa oranges, grapefruit, uglis (a cross between the tangerine and grapefruit), lemons and limes.

sized orange contains about forty Calories.

The taste of a citrus fruit is unmistakable, but within the group there is a delectable range of flavours. These depend on the proportions of sugars and acids in the juice. In most species, most notably oranges, there is a preponderance of sugar, while in lemons and limes there is more acid. There are, however, bitter oranges—the bigarades, or Seville oranges (*Citrus aurantium*), which the Arabs took from Asia to Spain. These have thick aromatic peel, little and sour juice and innumerable pips.

There are dozens of varieties of sweet oranges

Grapefruit (above) are overrated as an aid to dieting. Although low in sugar their fruit acid content is calorific. Three and a half ounces (100 g) provide about 22 Calories.

(*Citrus sinensis*) and some of them are worldwide household names. Jaffa oranges from Israel are large, oval, juicy and sweet. Valencias are round, thin-skinned, almost pipless and full of sweet juice. Washington navel oranges are large, seedless, easy to recognize from their navel-like protrusion and satisfyingly easy to peel. They originated in Brazil, and their introduction into the United States by Mrs Eliza Tibbets in 1873 is commemorated by a monument in her memorial park at Riverside, California. The rough-skinned Malta oranges get their popular name of blood oranges from the colour of their sweet and juicy flesh.

A whole group of deliciously sweet oranges is related to the Chinese Mandarin orange (*Citrus reticulata*). They are smaller than the sweet orange, all have loose, easy-to-peel skins, and many suffer from an inordinate number of pips. The tangerine, a darker-skinned variety than those usually sold as mandarins, is full of pips. Many people prefer a pipless Spanish variety called the satsuma, even though its greenish skin is less attractive. The clementine, ortanique and

tangor (the Temple orange of the United States) are crosses between the orange and the tangerine. Both tangelos and uglis are also hybrids.

A Captain Shaddock gave his name to a coarse citrus fruit which he took to Barbados in the West Indies at the end of the seventeenth century. The more familiar grapefruit (*Citrus paradisi*) was developed from it, but did not become popular until the twentieth century. As well as popularity it has gathered some of the more weird of the modern dietary myths—the most absurd being that it actually burns up fat in the body. There is, however, no argument that grapefruit is a pleasant source of vitamin C, and the pink-fleshed varieties also contain some carotene.

Lemons (*Citrus limon*) and limes (*Citrus aurantifolia*) are too acid to eat, but their very acidity makes them invaluable in cooking. The two species are closely related and during a long history of some four thousand years they have often been confused. The lime, however, is a tropical fruit, while the lemon grows in areas with a subtropical or Mediterranean-type climate. Both were used for centuries to prevent sailors from dying of scurvy on lengthy sea voyages, long before the cause of the disease— lack of vitamin C—was understood.

Like limes and lemons, the citron (*Citrus medica*) is too sour to eat, but its thick rough skin can be wonderfully transformed into candied peel. The kumquat (*Fortinella species*) is not a true citrus, although it looks like a small orange.

The Nutrients in Citrus Fruits
Citrus fruits are rich in vitamin C and a three-and-a-half-ounce (100 g) orange provides 40 Calories.

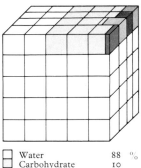

☐ Water	88	%
☐ Carbohydrate	10	
☐ Protein	0.75	
☐ Fibre	0.50	
☐ Vitamins and minerals	0.50	
☐ Fat	0.25	

FRUIT IN YOUR JUICE

No commercial drink matches freshly squeezed juice for flavour or for naturally occurring vitamin C. Some fruit-flavoured drinks are not made from fruit at all, but contain artificial ingredients. The description "whole fruit" drink is also deceptive, implying goodness but in fact meaning a drink whose fruit content has been strained from the fruit pulp instead of containing a definite proportion of real fruit juice. The fruit content of various drinks varies and is compared below. Most of them also contain artificial sweeteners.

FRUIT JUICES

Fresh fruit juice is full of vitamin C. A small wine glass of fresh orange juice can supply the total day's requirement. Canned or bottled juices provide about the same amount of vitamin C.

SQUASHES

Squashes contain far less vitamin C than "pure" juices —in Britain, for example, the legal lower limit is twenty-five per cent fruit juice before dilution. The same limit applies to cordials.

FIZZY DRINKS

Carbonated drinks need not by law contain any fruit at all—in Britain, for example, a drink is called -*ade* or fruit *flavoured* if it contains less than ten per cent fruit or has only artificial flavouring.

MARMALADE IS A JAM MADE WITH CITRUS FRUIT. It should have a good bright colour, a fresh fruity flavour and should set well and keep well. Basically all jams are made by boiling fruit with sugar until the mixture sets lightly when it is cold.

SUGAR

Use preserving or lump sugar for marmalade. To help the sugar dissolve more rapidly, warm it in a slow oven before adding it to the fruit.

TO TEST FOR SETTING

Chill some small plates in the refrigerator beforehand. Remove the pan from the heat and put a little marmalade on a cold plate and let it cool. If it wrinkles when pushed with your finger it is ready.

A faster and more reliable method is to use a sugar thermometer. Keep the thermometer in hot water in between testings. Stir the marmalade and insert the thermometer into the centre without touching the bottom of the pan. The temperature needed for a set is 220°F (104°C), but sometimes 222°F (105°C) will give better results.

STORING

When the marmalade is ready skim off the scum. Let the marmalade cool for about 15 minutes, or until a skin forms. This gives the marmalade time to thicken to suspend the fruit evenly. Stir the marmalade, then pour into clean, dry, warm jars.

Wipe the necks of the jars. Cover first with waxed discs, wax side down, and then with transparent cellulose covers that have been wiped with a damp cloth. Secure with rubber bands. Label, date and store in a cool, dark, ventilated cupboard.

There are few more satisfying sights than shelves well stocked with such preserves as dark and light Orange Marmalade, Lemon Honey and Ginger Marmalade and Grapefruit Marmalade.

TO PRESERVE SLICED CITRUS FRUIT

Sliced oranges, lemons, grapefruits and limes may be preserved in syrup or alcohol; use honey or sugar, brandy or wine.

Try pickling citrus fruit in a spiced wine vinegar syrup. The addition of such spices as cloves, cinnamon and mace produces unusual preserves which can be served with cold duck or turkey.

Lime Marmalade

This recipe makes a clear marmalade in which there are shreds of peel. To make a somewhat cloudier marmalade with slices of the fruit use the same quantities, but boil the whole limes in the water for 1½ to 2 hours, or until they are very soft. Remove the limes from the pan and slice them very thinly, discarding the pips. Return the sliced fruit and the juice to the pan. Then add the sugar.

Wash 1½ pounds (700 g) of limes. Thinly peel them. Cut the peel into thin shreds and put into a preserving pan or a large saucepan.

Cut the limes into halves and squeeze the juice. Strain the juice into the pan. Tie the pips and the lime pulp in a piece of muslin and add it to the pan with 3 pints (1.60 litres) of water. Bring to the boil. Reduce the heat and simmer gently for 1½ hours, or until the peel is very soft and the contents of the pan have reduced by about half.

Remove the muslin bag, squeezing all the juice into the pan.

Add 3 pounds (1.40 kg) of preserving sugar and stir until it is dissolved.

Boil rapidly until the setting point is reached, 220°F (104°C) on a sugar thermometer.

When the marmalade is set let it cool for 15 to 20 minutes, then pour it into jars. Seal and store.

INGREDIENTS TO MAKE ABOUT FIVE POUNDS (2.35 KG) OF MARMALADE :
1½ lb (700 g) limes
3 lb (1.40 kg) preserving sugar

Orange Marmalade

For a darker marmalade simmer the peel longer, so that the water reduces and becomes darker. Then add only 4½ pounds (2 kg) of preserving sugar and simmer until the setting point is reached and the marmalade has darkened. This will make about 8 pounds (3.60 kg) of marmalade. For an even darker marmalade 2 tablespoons (30 ml) of black treacle may be added with the sugar.

Wash 3 pounds (1.40 kg) of Seville oranges and 2 large lemons. Cut the oranges and lemons into halves. Squeeze the juice and strain it into a preserving pan or a large saucepan. Tie the pips in a piece of muslin and add them to the pan.

Shred the orange rinds finely or coarsely, depending on taste.

Add the shredded peel to the pan with 6 pints (3.50 litres) of water. Bring to the boil, then reduce the heat and simmer for 1½ hours, or until the peel is very soft when squeezed between the fingers.

Remove the muslin bag, squeezing all the juice into the pan.

Add 6 pounds (2.80 kg) of preserving sugar. Cook over low heat, stirring constantly, until the sugar is dissolved. Then boil until the setting point is reached, 220°F (104°C) on a sugar thermometer.

When the marmalade is set let it cool for 15 minutes before pouring it into jars.

INGREDIENTS TO MAKE ABOUT TEN POUNDS (4.70 KG) OF MARMALADE :
3 lb (1.40 kg) Seville oranges
2 large lemons
6 lb (2.80 kg) preserving sugar

Well worth the time involved in making them are, clockwise, Lemon Curd, Limes Preserved in Honey Syrup, Lime Marmalade, Spiced Pickled Oranges and Oranges Preserved in Brandy.

Lemon, Honey and Ginger Marmalade

This tart marmalade is set with honey instead of sugar.

Wash 8 large lemons. Cut them into halves and squeeze the juice. Strain the juice into a preserving pan or a large saucepan. Tie the pips in a piece of muslin with 1 ounce (25 g) of peeled and sliced root ginger. Add the muslin bag to the pan.

Cut the lemon rinds in half again, then cut the rinds into thin strips and add to the pan with 2 pints (1 litre) of water.

Bring to the boil, then reduce the heat and simmer gently for 1½ hours, or until the peel is very soft when pressed between the fingers.

Remove the muslin bag, squeezing out all the juice into the pan.

Coarsely chop ½ pound (250 g) of preserved ginger and add it to the pan with 3 pounds (1.40 kg) of honey.

Cook over low heat until the honey is dissolved. Then boil rapidly until setting point is reached, 220°F (104°C) on a sugar thermometer.

When the marmalade is set let it cool for 15 minutes before pouring it into jars.

INGREDIENTS TO MAKE ABOUT FIVE POUNDS (2.35 KG) OF MARMALADE:
8 large lemons
1 oz (25 g) root ginger
½ lb (250 g) preserved ginger
3 lb (1.40 kg) honey

Lemon Curd

This lemon curd has a strong flavour because it uses less sugar than most curd recipes. Orange can be substituted for the lemons to make a flavoursome orange curd.

Put the grated rind and juice of 4 large lemons into a mixing bowl. Add ¼ pound (100 g) of margarine or butter and ½ pound (250 g) of sugar.

Whisk 4 eggs, then strain them into the bowl.

Put the bowl over a pan of simmering water. Stir until the sugar has dissolved and the margarine or butter has melted.

Continue to cook, stirring constantly, until the curd thickens and coats the back of a spoon. It will thicken more when it cools.

Pour the curd into clean, dry, warm jars and cover as for marmalade. It will keep in a cool place for up to 1 month.

INGREDIENTS TO MAKE ONE TO ONE AND A HALF POUNDS (500 G TO 700 G) OF CURD:
4 large lemons
¼ lb (100 g) margarine or butter
½ lb (500 g) sugar
4 eggs

Grapefruit Marmalade

The proportion of sugar to fruit is comparatively low in this recipe, so the grapefruit flavour is concentrated and the marmalade is not too sweet.

Wash 2 large grapefruits and 4 large lemons. Using a potato peeler thinly peel the fruit. Cut the peel into narrow strips and put it into a preserving pan or a large saucepan.

Cut the pith from the fruit with a sharp knife. Coarsely chop the fruit and add it to the pan with any juice. Tie the pips and the pith in a large piece of muslin and put it into the pan. Add 3 pints (1.60 litres) of water.

Bring to the boil, then reduce the heat and simmer gently for 1 to 1½ hours, or until the contents of the pan are reduced by about half.

Remove the muslin bag, squeezing all the juice into the pan.

Add 3 pounds (1.40 kg) of preserving sugar and cook over low heat, stirring, until it has dissolved. Boil rapidly until the setting point is reached, 222°F (104°C) on a sugar thermometer.

Let the marmalade cool for 15 minutes before pouring it into jars.

INGREDIENTS TO MAKE ABOUT SIX POUNDS (2.80 KG) OF MARMALADE:
2 large grapefruits
4 large lemons
3 lb (1.40 kg) preserving sugar

Pork Chops Braised with Cabbage and Grapefruit

Preheat the oven to 375°F (190°C, Gas Mark 5).

Shred ¾ pound (350 g) of red cabbage into an ovenproof dish or casserole.

Peel and remove the pith from 2 small grapefruits. Working over the dish, cut the membrane away from the segments of fruit. Add the grapefruit segments, 2 ounces (50 g) of sultanas, salt and pepper to the cabbage and mix well.

Trim the fat from 4 pork loin chops. Arrange the chops on top of the cabbage and grapefruit mixture.

Cover the dish and bake for 45 to 60 minutes, or until the pork is tender and the cabbage is cooked but still crisp.

INGREDIENTS TO SERVE FOUR:
¾ lb (350 g) red cabbage
2 small grapefruits
2 oz (50 g) sultanas
salt
pepper
4 pork loin chops

Baked Spiced Grapefruit

These spiced hot grapefruit halves make a refreshing start or finish to a meal.

Preheat the oven to 400°F (200°C, Gas Mark 6).

Cut 2 grapefruits in half horizontally. Using a grapefruit knife, cut around the segments to loosen them. Remove and discard the pips.

Put the grapefruit halves on to a baking sheet. Sprinkle with 2 tablespoons (30 ml) of medium sherry.

Mix 1 ounce (25 g) of soft brown sugar with ½ teaspoon (2.5 ml) of ground mixed spice and sprinkle over the grapefruit halves.

Bake for 10 minutes, or until heated through. Serve hot.

INGREDIENTS TO SERVE FOUR:
2 grapefruits
2 tablespoons (30 ml) medium sherry
1 oz (25 g) soft brown sugar
½ teaspoon ground mixed spice

PREPARING GRAPEFRUIT

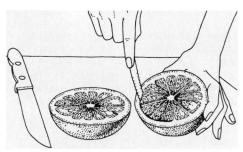

Cut between the flesh and skin of a grapefruit.

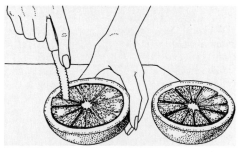

Cut between each segment. Use a serrated knife.

Grapefruit Mousse

Put ¼ pound (100 g) of castor sugar and 4 egg yolks into a bowl with the grated rind of 1 large grapefruit and the juice of ½ grapefruit.

Put the bowl over a pan of simmering water and whisk until the mixture is pale and thick. Remove from the heat.

Squeeze ½ grapefruit and pour the juice into a small bowl. Sprinkle ½ ounce (15 g) of powdered gelatine into the grapefruit juice. Stand the bowl in a pan of hot water and stir until the gelatine has dissolved.

Stir ¼ pint (150 ml) of yogurt and the dissolved gelatine into the egg mixture.

Cut the peel and pith from 1 grapefruit and cut the membrane away from the segments of fruit. Coarsely chop the segments and stir into the mousse.

Let the mousse cool until it is just beginning to set. Whisk 4 egg whites until just stiff, then fold them into the mousse.

Transfer the mousse to a serving bowl. Refrigerate for at least 2 hours before serving.

INGREDIENTS TO SERVE SIX:
¼ lb (100 g) castor sugar
4 large eggs
2 large grapefruits
½ oz (15 g) powdered gelatine
¼ pint (150 ml) yogurt

Orange Soufflé

Preheat the oven to 350°F (180°C, Gas Mark 4).

Melt 1 ounce (25 g) of margarine or butter in a large saucepan. Add 1 ounce (25 g) of flour and cook over low heat, stirring constantly, for 1 minute. Stir in the grated rind and juice of 3 oranges and 1 lemon. Bring to the boil and cook, stirring constantly, until the mixture is thick and smooth. Stir in 2 tablespoons (30 ml) of brandy or orange liqueur and 2 ounces (50 g) of castor sugar. Let the mixture cool slightly.

Beat 4 egg yolks into the orange mixture.

Cut the peel and pith from 1 orange. Cut the membrane away from the segments of fruit. Stir the orange segments into the orange mixture. (The soufflé may be made in advance up to this point.)

Whisk 5 egg whites until stiff, then fold them into the orange mixture. Pour into a 2-pint (1-litre) soufflé dish.

Bake for 45 minutes, or until the soufflé is well risen, set and the top is golden brown.

INGREDIENTS TO SERVE FOUR:
1 oz (25 g) margarine or butter
1 oz (25 g) flour
4 oranges
1 lemon
2 tablespoons (30 ml) brandy or orange liqueur
2 oz (50 g) castor sugar
4 egg yolks
5 egg whites

Orange and Green Pepper Salad

Wash 2 medium-sized green peppers and cut them into thin rings. Cut away the white pith and the seeds.

Using a serrated knife and a sawing motion, cut away the peel, pith and outer membrane from two large seedless oranges. Slice the oranges.

Arrange the pepper and orange slices on 4 individual salad plates or 1 serving dish.

For the dressing, combine 4 tablespoons (60 ml) of corn oil with the juice of 1 orange, 1 crushed garlic clove and salt to taste. Mix well.

Pour the dressing over the salad just before serving.

INGREDIENTS TO SERVE FOUR:
2 medium-sized green peppers
3 large seedless oranges
4 tablespoons (60 ml) corn oil
1 garlic clove
salt

SEPARATING ORANGE SEGMENTS

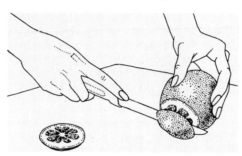

Slice the top and bottom off an orange.

Cut away the peel and pith in strips.

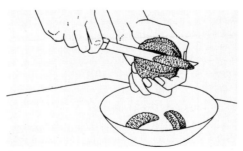

Cut away the membrane from the segments of fruit.

Oranges in Wine

Using a potato peeler, thinly peel 3 large, seedless oranges. Cut the peel into thin strips and put it into a small saucepan. Cover with cold water, bring to the boil and then drain. (This initial blanching will remove the bitterness from the peel.) Cover the orange shreds with clean cold water and bring to the boil. Reduce the heat and simmer for 20 minutes. Drain well.

Cut the pith and outer membrane from the oranges and the peel, pith and membrane from 3 more oranges. Slice the oranges and put them into a serving bowl.

Pour ¼ pint (150 ml) of red or white wine into a saucepan. Add the juice of 1 orange, 1 tablespoon (15 ml) of red currant jelly, 1 stick of cinnamon and the shredded peel. Cook over low heat until the jelly has dissolved, then bring to the boil. Remove the cinnamon stick and pour the sauce over the oranges.

Serve chilled.

INGREDIENTS TO SERVE FOUR TO SIX:
7 large seedless oranges
¼ pint (150 ml) red or white wine
1 tablespoon (15 ml) red currant jelly
1 cinnamon stick

Avgolemeno

Put 2 pints (1 litre) of well-seasoned chicken stock into a saucepan. Add 2 ounces (50 g) of brown rice, the grated rind of 1 large lemon, 1 sprig of thyme and 1 sprig of parsley.

Cover the pan and bring to the boil. Reduce the heat and simmer for 30 minutes, or until the rice is tender. Remove the herbs.

In a bowl beat 2 eggs until they are light and frothy. Beat in the juice of the lemon. Stir in a little hot soup, then pour into the pan. Season to taste with salt and pepper.

Reheat, stirring constantly. It must not boil or the egg will curdle.

Serve hot.

INGREDIENTS TO SERVE FOUR:
2 pints (1 litre) chicken stock
2 oz (50 g) brown rice
1 large lemon
1 thyme sprig
1 parsley sprig
2 eggs
salt
pepper

MORE GRAPES ARE GROWN than any other fruit. Most of them we consume as wine, and even those that are eaten as fruit are about eighty per cent water. The melon, another fruit that grows on a vine, can beat that, with more than ninety per cent water. What makes both fruits so desirable is the flavour of that water; their juices are among the most agreeable means imaginable of getting our quota of minerals, particularly potassium. Unfortunately, melons will not grow without warmth and grapes will not ripen without sun—therefore they are a luxury in the colder parts of the world.

Most of the grapes we eat or drink belong to the species *Vitis vinifera*, known as the European grape vine, although it probably originally came from western Asia. It is one of the most venerable of food plants, for it has been in cultivation for at least six thousand years.

There are American species, among them *Vitis labrusca* (Fox grapes) and *Vitis rotundifolia* (muscadine grapes), but they do not have the standing of *Vitis vinifera*. Vinifera grapes may be white, which is anything from green to yellow, or black, which may be various shades of red or purple. Some varieties are better for dessert, others for wine-making, but the flavour is affected to an extraordinary degree by the soil in which the vines are grown and by the climate.

The British have to rely on Spain and South Africa for most of their grapes, but in their own hothouses they produce the most succulent, and possibly the most expensive grapes in the world. There is no need for Americans to import grapes, but although grapes grow in many parts of the United States about ninety per cent of dessert grapes come from California.

Some of the best varieties of grapes have been around for centuries. Of those grown in Britain the best known is Black Hamburgh, which arrived from Germany more than two hundred years ago and already had a long history. It is black, large, sweet and tender. Muscat of Alexandria, a pale amber grape with a strong, sweet, muscat flavour, came by way of France and

THIRST-QUENCHING MELONS

Melons are more than ninety per cent water and it is this that makes them refreshing and low in calories. Melons are also a reasonable source of vitamin C and in addition yellow melons provide carotene. On the left is a watermelon with its distinctive red flesh and an ogen melon from Israel. On the right is the thicker skinned winter melon.

Spain two and a half centuries ago. Just as old is Royal Muscadine, alias French Chasselas de Fontainebleau, which has small golden berries.

The flesh of ripe melon tastes sweeter than that of grapes even though it contains far less sugar: five per cent as against about seventeen per cent. A melon contributes a whole range of minerals and vitamin C and yellow melons are a useful source of carotene.

India, tropical Africa and Iran have all been credited with being the original home of melons. Today they are grown in many of the warm temperate, subtropical and tropical parts of the world. They are annual and, like their relatives the cucumbers, have tendrils which they attach to anything that will support them.

Melons are to be found in all shapes and sizes and have different star ratings for lusciousness. The most popular types are cantaloupe and musk melons, but, confusingly, musk melons are often called cantaloupes in the United States. The cantaloupe, which was developed in Cantalupo in Italy in the seventeenth century, has a warty and often grooved skin and sweet juicy flesh, which is usually orange coloured. Charentais melons are a small aromatic type of cantaloupe which are becoming increasingly popular in Europe. A recent addition has been the ogen melon, an Israeli variety named after the kibbutz where it was developed. This has an orange skin and sweet green flesh.

Musk melons may be spherical or oval (hence their other name—nutmeg melons), the skin yellow or green and the flesh anything between pale green and red. What they have in common is that the skin is covered with a raised lacy network, hence yet another name—netted melons.

Other familiar names are honeydew and winter melons, both used somewhat indiscriminately. They are thick-skinned and the flesh is not strongly aromatic. The real honeydew has a creamy or yellowish skin and pale green flesh. One winter melon that is often miscalled honey dew has dark green corrugated skin and creamy insipid flesh. Because these melons travel well they persistently make the journey from Spain to Britain, deceiving the natives by their false name.

All these melons are varieties of *Cucumis melo*, but the watermelon is *Citrullus vulgaris*. It is common in the warmer parts of Europe and Asia and Africa; in Britain it needs to be grown in glasshouses, and is not considered worth the effort. The early colonists took watermelons to America and they are now grown in about half of the states, but mainly in California, Florida, Texas, Georgia and South Carolina. They are juicily refreshing when ripe and as they are often sold in slices it is possible to judge their ripeness. The flesh should be red and firm and the seeds brown or black, not white and immature.

Grapes are more than eighty per cent water, which makes them equally as refreshing as melons. They are, however, more calorific because they contain more sugars. Their sweet flavour is due to the fact that they contain not only glucose but fructose. This is more than twice as sweet as most sugars. They also provide useful amounts of vitamin C and small amounts of such minerals as potassium. The most widely cultivated grapes are those of the species *Vitis vinifera* (shown in the vineyard above and the inset bottom right). Most American dessert grapes of the species *Vitis labrusca* and *Vitis rotundifolia* are grown in California, but the dark purple Concord grapes (inset top right) are popular in New York State. All the varieties of dessert grapes make succulent additions to both vegetable and fruit salads, and are also delicious with cheese.

The Nutrients in Grapes
Grapes are mostly water and contain the sugars glucose and fructose. Three and a half ounces (100 g) provide about 75 Calories.

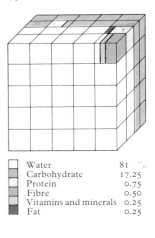

Water	81 %
Carbohydrate	17.25
Protein	0.75
Fibre	0.50
Vitamins and minerals	0.25
Fat	0.25

The Nutrients in Melons
Melons contain a high percentage of water and are low in calories. Three and a half ounces (100 g) provide about 25 Calories.

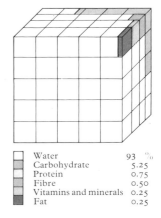

Water	93 %
Carbohydrate	5.25
Protein	0.75
Fibre	0.50
Vitamins and minerals	0.25
Fat	0.25

Grapes Baked with Oranges

Preheat the oven to 350°F (180°C, Gas Mark 4).

Remove the pips from 1 pound (500 g) of green grapes, keeping them whole if possible. (This is easily done with a tapestry or carpet needle.) Put the grapes into an ovenproof dish.

Pour in the juice of 2 oranges.

Cut the peel and pith from 2 more oranges. Working over the dish, cut the membrane away from the segments of fruit. Put the orange segments into the dish.

Cover the dish and bake for 15 to 20 minutes, or until the grapes are hot but not cooked enough to wrinkle.

Serve hot.

INGREDIENTS TO SERVE FOUR:
1 lb (500 g) green grapes
4 oranges

PITTING GRAPES

Cut grapes in half and remove the pips.

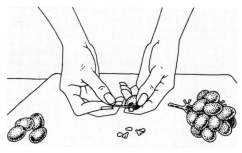

Remove grape pips with the eye of a large needle.

Grape and Grapefruit Flan

Make 6 ounces (150 g) of biscuit crust (see orange and lemon cheesecake, page 97). Use to line an 8-inch (20-cm) pie dish. Refrigerate.

Squeeze the juice of 1 large grapefruit and add water to bring it up to ¼ pint (150 ml). Pour into a saucepan and heat to just below boiling point.

In a mixing bowl beat 1 egg, then stir in 1 tablespoon (15 ml) of cornflour and 2 tablespoons (30 ml) of castor sugar. Stirring constantly, gradually add the hot liquid. Pour the mixture into the pan. Bring to the boil, stirring constantly, until the custard

thickens and boils. Remove from the heat and whisk in 5 tablespoons (75 ml) of yogurt. Cover the pan and leave the custard to cool, whisking occasionally to prevent a skin from forming.

Spoon the cooled custard into the flan case.

Cut ¾ pound (350 g) of grapes into halves and remove the pips. Put the halved grapes on top of the custard.

For the grapefruit glaze, heat the juice of 1 grapefruit in a small saucepan to just below boiling point. In a small bowl blend 1 teaspoon (5 ml) of arrowroot with 1 to 2 tablespoons (15 to 30 ml) of castor sugar and a little of the fruit juice, then stir in the remainder of the hot grapefruit juice. Return the mixture to the pan and bring to the boil, stirring constantly, until the glaze thickens and clears. Pour the glaze over the grapes in the flan. Refrigerate for at least 2 hours before serving.

INGREDIENTS TO SERVE SIX:
6 oz (150 g) biscuit crust (see orange and lemon cheesecake, page 97)
2 grapefruits
1 egg
1 tablespoon (15 ml) cornflour
3 to 4 tablespoons (45 to 60 ml) castor sugar
5 tablespoons (75 ml) yogurt
¾ lb (350 g) grapes
1 teaspoon (5 ml) arrowroot

Grape Snow

Reserving a few whole grapes for decoration cut 1 pound (500 g) of grapes into halves and remove the pips. Finely chop half of the grapes.

Just before serving, whisk 2 egg whites until stiff. Fold in ½ pint (300 ml) of yogurt with the grated rind of 1 orange and the chopped grapes. Add sugar to taste.

In individual glasses arrange the halved grapes in layers with the grape snow.

Decorate with the reserved whole grapes and serve immediately.

INGREDIENTS TO SERVE FOUR:
1 lb (500 g) grapes
2 egg whites
½ pint (300 ml) yogurt
1 orange
sugar

Grape Wine Jelly

Pour 1 pint (600 ml) of sweet white wine into a saucepan. Add ½ ounce (15 g) of powdered gelatine, 1 ounce (25 g) of castor sugar and the grated rind and juice of 1 lemon. Cook over low heat, stirring constantly, until the sugar and gelatine have dissolved, then bring

to the boil and remove the pan from the heat. Strain into a jug. Stand the jug in a pan or bowl of hot water to keep the jelly from setting.

Rinse out a 1½-pint (850-ml) jelly mould with cold water, then pour in a layer of jelly about ½ inch (1 cm) deep.

Halve ½ pound (250 g) of grapes and remove the pips.

Arrange a layer of grapes over the jelly and put the mould into the refrigerator for 10 to 15 minutes, or until the jelly begins to set.

Continue making layers of jelly and grapes, refrigerating between each layer, so that the grapes will be distributed evenly.

Finish with a layer of jelly and refrigerate until completely set. To serve, dip the mould in hot water for a few seconds, place a serving plate on top of the mould and invert.

INGREDIENTS TO SERVE SIX:
1 pint (600 ml) sweet white wine
½ oz (25 g) powdered gelatine
1 oz (25 g) castor sugar
1 lemon
½ lb (250 g) grapes

Grape Mincemeat

This deliciously moist traditional Christmas preserve may be stored for only 2 weeks.

Put ¼ pound (100 g) of seedless raisins, ¼ pound (100 g) of sultanas and ¼ pound (100 g) of currants into a mixing bowl.

Add 2 ounces (50 g) of chopped mixed peel, 2 ounces (50 g) of flaked almonds, ¼ lb (100 g) of demerara sugar and the grated rind and juice of ½ lemon.

Peel and core ½ pound (250 g) of cooking apples. Coarsely grate the apples into the bowl. Cut ½ pound (250 g) of grapes into halves and remove the pips. Cut the grapes into halves again and add them to the mincemeat with ½ teaspoon (2.5 ml) of ground mixed spice, ¼ teaspoon (1 ml) of grated nutmeg and 2 tablespoons (30 ml) of brandy. Stir the mincemeat well.

Cover the bowl and leave overnight. Pack the mincemeat into clean dry jars and cover as for marmalade (see page 178).

INGREDIENTS TO MAKE TWO AND A HALF POUNDS (1.20 KG) OF MINCEMEAT:
¼ lb (100 g) seedless raisins
¼ lb (100 g) sultanas
¼ lb (100 g) currants
2 oz (50 g) mixed peel
2 oz (50 g) flaked almonds
¼ lb (100 g) demerara sugar
½ lemon
½ lb (250 g) cooking apples
½ lb (250 g) grapes
½ teaspoon (2.5 ml) ground mixed spice
¼ teaspoon (1 ml) grated nutmeg
2 tablespoons (30 ml) brandy

Grape and Lemon Layer Pudding

Preheat the oven to 350°F (180°C, Gas Mark 4).

Cut ½ pound (250 g) of green grapes into halves and remove the pips. Arrange the halved grapes in the bottom of an ovenproof dish.

Cream 2 ounces (50 g) of margarine with 2 ounces (50 g) of castor sugar and the grated rind of 1 large lemon. Beat until pale and fluffy.

Separate 2 eggs. Add the yolks to the creamed mixture and beat well. Stir in ½ pint (300 ml) of milk, the juice of the lemon and 2 ounces (50 g) of self-raising flour. The consistency will be like curds.

Whisk the 2 egg whites until just stiff, then fold into the mixture. Spoon it on top of the grapes.

Put the dish into a roasting tin half-filled with hot water and bake for 40 to 45 minutes, or until the top is set, firm to the touch and golden brown.

INGREDIENTS TO SERVE FOUR:
½ lb (250 g) green grapes
2 oz (50 g) margarine
2 oz (50 g) castor sugar
1 large lemon
2 eggs
½ pint (300 ml) milk
2 oz (50 g) self-raising flour

Grape Stuffed Onions

Preheat the oven to 375°F (190°C, Gas Mark 5).

Peel 4 large onions and put them into a saucepan. Pour in 1 pint (600 ml) of boiling water. Cover the pan, reduce the heat and simmer the onions for 25 minutes. Drain the onions and set them aside until they are cool enough to handle.

Cut ¼ pound (100 g) of green grapes into halves and remove the pips. Put the grapes into a mixing bowl with 1 ounce (25 g) of blanched almonds, 2 tablespoons (30 ml) of yogurt and salt and pepper to taste. Mix well.

Cut a slice off the top of each of the onions. Carefully remove the centres, leaving ½ inch (1 cm) thick shells. (Reserve the centres of the onions for another dish.)

Spoon the filling into the centres of the onions. Put the onions into an ovenproof dish and bake for 20 to 30 minutes, or until the onions are tender. Serve hot.

INGREDIENTS TO SERVE FOUR:
4 large onions
¼ lb (100 g) green grapes
1 oz (25 g) blanched almonds
2 tablespoons (30 ml) yogurt
salt
pepper

Melon and Grape Salad

Cut a slice for the lid from the top of 1 ripe, medium-sized honeydew melon. Cut a thin slice off the bottom so that the melon will stand upright.

Scoop out and discard the seeds. Cut out the fruit and then dice it or scoop it out in balls. Put the melon into a mixing bowl.

Cut ½ pound (250 g) of green grapes into halves and remove and discard the pips. Add the grapes to the melon with the grated rind and juice of 1 large orange and 1 tablespoon (15 ml) of chopped mint. Toss lightly but well.

Spoon the melon and grape mixture into the melon shell. Sprinkle with ½ ounce (15 g) of blanched and split pistachio nuts and a sprig of mint.

Replace the melon lid and chill well before serving.

INGREDIENTS TO SERVE FOUR:
1 ripe medium-sized honeydew melon
½ lb (250 g) green grapes
1 large orange
mint sprigs
½ oz (15 g) split blanched pistachio nuts

MAKING MELON BALLS

Cut the top off a melon and scoop out the seeds.

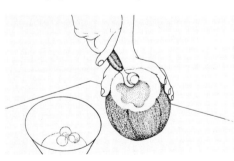

Use a small scoop to remove the fruit in balls.

Melon and Prawn Cocktail

Melon and prawns, with a dressing of grapefruit juice, make this a refreshing starter.

Cut 1 ripe small honeydew melon into quarters. Discard the seeds and cut the melon into ½-inch (1-cm) dice. Put the melon into a mixing bowl.

Peel and devein ¾ pound (350 g) of cooked prawns and add them to the melon pieces.

Pour the juice of 1 grapefruit over the melon and prawns and toss lightly.

Shred ½ small head of lettuce. Divide the lettuce between 6 individual serving glasses. Spoon the melon and prawns on top, pouring in any grapefruit juice from the bowl.

Serve chilled.

INGREDIENTS TO SERVE SIX:
1 ripe small honeydew melon
¾ lb (350 g) cooked prawns
1 grapefruit
½ small lettuce head

Melon and Ginger Sorbet

Cut 1 small honeydew melon into quarters. Remove the seeds and the skin. Coarsely chop the melon and put it into a saucepan with 1 teaspoon (5 ml) of ground ginger, 2 tablespoons (30 ml) of soft brown sugar and the grated rind and juice of 1 small lemon.

Cover the pan and cook over low heat for 10 to 15 minutes, or until the melon is soft. Pour the contents of the pan into a liquidizer and blend until smooth. Pour the puréed melon into a bowl. Put it into the freezer until it is half frozen.

Whisk 2 egg whites until stiff, then whisk the melon purée. Fold the whites into the purée and transfer to a rigid container. Return the purée to the freezer until solid.

Cover, seal and label the sorbet and store in the freezer until required.

INGREDIENTS TO SERVE FOUR TO SIX:
1 small honeydew melon
1 teaspoon (5 ml) ground ginger
2 tablespoons (30 ml) soft brown sugar
1 small lemon
2 egg whites

The Nutrients in Exotic Fruits

These fruits are high in sugar. A three-and-a-half-ounce (100-g) banana, for example, provides about 80 Calories.

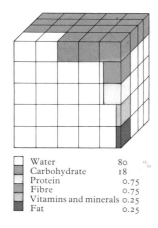

Water	80	%
Carbohydrate	18	
Protein	0.75	
Fibre	0.75	
Vitamins and minerals	0.25	
Fat	0.25	

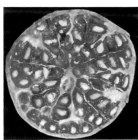

The refreshing juice of the pomegranate makes it worth the tedium of sucking the flesh from hundreds of tiny seeds (above).

NO PRECISE DEFINITION OF EXOTIC is possible. One man's exotica in one corner of the earth may be another man's commonplace elsewhere. To people who live in temperate zones the fruits that will grow only in the tropics seem particularly desirable (or outlandish). Some of the exotic image persists even when a tropical fruit becomes a regular part of Western diet. If you live in a skyscraper you might imagine a garden of your own filled with strawberries, raspberries and apples, but not with bananas, although they are the third most popular fruit in the world.

From being rare and expensive at the beginning of the twentieth century, bananas have now become a cheap product of agribusiness. America is supplied by Central America ("the banana republics") and the West Indies. Europeans get theirs from the Caribbean and West Africa. Almost all the imports are of dessert bananas, which have a high sugar content of between seventeen and twenty per cent. Cooking bananas, often called plantains, which are a staple food in some African countries, have more starch and less sugar.

There are numerous varieties of bananas, but only the very few which travel well and ripen in storage appear in the shops. A banana is at its best when it is entirely yellow with a few brown specks. Bananas with tips that are still green will ripen in a day or two at room temperature. Canary bananas, which grow in such sub-tropical climates as the Canary Islands and Israel, are small, thin-skinned, curved and very sweet with a real banana fragrance. The only drawback to them is that they tend to make you dissatisfied with other bananas. Nutritionally there is little to choose between the different varieties. They are all reasonable sources of the vitamins C, carotene and riboflavin.

The succulence of a ripe pineapple is hard to beat, but also hard to experience. Unlike the banana the pineapple will not ripen satisfactorily except on the plant, where it may even double its sugar content in the final stage of ripening. Then it has to face a long journey to the markets from its tropical homelands.

The pineapple is a native of South America, but more than half of the pineapples we eat come from Hawaii, where until less than a century ago the plant was regarded as a pernicious weed. Although fresh pineapples travel badly, they are still agreeable when canned, as most of them are. In canning, however, two-thirds of their rich supply of vitamin C is lost.

Other exotic fruits are more likely to add variety than nourishment to our diet, since they are generally too expensive to be eaten in quantity. Such is the mango, the fruit most commonly eaten in the tropics, but a luxury in the West. It has a marvellously delicate flavour—hard to pin down—with perhaps a hint of pear or melon, or perhaps pineapple or apricot. In other words, it tastes like a mango. Eaten in the kind of quantities that one would like, mangoes would be a good source of carotene.

Lychees, natives of China and now grown in many tropical countries, are becoming more available and fashionable. They look like plums that are covered in warts, but their sweet flesh is jelly-like. Lychees travel well, and even benefit from travel because their flavour becomes more aromatic.

It is a game of chance, with the odds heavily against you, to buy a fresh fig at that critical stage when its ripeness is just bursting through the skin. The chances are more in your favour if you travel to your figs instead of having them brought to you. (Try Provence, Sicily or Smyrna, for example.) Alternatively you can eat them canned or preserved.

The curse of figs is seeds and these, unfortunately, afflict some other pleasant exotic

fruits. The purple, plum-sized passion fruit has sweet (even too sweet) juicy pulp riddled with small blackish seeds. The fruit was given its name by Jesuits who arrived in South America in the sixteenth century and saw in the flower symbols of the passion of Christ, the five stamens representing his five wounds, the stigma the three nails and the ten sepals and petals the faithful disciples. The guava has no legend to distinguish it, but it does have a notably high content of vitamin C—even higher than that of citrus fruits. Whether this makes up for the mass of seeds embedded in the slightly sharp pulp is another matter. As for the pomegranate, the two Latin words that make up its name give it away— "the many-seeded apple". There are so many seeds in it that the fruit inevitably became a symbol of fertility.

The Japanese persimmon presents a different problem, for when it is unripe it is extremely sour and when it is ripe it can be cloyingly sweet. For centuries the Japanese persimmon has been cultivated in Japan, China and in Mediterranean countries and now it is grown in the United States.

There are hundreds more exotic tropical fruits that are popular where they grow, but impossible to market abroad in perfect condition. There is no better example than the durian, a large and prickly Malaysian fruit with creamy flesh, which when ripe is said to taste of rich cheese, peanuts, garlic, pineapple, apricots and sherry, but when overripe suggests nothing but sewage. It would be exciting however, to have the fruit of *Monstera deliciosa* (the ubiquitous potted plant which will not fruit in captivity), for its flavour is said to be a combination of all the most beautiful fruits.

Guavas (below) are extremely rich in vitamin C. Like black currants they have four times as much vitamin C as oranges. The juicy fruit, which turns from green to light yellow as it ripens, has a slightly sharp flavour and is, therefore, often stewed or made into jam or jelly.

Exotic fruits have intriguing flavours, are high in carbohydrate and are a source of vitamins and minerals. Chinese gooseberries, for example, are high in vitamin C and persimmons and mangoes are rich in carotene. Dates have an exceptionally high sugar content of more than sixty per cent and contain carotene, B vitamins and minerals. Left, clockwise, are: a pineapple, a mango, Chinese gooseberries, a papaya, passion fruits, rambutans and bananas. In the foreground are a date, a persimmon, a cut passion fruit and rambutans.

Baked Spiced Pineapple

Preheat the oven to 350°F (180°C, Gas Mark 4).

Cut the skin from 1 small pineapple. Slice the pineapple and remove the core. Arrange the rings in an ovenproof dish.

Mix the juice of 1 large orange with 2 tablespoons (30 ml) of brandy and 1 to 2 tablespoons (15 to 30 ml) of sugar. Pour over the pineapple rings and add 1 stick of cinnamon and 2 cloves to the dish.

Bake for 20 minutes. Serve hot or cold.

INGREDIENTS TO SERVE FOUR:
1 small pineapple
1 large orange
2 tablespoons (30 ml) brandy
1 to 2 tablespoons (15 to 30 ml) sugar
1 cinnamon stick
2 cloves

PREPARING PINEAPPLE

Slice the top, bottom and skin from pineapple.

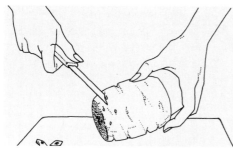

Cut any remaining eyes out with spiralling cuts.

Slice the pineapple and remove the core.

Pineapple Mousse

Separate 4 eggs. Put the egg yolks into a bowl and add ¼ pound (100 g) of castor sugar. Put the bowl over a pan of hot water and whisk until pale and thick.

Cut the skin from 1 medium-sized pineapple. Slice the pineapple and remove the central core. Reserving 1 slice for decoration, coarsely chop the pineapple then liquidize to a frothy purée.

Beat the pineapple purée into the egg yolks and sugar.

In a cup set in a pan of hot water dissolve ½ ounce (15 g) of powdered gelatine in the juice of 1 large lemon. Pour the dissolved gelatine into the pineapple mixture and beat well.

When the pineapple mousse is just beginning to set, whisk the 4 egg whites until just stiff, then fold in.

Pour into a serving dish and chill until set. Decorate with the reserved pineapple.

INGREDIENTS TO SERVE SIX:
4 eggs
¼ lb (100 g) castor sugar
1 medium-sized pineapple
½ oz (15 g) powdered gelatine
1 large lemon

Pineapple Sorbet

Cut the skin from 1 small pineapple. Slice the pineapple and remove the core. Coarsely chop the pineapple and then liquidize to a purée.

Pour the pineapple purée into a bowl. Stir in the juice of 1 large lemon and 1 large orange. Add sugar to taste.

Put into the freezer until the mixture is half-frozen.

Whisk 2 egg whites until stiff. Remove the half-frozen pineapple purée from the freezer and whisk well, then fold in the egg whites. Pour into a rigid container and freeze until solid.

Cover, seal and label and store in the freezer until required.

INGREDIENTS TO SERVE FOUR TO SIX:
1 small pineapple
1 large lemon
1 large orange
sugar
2 egg whites

Pineapple in Kirsch

This classic French way of serving a pineapple could not be simpler—soaked in kirsch and mixed with oranges and cherries.

Cut the skin from 1 small pineapple, then cut the pineapple into slices. Remove the central core and put the pineapple rings into a serving bowl. Pour over 3 tablespoons (45 ml) of kirsch and leave to soak for at least 1 hour.

Cut the peel and pith from 2 large oranges. Slice the oranges and arrange on top of the pineapple rings.

Stone ¼ pound (100 g) of cherries and arrange the cherries on top.

INGREDIENTS TO SERVE SIX:
1 small pineapple
3 tablespoons (45 ml) kirsch
2 large oranges
¼ lb (100 g) cherries

Frozen Banana and Hazelnut Yogurt

Peel 4 medium-sized bananas. Put them into a bowl and mash them well. Beat in the grated rind and juice of 1 lemon and 1 to 2 tablespoons (15 to 30 ml) of rum.

Add ½ pint (300 ml) of yogurt and 2 tablespoons (30 ml) of soft brown sugar. Mix well.

Whisk 2 egg whites until stiff, then fold into the banana mixture.

Put the bowl into the freezer until the mixture is half-frozen.

Remove from the freezer and whisk well. Stir in 2 ounces (50 g) of chopped toasted hazelnuts. Spoon into a rigid container and return to the freezer until frozen solid.

Cover, seal and label and store in the freezer until required.

INGREDIENTS TO SERVE FOUR:
4 medium-sized bananas
1 lemon
1 to 2 tablespoons (15 to 30 ml) rum
½ pint (300 ml) yogurt
2 tablespoons (30 ml) soft brown sugar
2 egg whites
2 oz (50 g) toasted hazelnuts

Baked Stuffed Bananas

Preheat the oven to 375°F (190°C, Gas Mark 5).

Slit the skins of 4 bananas along the length of the inside curve. Carefully remove the bananas, keeping the skins whole.

Put the bananas into a mixing bowl and mash them well. Stir in the grated rind and juice of ½ lemon, ¼ teaspoon (1 ml) of ground mixed spice and 1 ounce (25 g) of sultanas.

Whisk 1 egg white until stiff, then fold into the banana mixture.

Open out the banana skins and spoon in the filling. Put the bananas into an ovenproof dish, slit side upwards. Put them close together to prevent them falling over.

Bake for 15 minutes, or until the filling is puffed up and lightly browned.

Serve at once.

INGREDIENTS TO SERVE FOUR:
4 bananas
½ lemon
¼ teaspoon (1 ml) ground mixed spice
1 oz (25 g) sultanas
1 egg white

Caribbean Baked Bananas

Preheat the oven to 375°F (190°C, Gas Mark 5).

Peel 4 large bananas. Cut them into halves lengthways and put them into an ovenproof dish.

Mix the juice of 2 oranges with ¼ teaspoon (1 ml) of ground cinnamon and 1 tablespoon (15 ml) of rum and pour over the bananas.

Sprinkle with 1 ounce (25 g) of shredded coconut.

Bake for 15 minutes, or until the bananas are soft and heated through.

Serve immediately.

INGREDIENTS TO SERVE FOUR:
4 large bananas
2 oranges
¼ teaspoon (1 ml) ground cinnamon
1 tablespoon (15 ml) rum
1 oz (25 g) shredded coconut

Banana Cheese Whip

Peel 4 bananas and mash them well with the juice of 1 orange.

Beat ¼ pint (150 ml) of yogurt into ½ pound (250 g) of curd cheese until smooth. Beat the cheese mixture into the mashed bananas. Add honey to taste.

Spoon into individual dishes or glasses. Serve chilled.

INGREDIENTS TO SERVE FOUR:
4 bananas
1 orange
¼ pint (150 ml) yogurt
½ lb (250 g) curd cheese
honey

Papaya and Lime Mousse

Cut 1 medium-sized papaya into halves and remove the black seeds. Scoop out the fruit, scraping it away from the skin.

Mash the papaya with the juice of 1 large lime. Beat in ¼ pint (150 ml) of yogurt. Alternatively, put the papaya fruit into a liquidizer with the lime juice and yogurt and blend until smooth. Add sugar to taste.

In a cup set in a pan of hot water dissolve 2 teaspoons (10 ml) of powdered gelatine in 2 tablespoons (30 ml) of water. Stir the dissolved gelatine into the mousse.

When the mousse is beginning to set, whisk 2 egg whites until just stiff then fold them in.

Spoon into 4 individual dishes and chill for at least 3 hours before serving.

INGREDIENTS TO SERVE FOUR:
1 medium-sized papaya
1 large lime
¼ pint (150 ml) yogurt
sugar
2 teaspoons (10 ml) powdered gelatine
2 egg whites

PREPARING PAPAYA

Cut papaya into halves and scoop out the seeds.

Scoop the flesh out, down to the skin.

Balinese Fruit Salad

Cut ½ pineapple into ½-inch (1-cm) slices, cut off the skin and remove the central core. Cut the pineapple into chunks.

Slice 1 small mango, peel off the skin and remove the stone. Cut the fruit into cubes.

Cut the peel and pith from 1 pomelo, or 1 large grapefruit. Divide the fruit into segments.

Remove the seeds and peel from ½ small papaya and dice the fruit.

Cut 1 star fruit crossways into thin slices.

Remove the red prickly skin from 2 rambutans. Cut the fruit into sections, discarding the large seed.

Cut 1 passion fruit in half and scoop out the flesh with the seeds.

Peel and slice 2 bananas.

Put all the fruit into a large bowl. Pour in the juice of 2 large limes and sugar to taste. Toss lightly to coat the fruit.

INGREDIENTS TO SERVE SIX:
½ pineapple
1 small mango
1 pomelo or large sweet grapefruit
½ small papaya
1 star fruit
2 rambutans
1 passion fruit
2 bananas
2 large limes
sugar

Mango Fool

Peel 2 medium-sized mangoes.

Cut the fruit away from the stone and put the fruit into a mixing bowl. Mash the mango until smooth, then beat in the juice of 1 large lime or 1 small lemon and ¼ pint (150 ml) of yogurt. Alternatively, liquidize the mango with the lime juice and yogurt.

Spoon into 4 individual dishes and chill.

INGREDIENTS TO SERVE FOUR:
2 medium-sized mangoes
1 large lime or 1 small lemon
¼ pint (150 ml) yogurt

Figs with Yogurt and Honey

Cut the stems from 1 pound (500 g) of ripe figs. Cut the figs into quarters, or sixths if they are large, and put them into a glass serving bowl.

Put ½ pint (300 ml) of yogurt into a mixing bowl and stir in the grated rind of 1 lemon and 2 tablespoons (30 ml) of honey. Pour the yogurt mixture over the figs and sprinkle with 1 tablespoon (15 ml) of soft brown sugar. Chill before serving.

INGREDIENTS TO SERVE FOUR:
1 lb (500 g) ripe figs
½ pint (300 ml) yogurt
1 lemon
2 tablespoons (30 ml) honey
1 tablespoon (15 ml) soft brown sugar

BOTANICALLY a berry is a fruit with seeds enclosed in pulp, and by that definition the banana is included. But most people associate the word berry with the lush fruits of summer and autumn —strawberries, raspberries, black and red currants and blackberries, although many of them are not true berries. They are the exotic fruits of temperate climates.

Much of a berry is water—between eighty and ninety per cent—and which berry you prefer depends how you like your water flavoured. Besides water, most of the berries are quite prodigal with the vitamins C, carotene, thiamine and riboflavin. Strawberries and raspberries have niacin as well. Berries also provide reasonable amounts of such minerals as potassium.

Cultivated strawberries have two American species as parents, but it was not until they were introduced into Europe that they were interbred. The first species to arrive, in the seventeenth century, was *Fragaria virginiana* from the woodlands of the eastern states. A century later *Fragaria chiloensis* followed from the west coast. In America they had been separated by mountains, but in Europe innumerable hybrids were bred from them during the nineteenth century. Scientific breeding in the twentieth century put more emphasis on productivity, ability to travel and resistance to disease, than on flavour and texture. Nevertheless a freshly picked ripe strawberry is still something to savour.

Growing your own strawberries can give a wider range of flavours than buying them in the shops. When they are unripe all strawberries tend to be acid, but when ripe there are considerable differences from variety to variety in the degree and character of their sweetness. In some varieties, along with the strawberry flavour, is a background of pineapple, a trait for which the west coast ancestor is responsible. Although strawberries are conventionally served with sugar and cream, the flavour of ripe sweet berries is remarkably enhanced by a few drops of wine vinegar.

Wild strawberries have a more pronounced flavour and something of the same richness and sweetness is found in the small Alpine strawberries. Both are extravagantly improved if champagne is poured over them.

Out-of-season strawberries are a disappointing luxury. It is axiomatic that the sooner ripe strawberries are eaten after being picked the better they will be, so they inevitably suffer on a flight of several thousand miles. These imported strawberries also diminish the longing for the first strawberries of the season without satisfying the craving for them. But Remontant varieties do fruit into very late autumn and they help to fill the time gap naturally.

Raspberries have a less aggressive, more velvety flavour than strawberries, and raspberry addicts

raspberries

blueberries

blackberries

strawberries

Berries are a flavourful gift of summer. Although almost ninety per cent water, they are relatively rich in such minerals as calcium, and in the vitamins thiamine, riboflavin and carotene. They are a good source of vitamin C—black currants have four times as much as citrus fruits. Strawberries have less vitamin C, but like raspberries they contain niacin. Blackberries have the least vitamin C, but they are a source of calcium.

gooseberries

bilberries

red currants

black currants

never understand why strawberries are more popular. One reason is simple and unavoidable; raspberries need to be eaten as soon as they are picked because their delicate flavour begins to evaporate after even a few hours. Wild raspberries are richer but less fleshy, and many of the modern varieties have lost in flavour what they have gained in size. There are many summer- and fewer autumn-fruiting raspberries and while most are red there are particularly sweet yellow or black varieties.

Like strawberries and raspberries, the wild blueberry tastes better than the cultivated one, but cannot compete for size. Only since it was bred for plumpness in the last fifty years has it achieved its current American popularity. Those who prefer the wild blueberry can still find it growing in many of the barren places of the world, from the Arctic to South America.

Both the English and the American species of blackberry are indubitably better wild, for even when they are ripe the cultivated varieties retain a certain acidity. The loganberry, which is almost certainly a cross between a blackberry and a raspberry, is even more acid. Other hybrids have proliferated, differing more in their names than in their characteristics. Of these the boysenberry is probably the best known.

The other berries—black and red currants and gooseberries—are used more for cooking than as

dessert, although all of them become sweet enough to eat raw if they are left on the bushes longer than usual. Gooseberries have been popular in Britain since the Middle Ages, and in the north of England in Victorian times there was a craze for gooseberry clubs, which competed to grow the most gigantic berries. A few of these clubs still exist. As well as being rich in vitamins C and thiamine and a moderate source of carotene, gooseberries have the virtue of being the earliest soft fruit of the year.

The most health-giving berries are black currants because of their wealth of vitamin C and minerals. In Britain they are the most popular of the currants, whereas the less nutritious red and white currants are more popular in the United States.

One ancient berry enjoyed by the Romans is seldom grown today. This is the black mulberry. James I planted several hundred acres of mulberries in the heart of London at the beginning of the seventeenth century, and one tree survives in the gardens of Buckingham Palace. His idea was to establish a silkworm industry in Britain. But it is the leaves of the white mulberry on which the silkworm feeds, and King James had mistakenly planted the black variety. Mulberries are used in similar ways to blackberries, but they must be eaten at just the right moment—when they are falling off the trees with ripeness.

The Nutrients in Berries
Berries are a source of minerals and three and a half ounces (100 g) of strawberries, for example, provide 40 Calories.

Water	87	%
Carbohydrate	8	
Fibre	3	
Protein	1	
Fat	0.75	
Vitamins and minerals	0.25	

Blueberry Pie

Bilberries, blackberries, huckleberries or whortle berries may be substituted for blueberries in this recipe.

Preheat the oven to 400°F (200°C, Gas Mark 6).

Wash 1 pound (500 g) of blueberries and remove the stems. Put the blueberries into a 1½-pint (850-ml) pie dish. Sprinkle with 2 to 4 tablespoons (30 to 60 ml) of sugar depending on how tart the berries are.

Make 6 ounces (150 ml) of sweet flan pastry with wholewheat flour (see page 35). On a lightly floured surface roll out the pastry to

Cut a strip from around the edge of the pastry.

Press the strip onto the rim of the dish.

Cover with the remaining pastry.

Flute the edges of the pastry to seal.

½ inch (1 cm) larger in diameter than the top of the pie dish. Cut a ½-inch (1-cm) strip from around the edge of the pastry. Dampen the rim of the pie dish and press the strip of pastry on to it. Dampen the strip of pastry and cover the pie dish with the remaining pastry. Trim and press the edges of the pastry together. Flute to seal.

Cut any pastry trimmings into leaves and use to decorate the top of the pie. Brush the pastry with beaten egg to glaze.

Bake for 30 to 35 minutes, or until the pastry is crisp and brown on top.

Serve warm or cold.

INGREDIENTS TO SERVE SIX:
1 lb (500 g) blueberries
2 to 4 tablespoons (30 to 60 ml) sugar
6 oz (150 ml) sweet flan pastry made with wholewheat flour (see page 35)
1 egg

Spiced Cranberry Sauce

Grate the rind of 1 orange into a saucepan. Add the juice of 2 oranges, ¼ pound (100 g) of soft brown sugar, 1 stick of cinnamon, 1 clove and a pinch of grated nutmeg. Cook over very low heat until the sugar dissolves, then bring to the boil.

Add ½ pound (250 g) of cranberries and continue to boil, uncovered, for 5 to 10 minutes, or until the cranberries have burst and the liquid has thickened slightly.

Remove the cinnamon and clove and leave to cool. Serve chilled.

INGREDIENTS TO SERVE FOUR TO SIX:
2 oranges
¼ lb (100 g) soft brown sugar
1 cinnamon stick
1 clove
grated nutmeg
½ lb (250 g) cranberries

Gooseberry and Almond Sauce

Serve this tart sauce with oily fish, such as mackerel and trout, or with duck, goose or pork.

Top and tail ½ pound (250 g) of gooseberries and put them into a saucepan. Pour in ½ pint (300 ml) of water. Cover the pan and bring to the boil. Reduce the heat and simmer for 5 minutes, or until the gooseberries are tender.

Liquidize the gooseberries with the cooking liquor, then sieve them.

Melt 1 ounce (25 g) of margarine or butter in a saucepan. Add 2 ounces (50 g) of coarsely chopped blanched almonds and fry gently until they are golden brown. Stir in 1 tablespoon (15 ml) of flour and then the gooseberry purée. Heat gently, stirring

constantly, until the sauce thickens and boils. Simmer for 1 minute. Add salt and pepper to taste and a pinch of grated nutmeg.

Serve hot or cold.

INGREDIENTS TO SERVE FOUR:
½ lb (250 g) gooseberries
1 oz (25 g) margarine or butter
2 oz (50 g) blanched almonds
1 tablespoon (15 ml) flour
salt
pepper
grated nutmeg

PREPARING GOOSEBERRIES

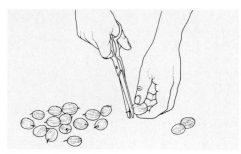
Trim gooseberries with scissors.

Gooseberry Fool

Top and tail 1 pound (500 g) of gooseberries and put them into a saucepan with 4 tablespoons (60 ml) of sugar and 4 tablespoons (60 ml) of water. Cover the pan and cook over low heat for 15 minutes, or until the gooseberries are tender.

Make ¼ pint (150 ml) of confectioner's custard (see page 93). Let the custard cool slightly, then beat in ¼ pint (150 ml) of yogurt.

Sieve the gooseberries into a mixing bowl. Add the custard to the gooseberry purée and mix well. Turn into 1 large serving bowl or 4 individual glasses or dishes.

Chill before serving.

INGREDIENTS TO SERVE FOUR:
1 lb (500 g) gooseberries
4 tablespoons (60 ml) sugar
¼ pint confectioner's custard (see page 93)
¼ pint (150 ml) yogurt

Gooseberry and Orange Compote

Top and tail 1 pound (500 g) of gooseberries. Put them into a saucepan with the grated rind of 1 orange, the juice of 2 oranges and 2 ounces (50 g) of sugar. Cover the pan and cook over low heat until the juice simmers. Continue to simmer very gently for about 3 minutes, or until the gooseberries are just tender.

Remove the peel and pith of 2 more oranges. Working over the pan, cut the membrane away from the segments of fruit. Carefully stir the orange segments into the gooseberries and leave to cool.

Transfer to a serving dish and chill. Serve cold.

INGREDIENTS TO SERVE SIX:
1 lb (500 g) gooseberries
4 oranges
2 oz (50 g) sugar

Gooseberry Squares

Preheat the oven to 400°F (200°C, Gas Mark 6).

Top and tail ½ pound (250 g) of gooseberries. Wash and drain them and put them into a large saucepan with 2 ounces (50 g) of castor sugar and 3 tablespoons (45 ml) of white wine. Heat the gooseberries gently, stirring occasionally, until they have reduced to a purée.

Add the grated rind of 1 lemon and 2 ounces (50 g) of split blanched almonds and mix well.

Make and roll out thinly ¾ pound (375 g) of cheese pastry (see quiche lorraine, page 89). Cut eight 4-inch (10-cm) squares out of the pastry. Transfer 4 squares to a greased baking sheet.

Spoon the gooseberry mixture on to the squares on the baking sheet. Dampen the edges of the pastry. Use the remaining squares to cover the gooseberry mixture. Press the edges of the pastry squares together to seal them. Cut a slit in the top of each square and brush the lids with beaten egg.

Bake for 15 to 20 minutes, or until the pastry is crisp and golden.

Serve immediately.

INGREDIENTS TO SERVE FOUR:
½ lb (250 g) gooseberries
2 oz (50 g) castor sugar
3 tablespoons (45 ml) white wine
1 lemon
2 oz (50 g) split blanched almonds
¾ lb (375 g) cheese pastry (see quiche lorraine, page 89)
1 egg

Strawberry Yogurt Whip

This light, fluffy dessert may be made just before serving or in advance and set with gelatine. Dissolve 2 teaspoons (10 ml) of powdered gelatine in the orange or lemon juice and add to the strawberry purée with the yogurt. Chill until set and decorate with the reserved whole strawberries before serving.

Hull ½ pound (250 g) of strawberries and, reserving a few for decoration, sieve or liquidize them to a purée. Add the grated rind of ½ orange or lemon.

Stir in ½ pint (300 ml) of yogurt and the juice of ½ orange or lemon. Add 1 tablespoon (15 ml) of sugar. Beat the mixture thoroughly adding more sugar if desired.

Whisk 2 egg whites until stiff, then fold into the strawberry mixture.

Serve at once decorated with the reserved whole strawberries.

INGREDIENTS TO SERVE FOUR:
½ lb (250 g) strawberries
½ orange or lemon
1 tablespoon (15 ml) sugar
½ pint (300 ml) yogurt
2 egg whites

HULLING STRAWBERRIES

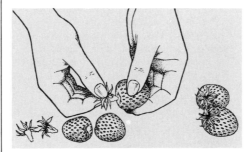

Pull leaves, stalk and soft centre from strawberries.

Strawberry Crème Brûlée

A traditional crème brûlée is a rich custard made with cream and egg yolks and topped with burnt sugar. This custard is made with yogurt and eggs, poured over strawberries. It has a tangy flavour and a rich texture.

Hull and slice ½ pound (250 g) of strawberries. Divide them among 4 individual ovenproof dishes.

To make the custard, put 1 pint (600 ml) of yogurt into a mixing bowl. Add ½ vanilla pod or 1 teaspoon (5 ml) of vanilla essence and a pinch of grated nutmeg.

Put the bowl over a pan of simmering water and heat the yogurt until it is lukewarm.

Beat 4 egg yolks with 1 ounce (25 g) of castor sugar and stir into the warm yogurt. Continue to heat, stirring constantly, until the custard thickens and coats the back of a spoon.

Strain the custard over the strawberries. Chill for at least 2 hours. The custard will set and thicken as it cools.

Sprinkle 2 tablespoons (30 ml) of demerara or soft brown sugar over the custard. Stand the dishes in a baking tin filled with ice cubes and put under a hot grill for 1 to 2 minutes, or until the sugar browns and caramelizes. Return the dishes to the refrigerator and chill before serving.

INGREDIENTS TO SERVE FOUR:
½ pound (250 g) strawberries
1 pint (600 ml) yogurt
½ vanilla pod or 1 teaspoon (5 ml) vanilla essence
grated nutmeg
4 egg yolks
1 oz (25 g) castor sugar
2 tablespoons (30 ml) demerara or soft brown sugar

Strawberry Cloud

Hull and slice 1 pound (500 g) of strawberries. Put the strawberries into a serving bowl. Sprinkle with 2 tablespoons (30 ml) of Grand Marnier.

Just before serving, whisk 2 egg whites until stiff. Carefully fold in ½ pint (300 ml) of yogurt, the grated rind of ½ lemon and 1 tablespoon (15 ml) of castor sugar. Fold in the strawberries.

Sprinkle with 1 ounce (25 g) of toasted flaked almonds and serve.

INGREDIENTS TO SERVE FOUR:
1 lb (500 g) strawberries
2 tablespoons (30 ml) Grand Marnier
2 egg whites
½ pint (300 ml) yogurt
½ lemon
1 tablespoon (15 ml) castor sugar
1 oz (25 g) toasted flaked almonds

Strawberries à l'Orange

Hull 1 pound (500 g) of strawberries. Cut them into halves and put them into a serving bowl.

Cut ¼ pound (100 g) of grapes into halves, remove the pips and add to the strawberries.

Cut the peel and pith from 2 oranges. Working over the bowl, cut the membrane away from the segments of fruit. Add the orange segments to the strawberries.

Mix the juice of 1 large orange with 3 tablespoons (45 ml) of Grand Marnier or brandy. Stir in sugar to taste, then pour over the strawberries.

Refrigerate for at least 1 hour before serving.

INGREDIENTS TO SERVE FOUR:
1 lb (500 g) strawberries
¼ lb (100 g) green grapes
3 oranges
3 tablespoons (45 ml) Grand Marnier
**   or brandy**
sugar

Strawberry and Cheese Tartlets

This recipe may be used to make one 8-inch (20-cm) flan instead of tartlets.

Preheat the oven to 400°F (200°C, Gas Mark 6).

Make 6 ounces (150 g) of almond pastry with wholewheat flour (see page 35). Roll out the pastry on a lightly floured surface. Using a 2½-inch (6-cm) round fluted cutter, cut out 18 circles and use them to line tartlet tins. Prick the pastry well with a fork and bake blind for 10 minutes. Leave to cool.

For the filling, put ½ pound (250 g) of curd cheese into a mixing bowl. Beat in 4 tablespoons (60 ml) of yogurt, 1 tablespoon (15 ml) of honey and the grated rind of 1 lemon.

Divide the filling among the baked pastry cases.

Hull ½ pound (250 g) of strawberries, cut them into halves if they are large and arrange on top of the tartlets.

For the glaze, put 2 tablespoons (30 ml) of red currant jelly into a small saucepan with the juice of 1 lemon. Cook over low heat until the jelly has dissolved, then spoon the glaze over the strawberries.

INGREDIENTS TO MAKE EIGHTEEN TARTLETS:
6 oz (150 g) almond pastry made with
**   wholewheat flour (see page 35)**
½ lb (250 g) curd cheese
4 tablespoons (60 ml) yogurt
1 tablespoon (15 ml) honey
1 lemon
½ lb (250 g) strawberries
2 tablespoons (30 ml) red currant jelly

Strawberry Wine Punch

Squeeze the juice of 4 lemons into a large punch bowl. Hull 1 pound (500 g) of strawberries and cut them into halves. Peel and remove the pips from 1 medium-sized melon. Cut the melon into 1-inch (2-cm) cubes. Add the strawberries and melon to the bowl and toss the fruit in the lemon juice.

Sprinkle 2 ounces (50 g) of castor sugar over the fruit and squeeze in the juice of 4 oranges. Pour 1 bottle of red wine and 1 pint (600 ml) of soda water into the bowl. Mix well and chill thoroughly.

Thinly slice 1 orange and 1 lemon and add them to the bowl. Serve immediately.

INGREDIENTS TO MAKE ABOUT 4 PINTS OF PUNCH:
5 lemons
1 lb (500 g) strawberries
1 medium-sized melon
2 oz (50 g) castor sugar
5 oranges
1 bottle red wine
1 pint (600 ml) soda water

Raspberry Sorbet

Reserving a few for decoration, sieve ½ pound (250 g) of raspberries, or liquidize and then sieve them to remove the seeds. Stir in ½ pint (300 ml) of yogurt, the juice of ½ lemon and 2 tablespoons (30 ml) of castor sugar. Put the purée into the freezer until it is half-frozen.

Whisk 2 egg whites until stiff. Whisk the half-frozen purée, then fold in the egg whites.

Return the sorbet to the freezer and freeze until firm.

Serve decorated with the reserved raspberries.

INGREDIENTS TO SERVE FOUR TO SIX:
½ lb (250 g) raspberries
½ pint (300 ml) yogurt
½ lemon
2 tablespoons (30 ml) castor sugar
2 egg whites

The season of berries is short and they are at their best for only a brief time, but during that time we can enjoy such memorable dishes as Strawberry à l'Orange, left, Raspberry Sorbet, right, and Summer Pudding, far right.

Raspberry Curd Fool

Put 1 pound (500 g) of raspberries into a mixing bowl, reserving a few for decoration. Mash the raspberries, then beat in ½ pound (250 g) of curd cheese and ½ pint (300 ml) of yogurt. Add 1 to 2 tablespoons (15 to 30 ml) of sugar to taste.

Just before serving, whisk 2 egg whites until stiff, then fold into the raspberry mixture. Spoon into 4 individual serving dishes or 1 large serving bowl and decorate with the reserved raspberries.

Serve immediately.

INGREDIENTS TO SERVE FOUR TO SIX:
1 lb (500 g) raspberries
½ lb (250 g) curd cheese
½ pint (300 ml) yogurt
1 to 2 tablespoons (15 to 30 ml) sugar
2 egg whites

Summer Pudding

This is a glorious pudding, incorporating as many different soft summer fruits as you care to include.

Lightly grease a 1½-pint (850-ml) pudding basin.

Cut the crust from 1 small loaf of thinly sliced white bread. Cut 1 slice of bread into a round to fit the bottom of the basin. Line the sides of the basin with bread slices, shaping them so that they fit close together.

Wash and hull 1½ pounds (700 g) of soft summer fruit, using a mixture of raspberries, strawberries, cherries and currants. Cut large strawberries into halves and pit the cherries.

Put the fruit into a saucepan with 2 ounces (50 g) of sugar, the grated rind and juice of ½ lemon and 2 tablespoons (30 ml) of water. Cover the pan and bring to the boil slowly. Reduce the heat and simmer for 1 minute.

Reserving 3 tablespoons (45 ml) of the juice, spoon the contents of the pan into the bread-lined basin.

Cover the fruit with the remaining slices of bread, trimming the edges to fit the top of the basin.

Put a small plate on top and then weight it with a heavy can. Refrigerate, preferably overnight. Turn the pudding out on to a serving plate.

Pour the reserved juice over any parts of the bread that have not been soaked through and coloured by the fruit juices and serve immediately.

INGREDIENTS TO SERVE FOUR TO SIX:
1 small thinly sliced white loaf
1½ lb (700 g) mixed soft summer fruits
2 oz (50 g) sugar
½ lemon

Frozen Raspberry Yogurt

Frozen flavoured yogurt is a marvellous substitute for ice-cream. Other fruits may be substituted for the raspberries in this recipe. The sugar must then be adjusted to taste.

Sieve ½ pound (250 g) of raspberries or liquidize and then sieve to remove the seeds.

Stir 1 pint (600 ml) of yogurt and 2 tablespoons (30 ml) of sugar into the purée. Mix well.

Pour into a polythene container, seal, label and freeze until firm.

Store in the freezer until required.

INGREDIENTS TO SERVE FOUR TO SIX:
½ lb (250 g) raspberries
1 pint (600 ml) yogurt
2 tablespoons (30 ml) sugar

Raspberry Melba Sauce

This sharp, colourful sauce is particularly good with peaches and strawberries.

Put ½ pound (250 g) of raspberries into a saucepan with the grated rind and juice of ½ lemon and 4 tablespoons (60 ml) of red currant jelly.

Cover the pan and cook over low heat until the jelly melts and the juices run from the raspberries. Uncover and continue to cook, stirring constantly, until the raspberries are mushy.

Sieve the raspberries and return to the pan.

Thicken the sauce a little by blending 1 teaspoon (5 ml) of arrowroot with 1 tablespoon (15 ml) of water and adding it to the sauce. Reheat, stirring constantly, until the sauce is thick and clear.

Serve hot or cold.

INGREDIENTS TO SERVE FOUR:
½ lb (250 g) raspberries
½ lemon
4 tablespoons (60 ml) red currant jelly
1 teaspoon (5 ml) arrowroot

Raspberry Zabaglione

Sieve ½ pound (250 g) of raspberries into a pudding basin. Add 4 egg yolks, 3 ounces (75 g) of castor sugar and ¼ pint (150 ml) of white wine.

Put the bowl over a pan of simmering water and whisk the custard until it is very foamy and thick.

Pour into 4 individual dishes or glasses and serve immediately.

INGREDIENTS TO SERVE FOUR:
½ lb (250 g) raspberries
4 egg yolks
3 oz (75 g) castor sugar
¼ pint (150 ml) white wine

Chilled Raspberry Soufflé

Reserving a few berries for decoration, sieve 1 pound (500 g) of raspberries, or liquidize and then sieve them to remove the seeds.

Separate 4 eggs. Put the yolks into a mixing bowl and add 3 ounces (85 g) of castor sugar and the grated rind of 1 lemon. Put the mixing bowl over a pan of hot water and whisk until the mixture is thick. Remove from the heat and whisk until cool.

Stir in the raspberry purée and ¼ pint (150 ml) of yogurt. Mix well.

Squeeze the juice from the lemon into a small bowl set in a pan of hot water. Sprinkle ½ ounce (15 g) of powdered gelatine into the lemon juice and stir until dissolved, then stir into the raspberry mixture.

When the mixture is beginning to set whisk the egg whites until just stiff and fold them in.

Tie a band of greaseproof paper around a 1½-pint (850-ml) soufflé dish so that it stands 2 inches (5 cm) above the rim and pour in the soufflé mixture. Alternatively, pour into a serving bowl. Refrigerate for at least 2 hours before serving.

To serve, carefully remove the greaseproof paper and decorate with the reserved raspberries.

INGREDIENTS TO SERVE FOUR TO SIX:
1 lb (500 g) raspberries
4 eggs
3 oz (75 g) castor sugar
1 lemon
¼ pint (150 ml) yogurt
½ oz (15 g) powdered gelatine

Raspberries and Peaches in Wine

Put 1 pound (500 g) of raspberries into a serving bowl.

Blanch and peel 2 peaches. Cut the peaches into halves and remove the stones. Slice the peaches into the bowl of raspberries.

Pour in ¼ pint (150 ml) of white wine and toss lightly to mix. Add sugar to taste.

Chill for at least 1 hour before serving.

INGREDIENTS TO SERVE FOUR:
1 lb (500 g) raspberries
2 peaches
¼ pint (150 ml) white wine
sugar

Hot Raspberry Snow

Preheat the oven to 400°F (200°C, Gas Mark 6).

Put 1 pound (500 g) of raspberries into an ovenproof dish. Sprinkle with 1 tablespoon (15 ml) of sugar.

Put ¼ pint (150 ml) of yogurt into a mixing bowl. Separate 2 eggs. Beat the egg yolks into the yogurt with ½ ounce (15 g) of flour and 1 ounce (25 g) of ground almonds.

Whisk the egg whites until they are stiff. Fold them into the yogurt mixture.

Spoon the topping over the raspberries and sprinkle with 2 tablespoons of soft brown sugar.

Bake for 15 to 20 minutes, or until the topping has risen and is lightly browned.

INGREDIENTS TO SERVE FOUR TO SIX:
1 lb (500 g) raspberries
1 tablespoon (15 ml) sugar
¼ pint (150 ml) yogurt
2 eggs
½ oz (15 g) flour
1 oz (25 g) ground almonds
2 tablespoons (30 ml) soft brown sugar

Red Fruit Compote

Wash ½ pound (250 g) of red currants and strip them from their stems. Put the currants into a saucepan.

Pit ½ pound (250 g) of cherries and add them to the pan with the juice of 1 orange and 2 tablespoons (30 ml) of red currant jelly. Add 1 to 2 tablespoons (15 to 30 ml) of sugar.

Cover the pan and cook over low heat until the juices come to the boil. Remove the pan from the heat and set aside for 10 minutes to soften the fruit.

Carefully stir in 1 pound (500 g) of raspberries, spoon into a serving dish and serve chilled.

INGREDIENTS TO SERVE FOUR TO SIX:
½ lb (250 g) red currants
½ lb (250 g) cherries
1 orange
2 tablespoons (50 ml) red currant jelly
1 to 2 tablespoons (15 to 30 ml) sugar
1 lb (500 g) raspberries

Red Currant Jelly

Red currant jelly is very good to have on hand. It can be used to sweeten, flavour and glaze numerous dishes. The yield will vary according to the ripeness of the fruit and the length of time it is left to strain.

Wash 3 pounds (1.40 kg) of red currants. It is not necessary to remove the stems.

Put the red currants into a saucepan with 1 pint (600 ml) of water. Bring to the boil, reduce the heat and simmer gently until the currants are reduced to a pulp. They must be thoroughly cooked in order to extract as much juice as possible.

Strain the currants through a jelly bag, preferably overnight, until all the juice has dripped through. Do not squeeze the bag of fruit because this will make the jelly cloudy. A clean tea-towel or a piece of muslin cloth may be used instead of a jelly bag.

Measure the juice and pour it into a saucepan. For every pint (600 ml) of juice add 1 pound (500 g) of preserving sugar. Cook over low heat, stirring constantly, until the sugar has dissolved. Boil rapidly until the setting point is reached (see marmalade, page 178).

Skim the jelly then pour at once into clean, dry, warm jars. Wipe the jars and cover.

INGREDIENTS:
**3 lb (1.40 kg) red currants
preserving sugar**

STRAINING RED CURRANT JELLY

Strain the juice of red currants through a jelly bag.

Cumberland Sauce

This red currant sauce is traditionally served with ham, but it is also good with lamb and game.

Cut the peel thinly from 2 large oranges and 1 large lemon, then cut the peel into thin strips. Put the peel into a small saucepan, cover with water and bring to the boil. Reduce the heat and simmer for 15 minutes. Drain well.

Squeeze the juice from the oranges and lemon into another saucepan. Add ½ pound (250 g) of red currant jelly. Cook over low heat until the jelly melts, then bring to the boil.

Blend 2 teaspoons (10 ml) of arrowroot with 4 tablespoons (60 ml) of port. Stir the mixture into the sauce. Stirring constantly, bring to the boil and cook until the sauce thickens and clears.

Add the orange and lemon peel, reduce the heat and simmer for 5 minutes.

Serve warm or cold.

INGREDIENTS TO SERVE FOUR:
**2 large oranges
1 large lemon
½ lb (250 g) red currant jelly
2 teaspoons (10 ml) arrowroot
4 tablespoons (60 ml) port**

Rødgrød

This delicious Danish red fruit pudding is a purée of mixed fruits.

Put 2 pounds (1 kg) of mixed red fruits (red or black currants, raspberries and strawberries) into a saucepan. Add the grated rind and juice of 1 lemon. Cover the pan and slowly bring to the boil. Simmer gently for 5 minutes, or until the fruit is just soft.

Sieve the fruit with the juices or liquidize and then sieve it. Return the fruit purée to the saucepan.

Blend 2 tablespoons (30 ml) of arrowroot with a little of the purée, then stir it into the pan. Bring to the boil, stirring constantly, until the mixture thickens. Add sugar to taste, reduce the heat and simmer for 2 minutes.

Let the rødgrød cool, then spoon it into individual serving dishes or glasses and decorate with 1 ounce (25 g) of flaked almonds.

INGREDIENTS TO SERVE SIX:
**2 lb (1 kg) mixed red fruits
1 lemon
2 tablespoons (30 ml) arrowroot
sugar
1 oz (25 g) flaked almonds**

Currant Cottage Cheese Delight

Wash 1 pound (500 g) of red or white currants, or a mixture of both, and remove the stems.

Put ¾ pound (350 g) of cottage cheese, ¼ pint (150 ml) of yogurt and 2 tablespoons (30 ml) of honey into a liquidizer and blend until smooth. Alternatively, sieve the cottage cheese, then stir in the yogurt and honey.

Fold in the currants and the grated rind of 1 lemon.

Pile into a serving dish and chill well before serving.

INGREDIENTS TO SERVE FOUR:
**1 lb (500 g) red or white currants
¾ lb (350 g) cottage cheese
¼ pint (150 ml) yogurt
2 tablespoons (30 ml) honey
1 lemon**

Blackcurrant Mousse

Remove the stems from 1 pound (500 g) of black currants. Put the fruit into a saucepan with the grated rind and juice of 1 large orange and 2 sprigs of mint. Cover the pan and cook over low heat until the juices come to the boil. Reduce the heat and simmer gently for 5 minutes, or until the currants are soft.

Separate 3 eggs. Add 3 ounces (75 g) of castor sugar to the yolks and whisk until thick and pale. Add the cooked black currants while they are still warm and whisk well. (The black currants may be liquidized or sieved for a smoother texture.)

In a cup set in a pan of hot water dissolve 2 teaspoons (10 ml) of powdered gelatine in 1 tablespoon (15 ml) of water. Stir the dissolved gelatine into the blackcurrant mixture. Add ¼ pint (150 ml) of yogurt and mix well.

When the mousse begins to set, whisk the egg whites until just stiff, then fold in.

Pour into a serving dish and chill for at least 2 hours before serving.

INGREDIENTS TO SERVE FOUR TO SIX:
**1 lb (500 g) black currants
1 large orange
2 mint sprigs
3 eggs
3 oz (75 g) castor sugar
2 teaspoons (10 ml) powdered gelatine
¼ pint (150 ml) yogurt**

The Nutrients in Nuts
Nuts are high in protein
and energy and three
and a half ounces (100 g) of
almonds, for example,
provide about 600 Calories.

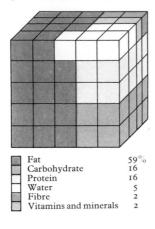

■ Fat	59%
■ Carbohydrate	16
□ Protein	16
□ Water	5
■ Fibre	2
□ Vitamins and minerals	2

The coconut (right) is the
most versatile of nuts. It
supplies milk as well as
"meat". Coconut milk is
easily digested and is low in
calories, but the meat is full of
energy-giving oil and contains
such minerals as iron.
Desiccated coconut is used in
cooking to add flavour and
texture. Oil, for cooking and
to make margarine, is
extracted from the meat.

MANKIND HAS BEEN EATING NUTS from time immemorial. Archaeological sites in the Near East indicate that pistachio nuts and acorns were being eaten in about 10,000 BC, possibly because other food was scarce. Today people in the West would eat acorns only out of dire necessity, while pistachios suggest cocktail-hour affluence.

There is a bewildering variety of nuts, but not all are used as food. Some are used as beads, some are made into varnish, hair oil or soap, and the *Ophiocaryon paradoxum* from Guiana has a reputation as a charm against snake bites. The most important edible nuts are filberts and hazels, pecans, walnuts, almonds, cashews, Brazils, peanuts, chestnuts, pistachios and macadamias.

Vegetarians apart, people in the West eat few nuts. Most people think nuts are something to nibble, rather than a serious food. But nuts are staggeringly nutritious and even a nibble provides a considerable amount of protein and fat and a wide range of minerals. Vegetarians would have a lean time without them, and there is no

NUTS FROM THE GROUND

Not true nuts, peanuts are actually the pods of a leguminous plant of South American origin. Because of the curious way in which they grow they have earned their other names—groundnuts and earthnuts. After the plant's flowers have been pollinated the stalks bearing them bend to the ground and grow longer, forcing the young pods into the soil. There, as illustrated left, they mature to produce two, three or four nuts within each shell. These nuts are a precious food because they are very rich in protein, fat, thiamine and niacin.

reason why they should cover up their delicious natural flavours by turning them into imitation meat dishes.

The nutritional value of different nuts varies considerably. Most are outstandingly rich in protein: almonds have twenty per cent, cashews seventeen per cent, Brazils thirteen per cent and walnuts twelve per cent. Even richer are pine nuts and peanuts, although neither of them is, botanically, a nut.

Pine nuts, or kernels, the seeds of the Stone Pine, may reach a surprising thirty one per cent protein and only a few meats achieve or excel that. They have something of an almond flavour, but are softer than true dessert nuts.

Peanuts may be twenty-eight per cent protein. They are eaten raw, or roasted and ground to make peanut butter. Oil extracted from them is used in cooking or for making margarine.

Strictly speaking, neither almonds nor Brazils are nuts either. The Brazil is a seed and an almond is a drupe, that is, a fleshy fruit enclosing a stone in which is a kernel. There are sweet and bitter almonds, but the bitter almonds are so bitter as to be inedible—fortunately so, since they contain a poison called prussic acid. After refining, however, the flavouring oil made from the kernels is perfectly safe and is widely used in cooking. Sweet almonds are equally delicious eaten raw, roasted, toasted or fried and used in either sweet or savoury dishes, especially with fish and chicken.

A very tall South American forest tree produces the very odd fruit that provides the highly desirable Brazil nuts. The fruit itself is a large woody sphere, weighing several pounds, which crashes to the ground when it is ripe and is hazardous to harvesters. Inside are about twenty of the familiar nuts, tightly packed like the segments of an orange. These are the shells with which we struggle to reach the large creamy coloured kernel within.

Walnuts are true nuts and among the most distinguished. The best flavoured is the English (alias Persian) walnut from the beautiful *Juglans regia* tree, which grows throughout Europe and Asia. The black walnut (*Juglans nigra*) is a native of North America and the kernel, when you get to it through the immensely hard shell, has a stronger flavour than the English walnut. When they are ripe walnuts are usually used in sweet, rather than savoury, cooking. Pickled walnuts, made from the whole walnuts before the shell has hardened (around midsummer), have no rival as companions to cold meats and cheese.

Two nuts in growing demand in the West are the pistachio and the macadamia. The pistachio is a pretty green, mild in flavour, unusually rich in iron and expensive. The macadamia, a native of Australia, which looks like a large hazelnut, has become popular in the United States. Although not rich in protein as nuts go, it is notable for its fat content of more than seventy per cent.

Another cocktail-belt nut is the cashew, less plebeian than the peanut, but the way in which it grows is equally singular. The tropical tree produces a crop of fleshy fruits and from the base of each hangs a single olive-coloured nut. This contains a particularly irritant oil, which has to be driven off by roasting before the nut is shelled to release the sweet kernel.

The most famous nuts of temperate climates are filberts, the related hazels, or cobs, and sweet chestnuts. The wild hazel is one of the most ancient of nuts, but its cultivation is comparatively recent. In Britain there are still many wild hazels in the hedgerows and they are also cultivated commercially. Because they contain more moisture—about forty per cent—than the hazels and filberts grown in Spain, Italy and Turkey, they are not as rich in protein and fat.

The names hazel and filbert are often used indiscriminately, and the justly famous Kentish cob is in fact a filbert. It is possible to distinguish between them. The hazel is more likely to be round and the filbert oval, but the husk is the more reliable indicator; the filbert's is longer than the cob's and it folds over and hugs the top of the nut closely.

The sweet, or Spanish, chestnut is a nut with a high moisture content—about fifty per cent —even when grown in sunny climates. It contains little more than two per cent protein and about the same amount of fat, so it is far less fattening than most nuts. Chestnuts have innumerable uses in cooking. They associate well with poultry, game and many other meats, as well as with the cabbage tribe. The French cook them in sugar to make marrons glacés, or purée them with ice-cream to make the exotic Nesselrode pudding. The Italians cook them in wine. The British like them roasted, and as winter approaches hot-chestnut vendors do a brisk trade roasting and selling them in the streets.

Nuts are a highly concentrated source of energy. They can be as much as seventy per cent fat and some nuts are as high as meat in carbohydrate and protein. They also contain B vitamins and such minerals as iron. Clockwise below from top left: pecans, very high in fat; Brazil nuts, a good source of niacin; pistachios, rich in iron; almonds, a source of calcium; and walnuts, which, unlike most other nuts, have more polyunsaturated than saturated fat.

Nut Pâté

Preheat the oven to 375°F (190°C, Gas Mark 5).

Chop 2 ounces of bacon. Peel and chop ½ pound (250 g) of onions.

Heat 1 tablespoon (15 ml) of corn oil in a saucepan and fry the bacon, the onions and 1 crushed garlic clove for 5 minutes, or until the onions are lightly browned.

Remove the pan from the heat and stir in ½ pound (250 g) of chopped mixed nuts (cashews, almonds, Brazil nuts and walnuts).

Add ¼ pound (100 g) of fresh wholewheat breadcrumbs, 1 tablespoon (15 ml) of chopped parsley, 1 tablespoon (15 ml) of chopped sage, salt and pepper. Stir well. Beat 1 egg then stir it into the mixture.

Turn into a lightly greased 1-pound (500-g) loaf tin. Alternatively, shape into a loaf on a greased baking sheet.

Bake for 40 to 45 minutes, or until brown.

Turn out on to a serving dish and serve immediately, or allow it to cool in the tin first and serve cold.

INGREDIENTS TO SERVE FOUR TO SIX:
2 oz (50 g) bacon
½ lb (250 g) onions
1 tablespoon (15 ml) corn oil
1 garlic clove
½ lb (250 g) mixed nuts
¼ lb (100 g) fresh wholewheat breadcrumbs
1 tablespoon (15 ml) chopped parsley
1 tablespoon (15 ml) chopped sage
salt
pepper
1 egg

Pork Saté

This speciality of Southeast Asia makes an unusual cocktail snack or first course. The strips of pork, marinated, cooked and served on bamboo sticks or small skewers, are dipped into a spicy sauce.

Cut 1 pound (500 g) of pork fillet or boned pork chops into slices ¼ inch (6 mm) thick. Cut the slices into strips about 1 inch (2 cm) long and ½ inch (1 cm) wide. Skewer 3 to 4 pieces of meat close together on the end of a bamboo stick. (You will need about 30 sticks.) Lay the sticks in a shallow bowl.

To make the marinade, in a small bowl combine 1 tablespoon (15 ml) of clear honey, 1 tablespoon (15 ml) of soy sauce, 1 teaspoon (5 ml) of peanut oil, 1 teaspoon (5 ml) of water, 1 teaspoon (5 ml) of grated onion, 1 crushed garlic clove, salt and pepper. Mix well. Pour the marinade over the meat. Marinate for at least 1 hour at room temperature or overnight in the refrigerator. Turn the sticks occasionally.

For the sauce, heat 1 tablespoon (15 ml) of peanut oil in a small saucepan. Add

1 crushed garlic clove and fry, stirring constantly, until it is lightly browned. Stir in ½ teaspoon (2.5 ml) of chilli powder and fry for 1 minute. Finely chop or grind ¼ pound (100 g) of roasted salted peanuts and add to the pan. Stir in ¼ pint (150 ml) of water and 1 tablespoon (15 ml) of lemon juice. Bring to the boil, stirring constantly. Reduce the heat and simmer gently for 5 minutes, or until the sauce has thickened enough to coat the back of a spoon. Season to taste with salt and pepper. Keep hot.

Remove the meat from the marinade and cook over a charcoal fire or under a moderate grill, turning the sticks frequently, for 4 to 5 minutes, or until the meat has browned.

Pour the hot sauce into a bowl. Pile the saté on a shallow serving dish. Garnish with wedges of cucumber and serve immediately.

INGREDIENTS TO SERVE SIX:
1 lb (500 g) pork fillet or boned pork chops
1 tablespoon (15 ml) clear honey
1 tablespoon (15 ml) soy sauce
4 teaspoons (20 ml) peanut oil
1 teaspoon (5 ml) grated onion
2 garlic cloves
salt
pepper
½ teaspoon (2.5 ml) chilli powder
¼ lb (100 g) roasted salted peanuts
1 tablespoon (15 ml) lemon juice
cucumber wedges

MAKING SATÉ

Cut lean pork into thin strips.

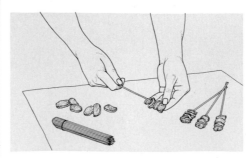

Thread the pork on to bamboo sticks.

Brazil Patties

Ground Brazil nuts flavoured with thyme make a tasty and satisfying meal. The patties may be fried or baked. Serve them with a mushroom sauce or a tomato sauce.

Coarsely grind ½ pound (250 g) of shelled Brazil nuts in a liquidizer, or chop them very finely, and put them into a mixing bowl.

Add 2 ounces (50 g) of fresh wholewheat breadcrumbs, 1 tablespoon (15 ml) of chopped thyme, salt and pepper and mix well. Beat 1 egg and stir it in.

Divide the mixture into 4 and shape into cakes about ½ inch (1 cm) thick and 3 inches (8 cm) in diameter.

Fry the patties in a little corn oil for 5 minutes, turning once so that both sides brown. Alternatively, put them on a lightly greased baking sheet and bake at 400°F (200°C, Gas Mark 6) for 20 minutes.

Serve hot or cold.

INGREDIENTS TO SERVE FOUR:
½ lb (250 g) shelled Brazil nuts
2 oz (50 g) fresh wholewheat breadcrumbs
1 tablespoon (15 ml) chopped thyme
salt
pepper
1 egg
corn oil

Walnut, Cheese and Tomato Loaf

Serve this dish as a starter or as a light main dish.

Preheat the oven to 400°F (200°C, Gas Mark 6).

Grind ½ pound (250 g) of shelled walnuts in a liquidizer. Put the nuts into a large mixing bowl.

Blanch and peel ½ pound (250 g) of tomatoes. Slice them thinly and add to the ground walnuts with ¼ pound (100 g) of grated Cheddar cheese, 1 grated onion, 1 tablespoon (15 ml) of chopped marjoram or oregano, salt and pepper. Mix well. Beat 1 egg and stir it in.

Spoon the mixture into a lightly greased 1-pound (500-g) loaf tin and press down well. Bake for 30 to 40 minutes, or until brown on top.

Cool the loaf in the tin and then turn it out on to a serving dish.

INGREDIENTS TO SERVE FOUR TO SIX:
½ lb (250 g) shelled walnuts
½ lb (250 g) tomatoes
¼ lb (100 g) grated Cheddar cheese
1 onion
1 tablespoon (15 ml) chopped marjoram or oregano
salt
pepper
1 egg

Mushroom and Nut Loaf

Preheat the oven to 350°F (180°C, Gas Mark 4).

Chop ½ pound (250 g) of onions. Chop ½ pound (250 g) of mushrooms. Coarsely grind ½ pound (250 g) of shelled Brazil nuts.

Heat 2 tablespoons (30 ml) of corn oil in a large saucepan. Add the onions and fry, stirring frequently, for 3 minutes. Add the mushrooms and fry for 2 minutes more.

Remove the pan from the heat and stir in the Brazil nuts and ¼ pound (100 g) of fresh wholewheat breadcrumbs.

Beat 1 egg with 2 teaspoons (10 ml) of Worcestershire sauce, salt and pepper and add to the mushroom and nut mixture. Mix well. Press the mixture into a lightly greased 1-pound (500-g) loaf tin.

Bake for 1 hour, or until the loaf is lightly browned.

Turn out of the tin and serve hot. To serve cold, cool in the tin and then turn out.

INGREDIENTS TO SERVE SIX:
**½ lb (250 g) onions
½ lb (250 g) mushrooms
½ lb (250 g) shelled Brazil nuts
2 tablespoons (30 ml) corn oil
¼ lb (100 g) fresh wholewheat
    breadcrumbs
1 egg
2 teaspoons (10 ml) Worcestershire
    sauce
salt
pepper**

Filbert and Apricot Stuffing

This dried apricot and filbert stuffing can be used for chicken, turkey or a rolled pork roast.

Chop ¼ pound (100 g) of dried apricots and put them into a mixing bowl.

Chop or coarsely grind ¼ pound (100 g) of filberts and add to the apricots with 2 ounces (50 g) of fresh wholewheat breadcrumbs, the grated rind of ½ lemon, ¼ teaspoon (1 ml) of ground mixed spice, salt and pepper. Mix well, then stir in 1 beaten egg to bind the stuffing.

INGREDIENTS TO MAKE 10 OUNCES (250 G) OF STUFFING:
**¼ lb (100 g) dried apricots
¼ lb (100 g) filberts
2 oz (50 g) fresh wholewheat
    breadcrumbs
½ lemon
¼ teaspoon (1 ml) ground mixed spice
salt
pepper
1 egg**

Walnut and Dried Fruit Stuffing

Use this unusual crunchy stuffing for chicken, duck or a rolled joint of pork or lamb.

Finely chop ¼ pound (100 g) of walnuts and put them into a mixing bowl.

Add ¼ pound (100 g) of sultanas and 2 ounces (50 g) of fresh wholewheat breadcrumbs.

Peel, core and finely chop 1 small dessert apple and add it to the stuffing with 2 chopped spring onions. Season to taste with salt and pepper. Mix well.

Bind the stuffing with 1 to 2 tablespoons (15 to 30 ml) of chicken stock.

INGREDIENTS TO MAKE THREE-QUARTERS OF A POUND (300 G) OF STUFFING:
**¼ lb (100 g) walnuts
¼ lb (100 g) sultanas
2 oz (50 g) fresh wholewheat
    breadcrumbs
1 small dessert apple
2 spring onions
salt
pepper
1 to 2 tablespoons (15 to 30 ml) chicken
    stock**

Cream of Peanut Soup

Chop 1 onion and put it into a saucepan with 1 pint (600 ml) of chicken stock. Cover the pan and bring to the boil. Reduce the heat and simmer for 10 minutes, or until the onion is soft.

Grind or finely chop ¼ pound (100 g) of salted peanuts and add to the pan with ½ pint (300 ml) of milk. Bring to the boil, stirring constantly.

Liquidize the soup and then return it to the pan.

Blend 2 teaspoons (10 ml) of cornflour with 3 tablespoons (45 ml) of dry sherry and add it to the soup. Bring to the boil, stirring constantly, until the soup has thickened. Season to taste with salt and pepper and simmer for 1 minute.

Serve hot, sprinkled with 1 ounce (25 g) of chopped salted peanuts.

INGREDIENTS TO SERVE FOUR TO SIX:
**1 onion
1 pint (600 ml) chicken stock
5 oz (125 g) salted peanuts
½ pint (300 ml) milk
2 teaspoons (10 ml) cornflour
3 tablespoons (45 ml) dry sherry
salt
pepper**

Bakewell Tart

Preheat the oven to 400°F (200°C, Gas Mark 6).

Make 6 ounces (150 g) of shortcrust pastry with wholewheat flour (see page 34) and line a 7- to 8-inch (18- to 20-cm) flan ring or dish. Bake blind for 15 minutes. Remove the baking paper and the beans and bake for 5 minutes more.

Spread the bottom of the pastry case with 2 tablespoons (30 ml) of lemon curd.

Cream 2 ounces (50 g) of margarine with 2 ounces (50 g) of soft brown sugar until pale and fluffy.

In a small bowl beat 1 egg with 1 ounce (25 g) of flour and ½ teaspoon (2.5 ml) of baking powder.

Stir in ¼ pound (100 g) of ground almonds and the grated rind and juice of 1 lemon.

Whisk 1 egg white until stiff, then carefully fold it into the filling. Spoon the filling into the pastry case and bake for 10 minutes.

Reduce the oven temperature to 350°F (180°C, Gas Mark 4) and continue to bake for 15 to 20 minutes more, or until the filling has risen and is golden brown.

Serve hot or cold.

INGREDIENTS TO SERVE SIX:
**6 oz (150 g) shortcrust pastry made with
    wholewheat flour (see page 34)
2 tablespoons (30 ml) lemon curd
2 oz (50 g) margarine
2 oz (50 g) soft brown sugar
1 egg
1 oz (25 g) flour
½ teaspoon (2.5 ml) baking powder
¼ lb (100 g) ground almonds
1 lemon
1 egg white**

BLANCHING ALMONDS

Pour boiling water over the almonds.

Slide the skins off.

FOR MANY THOUSANDS OF YEARS the only way to hoard food for the winter was to dry it. The principle behind drying is simple—bacteria need moisture to grow and as moisture content is reduced bacterial growth is inhibited. It was discovered that meat and fish were best dehydrated in a cold wind, and fruit was best dried by the heat of the sun. One early simple method was to bury dates and figs in the hot desert sand.

Most fruit is still dried by warmth, much of it in the natural heat of the sun, but more, with all the benefits of modern technology, by artificial heat. It is now possible, however, to dry fruit by freezing it at very low temperatures. It is then transferred to a vacuum chamber, where the ice crystals turn into vapour without first becoming liquid. The finished product is not frozen but dried, with a moisture content that may sometimes be as low as two per cent.

The most ancient and still most popular dried fruits are dates, figs and dried grapes (raisins, sultanas, or white seedless raisins, and currants).

The origin of the date palm is lost in time, but it has been in cultivation for more than five thousand years. It is the universal provider of the Arab world. The fruit is delicious eaten ripe straight from the palm, and many dates keep well when dried. Sugar and wine are made from the tree's sap, oil from the seeds and rope from the fibres. The palm fruits prodigiously, more than a hundred pounds (45 kg) of dates a year, and a tree may live for a century.

The world's most popular date is the variety Deglet Noor. This is the one that was introduced to California in the early years of the twentieth century and is now the variety most grown in the United States. When fresh and ripe it is amber in colour, but it is a darker brown when dried. Deglet Noor dates are exported in large quantities from North Africa and often sold in the familiar round-ended box with the soft and juicy fruit still attached to a stalk. Two-thirds or more of a date is sugar, so it is a fruit to be enjoyed in moderation, in spite of the natural temptation to sneak just one more. Like most other dried fruits dates are rich in niacin, and also have some carotene, thiamine and riboflavin.

The fig tree is less versatile than the date palm and, except for Adam and Eve and sculptors, interest in it is confined to the fruit. Fresh figs are thin-skinned and suffer if they have to travel, but there are no problems when they have been dried. This is usually done in the sun, and a deposit of sugar (sugar makes up half of a dried fig) appears on the skin. As well as being rich in sugar figs are notably rich in a whole range of minerals (the iron content, for example, is four milligrams in one hundred grams), and raw or stewed they are often included in the diet to be used as a pleasant and gentle laxative.

The Nutrients in Dried Fruits

Dried fruits are a good source of energy. Three and a half ounces (100 g) of raisins provide about 300 Calories.

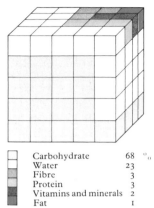

Carbohydrate	68 %
Water	23
Fibre	3
Protein	3
Vitamins and minerals	2
Fat	1

A selection of the more familiar dried fruits are shown in the jar (left).

Dried figs are high in fibre and protein as well as in B vitamins. Their gentle laxative action adds to their health-giving properties.

Dates are the sweetest of all the dried fruits but are no more calorific.

Apples are one of the few fruits that retain all their vitamin C when dried.

Prunes, or dried plums, contain less sugar than most other dried fruits and half the number of calories.

Sultanas are dried seedless white grapes.

Dried pears provide about six times as many calories as their fresh counterparts.

Seedless raisins, like dried currants, are only shrivelled grapes. Nutritionally raisins and currants are the same.

Dried apricots are a good source of vitamin C with twelve milligrams in three and a half ounces (100 g).

Currants, not to be confused with fresh red currants, white currants and black currants, have a reasonably high content of iron, but unfortunately this is poorly absorbed by the body.

Grapes when they are dried may be raisins, sultanas or currants, depending on which varieties of vines are used. Many are sun-dried. The best dessert raisins, large and sweet, are the so-called Malaga raisins, which are dried muscat grapes. Many are dried in the sun, the branches either left on the vine with the stalks partially severed or, more generally, spread out in the sun. Wine grapes are most commonly used for drying because they contain more sugar. Sultanas are dried white seedless grapes. The best sultanas come from Turkey, but they are cultivated in many parts of the Near East and in Australia and South Africa. In the United States the variety most widely grown for drying is Thompson Seedless. Although they are sweet and juicy sultanas are used most in cookery. Currants are dried small black grapes, which have been grown in Greece since classical times. They were long known as raisins of Corinth and in French still are, but in English Corinth has been corrupted to currant. Although currants taste more tart than raisins or sultanas they all contain similar amounts of sugar—about seventy per cent. They are all fairly rich in minerals, although they have only half as much iron as figs.

Prunes are made from plums with a high sugar content which can be dried without removing the stone; many plums ferment if they are dried unstoned. The United States is a major producer of prunes, either by sun-drying, as in California, or by artificial heat. Most American varieties are of European origin, the plums taken over by the early settlers. Prunes have only about half as much sugar as dates, figs and raisins and only half as many calories. Like figs they have a following for their laxative effect among those haunted by constipation.

Other dried fruits are of lesser importance. Dried apricots have a most delicious flavour and contain more protein than any other dried fruit.

Dates are still prepared by the traditional method of drying in the sun. Using this method most of the vitamin C in the dates is destroyed by oxidation. Modern factory drying in ovens or in streams of air results in fresher flavour and less vitamin C loss.

Peaches are less attractive when dried, but for dried fruit they contain an astonishing amount of iron (nearly seven milligrams in a hundred grams compared with the one and a half milligrams in raisins). Dried bananas ("banana figs") are often to be found in health-food shops. Apples (peeled, cored and cut into rings) and dessert pears (halved) are easily dried at home. Put them on racks in a very slow electric oven (not more than 150°F, 65°C) for several hours with the oven door slightly ajar.

GRAPES VERSUS CURRANTS

When dried, a pound of grapes reduces to about three and a half ounces (100 g) of currants. The three and a half ounces (100 g) of currants shown on the right-hand side of the balance provide more than 240 Calories, while the same weight of grapes shown on the left-hand side of the balance provides a mere 60 Calories. This is because grapes contain more than eighty per cent water, which provides no calories at all. Currants, however, contain only twenty per cent water—the rest is mostly sugar.

Stuffed Dates

Fresh or dried dates can be stuffed with this cheese and herb mixture, but the fresh dates are plumper and easier to handle.

Slit ½ pound (250 g) of dates and carefully remove the stones.

For the stuffing, put ¼ pound (100 g) of curd cheese into a bowl. Beat in 2 to 3 tablespoons (30 to 45 ml) of yogurt. The consistency should be thick and creamy.

Finely chop 2 spring onions or 1 small bunch of chives and beat into the cheese with 1 tablespoon (15 ml) of chopped parsley, 1 tablespoon (15 ml) of chopped sage and the grated rind of 1 orange. Mix well. Stuff the mixture into the stoned dates.

INGREDIENTS TO MAKE ABOUT 30 STUFFED
DATES:
½ lb (250 g) dates
¼ lb (100 g) curd cheese
2 to 3 tablespoons (30 to 45 ml) yogurt
2 spring onions or 1 small chives bunch
1 tablespoon (15 ml) chopped parsley
1 tablespoon (15 ml) chopped sage
1 orange

Spiced Raisins and Wine Sauce

Raisins cooked in spiced red wine make a delicious sauce to serve with pork and ham.

Put ¼ pound (100 g) of seedless raisins into a saucepan with 2 cloves, 1 stick of cinnamon, ½ pint (300 ml) of red wine and ¼ pint (150 ml) of water.

Cover the pan and bring to the boil. Reduce the heat and simmer gently for 10 minutes. Remove the cloves and the cinnamon.

In a small bowl blend 2 teaspoons (10 ml) of cornflour with 2 tablespoons (30 ml) of soft brown sugar and 2 tablespoons (30 ml) of lemon juice. Stir the mixture into the sauce. Bring to the boil, stirring constantly. Boil until the sauce thickens then reduce the heat and simmer for 2 minutes.

Serve hot or cold.

INGREDIENTS TO MAKE ¾ PINT (450 ML) OF
SAUCE:
¼ lb (100 g) seedless raisins
2 cloves
1 cinnamon stick
½ pint (300 ml) red wine
2 teaspoons (10 ml) cornflour
2 tablespoons (30 ml) soft brown sugar
2 tablespoons (30 ml) lemon juice

Devils on Horseback

Prunes stuffed with almonds, wrapped in bacon and grilled can be served as a snack.

Remove the stones from 8 large prunes. Stuff each prune with 1 blanched almond.

Stretch 4 rashers of streaky bacon with the back of a knife, then cut them into halves.

Wrap 1 half-slice of bacon around each prune and secure with a cocktail stick.

Grill, turning frequently, for about 5 minutes, or until the bacon is crisp and brown. Serve immediately.

INGREDIENTS TO SERVE FOUR:
8 large prunes
8 blanched almonds
4 streaky bacon rashers

MAKING DEVILS ON HORSEBACK

Carefully remove the stones from large prunes.

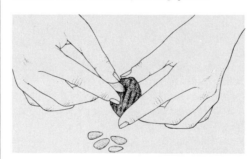

Fill each prune with a blanched almond.

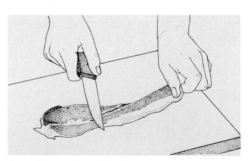

Stretch bacon slices with the back of a knife.

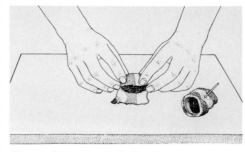

Wrap each prune in a half-slice of bacon.

Spinach and Prune Beef Stew

Heat 1 tablespoon (15 ml) of corn oil in a large saucepan. Add 1 chopped large onion and fry for 3 minutes.

Cut any excess fat from 1 pound (500 g) of chuck steak. Cut the steak into 2-inch (5-cm) cubes. Add the cubes to the pan and fry for 3 minutes, stirring constantly, until they are brown on all sides.

Add ½ pint (300 g) of beef stock, the grated rind and juice of 1 lemon, ¼ teaspoon (1 ml) of grated nutmeg, salt and pepper. Bring to the boil, stirring constantly, then add ¼ pound (100 g) of stoned prunes. Cover the pan, reduce the heat and simmer gently for 1½ to 2 hours, or until the meat is tender.

Meanwhile, thoroughly wash ½ pound (250 g) of spinach and drain it well. Coarsely chop the large spinach leaves leaving the small leaves whole. Press the spinach into the pan on top of the beef stew. Cover the pan and cook for 10 minutes more, so that the spinach cooks in the steam from the stew.

Stir the spinach into the stew and serve immediately.

INGREDIENTS TO SERVE FOUR:
1 tablespoon (15 ml) corn oil
1 large onion
1 lb (500 g) chuck steak
½ pint (300 ml) beef stock
1 lemon
¼ teaspoon (1 ml) grated nutmeg
salt
pepper
¼ lb (100 g) stoned prunes
½ lb (250 g) spinach

Dried Fruit Compote

Put 1 pound (500 g) of mixed dried fruit into a bowl. (Use dried apricots, prunes, peaches, pears, apples, figs and sultanas.)

Pour in 1 pint (600 ml) of water and add 1 large strip of lemon peel, 1 clove and 1 stick of cinnamon. Leave to soak overnight.

Transfer the fruit, liquid and spices to a saucepan. Cover and bring to the boil. Reduce the heat and simmer gently for 20 minutes, or until the fruit is tender, adding more water if the syrup is absorbed.

Remove the peel, clove and cinnamon. Serve the compote warm or cold.

INGREDIENTS TO SERVE FOUR TO SIX:
1 lb (500 g) mixed dried fruit
1 large strip lemon peel
1 clove
1 cinnamon stick

Christmas Pudding

Put $\frac{1}{4}$ pound (100 g) of fresh wholewheat breadcrumbs into a large mixing bowl with $\frac{1}{4}$ pound (100 g) of wholewheat flour, 1 teaspoon (5 ml) of baking powder, 2 ounces (50 g) of soft brown sugar, $\frac{1}{2}$ teaspoon (2.5 ml) of ground mixed spice, $\frac{1}{2}$ teaspoon (2.5 ml) of ground ginger, $\frac{1}{2}$ teaspoon (2.5 ml) of ground cinnamon and $\frac{1}{4}$ teaspoon (1 ml) of ground nutmeg. Mix well.

Stir in $\frac{1}{2}$ pound (250 g) of seedless raisins, $\frac{1}{4}$ pound (100 g) of sultanas, 2 ounces (50 g) of currants, 2 ounces (50 g) of chopped mixed peel and 2 ounces (50 g) of ground almonds.

Peel and core $\frac{1}{2}$ pound (250 g) of cooking apples. Coarsely grate the apples into the bowl. Add the grated rind of 1 orange and 1 lemon.

Squeeze the juice from the orange and lemon into a bowl. Beat in 1 large egg, 2 tablespoons (30 ml) of milk and 2 tablespoons (30 ml) of brandy. Pour into the dry ingredients and mix well.

Spoon the mixture into a 2-pint (1-litre) pudding basin which has been lightly greased. The mixture should fill about three-quarters of the basin.

Cover the basin with greaseproof paper or foil, allowing room for the pudding to rise, and seal.

Put the basin into a saucepan half-full of simmering water. Cover the pan and steam the pudding for 4 to 5 hours, adding more water when necessary.

Allow the pudding to cool in the basin. Cover with new foil or cloth and store in a cool place until required.

Steam the pudding for 2 hours before serving, then turn out onto a serving plate and serve hot.

INGREDIENTS TO SERVE SIX:
**$\frac{1}{4}$ lb (100 g) fresh wholewheat
  breadcrumbs
$\frac{1}{4}$ lb (100 g) wholewheat flour
1 teaspoon (5 ml) baking powder
2 oz (50 g) soft brown sugar
$\frac{1}{2}$ teaspoon (2.5 ml) ground mixed spice
$\frac{1}{2}$ teaspoon (2.5 ml) ground ginger
$\frac{1}{2}$ teaspoon (2.5 ml) ground cinnamon
$\frac{1}{4}$ teaspoon (1 ml) ground nutmeg
$\frac{1}{2}$ lb (250 g) seedless raisins
$\frac{1}{4}$ lb (100 g) sultanas
2 oz (50 g) currants
2 oz (50 g) chopped mixed peel
2 oz (50 g) ground almonds
$\frac{1}{2}$ lb (250 g) cooking apples
1 orange
1 lemon
1 large egg
2 tablespoons (30 ml) milk
2 tablespoons (30 ml) brandy**

Wholewheat Apricot Eclairs

Put $\frac{1}{4}$ pound (100 g) of dried apricots into a small bowl with 1 pint (600 ml) of water. Soak the apricots overnight.

Preheat the oven to 425°F (220°C, Gas Mark 7). Grease a large baking sheet.

Make 2$\frac{1}{2}$ ounces (75 g) of choux pastry with wholewheat flour (see page 35). Pipe strips of pastry, about 3 inches (8 cm) long, on to the prepared baking sheet. Bake for 20 minutes. Slit the éclairs, lower the oven temperature to 375°F (190°C, Gas Mark 5) and continue baking for a further 10 minutes. Cool the éclairs on a wire rack.

Fill the éclairs with $\frac{1}{2}$ pound (250 g) of yogurt cheese (see page 100).

Put the apricots and water into a saucepan and bring to the boil. Cover the pan, reduce the heat and simmer for 1 hour, or until the apricots are tender and almost all the water has evaporated. Liquidize the apricots to a smooth purée. Spread the purée along the tops of the éclairs and leave to set.

INGREDIENTS TO MAKE TWELVE ECLAIRS:
**$\frac{1}{4}$ lb (100 g) dried apricots
2$\frac{1}{2}$ oz (75 g) choux pastry (see page 35)
$\frac{1}{2}$ lb (250 g) yogurt cheese (see page 100)**

FILLING A PIPING BAG

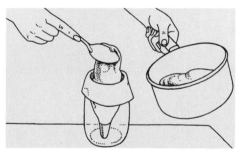

Support the bag in a jar and spoon in the dough.

Winter Salad

Put $\frac{1}{4}$ pound (100 g) of sultanas into a salad bowl. Add the juice of 1 large orange. Season with salt and pepper and mix well. Let the sultanas soak for at least 30 minutes.

Slice 2 sticks of celery and add to the sultanas. Peel, core and chop, or coarsely grate, 1 large dessert apple and add to the salad.

Toss lightly but well. Top with 1 ounce (25 g) of chopped walnuts and serve.

INGREDIENTS TO SERVE FOUR:
**$\frac{1}{4}$ lb (100 g) sultanas
1 large orange
salt
pepper
2 celery sticks
1 large dessert apple
1 oz (25 g) chopped walnuts**

Apricot Soufflé

Put 6 ounces (150 g) of dried apricots into a bowl. Add the grated rind and juice of 1 lemon and $\frac{1}{2}$ pint (300 ml) of water. Soak the apricots overnight.

Preheat the oven to 400°F (200°C, Gas Mark 6).

Put the apricots and the soaking liquid into a saucepan, cover and bring to the boil. Reduce the heat and simmer gently for 20 minutes, or until the apricots are tender.

Drain the apricots and reserve the liquid. If necessary add water to make the liquid up to $\frac{1}{4}$ pint (150 ml). Put the apricots and liquid into a liquidizer and blend to a purée.

Sweeten to taste with a little sugar.

Whisk 4 egg whites until just stiff and then fold them into the apricot purée.

Pour into a soufflé dish and bake for 20 minutes, or until the soufflé has risen and the top is lightly browned. Serve at once.

INGREDIENTS TO SERVE FOUR TO SIX:
**6 oz (150 g) dried apricots
1 lemon
sugar
4 egg whites**

Khoshaf

This Middle-Eastern fruit salad is made of dried apricots, prunes, raisins and figs that are soaked in scented water for 2 days.

Put $\frac{1}{4}$ pound (100 g) of dried apricots, $\frac{1}{4}$ pound (100 g) of prunes, $\frac{1}{4}$ pound (100 g) of seedless raisins and $\frac{1}{4}$ pound (100 g) of dried figs into a large bowl.

Pour in 1 pint (600 ml) of water and 1 tablespoon (15 ml) of rose water or orange blossom water.

Leave the fruit to soak for at least 2 days, when the syrup will be rich and golden.

Sprinkle with 2 ounces (50 g) of flaked blanched almonds and 1 ounce (25 g) of split pistachio nuts before serving.

INGREDIENTS TO SERVE FOUR TO SIX:
**$\frac{1}{4}$ lb (100 g) dried apricots
$\frac{1}{4}$ lb (100 g) prunes
$\frac{1}{4}$ lb (100 g) seedless raisins
$\frac{1}{4}$ lb (100 g) dried figs
1 tablespoon (15 ml) rose water or
  orange blossom water
2 oz (50 g) flaked blanched almonds
1 oz (25 g) split pistachio nuts**

HERBS ARE BACK IN FASHION, although sometimes it seems that people are more eager to read about them than actually use them. It is not surprising in view of all the dire warnings about using herbs with discretion. The proper way to use herbs is with common sense. Start with a little, nothing more than the proverbial pinch, adding more the second time you make the same dish until you find the level that you and your family enjoy. Common sense will tell you when you are spoiling the flavour of the food itself, and you will then know when to cut down.

Furthermore, as you gain confidence, do not be rigidly bound by someone else's "rules" about which herbs go with which foods—experiment. You may make a minor mistake, or discover a new and exciting combination of flavours. Parsley sauce, for example, goes with fish and, therefore, it keeps on and on going with fish. But there are such other herbs as fennel, chervil, dill leaves, chives, basil or sage which, used creatively, will go just as well.

The safer herbs—those which give a wide margin of error in the quantities used—are

The Nutrients in Herbs
Herbs are not eaten in enough quantity to be a great source of nutrients, but they do contain some valuable vitamins and minerals.

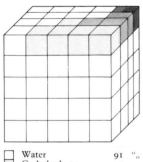

Water	91	"₀
Carbohydrate	5	
Protein	2	
Fibre	1	
Fat	0.5	
Vitamins and minerals	0.5	

THE USE OF HERBS IN MEDICINE

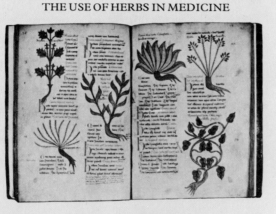

Herbs have long been used for treating various ailments. The seventeenth-century German illustration below shows a scholarly discussion of their merits. The twelfth-century herbal above recommends, for example, catmint for upset stomachs and *Cynoglossa*, or hound's tooth, for bruises or coughs.

Parsley contains almost as much protein as peas, but is low in carbohydrate. It has a wealth of carotene, vitamin C, iron, potassium and phosphorus. But it also contains apiol, a narcotic substance, which rules it out as a major vegetable. In small amounts, however, it is a garnish worth eating. Flat-leaved parsley has a stronger flavour than curly-leaved varieties.

Sweet basil is an annual with shiny green, slightly hairy leaves. These have a strong, sweet aroma and a powerful, spicy flavour. Delicious with tomato salads, basil is used in Italy for making the distinctive green sauce called *pesto* that is served with pasta. It can also be used with meats and fish.

Dill is a hardy annual. The leaves taste somewhat like parsley with a hint of orange peel, and the more pungent seeds are like those of caraway. Dill goes well with fish, and dill sauce is eaten with roast meat. The seeds are used in pickling, especially for pickled cucumbers.

Sweet marjoram has the more distinctive flavour, but pot marjoram is hardier. The greyish-green, slightly hairy leaves of sweet marjoram are sweet and spicy, with a hint of nutmeg. Used sparingly, marjoram goes well with pork, poultry and game and enhances sausages and rissoles. In stuffings for veal and poultry it keeps its savour and penetrates the meat, but in soups and stews the flavour tends to get lost.

Common thyme, an evergreen with narrow leaves, has a strong, sweet, clove-like flavour. It can easily dominate other herbs, but it complements thick stews, baked fish and roasts, and is useful in stuffings for poultry and veal. Lemon thyme (bottom left) has wider, lemon-scented leaves and adds flavour to custards.

Sage, a perennial with greyish-green, often furry leaves, has a strong, slightly bitter flavour. In forcemeat, it traditionally accompanies pork and duck and it is also used with liver and veal, stews and bean dishes. But try fresh sage with eel, or between the pieces of meat in kebabs, or sprinkled discreetly over a salad.

The mint family contains several subtly different flavours, but the most common is spearmint. Mint sauce, or jelly, is the traditional accompaniment to lamb, and sprigs of mint enhance the flavour not only of peas and new potatoes but also of baby carrots and French beans.

Evergreen rosemary has pale flowers, a fragrant aroma and needle-like green-grey leaves. These contain a volatile oil, comparable to eucalyptus oil, with a powerful flavour. The Italians like rosemary with young lamb and sucking pig. Elsewhere it is widely used in stuffings or in marinades for meat and strong-flavoured fish. It can be sprinkled lightly over poultry or other meats before roasting, or over cooked cauliflower and baked potatoes. And it can even be used in a claret cup.

parsley, chives and lemon thyme. Common thyme, sage, marjoram, garlic, rosemary, bay, lovage, tarragon and chervil are strongly flavoured. Dried herbs have a more definite flavour than fresh herbs, but the flavour of dried herbs is never the same as that of fresh herbs. If you have a garden it is foolish not to grow some herbs. A window box or indoor pots may also be used. Nevertheless, you cannot hope to have fresh herbs all the year round, and you will have to fall back on dried herbs or, in some instances, frozen herbs, which have even less flavour.

In classic cuisine *bouquet garni* used in soups, stews and meat dishes means three sprigs of parsley, one sprig of thyme and a bay leaf tied together so that they can be removed when the dish is ready to serve. But there is nothing to stop you from adding others—basil, chervil, marjoram, rosemary or tarragon, for example. *Fines herbes* usually means a mixture of parsley, chervil, tarragon and chives and is used for flavouring omelettes, chicken, grilled fish and steak. Dried mixed herbs are most likely to be a combination of parsley, thyme, marjoram and savory.

A GUIDE TO HERBS

Your choice of herbs is a matter of personal taste, but as a guide here are some frequently used combinations of foods and herbs.

Lamb: *rosemary, garlic, dill, bay*

Beef: *horseradish, marjoram, thyme, basil*

Veal: *lemon thyme, rosemary, sage*

Pork: *sage, chives, parsley, basil, bay*

Casseroles: *parsley, thyme, chives, garlic, sage, rosemary, bay, dill, marjoram, tarragon*

Poultry: *parsley, thyme, fennel, rosemary, sage, tarragon*

White fish: *parsley, chervil, dill, savory*

Oily fish: *basil, bay, fennel, marjoram, rosemary, tarragon, sage, balm, thyme*

Pasta: *parsley, thyme, mint, garlic, basil*

Salads: *parsley, chives, fennel, garlic, dill, mint*

French or yogurt dressings: *chives, tarragon, chervil, garlic*

Vinegars: *tarragon, garlic, sage, rosemary*

Jellies: *mint, parsley, lemon verbena*

Sour fruits: *sweet cicely, angelica, lemon balm*

INDIAN CURRY SPICES

Indian curries are made with a blend of up to thirty spices including turmeric, cinnamon, cumin, cloves, mace, coriander, chillies, cardamom, ginger, saffron and peppercorns. These spices not only tempt appetites jaded by the heat but also act as a food preservative. Right: spices being sold in Panjim.

Some of the wonderful range of spices that add subtle or rich flavours to savoury and sweet dishes. Top row, left to right: cinnamon sticks, aniseed, peppercorns, cloves. Middle row: caraway seeds, coriander seeds, sea salt. Front row: mustard seeds, mace, chilli powder. In the foreground, clockwise: sesame seeds (in the scoop), allspice, nutmeg and turmeric.

AROMATIC PLANTS ARE THE SOURCE of the spices and herbs that are so important in cookery for their flavour and aroma. The distinction usually made between them is that spices come from the tropics and culinary herbs come from temperate regions. The original home of almost all spices was the Orient, and the Western Hemisphere has contributed only three of importance—allspice, chillies and vanilla.

The history of spices in the Far East goes back at least four thousand years. In pre-Christian times the Arabs grew rich by their monopoly of the trade in spices from the East. The Romans broke this monopoly in the first century AD when they realized that, with the help of the monsoon winds, they could sail from Egypt to India and back in less than a year, while the Arab's overland camel route took at least two years.

With the fall of the Roman Empire the spice trade also collapsed. It was revived in the Middle Ages by the Crusaders, who were more effective in introducing their fellow Christians to spices than the infidels to Christianity.

The spices for which the world was explored, wars fought and people enslaved have been used for preserving food, for embalming, as perfumes and as medicines attributed with almost magical qualities, but, above all, they have been used to add flavour to our food. Throughout history and throughout the world pepper has always been, and still is, the most important spice. In the West pepper is closely followed by mustard. Cloves, cinnamon, ginger and nutmeg complete the list of the top six spices.

If possible it is wiser not to buy spices as powder. When ground they lose aroma and flavour more rapidly. Moreover, it is impossible to judge their quality, and spices have a bad record of adulteration. Always try to buy whole peppercorns, nutmegs, allspice and sticks of cinnamon, for example, and grind them yourself.

The nutritional value spices have is almost irrelevant because of the small amounts we eat. Mustard is almost one-third protein and one-third fat, but that still adds up to almost nothing in the smear we put on our food. The preservative qualities of spices are also meaningless in the quantities we usually use in the West, and their medicinal virtues are debatable. But certainly the aroma and flavour of spices do increase the flow of saliva and gastric juices. And spices can make uninteresting but otherwise wholesome food more appetizing.

Salt is not a spice, however indissolubly wedded pepper and salt are in our minds. It is a mineral called sodium chloride, which is obtained by evaporating sea water (sea salt), or by mining the crystalline deposits in the earth (rock salt). Salt may be mixed with ground dehydrated herbs (celery salt, garlic or onion salt, for example) or with spices. Although salt does not, strictly speaking, enhance the flavour of food, many people find that without salt some food tastes flat. Salt, which is an essential part of the diet, exists, however, in many foods without our adding it to them. Spices (excluding allspice or mace) may be used instead of salt to add interest to a salt-restricted diet.

Monosodium glutamate (MSG), a salt of glutamic acid, although almost flavourless itself, does enhance the flavour of food, especially meats, by making our taste buds more sensitive. It has little effect on sweet flavours. It is widely used in Chinese and Japanese cookery, but some people are allergic to it.

The old spice wars between nations are things of the past; the battle is now between the genuine spices and synthetic flavourings. There are thousands of them, made out of wood pulp, coal tar and a whole gamut of chemicals. They cannot totally achieve the flavour of the natural spice, but they often get near enough to fool us. These are the substances that put the taste of butter into margarine and the vanilla into ice-cream. St Anthony was once the patron saint of the ancient guilds of spicers, pepperers and grocers. Today we have the International Organization of the Flavour Industry.

Yeast, mainly used in baking and brewing, also adds flavour to all sorts of savoury dishes. Extremely rich in protein, minerals and such B vitamins as thiamine, niacin and riboflavin, it can be eaten in powdered form—added to drinks or sprinkled on cereals —or as liquid yeast extract. Both fresh and dried baker's yeast is nutritionally inferior but has a valuable role in bread-making. Without yeast, bread would be unattractively flat and hard, or "unleavened".

fresh baker's yeast

dried baker's yeast

powdered yeast

yeast extract

SUGARS /The Dangerous Seducers

WHOEVER COINED THE PHRASE "I have a sweet tooth" has a lot to answer for. Those who repeat it seem to regard it as total justification for shovelling sugar into coffee and tea, using it lavishly in cooking and cramming themselves with ice-cream, cakes, biscuits, sweets and chocolates. If there were such a thing as a sweet tooth, and it could be located, the right course would be to have it extracted.

Sweetness is the great seducer and in this context a little seduction should go a long way. But in practice it does not. On average sugar consumption in Britain works out at about two pounds a week for every man, woman and child. In the United States it is minimally less, because Americans are not quite as addicted to sweets as the British, the world's greatest sweet-eaters.

Those two pounds of sugar provide about 4,000 Calories, or almost 600 Calories a day, and this is between one-quarter and one-sixth of the daily energy requirement of most people. It would not matter if sugar were a balanced food. However, it is the most unbalanced food there is because it provides nothing but energy. For proteins, fats, minerals and vitamins it is necessary to turn to other foods, and since these also provide energy, if people are also eating sweets they are consuming more calories than they need.

There are, unfortunately, other ways in which sugar plays the villain. It increases the amount of triglycerides in the blood and, therefore, may be associated with coronary heart disease. It may raise the amount of uric acid in the blood and increase the risk of gout. It encourages dental decay, the metaphorical sweet tooth thus destroying the real ones.

There is certainly a strong case for reducing the amount of sugar in the diet. With comparatively little will power sugar intake can be cut by a third or a half. Like giving up smoking it is difficult and unpleasant to begin with, but before long the palate adjusts and very sweet dishes can even become nauseating. When you reduce the amount of sugar you use, you discover the real flavours of foods, for they are no longer lost under a predominant sugariness.

Home-made puddings and other desserts often have more sugar in them than is good for either their flavour or your health. Their sugar content is, however, under our control, but if we buy processed food we have no say. Food manufacturers are mistakenly liberal in their use of sugar, which is cheap, and they are as likely to add it to soup as to a pudding. The alternative is, of course, wholesome home cookery in which sugar is used sparingly.

Constant consumption of biscuits, sticky buns, chocolate cakes and sweets often has nothing to do with hunger and a lot to do with habit. It is, of course, impossible to totally remove sugar from

our diet, because it occurs naturally in foods. It is also sensible to use it to make acceptable those foods that would be too sour without it. And it makes beautiful preserves. It is not deprivation that is needed but discrimination.

More nonsense is written about honey than about any other food. In a strict sense it is hardly the "natural" food that health food devotees revere; it has been elaborately processed by bees. The nectar of flowers, which is mainly sucrose (sugar), is converted by enzymes in the body of the bee into fructose and glucose. Because it does not need further digestion, this "invert" sugar provides instant energy for humans. Honey is seventy to eighty per cent invert sugar.

But honey is also the most beautiful of all sweeteners. The flavours of the seasons—some subtle, some rich—may be captured in it: heather, wild rose, clover, lavender, lime, orange blossom, hawthorn. It is worth cutting down on other sugars to be able to spread this delicious food on your bread.

Inevitably, to avoid the excessive use of sugar, synthetic sweeteners have been invented. These have proved as controversial as sugar itself. Saccharin (ortho-sulphobenzimide), an American discovery of the late nineteenth century, is five hundred to six hundred times sweeter than sugar. Its disadvantage is that it leaves a slightly bitter after-taste. Cyclamate, another American discovery, is only about thirty times as sweet as sugar, but it has no bitter after-taste. Cyclamates were first used in the United States in 1950 and in Britain in 1964, but after American research showed that in high doses they could produce bladder cancer in rats they were banned in 1969 in the United States and Britain, as well as in several other countries. After similar research with saccharin, the United States has imposed limits on its use, and even proposed a ban. Many people, however, feel that saccharin, which is still widely used in Britain, is less harmful than the excessive use of sugar.

Dioscoreophyllum berries

Thaumatococcus seeds

MIRACLE FRUITS

Chemists have now discovered some surprising natural alternatives to sugar. Among the most promising are thaumatin and monellin, which are proteins that have been isolated from the African *Thaumatococcus* and *Dioscoreophyllum* berries respectively. Thaumatin is more than four thousand times as sweet as sugar. If these natural, low-calorie sweeteners can be isolated they could provide a satisfactory alternative to sugar.

Whether white or brown, sugar is just sucrose. Brown sugar boasts slightly more minerals than white, but both contain virtually nothing except calories (about 400 Calories in one hundred grams). Syrup—a thick solution of partially refined sugar—has fewer calories (300 Calories in one hundred grams) simply because it contains more water; molasses, with 230 Calories in one hundred grams, is even more dilute. However, you will not save calories by using syrup instead of sugar because syrup tastes less sweet and you will probably use more. The exception is honey which, calorie for calorie, is sweeter than sucrose and contains detectable amounts of essential fatty acids, minerals and vitamin C. Left, clockwise: a honeycomb, demerara (coarse-grained brown) sugar, granulated sugar, unrefined brown sugar and soft fine-grained brown sugar. In the centre: molasses (unrefined sugar syrup).

210

THE REASONS why we should limit the amount of sugar we eat are simple, but the reasons why we should cut down on fat are more complicated.

The difference between fats may be described in several ways. They may be animal or vegetable. They may be visible, like butter or the fat on a chop, or invisible, as is the considerable amount in nuts or the trace in most vegetables. They may also be described as fats or oils according to whether solid or liquid at room temperature.

The distinction increasingly made in recent years, however, is between polyunsaturated fats, which have gained the reputation of "goodies", and saturated fats, which are the "baddies". As it happens most animal fats are high in saturated fatty acids and most vegetable fats are higher in polyunsaturated acids. Consequently, animal fats have been dubbed bad and most vegetable fats have been extolled as virtuous.

The current preoccupation with fats in the diet is the result of the fearful increase in deaths, in the past twenty-five years in many parts of the West, from what is loosely called heart disease. Many causes have been suggested, among them smoking, obesity, high blood pressure, lack of exercise, heredity, stress and diet. In the diet the main villains are considered to be an excess of sugar or of fats, especially of saturated fats, or a combination of both.

The so-called experts often disagree about which is the most important causal factor, but there is statistical evidence that heart attacks are associated with a high level of blood fats—triglycerides and cholesterol—and the accumulation of fat on the inner walls of the arteries. Saturated fats—the solid fats—increase the level of cholesterol and triglycerides in the blood and lead to deposits in the arteries. Polyunsaturated fats—the soft fats or oils of fish and vegetables—cause blood cholesterol to fall. Hence the advice to eat fewer saturated fats and increase the proportion of polyunsaturated fats.

It is impossible to eat only fat that is completely unsaturated—because all fat includes both saturated and unsaturated fatty acids, and it is the proportions of each that vary. Although the more unsaturated the fat the lower its calorific value, both types of fat are high in calories, so you can

Corn oil has about forty per cent of linoleic acid, which makes it sixty per cent saturated. In the polyunsaturate league it trails well behind sunflower oil and safflower oil (both of which contain more than sixty per cent linoleic acid).

Peanut oil, with only thirty per cent linoleic acid, is well down in the vegetable oil league for polyunsaturation. Unlike such oils as safflower oil it has its own definite taste, which is not always acceptable. Some peanut oil, however, has been deodorized.

Soya bean oil is not only a good polyunsaturated oil with about sixty per cent linoleic acid but it is relatively cheap because of the high productivity and fat content of the soya bean. It is the third most favourable oil in terms of polyunsaturation.

Coconut oil is the villain of vegetable oils, with only two per cent linoleic acid. Although a saturated fat it is liquid because its saturated fatty acids are in shorter chains than in other oils. It is especially likely to cause heart disease.

Olive oil, with about ten per cent linoleic acid, is mostly rich in monounsaturated fatty acids, which do not contribute to heart disease. Its popularity as an ingredient of salad dressing is rivalled by the equally palatable safflower seed oil.

put on weight if you eat too much of either. The widely quoted recommendations of the American Heart Association to people with a high level of blood fats are that the total amount of fat in the diet should not account for more than thirty-five per cent of an individual's energy intake, and that the saturated fats should be less than ten per cent.

The most delicious of all fats is an animal fat—butter. It accounts for about a quarter of the world's fat consumption. It is still the favourite fat of the English, who eat almost twice as much butter as they do margarine. The Americans, however, have made a remarkable switch in the last twenty-five years. From eating almost twice as much butter as margarine they are now eating more than twice as much margarine as butter. Such has been the effect of all the publicity about heart disease.

For people in good health the flavour of butter is something not to be willingly sacrificed. Once again a compromise is necessary; polyunsaturated types of margarine can be used for cooking, and the butter used at the table can be offset by cutting down on more expendable saturated fats.

Butter is an ancient food, but margarine is little more than a century old. It was invented by a French chemist's assistant, Hippolyte Mège Mouriès, and consisted largely of beef suet, under the mistaken belief that this was the basis of cow's milk. Only after the process of hydrogenation had been discovered early in the twentieth century was it possible to harden almost any oil to produce a substance with the consistency of butter. But hydrogenation produces a saturated margarine, and it was not until the 1960s that soft margarine, which has a fair proportion of poly-unsaturated fat, was invented. There is no point in changing from butter to hard margarine. And even in the soft margarines the proportion of saturated fats ranges from just below sixty per cent to eighty per cent.

Fat accounts for much of the flavour in meat, but most people now prefer their meat lean, and animals are bred that way. Even the amount of marbling in the meat of intensively reared animals has decreased since the 1960s. The leanest meat, with the highest proportion of polyunsaturated fat, is, however, from "free-range" animals.

Vegetable oils can certainly be used for cooking, but some oils are considered to be more virtuous than others. They can be rated according to their richness in linoleic acid, a polyunsaturated fatty acid that cannot be synthesized in the body, and must be absorbed from the food we eat.

Safflower oil, bland and almost without odour, has, for example, between seventy and eighty per cent linoleic acid. Coconut oil, on the other hand, is a vegetable oil to avoid; although vegetable and liquid it is heavily saturated, with only a miserable two per cent linoleic acid.

SOFT MARGARINES—WATCH THE LABEL!

Margarine was originally made of hardened vegetable oils, but with the evidence linking polyunsaturation to heart disease manufacturers started making some margarines only from unhardened, unsaturated oils. These are the more healthy polyunsaturated margarines that are soft at fridge temperature. There are, however, ways of making soft, but more saturated, margarines, such as mixing hard margarine and water ("low calorie spreads") or by chemically adjusting hard margarines. Polyunsaturated margarines are always labelled as such.

Animal fats vary in their degree of saturation. Fish oils are as healthy as vegetable oils, but butter (above left) is about ninety-five per cent saturated and beef dripping, or unprocessed lard (above right), averages about ninety per cent. Unfortunately, manufacturers harden lard to give totally saturated, rock-hard suets (bottom).

HAMLET was thoroughly wide of the mark when he complained of his "too, too solid flesh". He was, like the rest of us are, at least two-thirds, and maybe three-quarters, water. It is much the same with our food. With few exceptions much of it, or most of it, is drink.

Deprived of water for only a few days, a human being dies. Without food most people could survive for several weeks. The functioning of the body depends on water, both within the cells and outside them. The fluid within the cells accounts for most of the water in the body, up to fifty-two pints (30 litres). Another seventeen pints (10 litres) surround the cells. In the blood plasma there are three and a half pints (2 litres). The total amount of body water is therefore more than seventy-two pints (42 litres).

The level of water within the body remains remarkably constant. It is lost through the breath and in urine and sweat. It is replaced by the liquids that we drink when we are thirsty, by the water in our food and the water formed during respiration. This may total more than five pints (3 litres) a day. For no apparent reason some people drink more than others. Some drink more because they sweat more and everyone drinks more in hot weather.

Natural thirst is a fairly reliable indicator of the amount of water we need, but it tends to be over-ruled when it comes to sweet or alcoholic drinks. The kidneys very efficiently rid the body of any excess fluid, along with sodium and other minerals, but they cannot prevent the obesity created by too many carbohydrate-rich drinks.

Except in certain rare diseases water is not responsible for overweight; fat is the cause. Restricting intake of water will not make people slim. On the other hand, cutting down on spirits, beer, wine and sweet soft drinks will certainly help.

According to its source water acquires different characteristics and flavours. Rain is contaminated as it falls through an atmosphere polluted by industry. If the gathering grounds for reservoirs are peaty the water will be soft and acid (and soft water is now being suggested as yet another predisposing factor in heart disease). If the water has run through limestone country it will be hard and alkaline, providing a source of calcium for the body. Other minerals become dissolved in it as it passes through the soil; the most common are sodium chloride and carbonates of sodium, calcium and magnesium. A little of such minerals add to the palatability of water, but some waters taste more like medicine and they are either drunk as such or bathed in.

The sparkle in mineral waters is caused by the presence of carbon dioxide. It can also be created artificially by impregnating ordinary water with carbon dioxide. The natural mineral waters are superior because although they are less fizzy to

begin with, they retain their fizziness longer.

The addition of one mineral—fluoride—to ordinary drinking water is the cause of endless controversy. Fluoride is being added to water supplies in many parts of the world in order to arrest tooth decay. Those opposed to fluoridation argue that it is not as effective as claimed, may be harmful and in any event enforced medication is an infringement of personal liberty.

Fluoride is found naturally in our bones and teeth. Adding more to a diet low in fluoride reduces tooth decay in the very young, far less in those children who are ten years old and over and very little in adults. Beyond a certain concentration in the body fluoride can produce unsightly mottling of the teeth.

Water is one of our most essential foods. Impure water can start deadly epidemics, but the only water that is totally pure—distilled water —is undrinkably boring. The piped water of the Western World is quite safe to drink, however, after it has been carefully filtered and chlorinated. Chlorine is added to water to kill germs, and then as much as possible is extracted to remove the unpleasant taste.

Spas became fashionable in the eighteenth and nineteenth centuries. The water at Bath spa, illustrated in this eighteenth-century cartoon "Comforts of Bath" (inset) by the satirist John Rowlandson, had a clear, bitter taste and was recommended for the cure of gout. While there is scant scientific evidence to support the value of spa waters as medicine, drinking calorie-free water is bound to be a beneficial alternative to drinking wine with its attendant dangers of obesity.

MINERAL WATERS

All water except distilled water contains some minerals and without them it is unpalatable. Some mineral water, such as that near Biarritz (left), is protected for local consumption. Bottled mineral waters are drunk by people who distrust the local water supply, or who drink them to help their digestion. These mineral waters vary considerably in taste. The popular French Vichy water, for example, contains about forty minerals, especially sodium bicarbonate, and has a markedly salty taste. In contrast, English Malvern water is very pure and absolutely tasteless.

Most foods contain only minute amounts of fluoride; water in some areas has scarcely any, but at the other extreme there may be fourteen parts of fluoride in a million parts of water. Adding fluoride to drinking water to ensure that there is one part per million of fluoride in the water would roughly double the average intake of fluoride without in general making it excessive.

Tea contains an unusually large amount of fluoride and several cups of strong tea a day would probably provide adequate amounts in the diet. But such avid tea drinkers are unlikely to be of the age when it will benefit their teeth. The alternative to fluoridation, of course, is to avoid the sugar that is responsible for tooth decay in the first place.

STIMULATION WITHOUT INEBRIATION is the function that coffee and tea have in common. The mild stimulants that are responsible, and that also stir up a certain amount of controversy, are theophylline and caffeine. Most people enjoy their effect, others complain of all kinds of side-effects, particularly insomnia. These drinks are, therefore, best avoided on medical grounds by certain people (those with peptic ulcers, for example), but in general they are pleasantly harmless.

Coffee contains the greatest amount of caffeine, which stimulates the brain. Tea may have only half as much caffeine, but it is richer in theophylline, which increases the heart rate and acts as a diuretic. However, we absorb so little of the stimulants in coffee or tea that we would have to drink a great deal, or be unusually sensitive, to be upset by them. Coffee can be bought, at an even higher price, decaffeinated, but that seems rather like dealcoholizing beer.

Cocoa has gained the reputation of being a more innocuous drink than coffee or tea. It does, however, contain mild stimulants, but unlike tea and coffee it does not keep you awake because the body does not absorb them. There is, on the other hand, no substance in cocoa (except, perhaps, the added milk) to send you to sleep.

Coffee is like the famous little girl who had a little curl: "When she was good she was very, very good, but when she was bad she was horrid." There is no point wasting time making horrid coffee when with a little more care it can be made to perfection. The steps to success are to buy good fresh coffee beans, roasted to the degree you want,

to grind them as you need them and to brew the coffee with care.

There are more than a hundred types of coffee beans, but they are usually sold blended. There is also a bewildering range of roasts, from those that are light and thin-tasting, to the darkest Italian or espresso. Experiment until you get the combination you most enjoy.

Roasted beans will remain reasonably fresh if they are kept in a tightly sealed jar in the refrigerator. They will keep fresh for two or three months in sealed jars in a freezer, but to avoid wastage use several small jars and not one large one because once removed from the freezer the beans are likely to go mouldy if they are put back again. They can, however, be stored in the refrigerator. Once a tin of vacuum-packed ground coffee has been opened even if it is stored in the refrigerator the flavour is lost in about a week.

HERBAL TEAS, OR TISANES

Infusions made from fresh or dried herbs have long been attributed with health-giving properties and are particularly good for the digestion. Providing a vast range of interesting flavours, herbal teas, for example mint, lavender and camomile, should be left to infuse for about six minutes and then served without milk, although they may be flavoured with a thin slice of lemon or orange.

Camomile tea, recommended for soothing the nerves, has a slightly bitter tang.

Peppermint leaves make a very refreshing tea that is said to relieve indigestion.

Lemon balm tea is tasty and fragrant. It is excellent after a heavy, rich meal.

Rose petals are used to make a pleasantly sweet tisane that is said to relieve headaches.

Lavender makes a highly aromatic infusion that is recommended as a tonic.

powder was made may have contained thirty per cent more soluble solids than the optimum. In some processing all the aroma vanishes but is put back artificially so that for a short time after the jar is opened there is at least a smell of coffee.

It is easier to make a good cup of tea than good coffee, as long as you buy good tea in the first place. While many British people reject instant tea, more than a third of the tea drunk in the United States is instant. Excellent tea can be made with tea bags if the tea in them is excellent. But most mass-marketed tea bags are filled with blends that vary between nondescript and vicious. It is safer to use loose tea.

There are three main kinds of loose tea: black tea has been fermented, green tea has not and oolong tea is halfway between the two. Such names as Pekoe, Orange Pekoe, Broken Orange Pekoe and Souchong given to black teas indicate only leaf sizes and not flavour. The pungent unblended Indian teas are likely to be from Assam and Darjeeling. Ceylon teas are gentler; they sometimes form the base of the famous Earl Grey tea, which is scented with bergamot.

To make good tea, first warm the teapot by rinsing it with boiling water and then put in one teaspoon (or tea bag) for every cup of tea you need. Pour boiling water on the tea and leave it to stand for three to five minutes: the smaller the leaf the shorter the infusion time. As the tea stands, caffeine and flavour are dissolved; left longer the tannin will build up and make the tea bitter. If you want a second cup that is as good as the first make another brew.

Coffee and tea make refreshing and stimulating drinks and are a rich source of niacin. They also contain some riboflavin and thiamine and without milk or sugar they have no calories. From left to right: a box of Ceylon tea, a bag of coffee beans, a caddy of Jasmine tea and, in the grinder, roasted coffee beans.

The fineness of the grind depends on how the coffee is to be brewed. There are many types of coffee pots, but basically there are only two methods of brewing; decoction, in which the coffee is boiled in the water, and infusion, in which the hot water is poured on the coffee, which is allowed to steep.

The purpose of brewing is to dissolve the soluble solids in the beans. Those which give coffee its pleasant flavour and aroma are the first to be dissolved. The coffee that is most generally acceptable contains not more than twenty per cent of these dissolvable solids, and extraction beyond that makes the coffee bitter.

In the presence of lovingly prepared coffee it is almost blasphemous to mention instant coffee. It has nothing to recommend it except convenience. In the first place instant coffee is not made from the best beans and the brew from which the

To make cocoa powder, cocoa beans (left) are fermented under palm leaves (above) before being dried, roasted and ground. Although some of the calorific cocoa butter fat is removed during this process, the amount of powder used to make one cup of cocoa provides up to 50 Calories. As many as 200 extra Calories may be provided by the sugar and milk that are added to the powder.

Spiced Tea

Tea flavoured with spices, orange and lemon makes a refreshing hot or cold drink.

Put 2 tablespoons (30 ml) of tea leaves into a tea pot.

Pour 2 pints (1 litre) of water into a saucepan. Add the juice of 1 large orange and 1 large lemon, 1 stick of cinnamon and 2 cloves. Bring to the boil and then pour on to the tea leaves.

Leave to infuse for 3 to 5 minutes, then serve hot with slices of orange and lemon.

To serve cold, allow the tea to cool. Strain into a jug and chill until ready to serve. Pour into glasses filled with ice cubes and decorate with slices of orange and lemon.

INGREDIENTS TO SERVE SIX:
2 tablespoons (30 ml) tea leaves
1½ large oranges
1½ large lemons
1 cinnamon stick
2 cloves

Mint Tisane

Coarsely chop 8 large sprigs of mint, including the stalks and put into a jug.

Pour in 1 pint (600 ml) of boiling water. Cover and leave to infuse for 3 minutes.

Strain out the mint leaves and serve hot.

INGREDIENTS TO MAKE 1 PINT (600 ML):
8 large mint sprigs

MAKING HERBAL TISANES

Pour boiling water over the chopped herbs.

Infuse, then strain before serving.

Irish Brack

Dried fruit that has been soaked in cold tea gives this traditional Irish teabread its moist texture.

Put 1 pound (500 g) of mixed dried fruit into a large bowl and pour ½ pint (300 ml) of cold strong tea over it. Leave the fruit to soak for at least 12 hours.

Preheat the oven to 350°F (180°C, Gas Mark 4). Grease a 7-inch (18-cm) square cake tin and line it with greaseproof paper. Grease the paper.

Meanwhile, in another bowl beat 2 ounces (50 g) of soft brown sugar and 1 egg together. Stir ½ pound (250 g) of self-raising flour into the egg and sugar mixture. Add the soaked fruit and mix well.

Spoon the mixture into the prepared cake tin. Bake the brack for 1¼ to 1½ hours, or until it is brown and firm to the touch. Remove the brack from the oven and turn it out of the tin on to a wire rack to cool.

INGREDIENTS TO MAKE ONE SMALL TEABREAD:
1 lb (500 g) mixed dried fruit
½ pint (300 ml) strong cold tea
2 oz (50 g) soft brown sugar
1 egg
½ lb (250 g) self-raising flour

Chocolate and Ginger Custard

Preheat the oven to 350°F (180°C, Gas Mark 4).

Break up ¼ pound (100 g) of plain chocolate and put it into a bowl over a pan of boiling water. Heat gently, stirring occasionally, until the chocolate has melted, then remove from the heat.

In a small saucepan heat ½ pint (300 ml) of milk until lukewarm.

Beat 2 eggs. Stir them into the melted chocolate with 1 tablespoon (15 ml) of soft brown sugar and the warm milk. Mix well.

Finely chop 2 pieces of preserved stem ginger and stir into the chocolate custard.

Spoon into 4 individual ovenproof dishes. Put the dishes into a baking tin and pour in enough hot water to come halfway up the sides of the dishes.

Bake for 35 to 40 minutes, or until the custards are set. Allow to cool.

Serve chilled.

INGREDIENTS TO SERVE FOUR:
¼ lb (100 g) plain chocolate
½ pint (300 ml) milk
2 eggs
1 tablespoon (15 ml) soft brown sugar
2 pieces preserved stem ginger

Chocolate and Orange Mousse

If you cannot resist chocolate mousse, then try this one, which is made without cream, butter or egg yolks. It can be made several hours in advance but if it is made the day before, a little of the egg white may separate out.

Break up 6 ounces (150 g) of plain chocolate. Put it into a mixing bowl with the grated rind and juice of 1 orange. Put the bowl over a pan of boiling water. Heat gently, stirring occasionally, until the chocolate has melted.

Remove from the heat and stir in 1 tablespoon (15 ml) of brandy. Leave the mixture to cool and thicken slightly.

Whisk 4 egg whites until stiff, then carefully fold them into the chocolate mixture.

Spoon the mousse into 4 serving dishes.

Refrigerate for at least 1 hour before serving.

INGREDIENTS TO SERVE FOUR:
6 oz (150 g) plain chocolate
1 orange
1 tablespoon (15 ml) brandy
4 egg whites

Chocolate Cake

This rich moist cake may be served plain or split into halves and filled with mashed strawberries, bananas or pears. Decorate the top with sliced fruit.

Preheat the oven to 350°F (180°C, Gas Mark 4).

In a large mixing bowl cream ¼ pound (100 g) of margarine with ¼ pound (100 g) of dark soft brown sugar.

Separate 2 eggs and add the yolks to the creamed mixture. Stir in 2 ounces (50 g) of ground almonds and beat well.

Dissolve 2 tablespoons (30 ml) of unsweetened cocoa powder in 4 tablespoons (60 ml) of boiling water and mix until smooth. Add to the creamed mixture and beat well.

Fold in 1 teaspoon (5 ml) of baking powder mixed with ¼ pound (100 g) of wholewheat flour.

Whisk the 2 egg whites until stiff and then fold into the cake mixture.

Transfer to a 7- or 8-inch (18- or 20-cm) cake tin.

Bake for 30 minutes, or until the cake has risen and is firm to the touch.

INGREDIENTS TO MAKE ONE SMALL CAKE:
¼ lb (100 g) margarine
¼ lb (100 g) dark soft brown sugar
2 eggs
2 oz (50 g) ground almonds
2 tablespoons (30 ml) unsweetened cocoa powder
1 teaspoon (5 ml) baking powder
¼ lb (100 g) wholewheat flour

Mocha Raspberry Roulade

Preheat the oven to 375°F (190°C, Gas Mark 5). Line a 13- by 9-inch (32- by 23-cm) baking sheet with a raised rim with greaseproof paper and brush lightly with oil.

Break ¼ pound (100 g) of plain chocolate into a mixing bowl. Add 2 tablespoons (30 ml) of strong black coffee. Put the bowl over a pan of boiling water. Heat gently, stirring occasionally, until the chocolate has melted.

Put 4 egg yolks into a large mixing bowl. Add ¼ pound (100 g) of soft brown sugar to the egg yolks and beat well. Beat in the melted chocolate. Stir in 2 ounces (50 g) of ground almonds.

Whisk 4 egg whites until stiff. Beat 2 tablespoons (30 ml) into the chocolate mixture, then fold in the rest.

Spoon the chocolate mixture into the prepared tin. Level the surface.

Bake for 15 minutes, or until the roulade has risen and is just firm to the touch.

Cover the roulade with a clean dampened tea-towel to prevent a crust from forming. Leave until cold.

Lightly sprinkle a large sheet of greaseproof paper with sugar. Turn the roulade out on to the paper. Peel off the baking paper.

Scatter ½ pound (250 g) of raspberries over the roulade. Roll the roulade up like a Swiss roll by lifting up the greaseproof paper at one end so that it falls into a roll. Chill for at least 1 hour before serving.

INGREDIENTS TO SERVE SIX:
¼ **lb (100 g) plain chocolate**
2 tablespoons (30 ml) strong black coffee
4 eggs
¼ **lb (100 g) soft brown sugar**
2 oz (50 g) ground almonds
½ **lb (250 g) raspberries**

Frozen Coffee and Almond Yogurt

Pour ½ pint (300 ml) of yogurt into a mixing bowl. Stir in 2 tablespoons (30 ml) of very strong black coffee and 2 tablespoons (30 ml) of dark soft brown sugar.

Whisk 2 egg whites until stiff, then fold into the coffee yogurt with 2 ounces (50 g) of toasted flaked almonds.

Pour into 4 individual dishes and freeze until firm.

Put the dishes into the refrigerator for 30 minutes before serving.

INGREDIENTS TO SERVE FOUR:
½ **pint (300 ml) yogurt**
2 tablespoons (30 ml) very strong black coffee
2 tablespoons (30 ml) dark soft brown sugar
2 egg whites
2 oz (50 g) toasted flaked almonds

Coffee Bavarois Ring

Pour ¾ pint (450 ml) of milk into a saucepan. Add 2 tablespoons (30 ml) of medium-ground coffee and bring to the boil. Remove the pan from the heat and stir well. Leave to infuse for 15 minutes.

Separate 2 eggs, put the yolks into a large mixing bowl.

Add 2 tablespoons (30 ml) of soft brown sugar to the egg yolks and beat well. Strain the milk into the bowl and stir until well blended.

Pour the custard mixture into a saucepan and cook over low heat, stirring constantly, until the custard thickens slightly. Do not let it boil or the eggs may curdle.

In a cup set in a pan of hot water dissolve ½ ounce (15 g) of powdered gelatine in 2 tablespoons (30 ml) of water. Stir the gelatine into the custard.

Leave to cool, stirring occasionally, until the custard thickens and begins to set.

Whisk the 2 egg whites until stiff and then fold into the coffee custard.

Pour into a 1½-pint (850-ml) ring mould and chill for at least 2 hours.

To serve, loosen the edges of the mould with a knife, then dip the mould into hot water for a few seconds and immediately invert on to a plate and remove the mould.

INGREDIENTS TO SERVE FOUR TO SIX:
¾ **pint (450 ml) milk**
2 tablespoons (30 ml) medium-ground coffee
2 eggs
2 tablespoons (30 ml) soft brown sugar
½ **oz (15 g) powdered gelatine**

Irish Coffee Sorbet

Put 2 ounces (50 g) of medium-ground coffee into a saucepan. Pour in 1 pint (600 ml) of water and bring to the boil. Remove the pan from the heat and leave the coffee to infuse for 15 minutes.

Strain the coffee into a bowl. Stir in ¼ pound (100 g) of soft brown sugar and 2 tablespoons (30 ml) of Irish whiskey or brandy. Put the bowl into the freezer until the sorbet is almost frozen.

Whisk 2 egg whites until stiff. Whisk the coffee mixture and then fold in the whisked egg white.

Pour the sorbet into a rigid container and return to the freezer until it is solid. Cover, seal, label and store in the freezer until required.

INGREDIENTS TO SERVE FOUR:
2 oz (50 g) medium-ground coffee
¼ **lb (100 g) soft brown sugar**
2 tablespoons (30 ml) Irish whiskey or brandy
2 egg whites

Coffee Swiss Roll

A delicious confection of coffee-flavoured sponge roll filled with confectioner's custard.

Preheat the oven to 425°F (220°C, Gas Mark 7). Line a Swiss-roll tin, 12 by 9 inches (30 by 23 cm), with greaseproof paper and brush lightly with oil.

Put 3 eggs into a mixing bowl with 3 ounces (75 g) of soft brown sugar. Put the bowl over a pan of simmering water and whisk until the mixture is thick and pale.

Add 1 tablespoon (15 ml) of coffee essence and whisk until well blended.

Carefully fold in 3 ounces (75 g) of wholewheat flour.

Spoon the cake mixture into the prepared tin and level the surface.

Bake for 10 minutes, or until the cake is well risen, golden brown and springy to the touch.

Lightly sprinkle a large sheet of greaseproof paper with sugar. Turn the cake out on to the paper. Peel off the baking paper. Trim off the crusty edges of the cake on the long sides so that it will roll up easily.

Put a sheet of greaseproof paper on top of the cake and, with the paper inside, roll the cake up loosely by lifting up the bottom piece of paper so that the cake falls into a roll.

For the filling make ¼ pint (150 ml) of confectioner's custard (see page 93) and beat in 1 teaspoon (5 ml) of coffee essence.

When the cake is cold unroll it and remove the paper. Spread with the filling and roll up again. Carefully transfer the roll to a serving plate and serve.

INGREDIENTS TO SERVE SIX TO EIGHT:
3 eggs
3 oz (75 g) soft brown sugar
4 teaspoons (20 ml) coffee essence
3 oz (75 g) wholewheat flour
¼ **pint (150 ml) confectioner's custard (see page 93)**

PREPARING SWISS ROLL

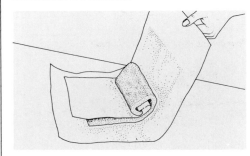

Roll up a Swiss roll with paper inside, allow to cool.

BEERS, WINES AND SPIRITS /Drink to Your Health

IT WAS INEVITABLE that man should learn to make alcohol, since fermentation, in which alcohol is produced through the reaction of sugar and yeasts in the presence of moisture, is a fundamental natural process.

The grape is a do-it-yourself wine-maker, for it has both the necessary sugar and the natural yeasts. To make wines from other fruits and to make beer from grains, either sugar or yeast, or both, have to be added. Natural fermentation continues until the level of alcohol reaches fourteen to fifteen per cent, then the yeast stops working. To reach a higher level of alcohol, distillation is needed and the more potent product is drunk as spirits, or added to some wines to make them stronger. These so-called fortified wines, which include port, sherry and vermouths such as Martini, Cinzano, Noilly Prat and Dubonnet, have an alcohol content of fifteen per cent. Ordinary table wines usually have no more than ten or eleven per cent alcohol. Beers range from two and a half to six per cent and spirits are thirty to forty per cent alcohol.

Alcoholic drinks are high in calories. Pure alcohol provides about 160 Calories per fluid ounce. One fluid ounce (30 ml) of wine provides about 20 Calories, one fluid ounce of fortified wine between 35 and 45 Calories and one fluid ounce of seventy degree proof spirit about 70 Calories. This is one reason why you should keep a sharp watch on how much you drink: from the point of view of obesity alcohol is even more dangerous than sugar. But beer and wines, unlike sugar, do contain some minerals and vitamins. Spirits have no vitamins and precious few minerals. Depending to any degree on alcoholic drinks for energy throws a diet entirely out of balance. This is quite apart from the more obvious disadvantage of hangovers, and the possible psychological and physical disasters of alcoholism. As with eating, so with drinking—the fault is in the excess.

On the other hand, drinking in moderation, especially at meals, is enjoyable. And because it depresses the centres of anxiety in the brain it can be an aid to relaxation.

There is, too, everything to be said for using beer and wine in cookery, for while all the alcohol will evaporate delicious flavours will be left behind. Beer and cider add a rich flavour to stews and make good marinades. Wine does not add its own flavour to food, but rather makes the dish richer. Spirits are less often used in cooking. Brandy, however, provides flavour and, in flambéing, an opportunity for the exhibitionist to perform.

Pinot Noir grapes (right), are carried in willow baskets to the presses to make champagne. The juice of these dusky skinned grapes, which are grown near Rheims, is white.

WINE

Wine can be made from the fermented juice of any fruit. The grape, however, is unique in producing within it the sugar and, on its skin, the natural yeasts needed for fermentation. Crushing grapes begins the process. White wine can be made from white grapes, black grapes or a mixture of both, since only the almost colourless juice is fermented. To make red wine, both the skins and juice are present during fermentation. Rosé wine is made either by leaving some skins with the juice or by adding a red wine to a white one. To produce a sparkling wine, such as champagne, the wine is bottled before fermentation is finished and natural carbon dioxide is still being produced. Fortified wines have brandy or pure alcohol added. To make port, brandy is added to stop the fermenting process; to make sherry pure alcohol is added afterwards. One fluid ounce (30 ml) of wine provides about 20 Calories, one fluid ounce of sherry about 35 Calories and one fluid ounce of port about 45 Calories.

SPIRITS

Most spirits are distilled from the alcohol made from grains, grapes and sugar cane and its products. The fermented brew is heated in a still to separate the alcohol from the water. Above 173 F (78 C) but below 212 F (100 C) the alcohol becomes a vapour, but the water does not boil. The alcohol vapour is collected and cooled back into a liquid.

The malt whiskies of Scotland are made entirely from malted barley. Blended Scotch whisky, which includes other unmalted grains, must by law be matured for three years, but in practice five years is often the minimum. Irish whiskey is made from a mixture of barley, wheat, rye and oats, and is matured for at least seven years. Bourbon, the American whiskey (above) must include at least fifty-one per cent maize in its mash; other components are barley and rye, and it is aged for at least four years. Rye whiskey must be made from at least a fifty-one per cent rye base.

Gin is a highly refined spirit, slightly flavoured with such spices as juniper, coriander or cassia. It needs no maturing.

Vodka can be made from potatoes, but wheat or rye are usually used.

Rum is distilled from fermented molasses. Most comes from the Caribbean: light rums from Cuba, dark rums from Jamaica and aromatic rums from Barbados, Puerto Rico and Martinique. One fluid ounce (30 ml) of 70 proof spirit provides about 70 Calories; 90 proof more than 100 Calories.

LIQUEURS AND APERITIFS

By distilling wine, brandy is obtained. Although French brandies such as Cognac and Armagnac are the most famous, there are many others. More brandy is, in fact, distilled in California than in France. Brandies are made from fruits other than grapes. Normandy's Calvados and American applejack are made from apples, Yugoslav slivovitz from plums and German kirsch from cherries.

Most liqueurs are made from sweetened and flavoured brandy. Bénédictine and Chartreuse, both devised by monks, are cognacs flavoured with secret mixtures of innumerable herbs. Green Chartreuse is stronger; yellow is sweeter. Crème de menthe is flavoured with peppermint, Kummel with caraway seeds, and Curaçao, Cointreau (above) and Grand Marnier with orange peel. Other fruit-flavoured liqueurs are apricot brandy and cherry brandy. Drambuie, however, is based not on brandy but on Scotch whisky flavoured with honey and herbs. One fluid ounce (30 ml) of liqueur provides approximately 70 Calories.

Of the popular apéritifs, vermouths, such as Martini, Cinzano, and Noilly Prat, are made from a mixture of wine, grape spirit and herbs; Dubonnet is a sweetened fortified wine flavoured with quinine and bittersweet Campari is more heavily fortified and flavoured with herbs. One fluid ounce (30 ml) of dry vermouth provides about 33 Calories.

BEER

Most beer is made from barley, hops, sugar, yeast and water. The barley is first soaked in water, allowed to germinate and then dried. The result is malt. This is then milled, made into a mash with water and cooked until the malt is further broken down into its component sugars. The liquid, called wort, is run off and boiled with hops. When it cools, yeast is added to cause fermentation, which converts the sugars into alcohol and carbon dioxide. Most beers are then pasteurized.

Two types of fermentation are used in beer-making. British beers, or ales, are made by top fermentation —the spent yeast rises to the top of the brew—and the beer is drunk fresh. American beer, or lager, is made by bottom fermentation— the spent yeast sinks to the bottom —and the beer is refrigerated for several weeks or even months to mellow it. Differences of flavour in beer are determined by the proportions of malt and hops—the more hops the more bitter the brew. And beer varies in colour, from pale ale to almost black stout, according to the temperatures used in malting the barley. The amount of froth depends on how much carbon dioxide has been put into it.

Twelve fluid ounces (just over half a pint) of beer provide between 100 and 250 Calories depending on its strength.

Coq au Vin

Preheat the oven to 350°F (180°C, Gas Mark 4).

Cut a 2½-pound (1.20-kg) chicken into 8 pieces. Chop ¼ pound (100 g) of bacon. Peel ½ pound (250 g) of button onions.

Heat 1 tablespoon (15 ml) of corn oil in a large saucepan and fry the bacon over low heat until the fat runs. Add the chicken pieces and fry quickly to brown them lightly on all sides. Using a slotted spoon remove the chicken from the pan and put it into a casserole.

Add the onions to the pan and fry until lightly browned. Add 1 crushed garlic clove and cook for 1 minute more.

Stir in 1 tablespoon (15 ml) of flour. Stirring constantly, gradually add ½ pint (300 ml) of dry red wine and ¼ pint (150 ml) of chicken stock. Bring to the boil. Season with salt, pepper and a little grated nutmeg.

Pour the wine sauce over the chicken. Add 1 bouquet garni, consisting of 1 bay leaf and sprigs of parsley and thyme.

Cover the casserole and bake for 45 minutes, or until the chicken is tender.

Stir in ¼ pound (100 g) of button mushrooms and bake for 10 to 15 minutes more, or until the mushrooms are cooked.

Remove the bouquet garni and serve sprinkled with 2 tablespoons (30 ml) of chopped parsley.

INGREDIENTS TO SERVE FOUR:
2½-lb (1.20-kg) chicken
¼ lb (100 g) bacon
½ lb (250 g) button onions
1 tablespoon (15 ml) corn oil
1 garlic clove
1 tablespoon (15 ml) flour
½ pint (300 ml) dry red wine
¼ pint (150 ml) chicken stock
salt
pepper
grated nutmeg
1 bouquet garni, consisting of 1 bay leaf
   and parsley and thyme sprigs
¼ lb (100 g) button mushrooms
2 tablespoons (30 ml) chopped parsley

Carbonnade of Beef

Preheat the oven to 325°F (170°C, Gas Mark 3).

Peel and slice 1 pound (500 g) of onions. Trim any fat from 1½ pounds (700 g) of lean chuck steak and cut into 2-inch (5-cm) cubes.

Heat 2 tablespoons (30 ml) of corn oil in a large saucepan. Add the onions to the pan and fry until lightly browned. With a slotted spoon remove the onions from the pan and put them into a casserole.

Add the meat to the pan and fry over high heat until it is lightly browned.

Remove the meat from the pan and put it into the casserole. Stir 1 tablespoon (15 ml) of flour into the remaining oil in the pan. Cook over low heat, stirring, for 1 minute. Stirring constantly, gradually add 1 pint (600 ml) of beer. Bring to the boil. Season with salt and pepper and pour over the beef and onions in the casserole.

Cover and bake for 2 to 2½ hours, or until the meat is tender.

INGREDIENTS TO SERVE FOUR:
1 lb (500 g) onions
1½ lb (700 g) chuck steak
2 tablespoons (30 ml) corn oil
1 tablespoon (15 ml) flour
1 pint (600 ml) beer
salt
pepper

Guinness Cake

Preheat the oven to 325°F (170°C, Gas Mark 3). Grease an 8-inch (20-cm) cake tin and line with greaseproof paper. Grease the paper.

In a large mixing bowl combine ½ pound (250 g) of wholewheat flour with 2 teaspoons (10 ml) of baking powder and 1 teaspoon (5 ml) of ground mixed spice.

Rub in ¼ pound (100 g) of margarine and then stir in ¼ pound (100 g) of soft brown sugar.

Add ¼ pound (100 g) of seedless raisins, ¼ pound (100 g) of sultanas, ¼ pound (100 g) of chopped walnuts and 2 ounces (50 g) of chopped mixed peel. Mix well.

Beat 2 eggs with ¼ pint (150 ml) of Guinness. Pour it into the flour mixture and blend thoroughly. Spoon into the prepared tin and level the surface.

Bake for 1½ to 2 hours, or until the top of the cake is brown and firm to the touch.

Let the cake cool and then remove it from the tin. Turn the cake upside down. With a fork prick the bottom of the cake, then pour 4 tablespoons (60 ml) of Guinness over it.

INGREDIENTS TO MAKE ONE SMALL CAKE:
½ lb (250 g) wholewheat flour
2 teaspoons (10 ml) baking powder
1 teaspoon (5 ml) ground mixed spice
¼ lb (100 g) margarine
¼ lb (100 g) soft brown sugar
¼ lb (100 g) seedless raisins
¼ lb (100 g) sultanas
¼ lb (100 g) chopped walnuts
2 oz (50 g) chopped mixed peel
2 eggs
¼ pint plus 4 tablespoons (210 ml)
   Guinness

Grand Marnier Soufflé

Preheat the oven to 350°F (180°C, Gas Mark 4).

Melt 1 ounce (25 g) of margarine in a saucepan. Stir in 1 ounce (25 g) of flour, then pour in ¼ pint (150 ml) of milk. Bring to the boil, stirring, until the sauce thickens. Reduce the heat, stir in the finely grated rind and juice of 1 orange and simmer for 1 minute. Leave to cool slightly.

Add 4 egg yolks to the saucepan. Beat well and then beat in 3 tablespoons (45 ml) of Grand Marnier.

Beat 5 egg whites until stiff. Stir 2 tablespoons (30 ml) of the egg whites into the pan, then fold in the remaining whites until well blended.

Pour the soufflé mixture into a 2-pint (1-litre) soufflé dish.

Bake for 45 minutes, or until the soufflé is well risen, set and golden brown.

Serve immediately.

INGREDIENTS TO SERVE FOUR:
1 oz (25 g) margarine
1 oz (25 g) flour
¼ pint (150 ml) milk
1 orange
4 egg yolks
3 tablespoons (45 ml) Grand Marnier
5 egg whites

Crème de Menthe Mousse

Put 2 ounces (50 g) of castor sugar into a mixing bowl.

Separate 4 eggs. Add the yolks to the sugar.

Put the bowl over a pan of simmering water and whisk until thick. Remove from the heat and whisk until cool.

Add 2 tablespoons (30 ml) of crème de menthe liqueur and ¼ pint (150 ml) of yogurt and whisk until well mixed.

In a cup set in a pan of hot water dissolve ½ ounce (15 g) of powdered gelatine in 3 tablespoons (45 ml) of water. Stir into the mousse.

When the mousse is just beginning to set, whisk the 4 egg whites until stiff and then fold them into the mousse.

Pour the mousse into 1 glass serving dish or 4 individual glasses and chill until set.

INGREDIENTS TO SERVE FOUR:
2 oz (50 g) castor sugar
4 eggs
2 tablespoons (30 ml) crème de menthe
   liqueur
¼ pint (150 ml) yogurt
½ oz (25 g) powdered gelatine

Rum Sauce

This sauce is traditionally served at Christmas with mince pies and Christmas pudding. It may be made with brandy instead of rum.

Put ¼ pound (100 g) of margarine into a mixing bowl with ¼ pound (100 g) of soft brown sugar and the grated rind of 1 lemon. Beat until the mixture is pale and creamy.

Gradually beat in 2 tablespoons (30 ml) of rum.

Transfer to a serving bowl and chill well.

INGREDIENTS TO SERVE FOUR TO SIX:
¼ lb (100 g) margarine
¼ lb (100 g) soft brown sugar
1 lemon
2 tablespoons (30 ml) rum

Orange and Madeira Sauce

Serve this richly flavoured sauce with duck, veal, ham or pork.

Put 4 tablespoons (60 ml) of soft brown sugar into a saucepan with 5 tablespoons (75 ml) of wine vinegar. Cook over low heat until the sugar has dissolved. Boil for 2 to 3 minutes, until the syrup is brown and thick.

Remove the pan from the heat and stir in ¼ pint (150 ml) of chicken stock, ¼ pint (150 ml) of madeira and the grated rind and juice of 2 large oranges.

Bring to the boil then reduce the heat and simmer gently for 15 minutes.

Blend 2 teaspoons (10 ml) of cornflour with 1 tablespoon (15 ml) of water and add it to the sauce. Bring to the boil, stirring constantly.

Peel and remove the pith from 1 orange. Cut the membrane away from the segments of fruit. Add the orange segments to the sauce and simmer for 5 minutes.

Serve hot.

INGREDIENTS TO MAKE ONE HALF PINT (300 ML) OF SAUCE:
4 tablespoons (60 ml) soft brown sugar
5 tablespoons (75 ml) wine vinegar
¼ pint (150 ml) chicken stock
¼ pint (150 ml) madeira
3 large oranges
2 teaspoons (10 ml) cornflour

Wine Sorbet

This sorbet is particularly good if it is served layered with strawberries.

Grate the rind of 2 oranges and 2 lemons into a saucepan and then add the juices and ¼ pound (100 g) of sugar. Cook over low heat until the sugar has dissolved, then simmer gently for 3 minutes. Remove the pan from the heat and leave to cool.

Pour 1 pint (600 ml) of medium or sweet white wine into a bowl. Strain in the fruit

juice mixture. Put the bowl into the freezer until the sorbet is half-frozen.

Whisk 2 egg whites until stiff, then whisk the sorbet to break down the ice crystals. Fold in the egg whites and blend well.

Pour the sorbet into a rigid container for freezing and return to the freezer until solid. Cover, seal and label and store in the freezer until required.

INGREDIENTS TO SERVE FOUR TO SIX:
2 oranges
2 lemons
¼ lb (100 g) sugar
1 pint (600 ml) medium or sweet white wine
2 egg whites

MAKING SORBET

Whisk the sorbet to break down the ice crystals.

Fold in stiffly whisked egg whites.

Pour into a rigid container and freeze.

Mulled Wine

Pour ½ pint (300 ml) of water into a large saucepan. Add ¼ pound (100 g) of soft brown sugar, 2 sticks of cinnamon, 4 cloves, 1 thinly sliced lemon and 1 thinly sliced orange.

Cook over low heat until the sugar has dissolved and then bring to the boil. Leave to stand for at least 10 minutes for the flavours to develop.

Pour in 1 bottle of red wine and heat to just below boiling point. Remove the pan from the heat and stir in 2 tablespoons (30 ml) of brandy. Serve hot.

INGREDIENTS TO SERVE EIGHT LARGE GLASSES:
¼ lb (100 g) soft brown sugar
2 cinnamon sticks
4 cloves
1 lemon
1 orange
1 bottle red wine
2 tablespoons (30 ml) brandy

Wassail Cup

Serve this hot spiced ale at winter parties.

Pour 2 pints (1 litre) of brown ale into a large saucepan.

Thinly peel 1 lemon and add the peel to the pan with the juice of the lemon, 2 ounces (50 g) of soft brown sugar, ¼ teaspoon (1 ml) of ground nutmeg, ¼ teaspoon (1 ml) of ground ginger and 1 stick of cinnamon.

Cut 1 dessert apple into quarters and remove the core. Thinly slice the apple into the pan.

Stir in ¼ pint (150 ml) of brandy or rum.

Cook over low heat until the sugar has dissolved, then bring to just below boiling point.

Serve hot.

INGREDIENTS TO SERVE TEN TO TWELVE GLASSES:
2 pints (1 litre) brown ale
1 lemon
2 oz (50 g) soft brown sugar
¼ teaspoon (1 ml) ground nutmeg
¼ teaspoon (1 ml) ground ginger
1 cinnamon stick
1 dessert apple
¼ pint (150 ml) brandy or rum

No recommendations exist for the growth rate of children, but the average growth rate found in a survey of American female children is illustrated right. The graph shows average weights and heights at each age and the columns indicate daily calorie requirements. While different children may grow faster or slower at different ages, their weight and height should remain the same proportionately. Weights given include light clothing.

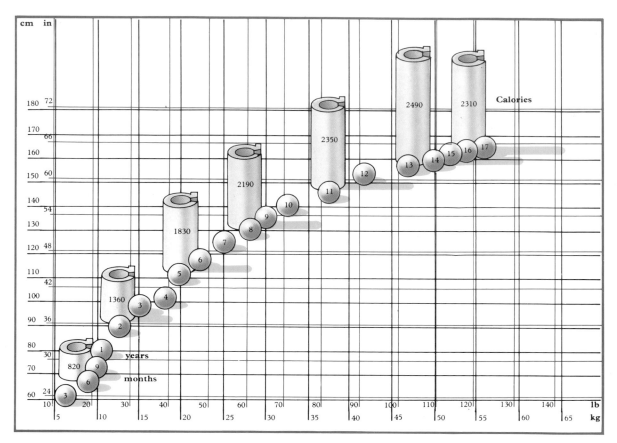

The graph right shows the average growth rates found in a survey of American male children. The graph shows average weight and height at each age and the columns indicate daily calorie requirements. Weights given include light clothing.

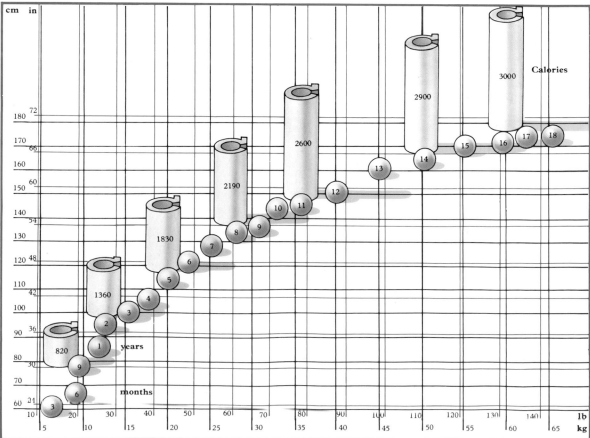

This graph shows ideal weights for adult females at each height and for each build. The weights include light clothing, and heights assume two-inch (5-cm) heels.

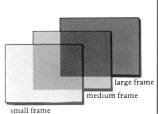

large frame

medium frame

small frame

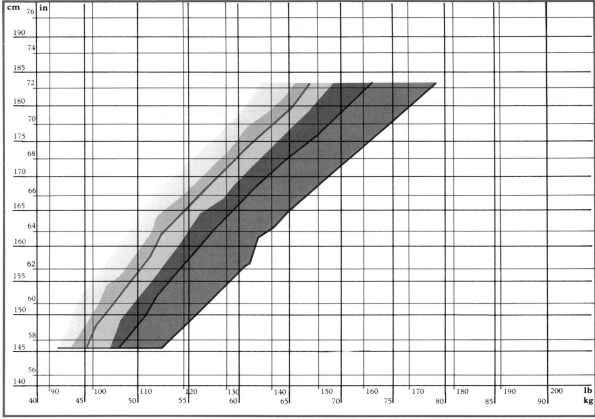

This graph shows ideal weights for adult males at each height and for each build. The weights include light clothing and heights assume one-inch (2.5-cm) heels.

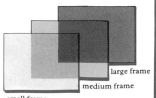

large frame

medium frame

small frame

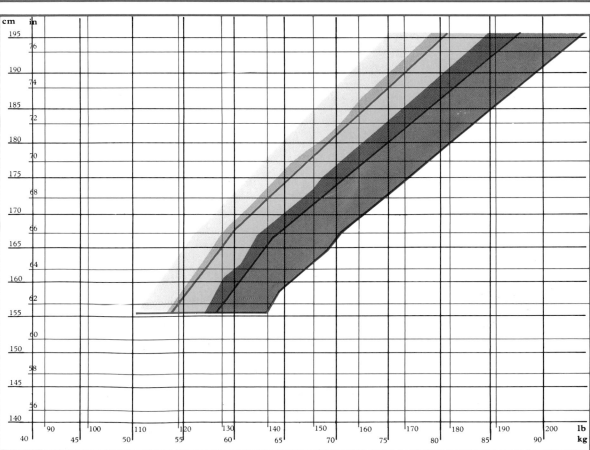

Calories are easy to come by and hard to spend. Every little snack provides us with some, and, as the chart illustrates, exercise costs us far fewer than is usually realized. The nine dishes shown are recipes given in this book. The calories provided by a single portion of each dish increase from Mushrooms and Eggs en Cocotte (113 Calories) to Dutch Apple Cake (550 Calories). Also shown are eight levels of activity which cost progressively more energy. And the clocks indicate the hours and minutes of each activity that are needed to dispose of the calories in each portion of food.

Mushrooms and Eggs en Cocotte

Raw Spinach Salad

Apple and Ginger Mousse

Orange Capered Skate

113

Calories per portion

141

Calories per portion

178

Calories per portion

211

Calories per portion

Activity	Mushrooms and Eggs en Cocotte — men	women	Raw Spinach Salad — men	women	Apple and Ginger Mousse — men	women	Orange Capered Skate — men	women
Sleeping	1 hr 45 min	2 hr 6 min	2 hr 11 min	2 hr 17 min	2 hr 45 min	3 hr 18 min	3 hr 15 min	3 hr 54 min
Sitting quietly	1 hr 21 min	1 hr 38 min	1 hr 41 min	2 hr 8 min	2 hr 8 min	2 hr 35 min	2 hr 32 min	3 hr 3 min
Driving	1 hr 11 min	1 hr 26 min	1 hr 28 min	1 hr 47 min	1 hr 51 min	2 hr 15 min	2 hr 12 min	2 hr 40 min
Cooking	55 min	1 hr 6 min	1 hr 8 min	1 hr 23 min	1 hr 26 min	1 hr 45 min	1 hr 42 min	2 hr 4 min
Walking	31 min	38 min	38 min	47 min	48 min	59 min	57 min	1 hr 10 min
Doing housework	26 min	32 min	33 min	40 min	41 min	51 min	49 min	1 hr
Playing tennis	18 min	23 min	23 min	28 min	28 min	36 min	34 min	42 min
Chopping wood	13 min	16 min	16 min	20 min	21 min	26 min	25 min	31 min

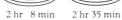

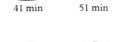
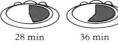

Chinese Fried Rice		**Baked Cheese Soufflé Potatoes**		**Steak with Mushrooms**		**Blueberry Pie**		**Dutch Apple Cake**	

225		**248**		**352**		**414**		**550**	
Calories per portion		Calories per portion		Calories per portion		Calories per portion		Calories per portion	
men	women	men	women	men	women	men	women	men	women
3 hr 28 min	4 hr 10 min	3 hr 50 min	4 hr 36 min	5 hr 26 min	6 hr 31 min	6 hr 23 min	7 hr 40 min	8 hr 29 min	10 hr 11 min
2 hr 42 min	3 hr 16 min	2 hr 58 min	3 hr 36 min	4 hr 13 min	5 hr 6 min	4 hr 58 min	6 hr	6 hr 36 min	7 hr 58 min
2 hr 21 min	2 hr 50 min	2 hr 35 min	3 hr 8 min	3 hr 40 min	4 hr 27 min	4 hr 19 min	5 hr 14 min	5 hr 44 min	6 hr 57 min
1 hr 49 min	2 hr 12 min	2 hr	2 hr 26 min	2 hr 50 min	3 hr 27 min	3 hr 20 min	4 hr 4 min	4 hr 26 min	5 hr 23 min
1 hr 1 min	1 hr 15 min	1 hr 7 min	1 hr 23 min	1 hr 35 min	1 hr 57 min	1 hr 52 min	2 hr 18 min	2 hr 29 min	3 hr 3 min
52 min	1 hr 4 min	58 min	1 hr 11 min	1 hr 22 min	1 hr 41 min	1 hr 36 min	1 hr 58 min	2 hr 8 min	2 hr 37 min
36 min	45 min	40 min	50 min	56 min	1 hr 10 min	1 hr 6 min	1 hr 23 min	1 hr 28 min	1 hr 50 min
26 min	33 min	29 min	36 min	41 min	51 min	48 min	1 hr	1 hr 4 min	1 hr 20 min

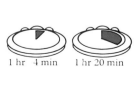

227

Vitamins are sensitive chemicals and the destructive barrage of conditions to which we subject them in preparing and cooking food is designed for our palate and not their survival. Cooking, processing and letting food stand can all contribute to the loss of vitamins. This can be illustrated if we take as a standard an extremely simple meal of, for example, fresh fruit juice, steak tartare, spinach salad, tomato salad, bread and fresh pineapple—the most vitamin-rich preparation of each food that is palatable—and then consider the alternative preparations for each food. With each variation some vitamins will be lost. The loss is represented as a percentage of the amount of the vitamin in the standard meal.

Fruit juice
Freshly squeezed

vitamin C
folic acid

Meat
Steak tartare

thiamine
folic acid

Spinach
Freshly prepared whole-leaf spinach salad

vitamin C
folic acid
thiamine

Tomatoes
Freshly prepared tomato salad

vitamin C
folic acid

Canned juice

100% loss of folic acid
20% loss of vitamin C

Grilled meat

65% loss of folic acid
35% loss of thiamine

Shredded spinach salad

no loss of thiamine
25% loss of folic acid
30% loss of vitamin C

Grilled tomatoes

50% loss of folic acid
50% loss of vitamin C

Frozen juice

100% loss of folic acid
20% loss of vitamin C

Roast meat

65% loss of folic acid
35% loss of thiamine

Steamed spinach

30% loss of thiamine
75% loss of folic acid
50% loss of vitamin C

Boiled canned tomatoes

90% loss of folic acid
50% loss of vitamin C

Stewed meat

50% loss of folic acid
20% loss of thiamine

Boiled spinach

100% loss of thiamine
100% loss of folic acid
100% loss of vitamin C

Bread
Fresh wholewheat bread

niacin

thiamine

folic acid

Pineapple
Freshly sliced pineapple

carotene

thiamine

folic acid

vitamin C

Fresh white bread

50% loss of niacin
10% loss of thiamine
60% loss of folic acid

Canned pineapple

40% loss of carotene

40% loss of thiamine
90% loss of folic acid
70% loss of vitamin C

Toasted white bread

50% loss of niacin
15% loss of thiamine
60% loss of folic acid

The amount of cholesterol eaten may not cause heart disease, but it does nothing to prevent it either. Medical opinion is divided on the significance of dietary cholesterol since we make it in our bodies as well as eat it. But few experts would disagree that the beginning of heart disease is caused by too much cholesterol in the blood. Thus if the disease occurs merely because our bodies make too much, eating even more will hardly help. In this chart the cholesterol content of some common foods is given as milligrams of cholesterol per hundred grams of food. Vegetable foods contain no cholesterol. Animal products, the sole dietary source of cholesterol, range from fifteen milligrams in cottage cheese to two thousand in brains. If you aim to keep your cholesterol intake below three hundred milligrams a day, then one egg, for example, is enough.

Dairy products

Meat

mg/100g

brains

2000

1900

1800

1700

1600

1500

egg yolk

1400

Miscellaneous foods **Fish and Shellfish**

1300

1200

1100

1000

900

800

700

600

500

kidney

pig liver

400

oysters

caviare

ox liver

butter

chicken liver

300

lobster

crab

beef

Cheddar cheese

cream

pork

shrimps

sardines

veal

200

salmon

halibut

cottage cheese

ice-cream

chicken

turkey

herring

milk

lamb

cod

trout

egg white

100

vegetable oils

margarine

cereals

fruits

0

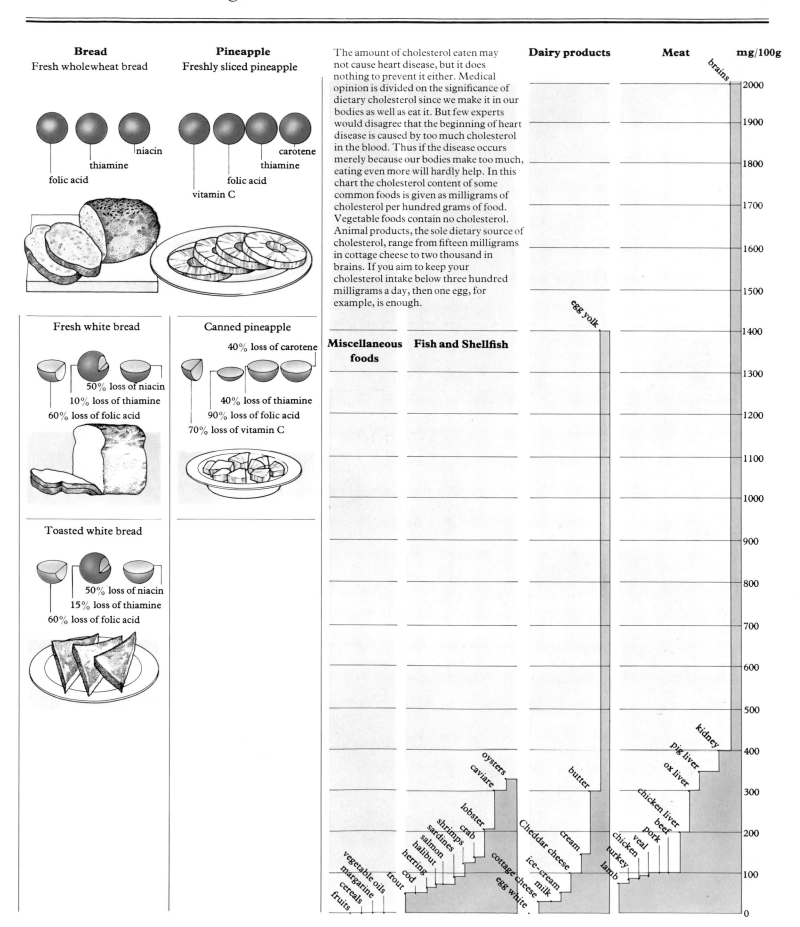

Storing wholefood is not encouraged, but there are occasions when it may be necessary. The chart, right, is therefore a guide to how long various wholesome foods can be stored in a cool larder, a refrigerator or a freezer. Times are approximate and assume that the food is in good condition to begin with. Fruit storage times are for whole fruit. Always clean shellfish, fish and poultry. Do not store French bread—it always deteriorates. Wash leaf vegetables and herbs before storage, but not root vegetables or soft fruit. Store root vegetables, leaf vegetables and milk in a cool place away from the light. Only freeze fruit and vegetables if they are cooked or blanched. Store eggs pointed end down. Only freeze yogurt if sugar has been added. Oils will vary in the length of time they can be stored according to the degree of saturation—the more saturated they are the longer they keep.

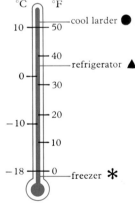

°C	°F	
10	50	cool larder ●
	40	refrigerator ▲
0	30	
	20	
−10	10	
−18	0	freezer ✱

Bread
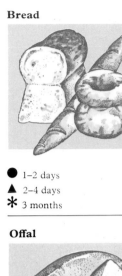

● 1–2 days
▲ 2–4 days
✱ 3 months

Fish

● not recommended
▲ 1–2 days
✱ 3–6 months

Cooked fish
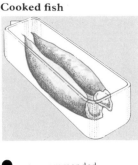

● not recommended
▲ 3–4 days (covered)
✱ 3–4 months

Smoked fish

● 2 days
▲ 2–4 days (covered)
✱ 6-12 months

Offal
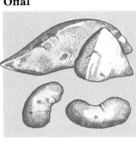

● not recommended
▲ 1–2 days
✱ 3–4 months

Smoked bacon

● 5–7 days
▲ 10–14 days
✱ 6 months

Cooked meat
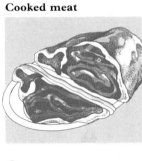

● 1 day
▲ 5 days
✱ 2 months

Eggs

● 1–2 weeks
▲ up to 4 weeks
✱ not recommended

Soft cheese

● 4–5 days
▲ 7–10 days
✱ 1 month

Cream and cottage cheese

● not recommended
▲ 1 week (covered)
✱ not recommended

Vegetable fruit

● 2–4 days
▲ 1 week (covered)
✱ 2 months (blanched)

Tomatoes

● until ripe
▲ 7–14 days (covered)
✱ not recommended

Mushrooms
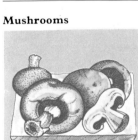

● 1 day
▲ 2–3 days (covered)
✱ 3–4 months (blanched)

Apples

● until ripe
▲ not recommended
✱ not recommended

Orchard fruit

● 1–3 days
▲ 3–7 days (covered)
✱ 6–9 months

Citrus fruit

● 2 weeks
▲ 2–3 weeks (covered)
✱ 3–6 weeks

Melons

● until ripe
▲ 1 week (covered)
✱ not recommended

Shellfish

● not recommended
▲ 1 day
✱ 1 month

Chicken

● 2 days
▲ 3–4 days
✱ 10–12 months

Large pieces of meat

● 1 day (covered)
▲ 4 days
✱ 6–8 months

Small cuts of meat

● 1 day (covered)
▲ 2–3 days
✱ 4 months

Minced meat

● not recommended
▲ 2–4 days
✱ 3 months

Hard-boiled eggs in shell

● 1 day
▲ 5–7 days
✱ not recommended

Milk

● 1 day (in dark)
▲ 3–4 days
✱ 2 months (homogenized)

Yogurt

● not recommended
▲ 7 days
✱ 2 months (sugar added)

Hard cheese

● 5–10 days (covered)
▲ 1–4 weeks (covered)
✱ 3 months

Grated cheese

● 2–3 days (covered)
▲ 1–2 weeks (covered)
✱ 4–6 months

Stalks and shoots

● 2–4 days
▲ 5–7 days (covered)
✱ 2 months (blanched)

Brassicas and leaf vegetables

● 1 day (in dark)
▲ 5 days (covered)
✱ 6–9 months

Potatoes and root vegetables

● 1 week (in dark)
▲ not recommended
✱ 6–9 months (carrots only)

Pods and seeds

● 1 day (unshelled)
▲ 1–2 days (shelled)
✱ 6–9 months (blanched)

Salad leaves

● 1 day (covered)
▲ 3–7 days (covered)
✱ not recommended

Pineapples

● until ripe
▲ 10 days (covered)
✱ not recommended

Soft fruit

● 1 day
▲ 2–3 days (not bananas)
✱ 7–9 months (not bananas)

Fresh herbs

● 1–2 days (in water)
▲ 1 week (covered)
✱ 6–9 months

Butter and margarine

● 3–7 days
▲ 7–14 days
✱ 1 month

Oils

● up to 6 months
▲ not recommended
✱ not recommended

RECIPE INDEX

The recipes are listed under their main ingredients, with the exception of bread, cakes, salad dressings and pastry.

239

The publishers wish to acknowledge the following people: A.E. Bicknell, Lis Blackburn, Andrew Duncan, Joan Faller, Mike Janson, Ethne Rose

Indexer: Donald Cameron

Artists: Javed Badar, David Baxter (The Garden Studio), Ray Burrows, Patricia Capon (Joan Farmer), Lyn Cawley, Richard Corfield (John Martin and Artists Ltd), Patrick Cox, Brian Delf, Chris Forsey, Gary Hincks, Ingrid Jacob, Richard Jacobs, Coral Milla, Marion Mills (Joan Farmer), Peter Morter, Keith Palmer (Arka Graphics), Andrew Popkiewicz, Christine Robins (The Garden Studio), Philip Rymer (The Garden Studio), Posy Simmonds, Glen Stewards (John Martin and Artists Ltd), David Watson (The Garden Studio), Sidney Woods

Fact Finder charts designed by Mike Blore

Photographic stylists: Maggi Heinz, Roisin Nield

Studio services: Face Photosetting, J.D. Colour Studios, Mitchell Beazley Studio, Negs Photography, PLS Typesetters, Sally Slight, Summit Art Studios

Original photography: Frank Apthorp 86, 102-3, 106-7, 112-13, 119 bottom left, 118-19, 126-7, 133, 138, 176, 182 bottom left, 2nd bottom right; Bryce Attwell 17 top left, 19 top right, 20 far left, 38 far left, 66-7, 70, 74-5, 95, 98-9, 110 bottom left, 110-11, 114 bottom left, 114-15, 122-3, 149, 150-1, 166-7, 171 bottom right, 174 bottom left, 175, 178-9, 186-7, 194-5, 199, 202, 203 bottom, 208 top, 209, 211, 212-13, 216 bottom left, 216-17; Steve Bicknell cover, 12 top right, 46-7, 52; Michael Freeman 13 top right, 21 far left, 70-1, 78-9 top right, 162-3; Michael Kaye 27 bottom left, bottom right and centre right

Additional photographs: A-Z Botanical Collection 187 top right; Ardea, London (Photo: John Mason) 186 top left; Barnaby's Picture Library 155, 203 top right; Battle Creek Sanitarium Hospital 22; The Bettmann Archive 206 bottom left; Bodleian Library, Oxford, from colour film strip 186 H, Ms. Ashmole 1462, folio 37v and 38, 206 top left; Cadbury Limited 217 bottom left and far right; Camera Press 23; Kay Casebourne 15 top right; Bruce Coleman 10 centre (Photo: C.B. Frith), 20 top left (Photo: Hans Reinhard), 71 left inset (Photo: Hans Reinhard), 182-3 centre (Photo: Sandro Prato), 183 bottom inset (Photo: Sandro Prato); Colorific 10 left (Photo: Penny Tweedie); Douglas Dickins 58, 198 bottom; Robert Estall 71 bottom right inset; Mary Evans Picture Library 18 top centre, 59; Explorer 8 far left, 8-9; Werner Forman Archive 47 top right; Archiv Gerstenberg 207; Robert Harding Associates 79 left inset, 220-1; Alan Hutchison 208 bottom; Imperial Chemical Industries Limited 20 inset; King Features (Walter Tuckwell and Associates) 15 top far left; The Mansell Collection 18 top right, 215 inset; Mitchell Beazley Archive 27 top right inset; Natural History Photographic Agency (Photo: Joe Blossom) 71 top right inset; New Zealand Dairy Board 20 centre top; Picturepoint 13 bottom right, 26-7, 163 inset, 177, 183 top right inset, 186 bottom left, 215 bottom left; Jean Ribière 18 top left; Harry Smith Horticultural Collection 138-9; Sofia Press, Bulgaria 94; Spectrum 112 bottom left, 214-15; *The Sunday Times Magazine* 9 far right; Tate & Lyle 210; Michael Warren 107; ZEFA 10 right, 47 top left, 71 centre inset, 113 bottom right, 162

The publishers also wish to acknowledge the kind co-operation of the following organizations for the loan of various items for use in photography and for reference for artwork: The Conran Shop, London SW3; The Craftsmen Potters Shop, London W1; Cucina, London NW3; Elizabeth David, London W1; Dodo Old Advertising, London W11; Habitat, London SW3; David Mellor, London SW1; Richard Morris, London SW6; The New Neal Street Shop, London WC2; Old Pine, London SW6; The Pine Mine, London SW6; The Potshop, London NW3; Thompson & Morgan, Ipswich; The Warehouse, London WC2; World's End Tiles and Flooring Ltd, London SW10